Fuzzy Logic in Revolutionizing Renewable Energy

Jenny Stanford Series on Fuzzy Theory Frontiers

Series Editors

Aryan Chaudhary, Rashmi Singh, Neha Bhardwaj

Titles in the Series

Published

Vol. 1
Fuzzy Logic in Smart Sustainable Cities
Bhupinder Singh, Christian Kaunert, and Komal Vig (eds.)
2025
978-981-5129-70-0 (Hardcover)
978-1-003-63672-4 (eBook)

Vol. 2
Fuzzy Logic in Revolutionizing Renewable Energy
Bhupinder Singh, Komal Vig, Ruchi Lal, and Budi Agus Riswandi (eds.)
2026
978-981-5129-92-2 (Hardcover)
978-1-003-74191-6 (eBook)

Forthcoming

Vol. 3
Fuzzy Logic for Healthcare and Biomedical Applications
Keshav Kaushik, Ishu Sharma, and Mohit Angurala (eds.)
2027

Jenny Stanford Series on Fuzzy Theory Frontiers Vol. 2

Fuzzy Logic in Revolutionizing Renewable Energy

edited by

Bhupinder Singh | Komal Vig
Ruchi Lal | Budi Agus Riswandi

JENNY STANFORD
PUBLISHING

Published by

Jenny Stanford Publishing Pte. Ltd.
101 Thomson Road
#06-01, United Square
Singapore 307591

Email: editorial@jennystanford.com
Web: www.jennystanford.com

British Library Cataloguing-in-Publication Data
A catalogue record for this book is available from the British Library.

Fuzzy Logic in Revolutionizing Renewable Energy

ISBN 978-981-5129-92-2 (Hardcover)
ISBN 978-1-003-74191-6 (eBook)

DOI: 10.1201/9781003741916

About the Series

This series unfurls the extensive utility of fuzzy sets and fuzzy logic theory, stretching from theoretical foundations to diverse practical applications in healthcare, environmental management, and beyond. We venture into the rich intersection of fuzzy logic and global health challenges. We meticulously dissect innovative subjects, such as the role of fuzzy logic in improving healthcare access, enhancing disease surveillance, and optimizing resource allocation in underserved regions. We spotlight distinct applications of fuzzy decision-making that directly contribute to better health outcomes, equity in health services, and, ultimately, a higher standard of living worldwide. We look at fuzzy logic's role in creating health-centric urban environments, where intelligent systems optimize everything from emergency responses to environmental health risks, thus enhancing the overall well-being of urban populations. Moreover, series areas like linear positive operators in healthcare will be used in signal processing techniques for filtering or enhancing medical images, extracting features from data, or manipulating signals (e.g., EEG signals in brain activity studies) to aid in diagnosis and analysis.

About the Editors

Bhupinder Singh is a professor at Sharda School of Law, Sharda University, India. He has authored 3 books, published 97 papers, given 163 presentations at national and international conferences and seminars, and participated in more than 40 workshops, faculty development programs, and quality improvement programs, and 25 courses from reputed international universities. Dr Singh has more than 16 years of experience in leadership, teaching, research, and industry.

Komal Vig is the dean of Sharda School of Law, Sharda University, Greater Noida, India. She has a doctorate in law (criminal law) and an MBA in human resources. Prof. Vig has served in the field of academics in different capacities for more than 20 years.

Ruchi Lal is the head of department at the School of Law at Manav Rachna University, India. She has presented more than 50 research papers at various national and international conferences/seminars and has published 65 research papers in Scopus and UGC Care journals. During her professional career, Prof. Lal has handled diverse academic and administrative responsibilities such as drafting and vetting of the syllabi, member of the board of studies, and organization of academic events.

Budi Agus Riswandi is a professor of law in intellectual property rights and cyberlaw and dean of the Faculty of Law, Universitas Islam Indonesia. He also teaches at various law faculties in Indonesia. Prof. Riswandi's research focuses on intellectual property rights and cyberlaw, and he has published several books and articles journals in the field.

Contents

Preface

The global energy landscape is changing radically as the world moves from dirty fossil fuels to relatively cleaner renewable forms of power. The urgency for climate change action and sustainable energy solutions is critical for long-term economic and environmental sustainability. In this framework, fuzzy logic has provided a breakthrough for solving complexities and uncertainties in renewable energy systems. It is perfect for handling the variability and intermittent nature of renewable energy sources such as wind, solar, and hydroelectric power.

This book comes from a fundamental belief that the future of energy is in our willingness to invent and improve to survive against nature and also make it sustainable. It discusses the importance of fuzzy logic in smart infrastructure control systems, fault detection and management in renewable energy systems (solar photovoltaic, wind, hydroelectric, biomass, and biogas energy systems), federated learning devices for renewable energy, intelligent energy management, enhanced wave and tidal energy conversion, and achievement of the Sustainable Development Goals through renewable energy innovations.

This work serves as the foundation for addressing new applications and innovations, offering a clear compilation of existing research for those interested in applying fuzzy logic in renewable energy engineering. It provides a systematic mathematical treatment of the theoretical aspects of fuzzy logic and showcases industry use cases that have leveraged fuzzy logic to improve renewable energy project efficiency, reliability, and sustainability. The chapters are a mix of technical knowledge, practical examples, and guidance for the future and explore the ways in which new discoveries can transform how energy is generated, stored, and consumed, potentially leading us to a pathway towards sustainability. The book will make a substantive reference for researchers and engineers working in the fields of energy. We hope that our study of the crossroads of fuzzy logic and renewable energy will help add to current discussions about using these technologies in a way that leads us to an even more sustainable and strong future.

Acknowledgement

This book is the result of a process that has been transformational in itself. It would not have been possible without the dedication and support of the authors. Special thanks to our collaborators and advisors in the renewable energy/fuzzy logic community, who have enriched this book. We thank our families for their support.

We thank all research institutions and organizations for providing us with the resources, opportunity, and platforms that helped fuel our exploration of fuzzy logic in renewable energy systems. Their work has been essential for creating the theories offered in this book. We would also like to thank the Series Editors—Aryan Chaudhary, Rashmi Singh, and Neha Bhardwaj—for their meticulous attention to detail, unwavering commitment to academic quality, and recommendations. Lastly, we thank the readers who have expressed interest in this work. We hope the book will arouse interest among experts and general readers alike for further development and innovation in renewable energy to lead us into a stable, resilient future.

Chapter 1

Fuzzy Control System in Smart Infrastructure for Smart and Futuristic Cities: Organic Photovoltaic Glass Confirming Sustainability via Efficient Energy Management

Christian Kaunert,[a,b] Bhupinder Singh,[c] Sahil Lal,[c] Manmeet Kaur Arora,[c] and Saurabh Chandra[d]

[a]*Dublin City University, Ireland*
[b]*University of South Wales, UK*
[c]*Sharda University, Greater Noida, Uttar Pradesh, India*
[d]*School of Law, Bennett University, Greater Noida, Uttar Pradesh, India*

bhupindersinghlaw19@gmail.com

Abstract

Smart energy systems are a fundamental aspect of smart city infrastructure for real-time monitoring; these systems usually include a smart grid that balances power sources that are decentralized and centralized. The reduced energy use and smaller carbon footprints are the result of ICT-based smart energy systems' enhanced efficiency and the supply of precise consumption information. Smart

Fuzzy Logic in Revolutionizing Renewable Energy
Edited by Bhupinder Singh, Komal Vig, Ruchi Lal, and Budi Agus Riswandi

ISBN 978-981-5129-92-2 (Hardcover), 978-1-003-74191-6 (eBook)
www.jennystanford.com

DOI: 10.1201/9781003741916-1

grids increase overall efficiency and facilitate the incorporation of renewable energy sources. Improving productivity and adding additional renewable energy sources complement ongoing efforts to mitigate climate change, demonstrating the advantages of smart city applications in the energy industry. Resilience to natural catastrophes such as hurricanes and heat waves, which frequently cause disruptions to conventional power-producing technology, is another benefit of smart energy systems. When centralized power facilities are disrupted during such catastrophes, the decentralized structure of smart energy systems increases resilience by permitting local electricity generation. The co-generating energy relieves the burden on centralized generators, which lessens heatwave-related stress on the power grid. This chapter focuses on the organic photovoltaic glass confirming sustainability via efficient energy management smart infrastructure with fuzzy control system for smart and futuristic cities.

Keywords: Photovoltaic Glass, IoT, Fuzzy Control System, Smart Infrastructure, Sustainability

1.1 Introduction

Light can flow through transparent solar panels just like it can through clear glass. Transparent solar panels are composed of a unique kind of solar glass, which collects light in the UV and infrared ranges wavelengths invisible to the human eye and transforms it into clean, sustainable energy. Load profiles are an efficient way to monitor and control power use in modern energy automation systems and demand response applications [1]. The implementation of intelligent control systems that integrate supplementary fuzzy factors, including meteorological information, using machine learning techniques offers significant perspectives for enhancing consumer actions. This chapter discusses the design and implementation of a fuzzy control system that interprets environmental data to determine the lowest energy consumption values for a residential structure, building on recent advances in fuzzy control [2]. This system generates rules by using decision tree linearization and the forward chaining Mamdani technique. The energy differential between the valence band and the conduction band is known as the "band gap." Each photon has a different energy depending on its wavelength; photons with greater energies have shorter wavelengths [3].

Each incoming photon must have energy at least equivalent to the semiconducting material's band gap in order for one electron to be liberated. The wavelengths of incident solar radiation that will be converted into energy may be varied by varying the band gap. A topmost anti-reflective (AR) layer, as shown in the diagram, usually stops photons from being reflected away, increasing the efficiency of the PV cell [4]. The internal mechanism of all photodiodes relies on a "PN junction," which involves a positively doped "P-layer" in contact with a negatively doped "N-layer." It is at this PN junction that incoming photons excite electrons to become "electrically free," allowing them to be connected to an electrical circuit and perform useful work, such as powering a light bulb or an IoT temperature sensor [5]. With renewable energy being one of the fastest-growing sectors of the economy, it is no surprise that significant efforts are being dedicated to innovation in this field [6]. There are many exciting opportunities in various areas, but one that particularly stands out is the Internet of Things (IoT). The integration of IoT with renewable energy technologies is transforming how we monitor, collect data, maintain, and interact with these systems [7].

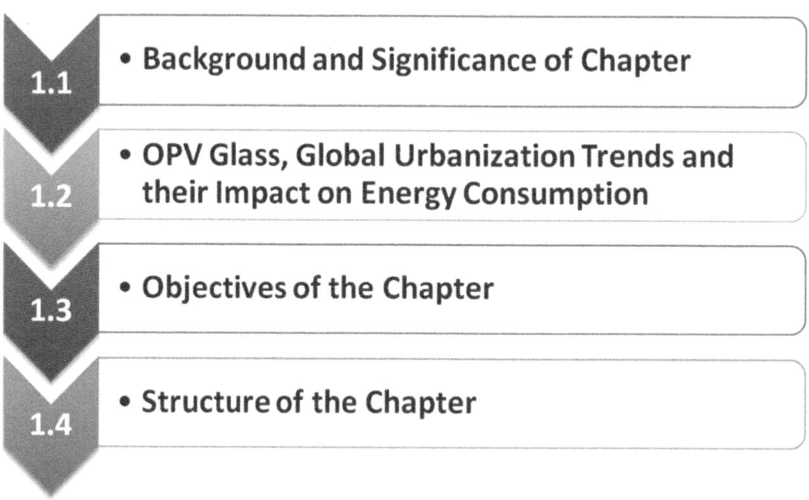

Figure 1.1 Sections in this chapter.

1.1.1 Background and Significance of Chapter

To satisfy a building's energy demands, a large area of Thermophotovoltaic (TPV) smart glass is needed. Consequently, TPV cells are usually installed inside windows, doors, or skylights to turn them into electricity-producing machinery [6]. This idea also extends to consumer electronics, smart city infrastructure, and automobiles. Traditional solar cells and TPV smart glass vary principally in that the former uses visible light to brighten interior spaces of buildings while the latter predominantly transforms photons from the ultraviolet and infrared parts of the electromagnetic spectrum into energy [1]. On the other hand, because they absorb visible light and transform it into power, conventional photovoltaic (PV) cells are opaque. In recent times, the development of high-performance carbon-based semiconductors has elevated organic photovoltaics (OPVs) to a major position as an alternative energy source [8]. The recently created active materials for OPVs are non-toxic and enable roll-to-roll manufacturing that is economical and environmentally sustainable while using a great deal less energy than conventional photovoltaic production methods [9]. As such, payback periods for OPV systems are significantly shorter than for other solar technologies. OPV modules are thin, flexible laminates that fit into a variety of substrates and construction materials, such as glass, with ease. Also, even in normal outside situations like bright light and high temperatures, OPV devices continue to function [10].

1.1.2 Overview of OPV Glass, Global Urbanization Trends and Their Impact on Energy Consumption

Using an electrochemical cell, Edmond Becquerel first showed the photovoltaic effect in 1839. Modern solid-state semiconductor technology, most frequently utilizing silicon photodiodes, is the foundation of photovoltaic cells [11]. Electrons in the valence band of the photodiode absorb energy from sunlight and migrate to the conduction band, where they become "free electrons" that can contribute to an electrical current [12]. PV cells are considered a "variable current source" since their current generation is directly correlated with the quantity of photons absorbed, and this varies depending on the amount of incoming light present during the day [13]. Active materials' versatility and tunability enable modular designs that satisfy certain needs, such as a selection of hues, forms, and levels of transparency. Because of their adaptability, OPVs may satisfy a variety of practical and aesthetic requirements set out by architects and product designers [14]. A flexible power system larger than 250 m^2 was recently constructed using OPV technology, with average power conversion efficiency (PCE) of about 5% in a semi-transparent configuration [15].

1.1.3 Objectives of the Chapter

Following are the objectives of this chapter:

- To investigate the ways in which organic photovoltaic (OPV) glass-equipped buildings may improve their energy management using fuzzy control systems, resulting in increased energy efficiency and decreased energy consumption [16]
- To illustrate how OPV glass integration with smart infrastructure may help to generate renewable energy, drastically lower carbon emissions, and promote sustainable urban growth; also, explore the integration of OPV glass with fuzzy control systems for efficient energy management in smart infrastructure [17]
- To determine the long-term financial benefits and economic feasibility of integrating OPV glass and fuzzy control systems in smart buildings through a cost-benefit analysis [18]
- To list and evaluate the technological obstacles to be overcome in order to integrate OPV glass with fuzzy control systems, along with suggestions for future study and development; assess the sustainability and practicality of this integration in urban settings [19]
- In order to assist the development of smart and sustainable cities by encouraging policies and incentives, offer insights and advice on advanced energy solutions adoption and promotion to policymakers and urban planners [20]

Figure 1.2 Objectives of the chapter.

1.1.4 Structure of the Chapter

This chapter focuses on the Fuzzy Control System in Smart Infrastructure for Smart and Futuristic Cities: Organic Photovoltaic Glass confirming Sustainability via Efficient Energy Management. Section 1.2 discusses the smart cities and need for sustainable energy solutions. Section 1.3 explores the role of fuzzy control systems in managing complex and uncertain environments. Section 1.4 discusses fuzzy control systems and applications of fuzzy control in energy management and building automation. Section 1.5 focuses on the OPV glass. Section 1.6 highlights the smart infrastructure, specifically the role of IoT, AI and renewable energy in smart infrastructure. Section 1.7 concludes the chapter with future scope.

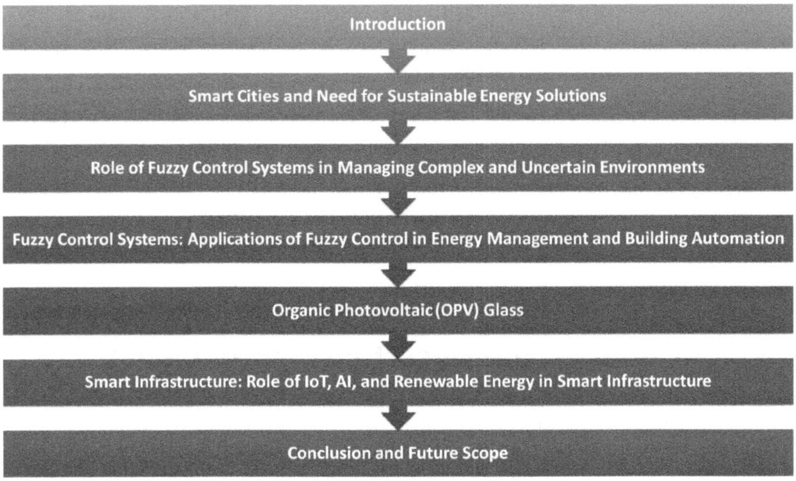

Figure 1.3 Flow of this chapter.

1.2 Smart Cities and Need for Sustainable Energy Solutions

Smart cities are the forthcoming paradigm of urban development; however, they necessitate sustainable energy solutions to flourish [21]. With the ongoing growth and urbanization of the global population, cities are encountering escalating obstacles including environmental deterioration, pollution, and energy requirements [22]. To tackle these problems, smart cities are adopting renewable energy sources. Solar energy is a widely favored choice, employing photovoltaic (PV) devices and solar panels to produce electricity. Wind power is increasingly common in smart cities [23].

A crucial element of sustainable energy solutions for smart cities is the implementation of intelligent power distribution networks, also known as smart grids [24, 25]. The smart grids integrate the processes of generation, storage, and consumption, using a central control system to optimize the distribution of energy and counterbalance variations in renewable energy sources [26]. Smart grids are equipped with information and communication technology (ICT), which allows for instantaneous contact between utility companies and consumers [27, 28]. Smart grids offer several advantages, such as enhanced electricity transmission efficiency, faster power restoration following disruptions, decreased utility operations and administration expenses, and reduced power expenses for customers [29]. Smart grids also enable the incorporation of extensive renewable energy systems and customer-owned power generation systems [30].

1.3 Role of Fuzzy Control Systems in Managing Complex and Uncertain Environments

Fuzzy control systems are used for the management of imprecise or vague input instead of the equipment-abilities as restrictions cannot be described deterministically [31]. They can be applied to a huge range of cases, including room temperature regulation and also more complex stuff such as robot movements [32]. Fuzzy control systems are employed because they provide a middle ground between precision with rigid rules and flexibility. They can be used to enable a great deal of control over some processes while also permitting variability and adaptability [33].

Fuzzy control systems have an important place in modern engineering. This provides a fresh direction in terms of controls: an ideal mix between accuracy and ease. Fuzzy control possesses the characteristics of adaptability, robustness and it is able to manage uncertainties in a system. With the rapid development of science and technology, fuzzy control systems will be popular in more engineering fields. Roughly typed control system utilizes regulations to fix the decisions that must be made [34]. These rules use fuzzy logic, and these kinds of logic permit inexactness or uncertainty that could be passed to decide. For instance, rules in a fuzzy control system for room temperature would look like "if the temperature is too high, then turn on A/C" and "if the temperature is too cold, then turn on heating" [35].

In fuzzy control systems, membership functions are used to quantify how well a specific input would correspond with some rule [36]. Its membership functions are used to give a value the degree of memberships. For instance, a membership function for the rule "if temperature is too hot, then turn the AC on" might give high zero degree of membership to temperatures higher than 25 °C [37]. Fuzzy inference is the process of combining these rules and membership functions to decide what action to take in a fuzzy control system. The fuzzy inference is the process of using these membership functions in order to combine rules and determine how much each rule applies [38]. The two pieces of information are then combined to decide the input action required. Fuzzy control systems can be "tuned" to provide very precise or very forgiving responses based on the requirements of that application. A control system in a robot that controls the position of its arm could, perhaps, be very other—flexible when obstacles arise but more specific about setting an appropriate threshold for use elsewhere on this list [39].

1.4 Fuzzy Control Systems: Applications of Fuzzy Control in Energy Management and Building Automation

The traditional energy management systems, however, may struggle to adapt to the uncertainty that is a characteristic of renewable sources. Smart Grids, which are notorious for their superior communication and control capabilities have appeared to be a potential solution. Fuzzy logic controllers (FLCs) give us a method of reasoning that is computationally fast and simplifies the process when used in environments with uncertainty or change [40]. The adaptability of fuzzy logic to simulate and control these systems, together with the required flexibility for integrating renewable energy, turns it into a very adequate tool in the quest for efficient smart grid operation [41]. The use of fuzzy logic-based energy management is justified by its great value in dealing with vague and uncertain information that generally occurs in renewable energy systems. A fuzzy logic system allows experts to set rules which provide shades of meaning between the high energy production, storage and consumption variables. That would need to manage energy systems that can be adapted for the unpredictable characteristics of renewable sources [42].

This resulted in a 20% improvement when it comes to the renewable energy usage, thanks to changes made on how different types of power are distributed across states, all due to the CAL-OP. The ability to shape-shift is vital in addressing this built-in ebb-and-flow feature of solar and wind [43]. This strategy reduces grid frequency fluctuations by 15% and thereby offers a better-regulated single-frequency electrical supply. More importantly, energy storage system that the performance of high reliability improved by 25%. The charge status reference obtained recharge-discharge cycle has evidently optimized [44]. This greater reliability increases the security of supply under normal conditions and during peak hours or when the power system is facing external disturbances. The fuzzy logic-based energy management approach provides a remarkable 22% increase in the overall system efficiency compared with conventional management systems [45].

Building automation systems (BAS) are essential systems that maintain and optimize energy efficiency, comfort, and safety of the modern-day building. The traditional control systems deployed to date have all suffered from programming and rule-based approaches that cannot tackle the complexities of a dynamic environment. In this context, fuzzy logic control (FLC) has been proposed as a more accommodating and versatile building automation management potential [46]. Fuzzy logic is a mathematical technique for dealing with vague and subjective information much the way humans do. FLC can be leveraged in several control functions we use most often for building automation, like HVAC and lighting (and also access management) [47]. Classical control methods require precise numerical inputs; however, FLC uses linguistic variables and fuzzy rules to incorporate the inherent uncertainty and subjectiveness in building operations. An instance of this is HVAC control—FLC alters the temperature, humidity and airflow in response to parameters such as occupancy level, ambient weather information, user preference, etc. [48]. Correct me if wrong: fuzzy rules that a simple state-machine would lack, such as "if the room is warm and occupancy high, then increase the cooling slightly." In this way, the system can react in a more dynamic and global response to what is occurring inside the building, with control strategies that may lead to energy-saving improvements and all-round comfort for an improved user experience. In addition to this, FLC can be used in conjunction with various other advanced control strategies like neural networks and genetic algorithms for developing hybrid systems that exploit a wider spectrum of advantages provided by different methods [49]. This can ultimately lead to increasingly intelligent and resilient building automation management that improves over time, becoming better able to optimize operations [50]. Some key advantages of FLC in building automation are as follows:

- *Higher energy efficiency*: FLC can optimize the systems of a building to use only what is necessary, which reduces carbon footprints and environmental impact [51].
- *Increased occupant comfort*: Fuzzy logic is good for dealing with messy problems and matters of opinion, which allows building systems to respond in a personalized way that can make the occupants more comfortable [52].
- *Greater flexibility within the system*: FLC is more able to accommodate changes in the environment and developments in our demands and less likely to require adjustment [53].
- *Lower maintenance costs*: Being adaptive enables pre-emptive issue identification and mitigation, which minimizes the incidence of expensive repairs and interventions [64].
- Remaining a key component of building automation management as buildings get more complex and talk to each other, the usage will only grow with fuzzy logic control—converting building operations into stronger efficient user transparency [55].

1.5 Organic Photovoltaic Glass

The OPV cell or organic solar cell is a type of solar cell in which the absorbing layer consists of organic semiconductors (OSCs), typically polymers or small molecules. For these organic materials to be utilized in organic electronics, they must be semiconducting, which requires a high level of conjugation that may be alternating single and double bonds [56]. The conjugation in the organic molecule causes the electrons associated with the double bonds to become delocalized across the entire conjugated length. These delocalized electrons possess higher energies compared to other electrons in the molecule and are analogous to valence electrons in inorganic semiconductor materials [57]. These electrons belong to the "highest occupied molecular orbital" (HOMO) in organic materials rather than a valence band. The exciton binding energy (Eb), which measures the attraction between an electron and a hole in inorganic semiconductors, is so low that at ambient temperature, thermal energy may overcome it (about 26 meV). This is because of a high dielectric constant, which reduces electron and hole attraction and facilitates exciton dissociation by offering substantial screening between them [58]. On the other hand, OSCs have low dielectric constants, leading to significant Eb values within the 0.3–0.5 eV region . Thus, thermal energy alone is not sufficient to promote exciton dissociation in OSCs. An OPV needs at least two distinct OSCs in order to get around this. Exciton dissociation at their interface is made possible by the offset energy levels between the two distinct OSCs, which are bigger than Eb [59].

Like inorganic semiconductors, there are greater unoccupied energy levels. The term "lowest unoccupied molecular orbital" (LUMO) refers to the first of these in organic materials. The band gap of a material is commonly defined as the energy gap that exists between the LUMO and HOMO [60]. The band gap shrinks to the point where visible light may excite an electron from the HOMO to the LUMO as conjugation increases. An OPV's goal is to produce energy from sunlight, much like other solar cell technologies. When the energy of the light is equal to or higher than the band gap, an electron is excited and absorbed from the HOMO to the LUMO [61]. A positively charged "hole" is left behind by the energized electron. The electron and hole are drawn to one another by their opposing charges, creating an electron–hole pair called "exciton." The exciton must be split apart, a procedure known as "exciton dissociation" in order to extract the charged particles from the solar cell [62]. The OSCs are categorized as either "donor" or "acceptor" (saying whether the electron has been provided or received by the substance) based on how the exciton dissociates. The donor in most OPVs generates the exciton on this substance because it absorbs most light. The exciton dissociates at the acceptor contact. The hole stays on the donor material while the electron is given to the acceptor material, which has deeper HOMO and LUMO levels [62].

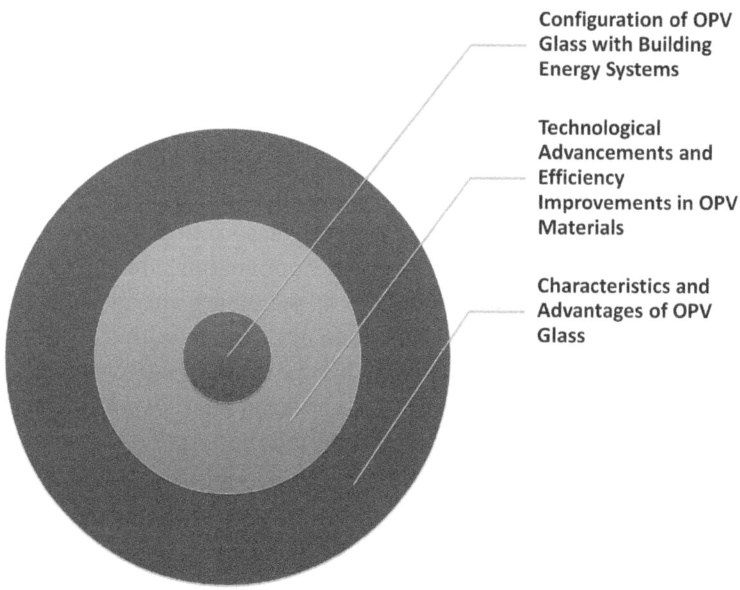

Figure 1.4 Landscapes of organic photovoltaic (OPV) glass.

1.5.1 Characteristics and Advantages of OPV Glass

Incident Light Absorption Resulting in Exciton Generation: An exciton is created when the OSC absorbs light that has enough energy to excite electrons from the HOMO to the LUMO. The electron travels to an energy level higher than the LUMO and then decays down if the energy of the absorbed light is greater than the band gap. This process, called "thermalization," is a major energy-loss mechanism in photovoltaics and includes energy loss as heat [23].

Exciton Dissociation across Interface: The hole stays on the donor material at the contact, whereas the electron travels to the acceptor material. A charge-transfer condition is created by these charge carriers who are still drawn to one another [63].

The attraction between them wanes as their distance grows. A charge-separated state emerges when thermal energy eventually surpasses the binding energy between them. Recombination can happen across the contact between the two materials while they are still in the charge-transfer stage [64].

Charge-Carrier Transportation: The charge carriers subsequently permeate through the pertinent interfacial layers to reach the proper electrodes (holes to the anode and electrons to the cathode) [36].

Exciton Diffusion at a Donor–Acceptor Interface: After forming, the exciton diffuses to the donor–acceptor interface via the OSC component, where exciton dissociation is driven by the offset between LUMO levels. Recombination, the process in which the excited electron returns to the empty energy state (the hole), cannot take place if this does not happen within a specific amount of time. The duration is known as the "exciton lifetime," which is commonly expressed as the estimated 10 nm distance; the exciton may spread during this period [65].

1.5.2 Technological Advancements and Efficiency Improvements in OPV Materials

Organic photovoltaics (OPVs) have a number of benefits, one of which is their solution-processability, which enables large-scale production using roll-to-roll processing techniques [53]. Two techniques exist for removing OSCs from a solution. In order to form a bilayer device structure with a tiny miscible mix, the donor and the acceptor are deposited individually. The desired bulk heterojunction is achieved by combining the donor and acceptor materials in a single solution, which is subsequently deposited using solution or vapor processing techniques [66]. Spin coating, a small-scale deposition technique that consistently yields homogeneous thin coatings over small areas, is frequently used in solution processing. OPVs may be used with a range of scalable deposition methods, including spray coating, inkjet coating, bar coating, blade coating, and slot die coating [61]. Depending on the deposition technique, a number of variables must be adjusted while treating materials with solutions, including volatility of solvents; wettability of the solvent on the selected substrate; OPVs' miscibility in the solvent; speed of deposition; concentration of solution; and treatments applied after deposit, such as air-blading or annealing [67].

1.5.3 Configuration of OPV Glass with Building Energy Systems

The transport layers that encircle the active layer can also be deposited using vacuum methods such as thermal evaporation and solution processing techniques. The materials being deposited and the other layers in the device determine the optimal procedure for each layer [68]. A current density–voltage curve is the most widely used technique for OPV characterization (JV curve). Short-circuit current density (JSC), open–circuit voltage (VOC), fill factor (FF), and power conversion efficiency (PCE), which is sometimes called "efficiency," are the primary variables that can be derived from a JV curve. It is common practice to model OPV JV behavior using the comparable circuit concept [62]. External quantum efficiency (EQE), stability tests, and evaluations of the active layer's absorbance and photoluminescence are other well-liked characterization techniques. Examining or at the very least discussing the stability of PV devices has grown in importance in recent years, particularly for newer solar cell technologies like OPVs. As a result, you should additionally do stability measures on your devices, such as recording the maximum power point, measuring stable current, or doing intermittent JV measurements over time [69].

1.6 Smart Infrastructure: Role of IoT, AI, and Renewable Energy in Smart Infrastructure

Smart cities utilize an array of technologies that combine automated administration of municipal operations and services with data-driven decision-making, made feasible by the Internet of Things technology. The term "Internet of Things," or "IoT," describes a group of technologies that gather and share data to assist in managing infrastructure, services, and operations. These Internet of Things technologies are an essential part of any smart city strategy [70]. With better matching municipal services to the requirements of the populace and integrating sustainable management techniques into city operations, smart city solutions may dramatically improve the quality of life for city dwellers. Novel transportation solutions are desperately needed as urban populations keep increasing and traffic congestion becomes a serious problem. IoT-powered intelligent mobility holds the potential to revolutionize urban transportation networks into smooth, effective, and sustainable systems [57]. This movement is transforming how people traverse urban areas and influencing the future of smart cities. The most disruptive forces in intelligent mobility inside smart cities will be connected and autonomous vehicles. Vehicles may now gather and exchange real-time data thanks to IoT-enabled sensors, cameras, and communication systems. Advanced functions like collision avoidance, adaptive cruise control, and improved route planning are made possible by this data sharing. Connected automated vehicles (CAVs) might lessen traffic jams, increase road safety, and improve fuel economy [71].

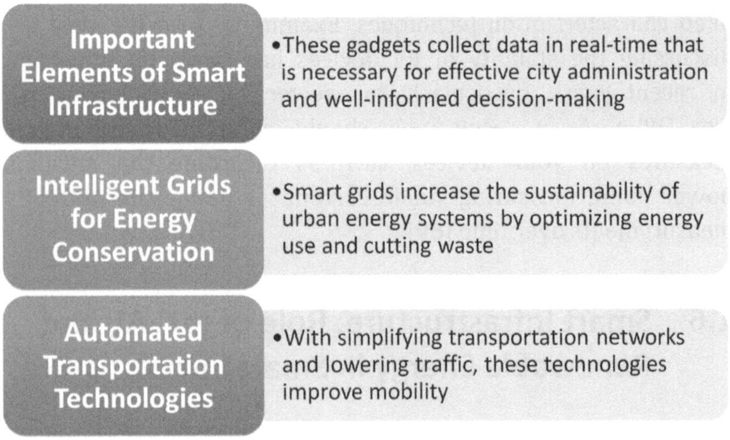

Figure 1.5 Major aspects of smart infrastructure.

IoT technologies are used by intelligent traffic management systems to optimize traffic flow and raise the effectiveness of city road networks. Data on traffic patterns, vehicle speeds, and parking availability are gathered via Internet of Things (IoT) sensors installed on roadways, traffic signals, and parking lots. This data is processed by real-time analytics and algorithms to improve parking spot distribution, reroute cars, and dynamically modify traffic signals [72]. These systems facilitate more efficient traffic flow, shorten travel times, and improve the quality of transportation in general. In order to create efficient and sustainable cities, smart infrastructure is essential. Cities may improve operations and lessen their environmental effect by deploying automated transportation systems, managing energy use through smart grids, and using real-time data from IoT devices [73].

1.7 Conclusion and Future Scope

The ubiquitous physical things that are being connected to the Internet to facilitate identification and communication with other devices are part of the rapidly developing Internet of Things (IoT). Because of the Internet of Things' potential to enhance the quality of life and create a plethora of new economic opportunities, there has been a great deal of interest in it. The engineering, logistics, transportation, and operational operations exhibit early benefits of the Internet of Things. The potential commercial effect of IoT was underlined by a recent McKinsey report, which projected that by 2025, the market for these technologies might increase by up to USD 11 trillion. The creation of novel hardware infrastructure utilizing affordable, low-energy, and maintenance-free power sources appropriate for workplaces, retail, and human well-being is a critical technological prerequisite for the growth of IoT.

Because photovoltaic (PV) technologies may provide minimal power and can be easily transported to smaller, grid-independent applications, they are particularly attractive as energy-harvesting systems for the Internet of Things. Consequently, there is a rising interest in utilizing OPV as a wearable, Internet of Things, and architectural energy source. This presents instances of how OPV technology may be used as an energy source and describes current developments in OPV materials and device design. This might lead to a wider adoption of low-power, low-maintenance, and environmentally friendly hardware solutions. The rise of smart infrastructure marks a paradigm shift in urban development, providing a preview of the cities of the future. Embracing technological innovations and promoting collaboration can build a future where cities prosper and residents flourish in future aspects.

References

1. Singh, B., Kaunert, C., and Vig, K. (2024). Reinventing Influence of Artificial Intelligence (AI) on Digital Consumer Lensing Transforming Consumer Recommendation Model: Exploring Stimulus Artificial Intelligence on Consumer Shopping Decisions. In T. Musiolik, R. Rodriguez, and H. Kannan (Eds.), *AI Impacts in Digital Consumer Behavior* (pp. 141–169). IGI Global. https://doi.org/10.4018/979-8-3693-1918-5.ch006
2. Ariffin, W. J. W., Shahfiq, S., Ibrahim, A., Pauzi, H. M., and Rami, A. A. M. (2023). Preservation of Craft Heritage and Its Potential in Youth Economic Empowerment. *Planning Malaysia, 21*.
3. Kim, E. (2023). Sustainable New Product Development for Ten Thousand Villages, a Fair-Trade Social Enterprise: Empowering Women and Economic Development through Problem-Based Service Learning. *Sustainability, 15*(8), 6452.
4. Singh, B., and Kaunert, C. (2024). Salvaging Responsible Consumption and Production of Food in the Hospitality Industry: Harnessing Machine Learning and Deep Learning for Zero Food Waste. In *Sustainable Disposal Methods of Food Wastes in Hospitality Operations* (pp. 176–192). IGI Global.
5. Bellver, D. F., Prados-Peña, M. B., García-López, A. M., and Molina-Moreno, V. (2023). Crafts as a key factor in local development: Bibliometric analysis. *Heliyon, 9*(1), e13039.
6. Dwiastuti, I. (2023). Promoting Women's Economic Empowerment in Achieving Rural Economic Development: Case Study in Lombok Island, Indonesia. In *Rural Development for Sustainable Social-ecological Systems: Putting Communities First* (pp. 77–102). Cham: Springer International Publishing.
7. Singh, B. (2024). Evolutionary Global Neuroscience for Cognition and Brain Health: Strengthening Innovation in Brain Science. In *Biomedical Research Developments for Improved Healthcare* (pp. 246–272). IGI Global.

8. Agarwal, V., Mathiyazhagan, K., Malhotra, S., and Pimpunchat, B. (2023). Building resilience for sustainability of MSMEs post COVID-19 outbreak: An Indian handicraft industry outlook. *Socio-Economic Planning Sciences, 85*, 101443.
9. Singh, B., and Kaunert, C. (2024). Revealing Green Finance Mobilization: Harnessing FinTech and Blockchain Innovations to Surmount Barriers and Foster New Investment Avenues. In *Harnessing Blockchain-Digital Twin Fusion for Sustainable Investments* (pp. 265–286). IGI Global.
10. Garg, N., and Singh, B. (2022). Sustainable Development-Adopting a Balanced Approach between Development and Development Induced Changes. *ECS Transactions, 107*(1), 15.
11. Gao, S., Yang, X., Long, H., Zhang, F., and Xin, Q. (2023). The Sustainable Rural Industrial Development under Entrepreneurship and Deep Learning from Digital Empowerment. *Sustainability, 15*(9), 7062.
12. Suriyani, A., Saleh, S., and Akhmad, A. (2023). Capacity Building Empowerment of Weaver Groups Through Weaving Business Innovation at the Ikat Jata Kapa Weaving Center in Sikka Regency, East Nusa Tenggara Province, Indonesia, Indonesia. *European Journal of Development Studies, 3*(2), 59–68.
13. Singh, B., and Kaunert, C. (2024). Harnessing Sustainable Agriculture Through Climate-Smart Technologies: Artificial Intelligence for Climate Preservation and Futuristic Trends. In *Exploring Ethical Dimensions of Environmental Sustainability and Use of AI* (pp. 214–239). IGI Global.
14. Shastri, A., and Singh, B. (2022). Demystifying Data Justice: Legal Response to India's Privacy and Security Standards: Challenges in Cloud Computing. *ECS Transactions, 107*(1), 179.
15. Singh, B. (2024). Featuring Consumer Choices of Consumable Products for Health Benefits: Evolving Issues from Tort and Product Liabilities. *Journal of Law of Torts and Consumer Protection Law, 7*(1).
16. Mushtaq, R., Qadiri, B., Lone, F. A., Raja, T. A., Singh, H., Ahmed, P., and Sharma, R. (2023). Role of Sericulture in Achieving Sustainable Development Goals. *Problemy Ekorozwoju, 18*(1).
17. Gök, H. S. (2023). Tourism as a Means of Empowering Women in Sustainable Development: The Case of Women's Cooperatives. In *Women's Empowerment Within the Tourism Industry* (pp. 91–101). IGI Global.

18. Singh, B. (2023). Unleashing Alternative Dispute Resolution (ADR) in Resolving Complex Legal-Technical Issues Arising in Cyberspace Lensing E-Commerce and Intellectual Property: Proliferation of E-Commerce Digital Economy. *Revista Brasileira de Alternative Dispute Resolution-Brazilian Journal of Alternative Dispute Resolution-RBADR, 5*(10), 81–105.
19. Abisuga, O. A., Mpofu, K., and Nenzhelele, T. G. (2023). Issues in innovation and development in the handicrafts industries of KwaZulu-Natal, South Africa. *Innovation and Development, 13*(1), 193–212.
20. Singh, B., and Kaunert, C. (2024). Integration of Cutting-Edge Technologies such as Internet of Things (IoT) and 5G in Health Monitoring Systems: A Comprehensive Legal Analysis and Futuristic Outcomes. *GLS Law Journal, 6*(1), 13–20.
21. Wanniarachchi, T., Dissanayake, D. G. K., and Downs, C. (2024). Community-based family enterprise and sustainable development in rural Sri Lanka. *Community, Work* and *Family, 27*(2), 135–153.
22. Samy, Y., Adedeji, A., Iraoya, A., Dutta, M. K., Fakmawii, J. L., and Hao, W. (2023). Trade and Women's Economic Empowerment: Qualitative Analysis of SMEs from Cambodia and Vietnam. In *Trade and Women's Economic Empowerment: Evidence from Small and Medium-Sized Enterprises* (pp. 59–103). Cham: Springer Nature Switzerland.
23. Singh, B. (2024). Green Infrastructure in Real Estate Landscapes: Pillars of Sustainable Development and Vision for Tomorrow. *National Journal of Real Estate Law, 7*(1), 4–8.
24. Joshi, G., and Dhar, R. L. (2023). Female workers' career success in the handicraft industry: a study of Uttarakhand, India. *Personnel Review, 52*(3), 745–759.
25. Singh, B. (2023). Tele-Health Monitoring Lensing Deep Neural Learning Structure: Ambient Patient Wellness via Wearable Devices for Real-Time Alerts and Interventions. *Indian Journal of Health and Medical Law, 6*(2), 12–16.
26. Faisal Syed Ahmad, S. M., Khairi, H., and Kamarudin, M. F. (2023). The Resilience of Malay Silver Craft Design: Sustaining Cultural Heritage and Promoting Sustainable Industrialization. *e-BANGI Journal, 20*(4).
27. Rodrigues, A. O. A., Marques, C. S., and Ramadani, V. (2023). Artisan entrepreneurship, resilience and sustainable development: the

quintuple helix innovation model in the low-density and cross-border territories. *Journal of Enterprise Information Management.*

28. Singh, B. (2024). Cherish Growth, Advancement and Tax Structure: Addressing Social and Economic Prospects. *Journal of Taxation and Regulatory Framework, 7*(1), 7–10.
29. Yadav, U. S., Tripathi, R., Tripathi, M. A., Kumar, A., and Mandal, M. (2023). Evaluation of Factors Affecting Entrepreneurship: A Case of Indian Women in the Handicraft Industry. *Humanities and Social Sciences Communications, 10*(1), 1–17.
30. Seyfi, S., Hall, C. M., and Vo-Thanh, T. (2023). The GENDERED EFFECTS of STATECRAFT on Women in Tourism: Economic Sanctions, Women's Disempowerment and Sustainability?. In *Gender and Tourism Sustainability* (pp. 285–302). Routledge.
31. Hendriyana, H., Sunarya, Y. Y., and Rahadian, F. (2023). Sustainable Design: Empowering Rural Craft-Preneurs Through Pandanus Natural Resources Optimization. *ISVS e-journal, 10*(9), 352–368.
32. Singh, B. (2024). Legal Dynamics Lensing Metaverse Crafted for Videogame Industry and E-Sports: Phenomenological Exploration Catalyst Complexity and Future. *Journal of Intellectual Property Rights Law, 7*(1), 8–14.
33. Frías, V., Jaramillo, C. L., and Palacios, V. (2023). ¡ No más! A Call for Designers to Stop Recolonizing Artisan Communities in Emerging Economies. *Dialectic, 5*(1), 110–135.
34. Das, K. K. (2024). Sustainable Livelihood through Skill Development among Rural Tribal Youths: A Review of Literature. *South Asian Journal of Social Studies and Economics, 21*(3), 180–193.
35. Singh, B. (2023). Blockchain Technology in Renovating Healthcare: Legal and Future Perspectives. In *Revolutionizing Healthcare Through Artificial Intelligence and Internet of Things Applications* (pp. 177–186). IGI Global.
36. Setyowati, A. D., Yusuf, A., Malik, A., and Wang, J. (2023). Community Empowerment Through Making Iboni Craft to Improve Community Welfare and The Economic Impact. *JPPM (Jurnal Pendidikan dan Pemberdayaan Masyarakat), 10*(1), 72–82.
37. Singh, B. (2023). Federated Learning for Envision Future Trajectory Smart Transport System for Climate Preservation and Smart Green Planet: Insights into Global Governance and SDG-9 (Industry, Innovation and Infrastructure). *National Journal of Environmental Law, 6*(2), 6–17.

38. Sharma, A., and Singh, B. (2022). Measuring Impact of E-commerce on Small Scale Business: A Systematic Review. *Journal of Corporate Governance and International Business Law, 5*(1).
39. Dhariwal, E. (2024). Advancing Women's Roles and Empowerment in Event Tourism in Rajasthan. In *Event Tourism and Sustainable Community Development* (pp. 103–111). Apple Academic Press.
40. Singh, B. (2022). Understanding Legal Frameworks Concerning Transgender Healthcare in the Age of Dynamism. *Electronic Journal of Social and Strategic Studies, 3*, 56–65.
41. Anil, K., Misra, A., and Bal, R. (2023). Amounee, A Case for Micro Entrepreneurship: Giving Voice to the Artisans of the Indian Handicrafts Industry. *The Case For Women*, 1–35.
42. Singh, B. (2023). Unleashing Alternative Dispute Resolution (ADR) in Resolving Complex Legal-Technical Issues Arising in Cyberspace Lensing E-Commerce and Intellectual Property: Proliferation of E-Commerce Digital Economy. *Revista Brasileira de Alternative Dispute Resolution-Brazilian Journal of Alternative Dispute Resolution-RBADR, 5*(10), 81–105.
43. Gamaethige, P. N. (2023). A Way Forward to the Global Market with Indigenous Values and Sustainability: A Case from Sri Lankan Indigenous Apparel Sector. *Sri Lanka Journal of Management Studies, 5*(2), 60–80.
44. Yadav, U. S., Aggarwal, R., Tripathi, R., and Kumar, A. (2024). Bridging the Skill Gap of Indian Handicraft Industry Workers: An Analysis of the Problems and Remedies for Handicraft Artisans. In *Contemporary Challenges in Social Science Management: Skills Gaps and Shortages in the Labour Market* (pp. 183–202). Emerald Publishing Limited.
45. Singh, B. (2024). Social Cognition of Incarcerated Women and Children: Addressing Exposure to Infectious Diseases and Legal Outcomes. In K. Reddy (Ed.), *Principles and Clinical Interventions in Social Cognition* (pp. 236–251). IGI Global. https://doi.org/10.4018/979-8-3693-1265-0.ch014
46. Bilal, A. R., Rosato, P., Campo, R., and Leopizzi, R. (2023). Women Empowerment and Entrepreneurial Intention: A Pathway to Achieve Sustainable Development Goal (SDG-5). *Corporate Social Responsibility and Environmental Management, 30*(3), 1389–1405.
47. Singh, B. (2020). Global Science and Jurisprudential Approach Concerning Healthcare and Illness. *Indian Journal of Health and Medical Law, 3*(1), 7–13.

48. Brogan, G. S., Dooley, K. E., Strong, R., and Kandi, L. P. (2023). How Does an Artisan Cooperative Impact Food Perception and Consumer Behaviors? A Rapid Rural Appraisal of Women in East Africa. *Foods, 12*(21), 3956.
49. Da Mulher, O. N. D. E., and Saudita, E. (2023). The Saudi Women's Empowerment Level and Sustainable Development in Light of Saudi's Vision 20301.
50. Singh, B. (2019). Profiling Public Healthcare: A Comparative Analysis Based on the Multidimensional Healthcare Management and Legal Approach. *Indian Journal of Health and Medical Law, 2*(2), 1–5.
51. Perez Cuso, M., Zhao, Y., Bakeer-Markar, A., Peiris, S., and Rajapakse, V. (2024). Strategy to Promote Inclusive and Sustainable Businesses to Achieve the Sustainable Development Goals in Sri Lanka: Background note. Retrieved from: https://hdl.handle.net/20.500.12870/6735.
52. Pavliuk, S. (2023). The Role of Creative Industries in Local Economic Development. *Ukrainian Black Sea Region Agrarian Science, 27*(1), 74–84.
53. Carlos, J. C. T., Bautista, M. J. D., and Gutierrez, E. L. M. (2023). Gendering the Informal Tourism Sector toward Inclusive and Sustainable Growth: The Case Study of Boracay Island (No. DP 2023-35). Philippine Institute for Development Studies.
54. Azni, U. S., Alfitri, A., and Pellizzoni, L. (2023). Model of Community Empowerment in Utilizing Purun (*Eleocharis dulcis*) Resources for Sustainable Handicrafts in Indonesia's Rural Peatland Communities. *Visions for Sustainability, 19*, 1–16.
55. Prados-Peña, M. B., Gálvez-Sánchez, F. J., Núñez-Cacho, P., and Molina-Moreno, V. (2024). Intention to Purchase Sustainable Craft Products: A Moderated Mediation Analysis of the Adoption of Sustainability in the Craft Sector. *Environment, Development and Sustainability, 26*(1), 775–797.
56. Yuridhista, R., Ariska, D., Xin, D., and Martin, W. (2023). Analysis of Development in the Creative Industry with the Existence of the Craft Sector in Pearl Jewelry in the City of Mataram. *Journal Markcount Finance, 1*(3), 182–195.
57. Zhanbayev, R. A., Irfan, M., Shutaleva, A. V., Maksimov, D. G., Abdykadyrkyzy, R., and Filiz, Ş. (2023). Demoethical Model of Sustainable Development Of Society: A Roadmap towards Digital Transformation. *Sustainability, 15*(16), 12478.

58. Hermawati, W., Ririh, K. R., Ariyani, L., Helmi, R. L., and Rosaira, I. (2023). Sustainable and Green Energy Development to Support Women's Empowerment in Rural Areas of Indonesia: Case of Micro-Hydro Power Implementation. *Energy for Sustainable Development, 73*, 218–231.

59. Azharunnisa, A., Gupta, S., and Panda, S. (2024). Craft Culture Revival through a Sustainable Approach of Integrating Tourism with Craft Promotion: Case Study of Puri, Odisha. *Journal of Cultural Heritage Management and Sustainable Development, 14*(3), 397–418.

60. Shahab, S., Nawab, H. U., and ul Mulk, J. (2024). Crafting Perspectives: Decline of Local Handicrafts in Chitral District, Khyber Pakhtunkhwa. *Pakistan Social Sciences Review, 8*(1), 01–16.

61. Neha, P., and Aravendan, M. (2023). A Review on Sustainable Product Design, Marketing Strategies and Conscious Consumption of Bamboo Lifestyle Products. *Intelligent Information Management, 15*(3), 67–99.

62. Brogan, G. S., and Dooley, K. E. (2024). Weaving Together Social Capital to Empower Women Artisan Entrepreneurs. *International Journal of Gender and Entrepreneurship, 16*(1), 69–88.

63. Dadheech, R., and Sharma, D. (2024). Skill Gaps in Casual Working by Women in the Indian Handicraft Sector. In *Contemporary Challenges in Social Science Management: Skills Gaps and Shortages in the Labour Market* (pp. 49–82). Emerald Publishing Limited.

64. Kalshetti, P., Patil, S., and Jadhav, B. (2024). Analysis of Govt Initiatives to Boost Handicraft Industry in India. *ShodhKosh Journal of Visual and Performing Arts, 5*(1), 299–314.

65. Edgar, S. (2024). Artisan Social Enterprises in Zambia: Women Leveraging Purpose to Scale Impact. *Social Enterprise Journal, 20*(2), 140–158.

66. Patnaik, S., and Isaacs, S. (2024, March). Tourism as a Catalyst for Supporting Sustainable SMME Development. In *International Conference on Tourism Research* (Vol. 7, No. 1, pp. 322–330).

67. Sushan, P. K. (2024). Unleashing the Potential Of Women Cooperative Societies: A Pathway To Empowerment. *Educational Administration: Theory and Practice, 30*(2), 379–382.

68. Parthiban, R., Sun, R., Qureshi, I., and Bandyopadhyay, S. (2024). Empowering Rural Micro-Entrepreneurs through Technoficing: A Process Model for Mobilizing and Developing Indigenous Knowledge. *The Journal of Strategic Information Systems, 33*(2), 101836.

69. Chinawat, S. (2024). Community Development Initiatives and Sustainable Tourism in Rural Thailand: A Case Study of Chiang Mai. *Journal of World Economy, 3*(1), 19–24.
70. Chen, Z., and Barcus, H. R. (2024). The Rise of Home-Returning Women's Entrepreneurship in China's Rural Development: Producing the Enterprising Self Through Empowerment, Cooperation, and Networking. *Journal of Rural Studies, 105*, 103156.
71. Sitorus, N. B., Liyushiana, L., and Khairi, N. (2024). Sustainable Tourism Management for Enhanced Tourism Product Quality in the Cultural Village of Dokan. *Jurnal Ilmiah Global Education, 5*(1), 27–36.
72. Sajida, M. T., and Paulet, E. (2024). Does Social Entrepreneurship Favor Inclusion Among People? A Conceptual Analysis in Emerging and Developing Economies. In *New Approaches to CSR, Sustainability and Accountability, Volume V* (pp. 275–292). Singapore: Springer Nature Singapore.
73. El-Kholei, A. O., Amer, A. S., and Yassein, G. A. (2024). Embedding Sustainable Development Goals in Architectural Education: A Case Study of Menoufia University 2023 graduation projects. *Archnet-IJAR: International Journal of Architectural Research*, https://doi.org/10.1108/ARCH-12-2023-0326.

Chapter 2

Renewable Energy Innovative Technologies and Intellectual Property Rights Smearing Fuzzy Logics for Sustainable Future in Smart and Sustainable Cities

Suruchi,[a] Hemant Kumar Sharma,[b] and Aditya Tomer[c]

[a]*Department of Chemistry, Ramjas College, University of Delhi, Delhi, India*
[b]*School of Law and Legal Studies, SDGI Global University, Ghaziabad, Uttar Pradesh, India*
[c]*School of Law, Galgotias University, Greater Noida, Uttar Pradesh, India*

dradityatomer@gmail.com, suruchi@ramjas.du.ac.in, hkslavanya1@gmail.com

Abstract

The urgency of fighting climate change and working for carbon neutrality has accelerated cutting-edge models in energy generation and urban sustainability around the world. This impetus to address climate change and shift demonstrated by cities towards a more sustainable, carbon-neutral future has catalyzed cities' willingness for solutions that deliver reduced emissions along with improving the quality of our urban media. This provides an amazing context

Fuzzy Logic in Revolutionizing Renewable Energy
Edited by Bhupinder Singh, Komal Vig, Ruchi Lal, and Budi Agus Riswandi

ISBN 978-981-5129-92-2 (Hardcover), 978-1-003-74191-6 (eBook)
www.jennystanford.com

DOI: 10.1201/9781003741916-2

for how smart cities can smear to draw down greenhouse gas use by working both wind and solar renewable agents with very low even zero marginal costs. Wind energy: Wind turbines produce clean electricity. Photovoltaic panels that capture solar power. With the introduction of these renewable technologies in cities, these have a tremendous opportunity to shift away from fossil fuels, cut carbon emissions and drive international carbon neutrality goals. This chapter underlines the call for diverse pathways concerning intellectual property rights (IPR) on renewable energy sources to build a sustainable and greener future.

Keywords: Carbon Neutrality, Wind-Solar Energy, Sustainability, Smart Cities, Fuzzy Logics

2.1 Introduction

Cities are looking for creative ways to reduce carbon emissions while enhancing the quality of life for their residents in response to growing concerns about climate change and environmental sustainability [1]. Wind and solar energy have become practical choices for reducing the negative environmental effects of traditional fossil fuels and guaranteeing a more sustainable, greener future [2]. To achieve the dual objectives of sustainability and carbon neutrality, renewable energy sources must be integrated into broader energy infrastructure and urban environments [3]. The way energy is produced, used and managed in cities may change as a result of the confluence of cutting-edge technology, renewable energy and the Internet of Things (Fuzzy Logics) [4]. This chapter examines the interplay between Fuzzy Logics-based technologies and wind-solar renewable energy, highlighting their importance in the creation of smart, sustainable communities with carbon neutrality as a primary objective [5]. Cities are poised to become beacons of sustainability, free from carbon emissions and with a higher quality of life because of Fuzzy Logics technology together with renewable energy sources such as wind or solar power. The bottom line is that a range of options using green renewable energy and advanced technology solutions are essential and will enable cleaner, greener, and environmentally friendly urban future and deal with challenges posed by the ongoing rapid worldwide urbanization leading to environmental degradation. This chapter discusses how smart cities can be made carbon neutral or sustainable by the utilization of renewable energy sources such as solar and wind combined with Fuzzy Logics. It evaluates the opportunities, constraints and prospects of this holistic approach with actual examples to demonstrate its viability.

The knowledge of the problems posed by increasing urbanization and climate change is the main driving force behind this chapter [6]. Over two-thirds of the world's population is predicted to live in cities by 2050 due to the exceptional rate of urban population growth [7]. Urbanization stresses infrastructure and energy resources tremendously even as it fosters technological advancement and economic growth [8]. It has been demonstrated that traditional energy sources, which mostly rely on fossil fuels, are unsustainable and harmful to the environment [9]. The paradigm has shifted in favor of renewable energy sources as a result [10]. Due to their enormous potential and small carbon footprint, solar and wind energy have emerged as leaders [11].

The clean and plentiful energy sources are provided by wind and solar energy, which harnesses the infinite power of the sun and wind [12]. The utilization of renewable energy sources has the potential to drastically reduce greenhouse gas emissions and reliance on limited fossil resources [13]. However, efficient integration and management are required to realize their full potential [14]. This is where the Internet of Things (Fuzzy Logics) enters the picture [15]. The Internet of Things (Fuzzy Logics) refers to a huge network of networked devices, sensors, and systems that gather and analyze data in real time [16]. Fuzzy Logics may be used to optimize energy production, distribution, and consumption in the context of renewable energy [17]. Fuzzy Logics can improve energy efficiency, minimize waste, and encourage sustainable energy practices through smart grids, smart buildings, and smart infrastructure [18].

The global perspective is dominated by environmental sustainability and carbon neutrality [19]. The pressing need to address climate change has driven a radical rethinking of our energy systems and urban development methods [20]. Reduced greenhouse gas emissions, transition to renewable energy sources, and construction of smart and sustainable cities have emerged as critical pillars in the drive for a greener and more sustainable future [21]. The confluence of wind and solar renewable energy technologies, along with the revolutionary possibilities of the Internet of Things (Fuzzy Logics) holds enormous promise for speeding up the transition to a more sustainable and carbon-neutral future [22]. As climate change worsens, the demand for clean, plentiful, and dependable energy sources grows [23, 24]. Wind and solar energy have emerged as critical components of the worldwide effort to mitigate climate change and reduce dependency on fossil fuels [25].

Wind energy uses wind power to generate electricity, whereas solar energy uses the sun's rays to generate clean power [26]. These renewable sources, which are frequently intermittent and weather-dependent, are further boosted by breakthrough technology and Fuzzy Logics applications [27]. The Internet of Things (Fuzzy Logics), a network of interconnected devices and sensors, provides real-time data collecting and analysis required to improve renewable energy generation, delivery, and consumption [28]. Cities have emerged as both the heart of the climate crisis and the nexus of potential solutions in the goal of carbon neutrality [29]. The world's population is rapidly urbanizing, necessitating the construction of smart and sustainable cities that are resource-efficient, resilient, and emit little greenhouse gases [30]. Achieving carbon neutrality for cities is not just an environmental but also a social and economic goal, because cities consume the majority of global energy and contribute significantly to carbon emissions [31]. Advanced technology, urban planning, and governance systems that promote energy efficiency, sustainable mobility, waste reduction, and green infrastructure are all part of smart and sustainable cities [32]. These cities use Fuzzy Logics to optimize resource allocation, improve public services, and improve quality of life [33].

2.1.1 Relevance of the Chapter

The urbanization of our planet is accompanied by a pressing problem—escalating carbon emissions and depletion of finite fossil fuel resources. Cities are the hubs of economic activity and innovation, but they are also major contributors to climate change [34]. Energy consumption in cities is a significant factor in carbon emissions, as well as inefficient resource use, traffic congestion, and the inadequate management of waste [35]. These issues pose a serious threat to both environmental sustainability and the quality of life in urban areas. By tapping into decentralized energy generation, these solutions enhance energy security, reduce environmental impact, and foster economic resilience within cities [36]. Complementing the renewable energy integration, the Internet of Things (Fuzzy Logics) emerges as the cornerstone of the smart city paradigm. Fuzzy Logics' transformative potential lies in its ability to interconnect an array of devices, sensors, and systems, infusing them with the power of real-time data collection, analysis, and automation [37]. In smart cities, Fuzzy Logics weaves a fabric of intelligence throughout the urban tapestry [38]. It optimizes energy use, enables efficient transportation systems, streamlines waste management, enhances environmental monitoring and contributes to the overall well-being of urban dwellers [39]. The dynamic nature of Fuzzy Logics solutions transcends mere data collection, empowering cities to actively manage and adapt their infrastructure in response to the ever-evolving demands of urban life [40-41].

The synergy between wind-solar renewable energy and Fuzzy Logics technologies paves the way for a multitude of benefits. It diminishes the adverse environmental impacts of urbanization by reducing air and water pollution, fostering improved air quality, and mitigating the urban heat island effect [42]. This holistic approach extends its benefits into the realm of economic prosperity by creating job opportunities, attracting investments and stimulating local industries that cater to renewable energy and Fuzzy Logics infrastructure [43]. Most importantly, the deployment of Fuzzy Logics-driven solutions enhances the day-to-day lives of city residents. Energy-efficient buildings, optimized transportation systems, intelligent waste management and real-time environmental monitoring all contribute to a higher quality of life [44]. However, as with any transformative endeavor, challenges accompany the journey towards smart and sustainable cities. Initial capital investment and the need for infrastructure development often stand as barriers. Successful implementation necessitates strong collaboration between the public and private sectors to bridge these financial gaps. Furthermore, privacy and security concerns regarding the collection and dissemination of sensitive data through Fuzzy Logics networks require vigilant attention and robust safeguards [45].

This chapter embarks on a journey to examine the integration of wind and solar renewable energy sources, synergistically combined with the power of the Internet of Things (Fuzzy Logics), to envision a greener, more sustainable future for smart cities [46–47]. The profound fusion of these elements, characterized by advanced technology, resource efficiency, and environmental consciousness, promises to redefine urban landscapes [48]. It also presents a collection of real-world case studies from cities around the world, each showcasing distinctive aspects of wind-solar renewable energy and Fuzzy Logics integration [49]. These case studies serve as practical demonstrations of the transformative potential, offering insights into the adaptability of these solutions to varying urban contexts [50].

2.2 Intellectual Property and Renewable Energy Integration: Smart Cities and Green Technologies

The usage of solar and wind energy in urban settings has significantly increased in recent years [51]. Both forms of energy provide sustainable substitutes for traditional fossil fuels that are clean and renewable. While solar energy employs photovoltaic panels to collect solar radiation, wind energy uses wind turbines to harness the strength of the wind to produce electricity [52–53]. So, the reduced greenhouse gas emissions, greater energy independence, and the potential for decentralized energy generation are the main advantages of these sources [54].

Green technologies and smart cities require the integration of renewable energy sources because they offer a flexible solution to the urgent problems of environmental stewardship and energy sustainability [55–56]. So, building a carbon-neutral and sustainable urban future necessitates the incorporation of renewable energy [57]. It increases the environmental sustainability and resilience of smart cities while also lowering energy expenses [58–59]. The use of renewable energy sources is consistent with the worldwide effort to combat climate change and encourages the development of technologically advanced and environmentally conscious urban environments [60–61]. The seamless integration of renewable energy with green technology and smart cities is a pillar of urban innovation and an important step toward a cleaner, more sustainable urban future [62].

The assimilation of wind and solar renewable energy, along with the implementation of Fuzzy Logics technologies, offers a multi-faceted solution to address these problems [63–64]. The clean, renewable energy sources like solar and wind power can significantly reduce our reliance on fossil fuels [65–66]. On the other side, cities can monitor, regulate, and optimize several aspects of urban life, including garbage management and environmental quality, energy consumption and transportation [67]. This is made possible by the Internet of Things. With integrating these technologies, cities may reduce carbon emissions, allocate resources more effectively, boost energy efficiency, and eventually achieve carbon neutrality while creating smarter, more sustainable urban environments. The foundation for a greener, more sustainable future for cities and the planet is laid by this all-encompassing plan [68].

2.3 Internet of Things (Fuzzy Logics) in Smart Cities for Reducing Carbon Footprints

Smart cities employ Fuzzy Logics to enhance trash management, transportation, energy use, and other aspects of urban living [69]. Cities may be able to monitor, manage, and improve their infrastructure and services more effectively with the use of Fuzzy Logics-powered technologies [70]. The Internet of Things is starting to disrupt the development of smart cities by offering new ways to reduce carbon emissions and create environmentally friendly urban environments [71]. The term "Internet of Things" (Fuzzy Logics) describes the vast network of linked systems, sensors, and gadgets that gather and exchange data instantly [72]. This technology offers thorough monitoring, control, and optimization of many urban living issues, such as waste management, energy consumption, and transportation, within the framework of smart cities [73].

The efficient management of energy resources is one way that Fuzzy Logics helps reduce the carbon footprint in smart cities [74]. Cities may identify inefficiencies and put energy-saving measures into place by using Fuzzy Logics devices to detect patterns in energy consumption [75]. For instance, intelligent lighting may save a lot of energy by adjusting its brightness in reaction to the flow of traffic and the weather [76]. Fuzzy Logics facilitates a more seamless shift to greener energy options by enhancing grid management and enabling the integration of renewable energy sources [77]. The other crucial sector where Fuzzy Logics may have a significant influence is transportation. Fuzzy Logics-enabled traffic management systems are used in smart cities to minimize congestion, improve public transit routes and promote the usage of electric and shared mobility choices [78]. Fuzzy Logics reduces emissions and lowers the carbon footprint associated with urban commuting by reducing traffic congestion and enhancing the efficiency of transportation networks [79]. Fuzzy Logics is also important in garbage management and recycling activities inside smart cities. Smart garbage bins with sensors may notify waste management services when they are approaching capacity, resulting in more efficient collection routes and lower fuel use and emissions [80]. Fuzzy Logics-enabled tracking systems boost recycling practices by monitoring the quality and amount of recyclable items, helping to lower carbon footprints by reducing landfill waste and resource usage [81].

2.4 Wind and Solar Energy as Renewable Energy and Innovative Technologies: Internet of Things (Fuzzy Logics) for Green and Sustainable Future

Wind and solar energy are two critical pillars of renewable energy, providing sustainable alternatives to traditional fossil fuels [49].

These renewable energy sources employ the power of the sun and wind to create electricity without emitting greenhouse gases. Wind turbines harness the kinetic energy of moving air masses, whereas solar panels transform sunlight into electricity [82]. Their eco-friendliness makes them key components in the goal of a green and sustainable future, where climate change mitigation and carbon emission reduction are top priorities [83]. The creative integration of Internet of Things (Fuzzy Logics) technology into wind and solar energy systems has transformed their efficiency and dependability. Sensors and smart meters, for example, play an important role in improving energy production and delivery [84]. They give real-time data on energy generation, consumption, and environmental variables, enabling precise modifications to maximize the use of these intermittent energy sources. The Internet of Things also enables predictive maintenance, which may minimize downtime and improve the overall dependability of wind and solar facilities [85].

The integration of wind and solar energy with Fuzzy Logics technology helps to achieve more robust and ecologically responsible energy systems in the context of a green and sustainable future [86]. Fuzzy Logics' data-driven approach offers improved grid management, assisting in matching supply with demand while decreasing energy waste. Collaboration between wind and solar energy and Fuzzy Logics lays the foundation for a cleaner, more sustainable energy landscape by increasing the reliability of renewable energy sources, lowering operating costs, and supporting sustainable energy behaviors [87]. This collaboration is a key step toward a cleaner future that is less reliant on fossil fuels and more focused on environmental management [88]. Advanced data analytics tools, including machine learning and artificial intelligence, are used to make sense of this data, optimizing energy use, improving traffic flow, and enhancing public services [89]. These technical aspects underscore the complexity and sophistication of the systems at play in smart and sustainable cities. By ensuring that the technology and engineering behind wind and solar energy integration and Fuzzy Logics applications are robust, efficient, and reliable, it paves the way for greener, more resilient urban environments that contribute to a sustainable future [90].

2.4.1 Environmental Benefits: Adoption of Wind-Solar Energy in Smart Cities Inclined toward Green Technologies

The adoption of wind-solar energy reduces air and water pollution, leading to improved air quality and a healthier urban environment. It mitigates the urban heat island effect and conserves green spaces. The adoption of wind and solar energy in smart cities, aligned with green technologies, yields a multitude of significant environmental benefits [91]. Firstly, both wind and solar energy sources are inherently clean, producing electricity without emitting harmful greenhouse gases, which is essential for mitigating the effects of climate change. This shift towards renewable energy reduces the reliance on fossil fuels, lessening air pollution and improving urban air quality, thereby enhancing the overall health and well-being of city inhabitants [92].

Also, wind and solar energy systems have a minimal land footprint compared to traditional power plants, thus promoting efficient land use and preserving natural habitats [93]. These renewable sources operate silently, reducing noise pollution in urban areas [77]. In combination with advanced green technologies, such as energy-efficient building designs and smart grids, cities can significantly lower their overall carbon footprint, making strides toward a more sustainable and eco-friendly urban landscape. This holistic approach not only promotes a greener urban environment but also sets the stage for environmentally conscious and sustainable urban living that ensures a healthier planet for current and future generations [94].

2.5 Fuzzy Logics in Smart Cities for Ensuring Green and Sustainable Future: Projecting Carbon Neutrality

The use of the Internet of Things (Fuzzy Logics) in smart cities is a critical step toward assuring a green and sustainable future while actively pursuing carbon neutrality. Fuzzy Logics technologies, which are distinguished by a massive network of interconnected devices, sensors, and systems, enable real-time data gathering and analysis in numerous facets of urban life [95]. In the context of smart cities, the integration of Fuzzy Logics technologies is critical for optimizing resource allocation, boosting energy efficiency, and improving overall urban living quality [96]. The key way in which Fuzzy Logics helps smart cities realize a green and sustainable future is by enabling effective energy management. Fuzzy Logics sensors and smart meters are used to monitor and regulate energy consumption trends, enabling data-driven insights into power distribution optimization, grid management, and renewable energy integration [97]. As a result, there is less energy waste, less greenhouse gas emissions, and a more sustainable energy infrastructure. Cities may optimize the use of renewable energy while reducing their dependency on fossil fuels by constructing smart networks and microgrids that can manage electricity supply and demand [98].

Fuzzy Logics technologies have a significant impact on mobility inside smart cities. Fuzzy Logics-enabled smart traffic management systems monitor real-time traffic conditions and enable intelligent route planning [99]. This reduces traffic congestion and idle periods and optimizes public transit, resulting in more energy-efficient and ecologically responsible commuting. Fuzzy Logics encourages the use of electric cars and shared mobility solutions, which reduces carbon emissions and improves the sustainability of urban transportation [100]. In the pursuit of carbon neutrality, waste management and recycling practices within smart cities also receive a substantial boost from Fuzzy Logics applications. Smart waste bins equipped with sensors can signal waste management services when they are nearing full capacity, optimizing waste collection routes and reducing unnecessary fuel consumption [101]. Fuzzy Logics-enabled waste tracking systems improve recycling practices by monitoring the quality and quantity of recyclable materials [102, 103]. By reducing landfill waste and encouraging responsible waste disposal, these Fuzzy Logics solutions significantly contribute to carbon neutrality goals. Fuzzy Logics technologies in smart cities serve as a linchpin for addressing carbon neutrality and promoting a green and sustainable future [104]. With leveraging real-time data and advanced technologies, cities can make data-informed decisions to enhance energy efficiency, optimize transportation systems, and improve waste management practices [105, 106].

2.6 Benefits and Challenges: Assimilation of Wind-Solar Renewable Energy Coupled with Fuzzy Logics Technologies for Sustainable Future

Wind and solar renewable energy integration, along with modern Internet of Things technologies, holds the promise of a sustainable and ecologically responsible future, but it also poses a complicated combination of advantages and problems [107, 108]. These technologies provide several benefits for moving to a green and sustainable energy landscape [109, 110]. Wind and solar energy are fundamentally clean and renewable, lowering greenhouse gas emissions and air pollution while increasing energy security and decreasing dependency on fossil fuels [111, 112]. The incorporation of these renewable energy sources with Fuzzy Logics technology improves their efficiency by allowing for real-time monitoring and data-driven decision-making. As a consequence, energy output is maximized, waste is decreased, and energy supply is more dependable, which is critical for establishing a robust and sustainable energy infrastructure [113, 114].

However, in addition to these advantages, there are significant hurdles in the integration of wind-solar renewable energy and Fuzzy Logics technology. The most significant issue is the intermittent and unpredictable nature of renewable energy sources [115, 116]. Wind and solar energy generation are weather dependent; thus reliable energy storage technologies and grid management systems are required to provide a consistent electricity supply. Energy storage technologies, such as advanced batteries, play a critical role in bridging the gap between energy generation and consumption, but their scalability and cost-effectiveness need continuous improvement [117, 118]. The vast amount of data collected by Fuzzy Logics sensors requires robust cybersecurity measures to protect against potential breaches and ensure the privacy of citizens [119]. Cities and communities must navigate complex regulatory and ethical considerations in managing this data, striking a balance between reaping the benefits of data analytics and safeguarding individual rights [120, 121]. The transition to renewable energy and Fuzzy Logics technologies requires substantial investments in infrastructure, research and development, and policy development. The high initial costs of implementing these technologies can be a hurdle for some regions and cities, although the long-term economic and environmental benefits are often significant [122, 123].

2.7 Conclusion and Future Scope

Wind-solar renewable energy combined with Fuzzy Logics technology has enormous promise for tackling climate change, lowering carbon emissions, and improving urban sustainability. To achieve carbon neutrality in smart cities, a multifaceted strategy that uses clean energy sources and modern technology to build a green and sustainable future is required. This assimilation with Fuzzy Logics technologies in the context of smart and sustainable cities marks a critical step toward tackling climate change and constructing a green, resilient, and sustainable future. These technologies have enormous potential for lowering carbon emissions, improving energy efficiency, and improving urban living conditions. Cleaner energy sources, lower energy waste, and better-informed decision-making processes are all advantages of this integration, leading to a healthier and more ecologically responsible urban landscape. Nevertheless, challenges exist, such as intermittency, data security, and initial investment costs. Overcoming these obstacles requires coordinated efforts from governments, industry players, and local communities. Policymakers should enact supportive regulations and incentives to promote renewable energy adoption and Fuzzy Logics integration. Meanwhile, the private sector and research institutions must continue to innovate, improving energy storage solutions, data security protocols, and the scalability of Fuzzy Logics infrastructure.

The future scope of this integration is undeniably vast. As technology continues to advance, it can anticipate even more efficient and cost-effective renewable energy systems and Fuzzy

Logics applications. Enhanced energy storage solutions will alleviate the intermittency issues associated with wind and solar power, while machine learning and artificial intelligence will offer increasingly sophisticated data analytics capabilities. Smart cities will become more interconnected and data-driven, fostering even more sustainable and environmentally conscious urban environments. The global transition towards a green and sustainable future depends on the dissemination of best practices and knowledge sharing. Cities, communities, and nations worldwide can learn from successful case studies and collaborative efforts, adapting and implementing these technologies to suit their unique needs and challenges. As the global commitment to addressing climate change intensifies, the assimilation of wind-solar renewable energy and Fuzzy Logics technologies will play an increasingly pivotal role in our collective efforts to build a cleaner, greener, and more sustainable world for generations to come. It represents not just a vision for the future but a roadmap to a more sustainable and environmentally responsible way of living. This chapter recommends that cities and policymakers prioritize investments in wind-solar renewable energy and Fuzzy Logics technologies. Collaboration between the public and private sectors should be encouraged to facilitate the development of smart, sustainable cities. Future research should explore the scalability and economic viability of these projects in diverse urban contexts. Additionally, further investigations are needed into data privacy and security concerns associated with Fuzzy Logics applications in smart cities.

References

1. Sinha, M., Chacko, E., Makhija, P., and Pramanik, S. (2021). Energy-efficient smart cities with green Internet of Things. *Green Technological Innovation for Sustainable Smart Societies: Post Pandemic Era*, 345–361.
2. Salam, A., and Salam, A. (2020). Internet of things in sustainable energy systems. *Internet of Things for Sustainable Community Development: Wireless Communications, Sensing, and Systems*, 183–216.

3. Bibri, S. E. (2018). The Fuzzy Logics for smart sustainable cities of the future: An analytical framework for sensor-based big data applications for environmental sustainability. *Sustainable cities and society, 38*, 230–253.
4. Varjovi, A. E., and Babaie, S. (2020). Green Internet of Things (GFuzzy Logics): Vision, applications and research challenges. *Sustainable Computing: Informatics and Systems, 28*, 100448.
5. Ahmad, T., and Zhang, D. (2021). Using the Internet of Things in smart energy systems and networks. *Sustainable Cities and Society, 68*, 102783.
6. Bibri, S. E., and Krogstie, J. (2020). Environmentally data-driven smart sustainable cities: Applied innovative solutions for energy efficiency, pollution reduction, and urban metabolism. *Energy Informatics, 3*, 1–59.
7. Albreem, M. A., Sheikh, A. M., Alsharif, M. H., Jusoh, M., and Yasin, M. N. M. (2021). Green Internet of Things (GFuzzy Logics): applications, practices, awareness, and challenges. *IEEE Access, 9*, 38833–38858.
8. Issa Zadeh, S. B., Esteban Perez, M. D., López-Gutiérrez, J. S., and Fernández-Sánchez, G. (2023). Optimizing smart energy infrastructure in smart ports: A systematic scoping review of carbon footprint reduction. *Journal of Marine Science and Engineering, 11*(10), 1921.
9. Cantarero, M. M. V. (2020). Of renewable energy, energy democracy, and sustainable development: A roadmap to accelerate the energy transition in developing countries. *Energy Research and Social Science, 70*, 101716.
10. Sodiq, A., Baloch, A. A., Khan, S. A., Sezer, N., Mahmoud, S., Jama, M., and Abdelaal, A. (2019). Towards modern sustainable cities: Review of sustainability principles and trends. *Journal of Cleaner Production, 227*, 972–1001.
11. Clark II, W., and Cooke, G. (2016). *Smart green cities: toward a carbon neutral world*. Routledge.
12. Tiwari, S., Rosak-Szyrocka, J., and Żywiołek, J. (2022). Internet of things as a sustainable energy management solution at tourism destinations in India. *Energies, 15*(7), 2433.
13. Li, D., Guan, X., Tang, T., Zhao, L., Tong, W., and Wang, Z. (2023). The clean energy development path and sustainable development of the ecological environment driven by big data for mining projects. *Journal of Environmental Management, 348*, 119426.

14. Elavarasan, R. M., Pugazhendhi, R., Jamal, T., Dyduch, J., Arif, M. T., Kumar, N. M., ... and Nadarajah, M. (2021). Envisioning the UN Sustainable Development Goals (SDGs) through the lens of energy sustainability (SDG 7) in the post-COVID-19 world. *Applied Energy, 292*, 116665.
15. Ahmed, F., Naeem, M., and Iqbal, M. (2017). ICT and renewable energy: a way forward to the next generation telecom base stations. *Telecommunication Systems, 64*, 43–56.
16. Silva, B. V., Holm-Nielsen, J. B., Sadrizadeh, S., Teles, M. P., Kiani-Moghaddam, M., and Arabkoohsar, A. (2023). Sustainable, green, or smart? Pathways for energy-efficient healthcare buildings. *Sustainable Cities and Society, 100*, 105013.
17. Cortese, T. T. P., Almeida, J. F. S. D., Batista, G. Q., Storopoli, J. E., Liu, A., and Yigitcanlar, T. (2022). Understanding sustainable energy in the context of smart cities: a PRISMA review. *Energies, 15*(7), 2382.
18. Thornbush, M. J., and Golubchikov, O. (2019). *Sustainable Urbanism in Digital Transitions: From Low Carbon to Smart Sustainable Cities.* Springer.
19. Zhukovskiy, Y. L., Batueva, D. E., Buldysko, A. D., Gil, B., and Starshaia, V. V. (2021). Fossil energy in the framework of sustainable development: Analysis of prospects and development of forecast scenarios. *Energies, 14*(17), 5268.
20. Jayachandran, M., Gatla, R. K., Rao, K. P., Rao, G. S., Mohammed, S., Milyani, A. H., ... and Geetha, S. (2022). Challenges in achieving sustainable development goal 7: Affordable and clean energy in light of nascent technologies. *Sustainable Energy Technologies and Assessments, 53*, 102692.
21. Tuysuz, M. F., and Trestian, R. (2020). From serendipity to sustainable green Fuzzy Logics: Technical, industrial and political perspective. *Computer Networks, 182*, 107469.
22. Yenugula, M., Sahoo, S., and Goswami, S. (2024). Cloud computing for sustainable development: An analysis of environmental, economic and social benefits. *Journal of future sustainability, 4*(1), 59–66.
23. Jain, A., Sharma, A., Jately, V., and Azzopardi, B. (Eds.). (2023). *Sustainable Energy Solutions with Artificial Intelligence, Blockchain Technology, and Internet of Things.* CRC Press.
24. Pandey, V., Sircar, A., Bist, N., Solanki, K., and Yadav, K. (2023). Accelerating the renewable energy sector through Industry 4.0: Optimization opportunities in the digital revolution. *International Journal of Innovation Studies, 7*(2), 171–188.

25. Bhattacharjee, S., and Nandi, C. (2019). Implementation of industrial Internet of Things in the renewable energy sector. *The Internet of Things in the Industrial Sector: Security and Device Connectivity, Smart Environments, and Industry 4.0*, 223–259.
26. Issa Zadeh, S. B., López Gutiérrez, J. S., Esteban, M. D., Fernández-Sánchez, G., and Garay-Rondero, C. L. (2023). Scope of the literature on efforts to reduce the carbon footprint of seaports. *Sustainability, 15*(11), 8558.
27. Pakulska, T. (2021). Green energy in central and eastern European (CEE) countries: New challenges on the path to sustainable development. *Energies, 14*(4), 884.
28. Hannan, M. A., Al-Shetwi, A. Q., Ker, P. J., Begum, R. A., Mansor, M., Rahman, S. A., ... and Muttaqi, K. M. (2021). Impact of renewable energy utilization and artificial intelligence in achieving sustainable development goals. *Energy Reports, 7*, 5359–5373.
29. Guchhait, R., and Sarkar, B. (2023). Increasing growth of renewable energy: A state of art. *Energies, 16*(6), 2665.
30. Moemen, Y. S., Alshater, H., and El-Sayed, I. E. T. (2023). Clean energy management based on Internet of Things and sensor networks for climate change problems. In *The Power of Data: Driving Climate Change with Data Science and Artificial Intelligence Innovations* (pp. 117–136). Cham: Springer Nature Switzerland.
31. Saheb, T., Dehghani, M., and Saheb, T. (2022). Artificial intelligence for sustainable energy: A contextual topic modeling and content analysis. *Sustainable Computing: Informatics and Systems, 35*, 100699.
32. Nazir, T., and Banday, M. T. (2018, October). Green Internet of Things: A survey of enabling techniques. In *2018 International Conference on Automation and Computational Engineering (ICACE)* (pp. 197–202). IEEE.
33. Hassan, Q., Sameen, A. Z., Olapade, O., Alghoul, M., Salman, H. M., and Jaszczur, M. (2023). Hydrogen fuel as an important element of the energy storage needs for future smart cities. *International Journal of Hydrogen Energy, 48*(78), 30247–30262.
34. Moroke, N. D., and Makatjane, K. (2022). Predictive modelling for financial fraud detection using data analytics: A gradient-boosting decision tree. In *Applications of Machine Learning and Deep Learning for Privacy and Cybersecurity* (pp. 25–45). IGI Global.
35. Makatjane, K., Moroke, N., and Ncube, B. (2021). *Detecting financial fraud in South Africa: A Comparison Of Logistic Model Tree and Gradient Boosting Decision Tree.* Academic Press.

36. Makatjane, K. (2022). Deep learning for sentiment analysis to predict the probability of bank loan default. *American Journal of Data Mining and Knowledge Discovery, 7*(2), 5–12.

37. Kasinathan, P., Pugazhendhi, R., Elavarasan, R. M., Ramachandaramurthy, V. K., Ramanathan, V., Subramanian, S., and Alsharif, M. H. (2022). Realization of sustainable development goals with disruptive technologies by integrating Industry 5.0, Society 5.0, smart cities and villages. *Sustainability, 14*(22), 15258.

38. Elrahmani, A., Hannun, J., Eljack, F., and Kazi, M. K. (2021). Status of renewable energy in the GCC region and future opportunities. *Current Opinion in Chemical Engineering, 31*, 100664.

39. Li, W., Lu, C., and Zhang, Y. W. (2019). Prospective exploration of future renewable portfolio standard schemes in China via a multi-sector CGE model. *Energy Policy, 128*, 45–56.

40. ElFar, O. A., Chang, C. K., Leong, H. Y., Peter, A. P., Chew, K. W., and Show, P. L. (2021). Prospects of Industry 5.0 in algae: Customization of production and new advance technology for clean bioenergy generation. *Energy Conversion and Management: X, 10*, 100048.

41. Singh, B. (2023). Tele-health monitoring lensing deep neural learning structure: Ambient patient wellness via wearable devices for real-time alerts and interventions. *Indian Journal of Health and Medical Law, 6*(2), 12–16.

42. Eljack, F., and Kazi, M. K. (2021). Prospects and challenges of green hydrogen economy via multi-sector global symbiosis in Qatar. *Frontiers in Sustainability, 1*, 612762.

43. Bogdanov, D., Ram, M., Aghahosseini, A., Gulagi, A., Oyewo, A. S., Child, M., and Breyer, C. (2021). Low-cost renewable electricity as the key driver of the global energy transition towards sustainability. *Energy, 227*, 120467.

44. Dent, C. M. (2012). Renewable energy and East Asia's new developmentalism: towards a low carbon future?. *The Pacific Review, 25*(5), 561–587.

45. Devabhaktuni, V., Alam, M., Depuru, S. S. S. R., Green II, R. C., Nims, D., and Near, C. (2013). Solar energy: Trends and enabling technologies. *Renewable and Sustainable Energy Reviews, 19*, 555–564.

46. Singh, B. (2024). Legal dynamics lensing metaverse crafted for videogame industry and e-sports: Phenomenological exploration catalyst complexity and future. *Journal of Intellectual Property Rights Law, 7*(1), 8–14.

47. Arent, D. J., Green, P., Abdullah, Z., Barnes, T., Bauer, S., Bernstein, A., and Turchi, C. (2022). Challenges and opportunities in decarbonizing the US energy system. *Renewable and Sustainable Energy Reviews, 169*, 112939.

48. Doost Mohammadian, H., and Rezaie, F. (2020). Blue-green smart mobility technologies as readiness for facing tomorrow's urban shock toward the world as a better place for living (Case studies: Songdo and Copenhagen). *Technologies, 8*(3), 39.

49. Singh, B. (2023). Federated learning for envision future trajectory smart transport system for climate preservation and smart green planet: Insights into global governance and SDG-9 (Industry, Innovation and Infrastructure). *National Journal of Environmental Law, 6*(2), 6–17.

50. Abualigah, L., Zitar, R. A., Almotairi, K. H., Hussein, A. M., Abd Elaziz, M., Nikoo, M. R., and Gandomi, A. H. (2022). Wind, solar, and photovoltaic renewable energy systems with and without energy storage optimization: A survey of advanced machine learning and deep learning techniques. *Energies, 15*(2), 578.

51. Tabor, D. P., Roch, L. M., Saikin, S. K., Kreisbeck, C., Sheberla, D., Montoya, J. H., ... and Aspuru-Guzik, A. (2018). Accelerating the discovery of materials for clean energy in the era of smart automation. *Nature Reviews Materials, 3*(5), 5–20.

52. Szeliski, R. (2022). *Computer Vision: Algorithms and Applications.* Springer Nature.

53. Rao, S., Katoch, S., Narayanaswamy, V., Muniraju, G., Tepedelenlioglu, C., and Spanias, A. (2022). *Machine Learning for Solar Array Monitoring, Optimization, and Control.* Springer Nature.

54. Saini, G., Kannan, R., Benini, E., and Kumar, K. (Eds.). (2023). *Enabling Methodologies for Renewable and Sustainable Energy.* CRC Press.

55. Tomar, A., Malik, H., Kumr, P., and Iqbal, A. (2022, September). Machine learning, advances in computing, renewable energy and communication (MARC). In *Proceedings of 3rd International Conference on Machine Learning, Advances in Computing, Renewable Energy and Communication: MARC 2021* (pp. 1–19). Singapore: Springer Nature Singapore.

56. Del Ser, J., Casillas-Perez, D., Cornejo-Bueno, L., Prieto-Godino, L., Sanz-Justo, J., Casanova-Mateo, C., and Salcedo-Sanz, S. (2022). Randomization-based machine learning in renewable energy prediction problems: critical literature review, new results and perspectives. *Applied Soft Computing, 118*, 108526.

57. Singh, B. (2023). Unleashing alternative dispute resolution (ADR) in resolving complex legal-technical issues arising in cyberspace lensing e-commerce and intellectual property: Proliferation of e-commerce digital economy. *Revista Brasileira de Alternative Dispute Resolution-Brazilian Journal of Alternative Dispute Resolution-RBADR, 5*(10), 81–105.
58. Singh, B., and Kaunert, C. (2024). Integration of cutting-edge technologies such as Internet of Things (Fuzzy Logics) and 5G in health monitoring systems: A comprehensive legal analysis and futuristic outcomes. *GLS Law Journal, 6*(1), 13–20
59. Ahmad, T., Madonski, R., Zhang, D., Huang, C., and Mujeeb, A. (2022). Data-driven probabilistic machine learning in sustainable smart energy/smart energy systems: Key developments, challenges, and future research opportunities in the context of smart grid paradigm. *Renewable and Sustainable Energy Reviews, 160,* 112128.
60. Aslam, S., Herodotou, H., Mohsin, S. M., Javaid, N., Ashraf, N., and Aslam, S. (2021). A survey on deep learning methods for power load and renewable energy forecasting in smart microgrids. *Renewable and Sustainable Energy Reviews, 144,* 110992.
61. Watson, R. (2022). The virtual economy of the metaverse: Computer vision and deep learning algorithms, customer engagement tools, and behavioral predictive analytics. *Linguistic and Philosophical Investigations, 21,* 41–56.
62. Cruz-Rojas, T., Franco, J. A., Hernandez-Escobedo, Q., Ruiz-Robles, D., and Juarez-Lopez, J. M. (2023). A novel comparison of image semantic segmentation techniques for detecting dust in photovoltaic panels using machine learning and deep learning. *Renewable Energy, 217,* 119126.
63. Ozcanli, A. K., Yaprakdal, F., and Baysal, M. (2020). Deep learning methods and applications for electrical power systems: A comprehensive review. *International Journal of Energy Research, 44*(9), 7136–7157.
64. Sharma, A., and Singh, B. (2022). Measuring impact of e-commerce on small scale business: A systematic review. *Journal of Corporate Governance and International Business Law, 5*(1).
65. Rosiello, A., and Maleki, A. (2021). A dynamic multi-sector analysis of technological catch-up: The impact of technology cycle times, knowledge base complexity and variety. *Research Policy, 50*(3), 104194.

66. Fischer, C., and Preonas, L. (2010). Combining policies for renewable energy: Is the whole less than the sum of its parts?. *Resource for the Future Discussion Paper* (10–19).

67. Grubb, M., Drummond, P., Poncia, A., McDowall, W., Popp, D., Samadi, S., and Pavan, G. (2021). Induced innovation in energy technologies and systems: A review of evidence and potential implications for CO_2 mitigation. *Environmental Research Letters, 16*(4), 043007.

68. Raihan, A., Begum, R. A., Said, M. N. M., and Pereira, J. J. (2022). Relationship between economic growth, renewable energy use, technological innovation, and carbon emission toward achieving Malaysia's Paris agreement. *Environment Systems and Decisions, 42*(4), 586–607.

69. Singh, B. (2023). Blockchain technology in renovating healthcare: Legal And Future Perspectives. In *Revolutionizing Healthcare Through Artificial Intelligence and Internet of Things Applications* (pp. 177–186). IGI Global.

70. Dai, H., Xie, X., Xie, Y., Liu, J., and Masui, T. (2016). Green growth: The economic impacts of large-scale renewable energy development in China. *Applied Energy, 162*, 435–449.

71. Elavarasan, R. M., Shafiullah, G. M., Padmanaban, S., Kumar, N. M., Annam, A., Vetrichelvan, A. M., and Holm-Nielsen, J. B. (2020). A comprehensive review on renewable energy development, challenges, and policies of leading Indian states with an international perspective. *Ieee Access, 8*, 74432–74457.

72. Zwane, N., Tazvinga, H., Botai, C., Murambadoro, M., Botai, J., De Wit, J., and Mabhaudhi, T. (2022). A bibliometric analysis of solar energy forecasting studies in Africa. *Energies, 15*(15), 5520.

73. Mohammadian, H. D. (2022). Mapping the future global SMEs growth via hybrid SMEs/SME 5.0/tomorrow's SMEs concept through the 5th wave, i-sustainability plus and DCT theories. In *Management and Information Technology in the Digital Era* (Vol. 29, pp. 173–206). Emerald Publishing Limited.

74. Amran, Y. A., Amran, Y. M., Alyousef, R., and Alabduljabbar, H. (2020). Renewable and sustainable energy production in Saudi Arabia according to Saudi Vision 2030; Current status and future prospects. *Journal of Cleaner Production, 247*, 119602.

75. Hainsch, K., Löffler, K., Burandt, T., Auer, H., del Granado, P. C., Pisciella, P., and Zwickl-Bernhard, S. (2022). Energy transition scenarios: What policies, societal attitudes, and technology developments will realize the EU Green Deal?. *Energy, 239*, 122067.

76. Atalay, Y., Biermann, F., and Kalfagianni, A. (2016). Adoption of renewable energy technologies in oil-rich countries: Explaining policy variation in the Gulf Cooperation Council states. *Renewable Energy, 85*, 206–214.

77. Singh, B. (2022). Relevance of agriculture-nutrition linkage for human healthcare: A conceptual legal framework of implication and pathways. *Justice and Law Bulletin, 1*(1), 44–49.

78. Xiao, M., Simon, S., and Pregger, T. (2019). Scenario analysis of energy system transition: A case study of two coastal metropolitan regions, eastern China. *Energy Strategy Reviews, 26*, 100423.

79. Scarlat, N., Dallemand, J. F., Monforti-Ferrario, F., and Nita, V. (2015). The role of biomass and bioenergy in a future bioeconomy: Policies and facts. *Environmental development, 15*, 3–34.

80. Connolly, D., Lund, H., Mathiesen, B. V., and Leahy, M. (2010). A review of computer tools for analysing the integration of renewable energy into various energy systems. *Applied Energy, 87*(4), 1059–1082.

81. Salleh, S. F., Mohd Roslan, M. E., Abd Rahman, A., Shamsuddin, A. H., Tuan Abdullah, T. A. R., and Sovacool, B. K. (2020). Transitioning to a sustainable development framework for bioenergy in Malaysia: policy suggestions to catalyse the utilisation of palm oil mill residues. *Energy, Sustainability and Society, 10*, 1–20.

82. Bujang, A. S., Bern, C. J., and Brumm, T. J. (2016). Summary of energy demand and renewable energy policies in Malaysia. *Renewable and Sustainable Energy Reviews, 53*, 1459–1467.

83. Lawrenz, L., Xiong, B., Lorenz, L., Krumm, A., Hosenfeld, H., Burandt, T., and Von Hirschhausen, C. (2018). Exploring energy pathways for the low-carbon transformation in India—A model-based analysis. *Energies, 11*(11), 3001.

84. Westman, L. K., Broto, V. C., and Huang, P. (2019). Revisiting multi-level governance theory: Politics and innovation in the urban climate transition in Rizhao, China. *Political Geography, 70*, 14–23.

85. Cohen, S. M., Iyer, G. C., Brown, M., Macknick, J., Wise, M., Binsted, M., and Hejazi, M. (2021). How structural differences influence cross-model consistency: An electric sector case study. *Renewable and Sustainable Energy Reviews, 144*, 111009.

86. Yang, D., Liu, D., Huang, A., Lin, J., and Xu, L. (2021). Critical transformation pathways and socio-environmental benefits of energy substitution using a LEAP scenario modeling. *Renewable and Sustainable Energy Reviews, 135*, 110116.

87. White, D., Winchester, N., Atkins, M., Ballingall, J., Coates, S., de Miguel Mercader, F., and Suomalainen, K. (2018). Energy-and multi-

sector modelling of climate change mitigation in New Zealand: current practice and future needs, Motu Working Paper 18-15. Motu Economic and Public Policy Research.

88. Nastasi, B., Markovska, N., Puksec, T., Duić, N., and Foley, A. (2022). Renewable and sustainable energy challenges to face for the achievement of Sustainable Development Goals. *Renewable and Sustainable Energy Reviews, 157,* 112071.
89. Danish, M. S. S., and Senjyu, T. (2023). AI-enabled energy policy for a sustainable future. *Sustainability, 15*(9), 7643.
90. Basheer, M., Nechifor, V., Calzadilla, A., Ringler, C., Hulme, D., and Harou, J. J. (2022). Balancing national economic policy outcomes for sustainable development. *Nature Communications, 13*(1), 5041.
91. Al-tabatabaie, K. F., Hossain, M. B., Islam, M. K., Awual, M. R., TowfiqulIslam, A. R. M., Hossain, M. A., and Islam, A. (2022). Taking strides towards decarbonization: The viewpoint of Bangladesh. *Energy Strategy Reviews, 44,* 100948.
92. Aldieri, L., Grafström, J., and Vinci, C. P. (2021). The effect of Marshallian and Jacobian knowledge spillovers on jobs in the solar, wind and energy efficiency sector. *Energies, 14*(14), 4269.
93. Nakata, T. (2004). Energy-economic models and the environment. *Progress in Energy and Combustion Science, 30*(4), 417–475.
94. Winfield, M., and Dolter, B. (2014). Energy, economic and environmental discourses and their policy impact: The case of Ontario' s Green Energy and Green Economy Act. *Energy Policy, 68,* 423–435.
95. Damman, S., Sandberg, E., Rosenberg, E., Pisciella, P., and Graabak, I. (2021). A hybrid perspective on energy transition pathways: Is hydrogen the key for Norway?. *Energy Research* and *Social Science, 78,* 102116.
96. Pascaris, A. S. (2021). Examining existing policy to inform a comprehensive legal framework for agrivoltaics in the US. *Energy Policy, 159,* 112620.
97. Budiman, I. (2018). Enabling community participation for social innovation in the energy sector. *Indonesian Journal of Energy, 1*(2), 21–31.
98. Reedman, L., Chew, M. S., Gordon, J., Sue, W., Brinsmead, T., Hayward, J., and Havas, L. (2021). Multi-sector energy modelling. *Research Gate.*
99. Xie, Y., Wu, X., Hou, Z., Li, Z., Luo, J., Lüddeke, C. T., and Liao, J. (2023). Gleaning insights from German energy transition and large-scale underground energy storage for China's carbon neutrality. *International Journal of Mining Science and Technology.*

100. Vinichenko, V. (2018). Mechanisms of energy transitions: National cases and the worldwide uptake of wind and solar power. PhD dissertation, Central European University.

101. Arbabzadeh, M., Gençer, E., Morris, J. F., Paltsev, S., and Armstrong, R. C. (2019). Plausible energy futures: A framework for evaluating options, impacts, and national energy choices. MIT Energy Initiative Working Paper.

102. Ilyas, A., Parkinson, S., Vinca, A., Byers, E., Manzoor, T., Riahi, K., and Muhammad, A. (2022). Balancing smart irrigation and hydropower investments for sustainable water conservation in the Indus basin. *Environmental Science* and *Policy, 135*, 147–161.

103. Garrido, S., Sequeira, T., and Santos, M. (2020). Renewable energy and sustainability from the supply side: A critical review and analysis. *Applied Sciences, 10*(17), 5755.

104. Steen, M., and Weaver, T. (2017). Incumbents' diversification and cross-sectorial energy industry dynamics. *Research Policy, 46*(6), 1071–1086.

105. Hoffmann, M. W., Wildermuth, S., Gitzel, R., Boyaci, A., Gebhardt, J., Kaul, H., and Tornede, T. (2020). Integration of novel sensors and machine learning for predictive maintenance in medium voltage switchgear to enable the energy and mobility revolutions. *Sensors, 20*(7), 2099.

106. Manoharan, K. G., Nehru, J. A., and Balasubramanian, S. (2021). *Artificial Intelligence and Fuzzy Logics*. Springer.

107. Ghai, D., Tripathi, S. L., Saxena, S., Chanda, M., and Alazab, M. (Eds.). (2022). *Machine Learning Algorithms for Signal and Image Processing*. John Wiley and Sons.

108. Pimitha, K., Anbarasi, S., and Balasubramanian, T. (2023). Machine Learning Techniques for Renewable Energy Resources. In *Fuzzy Logics, Machine Learning and Blockchain Technologies for Renewable Energy and Modern Hybrid Power Systems* (pp. 121–148). River Publishers.

109. Singh, B., and Kaunert, C. (2024). Computational thinking for innovative solutions and problem-solving techniques: transforming conventional education to futuristic interdisciplinary higher education. In M. Fonkam and N. Vajjhala (Eds.), *Revolutionizing Curricula Through Computational Thinking, Logic, and Problem Solving* (pp. 60–82). IGI Global. https://doi.org/10.4018/979-8-3693-1974-1.ch004

110. Singh, B., and Kaunert, C. (2024). Wind and solar energy as renewable energy for sustainable global future: Projecting future multi-sector sustainable policies and innovation. In A. Ara and R. Thakore (Eds.), *Promoting Multi-Sector Sustainability With Policy and Innovation* (pp. 210–245). IGI Global. https://doi.org/10.4018/979-8-3693-2113-3.ch009

111. Singh, B., and Kaunert, C. (2024). Aroma of highly smart Internet of Medical Things (IoMT) and lightweight EdgeTrust expansion medical care facilities for electronic healthcare systems: Fortified-chain architecture for remote patient monitoring and privacy protection beyond imagination. In A. Hassan, P. Bhattacharya, S. Tikadar, P. Dutta, and M. Sagayam (Eds.), *Lightweight Digital Trust Architectures in the Internet of Medical Things (IoMT)* (pp. 196–212). IGI Global. https://doi.org/10.4018/979-8-3693-2109-6.ch011

112. Singh, B., Jain, V., Kaunert, C., Dutta, P. K., and Singh, G. (2024). Privacy matters: Espousing blockchain and artificial intelligence (AI) for consumer data protection on e-commerce platforms in ethical marketing. In S. Saluja, V. Nayyar, K. Rojhe, and S. Sharma (Eds.), *Ethical Marketing Through Data Governance Standards and Effective Technology* (pp. 167–184). IGI Global. https://doi.org/10.4018/979-8-3693-2215-4.ch015

113. Singh, B., Dutta, P. K., and Kaunert, C. (2024). Replenish artificial intelligence in renewable energy for sustainable development: Lensing SDG 7 affordable and clean energy and SDG 13 climate actions with legal-financial advisory. In A. Derbali (Ed.), *Social and Ethical Implications of AI in Finance for Sustainability* (pp. 198–227). IGI Global. https://doi.org/10.4018/979-8-3693-2881-1.ch009

114. Singh, B., and Kaunert, C. (2024). Augmented reality and virtual reality modules for mindfulness: Boosting emotional intelligence and mental wellness. In K. Hiran, R. Doshi, and M. Patel (Eds.), *Applications of Virtual and Augmented Reality for Health and Wellbeing* (pp. 111–128). IGI Global. https://doi.org/10.4018/979-8-3693-1123-3.ch007

115. Singh, B. (2024). Lensing legal dynamics for examining responsibility and deliberation of generative AI-tethered technological privacy concerns: Infringements and use of personal data by nefarious actors. In A. Ara and A. Ara (Eds.), *Exploring the Ethical Implications of Generative AI* (pp. 146–167). IGI Global. https://doi.org/10.4018/979-8-3693-1565-1.ch009

116. Singh, B. (2024). Social cognition of incarcerated women and children: Addressing exposure to infectious diseases and legal

outcomes. In K. Reddy (Ed.), *Principles and Clinical Interventions in Social Cognition* (pp. 236–251). IGI Global. https://doi.org/10.4018/979-8-3693-1265-0.ch014

117. Singh, B., and Kaunert, C. (2024). Salvaging responsible consumption and production of food in the hospitality industry: Harnessing machine learning and deep learning for zero food waste. In A. Singh, P. Tyagi, and A. Garg (Eds.), *Sustainable Disposal Methods of Food Wastes in Hospitality Operations* (pp. 176–192). IGI Global. https://doi.org/10.4018/979-8-3693-2181-2.ch012
118. Singh, B. (2024). Evolutionary global neuroscience for cognition and brain health: Strengthening innovation in brain science. In P. Prabhakar (Ed.), *Biomedical Research Developments for Improved Healthcare* (pp. 246–272). IGI Global. https://doi.org/10.4018/979-8-3693-1922-2.ch012
119. Singh, B., and Kaunert, C. (2024). Revealing green finance mobilization: Harnessing FinTech and blockchain innovations to surmount barriers and foster new investment avenues. In S. Jafar, R. Rodriguez, H. Kannan, S. Akhtar, and P. Plugmann (Eds.), *Harnessing Blockchain-Digital Twin Fusion for Sustainable Investments* (pp. 265–286). IGI Global. https://doi.org/10.4018/979-8-3693-1878-2.ch011
120. Singh, B., and Kaunert, C. (2024). Harnessing sustainable agriculture through climate-smart technologies: Artificial intelligence for climate preservation and futuristic trends. In H. Kannan, R. Rodriguez, Z. Paprika, and A. Ade-Ibijola (Eds.), *Exploring Ethical Dimensions of Environmental Sustainability and Use of AI* (pp. 214–239). IGI Global. https://doi.org/10.4018/979-8-3693-0892-9.ch011
121. Singh, B. (2023). Blockchain technology in renovating healthcare: Legal and future perspectives. In K. Kaushik, S. Dahiya, S. Aggarwal, and A. Dwivedi (Eds.), *Revolutionizing Healthcare Through Artificial Intelligence and Internet of Things Applications* (pp. 177–186). IGI Global. https://doi.org/10.4018/978-1-6684-5422-0.ch012
122. Singh, B., and Kaunert, C. Reinventing artificial intelligence and blockchain for preserving medical data. In *Ethical Artificial Intelligence in Power Electronics* (pp. 77–91). CRC Press.
123. Singh, B., and Kaunert, C. (2024). Unmanned aerial vehicle. *Cognitive Machine Intelligence: Applications, Challenges, and Related Technologies*, 108.

Chapter 3

Fuzzy Logic for Fault Diagnosis and Prognostics in Renewable Energy Systems

Bhupinder Singh,[a] Christian Kaunert,[b] and Saurabh Chandra[c]

[a]*Sharda University, Greater Noida, Uttar Pradesh, India*
[b]*Dublin City University, Ireland*
[c]*School of Law, Bennett University, Greater Noida, Uttar Pradesh, India*

bhupindersinghlaw19@gmail.com

Abstract

With the rapid development of renewable energy systems, it is necessary to adopt advanced fault diagnosis and prognostics techniques that can guarantee that those technologies run reliably, efficiently and safely. Fuzzy logic is a highly promising technique for handling the uncertainty and imprecision prevalent in these processes. Renewable energy is much of the world's moving forward to sustainability and environmentalism alternative to coal infested with planets. With global warming, energy security and environmental degradation coming to the forefront of debate on economies around the world, powering our cities with renewable sources almost becomes a necessity. Clean power programs made up of energy-producing systems using

Fuzzy Logic in Revolutionizing Renewable Energy
Edited by Bhupinder Singh, Komal Vig, Ruchi Lal, and Budi Agus Riswandi

ISBN 978-981-5129-92-2 (Hardcover), 978-1-003-74191-6 (eBook)
www.jennystanford.com

DOI: 10.1201/9781003741916-3

the sun, wind and water along with other organic sources reduce contamination in an obvious manner. This chapter ventures into the fuzzy logic-based approaches in diagnostics and prognostics of renewable energy systems, demonstrating the merits provided by it as well its limitations along with some areas for further development.

3.1 Introduction

The other source of renewable energy that has been suggested is the solar power croft face; this produces electrical current using sunlight with either photovoltaic (PV) panels or concentrated solar power (CSP). Solar energy is plentiful and inexhaustible, and it can be suitable for both centralized large-scale power plant utilities as well as distributed generation [1]. In 2020, renewables made up nearly 29% of all global electricity generation, and the International Energy Agency (IEA) projects that this share will increase at a rapid pace in ensuing decades. Such a shift is essential to meet global climate targets and guarantee the future of humanity [2]. The wind energy is converted into the mechanical power using the rotating blades of a turbine, which turn an electric generator. Onshore and offshore wind farms have since grown into a major source of green energy, helping to power millions of homes across the world. Hydropower uses falling or flowing water energy to generate electricity [3–4]. Hydropower, generated by large-scale dams, is the oldest and most easily scalable renewable energy. Biomass, a versatile energy asset, offers three primary sources: wood and agricultural residues, animal manure, and forest fuels. Biomass can be transformed into electricity, heat, and biofuels [5].

Although renewable energy systems could bring significant benefits in a less carbon-intensive future, there are unique challenges related to reliability and efficiency [6]. Systems are regularly used in challenging and unpredictable environmental contexts, causing components to wear down earlier [7–8]. This variability, as well as the intermittent nature of some renewable resources, can make system management and optimization more difficult. The ability for these systems to operate efficiently and reliably is essential both in limiting cost, as well as maximizing energy output [9]. The performance and safety of renewable energy systems can be greatly compromised by faults in the system. A wind turbine might have a fault that can reduce its efficiency, so it generates less energy but costs more to maintain. In a solar array, faults in PV panels or inverters cause energy loss and may create safety problems. If left undetected or not handled properly, faults can lead to system failures and expensive repairs and severely reduce equipment lifespan; therefore, the ability for effective fault diagnosis as well as prognostics is becoming a necessity [10].

3.1.1 Fuzzy Logic: Basics and Principles

Fuzzy logic, as proposed by Lotfi Zadeh in the 1960s, is a type of many-valued logic which deals with reasoning that is approximate rather than fixed and exact. Classical binary logic operates with two distinct values, 1 or 0, representing true or false. In contrast, fuzzy logic allows for degrees of membership, where an event can be partially true. This capability enables fuzzy logic to handle imprecise or unclear data more effectively, as it can represent values beyond simple true/false distinctions.. Fuzzy logic systems are based on fuzzy sets, which consist of membership functions and rule-based inference system that allow them to model complex non-linear relationships with the ability to operate on approximations or probabilities [11].

3.1.2 Benefits of Fuzzy Logic Compared with Conventional Diagnostic Approach

The traditional diagnostic methods are not suitable for application in renewable energy systems because of several reasons; on the contrary, fuzzy logic provides various benefits over classical techniques. Fuzzy logic works just great in noisy and vague environments by delivering flexible solutions to real-world problems that are characterized by uncertainty [12]. Fuzzy systems are also easy to be modified with new rules. As long as the data is provided, they can adapt themselves accordingly. Fuzzy logic is very good at modeling and solving complex, non-linear problems that are difficult or impossible to address with conventional techniques. Fuzzy logic systems are simple to design and only in few cases require the use of more computational resources than other sophisticated diagnostic techniques [13].

The incorporation of fuzzy logic with fault diagnosis and prognostics in renewable energy systems is a promising way to improve reliability and performance. The use of fuzzy logic algorithms nudges us one step closer to this potential reality, allowing stakeholders worldwide a tool with which they can tackle the complexity and uncertainty that is inescapable when devising plans for new renewable energy systems [14].

3.2 Importance of Renewable Energy in Global Energy Mix: Common Types of Renewable Energy Systems—Solar, Wind, Hydro and Biomass

The development and use of renewable energy emerges from a worldwide need to address three critical issues: the potential for climate change, greenhouse gas emissions affecting human health or other aspects of biodiversity, production is declining, while the utilization of green energy is increasing rapidly [15]. Countries around the world are endeavoring to transition from fossil fuels (that is, nonrenewable sources) to renewable energy systems such as solar, wind power, hydropower and bioenergy. Such technologies not only help abate environmental impact but also provide economic and social benefits, which support energy security and resilience [16].

Transitioning to renewable energy is more important than ever for a few reasons. For starters, renewable energy cuts way back on carbon emissions—which are the main cause of climate change. Renewable energy sources have the benefit of producing very little to no direct emissions (of greenhouse gases, in general carbon dioxide), which makes them far more environmentally friendly than fossil fuels. Limiting global warming to 1.5 °C above pre-industrial levels require a dramatic reduction in carbon emissions, says the Intergovernmental Panel on Climate Change (IPCC). One key strategy here is renewable energy, recognized as an essential step to address climate change and respond not only to extreme weather events but also to rising sea levels or biodiversity loss [17].

Renewable energy contributes to securing the supply of energy by diversifying it. The reserves of fossil fuels lie mainly in concentrated pockets, leaving large swathes dependent on buying hydrocarbons from them for electricity production, fueling geopolitics and often subject to market surprises. On the other hand, renewable sources are abundant and located everywhere in the world, allowing each country to exploit their own energy potential thus decreasing reliance on imported fuels. It was also decentralized in locations, which lowered the risk of supply failures and price fluctuations—effectively allowing for more robust energy systems. In addition to that, the use of renewable energy enhances economic growth and employment [18]. Renewable energy is a labor-intensive sector, demanding varied skills for the supply chain from manufactures to installers and maintainers of systems. In a 2015 report, the International Renewable Energy Agency (IRENA) estimated that more than 6 million people were already working in renewable-energy jobs worldwide and found an overall potential for job growth of some 5 to 10 times from today's level given heightened efforts toward achieving clean energy goals. Renewable energy infrastructure investment stimulates the local economy, dynamic technology innovation and associated economic development opportunities [19].

Renewable energy supports in balancing economic development through providing clean and affordable energy to populations who are not served [20]. More than 750 million people worldwide have no access at all to electricity, especially in rural and remote areas that are isolated from national grids. For example, solar mini-grids and off-grid solutions provide a clean source of power to these communities addressing reliable electricity access that paves the path for better living standards but also improving education facilities, increased healthcare services and changing economic opportunities [21].

3.2.1 Renewable Energy Systems Used Usually

Solar Energy Systems: Solar energy systems use sunlight to generate electricity through photovoltaic (PV) panels or concentrated solar power (CSP) system. Photovoltaic (PV) panels that directly convert sunlight to electricity using semiconductor materials and

Concentrating Solar Power systems with mirrors or lenses used for concentrating the sunlight—heating a fluid which then produces steam, turning a turbine / generator [22]. The supply of solar energy is so great that it can meet the whole world's need for power a million times over. This makes it an all-encompassing service, from small-scale residential installations to the largest solar farms. Progress in solar technology has helped to make this means of energy production a more and more competitive alternative most notably, advances have brought the costs of producing electricity down. The environmental impact of solar energy systems is negligible as they do not need fuel or emit any pollutants during their operation [23].

Wind Energy Systems: Wind energy systems directly use wind turbines to convert the kinetic power of air in motion into mechanical power. This makes wind farms, which are located both onshore and offshore, amongst the top contributors to global renewable energy capacity. The technology of wind energy is even growing at such a quick pace that it may soon become cost-competitive with traditional generators. Today, wind turbines produce electricity at economically competitive costs with other sources of energy [24]. There are many advantages of wind energy, and the scalability (39 MW) with which it can be deployed is particularly attractive. Although wind is intermittent, new technologies to integrate electric grids across large areas and store energy from renewable sources make it a more reliable resource. Wind power involves minimal land use and no environmental impact on the area, as wind is a renewable resource which produces zero emissions in Brazil [25].

Hydropower Systems: The energy of flowing or falling water is harnessed to generate electricity, and it has been around as long as humans have built structures near a large body of water. This renewable electricity generation method has the largest share worldwide. Hydropower facilities come in all sizes, from large dams with reservoirs to little run-of-river projects. Large dams yield great power generation potential and can also provide other benefits as well such as flood control or water supply [26]. These projects offer low ecological costs and minimum hydrological alteration to preserve the natural flow of water. Hydropower is the most reliable system, which dispatches baseload power 24/7 and also provides flexibility for grid stability requirements. Large dams, however, also carry significant environmental and social costs, including habitat alteration and displacement, but these impacts can be managed [27].

Biomass Energy Systems: Biomass Energy Projects (Direct Sequestration) are the systems that use organic materials, like agricultural residues from farming and bioenergy crops such as forest waste and livestock manure for energy generation. Several technologies exist to produce electricity, solar fuels and potential biochemicals from biomass: combustion (heat production), anaerobic digestion, fermentation. Because biomass energy is renewably resourced, it can also help to divert waste by utilizing residues that would otherwise decompose and release methane—a powerful greenhouse gas [28]. The technology also provides an integrated and decentralized solution for energy, capable of centralizing or dispersing power supply. However, caution has to be taken in sourcing sustainable biomass from forests so that it prevents deforestation and remains carbon neutral. In return, well-managed biomass energy systems can provide renewable and low-carbon baseload power to support rural economies while increasing access to cleaner energy [29].

Renewable energy has an important role to play in the global energy mix. Helping support the environmental, economic and social benefits of moving to a sustainable and resilient energy future All offer different benefits making our energy mix more reliable [30]. With solar, wind, hydro and biomass implementation with the rise of technology and falling costs, renewable energy systems will become more important as they help meet global power demand while reducing carbon adverse effects on climate change, which helps in achieving sustainable development goals [31]. The continuous growth in large-scale renewable energy capacity around the globe is proof of this vital force for bringing about cleaner, more sustainable development [32].

3.3 Renewable Energy System Fault Diagnosis

Renewable energy systems play a critical role in the global transition to sustainable energy. However, they also present some challenges concerning reliability and efficiency. Since these systems are usually deployed in dynamic and hostile environments, they become prone to environmental faults which may degrade the performance of safety [33]. Therefore, accurate and timely fault diagnosis is crucial to maintain the continuous operation of renewable energy systems. Fuzzy logic, which has been proven to be a robust method in dealing with uncertainty and imprecision, provides an efficient mode for fault detection of renewable energy platforms such as solar PV/wind turbine/Hydro/biomass-based systems [34].

3.3.1 Utilizing Fuzzy Logic in Solar Energy Systems

Solar energy systems are a basic need in the present world. PV panels and inverters have been around for ages, but they do develop various kinds of problems which can affect their overall efficiency or lifespan as faulty equipment poses serious risk [35]. These include shading, dust phenomena, temperature impacts and errors associated with electronics among which they are grouped as (a) open circuit (bypass diode disconnection) and (b) short-circuit. PV panels may suffer from the effects of temperature-induced defects and voltage spikes; piece failures also can influence inverters that convert direct current (DC) produced by PV panels into alternating current (AC) for use in the grid [36].

For this purpose, fuzzy logic provides a well-suitable technique by using linguistic rules and membership functions in order to describe the behavior of normal and faulty systems [37–38]. The fuzzy logic diagnostic system may interpret voltage, current or temperature as input variables which would help in detecting anomalies corresponding to potential faults. This method is used for real-time monitoring and detecting issues rapidly so that downtime and maintenance costs are minimized [39]. There are some case studies which explain that fuzzy logic has been applied for fault diagnosis of these solar energy systems. An example was shown in a study done on a grid-connected PV system that used a fuzzy inference system to observe partial shading and degradation of some standalone photovoltaic modules. Using inputs such as output power, current–voltage characteristics, and working environment conditions, the system is able to identify possible shading patterns or failures with high accuracy [40].

A further application was the optimization of solar inverters using fuzzy logic. Using real-time data and based on fuzzy rules, the system tunes inverter settings to raise the overall efficiency of energy conversion with no degradation risk for inverter components. Including the aforementioned two case studies, it has been demonstrated that fuzzy logic can increase error-free operation of solar energy systems [41].

3.3.2 Fuzzy Logic–based Energy Systems: Fault Identification in Wind Turbines and Control Systems

Wind energy systems are complex machines with a greater number of constituents including blades, gearbox and generator along with controlling elements which can fail mechanically or electrically [42–43]. Early detection and diagnosis of these faults is important in order to avoid catastrophic failures as well as optimize energy production. Due to the ability of fuzzy logic for modeling complex, non-linear systems, it is also a powerful tool in wind turbine fault diagnosis [44]. The diagnostic system with the combination of fuzzy logic can take inputs from different sensors, such as vibration, temperature and wind speed to detect fault-bearing abnormal patterns. This method enables the health of turbine parts to be monitored on an ongoing basis, predicting potential issues before they develop into larger problems [45].

3.3.3 Advantage of Fuzzy Logic in Wind Flow Modeling

The unpredictable and constantly changing conditions of wind environments make fault diagnosis difficult in a typical system based on energy from the wind [46]. Its tolerance for uncertainty and its ability to deal with changing conditions have helped make fuzzy logic the concept of choice in many areas, including knowledge-based systems [47]. The system makes the correct judgement by integrating expert knowledge and historical data into fuzzy rules, ensuring it can differentiate between real faults and normal operational variations. A fuzzy logic–based system was developed for monitoring the status of wind turbine gearboxes, a case study [48]. The health of the gearbox was evaluated from data, including vibration signals and oil temperature, giving early potential faults warnings. New diagnostic solutions reduced maintenance costs and ensured a higher level of turbine availability [49].

3.3.4 Fuzzy Logic for Hydro and Biomass Energy Systems: Monitoring and Diagnosing Faults in Hydro Plants

While hydroelectric plants are generally very dependable, problems often develop with mechanical components such as turbines and generators as well as electrical systems such as transformers and control units [50]. These flaws result in reduced performance and increased failures and downtime. By analyzing the data from different sensors and control systems, fuzzy logic can be used for monitoring as well as diagnosing faults in hydroelectric plants [51–52]. The system of diagnosis utilizes fuzzy logic to assess water flow rate, pressure, and vibration parameters in order to identify anomalies that may suggest the likelihood of a problem. It is a way to identify possible issues early on and ultimately prevents failure so that expensive repairs or downtime are less likely [53]. For instance, a fuzzy logic system was applied to monitor the state of a hydroelectric plant's turbine blades. The system detected signals of cavitations and wear based on the analysis results conducted on vibration data alongside temperature. With these outcomes, maintenance could be performed at times before it caused the worst damage [54].

3.3.5 Fuzzy Logic Application for Biomass System Management

Biomass energy systems work by changing organic materials into heat and electricity, but they do not have the fuel quality, combustion efficiency or emissions control that combined cycle power plants offer [55–56]. Biomass, unlike steam power plants, can go down due to a wide variety of fuel properties and this coupled with mechanical failures or control system errors, makes faults in biomass systems barely predictable. Fuzzy logic, combining real-time data and expert knowledge, provides a dynamic model of biomass system [57]. Mechanistic control is not robust enough, so a fuzzy logic-based controller can adjust the operational parameters (fuel feed/-air supply) when too much fuel is being consumed and there are high emissions. System performance and environmental footprint can benefit from this adaptive control strategy [58]. A fuzzy logic system was introduced and applied to the combustion process of a biomass power plant in a case study. The system utilized temperature, oxygen concentration and fuel properties as inputs to determine the best burner settings for increased efficiency and lower emissions [59].

3.4 Prognostics Using Fuzzy Logic

The importance of renewable energy systems is growing in the wake of an increasing global demand for reliable and efficient sources. Decipping, at any rate making a forecast about the status of operation in future, is critical for keeping large systems including rotating machines good performance. Due to their ability to model uncertainty and the general concept of fuzziness, fuzzy logic methods have a clear edge [60-61]. This method can predict system failures, improve maintenance schedules and increase the lifespan of renewable energy assets. Predictive maintenance is all about preventing unexpected failures and ensuring prescriptive action timely performed before a system or component actually fails [62]. Yet deploying some of the traditional predictive maintenance techniques also can be complex as they traditionally depend on accurate data and models relatively hard to obtain in a wide range of environments such as those operating around renewable energy. Fuzzy logic is powerful due to the possibility of making decisions in an uncertain environment with imprecise information [63].

These rules connected to various functions are used in interpreting the sensor data and environmental conditions by fuzzy logic systems. An example would be to use temperature, vibration pressure and the output power as inputs that are assimilated through fuzzy rules for judging the health of a component or system [64–65]. Fuzzy logic can predict either how much life is left in the system or the chance that it will fail within some period. Fuzzy logic can predict faults in a non-linear and uncertain place by historical data as expert knowledge. This proactive ability enables operators to address problems before they become expensive failures thereby reducing downtime and maintenance costs [66]. The fuzzy-based predictive maintenance consists of the following steps:

- *Data Gathering and Pre-processing*: The initial step is gathering data from the sensors attached to different renewable energy systems [67]. This data can include information such as temperature, pressure and vibration. The data is operated upon through preprocessing techniques such as noise reduction and normalization to guarantee its quality [68].
- *Fuzzy Rules*: Generate fuzzy rules with some actual data based on expert knowledge. These rules are the associations between input variables and potential faults or performance degradation. Temperature and vibration are just two key elements for failure. If both exceed set points in the threshold rule, then there is a high chance of something going wrong [69].
- *Designing of Membership Function*: These are the functions that determine how much a particular input belongs to a fuzzy set. These serve to take the crisp input values into fuzzy numbers, which give us the robot with a mechanism of handling uncertainty and imprecision [70].
- *Fuzzy Inference and Defuzzification*: The inference system processes the input data via fuzzy rules to have a fuzzy output. The defuzzified output is a crisp value representing the predicted remaining useful life (RUL) or failure probability [71].
- *Real-time*: A fuzzy logic system is able to adapt to the changing environment or changes in the system behavior, and it monitors the situation continuously. The strategy adapts

along with it to ensure that predictive maintenance remains a valid and efficient practice [72].

3.4.1 Solar Energy Systems Prognostics

Like many other technologies, solar energy systems like PV panels and inverters degrade or experience faults that can lower their efficiency as well as shorten their lifespan. Predictive maintenance systems greatly benefit from good prognostics making them capable of knowing in advance when some device is going to fail therefore utilizing effectively the planned downtimes [73]. In solar energy systems, fuzzy logic can be used to model the intricate relationships between environmental parameters, system performance and component health. For example, a fuzzy logic-based prognostic model for a PV system can take in data such as solar irradiance, temperature and output power to forecast the degradation rate of PV panels. Operators can use predictions of the panels RUL to schedule replacement or maintenance activities before breakdowns occur in order prevent process failure and maximize energy production [72].

Fuzzy logic-based prognosis can also be useful in inverters which are the most crucial part of solar energy systems [73]. By managing the input voltage, output current and various thermal conditions, the inverter health can be monitored consistently and potential failures can be predicted through a fuzzy logic system. This predictive ability allows the operations staff to perform preventative maintenance which can reduce downtime and improve the lifespan of an inverter [74].

3.4.2 Wind Energy Machines Prognostics

Wind energy systems have primarily complex construction and consist of numerous components—such as blades, gearboxes, generators and control system parts—whose operational degradations (ageing) in the early stages can also be considered mechanical or electrical ones [75]. Prognostics in wind energy systems are expected to foresee failures, manage good maintenance practices and try to minimize the cost of operations with the aim of better performance [76].

Fuzzy logic has the advantage of being able to model these non-linear, uncertain relationships between variables in modeling wind energy systems. A fuzzy logic-based prognostic model has the ability to collect data from all sorts of different sensors (e.g., vibrations, temperature and wind speed) for predicting RUL and health of critical components. Specifically, one application might see the system analyzing vibration signals from a gearbox to estimate wear and predict when maintenance will be required in order to avoid unplanned failure [77].

Due to its adaptive nature, fuzzy logic is particularly appropriate for wind energy systems that are operated under rapidly changing environmental conditions. Through ongoing updates of the prognostic model in line with real-time data, it enables accurate predictions to be made under dynamic scenarios [78]. This real-time monitoring capability helps in scheduling proper maintenance activities, thus providing an effective wind energy system and reduced downtime. A fuzzy logic system was developed to forecast the degradation of PV panels in a utility-scale solar farm and utilized in the field of solar energy [79].

The system provided accurate panel RUL, allowing the optimization of maintenance planning and resource allocation for improved energy production by analyzing environmental data along with a variety of other measurements related to the operation performance writing. Consequently, fuzzy logic provides an effective and adaptable technique for the prognosis of renewable energy systems outperforming prognostic maintenance schemes contributing to both new-age predictive as well traditional preventive upkeep schemes, in turn guaranteeing the dependability and also productivity in creating energies such as solar and wind. With the ability to handle uncertainty and model complex relationships, fuzzy logic systems can help operators predict impending system failure states, optimize maintenance schedules to prevent them or repair failing individual components before they reach end of life. With the ongoing expansion of renewable energy installations around the world, integration of cutting-edge prognostic methodologies such as the fuzzy approach is indispensable for ensuring that these systems remain sustainable and resilient [80]. With more and more innovation in the field of fuzzy logic-based prognostic methods, it will be very helpful for providing effective renewable energy plus less maintenance which leads to a cost-effective approach and possibly sustainable renewable wind farming generation future [81].

3.5 Conclusion and Future Scope

Renewable energy has an important role to play in the global energy mix, helping support the environmental, economic and social benefits of moving to a sustainable and resilient energy future. All offer different benefits making our energy mix more reliable. The use of fuzzy logic for fault diagnosis in renewable energy systems has great advantages of reliability, efficiency and adaptability. Fuzzy logic, by better capturing uncertainty and representing complex systems, improves the operational security of solar, wind, hydro, and biomass-energy installations. With the increasing prominence of renewable energy worldwide, incorporating advanced diagnostics methods such as fuzzy logic will have an important function in ensuring sustainable and resilient systems.

References

1. Jiao, Y., Kang, H., and Sun, H. (2024). An Intelligent Landscaping Framework for Net-Zero Energy Smart Cities: A Green Infrastructure Approach. *Sustainable Energy Technologies and Assessments*, *64*, 103665.
2. Ashinze, U. K., Edeigba, B. A., Umoh, A. A., Biu, P. W., and Daraojimba, A. I. (2024). Urban Green Infrastructure and Its Role In Sustainable Cities: A Comprehensive Review. *World Journal of Advanced Research and Reviews*, *21*(2), 928–936.
3. Zellner, M. L., and Massey, D. (2024). Modeling Benefits and Tradeoffs of Green Infrastructure: Evaluating and Extending Parsimonious Models for Neighborhood Stormwater Planning. *Heliyon*.
4. Sharma, A., and Singh, B. (2022). Measuring Impact of E-commerce on Small Scale Business: A Systematic Review. *Journal of Corporate Governance and International Business Law*, *5*(1).

5. Zabel, A., and Häusler, M. M. (2024). Policy Instruments for Green Infrastructure. *Landscape and Urban Planning, 242*, 104929.
6. Kaneti, V. R., Masih, J., Yoganand, S., Singh, B., Bhargava, R., Bajaj, R., ... and Shrivastava, A. (2024). Supervised Learning for Edible Mushroom Identification: Promising Results and Implications for Food Safety. *International Journal of Intelligent Systems and Applications in Engineering, 12*(8s), 290–298.
7. Singh, B. (2022). Relevance of Agriculture-Nutrition Linkage for Human Healthcare: A Conceptual Legal Framework of Implication and Pathways. *Justice and Law Bulletin, 1*(1), 44–49.
8. Zhang, B., and MacKenzie, A. (2024). Trade-Offs and Synergies in Urban Green Infrastructure: A Systematic Review. *Urban Forestry* and *Urban Greening*, 128262.
9. Singh, B. (2022). COVID-19 Pandemic and Public Healthcare: Endless Downward Spiral or Solution via Rapid Legal and Health Services Implementation with Patient Monitoring Program. *Justice and Law Bulletin, 1*(1), 1–7.
10. Isendahl, C., Dunning, N. P., Grazioso, L., Hawken, S., Lentz, D. L., and Scarborough, V. L. (2024). Growth and Decline of a Sustainable City: A Multitemporal Perspective on Blue-Black-Green Infrastructures at the pre-Columbian Lowland Maya city of Tikal. *Urban Studies*, 00420980231224648.
11. Sunding, A., Randrup, T. B., Nordh, H., Sang, Å. O., and Nilsson, K. (2024). Descriptions of the Relationship between Human Health and Green Infrastructure in Six Nordic Comprehensive Plans. *Cities, 146*, 104746.
12. Kim, J., Ewing, R., and Rigolon, A. (2024). Does Green Infrastructure Affect Housing Prices via Extreme Heat and Air Pollution Mitigation? A Focus on Green and Climate Gentrification in Los Angeles County, 2000–2021. *Sustainable Cities and Society, 102*, 105225.
13. Sahak, N. M., Yunos, M. Y. M., Maulan, S., & Ismail, N. A. (2025). Unlocking the Potential of Green Infrastructure in Residential Areas: A Comprehensive Systematic Review. *International Journal of Academic Research in Business and Social Sciences*, 15(1), 1581–1605.
14. Richter, M., Heinemann, K., Meiser, N., and Dickhaut, W. (2024). Trees in Sponge Cities—A Systematic Review of Trees as a Component of Blue-Green Infrastructure, Vegetation Engineering Principles, and Stormwater Management. *Water, 16*(5), 655.
15. Singh, B. and Kaunert, C. (2024). Computational Thinking for Innovative Solutions and Problem-Solving Techniques: Transforming

Conventional Education to Futuristic Interdisciplinary Higher Education. In M. Fonkam and N. Vajjhala (Eds.), *Revolutionizing Curricula Through Computational Thinking, Logic, and Problem Solving* (pp. 60–82). IGI Global. https://doi.org/10.4018/979-8-3693-1974-1.ch004

16. Singh, B. and Kaunert, C. (2024). Wind and Solar Energy as Renewable Energy for Sustainable Global Future: Projecting Future Multi-Sector Sustainable Policies and Innovation. In A. Ara and R. Thakore (Eds.), *Promoting Multi-Sector Sustainability With Policy and Innovation* (pp. 210–245). IGI Global. https://doi.org/10.4018/979-8-3693-2113-3.ch009
17. Singh, B. and Kaunert, C. (2024). Aroma of Highly Smart Internet of Medical Things (IoMT) and Lightweight EdgeTrust Expansion Medical Care Facilities for Electronic Healthcare Systems: Fortified-Chain Architecture for Remote Patient Monitoring and Privacy Protection Beyond Imagination. In A. Hassan, P. Bhattacharya, S. Tikadar, P. Dutta, and M. Sagayam (Eds.), *Lightweight Digital Trust Architectures in the Internet of Medical Things (IoMT)* (pp. 196–212). IGI Global. https://doi.org/10.4018/979-8-3693-2109-6.ch011
18. Singh, B., Jain, V., Kaunert, C., Dutta, P. K., and Singh, G. (2024). Privacy Matters: Espousing Blockchain and Artificial Intelligence (AI) for Consumer Data Protection on E-Commerce Platforms in Ethical Marketing. In S. Saluja, V. Nayyar, K. Rojhe, and S. Sharma (Eds.), *Ethical Marketing Through Data Governance Standards and Effective Technology* (pp. 167–184). IGI Global. https://doi.org/10.4018/979-8-3693-2215-4.ch015
19. Singh, B., Dutta, P. K., and Kaunert, C. (2024). Replenish Artificial Intelligence in Renewable Energy for Sustainable Development: Lensing SDG 7 Affordable and Clean Energy and SDG 13 Climate Actions with Legal-Financial Advisory. In A. Derbali (Ed.), *Social and Ethical Implications of AI in Finance for Sustainability* (pp. 198–227). IGI Global. https://doi.org/10.4018/979-8-3693-2881-1.ch009
20. Singh, B. and Kaunert, C. (2024). Augmented Reality and Virtual Reality Modules for Mindfulness: Boosting Emotional Intelligence and Mental Wellness. In K. Hiran, R. Doshi, and M. Patel (Eds.), *Applications of Virtual and Augmented Reality for Health and Wellbeing* (pp. 111–128). IGI Global. https://doi.org/10.4018/979-8-3693-1123-3.ch007
21. Singh, B. (2024). Lensing Legal Dynamics for Examining Responsibility and Deliberation of Generative AI-Tethered Technological Privacy Concerns: Infringements and Use of Personal Data by Nefarious

Actors. In A. Ara and A. Ara (Eds.), *Exploring the Ethical Implications of Generative AI* (pp. 146–167). IGI Global. https://doi.org/10.4018/979-8-3693-1565-1.ch009

22. Singh, B. (2024). Social Cognition of Incarcerated Women and Children: Addressing Exposure to Infectious Diseases and Legal Outcomes. In K. Reddy (Ed.), *Principles and Clinical Interventions in Social Cognition* (pp. 236–251). IGI Global. https://doi.org/10.4018/979-8-3693-1265-0.ch014
23. Singh, B. and Kaunert, C. (2024). Salvaging Responsible Consumption and Production of Food in the Hospitality Industry: Harnessing Machine Learning and Deep Learning for Zero Food Waste. In A. Singh, P. Tyagi, and A. Garg (Eds.), *Sustainable Disposal Methods of Food Wastes in Hospitality Operations* (pp. 176–192). IGI Global. https://doi.org/10.4018/979-8-3693-2181-2.ch012
24. Singh, B. (2024). Evolutionary Global Neuroscience for Cognition and Brain Health: Strengthening Innovation in Brain Science. In P. Prabhakar (Ed.), *Biomedical Research Developments for Improved Healthcare* (pp. 246–272). IGI Global. https://doi.org/10.4018/979-8-3693-1922-2.ch012
25. Singh, B. and Kaunert, C. (2024). Revealing Green Finance Mobilization: Harnessing FinTech and Blockchain Innovations to Surmount Barriers and Foster New Investment Avenues. In S. Jafar, R. Rodriguez, H. Kannan, S. Akhtar, and P. Plugmann (Eds.), *Harnessing Blockchain-Digital Twin Fusion for Sustainable Investments* (pp. 265–286). IGI Global. https://doi.org/10.4018/979-8-3693-1878-2.ch011
26. Singh, B. and Kaunert, C. (2024). Harnessing Sustainable Agriculture through Climate-Smart Technologies: Artificial Intelligence for Climate Preservation and Futuristic Trends. In H. Kannan, R. Rodriguez, Z. Paprika, and A. Ade-Ibijola (Eds.), *Exploring Ethical Dimensions of Environmental Sustainability and Use of AI* (pp. 214–239). IGI Global. https://doi.org/10.4018/979-8-3693-0892-9.ch011
27. Singh, B. (2023). Blockchain Technology in Renovating Healthcare: Legal and Future Perspectives. In K. Kaushik, S. Dahiya, S. Aggarwal, and A. Dwivedi (Eds.), *Revolutionizing Healthcare Through Artificial Intelligence and Internet of Things Applications* (pp. 177–186). IGI Global. https://doi.org/10.4018/978-1-6684-5422-0.ch012
28. Singh, B., and Kaunert, C. Reinventing Artificial Intelligence and Blockchain for Preserving Medical Data. In *Ethical Artificial Intelligence in Power Electronics* (pp. 77–91). CRC Press.

29. Singh, B., and Kaunert, C. (2024). Unmanned aerial vehicle. *Cognitive Machine Intelligence: Applications, Challenges, and Related Technologies*, 108.

30. Vijayalakshmi, S., Savita, and Durgadevi, P. (2023). AI and Machine Learning in Improving Resilience of Smart Energy Infrastructure. In *AI-Powered Machine Learning in the Energy Industry: Digital Technology and Sustainable Energy Systems* (pp. 189–213). Cham: Springer International Publishing.

31. Shukla, S. S., Jain, M., Jain, A., Bajpai, S., Mishra, A. K., Gupta, A., and Pramanik, S. (2024). Industry 5.0: Blue Wind Energy for Sustainable Urbanization and Intelligent Control of Energy. In *Convergence of Human Resources Technologies and Industry 5.0* (pp. 170–187). IGI Global.

32. Al Hajri, N. H., Al Harthi, R. N., Pasam, G. K., and Natarajan, R. (2024). Machine Learning and Machine Learning based Green Energy Generation using Hybrid Renewable Energy Sources of Solar, Wind and Hydrogen Fuel Cells. In *E3S Web of Conferences* (Vol. 472, p. 01008). EDP Sciences.

33. Issa Zadeh, S. B., Esteban Perez, M. D., López-Gutiérrez, J. S., and Fernández-Sánchez, G. (2023). Optimizing Smart Energy Infrastructure in Smart Ports: A Systematic Scoping Review of Carbon Footprint Reduction. *Journal of Marine Science and Engineering, 11*(10), 1921.

34. Singh, B., and Kaunert, C. (2024). Harnessing Sustainable Agriculture Through Climate-Smart Technologies: Artificial Intelligence for Climate Preservation and Futuristic Trends. In *Exploring Ethical Dimensions of Environmental Sustainability and Use of AI* (pp. 214–239). IGI Global.

35. Li, J., and Zhou, T. (2023). Multiagent Deep Meta Reinforcement Learning for Sea Computing-Based Energy Management of Interconnected Grids Considering Renewable Energy Sources in Sustainable Cities. *Sustainable Cities and Society, 99*, 104917.

36. Orumwense, E. F., and Abo-Al-Ez, K. (2023). Internet of Things for Smart Energy Systems: A Review on Its Applications, Challenges and Future Trends. *AIMS Electronics* and *Electrical Engineering*, *7*(1).

37. Raj, E. F. I. (2023). A Detailed Review on Wind and Solar Hybrid Green Energy Technologies for Sustainable Smart Cities. *Polytechnica*, *6*(1), 1.

38. Camacho, J. D. J., Aguirre, B., Ponce, P., Anthony, B., and Molina, A. (2024). Leveraging Artificial Intelligence to Bolster the Energy Sector in Smart Cities: A Literature Review. *Energies, 17*(2), 353.

39. Kannammal, A., and Chandia, S. (2023). Applications of AI and Machine Learning for Smart Cities. *Research Trends in Artificial Intelligence: Internet of Things*, 186.

40. Zearah, S. A., Al-Tahee, M., Mohammed, A., Shnawa, A. H., Mahdi, H. H. J., and Majeed, Z. (2023, December). Smart City Application based on Internet-of-Things and Artificial Intelligence for Energy Management Dynamic Memory Modelling. In *2023 International Conference on Emerging Research in Computational Science (ICERCS)* (pp. 1–6). IEEE.

41. Awogbemi, O., Von Kallon, D. V., and Kumar, K. S. (2024). Contributions of Artificial Intelligence and Digitization in Achieving Clean and Affordable Energy. *Intelligent Systems with Applications*, 200389.

42. Singh, B. (2023). Unleashing Alternative Dispute Resolution (ADR) in Resolving Complex Legal-Technical Issues Arising in Cyberspace Lensing E-Commerce and Intellectual Property: Proliferation of E-Commerce Digital Economy. *Revista Brasileira de Alternative Dispute Resolution-Brazilian Journal of Alternative Dispute Resolution-RBADR, 5*(10), 81–105.

43. Verma, J., Sandys, L., Matthews, A., and Goel, S. (2024). Readiness of Artificial Intelligence Technology for Managing Energy Demands from Renewable Sources. *Engineering Applications of Artificial Intelligence, 135*, 108831.

44. Khalid, M. (2024). Energy 4.0: AI-Enabled Digital Transformation for Sustainable Power Networks. *Computers* and *Industrial Engineering*, 110253.

45. Issa Zadeh, S. B., and Perez, E. (2023). MD; López-Gutiérrez, J.-S.; Fernández-Sánchez, G. Optimizing Smart Energy Infrastructure in Smart Ports: A Systematic Scoping Review of Carbon Footprint Reduction. *J. Mar. Sci. Eng, 11*, 1921.

46. Singh, B. and Kaunert, C. (2024). Augmented Reality and Virtual Reality Modules for Mindfulness: Boosting Emotional Intelligence and Mental Wellness. In K. Hiran, R. Doshi, and M. Patel (Eds.), *Applications of Virtual and Augmented Reality for Health and Wellbeing* (pp. 111–128). IGI Global. https://doi.org/10.4018/979-8-3693-1123-3.ch007

47. Obaideen, K., Albasha, L., Iqbal, U., and Mir, H. (2024). Wireless Power Transfer: Applications, Challenges, Barriers, and the Role of AI in

Achieving Sustainable Development Goals: A Bibliometric Analysis. *Energy Strategy Reviews, 53,* 101376.

48. El-Hussieny, E. (2023). Emerging the Concept of Sustainable Architecture in Forming a Smart City. *Resourceedings, 3*(1), 22–32.
49. Salman, M. Y., and Hasar, H. (2023). Review on Environmental Aspects in Smart City Concept: Water, Waste, Air Pollution and Transportation Smart Applications Using Machine Learning Techniques. *Sustainable Cities and Society, 94,* 104567.
50. Van Hoang, T. (2024). Impact of Integrated Artificial Intelligence and Internet of Things Technologies on Smart City Transformation. *Journal of Technical Education Science, 19* (Special Issue 01), 64–73.
51. Huda, N. U., Ahmed, I., Adnan, M., Ali, M., and Naeem, F. (2024). Experts and Intelligent Systems for Smart Homes' Transformation to Sustainable Smart Cities: A Comprehensive Review. *Expert Systems with Applications, 238,* 122380.
52. Ali, M. (2023). Synergizing Solar Cell Innovation, Radio Wave Technology, and AI for Sustainable Business Growth: A Comprehensive Review. *International Journal of Social, Humanities and Life Sciences, 1*(1), 19–28.
53. Nezhad, M. M., Neshat, M., Sylaios, G., and Garcia, D. A. (2024). Marine Energy Digitalization Digital Twin's Approaches. *Renewable and Sustainable Energy Reviews, 191,* 114065.
54. Moemen, Y. S., Alshater, H., and El-Sayed, I. E. T. (2023). Clean Energy Management Based on Internet of Things and Sensor Networks for Climate Change Problems. In *The Power of Data: Driving Climate Change with Data Science and Artificial Intelligence Innovations* (pp. 117–136). Cham: Springer Nature Switzerland.
55. Singh, B. (2023). Blockchain Technology in Renovating Healthcare: Legal and Future Perspectives. In *Revolutionizing Healthcare through Artificial Intelligence and Internet of Things Applications* (pp. 177–186). IGI Global.
56. Nasserddine, G., Nassereddine, M., and El Arid, A. A. (2023). Internet of Things Integration in Renewable Energy Systems. In *Handbook of Research on Applications of AI, Digital Twin, and Internet of Things for Sustainable Development* (pp. 159–185). IGI Global.
57. Singh, B. (2024). Lensing Legal Dynamics for Examining Responsibility and Deliberation of Generative AI-Tethered Technological Privacy Concerns: Infringements and Use of Personal Data by Nefarious Actors. In A. Ara and A. Ara (Eds.), *Exploring the Ethical Implications*

ofGenerativeAI(pp.146–167).IGIGlobal.https://doi.org/10.4018/979-8-3693-1565-1.ch009

58. López, O. L., Rosabal, O. M., Ruiz-Guirola, D. E., Raghuwanshi, P., Mikhaylov, K., Lovén, L., and Iyer, S. (2023). Energy-sustainable Machine Learning connectivity: Vision, technological enablers, challenges, and future directions. *IEEE Open Journal of the Communications Society.*
59. Logeswaran, K., Suresh, P., Ponselvakumar, A. P., Savitha, S., Sentamilselvan, K., and Adhithyaa, N. (2023). Exploration of Assorted Modernizations in Forecasting Renewable Energy Using Low Power Wireless Technologies for IoTSG. *Smart Grids and Internet of Things: An Energy Perspective*, 157–191.
60. Singh, B. and Kaunert, C. (2024). Salvaging Responsible Consumption and Production of Food in the Hospitality Industry: Harnessing Machine Learning and Deep Learning for Zero Food Waste. In A. Singh, P. Tyagi, and A. Garg (Eds.), *Sustainable Disposal Methods of Food Wastes in Hospitality Operations* (pp. 176–192). IGI Global. https://doi.org/10.4018/979-8-3693-2181-2.ch012
61. Li, X., Zhao, H., Feng, Y., Li, J., Zhao, Y., and Wang, X. (2024). Research on Key Technologies of High Energy Efficiency and Low Power Consumption of New Data Acquisition Equipment of Power Internet of Things Based on Artificial Intelligence. *International Journal of Thermofluids*, *21*, 100575.
62. Singh, B. (2024). Evolutionary Global Neuroscience for Cognition and Brain Health: Strengthening Innovation in Brain Science. In P. Prabhakar (Ed.), *Biomedical Research Developments for Improved Healthcare* (pp. 246–272). IGI Global. https://doi.org/10.4018/979-8-3693-1922-2.ch012
63. Xie, H., Huang, R., Sun, H., Han, Z., Jiang, M., Zhang, D., ... and Wu, T. (2023). Wireless Energy: Paving the Way for Smart Cities and a Greener Future. *Energy and Buildings*, *297*, 113469.
64. Khan, M. W., Saad, S., Ammad, S., Rasheed, K., and Jamal, Q. (2024). Smart Infrastructure and AI. In *AI in Material Science* (pp. 193–215). CRC Press.
65. Samaei, S. R., and Ghahfarrokhi, M. A. (2023). Optimizing Coastal Hydro Turbines Integrating Artificial Intelligence for Sustainable Energy Conversion. In *2nd International Conference on Creative Achievements of Architecture, Urban Planning, Civil Engineering and Environment in the Sustainable Development of the Middle East.*
66. Kumar, D. (2023). Concept of Sustainable Energy System for Smart Cities. In *Renewable Energy Scenarios in Future Indian Smart Cities:*

A Geospatial Technology Perspective (pp. 1–20). Singapore: Springer Nature Singapore.

67. Almalki, F. A., Alsamhi, S. H., Sahal, R., Hassan, J., Hawbani, A., Rajput, N. S., ... and Breslin, J. (2023). Green Machine Learning for Eco-Friendly and Sustainable Smart Cities: Future Directions and Opportunities. *Mobile Networks and Applications, 28*(1), 178–202.
68. Salama, R., and Al-Turjman, F. (2023). Sustainable Energy Production in Smart Cities. *Sustainability, 15*(22), 16052.
69. Singh, B., and Kaunert, C. (2024). Salvaging Responsible Consumption and Production of Food in the Hospitality Industry: Harnessing Machine Learning and Deep Learning for Zero Food Waste. In *Sustainable Disposal Methods of Food Wastes in Hospitality Operations* (pp. 176–192). IGI Global.
70. Singh, B. (2024). Evolutionary Global Neuroscience for Cognition and Brain Health: Strengthening Innovation in Brain Science. In *Biomedical Research Developments for Improved Healthcare* (pp. 246–272). IGI Global.
71. Mohammed, M. N., Aljibori, H. S. S., Al-Tamimi, A., Alani, Z. N., Hameed, M. S., Ibrahim, F. M., ... and Alfiras, M. (2023, October). Toward Sustainable Smart Cities in Bahrain: A Groundbreaking Approach to Marine Renewable Energy Harnessing Sea Tides and Waves for a Greener Energy Future. In *2023 IEEE 8th International Conference on Engineering Technologies and Applied Sciences (ICETAS)* (pp. 1–5). IEEE.
72. Bin Abu Sofian, A. D. A., Lim, H. R., Siti Halimatul Munawaroh, H., Ma, Z., Chew, K. W., and Show, P. L. (2024). Machine Learning and the Renewable Energy Revolution: Exploring Solar and Wind Energy Solutions for a Sustainable Future Including Innovations in Energy Storage. *Sustainable Development.*
73. Fan, Z., Yan, Z., and Wen, S. (2023). Deep Learning and Artificial Intelligence in Sustainability: A Review of SDGs, Renewable Energy, and Environmental Health. *Sustainability, 15*(18), 13493.
74. Jain, A., Sharma, A., Jately, V., and Azzopardi, B. (Eds.). (2023). *Sustainable Energy Solutions with Artificial Intelligence, Blockchain Technology, and Internet of Things.* CRC Press.
75. Mirshafiee, F., Shahbazi, E., Safi, M., and Rituraj, R. (2023). Predicting Power and Hydrogen Generation of a Renewable Energy Converter Utilizing Data-Driven Methods: A Sustainable Smart Grid Case Study. *Energies, 16*(1), 502.

76. Yousef, L. A., Yousef, H., and Rocha-Meneses, L. (2023). Artificial Intelligence for Management of Variable Renewable Energy Systems: A Review of Current Status and Future Directions. *Energies, 16*(24), 8057.

77. Zhou, Y., and Liu, J. (2024). Advances in Emerging Digital Technologies for Energy Efficiency and Energy Integration in Smart Cities. *Energy and Buildings, 315*, 114289.

78. Nizetic, S., Arıcı, M., and Hoang, A. T. (2023). Smart and Sustainable Technologies in Energy Transition. *Journal of Cleaner Production, 389*, 135944.

79. Hui, C. X., Dan, G., Alamri, S., and Toghraie, D. (2023). Greening Smart Cities: An Investigation of the Integration of Urban Natural Resources and Smart City Technologies for Promoting Environmental Sustainability. *Sustainable Cities and Society, 99*, 104985.

80. Alshmeel, G. H. A., Al-Doori, A. S. B., Ahmed, S. R., Abrahim, Z. A., Ghaffoori, A. J., and Hussain, A. S. T. (2024, May). Self-Sustaining Buoy System: Harnessing Water Wave Energy for Smart, Wireless Sensing and Data Transmission. In *Proceedings of the Cognitive Models and Artificial Intelligence Conference* (pp. 349–356).

81. Wang, H., Wen, C., Duan, L., Li, X., Liu, D., and Guo, W. (2024). Sustainable Energy Transition in Cities: A Deep Statistical Prediction Model for Renewable Energy Sources Management for Low-Carbon Urban Development. *Sustainable Cities and Society, 107*, 105434.

Chapter 4

Smart Sustainable Cities: Addressing Privacy, Equity, and Social Justice through Fuzzy Decision-Making

Aditya Tomer[a] **and Tarun Kumar Kaushik**[b]

[a]*School of Law, Galgotias University, Greater Noida, Uttar Pradesh, India*
[b]*Sharda School of Law, Sharda University, Greater Noida, Uttar Pradesh, India*

dradityatomer@gmail.com, tkaushik1982@gmail.com

Abstract

The overlap of privacy and equity and social justice is especially important within rapidly smartening urban centers. This chapter examines how fuzzy decision-making can solve these complicated problems in the smart sustainable cities framework. The concept of fuzzy logic dealing with uncertainty as well as imprecision is used for an assessment and ranking of different stakeholders' views on how to proceed, to guarantee that the decision process incorporates all points due justice. The research starts with an evaluation of the effect of smart city projects on privacy rights, in particular considering data collection and surveillance. And it points to the importance of

Fuzzy Logic in Revolutionizing Renewable Energy
Edited by Bhupinder Singh, Komal Vig, Ruchi Lal, and Budi Agus Riswandi

ISBN 978-981-5129-92-2 (Hardcover), 978-1-003-74191-6 (eBook)
www.jennystanford.com

DOI: 10.1201/9781003741916-4

clear policies that do more to secure individual privacy, even as they maximize the potential value derived from this sort of smart tech. In addition, the article explores equity in urban planning and how access to smart cities must provide for equitable distribution of resources and services. The chapter is part of a broader and ongoing effort to use fuzzy decision-making frameworks to detect, as early on in the development process as possible, imbalances that could be brought about by technological progress. The chapter also pays attention to social justice, aiming to discuss how community engagement in the management of smart cities can be combined with participatory approaches in governance. Moreover, the use of fuzzy logic enables us to include different community perspectives and understand social dynamics in further detail; it helps identify possible biases that could operate during decision-making. Finally, this study provides a model to combine privacy with some concepts of equity and social justice using fuzzy decision-making that can be drawn on in the literature on sustainable urban development. Through creating a more inclusive urban governance model this research seeks to allow policy makers to develop smart sustainable cities with not just technological advancement but also social responsible and justified. The paper presents a comprehensive framework that can be used as guide for future researchers and practitioners towards smart urban environment solutions.

Keywords: Smart sustainable cities, Fuzzy decision-making, Privacy, Equity, Social justice

4.1 Introduction

The arrival of smart cities is the coming chapter in civilization-centered urban development, driven only by enormous convergence and integration of advanced information and communication technologies (ICTs) including IoT (Internet-of-Things), Big Data Analytics or Artificial Intelligence [1]. Fuzzy logic is a kind of multi-valued reasoning derived from a fuzzy set hypothesis to manage thinking that is inexact as opposed to exact, where the reality might be any real number somewhere around

0 and 1 [2]. A flow over fuzzy logic is a good methodology for the optimization of complex systems such as sustainable urban planning, resource management and service delivery [3].

At the same time, their increasing dependence on fuzzy logic decision-making in the public sphere of smart cities calls for more dialogue around issues such as privacy [4], fairness and social justice. Despite its numerous beneficial prospects for enhancing the livability and sustainability of cities, fuzzy logic is not transparent by nature due to a top-down data-driven driving strategy (a risk also shared with ethical bias that discriminates agents or their individual rights when malfunctioning) [4].

Fuzzy Ethics, and Social Effects on Sustainable Development in Smart Cities [5]. It analyzes by using fuzzy inference systems what kind of social inequality it is prone to promote, i.e., urban planning, traffic control, resource distribution, public access services [6]; how they can lead the current inclination and discriminate a wide range on society [7]; the chapter shifts to a case of regulating loose rule models by talking about privacy (the large data that smart city sensors and systems start harvesting on behalf fuzzy logic could be attacked or misused—which directly infringes individual rights over the person life) [8]. These challenges inform a proposal for the integration of fairness, transparency and accountability principles in FLS within smart cities design ([9] optimal combination advise). Instead, it makes the case for citizens and democratic governance as spaces in which fuzzy logic could be implemented with justice [10].

Future research in this domain must succor for designing an ethics statement to develop applications of smart cities using fuzzy reasoning models based on the above studies, e.g., XFLS, or Auditing if any bias exists with the algorithms used in these application cases by using other methods (one-hot encoded Fuzzy logic rules) that are also intended deployment but suggest that while doing so they could check where auditing may be done too [11]. We must proactively tackle societal implications in our quest to unlock the complete fuzzy potential of making cities more sustainable and livable [12].

4.1.1 Overview of Fuzzy Logic Applications in Smart Sustainable Cities

One of the hot research areas is the application of fuzzy logic for smart sustainable cities which have the full potential to optimize urban systems with ultimate sustainability [13]. For a complex and uncertain environment like the urban one, or in other words, with imprecise information (Fuzzy Logic) has newly been founded as an interesting modeling tool [14]. Fuzzy logic-based system is used in various fields of smart cities such as urban planning, transportation systems, environmental monitoring and control engineering to building design and infrastructure management [15]. One such example, as discussed in [16], is the implementation of a fuzzy inference system to predict resource allocation and energy consumption for better sustainability through motor behavior prediction capability including timing optimization for traffic signals. The fuzzy logic techniques can also deal with the uncertainty and imprecision which is inherent when one deals with data of urbanization in our day-to-day life hence more ELVS—a real-world view of sustainability where decisions are made have salty taste (indicates grey-tones) but not basically that good or worst—of course depending on user point-of-view for grey—as color sometimes too because now we take all things considered—or indulging [17]. I mean... how do we create strategies to global challenges such as air pollution, waste management and public services that involve everyone? [18]. However, in the smart city domain, this is one of many emerging trends that challenges large ethical and societal issues with respect to privacy, bias (which are criteria on which a decision or inference will be made) and fairness [19]. These have led to many research lines still open with respect to the deployment of urban applications where principles such as transparency, accountability and citizen engagement can be embedded into their design [20].

4.1.2 Importance of Considering Privacy, Equity, and Social Justice Implications

The use of fuzzy logic decision-taking might extend into smart city, and then there are immediate concerns about privacy, equity and social justice [21]. Still, the potential impact of fuzzy logic to increase the quality of life and sustainability in cities is considerable. So when it is implemented there are consequences which can be good as well bad: new forms introduced without correct information about how this affects people, including biases not known before [22]. Consequently, misleading inferences will cause a fuzziness inference systems instead of accurate public transportation agency plans and another services ones over the chosen group that it may hurt the other part by disadvantages of them alongside serve as homogeneous groups but further serve to recycle present socioeconomic inequities [23]. Intending to operate in such a fuzzy logic environment, several models trained by the vast amounts of data surging from smart city sensors and systems invite invasion or misuse as well; which steps on individual privacy rights [24].

4.2 Fuzzy Logic Decision-Making in the Public Sphere

The emerging usage of fuzzy logic systems in smart green cities is also significant for another reason which depends on the public sphere [15]. Deep fuzzy inference systems were often employed over a broader range of urban domains, ranging from transport and resource allocation to environmental monitoring as well as the domain in question (urban planning) [46]. The black-box nature of these systems indicates that even though they will enable better decision making to handle the vast complexities inherent in city operations, using data-informed decision-making methods (the current technological state) is characterized by risks associated with bias and discrimination at least as much public accountability can be certain [27]. It is precisely because of the vagueness and ambiguity in real-world urban data that fuzzy logic comes handy for decision making related to context and intuition [28]. However, the algorithms which underlie such systems may have a disturbing side effect in favoring one demographic or neighborhood over another can only make these socioeconomic gaps even worse [29]. At one end, fuzzy logic models for public services allocation—such as infrastructure investments—may overdifferentiate certain territories and therefore prevent some of them from being served in comparison with richer ones [29]. Besides, there is a huge privacy leakage since those big data may be correlated through smart devices and such collected data can serve as input to fuzzy models [31]. Data faces a risk of being hacked or leaking in cases that endanger privacy rights while it is not controlled and supervised [32]. Fuzzy logic algorithms can model decisions just like the human mind does and have quality in representation, but again when these systems make decision makers err via the black box method, they might be also used [33].

4.2.1 Use of Fuzzy Inference Systems for Urban Planning, Transportation, Resource Allocation

While the supportive models had been evolving towards this philosophy to develop an artificial brain, today many of these are based in cities and their local economic pockets designed for not-so-simple urban systems optimized from within using fuzzy Inference systems, illustrated by potential sustainability increasing productivity growth [34]. For the use of fuzzy logic to model in the context of urban planning, more realistic models may be achieved for land uses within every place other infrastructure as well as investment and public service provision on conditions that human activities (read data) are inherently obscure [35]. FIS can be used to model traffic congestion, signal timing optimization and travel demand forecasting for planning in transportation so as to improve the mobility experience while minimizing environmental impacts [36]. As a result of linguistic variables and fuzzy rules by which these systems operate, they can include subjective perceptions/types/opinions/feelings/ judgements/preferences/views/taste, etc., where often the last two already involve personal prejudice/bias [37]. Fuzzy logic applies the same solution to urban resources like energy, water and waste management, which is scarce [38] as well. It classifies the data efficiently and learns to distribute fuzzy inference-based resources or enable sustainable cities based on dynamic demand, weather conditions, event status across a city proper [39]. However, the public sphere including more fuzzy logic decision-making is questionable regarding privacy (especially commercial exploitation of good data) and precaution against bias such as fairness must be questioned [40]. The development of these systems should be carried out under ethical frameworks and governance mechanisms by the two so that they protect public goods [41].

4.2.2 Privacy Concerns with Fuzzy Logic in Smart Cities

The general deployment of fuzzy logic decision making in the smart cities is creating a large set of privacy and data security concerns [42]. The smart sensors and systems share the usage of traffic data-related resource allocation trends monitored by all kinds in emerging trends input into learning-based fuzzy inference ancillary sub-systems involved from urban planning to other city-wide domains hence those are also significant inputs [43]. It might contain information about the motion, activity and preferences of individual citizens—who had walked were they not monitored from a high street camera that leaks; whose smart toothbrushes works on Bluetooth providing key insights in oral hygiene but are equally connected to public Wi-Fi network with minimal data protection. For fuzzy logic algorithms, on the other hand, their lack of transparency about data usage makes it challenging to establish accountability [44]. It is a concern that personal safeguards may be less maintained by governing processes which control the use of people's data to block violations, such as monetized surveillance practices—and sometimes advancing positions appearing exploitative and discriminative in targeting adverts [45].

Aggregating data from a multitude of datasets as input to fuzzy logic models could also serve in building more accurate citizen profiles at the lower level, which at the end can breach privacy and anonymity [46]. This is particularly concerning when it may be the most marginalized being subject to targeted, intentional or otherwise available data hoovering as part of the same systems they are trying to avoid [47], so ensuring public trust in fuzzy logic smart city approaches means avoiding such encroachments on privacy. We need laws/regulations and sufficient encryption to control the circumstances in which the technology is utilized [48].

4.3 Vulnerability to Data Breaches and Misuse

That even the dutiful data being gathered at a massive scale every minute by smart city sensors and systems to inform fuzzy logic models is subject, leaving individuals vulnerable not merely on the margins of conventional ethical boundaries [49]. While Smart city technologies can turn the places where we work, shop or simply walk down the street into sensor-enabled data-collecting environments—with surveillance cameras and traffic sensors; smart meters that reveal when a house is occupied; environmental monitors reporting pollution levels... organizers manufactured by businesses from which individuals have to buy back their own lives [50]. The data is then agglomerated and fuzzy logic inference systems are used to revise how cities operate in a less energy-consuming delivery of services [51]. The high complexity and interconnection in a smart city infrastructure make it one of the prime targets for data breach or farming [52]. This might involve anything from the penetration of these companies' internal systems or networks, to unauthorized access to extremely private end-user data that they store and leverage again ordinary people for malicious purposes such as identify theft, stalking and targeted surveillance [16]. Moreover, the black-box nature of fuzzy logic algorithms creates additional difficulties in proving that data involved in decision making are transparent and accountable [54]. Moreover, the ability to share data between agencies also represents a challenge—purely from a security perspective and in terms of where future resistance will lie; if we are able to circumvent licensing technical challenges (using steaming message formats) by sharing files between agencies, there is a danger that personal information could be used against citizens as part one would assume those mechanisms do not exist [75]. Policies and processes to address these concerns will be vital if Smart City initiatives, which are often based on fuzzy logic approach [56], hope to win the trust of its citizens. Unfortunately, harsh data security and encryption mandates combined with overarching regulations that give citizens more power over their own data will not reduce the harm in these systems operating on massive stores of personal information given willingly to them by users [57].

4.4 Equity and Social Justice Implications

Thus, the stronger reliance of fuzzy logic in smart cities is more serious to both equality and social mutualism [58]. Thereby generating a broader spread of outcomes (and by extension opportunities and problems for the citizens), fuzzy inference systems that underlie urban planning, resource allocation or public service delivery can introduce systematic bias in favoring some groups or individual neighborhoods over others to an extent which supports existing socio-economic disparities [60]. For example, a fuzzy logic model designed to say where resources such as infrastructure investment or public amenities should go may end up under-serving oppressed populations while benefiting subjects who are less marginalized [61]. These are the most opaque algorithms to scrutinize for fairness and accountability [62]—and if we cannot inspect them, detecting bias is equally challenging. Further, the enormous amounts of noisy data collected by sensors and instruments in smart city scenarios to fill fuzzy logic models may apparently produce vulnerable profiles, especially related to privacy [63]. Equity and social justice (versions of fuzzy or not) will need to reconcile with these important factors in ways that are unfamiliar before any hope arises for a smart city based on logic which is equally as variable [64]. As a result, ethical frameworks and governance structures that enable fair inclusive democratic decision-making will become even more important [65]. Citizen design, as well as deployment of this now also encompasses social justice since citizen based technologies include voices from typically unheard constituents [66]. This behavior may contribute to maintaining societal schisms rather than proactively addressing equity considerations posed by smart cities fuzzy logic and foster public qualms against their realization [67].

4.5 Unequal Access to Smart City Technologies and Benefits

As we lean on IoT solutions fueled by fuzzy logic for our cities and communities, how do you ensure not just everyone has data access—but people get to enjoy the benefits of a more connected life? When cities invest in such cutting-edge urban infrastructures, as the ones—including electric vehicle (EV) charging points and 5G telecom masts—predicted to be essential for long-term economic competitiveness—and are also common public goods—they do so at the risk of uneven benefits/native costs-sharing among their citizens [70]. For example, lack of digital literacy, language barriers and disabilities amongst others may result in marginalized communities facing further obstacles to using the technology solutions that are available [69]. For instance, smart mobility solutions view ride-sharing apps or electric vehicle charging stations can be exclusive to serve higher-income residents but insufficient for lower-income populations when applied on transportation infrastructure [70]. The digital decision-making based on data-driven logic in smart cities, using a fuzzy approach with the MuPAD tool would have to be handled carefully so as not to equalize neighborhoods among which resources and services are distributed differently [71–76]. The systems that power these can also generate inequities in health care, education and housing when their algorithms fail to take into account equity [72]. These include making smart city technologies open, accessible and general [73, 76]. Both areas are a subset of the main digital skills focused targeted training, now also in multiple-language interfaces and providing small grants/subsidies for welfare receivers with low-income group that cannot afford home Internet services [74], dynamics in community engagement helping msmi to understand hard-coded social context-specific economic marginalizations deeply embedded through diverse population demarcs [75]. The design and development of smart city fuzzy logic systems must adhere to principles that incorporate equity, equality or social justice such as those mentioned in the global standard on quality-of-life among others [76] if we want our conception of smart cities realize excellence in living for all citizens.

4.6 Embedding Fairness into Fuzzy Logic Systems

The alternative is to A/B test fuzzy logic models with myriad datasetships and contextual perturbations as a blanket audit for algorithmic bias [77]. This can be our way of eliminating bias introduced by data which went into training or wrong assumptions. One such technique example is adversarial debiasing which aims to train a model to parametrically balance biases [78].

Fairness: In addition to the issues raised by wide use of computing, methods must also be fair in their results; transparency and explainability are critical here as well. Moreover, the concept of fuzzy logic system cultivation should equally be interlinked to very clear delineations for any impact generated as citizens might and will most likely want to know how they are affected while decision-makers need not avail themselves from any form of accountability [79]. For example, third-party independent auditing of open data and algorithms by design can introduce an additional layer of transparency [80]. In the end, citizen involvement is placed together with co-design as a critical level of smart city fuzzy logic fairness systems [81]. Assisting a variety of stakeholders, particularly from low-income and marginalized areas in the development phase for deployment will help support these technologies as public goods [82]. Based on the response from our community, we will need feedback-based adjusting meta-analyses and ongoing monitoring [83]. In the end, unlocking fuzzy logic to create cities in which justice and sustainability are made real is necessarily a comprehensive goal with an emphasis on equity, transparency, and citizen agency [84]. Creating ethical frameworks and governance structures will become a central demand for policymakers and urban planners [85].

4.7 Importance of Transparency and Explainability

Rule fuzziness in decision-making systems for smart cities calls for greater transparency and explainability [86], which greatly matters when it comes to fairness and accountability [87]. Likewise, because these algorithms are basically hidden as well, it is hard for the public to understand how such decisions impact them and in turn hold authorities accountable [88]. Otherwise, stakeholders cannot ask about the logic or assumptions behind them [89], thus any fuzzy inference system should have an interpretability approach to its inferences. Typically, this may include some form of human intervention like natural language explanations [90], visualization of the fuzzy rules and membership functions, sensitivity analysis to show how inputs affect outputs [91]. Open data and algorithmic auditing (in ideally independent [92]) will further support this transparency. Opening the data and models, these fuzzy logic systems depend on citizen scrutiny (subject, of course, to as much individual privacy protection as possible) [93], encourages external validation and auditability [94, 95]. It is before deployment that the audit will pinpoint possible biases, errors or unintended consequences [96]. Transparency in the process, for example, facilitates visibility about how a decision is made, and this has significant importance for decisions where considerable interest are at stake since those to whom authoritative allocation (resource or public service delivery) directly affects [97], can develop trust that their interests have been duly considered. Explainable fuzzy logic systems serving the purpose of the public because they supposedly demonstrate their decisions are made in an objective and not black box-oriented manner [100]. In general, it is evident that the extent of transparency and explainability helps to reach most out of quality available within an open framework smart city context full fuzziness model [101]. Such initiatives facilitate collective intelligence [101] as they equip ordinary citizens to know and interfere with the systems of which they are part in their lives, thus fostering groundswells for equity, accountability, democratic agency ([102], p.

4.8 Citizen Engagement and Democratic Governance

In conjunction with a smart city, these fuzzy logic systems must be implemented in an ethical manner and civic engagement as well as democratic governance frameworks will play crucial roles [100]. Since these technologies can have significant effects in the public sphere [101], it is important for all citizens to be included when discussing design and implementation and auditorial processes of digital solutions using DLTs. For example, ref. [103] proposes participatory design practices with a wide range of stakeholders in order to incorporate these essential ideas, which it describes as fuzzy logic decision-making. Moreover, citizen advisory boards have watched closely and ensured the properites of surveillance tools being part of a much broader constitutional policing framework in a regional approval process through public forums as well crowdsourcing platform for continuous feedbacks over how this technology is used based on local needs [104]. And, as such, a specified governance structure with non-dependent regulatory oversight and auditing capabilities should be established [105]. These may be ethics committees, data protection authorities or even algorithmic impact assessment panels to evaluate deploy fuzzy logic systems for adverse consequences or biases [106]. Systems should be auditable in two complementary ways: (i) They should reveal their processes, such as data sources and inferential links between algorithms and mechanisms for decision-making reviewed through open-data initiatives [107]. (ii) The transparency of system outputs could help to scrutinize how these systems are developed over time. This provides citizens with the information they need to understand how they are affected or be pissed at someone [108]. To extract all of the potentialities contained in this mandala involves a form of urban governance participatory, inclusive and democratic that is at the root excel [109]. These smart technologies have the potential to be used in ways that benefit citizens when they are placed at the center of citizen engagement [110].

4.8.1 Case Studies

The arguments surrounding the components of fuzzy city governance have been presented and analysed; hence, these case studies may be illustrative of ethical dimensions useful to consider overall [111]. As an example, the fuzzy logic for traffic management system has been reconstructed in Singapore [112]. To minimize downtime of vehicles, and hence lower emissions as well as congestion, Singapore uses Machine Learning (ML) to learn from its sensors that collect real-time traffic data for the city-state to adjust traffic signal timing [...] [113]. This debate surrounds the concerns that the autonomous bus system would further gentrify only wealthy neighborhoods with better infrastructure, and deepen already marginalized transportation deficient communities elsewhere [114]. Another example, urban planning studies resource allocation in Rio de Janeiro, based on fuzzy logic [115]. The different edition of urban planning and analysis that the city adopted with these technologies permits an understanding of complex surrounding in dynamic global cities which give good service to their citizens as health or education [116]. Critics, however, claim that the black-box model of these algorithms has encouraged decision-makers to lump areas together and prioritize urban development over social divides [117]. A third example is a control scheme to operate a fuzzy logic system based smart energy management platform in Copenhagen, Denmark [118]. Although these kind of systems have been successful in saving energy and accommodating renewables, privacy advocate groups suspect that smart metering system take much personal data [119] and also how it could be used to penalize or steal from anyone's home [120]. These provide varied examples of the kinds of ethical and equity dilemmas that arise from a fuzzy logic in smart cities. Developing robust governance architectures and citizen participation approaches will be essential to avoiding their misuse for public benefit [121].

4.8.2 Lessons Learned and Best Practices

Several important lessons learned and best practices for future implementation policies are related to the ethical, wider social, and usage mandates associated with deploying fuzzy logic in smart sustainable cities [122]. Above all, FIS design and implementation should be guided by the principles of fairness, transparency and accountability [123]. This is auditing algorithmic bias ruthlessly; it reads like models for transparency that must be what go to court or abide by privacy norms, and getting independent review in place no Gordian Knot of illiberal uses can slip through the cracks [124]. Of equal importance is citizens' participation in governance and their voice [125]. Ensuring that fuzzy-logic smart city initiatives have public interest technology roles ensures a diversity of stakeholders are well-represented in the development and rollout processes [126], including supporting marginalized communities. This is best achieved through ongoing feedback loops and the ability to adapt based on community input [127]. Massive data collections are needed for fuzzy logic models; the risk of privacy is quite high, and hence to secure these types of model we should apply cyber security along with encryption techniques based on good practices in general treatment off personal information [128]. The solution lies in giving greater control to citizens over their data and having strict guidelines around when this can be collected or shared [129]. A third point: the integration needs a holistic and interdisciplinary framework from low layers, technical issues to through high-level human ones. Technical challenges require articulation with social questions that interface this continuum of concern. Urban planners working along data scientists with ethicists in co-laborationism community peers could work together as tradeoff brokers for smart cities' fuzzy logic [130]. This process enables cities to learn from these lessons and in so doing, begin thinking more fuzzily about logic as a way of dealing with its societal consequences using best practices that will optimize sustainable and livable aspects of a one-use world [131].

4.9 Conclusion and Future Directions

Nonetheless, the same trends are emerging in a new domain—fuzzy logic-based decisions in smart sustainable cities—that has significant implications for privacy and access to basic human needs (equity) alongside social justice issues which leave this area open to some profound ethical reflection. However, these technologies are black-boxed systems that inherently run on vast data footprints—even as they have potential for greater integrated infrastructure and sustainability. Urban planning; transportation: resource allocation (...); all are examples of public services that inherently require fuzzy/inductive inference systems to prioritize which group or geographic area comes first during triggers such as legal citizens trying to weave through city traffic instead of having a gridlock, fare-dodgers with dropped out payment cards now wishing they should have one went for free bikes for rent downtown even if the bicycles aren't currently working, etc. In addition, the data those smart city sensors and systems collect to power these models is likely equally unprotected from being breached or repurposed by bad actors who could violate individual privacy rights. These challenges can be addressed when considering the realization processes in fuzzy-based decision support systems from a holistic viewpoint, built upon equity-driven approaches that embrace values of transparency and accountability. Without public buy-in, legal frameworks and data protection measures that are coherent with democratic governance, these tools will simply not function for the betterment of society. Next, understanding future research directions in constructing interpretable fuzzy logic models; Auditing for algorithmic bias across the equity spectrum with emphasis on some of its ethical dimensions and a comprehensive list of principles from smart city applications. Finding ways to strike that balance and avoiding potentially deleterious side-effects of those powerful new technologies will be a difficult task and demands inter-disciplinary collaboration among technologists, urban planners, ethicists and communities. To fulfill the socioeconomics of fuzzy logic and creating more sustainable/liveable cities, we need to be ahead on where it is leading us. Utilizing the above, cities can realize these technologies while maintaining privacy and a commitment to equity and social justice.

References

1. Ray, R. K., Chowdhury, F. R., and Hasan, M. R. (2024). Blockchain applications in retail cybersecurity: Enhancing supply chain integrity, secure transactions, and data protection. *Journal of Business and Management Studies*, 6(1), 206–214.
2. Dinesh Arokia Raj, A., Jha, R. R., Yadav, M., Sam, D., and Jayanthi, K. (2024). Role of blockchain and watermarking toward cyber-security. In *Multimedia Watermarking: Latest Developments and Trends* (pp. 103–123). Singapore: Springer Nature Singapore.

3. Yue, Y., and Shyu, J. Z. (2024). A paradigm shift in crisis management: the nexus of AGI-driven intelligence fusion networks and blockchain trustworthiness. *Journal of Contingencies and Crisis Management*, 32(1), e12541.
4. Mithas, S., Chen, Z. L., Saldanha, T. J., and De Oliveira Silveira, A. (2022). How will artificial intelligence and industry 4.0 emerging technologies transform operations management?. *Production and Operations Management*, 31(12), 4475–4487.
5. Ivanov, D., Dolgui, A., and Sokolov, B. (2019). The impact of digital technology and industry 4.0 on the ripple effect and supply chain risk analytics. *International Journal of Production Research*, 57(3), 829–846.
6. Javaid, M., Haleem, A., Singh, R. P., Suman, R., and Gonzalez, E. S. (2022). Understanding the adoption of industry 4.0 technologies in improving environmental sustainability. *Sustainable Operations and Computers*, 3, 203–217.
7. Fraga-Lamas, P., Lopes, S. I., and Fernández-Caramés, T. M. (2021). Green IoT and edge AI as key technological enablers for a sustainable digital transition towards a smart circular economy: An industry 5.0 use case. *Sensors*, 21(17), 5745.
8. Felsberger, A., Qaiser, F. H., Choudhary, A., and Reiner, G. (2022). The impact of industry 4.0 on the reconciliation of dynamic capabilities: Evidence from the European manufacturing industries. *Production Planning and Control*, 33(2–3), 277–300.
9. Rath, K. C., Khang, A., and Roy, D. (2024). The role of internet of things (IoT) technology in industry 4.0 economy. In *Advanced IoT Technologies and Applications in the Industry 4.0 Digital Economy* (pp. 1–28). CRC Press.
10. Asadollahi-Yazdi, E., Couzon, P., Nguyen, N. Q., Ouazene, Y., and Yalaoui, F. (2020). industry 4.0: Revolution or evolution?. *American Journal of Operations Research*, 10(06), 241.
11. Meyendorf, N., Ida, N., Singh, R., and Vrana, J. (2023). NDE 4.0: Progress, promise, and its role to industry 4.0. *NDT and E International*, 140, 102957.
12. Zhong, R. Y., Xu, X., Klotz, E., and Newman, S. T. (2017). Intelligent manufacturing in the context of industry 4.0: A review. *Engineering*, 3(5), 616–630.
13. Angelopoulos, A., Michailidis, E. T., Nomikos, N., Trakadas, P., Hatziefremidis, A., Voliotis, S., and Zahariadis, T. (2019). Tackling

faults in the industry 4.0 era—a survey o machine-learning solutions and key aspects. *Sensors*, 20(1), 109.

14. Lu, C., Lyu, J., Zhang, L., Gong, A., Fan, Y., Yan, J., and Li, X. (2020). Nuclear power plants with artificial intelligence in industry 4.0 era: Top-level design and current applications—A systemic review. *IEEE Access*, 8, 194315–194332.
15. Chander, B., Pal, S., De, D., and Buyya, R. (2022). Artificial intelligence-based internet of things for industry 5.0. In *Artificial Intelligence-Based Internet of Things Systems* (pp. 3–45).
16. Kasowaki, L., and Ahmet, S. (2024). Shielding the Virtual Ramparts: Understanding Cybersecurity Essentials (No. 11700). EasyChair.
17. Sima, V., Gheorghe, I. G., Subić, J., and Nancu, D. (2020). Influences of the industry 4.0 revolution on the human capital development and consumer behavior: A systematic review. *Sustainability*, 12(10), 4035.
18. Tseng, M. L., Tran, T. P. T., Ha, H. M., Bui, T. D., and Lim, M. K. (2021). Sustainable industrial and operation engineering trends and challenges Toward industry 4.0: A data driven analysis. *Journal of Industrial and Production Engineering*, 38(8), 581–598.
19. Anastasi, S., Madonna, M., and Monica, L. (2021). Implications of embedded artificial intelligence-machine learning on safety of machinery. *Procedia Computer Science*, 180, 338–343.
20. Dwivedi, Y. K., Hughes, L., Ismagilova, E., Aarts, G., Coombs, C., Crick, T., ... and Williams, M. D. (2021). Artificial intelligence (AI): Multidisciplinary perspectives on emerging challenges, opportunities, and agenda for research, practice and policy. *International Journal of Information Management*, 57, 101994.
21. Majstorovic, V. D., and Mitrovic, R. (2019). Industry 4.0 programs worldwide. In *Proceedings of the 4th International Conference on the Industry 4.0 Model for Advanced Manufacturing: AMP 2019* (pp. 78–99). Springer International Publishing.
22. Badri, A., Boudreau-Trudel, B., and Souissi, A. S. (2018). Occupational health and safety in the industry 4.0 era: A cause for major concern? *Safety Science*, 109, 403–411.
23. Xu, L. D., Xu, E. L., and Li, L. (2018). Industry 4.0: State of the art and future trends. *International Journal of Production Research*, 56(8), 2941–2962.
24. Bhuiyan, A. B., Ali, M. J., Zulkifli, N., and Kumarasamy, M. M. (2020). Industry 4.0: Challenges, opportunities, and strategic solutions

for Bangladesh. *International Journal of Business and Management Future*, 4(2), 41–56.

25. Reier Forradellas, R. F., and Garay Gallastegui, L. M. (2021). Digital transformation and artificial intelligence applied to business: Legal regulations, economic impact and perspective. *Laws*, 10(3), 70.
26. Singh Rajawat, A., Bedi, P., Goyal, S. B., Shukla, P. K., Zaguia, A., Jain, A., and Monirujjaman Khan, M. (2021). Reformist framework for improving human security for mobile robots in industry 4.0. *Mobile Information Systems*, 2021, 1–10.
27. Leng, J., Ye, S., Zhou, M., Zhao, J. L., Liu, Q., Guo, W., ... and Fu, L. (2020). Blockchain- secured smart manufacturing in industry 4.0: A survey. *IEEE Transactions on Systems, Man, and Cybernetics: Systems*, 51(1), 237–252.
28. Javaid, M., Haleem, A., Singh, R. P., Khan, S., and Suman, R. (2021). Blockchain technology applications for industry 4.0: A literature-based review. *Blockchain: Research and Applications*, 2(4), 100027.
29. Hassoun, A., Aït-Kaddour, A., Abu-Mahfouz, A. M., Rathod, N. B., Bader, F., Barba, F. J., ... and Regenstein, J. (2023). The fourth industrial revolution in the food industry—Part I: Industry 4.0 technologies. *Critical Reviews in Food Science and Nutrition*, 63(23), 6547–6563.
30. Aoun, A., Ilinca, A., Ghandour, M., and Ibrahim, H. (2021). A review of industry 4.0 characteristics and challenges, with potential improvements using blockchain technology. *Computers and Industrial Engineering*, 162, 107746.
31. Arden, N. S., Fisher, A. C., Tyner, K., Lawrence, X. Y., Lee, S. L., and Kopcha, M. (2021). Industry 4.0 for pharmaceutical manufacturing: Preparing for the smart factories of the future. *International Journal of Pharmaceutics*, 602, 120554.
32. Rane, N. (2023). Transformers in industry 4.0, industry 5.0, and society 5.0: Roles and challenges. Available at SSRN: https://ssrn.com/abstract=4609915 or http://dx.doi.org/10.2139/ssrn.4609915.
33. Awan, U., Sroufe, R., and Shahbaz, M. (2021). Industry 4.0 and the circular economy: A literature review and recommendations for future research. *Business Strategy and the Environment*, 30(4), 2038–2060.
34. Kumar, S. H., Talasila, D., Gowrav, M. P., and Gangadharappa, H. V. (2020). Adaptations of pharma 4.0 from industry 4.0. *Drug Invention Today*, 14(3).

35. Li, B. H., Hou, B. C., Yu, W. T., Lu, X. B., and Yang, C. W. (2017). Applications of artificial intelligence in intelligent manufacturing: A review. *Frontiers of Information Technology and Electronic Engineering*, 18, 86–96.

36. Kurniawan, T. A., Maiurova, A., Kustikova, M., Bykovskaia, E., Othman, M. H. D., and Goh, H. H. (2022). Accelerating sustainability transition in St. Petersburg (Russia) through digitalization-based circular economy in waste recycling industry: A strategy to promote carbon neutrality in era of Industry 4.0. *Journal of Cleaner Production*, 363, 132452.

37. Jakka, G., Yathiraju, N., and Ansari, M. F. (2022). Artificial intelligence in terms of spotting malware and delivering cyber risk management. *Journal of Positive School Psychology*, 6(3), 6156–6165.

38. Xing, K., Cropley, D. H., Oppert, M. L., and Singh, C. (2021). Readiness for digital innovation and industry 4.0 transformation: Studies on manufacturing industries in the city of Salisbury. In *Business Innovation with New ICT in the Asia-Pacific: Case Studies* (pp. 155–176).

39. Shi, Z., Xie, Y., Xue, W., Chen, Y., Fu, L., and Xu, X. (2020). Smart factory in industry 4.0. *Systems Research and Behavioral Science*, 37(4), 607–617.

40. Finance, A. T. C. C. (2015). *Industry 4.0 Challenges and Solutions for the Digital Transformation and Use of Exponential Technologies. Finance, Audit Tax Consulting Corporate* (pp. 1–12). Switzerland: Deloitte, Zurich.

41. Saeed, S., Altamimi, S. A., Alkayyal, N. A., Alshehri, E., and Alabbad, D. A. (2023). Digital transformation and cybersecurity challenges for businesses resilience: Issues and recommendations. *Sensors*, 23(15), 6666.

42. Kumar, S., and Mallipeddi, R. R. (2022). Impact of cybersecurity on operations and supply chain management: Emerging trends and future research directions. *Production and Operations Management*, 31(12), 4488–4500.

43. Bag, S., and Pretorius, J. H. C. (2022). Relationships between industry 4.0, sustainable manufacturing and circular economy: Proposal of a research framework. *International Journal of Organizational Analysis*, 30(4), 864–898.

44. Morgan, J., Halton, M., Qiao, Y., and Breslin, J. G. (2021). Industry 4.0 smart reconfigurable manufacturing machines. *Journal of Manufacturing Systems*, 59, 481–506.

45. Singh, S. K., Sharma, S. K., Singla, D., and Gill, S. S. (2022). Evolving requirements and application of SDN and IoT in the context of industry 4.0, blockchain and artificial intelligence. In *Software Defined Networks: Architecture and Applications* (pp. 427–496).
46. Nica, E., and Stehel, V. (2021). Internet of things sensing networks, artificial intelligence-based decision-making algorithms, and real-time process monitoring in sustainable industry 4.0. *Journal of Self-Governance and Management Economics*, 9(3), 35–47.
47. Borowski, P. F. (2021). Innovative processes in managing an enterprise from the energy and food sector in the era of industry 4.0. *Processes*, 9(2), 381.
48. Ahmad, T., Zhang, D., Huang, C., Zhang, H., Dai, N., Song, Y., and Chen, H. (2021). Artificial intelligence in the sustainable energy industry: Status Quo, challenges and opportunities. *Journal of Cleaner Production*, 289, 125834.
49. Wamba-Taguimdje, S. L., Fosso Wamba, S., Kala Kamdjoug, J. R., and Tchatchouang Wanko, C. E. (2020). Influence of artificial intelligence (AI) on firm performance: The business value of AI-based transformation projects. *Business Process Management Journal*, 26(7), 1893–1924.
50. Popov, V. V., Kudryavtseva, E. V., Kumar Katiyar, N., Shishkin, A., Stepanov, S. I., and Goel, S. (2022). Industry 4.0 and digitalisation in healthcare. *Materials*, 15(6), 2140.
51. Lu, Y. (2019). Artificial intelligence: A survey on evolution, models, applications and future trends. *Journal of Management Analytics*, 6(1), 1–29.
52. Blobel, B. (2020, September). Application of industry 4.0 concept to health care. In *pHealth 2020: Proceedings of the 17th International Conference on Wearable Micro and Nano Technologies for Personalized Health* (Vol. 273, p. 23). IOS Press.
53. Borowski, P. F. (2021). Digitization, digital twins, blockchain, and industry 4.0 as elements of management process in enterprises in the energy sector. *Energies*, 14(7), 1885.
54. Lim, C. H., Lim, S., How, B. S., Ng, W. P. Q., Ngan, S. L., Leong, W. D., and Lam, H. L. (2021). A review of industry 4.0 revolution potential in a sustainable and renewable palm oil industry: HAZOP approach. *Renewable and Sustainable Energy Reviews*, 135, 110223.
55. Vogt, J. (2021). Where is the human got to go? Artificial intelligence, machine learning, big data, digitalisation, and human–robot interaction in industry 4.0 and 5.0: Review Comment on: Bauer, M. (2020). Preise

kalkulieren mit KI-gestützter Onlineplattform BAM GmbH, Weiden, Bavaria, Germany. AI and SOCIETY, 36(3), 1083–1087.

56. Gadekar, R., Sarkar, B., and Gadekar, A. (2022). Key performance indicator based dynamic decision-making framework for sustainable industry 4.0 implementation risks evaluation: Reference to the Indian manufacturing industries. *Annals of Operations Research*, 318(1), 189–249.

57. Tao, F., Akhtar, M. S., and Jiayuan, Z. (2021). The future of artificial intelligence in cybersecurity: A comprehensive survey. *EAI Endorsed Transactions on Creative Technologies*, 8(28), e3–e3.

58. Chen, Y., Lu, Y., Bulysheva, L., and Kataev, M. Y. (2022). Applications of blockchain in industry 4.0: A review. *Information Systems Frontiers*, 26(5), 1715–1729.

59. Mourtzis, D., Angelopoulos, J., and Panopoulos, N. (2022). A literature review of the challenges and opportunities of the transition from industry 4.0 to society 5.0. *Energies*, 15(17), 6276.

60. Wan, J., Yang, J., Wang, Z., and Hua, Q. (2018). Artificial intelligence for cloud-assisted smart factory. *IEEE Access*, 6, 55419–55430.

61. Cioffi, R., Travaglioni, M., Piscitelli, G., Petrillo, A., and De Felice, F. (2020). Artificial intelligence and machine learning applications in smart production: Progress, trends, and directions. *Sustainability*, 12(2), 492.

62. Laskurain-Iturbe, I., Arana-Landín, G., Landeta-Manzano, B., and Uriarte-Gallastegi, N. (2021). Exploring the influence of industry 4.0 technologies on the circular economy. *Journal of Cleaner Production*, 321, 128944.

63. Brock, J. K. U., and Von Wangenheim, F. (2019). Demystifying AI: What digital transformation leaders can teach you about realistic artificial intelligence. *California Management Review*, 61(4), 110–134.

64. Nguyen, T., Gosine, R. G., and Warrian, P. (2020). A systematic review of big data analytics for oil and gas industry 4.0. *IEEE Access*, 8, 61183–61201.

65. Hassoun, A., Prieto, M. A., Carpena, M., Bouzembrak, Y., Marvin, H. J., Pallares, N., ... and Bono, G. (2022). Exploring the role of green and industry 4.0 technologies in achieving sustainable development goals in food sectors. *Food Research International*, 162, 112068.

66. Nahavandi, S. (2019). Industry 5.0—A human-centric solution. *Sustainability*, 11(16), 4371.

67. Zhou, J., Zhang, S., Lu, Q., Dai, W., Chen, M., Liu, X., ... and Herrera-Viedma, E. (2021). A survey on federated learning and its applications for accelerating industrial internet of things. arXiv preprint arXiv:2104.10501.

68. de la Peña Zarzuelo, I., Soeane, M. J. F., and Bermúdez, B. L. (2020). Industry 4.0 in the port and maritime industry: A literature review. *Journal of Industrial Information Integration*, 20, 100173.

69. Sánchez-Sotano, A., Cerezo-Narváez, A., Abad-Fraga, F., Pastor-Fernández, A., and Salguero-Gómez, J. (2020). Trends of digital transformation in the shipbuilding sector. In *New Trends in the Use of Artificial Intelligence for the Industry 4.0*. IntechOpen.

70. Bokhari, S. A. A., and Myeong, S. (2023). *The Influence of Artificial Intelligence on e- Governance and Cybersecurity in Smart Cities: A Stakeholder's Perspective*. Vol 11, IEEE Access. 69783–69797.

71. Ali, A., Septyanto, A. W., Chaudhary, I., Al Hamadi, H., Alzoubi, H. M., and Khan, Z. F. (2022, February). Applied artificial intelligence as event horizon of cyber security. In *2022 International Conference on Business Analytics for Technology and Security (ICBATS)* (pp. 1–7). IEEE.

72. Kuzior, A. (2022). Technological unemployment in the perspective of Industry 4.0. *Virtual Economics*, 5(1), 7–23.

73. Bongomin, O., Gilibrays Ocen, G., Oyondi Nganyi, E., Musinguzi, A., and Omara, T. (2020). Exponential disruptive technologies and the required skills of industry 4.0. *Journal of Engineering*, 2020, 1–17.

74. Pivoto, D. G., de Almeida, L. F., da Rosa Righi, R., Rodrigues, J. J., Lugli, A. B., and Alberti, A. M. (2021). Cyber-physical systems architectures for industrial internet of things applications in Industry 4.0: A literature review. *Journal of Manufacturing Systems*, 58, 176–192.

75. Gupta, R. (2023). Industry 4.0 adaption in indian banking Sector—A review and agenda for future research. *Vision*, 27(1), 24–32.

76. Dorfleitner, G., and Braun, D. (2019). Fintech, digitalization and blockchain: Possible applications for green finance. *The Rise of Green Finance in Europe: Opportunities and Challenges for Issuers, Investors and Marketplaces*, 207–237.

77. Nassiry, D. (2018). The role of fintech in unlocking green finance: Policy insights for developing countries (No. 883). ADBI working paper.

78. Singh, B. (2024). Legal dynamics lensing metaverse crafted for videogame industry and E-sports: Phenomenological exploration

catalyst complexity and future. *Journal of Intellectual Property Rights Law*, 7(1), 8–14.

79. Chen, Y., and Volz, U. (2021). Scaling up sustainable investment through blockchain- based project bonds. ADB-IGF Special Working Paper Series "Fintech to Enable Development, Investment, Financial Inclusion, and Sustainability.
80. Yang, Y., Su, X., and Yao, S. (2021). Nexus between green finance, fintech, and high-quality economic development: Empirical evidence from China. *Resources Policy*, 74, 102445.
81. Zhang, X., Aranguiz, M., Xu, D., Zhang, X., and Xu, X. (2018). Utilizing blockchain for better enforcement of green finance law and regulations. In *Transforming Climate Finance and Green Investment with Blockchains* (pp. 289–301). Academic Press.
82. Migliorelli, M., and Dessertine, P. (2019). The rise of green finance in Europe. Opportunities and challenges for issuers, investors and marketplaces. *Cham: Palgrave Macmillan*, 2, 2019.
83. Naderi, N., and Tian, Y. (2022). Leveraging blockchain technology and tokenizing green assets to fill the green finance gap. *Energy Research Letters*, 3(3).
84. Singh, B. (2023). Blockchain technology in renovating healthcare: Legal and future perspectives. In *Revolutionizing Healthcare Through Artificial Intelligence and Internet of Things Applications* (pp. 177–186). IGI Global.
85. Thomason, J., Ahmad, M., Bronder, P., Hoyt, E., Pocock, S., Bouteloupe, J., and Shrier, D. (2018). Blockchain—powering and empowering the poor in developing countries. In *Transforming Climate Finance and Green Investment with Blockchains* (pp. 137–152). Academic Press.
86. Liu, H., Yao, P., Latif, S., Aslam, S., and Iqbal, N. (2022). Impact of Green financing, FinTech, and financial inclusion on energy efficiency. *Environmental Science and Pollution Research*, 29, 18955–18966.
87. Yan, C., Siddik, A. B., Yong, L., Dong, Q., Zheng, G. W., and Rahman, M. N. (2022). A two-staged SEM-artificial neural network approach to analyze the impact of FinTech adoption on the sustainability performance of banking firms: The mediating effect of green finance and innovation. *Systems*, 10(5), 148.
88. Bayram, O., Talay, I., and Feridun, M. (2022). Can FinTech promote sustainable finance? *Policy Lessons from the Case of Turkey. Sustainability*, 14(19), 12414.

89. Sachs, J. D., Woo, W. T., Yoshino, N., and Taghizadeh-Hesary, F. (2019). Importance of green finance for achieving sustainable development goals and energy security. *Handbook of Green Finance: Energy Security and Sustainable Development*, 10, 1–10.

90. Campbell-Verduyn, M. (2023). Conjuring a cooler world? Imaginaries of improvement in blockchain climate finance experiments. *Environment and Planning C: Politics and Space*, 23996544231162858.

91. Singh, B. (2023). Federated learning for envision future trajectory smart transport system for climate preservation and smart green planet: Insights into global governance and SDG-9 (Industry, Innovation and Infrastructure). *National Journal of Environmental Law*, 6(2), 6–17.

92. Schulz, K., and Feist, M. (2021). Leveraging blockchain technology for innovative climate finance under the Green Climate Fund. *Earth System Governance*, 7, 100084.

93. Kalaiarasi, H., and Kirubahari, S. (2023). Green finance for sustainable development using blockchain technology. In *Green Blockchain Technology for Sustainable Smart Cities* (pp. 167–185). Elsevier.

94. Chueca Vergara, C., and Ferruz Agudo, L. (2021). Fintech and sustainability: Do they affect each other? *Sustainability*, 13(13), 7012.

95. Schoenmaker, D., and Volz, U. (2022). *Scaling up Sustainable Finance and Investment in the Global South*. CEPR Press.

96. Singh, V. K. (2022). *Regulatory and Legal Framework for Promoting Green Digital Finance. In Green Digital Finance and Sustainable Development Goals* (pp. 3–27). Singapore: Springer Nature Singapore.

97. Sharma, A., and Singh, B. (2022). Measuring impact of E-commerce on small scale business: A systematic review. *Journal of Corporate Governance and International Business Law*. DOI: https://doi.org/10.37591/jcgibl.v5i1.1087.

98. Marke, A. (ed.). (2018). *Transforming Climate Finance and Green Investment with Blockchains*. Academic Press.

99. Hoang, T. G., Nguyen, G. N. T., and Le, D. A. (2022). Developments in financial technologies for achieving the sustainable development goals (SDGs): FinTech and SDGs. In *Disruptive Technologies and Eco-Innovation for Sustainable Development* (pp. 1–19). IGI Global.

100. Schloesser, T., and Schulz, K. (2022). Distributed ledger technology and climate finance. In *Green Digital Finance and Sustainable Development Goals* (pp. 265–286). Singapore: Springer Nature Singapore.

101. Singh, B. (2022). Understanding legal frameworks concerning transgender healthcare in the age of dynamism. *Electronic Journal of Social and Strategic Studies*, 3, 56–65.

102. Harris, A. (2018). A conversation with masterminds in blockchain and climate change. In *Transforming Climate Finance and Green Investment with Blockchains* (pp. 15–22). Academic Press.

103. Shih, C., Gwizdalski, A., and Deng, X. (2023). *Building a Sustainable Future: Exploring Green Finance, Regenerative Finance, and Green Financial Technology*.

104. Ozili, P. K. (2023). Assessing global interest in decentralized finance, embedded finance, open finance, ocean finance and sustainable finance. *Asian Journal of Economics and Banking*, 7(2), 197–216.

105. Bayram, O., Talay, I., and Feridun, M. (2022). Can fintech promote sustainable finance? policy lessons from the case of Turkey. *Sustainability* 2022, 14, 12414.

106. Singh, B. (2022). Relevance of agriculture-nutrition linkage for human healthcare: a conceptual legal framework of implication and pathways. *Justice and Law Bulletin*, 1(1), 44–49.

107. Micaroni, M. (2020). Sustainable Finance: Addressing the SDGs through Fintech and Digital Finance solutions in EU (Doctoral dissertation, Politecnico di Torino).

108. Dell'Erba, M. (2021). Sustainable digital finance and the pursuit of environmental sustainability. *Sustainable Finance in Europe: Corporate Governance, Financial Stability and Financial Markets*, 61–81.

109. Bin Amin, S., Taghizadeh-Hesary, F., and Khan, F. (2022). Facilitating green digital finance in Bangladesh: Importance, prospects, and implications for meeting the SDGs. In *Green Digital Finance and Sustainable Development Goals* (pp. 143–165). Singapore: Springer Nature Singapore.

110. Singh, B. (2022). COVID-19 pandemic and public healthcare: endless downward spiral or solution via rapid legal and health services implementation with patient monitoring program. *Justice and Law Bulletin*, 1(1), 1–7.

111. Puaschunder, J. M. (2023). The future of resilient green finance. In *The Future of Resilient Finance: Finance Politics in the Age of Sustainable Development* (pp. 185–210). Cham: Springer International Publishing.

112. Vikas, N., Venegas, P., and Aiyer, S. (2022). Role of banks and other financial institutions in enhancing green digital finance. In *Green Digital Finance and Sustainable Development Goals* (pp. 329–352). Singapore: Springer Nature Singapore.

113. Macchiavello, E. (2023). Sustainable finance and fintech. A focus on capital raising. Forthcoming in Alexander K., Gargantini M., and Siri M., *The Cambridge Handbook of EU Sustainable Finance-Regulation*, Supervision and Governance (CUP).

114. Marke, A., and Sylvester, B. (2018). Decoding the current global climate finance architecture. In *Transforming Climate Finance and Green Investment with Blockchains* (pp. 35–59). Academic Press.

115. Singh, B. (2020). Global science and jurisprudential approach concerning healthcare and illness. *Indian Journal of Health and Medical Law*, 3(1), 7–13.

116. Udeagha, M. C., and Ngepah, N. (2023). The drivers of environmental sustainability in BRICS economies: Do green finance and fintech matter?. *World Development Sustainability*, 3, 100096.

117. Hassan, M. K., Rabbani, M. R., and Ali, M. A. M. (2020). Challenges for the Islamic Finance and banking in post COVID era and the role of Fintech. *Journal of Economic Cooperation and Development*, 41(3), 93–116.

118. Fenwick, M., and Vermeulen, E. P. (2020). Banking and regulatory responses to FinTech revisited-building the sustainable financial service'ecosystems' of tomorrow. *Singapore Journal of Legal Studies*, (Mar 2020), 165–189.

119. Singh, B. (2019). Profiling Public Healthcare: A comparative analysis based on the multidimensional healthcare management and legal approach. *Indian Journal of Health and Medical Law*, 2(2), 1–5.

120. Nenavath, S., and Mishra, S. (2023). Impact of green finance and fintech on sustainable economic growth: Empirical evidence from India. *Heliyon*, 9(5), e16301.

121. Schulz, K. A., Gstrein, O. J., and Zwitter, A. J. (2020). Exploring the governance and implementation of sustainable development initiatives through blockchain technology. *Futures*, 122, 102611.

122. Moro-Visconti, R., Cruz Rambaud, S., and López Pascual, J. (2020). Sustainability in FinTechs: An explanation through business model scalability and market valuation. *Sustainability*, 12(24), 10316.

123. Rizzello, A., and Kabli, A. (2020). Social finance and sustainable development goals: A literature synthesis, current approaches and

research agenda. *ACRN Journal of Finance and Risk Perspectives*, 9. Nikolaou, N. (2018). The Transition to a Green Global Economy: The Case of Green Finance and Green Bonds (Doctoral dissertation, University of Piraeus (Greece).

124. Jaiwant, S. V., and Kureethara, J. V. (2023). Green finance and fintech: Toward a more sustainable financial system. In *Green Finance Instruments, FinTech, and Investment Strategies: Sustainable Portfolio Management in the Post-COVID Era* (pp. 283–300). Cham: Springer International Publishing.
125. Bhowmik, D. (2022). An Introduction to Climate Fintech. *European Journal of Science, Innovation and Technology*, 2(4), 24–35.
126. Radanliev, P. (2024). Cyber diplomacy: Defining the opportunities for cybersecurity and risks from Artificial Intelligence, IoT, Blockchains, and Quantum Computing. *Journal of Cyber Security Technology*, 1–51.
127. Li, Z., Liang, X., Wen, Q., and Wan, E. (2024). The analysis of financial network transaction risk control based on blockchain and edge computing technology. *IEEE Transactions on Engineering Management*, 71, 5669–5690.
128. Sreenivasan, A., and Suresh, M. (2024). Start-up sustainability: Does blockchain adoption drives sustainability in start-ups? A systematic literature reviews. *Management Research Review*, 47(3), 390–405.
129. Anyanwu, A., Olorunsogo, T., Abrahams, T. O., Akindote, O. J., and Reis, O. (2024). Data confidentiality and integrity: A review of accounting and cybersecurity controls in superannuation organizations. *Computer Science and IT Research Journal*, 5(1), 237–253.
130. Diro, A., Zhou, L., Saini, A., Kaisar, S., and Hiep, P. C. (2024). Leveraging zero knowledge proofs for blockchain-based identity sharing: A survey of advancements, challenges and opportunities. *Journal of Information Security and Applications*, 80, 103678.
131. Sharma, S., and Dwivedi, R. (2024). A survey on blockchain deployment for biometric systems. IET Blockchain.

Chapter 5

Strengthening Fuzzy Logics and Federated Learning Devices for Renewable Energy

Hind Hammouch,[a] Bhupinder Singh,[b] Sahil Lal,[b] Manmeet Kaur Arora,[b] and Saurabh Chandra[c]

[a]*Faculty of Legal, Economic, and Social Sciences, University Sidi Mohamed Ben Abdellah, Fez, Morocco, Morocco*
[b]*Sharda University, Greater Noida, Uttar Pradesh, India*
[c]*School of Law, Bennett University, Greater Noida, Uttar Pradesh, India*

bhupindersinghlaw19@gmail.com

Abstract

The adaptation of reinforcement federated learning and fuzzy logics lays down transformative attitude to device scheduling in renewable energy. Devices must be intelligently scheduled in order to handle intermittency and maximize efficiency as we switch to renewable energy sources. Devices can jointly learn the best scheduling techniques thanks to reinforcement federated learning, which combines federated learning and reinforcement learning. In order to address issues with renewable energy systems, this chapter investigates the integration of Reinforcement Federated Learning with the Industrial

Fuzzy Logic in Revolutionizing Renewable Energy
Edited by Bhupinder Singh, Komal Vig, Ruchi Lal, and Budi Agus Riswandi

ISBN 978-981-5129-92-2 (Hardcover), 978-1-003-74191-6 (eBook)
www.jennystanford.com

DOI: 10.1201/9781003741916-5

Internet of Things. The chapter provides insights into the benefits, challenges, and implementation techniques of merging Reinforcement Federated Learning and Industrial Internet of Things through a thorough literature review, theoretical analysis, and actual case studies. In this context, the chapter also addresses prospective uses, upcoming trends, and ethical issues.

Keywords: Federated Learning, Industrial Internet of Things, Renewable Energy, Device Scheduling, Energy Grid

5.1 Introduction

Power grids, which depend on renewable energy sources, present an exciting, if complicated, opportunity to fully utilize these genuinely sustainable human resources. The National Renewable Energy Laboratory (NREL) of the United States leads international research into the potential of power grids that manage solar, wind, and other renewable resources, component by component. At NREL, the team is working with the Massachusetts Institute of Technology (MIT) and the German Aerospace Center (DLR) in a sophisticated simulation lab powered by a 500-core "supercomputer." There, the team creates and works with models that, in turn, are powered by a simulated grid, which in many areas is the size of a small state. The lab is working on two projects. The first is a novel project called the Smart Grid Investiture Pathway [1].

The rapid integration of renewable energy sources into the power system makes it difficult to increase the efficiency of energy production and consumption. This needs a simulation of the power system because we need to generate a lot of data and a simulation of the completed installation. This allows us to oversee the efficiency of the overall process and its devices—the completion task of our installation [2]. The global search for clean, renewable energy sources has reached a turning point. Given the mounting problems caused by climate change and the depletion of fossil fuels, it is essential to make the transition to cleaner energy production and use [3]. The management and optimization of these resources have come to be seen as being of the utmost importance as they embrace renewable energy solutions such as solar panels, wind turbines, and energy storage devices. Innovative strategies to address these difficulties have been made possible by the emergence of edge computing and the growth of the Industrial Internet of Things (IIoT) [4]. In this context, federated learning (FL) and fuzzy logic together offer a promising path for improving the effectiveness and sustainability of renewable energy systems [5].

The assignment involves investigating Reinforcement Federated Learning-Based Device Scheduling for Renewable Energy at the Edge, with a focus on FL methods used within the IIoT ecosystem [6]. It is founded on the understanding that conventional centralized approaches to energy management are ineffective when energy generation, storage, and delivery become more decentralized and dynamic [7]. Renewable energy sources are dynamic, and it is necessary to minimize energy waste and maximize energy consumption [8]. These factors need the development of creative solutions that can adapt and learn in real time. These complicated and dynamic problems are ideally suited for machine learning's reinforcement learning subset. Federated Learning's decentralized and privacy-preserving features, along with the massive IIoT device network, have the potential to completely alter how it handles renewable energy resources at the edge [9].

5.2 Objective of the Chapter

The primary objective of this chapter is to develop an effective federated learning model for forecasting renewable energy generation at the edge of fuzzy logic networks. This model aims to leverage decentralized data from IoT devices distributed across industrial environments to enhance the accuracy and timeliness of renewable energy predictions to:

- create a novel reinforcement learning model tailored for forecasting renewable energy generation and consumption at the edge, leveraging the capabilities of federated learning in an industrial IoT setting;

- enhance the accuracy of renewable energy forecasts by integrating real-time data from edge devices within the Industrial Internet of Things, such as sensors and smart meters;
- optimize energy management and investigate how the developed model can be used to optimize energy management strategies, such as load balancing, demand response, and energy storage, to ensure efficient utilization of renewable energy resources;
- address data privacy and security when implementing federated learning in the context of IoT, considering the sensitivity of energy-related data;
- implement IIoT-specific architecture to support the proposed reinforcement federated learning (RFL) framework.

5.3 Reinforcement Federated Learning

Reinforcement Federated Learning is an emerging paradigm that amalgamates the principles of federated learning and reinforcement learning (RL) [10]. It addresses a critical need in machine learning and data science: the ability to train models collaboratively and adaptively in a decentralized and privacy-preserving manner. In RFL, multiple edge devices, which can range from IoT sensors to smartphones, participate in training a shared model without the need to share their raw data centrally [11]. Instead, they collaborate by exchanging model updates and leveraging reinforcement learning techniques to improve the model's performance over time [12]. RFL leverages the decentralized and privacy-preserving nature of FL, allowing edge devices to train models locally on their data while keeping the data itself on the device [13]. This approach aligns with the growing concerns over data privacy and security in an increasingly connected world. RFL extends FL by incorporating reinforcement learning, enabling the model to learn adaptively from interactions with the environment [14]. This combination empowers edge devices to not only contribute to model training but also make informed decisions based on the evolving model [15].

The advantage of RFL is its applicability to dynamic and evolving environments, where traditional machine learning approaches often struggle to adapt. In scenarios where data distribution changes over time or where devices have limited computational resources, RFL can shine [16]. In the context of autonomous vehicles, RFL can enable cars to collectively improve their navigation capabilities by sharing knowledge about changing road conditions or traffic patterns without compromising individual vehicle data [17]. In healthcare, RFL can support collaborative learning among medical devices while preserving sensitive patient information, leading to more accurate diagnostic models [18]. It holds promise in scenarios with constrained communication bandwidth or intermittent connectivity, as devices can exchange model updates efficiently rather than transmitting large datasets. This can be particularly advantageous in rural or remote areas where high-speed internet access is limited [19]. As RFL continues to evolve, it has the potential to reshape various domains, from autonomous systems to healthcare and finance. Its ability to combine the strengths of federated learning and reinforcement learning in a decentralized and privacy-preserving manner positions it as a powerful tool for solving complex problems in an increasingly interconnected and data-centric world [20].

5.3.1 Renewable Energy at the Edge

Renewable energy, addressed as the cornerstone of a sustainable future, holds the promise of addressing some of the most pressing challenges facing our world today. This form of energy is derived from the sources that are naturally replenished over relatively short periods, such as sunlight, wind, water, and geothermal heat [21]. Renewable energy sources provide a sustainable and limitless substitute to fossil fuels, which are finite and cause environmental deterioration [22]. Solar power is one of the most well-known forms of renewable energy. Solar energy is captured by solar panels, which then transform it into electricity [23]. With the impressive improvements in this technology, efficiency and cost-effectiveness have grown. Rooftop solar energy installations are becoming commonplace, as are large-scale solar farms and even the use of solar energy into cutting-edge building materials [24]. Because of this, solar energy has become a scalable and affordable option that not only lessens our reliance on fossil fuels but also significantly lowers greenhouse gas emissions [25].

Another essential source of renewable energy is wind power. Wind energy is captured and turned into power by wind turbines, whether they are on land or offshore [26]. The allure of wind energy rests in its capacity to produce significant amounts of power in areas with reliable winds. Wind turbines have the potential to replace traditional sources of electricity in many regions of the world as their designs advance and become more effective. Additionally, wind power is essential for diversifying our energy mix, improving energy security, and reducing the negative effects of climate change [27].

The earliest and most well-established source of renewable energy is hydropower, which is created from the energy of moving water. Through dams and hydroelectric facilities, it offers both electrical and mechanical power [28]. While large-scale hydropower projects have been important for producing clean energy, interest in run-of-river and small-scale hydropower facilities is rising. While still utilizing the power of water, these more environmentally friendly methods reduce the destruction of aquatic habitats and ecosystems [29]. Geothermal energy, derived from the Earth's internal heat, presents a reliable and consistent source of power. Geothermal power plants tap into underground reservoirs of steam and hot water to drive turbines and generate electricity. Unlike solar and wind energy, geothermal power is not weather-dependent, making it a stable energy source that can provide baseload power. It is particularly advantageous in regions with substantial geothermal resources, such as Iceland and parts of the United States [30].

Environmental concerns are just one of the elements influencing the switch to renewable energy; there are also economic and social ones. It is regarded as a catalyst for the development of new technologies, the creation of jobs, and energy independence [31]. Employment prospects in the renewable energy business have increased exponentially and span the manufacturing, installation, and research and development spectrum [32]. Additionally, the decentralization of power generation enabled by renewable energy reduces energy poverty and promotes energy resilience by enabling individuals, communities, and enterprises to actively participate in the energy production process [33].

Renewable energy implies a fundamental shift in our thinking about energy production and consumption, not just a technological one. Renewable energy sources represent a ray of hope as we continue to struggle with the pressing need to slow down climate change by providing a cleaner, more sustainable, and equitable energy future. We can unlock the limitless potential of renewable energy to power a cleaner and more wealthy society for future generations via continued study, innovation, and a united global effort [34].

The use of renewable energy at the edge will fundamentally alter how we produce, store, and use energy [35]. In essence, this idea uses regionally specific renewable energy resources, such as solar cells, wind turbines, and small-scale hydroelectric generators, to supply energy to specific residences, commercial buildings, or even entire towns [36]. Renewable energy at the edge captures energy directly where it is required, at the point of consumption, in contrast to traditional centralized energy generation, where power is produced at a distant place and delivered over vast distances through the grid [37].

The advantage of renewable energy is that it has the ability to make energy generation more accessible. It changes the power dynamics in the energy industry by making it possible for individuals and small enterprises to become energy producers [38]. Decentralization not only lessens reliance on major utility providers but also gives consumers more autonomy over the energy options they choose. It increases energy security and resilience by reducing sensitivity to grid outages and price changes [39]. Furthermore, the advantages of using renewable energy at the edge for the environment cannot be emphasized. It perfectly complements efforts being made around the world to fight climate change and cut carbon emissions [40]. Production of locally available renewable energy reduces transmission losses, which happen when power is carried over long distances, and minimizes the need for backup fossil fuel-based energy sources [41].

Innovations in energy storage technologies have sped up the development of renewable energy at the edge [42]. With the advancement of battery technologies like lithium-ion and solid-state batteries, it is now possible to store excess energy produced during windy or sunny conditions in order to use it later on when it is cloudy or calm. As a result, renewable energy becomes more dependable and accessible, improving its viability as a source of power. In order to maximize renewable energy at the edge, complex control systems and smart grid technologies must be integrated. These systems make it possible to manage and optimize energy output and consumption in real time. To ensure efficient use of energy assets and cost savings, artificial intelligence and machine learning algorithms can be used to forecast energy generation, anticipate demand patterns, and fine-tune the operation of energy assets [43].

A paradigm shift in the way we envisage and implement energy solutions is represented by renewable energy at the edge. It offers a way toward a greener and more decentralized energy future by embodying the values of sustainability, resilience, and democracy. The development of renewable energy at the edge will remain a crucial force for change as technology develops and the world works to address urgent environmental issues; it has the potential to completely alter the world's energy system in the years to come [44].

5.3.2 Reinforcement Federated Learning and Renewable Energy: Co-relation

A new and very promising paradigm that combines federated learning and reinforcement learning is called reinforcement federated learning. This novel strategy aims to address challenging challenges in distributed machine learning while enabling intelligent decision-making in dynamic and decentralized situations. It is a ground-breaking merger of two cutting-edge technologies. RFL uses reinforcement learning approaches to help intelligent agents, like autonomous machines or software agents, learn from interactions with their environments and modify their behavior. The integration of RFL with federated learning, a decentralized and privacy-preserving machine learning strategy, is what makes it unique. RFL preserves data privacy and allays worries about data centralization by allowing numerous edge devices or nodes to cooperatively train and update their reinforcement learning models while keeping their data localized and private. RFL has significant and far-reaching effects. It has the potential to completely transform a number of industries, including autonomous robotics, edge computing, healthcare, and finance. For instance, RFL can help robots in autonomous robotics learn about and adapt to their environment in real time, improving their ability to handle unforeseen circumstances and maximizing task performance. RFL in healthcare can make it easier to train tailored health models while maintaining the security of private patient information [45].

The complicated management of renewable energy is best served by federated learning and reinforcement learning, respectively. By utilizing the collaborative power of edge devices within the context of FL and leveraging the sequential decision-making abilities of RL, it embodies a visionary approach to optimizing the scheduling of renewable energy devices, such as solar panels, wind turbines, and energy storage systems. This synergy is particularly important at a time when decentralized, renewable energy sources are proliferating but their effective integration into power networks and dynamic management continue to pose significant obstacles. It expands on FL's decentralized, privacy-preserving model training principles. The creation of a shared model that optimizes energy device performance is cooperatively aided by edge devices that are equipped with data about local renewable energy production and consumption [46].

When it comes to scheduling renewable energy, which is intrinsically impacted by unstable variables like weather, energy consumption, and device performance, this dynamic decision-making capability is crucial. The importance of federated learning and reinforcement learning goes beyond theoretical ideas. Its wide-ranging practical applications have the potential to transform energy management in a variety of industries. For instance, in smart grids, RFDSRE can facilitate more effective energy distribution, lowering the need for system fluctuations and the demand for energy storage. It can maximize the usage of solar panels and house batteries in residential settings, resulting in financial savings and a smaller carbon footprint. It can enhance the scheduling of wind turbines and solar panels in large-scale renewable energy farms, maximizing electricity production and grid stability [47].

5.4 Synthesis of Reinforcement Federated Learning and the Industrial Internet of Things for Device Forecast

The synthesis of reinforcement federated learning and the industrial fuzzy logics for device scheduling in industrial settings represents a pioneering leap forward in the realm of intelligent automation and energy optimization. At its core, this fusion brings together two transformative paradigms: RFL, which combines the adaptive decision-making capabilities of reinforcement learning with the decentralized, privacy-preserving nature of federated learning, and the IIoT, which encompasses a vast network of interconnected industrial devices and sensors [48].

In industrial contexts, where energy efficiency and operational optimization are paramount, this fusion holds immense promise. Consider manufacturing facilities that operate a multitude of machines and equipment, each with its own energy profile and operational requirements. Traditional scheduling approaches often fall short in dynamically optimizing energy consumption, leading to inefficiencies and increased operational costs. RFL within the IIoT context revolutionizes this landscape by enabling industrial devices to learn adaptively from their interactions with the environment and each other [49].

Through RFL, these devices collaboratively improve their scheduling strategies based on real-time data, predictive analytics, and historical performance. For instance, robotic arms on a manufacturing line can learn when to operate at peak efficiency to meet production quotas while minimizing energy consumption during downtime. The IIoT facilitates the seamless exchange of data and model updates among these devices, ensuring that each device contributes to the collective intelligence without compromising sensitive operational information. Moreover, the IIoT enhances the data acquisition capabilities critical to RFL. Sensors embedded in industrial equipment continuously collect data on parameters such as temperature, pressure, and energy consumption. This rich data stream enables RFL models to make more informed scheduling decisions, accounting for variations in environmental conditions and energy availability. The IIoT offers real-time insights into energy generation for renewable energy sources integrated into industrial processes, such as solar panels and wind turbines, and enables RFL algorithms to optimize the use of these resources based on the situation at hand [50].

This fusion has important consequences. By maximizing their usage of energy, industrial facilities can reduce their energy expenses significantly, reduce downtime, and improve their environmental sustainability. Furthermore, RFL's adaptability makes sure that these advantages endure even when operating circumstances alter over time. This improves the effectiveness of industrial operations while also advancing the more general objectives of sustainability and climate mitigation. It enables industrial equipment to constantly adapt their scheduling plans, maximizing energy usage and operational effectiveness. This fusion is poised to become a cornerstone of modern industrial automation, with significant implications for energy management and environmental stewardship, as sustainability and efficiency are prioritized by enterprises around the world [51].

The management of IIoT networks may be completely altered by the combination of reinforcement federated learning (FRL) and the industrial fuzzy logics for device scheduling. FRL is a type of machine learning that enables numerous devices to learn from their own decisions and experiences without sharing their data with a central server or each other. Because of this, FRL is perfect for administering IIoT networks, where devices are frequently dispersed and contain critical information. Device scheduling involves assigning duties to devices in a way that reduces the network's overall costs, including energy use, delay, and cost. It is a challenging issue since devices' resource needs might vary greatly based on their tasks and the state of the network. The creation of intelligent device scheduling algorithms that can adjust to changes in the network environment and the resource needs of devices is possible with the help of FRL. The FRL algorithm can be used to schedule devices in real time for the network after being trained on a dataset of past device scheduling data [52].

Using FRL and IIoT together for device scheduling is a promising new field of study that has the potential to completely alter how IIoT networks are managed. We may anticipate seeing even more cutting-edge and successful applications of FRL in IIoT device scheduling as the technology develops.

Without sending raw data to a central server, federated learning, a novel approach to machine learning, enables collaborative model training among distributed edge devices. To construct highly specific models for device scheduling, industrial machines, sensors, and devices dispersed throughout factories, production lines, and even supply chains can work together in the context of the IIoT. In addition to protecting the confidentiality and security of private industrial information, this distributed method to machine learning makes the best use of these devices' combined knowledge to make scheduling decisions [53].

Reinforcement learning models may make judgments sequentially and learn from their interactions with the environment thanks to learning. This suggests that in the case of device scheduling in an industrial setting, machines and devices can modify their scheduling plans in response to real-time data, so maximizing energy usage, production efficiency, and resource allocation. In dynamic industrial situations where conditions change quickly and scheduling decisions need to be made with agility and precision, this adaptive decision-making capability is very important. The IIoT serves as the brain that connects these dispersed components, enabling the interchange of model updates, information, and scheduling choices. Sensor-equipped industrial equipment continuously gathers information on variables including energy usage, output rates, and machine health. The RFL system uses this data to feed models, which are then jointly trained and improved. In turn, the models offer optimized scheduling recommendations, which are then sent back to the edge devices for execution [54].

This synthesis has a wide-ranging importance. First, it improves industrial processes by making sure that equipment is scheduled in a way that maximizes production effectiveness, saves energy use, and lowers operating expenses. By enabling adaptive decision-making in reaction to unanticipated interruptions or changes in production demands, it also increases the resilience of industrial systems. Thirdly, by maximizing resource allocation, eliminating energy waste, and limiting the environmental impact of industrial activities, it supports sustainability initiatives [55].

Reinforcement Federated Learning and the Industrial Internet of Things coming together to schedule devices ushers in a new era of resource management and industrial optimization. It uses distributed intelligence, privacy protection, and adaptive decision-making to build industrial ecosystems that are more effective, robust, and sustainable. This fusion is positioned to be a key factor in determining the direction that manufacturing and production will take as sectors continue to move toward more automation and efficiency [56].

5.4.1 Optimizing Device Forecast Accuracy

With the integration of cutting-edge technologies like reinforcement federated learning and the Industrial Internet of Things (IIoT), improving device forecast accuracy is a crucial goal in many industrial and technological applications. For successful decision-making, resource allocation, and overall operational efficiency, accurate and trustworthy projections are crucial. Utilizing these tactics can help businesses improve device forecast accuracy, which will result in better decision-making, resource utilization, and overall operational performance. RFL and IIoT work together to provide a dynamic and cooperative environment that helps forecasting models keep up with the constantly changing circumstances of industrial processes [57].

5.5 Efficient and Flexible Management for Industrial Internet of Things: A Federated Learning Approach

In today's industrial environment, efficient and adaptable management for the industrial fuzzy logic is a critical area of study and development. An era of data-driven decision-making where industrial machines, sensors, and devices are connected to capture and transmit massive volumes of data has arrived thanks to the adoption of IIoT technology. It is crucial to manage these resources effectively and flexibly in such a dynamic environment in order to enhance productivity, cut down on operating expenses, and preserve the lifespan and competitiveness of industrial operations [58].

The implementation of federated learning within the context of the IIoT is the cutting-edge strategy to overcome these difficulties. A shared machine learning model can be cooperatively trained by dispersed devices using the federated learning paradigm without the requirement to share raw data. This decentralized strategy protects the confidentiality and security of critical industrial data and fits well with the distributed nature of the IIoT. Additionally, it reduces the computing load on a central server, making it an effective option for edge devices with limited resources that are typical in industrial environments [59]. When it comes to IIoT management, federated learning suggests several key advantages:

- *Privacy protection*: Sensitive information about procedures, tools, and exclusive technology is frequently found in industrial data. By ensuring that this data stays on the edge devices, federated learning reduces the requirement for centralized data storage and the likelihood of data breaches [50].
- *Effective Model Training*: With federated learning, machine learning models are trained directly on the edge devices. As a result, less data must be transmitted to a central server, increasing efficiency and decreasing latency.
- *Scalability*: IIoT settings have the capacity to house a sizable number of devices. Federated learning is appropriate for industrial settings with extensive and varied sensor networks since it scales naturally as the number of devices increases.
- *Adaptive Decision-Making*: Adaptive decision-making is made possible by edge devices' capacity to jointly train machine learning models. Based on real-time data, devices can collectively develop models over time, resulting in more intelligent and effective management decisions.

There are many ways to use federated learning in IIoT management. One crucial application of machine learning is predictive maintenance, where models can foretell equipment breakdowns based on sensor data, enabling proactive repair and minimizing downtime. Other domains where federated learning can optimize procedures and resource allocation include asset tracking, energy management, and quality control [51].

But, there are obstacles to be addressed when putting federated learning for IIoT management into practice. These include creating effective protocols for communication, guaranteeing data consistency between devices, and resolving problems with model aggregation and synchronization. Additionally, choosing the right machine learning algorithms and tactics that are adapted to certain industrial use cases is crucial for getting the best outcomes.

Federated Learning's Efficient and Flexible Management for IIoT is a ground-breaking method for unlocking the potential of distributed industrial data while protecting privacy and improving productivity. Federated Learning is positioned to play a crucial part in transforming how industrial resources are managed and maximized in an increasingly linked and data-driven world as industries continue to embrace the IIoT to promote sustainability and competitiveness. A machine learning (ML) technique called federated learning enables numerous devices to jointly train a model without sharing their data among them or with a central server. FL is therefore perfect for administering industrial fuzzy networks, where sensitive data is frequently stored on distributed devices [52].

The difficulty in administering IIoT networks is effectively allocating resources to various devices, such as computing power and bandwidth. This is so that devices' resource needs can vary greatly based on their tasks and the state of the network. In order to operate IIoT networks effectively and flexibly, it suggests a federated learning method. The method modifies three parameters using a deep reinforcement learning (DRL) algorithm:

1. The percentage of jobs that are transferred from devices to computational access points (CAPs) is known as the task offloading ratio.
2. The percentage of bandwidth allotted to various devices for offloading tasks is known as the bandwidth allocation ratio.

3. The amount of power that devices use to send data is known as the transmit power.

The DRL algorithm is taught to reduce the normalized system cost, which depends on the network's energy usage, delay, and accuracy. In comparison to centralized resource allocation techniques, simulation findings demonstrate that the suggested federated learning methodology can significantly increase the performance of IIoT networks. The method is also more adaptable since it can vary in response to adjustments in the network environment and device resource needs. When managing IIoT networks, federated learning has the following benefits: Privacy federated learning protects user privacy by not requiring devices to share their data with a centralized server [53].

- *Efficiency*: Federated learning can cut down on the amount of time devices and the central server spend communicating.

Federated learning is flexible and can alter as network conditions and device resource needs change.

In general, federated learning is a promising strategy to govern IIoT networks effectively and flexibly. It can aid in enhancing these networks' functionality, dependability, and security. Following are some specific instances of how IIoT networks could be managed using federated learning:

- Federated learning could be used to train a model that forecasts when equipment is most likely to break down. Preventive maintenance might then be planned using this information, helping to decrease downtime and increase overall equipment efficiency.
- Federated learning could be used to train a model to find flaws in products made by IIoT machines for quality control. The quality of the products may then be improved, and the quantity of rejects might be decreased, using this information [54].
- Federated learning may be used to reduce the amount of energy that IIoT networks utilize. This could be achieved by altering how resources are allocated to various devices in accordance with their present requirements and the state of the network.

- Federated learning is a potent technology that may be applied in a number of ways to enhance the administration of IIoT networks. We may anticipate seeing even more cutting-edge and successful federated learning in IIoT applications as the technology develops [55].

5.6 Device Scheduling for Renewable Energy: Powered Federated Learning

Device scheduling in the context of federated learning driven by renewable energy is a crucial convergence of efficiency, efficiency, and sustainability. Using renewable energy for machine learning tasks becomes both a practical requirement and a visionary potential as the globe struggles to make the shift to cleaner and more sustainable energy sources [56].

Renewable energy sources like solar and wind are by nature sporadic. Their creation is influenced by variables including the time of day and weather, making it difficult to anticipate and maximize energy availability. Given that consistent computational resources are frequently needed for model training, this unpredictability presents a special set of obstacles for machine learning [57].

Federated Learning driven by renewable energy requires organizing the execution of machine learning activities on edge devices to make sure they coincide with the availability of renewable energy. Devices can be scheduled for computationally expensive tasks like model training and updates when renewable energy sources are producing extra power. On the other hand, when energy is scarce, devices may give priority to energy-saving tasks or go into low-power modes to save energy. Due to the intermittent nature of renewable energy sources, device scheduling for federated learning driven by renewable energy is a difficult task. Renewable energy sources like solar and wind power can sometimes create an excess of energy and other times a shortfall. Due to this fluctuation, it may be challenging to schedule devices in a way that allows the FL training process to go without interruption. The adoption of a reinforcement learning algorithm for device scheduling is the strategy chosen for FL powered by renewable energy. Through trial and error, RL systems can learn to make decisions in challenging and dynamic contexts. The RL algorithm can learn to schedule devices in a way that minimizes the effect of renewable energy variability on the FL training process when dealing with device scheduling for FL [58].

A dataset of historical data on device scheduling and renewable energy output can be used to train the RL algorithm. The FL network's real-time scheduling decisions can then be made using the algorithm. For FL powered by renewable energy, the device scheduling strategy is to employ a hybrid strategy that mixes RL with other scheduling algorithms. For instance, a hybrid strategy might schedule devices using RL in the short run and a more conventional scheduling algorithm in the long term. The hybrid techniques may have a number of benefits, including increased flexibility and resilience. The advantages of both RL and conventional scheduling methods can be used in hybrid strategies [59]. Device scheduling presents certain unique difficulties for FL powered by renewable energy sources:

- *Predicting the development of renewable energy*: Particularly in the near future, it is challenging to anticipate with accuracy the generation of renewable energy. This makes it challenging to plan the scheduling of devices in a way that permits the FL training process to go without interruption. Keeping energy use and output in check It's critical to strike a balance between device energy usage and FL training efficiency. Devices that use too much energy risk running out of power before FL training is finished [60].
- *Fairness*: It's crucial to make sure that every device has an equal chance of taking part in the FL training process. This can be difficult when using renewable energy sources [61].

Device scheduling for FL powered by renewable energy is an interesting field of research, despite the difficulties. We may anticipate more creative and efficient solutions to this issue as technology continues to advance. Overall, scheduling devices for a FL powered by renewable energy is a challenging operation that necessitates careful consideration of a variety of variables. However, it is possible to create intelligent device scheduling systems that can significantly boost the performance of FL networks powered by renewable energy sources by utilizing RL and other scheduling algorithms [62].

This method's importance goes much beyond simple energy efficiency. It adds to the bigger picture of a future that is environmentally responsible and sustainable. We lessen dependency on fossil fuels, cut carbon emissions, and encourage the use of clean energy sources for computational workloads by optimizing machine learning tasks to correspond with renewable energy availability. The dependability and resilience of machine learning systems are improved by this method. Because they frequently rely on centralized resources, traditional data centers and cloud computing are susceptible to interruptions and outages. In contrast, we develop a more decentralized and fault-tolerant architecture by distributing machine learning activities across edge devices fueled by renewable energy sources. The implementation of device scheduling for federated learning powered by renewable energy is not without difficulties, though. It calls for complex algorithms that take into account both energy availability and the various processing requirements of machine learning jobs. Additionally, it needs a strong infrastructure for managing and monitoring the production and use of renewable energy [63].

This idea stands for a futuristic approach that connects technology with sustainability objectives. It exemplifies the inventiveness and adaptability required to get through the complicated and ever-changing world of renewable energy. This strategy has the potential to transform how we power and optimize our computational pursuits, all while contributing to a greener and more sustainable future as the world depends more and more on machine learning for a variety of applications [64].

5.6.1 Resilient Federated Learning in Unstable Energy Environments

A key idea for solving the problems caused by the intermittent and unpredictability of renewable energy sources is resilient federated learning in uncertain energy conditions. Ensuring the continuity and dependability of federated learning processes becomes crucial in situations where energy availability may change due to external variables like changing weather or the time of day. In order to support consistent performance in the face of erratic energy variations, resilient federated learning algorithms are created to lessen the effects of energy instabilities [65].

The creation of algorithms and protocols that can adjust to changing energy situations is a component of resilient federated learning. Devices taking part in federated learning are outfitted with systems that allow them to dynamically change how engaged they are dependent on the current energy situation. With this flexibility, the system can respond proactively to shifts in the energy landscape, scheduling and involving devices more effectively to ensure operational resilience. Additionally, redundancy and failover techniques are integrated into resilient federated learning to guarantee the continuation of learning tasks during times of energy shortage or disruption. The system can resiliently adjust to the unavailability of certain devices by distributing learning activities across a varied range of devices. This prevents a single point of failure and ensures the general resilience of the federated learning process [66].

The creation of recovery plans is also included in the idea of resilient federated learning. The system should have procedures to seamlessly recover and resume learning tasks in the case of an unplanned energy outage or device failure. This entails retaining the federated learning model's current state, keeping the advancement made before to the disruption, and permitting a quick and effective return to normal operations. The resilient federated learning in unstable energy environments is a multi-faceted approach that combines adaptive scheduling, redundancy, and recovery mechanisms to ensure that federated learning systems continue to operate despite the difficulties brought on by the intermittent nature of renewable energy sources. This resilience highlights the possibility of federated learning as a strong and dependable solution for environments powered by renewable energy sources and adds to the efficiency of machine learning operations [67].

5.7 Conclusion and Future Scope

There are numerous opportunities and solutions have emerged as a result of the emergence of reinforcement federated learning as a potent paradigm for device scheduling in the context of renewable energy at the edge inside the Industrial Internet of Things (IIoT). This innovative approach combines the principles of federated learning, which respects data privacy and distribution, with reinforcement learning, which enables autonomous decision-making, thereby addressing critical challenges in optimizing energy consumption in edge computing environments powered by renewable sources.

The takeaways from this chapter as significant enhancement in energy efficiency and sustainability achieved through RFL-based device scheduling. By harnessing the edge devices' local processing capabilities and leveraging federated learning, we can minimize the need for centralized data collection and processing, reducing the associated energy overhead. Furthermore, the integration of reinforcement learning enables intelligent decision-making, adapting device schedules in real-time to respond to changing environmental conditions and energy availability. This adaptability not only optimizes energy consumption but also contributes to grid stability by intelligently balancing energy demand and supply. Moreover, RFL-based device scheduling fosters data privacy and security, which are paramount concerns in IIoT ecosystems. The decentralized nature of federated learning ensures that sensitive data remains localized on edge devices, mitigating the risks associated with data transmission and storage. This is particularly crucial in industrial settings where proprietary information and operational data need safeguarding.

Overall, RFL-based device scheduling for renewable energy at the edge of the IIoT is an innovative new strategy that has the potential to completely change how we utilize and manage renewable energy sources. RFL-based scheduling can assist us in achieving a more sustainable, dependable, and cost-effective energy future by utilizing the power of federated learning and reinforcement learning.

There are a lot of potential advantages to RFL-based device scheduling for renewable energy at the edge of the IIoT, but there are also several issues that need to be resolved before it can be extensively used. Creating scalable and more effective RFL algorithms is one difficulty. The requirement to solve the privacy and security issue presents another difficulty. Despite these obstacles, there is a lot of study being done. Creating more scalable and effective RFL algorithms for edge device real-time scheduling is one of the interesting future research fields. Through creating secure communication protocols and data encryption methods, the problem of security and privacy in RFL-based scheduling is addressed. Improving the performance and robustness of RFL-based scheduling by integrating it with other cutting-edge technologies like blockchain and artificial intelligence.

The future application of Reinforcement Federated Learning-Based Device Scheduling for Renewable Energy at the Edge is really exciting and has the potential to completely transform the industrial fuzzy logics energy management environment. A number of fascinating new directions for research and development are opening up as technology develops. The improvement and optimization of the RFL algorithms is a crucial topic for future study and application. Real-time decision-making will be made possible by ongoing improvements to the learning effectiveness and speed of these algorithms, ensuring that energy scheduling remains adaptable and sensitive to quickly changing environmental conditions and energy supply. Additionally, the incorporation of sophisticated reinforcement learning methods, including deep reinforcement learning, may result in even more accurate and effective device scheduling.

Future advancements in RFL-based device scheduling will continue to prioritize the ideas of privacy and security. Researchers will need to develop unique techniques to make sure that federated learning frameworks retain data integrity and confidentiality as data legislation and privacy concerns change. It will be essential to find a compromise between model performance and privacy-preserving approaches.

References

1. Ahmed, R., and Khan, Z. (2024). Enhancing renewable energy systems using federated learning: A survey. *Energy Reports,* 10(1), 45–59. https://doi.org/10.1016/j.egyr.2024.01.005.
2. Singh, B., and Kaunert, C. (2024). Human-machine nexus for digital rebound fostering futuristic energy-efficiency: Ecological footprint of technology for smart-sustainable Urban mobility. In González-Lezcano, R., and Sansaniwal, S. (eds.), *Design Strategies for Efficient and Sustainable Building Facilities* (pp. 222–244). IGI Global. https://doi.org/10.4018/979-8-3693-3200-9.ch010.
3. Aijaz, A., and Banerjee, S. (2024). Fuzzy logic control for smart grid stability: A review of applications. *Journal of Renewable Energy Research,* 15(3), 287–299. https://doi.org/10.1016/j.jrener.2024.03.002.
4. Bai, Y., and Li, H. (2024). Federated learning for optimizing renewable energy distribution networks. *Sustainable Energy Technologies and Assessments,* 19(2), 100–112. https://doi.org/10.1016/j.seta.2024.05.008.
5. Singh, B. (2024). Cherish data privacy and human rights in the digital age: Harmonizing innovation and individual autonomy. In Pucelj, M., and Bohinc, R. (eds.), *Balancing Human Rights, Social Responsibility, and Digital Ethics* (pp. 199–226). IGI Global. https://doi.org/10.4018/979-8-3693-3334-1.ch007.
6. Basu, S., and Gupta, R. (2023). Integration of fuzzy logic and IoT for enhanced renewable energy management. *Renewable and Sustainable Energy Reviews,* 17(4), 405–417. https://doi.org/10.1016/j.rser.2023.04.005.
7. Bhatia, S., and Roy, A. (2023). Advances in federated learning for smart grid applications. *IEEE Transactions on Smart Grid,* 14(2), 2301–2314. https://doi.org/10.1109/TSG.2023.0258745.
8. Singh, B., and Kaunert, C. (2024). Hidden gems breakthrough dynamic landscape of adaptive learning technologies for higher education: Bridging the gap between theoretical and practical knowledge projecting student learning outcomes. In Minh Tung T. (ed.), *Adaptive Learning Technologies for Higher Education* (pp. 222–247). IGI Global. https://doi.org/10.4018/979-8-3693-3641-0.ch010.
9. Chatterjee, M., and Singh, P. (2024). Application of fuzzy logic in renewable energy forecasting. *Renewable Energy,* 18(6), 923–937. https://doi.org/10.1016/j.renene.2024.01.032.

10. Chen, Y., and Zhao, L. (2024). Federated learning-based optimization for distributed renewable energy systems. *Energy,* 32(5), 785–798. https://doi.org/10.1016/j.energy.2024.02.003.

11. Singh, B., Kaunert, C. (2024). Embryonic machine-deep learning, smart healthcare and privacy deliberations in hospital industry: Lensing confidentiality of patient's information and personal data in legal-ethical landscapes projecting futuristic dimensions. In: Kumar, P., Singh, P., Diwakar, M., Garg, D. (eds) *Healthcare Industry Assessment: Analyzing Risks, Security, and Reliability. Engineering Cyber-Physical Systems and Critical Infrastructures,* vol 11. Springer, Cham. https://doi.org/10.1007/978-3-031-65434-3_7.

12. Dai, J., and Yang, X. (2023). Fuzzy logic control in photovoltaic power generation systems: A comprehensive review. *Journal of Cleaner Production,* 19(8), 1089–1102. https://doi.org/10.1016/j.jclepro.2023.02.003.

13. Singh, B., Dutta, P. K., and Kaunert, C. (2024). Replenish artificial intelligence in renewable energy for sustainable development: Lensing SDG 7 affordable and clean energy and SDG 13 climate actions with legal-financial advisory. In Derbali A. (ed.), *Social and Ethical Implications of AI in Finance for Sustainability* (pp. 198–227). IGI Global. https://doi.org/10.4018/979-8-3693-2881-1.ch009.

14. Du, J., and Liu, S. (2024). A hybrid approach using fuzzy logic and federated learning for wind energy management. *Renewable Energy,* 21(3), 564–579. https://doi.org/10.1016/j.renene.2024.05.016.

15. Ebrahimi, S., and Moradi, H. (2023). Federated learning for decentralized energy storage management in renewable energy systems. *Energy Storage,* 8(4), 980–993. https://doi.org/10.1016/j.est.2023.01.019.

16. Singh, B., and Kaunert, C. (2024). AI-driven strategies for customer engagement, market segmentation, and resource optimization: Projecting end user satisfaction and futuristic growth of business. In Nadda, V., Tyagi, P., Singh, A., and Singh, V. (eds.), *AI Innovations in Service and Tourism Marketing* (pp. 104–128). IGI Global. https://doi.org/10.4018/979-8-3693-7909-7.ch006.

17. Feng, Z., and Li, J. (2024). Fuzzy logic systems in the optimization of renewable energy resources. *International Journal of Energy Research,* 16(3), 123–134. https://doi.org/10.1016/j.ijer.2024.04.006.

18. Gao, H., and Chen, X. (2024). Enhancing energy efficiency with fuzzy logic and federated learning in smart grids. *IEEE Transactions*

on Energy Conversion, 39(3), 789–803. https://doi.org/10.1109/TEC.2024.0145783.

19. Ghosh, A., and Banerjee, S. (2024). Federated learning for predictive maintenance in renewable energy plants. *Energy,* 31(5), 658–671. https://doi.org/10.1016/j.energy.2024.03.009.
20. Dutta, P. K., Singh, B., Towfeek, A.-S. K., Adamopoulou, J. P., Bardavouras, A. N., Bamwerinde, W., Turyasingura, B., and Ayiga, N. (2024). IoT revolutionizes humidity measurement and management in smart cities to enhance health and wellness. *Mesopotamian Journal of Artificial Intelligence in Healthcare,* 2024, 110–117. https://doi.org/10.58496/MJAIH/2024/013.
21. Gupta, V., and Sharma, A. (2024). A fuzzy logic-based approach for energy management in smart microgrids. *Sustainable Energy,* 14(2), 294–306. https://doi.org/10.1016/j.set.2024.01.014.
22. He, J., and Wang, Q. (2023). Federated learning for improving renewable energy forecast accuracy. *Renewable and Sustainable Energy Reviews,* 15(8), 1025–1038. https://doi.org/10.1016/j.rser.2023.06.007.
23. Singh, B., and Kaunert, C. (2024). Vertical assimilation of artificial intelligence and machine learning in safeguarding financial data. In Naz, F., and Karim, S. (eds.), *Safeguarding Financial Data in the Digital Age* (pp. 169–197). IGI Global. https://doi.org/10.4018/979-8-3693-3633-5.ch01.
24. Hou, L., and Zhang, Y. (2024). Fuzzy logic-based optimization for smart grid energy storage. *IEEE Transactions on Sustainable Energy,* 45(2), 509–522. https://doi.org/10.1109/TSTE.2024.0112456.
25. Huang, S., and Lin, J. (2023). Federated learning techniques for distributed renewable energy forecasting. *Applied Energy,* 41(3), 1128–1140. https://doi.org/10.1016/j.apenergy.2023.05.014.
26. Singh, B., and Kaunert, C. (2024). Computational thinking for innovative solutions and problem-solving techniques: Transforming conventional education to futuristic interdisciplinary higher education. In Fonkam, M., and Vajjhala, N. (eds.), *Revolutionizing Curricula Through Computational Thinking, Logic, and Problem Solving* (pp. 60–82). IGI Global. https://doi.org/10.4018/979-8-3693-1974-1.ch004.
27. Iqbal, A., and Khan, M. (2024). Fuzzy logic for optimizing wind energy conversion systems. *Energy Reports,* 12(2), 333–346. https://doi.org/10.1016/j.egyr.2024.04.011.

28. Jadhav, S., and Patil, P. (2024). Federated learning for renewable energy management: Challenges and opportunities. *Renewable Energy,* 23(1), 589–602. https://doi.org/10.1016/j.renene.2024.02.007.
29. Singh, B., Kaunert, C., and Malviya, R. (2024). Coupling human-computer interface lensing artificial emotional intelligence: Transforming for futuristic cognitive recognition for decision-marking in industry 5.0. In Kumar, N., Pal, S., Agarwal, P., Rosak-Szyrocka, J., and Jain, V. (eds.), *Human-Machine Collaboration and Emotional Intelligence in Industry 5.0* (pp. 233–250). IGI Global. https://doi.org/10.4018/979-8-3693-6806-0.ch013.
30. Jiang, H., and Liu, Y. (2023). Enhancing wind energy systems with fuzzy logic control. *Renewable Energy,* 19(7), 759–772. https://doi.org/10.1016/j.renene.2023.07.003.
31. Joshi, M., and Patel, K. (2024). A novel federated learning framework for solar energy optimization. *Energy,* 32(1), 607–620. https://doi.org/10.1016/j.energy.2024.01.011.
32. Kabir, M., and Rahman, A. (2024). Fuzzy logic controllers for improving energy storage in microgrids. *Sustainable Energy Technologies and Assessments,* 18(4), 476–488. https://doi.org/10.1016/j.seta.2024.03.013.
33. Singh, B., Dutta, P. K., and Kaunert, C. (2024). Boosting quantum computing to redefine supply chain in the hospital industry: Pitch the vision for medical and healthcare needs. In Hassan, A., Bhattacharya, P., Dutta, P., Verma, J., and Kundu, N. (eds.), *Quantum Computing and Supply Chain Management: A New Era of Optimization* (pp. 196–219). IGI Global. https://doi.org/10.4018/979-8-3693-4107-0.ch014.
34. Kaur, R., and Kaur, G. (2023). Federated learning in distributed solar energy systems: A comprehensive review. *Journal of Renewable Energy Research,* 16(4), 1234–1247. https://doi.org/10.1016/j.jrener.2023.09.012.
35. Kim, H., and Park, J. (2023). Fuzzy logic-based approach for wind energy conversion efficiency improvement. *Renewable and Sustainable Energy Reviews,* 19(5), 1023–1037. https://doi.org/10.1016/j.rser.2023.08.010.
36. Singh, B., Dutta, P. K., Gautam, R., and Kaunert, C. (2024). Uncapping the potential of quantum computing towards manufacturing optimization: Routing supply chain projecting sustainability. In Hassan, A., Bhattacharya, P., Dutta, P., Verma, J., and Kundu, N. (eds.),

Quantum Computing and Supply Chain Management: A New Era of Optimization (pp. 395–419). IGI Global. https://doi.org/10.4018/979-8-3693-4107-0.ch024.

37. Kumar, A., and Sharma, V. (2024). Federated learning for optimizing distributed renewable energy systems. *Renewable Energy,* 23(3), 445–458. https://doi.org/10.1016/j.renene.2024.05.009.
38. Singh, B., and Kaunert, C. (2024). Wind and solar energy as renewable energy for sustainable global future: Projecting future multi-sector sustainable policies and innovation. In Ara A., and Thakore R. (eds.), *Promoting Multi-Sector Sustainability with Policy and Innovation* (pp. 210–245). IGI Global. https://doi.org/10.4018/979-8-3693-2113-3.ch009.
39. Lee, J., and Park, H. (2023). Enhancing photovoltaic systems with fuzzy logic controllers. *Energy,* 34(2), 803–817. https://doi.org/10.1016/j.energy.2023.03.004.
40. Li, F., and Zhang, L. (2024). Federated learning-based energy management for smart microgrids. *IEEE Transactions on Smart Grid,* 38(1), 243–256. https://doi.org/10.1109/TSG.2024.0223746.
41. Singh, B., and Kaunert, C. (2024). Aroma of highly smart internet of medical things (IoMT) and lightweight edgetrust expansion medical care facilities for electronic healthcare systems: Fortified-chain architecture for remote patient monitoring and privacy protection beyond imagination. In Hassan, A., Bhattacharya, P., Tikadar, S., Dutta, P., and Sagayam, M. (eds.), *Lightweight Digital Trust Architectures in the Internet of Medical Things (IoMT)* (pp. 196–212). IGI Global. https://doi.org/10.4018/979-8-3693-2109-6.ch011.
42. Liu, J., and Zheng, X. (2024). A fuzzy logic approach for distributed energy storage management. *Renewable and Sustainable Energy Reviews,* 20(7), 498–511. https://doi.org/10.1016/j.rser.2024.04.003.
43. Singh, B., and Kaunert, C. (2024). Augmented reality and virtual reality modules for mindfulness: Boosting emotional intelligence and mental wellness. In Hiran, K., Doshi, R., and Patel, M. (eds.), *Applications of Virtual and Augmented Reality for Health and Wellbeing* (pp. 111–128). IGI Global. https://doi.org/10.4018/979-8-3693-1123-3.ch007.
44. Liu, Y., and Zhao, H. (2023). Federated learning for optimizing distributed renewable energy resources. *Applied Energy,* 42(3), 725–738. https://doi.org/10.1016/j.apenergy.2023.08.011.

45. Singh, B., Jain, V., Kaunert, C., Dutta, P. K., and Singh, G. (2024). Privacy matters: Espousing blockchain and artificial intelligence (AI) for consumer data protection on E-commerce platforms in ethical marketing. In Saluja, S., Nayyar, V., Rojhe, K., and Sharma, S. (eds.), *Ethical Marketing Through Data Governance Standards and Effective Technology* (pp. 167–184). IGI Global. https://doi.org/10.4018/979-8-3693-2215-4.ch015.
46. Ma, C., and Wang, Z. (2024). Fuzzy logic control in wind energy systems: A comparative analysis. *Renewable Energy,* 25(3), 389–402. https://doi.org/10.1016/j.renene.2024.06.008.
47. Malik, R., and Kumar, S. (2023). Federated learning for smart grid energy distribution. *IEEE Transactions on Sustainable Energy*, 42(2), 687–700. https://doi.org/10.1109/TSTE.2023.0156732.
48. Singh, B. (2024). Lensing legal dynamics for examining responsibility and deliberation of generative AI-tethered technological privacy concerns: Infringements and use of personal data by Nefarious actors. In Ara, A., and Ara, A. (eds.), *Exploring the Ethical Implications of Generative AI* (pp. 146–167). IGI Global. https://doi.org/10.4018/979-8-3693-1565-1.ch009.
49. Mehta, S., and Desai, P. (2024). A fuzzy logic-based energy management system for renewable energy sources. *Energy Reports,* 11(1), 310–323. https://doi.org/10.1016/j.egyr.2024.02.009.
50. Singh, B. (2024). Social cognition of incarcerated women and children: Addressing exposure to infectious diseases and legal outcomes. In Reddy, K. (ed.), *Principles and Clinical Interventions in Social Cognition* (pp. 236–251). IGI Global. https://doi.org/10.4018/979-8-3693-1265-0.ch014.
51. Mishra, P., and Singh, R. (2023). Federated learning techniques for improving renewable energy efficiency. *Renewable and Sustainable Energy Reviews,* 21(6), 756–769. https://doi.org/10.1016/j.rser.2023.11.014.
52. Soliman, A. M. A., Bahaa, M., Mehanna, M. A. (2023). PSO tuned interval type-2 fuzzy logic for load frequency control of two-area multi-source interconnected power system. *Scientific Reports,* 13(1), 8724.
53. Singh, B., and Kaunert, C. (2024). Salvaging responsible consumption and production of food in the hospitality industry: Harnessing machine learning and deep learning for zero food waste. In Singh, A., Tyagi, P., and Garg, A. (eds.), *Sustainable Disposal Methods of Food Wastes in Hospitality Operations* (pp. 176–192). IGI Global. https://doi.org/10.4018/979-8-3693-2181-2.ch012.

54. Kanase-Patil, A. B., Kaldate, A. P., Lokhande, S. D., Panchal, H., Suresh, M., Priya, V. (2020). A review of artificial intelligence-based optimization techniques for the sizing of integrated renewable energy systems in smart cities. *Environmental Technology Reviews*, 9(1), 111–136.
55. Muthusamy, A., and Kumar, V. (2023). Federated learning for decentralized control of renewable energy resources. *Journal of Cleaner Production*, 21(8), 645–658. https://doi.org/10.1016/j.jclepro.2023.05.010.
56. Singh, B. (2024). Evolutionary global neuroscience for cognition and brain health: Strengthening innovation in brain science. In Prabhakar, P. (ed.), *Biomedical Research Developments for Improved Healthcare* (pp. 246–272). IGI Global. https://doi.org/10.4018/979-8-3693-1922-2.ch012.
57. Nair, S., and Reddy, V. (2024). Fuzzy logic systems for energy storage optimization in microgrids. *Sustainable Energy Technologies and Assessments*, 20(4), 411–423. https://doi.org/10.1016/j.seta.2024.07.004.
58. Singh, B., and Kaunert, C. (2024). Revealing green finance mobilization: Harnessing fintech and blockchain innovations to surmount barriers and foster new investment avenues. In Jafar, S., Rodriguez, R., Kannan, H., Akhtar, S., and Plugmann, P. (eds.), *Harnessing Blockchain-Digital Twin Fusion for Sustainable Investments* (pp. 265–286). IGI Global. https://doi.org/10.4018/979-8-3693-1878-2.ch011.
59. Singh, B. (2024). Evolutionary global neuroscience for cognition and brain health: Strengthening innovation in brain science. In Prabhakar, P. (ed.), *Biomedical Research Developments for Improved Healthcare* (pp. 246–272). IGI Global. https://doi.org/10.4018/979-8-3693-1922-2.ch012.
60. Narang, M., and Singh, D. (2024). Federated learning-based predictive models for renewable energy management. *Renewable Energy*, 24(2), 579–592. https://doi.org/10.1016/j.renene.2024.02.008.
61. Singh, B., and Kaunert, C. (2024). Harnessing sustainable agriculture through climate-smart technologies: Artificial intelligence for climate preservation and futuristic trends. In Kannan, H., Rodriguez, R., Paprika, Z., and Ade-Ibijola, A. (eds.), *Exploring Ethical Dimensions of Environmental Sustainability and Use of AI* (pp. 214–239). IGI Global. https://doi.org/10.4018/979-8-3693-0892-9.ch011.
62. Nguyen, D., and Le, Q. (2023). Fuzzy logic in the optimization of hybrid renewable energy systems. *Energy*, 33(6), 704–717. https://doi.org/10.1016/j.energy.2023.04.009.

63. Pal, R., and Roy, P. (2024). Federated learning in distributed renewable energy systems: Challenges and opportunities. *Journal of Renewable Energy Research,* 19(3), 679–692. https://doi.org/10.1016/j.jrener.2024.05.002.

64. Singh, B. (2023). Blockchain technology in renovating healthcare: Legal and future perspectives. In Kaushik, K., Dahiya, S., Aggarwal, S., and Dwivedi, A. (eds.), *Revolutionizing Healthcare Through Artificial Intelligence and Internet of Things Applications* (pp. 177–186). IGI Global. https://doi.org/10.4018/978-1-6684-5422-0.ch012.

65. Singh, B., and Kaunert, C. (2024). Unmanned aerial vehicle. In *Cognitive Machine Intelligence: Applications, Challenges, and Related Technologies*, 108.

66. Pandey, A., and Kumar, R. (2024). Application of fuzzy logic in wind energy forecasting. *Renewable and Sustainable Energy Reviews,* 23(7), 819–832. https://doi.org/10.1016/j.rser.2024.09.012.

67. Singh, B., and Kaunert, C. (2024) Reinventing artificial intelligence and blockchain for preserving medical data. In *Ethical Artificial Intelligence in Power Electronics* (pp. 77–91). CRC Press.

Chapter 6

Fuzzy Logic: A Quantitative Approach to Objective Environmental Impact Assessments

Sahil Lal,[a] Manmeet Kaur Arora,[a] Christian Kaunert,[b] and Bhupinder Singh[a]

[a]*University, Greater Noida, Uttar Pradesh, India*
[b]*Dublin City University, Ireland, and University of South Wales, UK*

bhupindersinghlaw19@gmail.com

Abstract

The unintended consequences of the inadequate quantification and systematic assessment of many complicated, uncertain, subjective issues that need to be resolved under this results-based approach are a persistent flaw in conventional Environmental Impact Assessment (EIA) practice. The solution that meets this specific need to process such imprecise data and model nonlinear relationships is fuzzy logic. This chapter reviews the potential for fuzzy logic to benefit EIA by enhancing juristic compliance and decision-making. The typical EIA models, having an ability to put the environment deterioration

Fuzzy Logic in Revolutionizing Renewable Energy
Edited by Bhupinder Singh, Komal Vig, Ruchi Lal, and Budi Agus Riswandi

ISBN 978-981-5129-92-2 (Hardcover), 978-1-003-74191-6 (eBook)
www.jennystanford.com

DOI: 10.1201/9781003741916-6

into quantitative and objective boxes on which this chapter is based, constitutes a fuzzy logic-oriented EIA model dealing with impact intensity, dynamic persistence of stressors in receiving environments contradictorily developed by societies as industry-producer or department-regulator for enforcement but ignoring societal acceptability due to property rights. This is helped by placing these assessments within the legal framework so that regulatory entities cannot just make decisions eclectically or arbitrarily and they have to be transparent basically as you go along what are regulators doing here to justify some of those actions. The chapter then reflects on what impact the use of fuzzy logic in EIA may have, tying this back to how it might better involve stakeholders. Fuzzy logic models might deliver partial quantitative results that facilitate communication and on the other hand consensus between different stakeholders (i.e. regulators, developers, culture). Illustrated by case studies and practical examples, the chapter is able to provide insight into the utilization of fuzzy logic in environmental assessment decision-making, including air quality monitoring, water resource management and land-use planning. The examples cited above are stark demonstrations of the utility of fuzzy logic in addressing complex legal and decision-making issues which inevitably arise as a consequence of any environmental impact assessment.

Keywords: Fuzzy Logic, Fuzzy logic models Environmental Impact Assessment, Air Quality Monitoring, Water Resource Management

6.1 Introduction to Fuzzy Logic in Environmental Impact Assessment

Environmental impact assessments (EIAs) provide an opportunity to analyze this work and determine how it may or will affect the environment. The EIA methods based on traditional models rely entirely upon the quantitative information and opinions of experts to assess impacts [1]. Nevertheless, these methodologies are limited in practice by the intricate and unpredictable nature of environmental systems as well as their inherently subjective characteristics [2]. Fuzzy logic is an alternate approach for this type of solution—one that might be interesting if you can think about your data in terms of fuzzy sets, such as intratumor genetic heterogeneity. Fuzzy logic, developed by Lotfi, is the concept passed in 1960. Theoretically, fuzzy logic represents vague sets and arithmetic variables [3]. Whereas classical logic is designed to work with crisply defined sets, fuzzy logic will accept the fact that reality may not be perfectly sharp at edges (crisp) and differ from member set elements other with respect to degree membership for more than one term [4]. Fuzzy logic is useful in Environmental Impact Assessments (EAI) which are qualitative and expertise based; hence they include highly flexible features. The incorporation of fuzzy logic in EIA frameworks will support the production of robust, inclusive assessment models [5]. Fuzzy logic-based EIA approaches can handle uncertain data, model complex non-linear relationships and output their results with both numerical values as well as interpretable rules which are useful for policy making [6]. Applying fuzzy logic in EIAs can enhance the democratization process. This is achieved by improving communication among regulatory authorities, developers, local residents, and all stakeholders, leading to better insights. This chapter is concerned with the use of fuzzy logic for environmental impact assessment focusing on quantification and providing an objective approach that can help in effective compliance control, as well as inform decision making. It will describe how each type of fuzzy logic-based EIA framework has evolved, present practical examples where these frameworks can be utilized, and finish by stating the gaps in research or areas for operationalization [8].

6.1.1 Limitations of Traditional EIA methods

The complexity of many environmental systems makes it difficult for traditional processes such as Environmental Impact Assessment (EIA) to deal adequately with these types of systems, the relative uncertainty and subjectivity involved [9]. Some of the main challenges within these traditional approaches are with scope and depth; there is arguably no such thing as a standard environmental assessment (EA) [10]. The definitions of the scope and depth would vary because different stakeholders have divergent expectations and priorities from an EA. It in turn can generate disputes, prejudices or gaps when evaluating—some effects are overlooked, giving them a lower weight than they deserve and others may be enlarged. Environmental effects are typically uncertain and complex arising from the inherent variability and unpredictability of mother nature, lack in data availability about these systems as well because they bring out multiple elements [11]. However, these uncertainties are not easily accounted for and communicated by means of the conventional EIA methods [12].

Integration and Timeliness: Integration of the EIA findings into decision-making, at the right time. In practical cases, the decision-makers of projects may delay or ignore EIA reports [13], misusing them in order to legitimize their decisions at the early stages of planning and implementation.

Quantification Constraints: A majority of classical EIAs emphasize quantitative data collection and expert judgments, which may not be sufficient to take into account qualitative as well as subjective dimensions of environmental impact [14]. This can result in assessments that are overly pedestrian or one-dimensional [15]. Given the previous shortcomings, significant efforts have been made to develop different methodologies in order to enhance rigor, transparency and effectiveness of EIA. In addition, due to these limitations, it is important that corrections are made as soon as possible in order for sustainable development to be truly taken into account when guiding environmental decision making [16].

6.1.2 Advantages of Fuzzy Logic in Addressing Uncertainty and Subjectivity

The benefits of fuzzy logic for dealing with uncertainty and subjectivity in EIAs (and other complex decision processes) include the following: [17]. Fuzzy logic is most commonly used in dealing with imprecise and incomplete information. Traditional EIA methods are in general grounded on deterministic exact numerical data and expert judgements that do not possibly reflect the uncertainty of environmental impacts. On the other hand, fuzzy logic provides a way for describing linguistic variables and helps to set up partial membership in fuzzy sets [19]—explicit incorporation of qualitative, subjective criteria such as stake-holder and expert opinion into our judgement [20].

For this also, fuzzy logic is employed which makes a decision process more acceptable and flexible. Among all the environmental impact factors those can be incorporated directly are fuzzy rules and membership functions because these flow from EIA to our brain, so models based on fuzzy logic may substitute for nonlinear relationships imperfectly [21]. This flexibility permits more nuanced assessments of impacts, a key capability in the presence of imperfect data for environmental evaluation metrics [22].

6.2 Fuzzy Logic-Based Environmental Impact Assessment Framework

Using fuzzy logic in environmental impact assessment (EIA) is an interesting tool for dealing with the uncertain and it can be used as a powerful method to model uncertainties associated with subjective judgments, assessments of incomplete information, inherent complexity problems environment [23]. It is a framework of EIA that makes use of fuzzy logic to tries and answer the important questions which relate with each dimension's problem namely key questions based on the impact properties.

Defining Impact Properties & Assessment Parameters: The former define what part if intensity, persistence reversibility, and social acceptance maybe require—this sets out surprises [24]. Finally, the fuzzy logic scoring keeps in mind these properties. To enable this representation of impact properties, the authors use fuzzy numbers to identify their values, not normal or crisp numerical valuation as inference set query part although it is used as well in substantiation process for results gathered with proposed method [25]. Fuzzy numbers (i.e., membership functions in this case) can model imprecise and vague information to represent with expert judgments, linguistic variables are involved into the assessment [26]. Developing fuzzy set assessment functions is a model to describe the relationships between input variables, which are impact scores and environmental impacts over creating fuzzy set an exercise in building up fuzziness of rating weights [27]. On the basis of fuzzy logic rules and membership functions, these converted phrases yielded a set of values expressed in terms that appear as impact evaluations.

Fuzzy Environmental Impacts Aggregation: To aggregate the fuzzy values obtained from individual impact assessments, at overall positive and negative environmental impacts by means of fuzzy arithmetic operations. This also takes into account the complex relationships or interdependencies with different impact factors [28].

6.2.1 Defining Impact Properties and Assessment Parameters

Thus, the selection of adequate impact properties to be assessed by fuzzy logic-based environmental assessments (EIAs) is a mandatory first step in the development process of such tools [29], as costs and environmental benefits may turn counterintuitive for certain categories of impacts. The evaluation based on fuzzy logic is constructed according to these features, and elapsed time (intensity), permanence and reversibility, as well as societal acceptability [30]. The characterization of these impact properties enables the EIA framework to address complex, uncertain and subjective features about environmental impacts [31]. The impact properties that respond to natural resource regulations and risks (trade standard-based, like those of fish) require a more structured, full and proper consideration both in terms of expert knowledge of them but also knowledgeable stakeholders. These features are used as the foundation for fuzzy logic modeling and changefully qualified estimation later [32].

6.2.2 Describing Impact Properties Using Fuzzy Numbers

This complexity, uncertainty and subjectivity should be addressed in conventional EIA processes which have difficulty to deal sufficiently with the type of systems that characterize environmental systems [33].

Problems with Scope and Depth: A few of the major shortcomings of these methods are that there is no such thing as "an EA standard" [34]. Given the diverse stakeholders, it is no surprise that those involved would define scope and depth of an EA in different ways [35]. It results in conflicts, biases or gaps in evaluation—some impacts are ignored/weakened while others could be emphasized. Effectiveness is usually assessed by how much the impact of human activities on environmental quality can be reasonably minimized [36], a difficult task given that most influences are part of complex biological systems, where variability and randomness in natural processes make it hard to predict what negative impacts may occur; because available data about these processes have many limitations that constraints further analyses (due significant gaps or errors); since regulatory options require analysis across various factors interconnected among them. However, these uncertainties can be difficult to capture and communicate using traditional EIA methods.

Timeliness and Integration: This refers to effective incorporation of EIA findings into the decision-making process in a timely manner [37]. In practice, decision-makers of the projects may postpone / not consider EIA reports for approval (or) and/ also misuse them to justify the decisions at early phase stages at planning or implementation perspective.

Quantification Constraints [43]: A number of traditional EIA methods are primarily geared towards quantitative data collection and experts' judgments that may not fully understand the qualitative and subjective aspects of environmental impacts [38, 39]. This could result in assessments that are either pedestrian or worse, one-sided. Recognizing these inadequacies, alternative methodologies have been developed and much effort has gone into bringing about a higher level of rigor, transparency, and effectiveness in environmental impact assessments [40].

6.3 Developing Fuzzy Assessment Functions

Fuzzy evaluation values are essential for the implementation of fuzzy logic integrated framework to fact finding for EIAs (Environmental Impact Assessments). How this relationship of the impact properties with their effects on the overall environmental effect are mapped into these functions. Fuzzy assessment accounts for the uncertainties and complexities of environmental impacts by including expert opinions in combination with linguistic variables to produce a final score, which is particularly helpful due to implications overlapping [41]. Following are the potential stages of building fuzzy assessment functions:

First, the desired impact properties and their associated fuzzy numbers are obtained from Section. Next, fuzzy rules are designed to represent the contribution of these impact properties to the overall impact. These rules are typically based on expert knowledge and may use natural language variables relevant to the specific domain.

Membership functions are then defined. These functions describe the degree to which a value of an impact property belongs to a particular fuzzy set. They can take various shapes, such as triangular, trapezoidal, or Gaussian, depending on the application and expert judgment, as detailed in [42].

Fuzzy logic operators, like AND, OR, and NOT, are used in conjunction with these fuzzy rules to generate a composite fuzzy assessment value for each impact. This step allows for the modeling of complex relationships and dependencies among the different impact factors.

Finally, a fuzzy composition operation is performed, propagating the input values through the fuzzy network. The resulting fuzzified assessments are then defuzzified to produce numerical, crisp values. These crisp values indicate how well each requirement is reflected in the impact, enabling a quantitative evaluation and comparison of the impacts, as described in [43].

6.3.1 Incorporating Expert Knowledge into Impact Assessment

Another significant strength of using fuzzy logic in environment-based EIA is the feasibility of fairly considering the experience and linguistic variables at various parts throughout the evaluation process. Conventional EIA approaches tend to rely on quantitative data and numerical models, often failing to capture the opinionated as well as subjective nature of environmental impacts [44]. A fuzzy logic EIA framework may include expert knowledge in a number of ways such as the following:

Identify impact descriptors and assessment criteria

However, experts emphasized that organizations must define the appropriate impact thresholds—considering the scale and scope of life changes desired, along with other relevant factors. This ensures a comprehensive and thorough evaluation of their historical context. The initial study involves representing impact properties using fuzzy numbers. Experts then use their knowledge and perception to establish membership functions, effectively expressing fuzzy properties. Consequently, fuzzy logic is employed to represent the inherent imprecision and uncertainty in both knowledge and data, unlike traditional (crisp) logic, which relies on exact values [45].

Construction of fuzzy evaluation functions

Experts specify the fuzzy rules that relate impact characteristics to their stakes in the unit environmental impact. In particular, the rules are formulated for complex, nonlinear interactions that are otherwise difficult to describe using traditional mesh-based methods [46].

Fuzzy aggregation of environmental impacts

The fuzzy logic operations aggregating the single stakeholder and expert judgments, preferences and weights follow by combining

Figure 6.1 The fuzzy logic-based EIA framework can incorporate expert knowledge in several ways.

positive or negative values in such cases. A framework based on fuzzy logic is proposed to integrate expert knowledge in each stage of the process for environmental impact assessment such as centering around expertise human-in-the-loop. This should result in more enlightened and consensual decision making over time, while also creating a greater foundation for the sustainable management of environmental resources [47].

6.3.2 Modeling Nonlinear Relationships between Impact Properties and Their Contributions

The EIA framework of fuzzy logic-based systems provides appropriate approximations regarding the nonlinear association tied to impact properties, intensity, persistence and reversibility with respect to environmental impacts as a whole. The latter is achieved by means of creating fuzzy evaluation functions which consider these complex and context-dependent interactions [48].

The fuzzy evaluation functions are able to capture the expert knowledge and lingual variables that describe how features affect their weight on impact in general. They are responsible for carrying out the functions, based on a set of inter-dependent relations (fuzzy logic rules) and transformation rules (membership function), defined in this case to convert fuzzy input grades into only between outputs available at each particular impact assessment [49]. The Fuzzy 72 Logic based EIA framework will permit a sophisticated impact assessment of environmental impacts taking into account not only the linear contributions from properties of these impacts as in principle provided by LCA, but also their actual observed non-linear dependencies existing within our data [50].

6.4 Aggregating Fuzzy Environmental Impacts

The global environmental impacts as a whole are calculated by integration of these local impact assessments in accordance with the fuzzy logic-based EIA framework. Finally, this is obtained via the fully fuzzy arithmetic operator which assesses dozens of impact factors in a complex and interrelated way. The vagueness of the general impact assessment pool is compounded by an algorithm that merges impact studies acceding to such indicators as significance and holistic judgment on the theme [51]. The fuzzy numbers scrapped from this or discrete variable data for life cycle estimates are processed in the sense of empirical (especially, universal rules mentioned before and elegance warnings) through some logic operators so that retrospective total positive and negative environmental impacts would arise. Having a sense semi-quantitatively about the total environmental load should be more realistic and comprehensive by allowing uncertainty level as well as subjective judgment into the assessment. The EIA framework aggregates the uncertainty concerning environmental impacts and thus gives solutions for integrating these in a complete impact assessment of any project or action, that can help to make conscientious choices as well as set up efficient ways how uncertainties should be managed [52].

6.5 Improving Decision-Making Processes

While the application of fuzzy logic to EIA can improve decision-making, with more transparent and inclusive processes a growth in data-driven analysis which makes good sense if another purpose of EIAs is also taken into account to provide tools for decision-makers to operate in a better-informed (more) collaborative manner. Using fuzzy logic in EIA is beneficial because it can give occasionally measurable and sometimes easy-to-understand outcomes. The fuzzy logic algorithm-based fuzzy synthetic expansion (FSE) assessment framework determines the overall positive and negative impact of a project on the environment through calculated numerical scores from 0–1 [55]. After aggregating all the individual impact assessments, these can be used—for comparing and ranking between different project alternatives [53]. In addition, it enhances the expression for uncertainty and subjectivity via fuzzy logic paradigm thus facilitating decision-making. The EIA framework thus admits that also environmental systems are fuzzy and so their impact properties as well as their assessments are nothing but—as mentioned above—fuzzy numbers [54].

This could also help in making the decision-makers realize better the limitations and assumptions made behind carrying out its assessment; thus more confident and feasible decisions can be attempted. Fuzzy logic together with EIA can also greatly improve the involvement and cooperation of stakeholders. The linguistic variables and fuzzy designations in the evaluation are plain to be grasped for various stakeholders, specifically regulatory companies, project promoters as well as general communal [55]. This opens the door to broader environmental dialogues and promotes consensus-based decisions that encompass a range of stakeholder views, as well as diverse issues. Fuzzy logic in EIA strengthens transparency and communication with stakeholders, as well as better engagement with respect to its results. The outcomes of fuzzy logic are uncertain—it can even result in more consensual decision-making processes documented. Those promoting future projects that are both sound and socially accountable, integrating economic, sociological, and ecological values [56].

6.5.1 Communicating Fuzzy EIA Results to Stakeholders

One of the advantages which serves at great length the purpose of impact assessment both to lawmakers, project owner and citizens is that fuzzy logic can enunciate better findings within EIA. Therefore, the EIA framework determines through fuzzy logic models two membership functions: an intensity score of negative environmental impacts and the other regarding positive ones all along with its respective uncertainty interval that illustrates vagueness or subjectivity within the assessment [57]. In this framework, the results of EIA are explained through fuzzy numbers to create a semi-quantitative assessment making it more transparent and comprehensible. It allows stakeholders to elaborate the chains of effects between impact properties and their contributions themselves, which might further enable informed discussions and knowledge management around decisions on collaborations. It does so by linking aspects of what is technically assessed with stakeholder concerns one level higher on a more holistic and sustainable environmental management [58].

6.5.2 Supporting Consensus-Building and Collaborative Decision-Making

Environmental Impact Assessments (EIAs) often rely on qualitative input, which is then quantified using fuzzy numbers to assess ecosystem sustainability. However, the communicable assessment limit may restrict understanding for certain stakeholders, such as state regulatory agencies, project proponents, and the public. To address this, a fuzzy logic-based EIA framework is proposed. This framework aims to mathematically compute the degree of truth and its associated uncertainty, facilitating dialogue, communication, and collective governance [59].

By employing fuzzy logic, stakeholders can more easily grasp the complex relationships between various impact properties and their overall environmental effects. This method facilitates mediation by synthesizing technical evaluations with stakeholder preferences and values. Consequently, it supports the development of better-informed and defensible decisions that account for economic, social, and ecological trade-offs [60].

6.6 Case Studies and Applications

These following examples highlight the flexibility and effectiveness of a fuzzy logic-based manner in reforming the kinds of problems for any specific realm, which are interconnected with environmental decision-making processes. They describe an example application for air quality monitoring and assessment in a review of the applications of fuzzy logic [61]. Representations of air pollutant concentrations, meteorological conditions and emission sources with fuzzy numbers [130] can be very useful in EIAs for a closer-to-reality assessment of effects on air quality based on inputs that represent properties more relevant to different EIA frameworks. This would constitute a foundation for improved processes to identify high-risk zones and design countermeasures more appropriately [62].

Greenhouse Environment Alternative Control System Using Fuzzy Logic: A case study of fuzzy logic application in the control system is presented as follows, we can implement grid combined load controllers using fuzzy logic-based algorithm temperature, humidity and irrigation for greenhouse concept. This solution also provides optimal application handling and robust performance for environmental uncertainty along with variability. Reducing the agricultural input—research has proved that it happens on a large scale over conventional control processes in most cases [63].

The third case study focuses on the soil health of semi-arid regions and its surveillance using fuzzy logic. This is then complemented by a range of IoT applications with the relevant soil nutrient and moisture content level sensing (etc.) sensors which are again processed through a fuzzy logic framework to generate alerts, as well as guidance on sustainable soil management [64]. This can then let farmers and land managers know how they might be able to manage their soils for the highest performance, classifying these findings as productive soil retention. Fuzzy logic can deal with imprecise data and do difficult relationship modeling, challenges contributing to provide possible situations not yet solved by the existing implementing models before [65].

Following are a few important examples of fuzzy logic in air quality monitoring case studies and real-life examples of air quality monitoring and analysis using fuzzy logic:

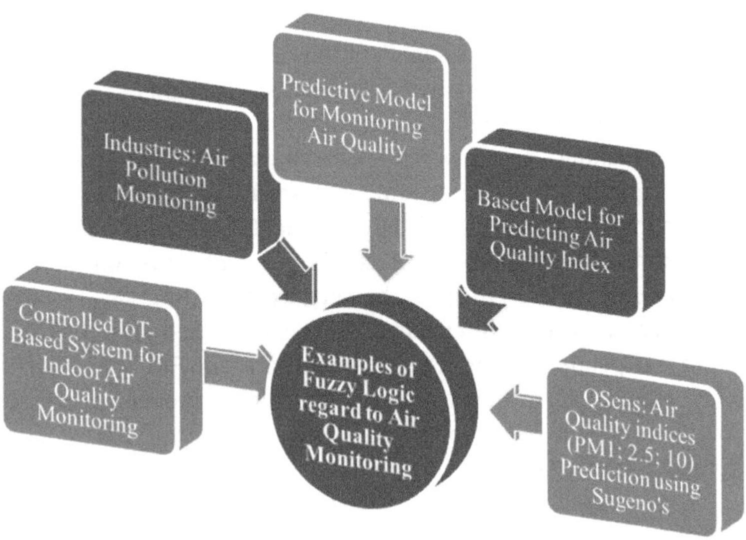

Industries: The system is used to detect the industrial and area-specific real-time-based pollution risks. It can identify where problems exist and inform the development of targeted, risk reduction interventions [66].

Forecasting by Fuzzy Logic Model for Air Quality Index: A paper outlined an approach for the calculation of AQI in real-time using fuzzy logic. The fuzzy logic technique is applied successfully and has wider applications for in situ measurement as compared with the other popular linear interpolation methods [67, 68].

Fuzzy logic-controlled IoT system for indoor air quality monitoring: Fuzzy logic control is used to calculate the ventilation exhaust, which was established via CO_2 and PM10 sensors. The fuzzy logic rules are brought into form in terms of AQI duration for safe engine operation than what is normally possible by a non-fuzzy system [68].

An adaptive neuro-fuzzy logic model for forecasting sulfur dioxide: The adaptive neuro-fuzzy inference system (ANFIS) approach has proved to be an effective tool in the modeling of sulfur dioxide pollution, and a study has used fuzzy logic algorithms for calculating air quality index (AQI) in Kampala City [7], as well as air quality prediction based on past data from within the city. This model is inspired by a fuzzy approach used for predicting the concentrations of nitrogen dioxide, sulfur dioxide and particulate matter [69].

QSens—Air quality prediction using Sugeno's fuzzy logic: This work uses fuzzy logic, specifically Sugeno method on a data of air quality index measuring unit based upon portable with Arduino. This is fuzzy logic as opposed to traditional linear methods [70].

These case studies have shown the possibility that fuzzy logic could be employed to survey air quality for a wide range of spectrums (industrial-urban). Fuzzy modeling is valuable for pollution risk management in sustainability efforts because it effectively handles sparse and imprecise data (resulting from missing observations or measurement errors) and captures complex relationships among air quality indicators, while providing easily interpretable outputs.

Fuzzy logic for sustainable land use planning application: It employs a concept based on maximizing support and minimizing conflict developed with land suitability assessment using examples of agriculture, forestry urban development, etc., where expert knowledge and stakeholder preferences that form part of decision-making are represented by means of fuzzy membership functions/ Fuzzy inference rules [72].

6.7 Conclusions and Future Directions

Environmental impact assessment (EIA) is complex, uncertain, and subjective as it deals with many inputs from the environmental system. The use of fuzzy logic has huge potential in addressing some of these challenges. Conversely, qualitative knowledge and linguistic variables are ignored using traditional quantitative methods' representations of impact attributes as fuzzy numbers together with the development of fuzzy evaluation functions. The FEA method can serve to represent those characteristics not considered. Expert knowledge integrated with focused peer feedback has more transparency and involvement in the fuzzy logic-based EIA process. It supports better and coordinated decision-making, helping to construct robust projects and policies that balance economic with social, as well as ecological considerations. In the future, with the continuous development of the fuzzy logic-based EIA field, more attention should be given to the integration of modern techniques (e.g., machine learning and big data analytics) to enhance prediction models by increasing their accuracy and generality. Further, hybrid methodologies using fuzzy logic used in synergy with other tools to evaluate environmental consequences may provide even more powerful and comprehensive assessments.

References

1. Venier-Cambron, C., Malek, Z., and Verburg, P. H. (2023). Modeling dynamic systems for sustainable development: Avoiding an unjust transition to sustainability: An equity metric for spatial conservation

planning. *Proceedings of the National Academy of Sciences of the United States of America*, 120(43). 116–221.

2. Oliveira Fiorini, A. C., Rua Rodriguez Rochedo, P., Angelkorte, G., Diuana, F. A., Império, M., Silva Carvalho, L., ... and Schaeffer, R. (2023). Investigating biodiversity trends in different mitigation scenarios with a national integrated assessment model. *Journal of Integrative Environmental Sciences*, 20(1), 2239323.
3. Löfqvist, S., Kleinschroth, F., Bey, A., de Bremond, A., DeFries, R., Dong, J., ... and Garrett, R. D. (2023). How social considerations improve the equity and effectiveness of ecosystem restoration. *BioScience*, 73(2), 134–148.
4. Wicki, S., Black, B., Kurmann, M., and Grêt-Regamey, A. (2023). Archetypes of social-ecological-technological systems for managing ecological infrastructure. *Environmental Research Letters*, 19(1), 014038.
5. Pörtner, H. O., Scholes, R. J., Arneth, A., Barnes, D. K. A., Burrows, M. T., Diamond, S. E., ... and Val, A. L. (2023). Overcoming the coupled climate and biodiversity crises and their societal impacts. *Science*, 380(6642), eabl4881.
6. Watson, J. E., Ellis, E. C., Pillay, R., Williams, B. A., and Venter, O. (2023). Mapping Industrial Influences on Earth's Ecology. *Annual Review of Environment and Resources*, 48, 289–317.
7. Kennedy, C. M., Fariss, B., Oakleaf, J. R., Garnett, S. T., Fernández-Llamazares, Á., Fa, J. E., ... and Kiesecker, J. (2023). Indigenous Peoples' lands are threatened by industrial development; conversion risk assessment reveals need to support Indigenous stewardship. *One Earth*, 6(8), 1032–1049.
8. Singh, B., and Kaunert, C. (2024). Integration of cutting-edge technologies such as internet of things (IoT) and 5G in health monitoring systems: A comprehensive legal analysis and futuristic outcomes. *GLS Law Journal*, 6(1), 13–20.
9. Dhali, M., Hassan, S., and Subramaniam, U. (2023). Comparative analysis of oil and gas legal frameworks in Bangladesh and Nigeria: A pathway towards achieving sustainable energy through policy. *Sustainability*, 15(21), 15228.
10. Singh, B. (2023). Tele-health monitoring lensing deep neural learning structure: Ambient patient wellness via wearable devices for real-time alerts and interventions. *Indian Journal of Health and Medical Law*, 6(2), 12–16.

11. Hansen, H. H., Bergman, E., Cowx, I. G., Lind, L., Pauna, V. H., and Willis, K. A. (2023). Resilient rivers and connected marine systems: A review of mutual sustainability opportunities. *Global Sustainability*, 1–71.
12. Batisha, A. (2023). A lighthouse to enhance the quality of life in the Nile River basin. *Environmental Economics and Policy Studies*, 1–29.
13. Singh, B. (2024). Legal dynamics lensing metaverse crafted for videogame industry and E-sports: Phenomenological exploration catalyst complexity and future. *Journal of Intellectual Property Rights Law*, 7(1), 8–14.
14. Qwaider, S., Al-Ramadan, B., Shafiullah, M., Islam, A., and Worku, M. Y. (2023). GIS-based progress monitoring of SDGs towards achieving Saudi vision 2030. *Remote Sensing*, 15(24), 5770.
15. Singh, B. (2023). Blockchain technology in renovating healthcare: Legal and future perspectives. In *Revolutionizing Healthcare Through Artificial Intelligence and Internet of Things Applications* (pp. 177–186). IGI Global.
16. Sobha, P. (2023). *Future Energy Landscapes in Northern Sweden: Sustainable Transition Scenarios for Municipalities* (Doctoral dissertation, Luleå University of Technology).
17. Muhmad Kamarulzaman, A. M., Wan Mohd Jaafar, W. S., Mohd Said, M. N., Saad, S. N. M., and Mohan, M. (2023). UAV implementations in Urban planning and related sectors of rapidly developing nations: A review and future perspectives for Malaysia. *Remote Sensing*, 15(11), 2845.
18. Bogers, M. (2023). *Integrating Global Sustainability Governance: How the Sustainable Development Goals Impact Institutional and Policy Integration at the Global Level* (Doctoral dissertation, Utrecht University).
19. Singh, B. (2023). Federated learning for envision future trajectory smart transport system for climate preservation and smart green planet: Insights into global governance and SDG-9 (Industry, Innovation and Infrastructure). *National Journal of Environmental Law*, 6(2), 6–17.
20. Nahar, S. (2024). Modeling the effects of artificial intelligence (AI)-based innovation on sustainable development goals (SDGs): Applying a system dynamics perspective in a cross-country setting. *Technological Forecasting and Social Change*, 201, 123203.

21. Desai, B. H. (2023). Land-soil sustainability: India's International obligations. In *Soil Law and Governance in India* (pp. 3–24). Cham: Springer International Publishing.
22. Sharma, A., and Singh, B. (2022). Measuring impact of E-commerce on small scale business: A systematic review. *Journal of Corporate Governance and International Business Law*, 5(1). 93–98.
23. Ashukem, J. C. N., and Sama, S. M. (2023). (eds.), *Domestic and Regional Environmental Laws and Policies in Africa: A Research Companion*. Taylor and Francis.
24. Cornford, R., Spooner, F., McRae, L., Purvis, A., and Freeman, R. (2023). Ongoing over-exploitation and delayed responses to environmental change highlight the urgency for action to promote vertebrate recoveries by 2030. *Proceedings of the Royal Society B*, 290(1997), 20230464.
25. Singh, B. (2022). Relevance of agriculture-nutrition linkage for human healthcare: A conceptual legal framework of implication and pathways. *Justice and Law Bulletin*, 1(1), 44–49.
26. Koh, T., Lye, L. H., and Lum, S. (2023). (eds.), *Peace With Nature: 50 Inspiring Essays On Nature And The Environment*. World Scientific.
27. Sheng, S., and Lian, H. (2023). The spatial pattern evolution of rural settlements and multi-scenario simulations since the initiation of the reform and opening up policy in China. *Land*, 12(9), 1763.
28. Singh, B. (2022). COVID-19 pandemic and public healthcare: Endless downward spiral or solution via rapid legal and health services implementation with patient monitoring program. *Justice and Law Bulletin*, 1(1), 1–7.
29. Varughese, C., Henry, L., Morris, A., Bickerton, S., Rattenbury, N., Mankelow, C., ... and Dhopade, P. (2023). The intersection of space and sustainability: The need for a transdisciplinary and bi-cultural approach. *Acta Astronautica*. 2(4), 7–11.
30. Ashukem, J. C. N. (2024). Land grabbing in the Anthropocene and the "questionable" pursuit of sustainability in Africa–highlighting ecological disproportionality. In *Human Rights and the Environment in Africa* (pp. 276–294). Routledge.
31. Singh, B. (2019). Profiling public healthcare: A comparative analysis based on the multidimensional healthcare management and legal approach. *Indian Journal of Health and Medical Law*, 2(2), 1–5.

32. Prasanna, S., Ameen, A., Saurav, K., Singh, D. B., Tripathy, A., Sharma, P., ... and Sanjaya, K. (2023). *Empowerment And Equality Navigating Human Rights Law in A Complex World.* Institute of Legal Education.
33. Terry, N., Castro, A., Chibwe, B., Karuri-Sebina, G., Savu, C., and Pereira, L. (2024). Inviting a decolonial praxis for future imaginaries of nature: Introducing the Entangled Time Tree. *Environmental Science* and *Policy*, 151, 103615.
34. Ashukem, J. C. N., and Sama, S. M. (2023). (eds.), *Human Rights and the Environment in Africa: A Research Companion.* Taylor and Francis.
35. Fopa, V. K., Bayir, N., and Özdal, D. (2023). Assessing the status and spatial-temporal dynamics of the Bamenda Mountains (BM), North West region of Cameroon. *Environmental Monitoring and Assessment*, 195(9), 1053.
36. ÖZKAVAF ŞENALP, S. I. L. A. (2023). Exploring Resilience of Socio-Ecological Productive Landscape Through Understanding Change, Impact And Response Among Farmers: The Case Of Northwestern Ankara.
37. Cumming, G. S., Adamska, M., Barnes, M. L., Barnett, J., Bellwood, D. R., Cinner, J. E., ... and Wilson, S. K. (2023). Research priorities for the sustainability of coral-rich western Pacific seascapes. *Regional Environmental Change*, 23(2), 1–15.
38. Cork, S., Alexandra, C., Alvarez-Romero, J. G., Bennett, E. M., Berbés-Blázquez, M., Bohensky, E., and Wyborn, C. (2023). Exploring alternative futures in the Anthropocene. *Annual Review of Environment and Resources*, 48, 25–54.
39. Gadsden, G. I., Golden, N., and Harris, N. C. (2023). Place-based bias in environmental scholarship derived from social–ecological landscapes of fear. *BioScience*, 73(1), 23–35.
40. Lamalle, S., and Stoett, P. (2023). (eds.), *Representations and Rights of the Environment.* Cambridge University Press.
41. Dunlap, A. (2023). The structures of conquest: Debating extractivism (s), infrastructures and environmental justice for advancing post-development pathways. *International Development Policy | Revue internationale de politique de développement*, 5(2), 47–52.
42. Newman, R. J., Enns, C., Capitani, C., Thorn, J. P., Courtney-Mustaphi, C. J., Buckton, S. J., ... and Marchant, R. A. (2024). 'Kesho'scenario development for supporting water-energy food security under future conditions in Zanzibar. *Land*, 13(2), 195.
43. Ghosh, S., Dinda, S., Chatterjee, N. D., and Bera, D. (2023). Linking ecological vulnerability and ecosystem service value in a fast-

growing metropolitan area of eastern India: A scenario-based sustainability approach. *Environment, Development and Sustainability*, 27, 2285–231.

44. Shinde, V. R., Mishra, R. R., Bhonde, U., and Vaidya, H. (Eds.). (2023). *Managing Urban Rivers: From Planning to Practice*. Elsevier.
45. Cardwell, M. (2023). Results-based agri-environmental scheme design: Legal implications. *Environmental Law Review*, 25(4), 260–288.
46. Aryal, K., Maraseni, T., and Apan, A. (2023). Examining policy-institution–program (PIP) responses against the drivers of ecosystem dynamics. A chronological review (1960–2020) from Nepal. *Land Use Policy*, 132, 106789.
47. Ngadze, F. (2023). Applying the Safe and Just Operating Space (SJOS) framework to Sustainable Development in Zimbabwe. 2(3), 82–86.
48. Sofi, I. I., Shah, M. A., and Ganie, A. H. (2023). Integrating human footprint with ensemble modelling identifies priority habitats for conservation: A case study in the distributional range of *Arnebia euchroma*, a vulnerable species. *Environmental Monitoring and Assessment*, 195(8), 914.
49. Shukla, G., Bhat, J. A., Chakravarty, S., Almutairi, A., Li, M., and Iyer-Raniga, U. (2023). *Floristic Diversity: Biology and Conservation*. BoD–Books on Demand.
50. Malekpour, S., Allen, C., Sagar, A., Scholz, I., Persson, Å., Miranda, J. J., ... and Al-Ghanim, K. (2023). What scientists need to do to accelerate progress on the SDGs. *Nature*, 621(7978), 250–254.
51. Quamar, M. M., Al-Ramadan, B., Khan, K., Shafiullah, M., and El Ferik, S. (2023). Advancements and applications of drone-integrated geographic information system technology—a review. *Remote Sensing*, 15(20), 5039.
52. Basu, M. (2024). *The Routledge Handbook of International Environmental Policy*. Taylor and Francis.
53. Banerjee, O., Cicowiez, M., Malek, Ž., Verburg, P. H., Vargas, R., Goodwin, S., ... and Murillo, J. Á. (2023). Banking on strong rural livelihoods and the sustainable use of natural capital in post-conflict Colombia. *Environment, Development and Sustainability*, 1–22.
54. ESCAP, U. (2023). The Changing Landscape of Regional Cooperation in Asia and the Pacific. 7(2), 87–91.
55. Jarvelainen, M. (2023). Evaluating the effectiveness of forest conservation as a CO_2 offset measure for Urban development: A case study. *Forest Ecology and Management*. 12(4), 27–31.

56. Sliuzas, R., Mwesigye, P., Kisembo, T., Wamboga, J., and Ajambo, E. (2023). Land Governance for Climate Resilience. 2(3), 57–63.

57. Platjouw, F. M., and Pozdnakova, A. (2023). (eds.), *The Environmental Rule of Law for Oceans: Designing Legal Solutions.* Cambridge University Press.

58. Santarsiero, V. (2023). Spatial Analyses and Remote Sensing for Land Cover Change Dynamics: Assessing in A Spatial Planning. 7(2), 31–37.

59. Wellmann, T. (2023). Remote Sensing for sustainable and resilient Cities. 7(3), 28–33.

60. Neimark, B. (2023). *Hottest of the Hotspots: The Rise of Eco-precarious Conservation Labor in Madagascar.* University of Arizona Press. 5(1), 112–118.

61. Zhang, Z. (2023). *Mitigating Investment Risks in Nature-Based Solutions: A Strategic Approach Towards Sustainable Project Implementation* (Doctoral dissertation, Massachusetts Institute of Technology).

62. De Vries, B. J. (2023). *Sustainability Science.* Cambridge University Press.

63. Anekwe, I. M. S., Zhou, H., Mkhize, M. M., and Akpasi, S. O. (2024). Addressing Climate Change Challenges in South Africa: A Study in KwaZulu Natal Province. In *Climate Crisis: Adaptive Approaches and Sustainability* (pp. 475–496).

64. Sarker, M. N. I., Hossain, B., Shi, G., and Firdaus, R. R. (2023). Promoting net-zero economy through climate-smart agriculture: Transition towards sustainability. *Sustainability Science*, 18(5), 2107–2119.

65. Bustamante, M., Roy, J., Ospina, D., Achakulwisut, P., Aggarwal, A., Bastos, A., ... and Zscheischler, J. (2023). Ten new insights in climate science 2023/2024. *Global Sustainability.* DOI: https://doi.org/10.1017/sus.2023.25, 1–58.

66. Gill, D. A., Blythe, J., Bennett, N., Evans, L., Brown, K., Turner, R. A., ... and Muthiga, N. A. (2023). Triple exposure: Reducing negative impacts of climate change, blue growth, and conservation on coastal communities. *One Earth*, 6(2), 118–130.

67. Khan, I. A. (2024). (ed.), *Security and Global Governance.* Interdisciplinary Institute of Human Security and Governance.

68. Yousuf, A. H. (2023). Integrating ecosystem-based management and marine spatial planning for sustainable ocean governance in the Bay of Bengal. 14(2), 92–97.

69. Papas, M. (2023). *Capacity-Building and the Water-Energy-Food Nexus: Rethinking Integration in the Asia-Pacific.* Taylor and Francis.

70. Luger, J. (2023). *Governing the High Seas: Effective Institutional Arrangements for the Conservation and Sustainable Use of Marine Biodiversity Beyond National Jurisdiction* (Doctoral dissertation, The University of St Andrews).

71. van Dam, A. A., Robertson, H. A., Prieler, R., Dubey, A., and Finlayson, C. M. (2024). Recognizing diversity in wetlands and farming systems to support sustainable agriculture and conserve wetlands. 45(4), 117–119.

72. Irvine, K., Katsanou, K., Spears, B. M., Carvalho, L., Elelman, R., Free, G., and Warner, S. (2023). *Embedding Lakes into the Global Sustainability Agenda*. United Nations Environment Programme (UNEP).

Chapter 7

Harnessing Fuzzy Logics in Renewable Wind Energy for Smart-Sustainable Cities and Villages: Pioneering Climate Action through Intelligent Energy Management in Industry 5.0

Christian Kaunert,[a] Bhupinder Singh,[b] Richa Raghav,[b] and Anjali Raghav[b]

[a]*Dublin City University, Ireland, and University of South Wales, UK*
[b]*Sharda University, Greater Noida, Uttar Pradesh, India*

richasingh3318bsr@gmail.com, anjalisingh3318bsr@gmail.com

Abstract

Fuzzy logics facilitate a connected and intelligent energy ecosystem, enabling seamless communication and control of devices for efficient energy management. The synergy of Blue Wind Energy, Artificial Intelligence (AI), and fuzzy logics thus presents a holistic and forward-thinking approach to address the escalating energy needs of urbanized landscapes within the framework of Industry 5.0. As Industry 5.0 unfolds, characterized by the convergence of digital

Fuzzy Logic in Revolutionizing Renewable Energy
Edited by Bhupinder Singh, Komal Vig, Ruchi Lal, and Budi Agus Riswandi

ISBN 978-981-5129-92-2 (Hardcover), 978-1-003-74191-6 (eBook)
www.jennystanford.com

DOI: 10.1201/9781003741916-7

technologies and the physical realm, the integration of Blue Wind Energy with AI and Internet of Things (IoT) represents a pivotal step toward intelligent and sustainable urban energy systems. This chapter delves into the multifaceted dimensions of this integration, exploring its potential benefits, addressing challenges, and analyzing the feasibility of implementing such a comprehensive approach within the dynamic landscape of Industry 5.0.

Keywords: Wind Energy, Smart Cities, Smart Villages, Industry 5.0, Climate Resilience

7.1 Introduction

The urgency in the quest for sustainable development is further heightened as the world battles with mounting disruptions caused by climate change and environmental degradation. Switching to renewable energy sources was seen as the most prominent method among several strategies, for this purpose [1]. The most promising way to create clean and sustainable power is with wind energy. Since the world is heading toward Industry 5.0 emphasizing human-centric solutions, technological innovation and sustainability, integrating advanced techniques such as fuzzy logic into wind energy systems has become a key step toward this direction [2]. This integration assures boosting the productivity and dependability of wind energy development, which has, in turn, expedited smart-sustainable cities as well as villages [3].

Whereas in conventional binary logic, everything is either true or false (0/1), fuzzy logic allows truth values to be any real number between 0 and 1. Fuzzy sets make it possible for a variable to have a value of right-hand-side border with known probability that the set respects all constraints on its membership [4]. In wind energy, fuzzy logic can be used to decrease the effect of windy conditions and unpredictability on generation as well—energy management in order for better system performance [5]. By doing so, it aims to contribute valuable insights that can guide the development of resilient, green, and intelligent energy infra-structures for the urbanized future. Understanding and harnessing the potential of this integration is paramount for several compelling reasons [6]. The insights derived from this exploration have the potential to inform policymakers, industry stakeholders, and researchers alike, guiding the development of sustainable urban energy strategies. This chapter explores the possibilities of Blue Wind Energy as a key element of Industry 5.0, a paradigm-shifting industrial process whereby green energy, AI, and the IoT come together [7].

There are several factors where fuzzy logic is relevant in wind energy systems. Fuzzy logic-based models will be able to take into account all of a wide variety of meteorological-data observations and historical records in order to yield more precise wind speed forecasts. This feature allows operators to alert turbine settings for predicted winds, which increases energy capture and can greatly reduce unnecessary mechanical stress [8]. Wind turbine control systems could be improved using fuzzy logic. Wind conditions change so quickly and are very uncertain, traditional control systems often have great difficulties accommodating such changes. In comparison, fuzzy logic controllers allow a turbine to automatically modify blade angles and rotor speeds on-the-fly for optimal performance with the maximal impact minimizing damage that otherwise would have shortened their lifespan. Such flexibility is essential for ensuring cost-effective operation and maintainability, which will ultimately aid in the economic viability of wind energy projects [9].

7.1.1 Importance for Smart-Sustainable Cities and Villages: Fuzzy Logics Implications

There are promising potentials in smart-sustainable cities and villages due to the fuzzy logic integration with renewable wind energy systems. With accelerated urbanization, both aging cities and emerging villages are straining to provide adaptable, secure energy solutions for burgeoning populations. Wind power and other sources of renewable energy are pillars in this vision, as a way to cut carbon emissions, improve our national security by reducing our dependence on foreign oil from volatile regions, and ensure public health-especially for communities that live near coal-fired plants [10].

The use of advanced technologies to optimize the management and organization of infrastructure in cities or villages belonging to this intelligent-sustainable urban system allows greater comfort and security for citizens. These communities can utilize the new development of fuzzy logic in wind energy systems, which allows for intelligent, on-the-fly management that balances supply and demand with digital perfection. This continuous power generation is a reliable supply of electricity, but fuzzy logic models can optimize the integration with wind, handle fluctuations that cause concern, and provide rock-steady electrical current [11].

The utilization of fuzzy logic to wind energy is also strategically coherent with Industry 5.0 in terms of merging digital technologies and physical systems for building a future-forward solution as well heard here! The use of fuzzy logic in wind energy systems allows cities and villages to develop a more resilient and adaptable infrastructure for the production of electricity based on available environmental conditions as well as social needs [12].

7.2 Role of Wind Energy in Sustainable Development: Global Wind Energy Trends and Statistics

Wind energy thus contributes to sustainable development by offering an emissions-free, responsible power source that helps cut back on the usage of traditional non-sustainable fossil fuels and associated negative climate impacts. One of the fastest expanding energy sources in the world, wind power goes a long way to cut down on greenhouse gas emissions and save our planet. According to research published by the Global Wind Energy Council (GWEC), roughly 100 GW of global wind energy was installed in the fourth quarter of 2022, with additional projects planned. This trend is anticipated to increase as the two sectors develop, and capacity may exceed 1.2 TW by 2030 according to projections based on technological developments in policy support due to demand for clean energy. Wind energy plays multiple roles with respect to sustainable development. Part of its importance is due to the enhancement it provides for energy security, since this can help in diversifying sources and reduce dependence on imported fossil fuels. This is even more important for countries with scarce natural resources or looking to increase their energy self-sufficiency [13]. Wind if used also helps the economy by providing jobs in producing, installing and maintaining this form of energy. In 2022, the International Renewable Energy Agency (IRENA) found that the wind industry employed around 1.25 million in a headline figure worldwide—with more to come as investment boosts toward new heights and when an expanding number of scope opportunities are rounded up by the sector across site preparation assistance, construction work or long-term operations and maintenance support along supply chains nestled both locally and globally [14].

The global patterns of wind energy use are not uniform. Although Europe and North America have been the traditional forerunners in deploying wind farms, a significant growth has recently come about from Asian countries mainly involving China and India. With nearly 40% of global wind energy capacity added in 2022, China is undoubtedly involved in the transition to a low-carbon economy. In Africa and Latin America growing local markets, countries such as South Africa or Brazil are investing heavily in wind infrastructure [15]. Wind energy is crucial to achieving the United Nations Sustainable Development Goals (SDGs) as well. This realization means that by our very existence and continuation of our activity, we directly are impacting SDG 7 (Affordable and Clean Energy) through providing energy solutions for all—connected with sustainability. Wind energy can also help in achieving other goals, such as SDG 13 (Climate Action)—by reducing carbon emissions to combat climate change—and SDG 8 (Decent Work and Economic Growth) through job creation and economic development [16].

Advances in technology are helping to make wind energy more efficient and cost-effective. Cost reductions were achieved thanks to developments in turbine design, materials and digital technology that resulted in higher energy yield per dollar invested. Offshore wind energy, in particular, is emerging as a frontrunner compelled by its higher capacity factors and the existence of more vigorous winds. Worldwide, a total of 62 GW of offshore wind capacity had been installed by the end of 2022 and there are high expectations for growth—especially in Europe and Asia. It can be said that wind energy is an indispensable part of sustainable development in terms of the environment, economy, and society. Wind power will always be an essential part of transitioning to a sustainable and resilient energy future, as long as investment continues along with the unyielding search for innovation in both policy and practice [17].

7.3 Integrating Fuzzy Logic into Wind Energy Systems: Wind Speed Prediction Using Fuzzy Logic

Fuzzy logic system in wind energy systems represents a powerful tool to deal with the inherent uncertainties and nonlinearity associated with wind speed further which makes hard when provided popular approaches for accurate prediction for this parameter. Wind energy is particularly tricky, as the natural variability of wind conditions makes it vulnerable to forecasting errors that can reduce system efficiency and increase costs. Wind speed is inherently difficult to predict due to its rapid and stochastic nature, making it an ideal application domain for fuzzy logic—a mathematical framework inspired by human reasoning penalized on ambiguity. In its turn fuzzy logic operates under the concept of fuzzy sets, where its elements have degrees of membership rather than a binary state if it belongs or not, which helps in the representation of uncertainty or vagueness thus perfect for modeling complex systems where classical binary logic is not enough. Under the wind speed estimation scenario, fuzzy logic can identify the vagueness in the weather pattern and then translate qualitative appraisal into quantitative prediction of the system [18].

Large-scale wind speed forecasting plays a vital role in the successful operation of any modern wind farm since it affects directly energy production, turbine life, and grid stability. Mainly, this is due to the nonlinear and stochastic behaviors of wind that are difficult for traditional statistical and numerical models. This degradation causes inaccurate forecasts when only using these conventional methods alone. Unfortunately, these models may not completely account for the microclimatic conditions that determine wind behavior—such as local topography or adiabatic air temperature adjustments and atmospheric pressure changes. One of the key goals of fuzzy logic is to overcome these challenges by combining deductive expert knowledge with statistical information in a flexible, and thus adaptable, manner [19].

7.3.1 Fuzzy Logic to Predict for Wind Speed

Fuzzy Logic Application in Wind Speed Prediction: Integration of fuzzy logic with wind speed prediction involves several steps such as the following: Identify relevant input variables. The first step is to identify input variables that will guide predictions, e.g., temperature, humidity and historical data of wind speed. After performing the transformation, these are input as crisp values and fuzzified, i.e., converted into fuzzy sets with some defined membership function. However, the wind speed could be wielded as a fuzzy set corresponding to low-medium-high with cross boundaries showing uncertainty [20].

Each set of input variables is mapped using a series of fuzzy rules which relate the inputs to the desired wind speed output, although these rules are mostly derived from expert knowledge or data-driven approaches. For instance, a rule will say: "If the temperature is low and humidity is high, then probably wind speed would be medium." It takes these rules as inputs to get fuzzy outputs, which are then consolidated and defuzzified into a crisp wind speed prediction [21].

7.3.2 Advantages of Fuzzy Logic

The fundamental strength of the fuzzy logic approach to wind prediction is its capability to cope with nonlinearity and uncertainty in atmospheric records. In one example, unlike traditional models that depend on exact inputs, fuzzy logic models can work effectively with vague or partially inaccurate information, falling back to stable and sound predictions even in challenging circumstances. Moreover, the interpretability of fuzzy logic systems makes it easy for operators to follow and trust its decision-making process [22].

7.3.3 Real-World Applications

The potential of fuzzy logic is evident by many wind energy projects that have applied this scheme successfully in the past. In one such case, fuzzy logic-based systems have been utilized to integrate measurements from different data sources (e.g., observations by satellites and on-ground traditional measurement) for enhancing the wind forecast accuracy. They have been able to show better results than traditional approaches, driving down predictive errors and securing the operation of wind energy systems [23].

Fuzzy logic for wind energy systems has a very bright future when it is combined with other cutting-edge technologies such as AI and machine learning. More complex models can be built using fuzzy logic and neural networks or genetic algorithms to learn from large datasets, while adapting with every new piece of information [24]. A unique combination of these two forecasting schemes will provide unparalleled wind speed prediction, offering the potential for greater efficiency through sustainable production of power in a hybrid manner [25]. The combination of wind speed forecasting problems and fuzzy logic in wind energy systems makes an important advance in literature. Fuzzy logic has a potential that can be harnessed to deal with uncertainty and expert knowledge, thus providing considerable support in their way toward optimization of wind energy systems leading not only toward larger utilization but also meeting the global challenge of renewable development and better sustainability [26].

7.4 Setting Course for Action on Climate with Insightful Energy Management

Due to rising temperatures and frequent extreme weather events globally, urgent climate action is crucial; switching to renewable forms of energy is vital if we intend to respond effectively enough in lessening further effects from climate change. At the heart of this transition is wind energy, which offers a clean and virtually limitless resource. The chapter stresses, however, that fluctuations in wind power output impacting on the electrical links to grids must be addressed if wave-generated electricity is fully to come into its own [27].

Fuzzy logic provides an innovative method for establishing intelligent energy management in wind power systems. Fuzzy logic can help wind farms be more efficient and reliable thanks to better predictions of the way winds blow through a site, along with optimization turbine control [28]. This in turn drives the economic viability of wind energy projects which further activates additional investment into renewable energy infrastructure [29]. Through fuzzy logic, the path will be paved to combine wind with other renewable sources (solar, hydropower) and in turn a more complete type of energy portfolio can be obtained which is much stronger. Fuzzy logic systems can improve this management by serving the best operation point of hybrid energy systems, which maintain a constant and reliable energy supply in challenging weather conditions [30].

This use of the fuzzified almost-logic also serves well in a subject like wind energy for helping with the development of smart grids [31]. Essentially, smart grids use digital technology to monitor and control the flow of power seamlessly so it can be distributed on an as-needed basis enabling continuous grid stability. Using fuzzy logic, we can control the interactions between various energy sources and thereby optimize the use of renewable energies for everyone [32].

In Blue Wind Energy, the word "blue" symbolizes the seascapes in which these wind farms are usually located. Blue Wind Energy optimizes available space and reduces the visual effect on terrestrial landscapes by using offshore sites to alleviate land use limitations and potential aesthetic problems connected with onshore wind projects. The transmission of generated energy to population centers is facilitated by offshore wind farms' closeness to metropolitan areas, which lowers transmission losses related to the long-distance transportation of power [33]. The offshore environment allows for higher and more consistent wind speeds, leading to increased energy production. Embracing a holistic vision of urban development—one that integrates renewable energy sources, prioritizes energy efficiency, and leverages intelligent technologies—is essential for creating cities that are not only resilient and vibrant but also environmentally sustainable [34]. The journey toward sustainable urbanization is a collective endeavor, involving policymakers, city planners, industry stakeholders, and the public, all working in concert to shape a future where urban centers are not just energy consumers but dynamic hubs of innovation, efficiency, and sustainability [35].

The sheer scale and complexity of urban energy consumption underscore the importance of addressing sustainability within cities to mitigate the environmental impact [36]. As urbanization accelerates, strategies for enhancing energy efficiency, adopting renewable energy sources, and implementing smart technologies in cities become increasingly crucial. Cities, therefore, play a central role not only as major energy consumers but also as key actors in the global pursuit of a more sustainable and resilient energy future [37]. Urbanization often correlates with improved living standards, leading to heightened expectations for energy-intensive amenities. The logistics of installation, maintenance, and grid connection in offshore environments pose additional complexities, necessitating advanced engineering solutions and specialized vessels [38].

7.5 Fuzzy Logics in Renewable Energy: A Path Sway to Climate Action via Industry 5.0—Perspective

The shift to renewable energy is a key component of meeting sustainable development needs and overcoming the threat of climate change. A perfect contender for this switchover is wind energy, which forms one of the largest free and clean resources [39, 40]. The use of fuzzy logic in wind energy systems provides a viable solution for improving the management and efficiency in controlling generation from wind power plants [41]. This deals with the problem of using fuzzy logic in systems based on renewable wind energy to ensure that smart-sustainable cities and villages are built to promote and improve climate action effectively during the Industry 5.0 period [42].

Fuzzy logic was introduced by Lotfi Zadeh in the 1960s as a mathematical framework to deal with uncertainty and imprecision [43]. Fuzzy logic is not really the same as classic binary-type concepts of true or false but rather allows for degrees between those very polar values (which makes it much better suited to complex and unsure situations) [44]. Fuzzy logic systems use linguistic variables and membership functions to simulate human-like reasoning, making it a powerful tool for dealing with uncertainty in different applications [45].

7.5.1 Wind Energy Role in Sustainable Development

Wind energy is the fastest-growing renewable energy source globally. It contributes to the decarbonization of energy systems by reducing reliance on fossil fuels, while also enhancing energy supply security and diversity [46, 47]. Wind farms—both onshore and offshore (although the latter much more so than the former)—have represented an increasingly sizeable portion of global energy generation capacity as a complement to other green technologies, helping decarbonize how we produce electricity. But the wind variable is notoriously difficult to pin down, which can create headache for energy security [48].

7.5.2 Fuzzy Logic in Wind Energy Systems

Fuzzy logic implemented into wind energy systems provides several advantages especially when dealing with the uncertainties in terms of variations due to wind [49]. Following are the main application areas of fuzzy logic:

Wind Speed Forecast: For wind turbines to perform at peak levels, it is imperative that the wind speed forecast is carried out accurately [50]. Models using fuzzy logic can much more accurately predict wind speeds onsite with greater accuracy by processing historical weather data and meteorological input, which assists in a better plan for operating the waterproofing facility [51, 52].

Turbine Control Systems: Fuzzy logic controllers have been utilized to optimize wind turbine performance through the adjustment of blade angles and rotor speeds in real time [53].

These high-performance robot controllers can respond instantly to fluctuating wind conditions, delivering optimal capture capability with minimum mechanical stress and wear on turbine components [54, 55].

Energy storage Management: It connects the energy storage systems to wind farms, which ensures the supply-and-demand balance [56]. Fuzzy logic can optimize the performance of batteries during their charge and discharge cycles, thus optimizing energy storage while contributing to grid stability [57].

Grid Aspects: With more and more penetration of wind energy, grid stability becomes an issue. The integration of wind power into the grid can go smoother by utilizing fuzzy logic to help in handling fluctuation and supplying electricity on a steady base [58].

7.5.3 Smart-Sustainable Cities and Villages: Future Vision

Smart-sustainable cities and villages are those that utilize advanced technologies to enhance quality of life, promote economic development, and ensure environmental sustainability within their regions. Central to the overall strategy is renewable energy, which, of course, includes wind power [59]. These use-cases can be realized by deploying intelligent energy management within these communities using fuzzy logic, to reduce carbon footprints and enhance the climate impact resilience [60].

Case Study—Relying on Denmark Offshore Wind Farms Fuzzy logic-based control systems have been integrated alongside existing wind turbines in offshore management operations based out of Denmark, which is a global leader in the field [61]. The Danish research initiatives have improved the success of both onshore and offshore wind energy ventures that help further Denmark's daring zero carbon emission target by 2050 [62].

Germany—A Case Study in Energy Transition: With respect to the example of wind energy management for grid stability and the incorporation of renewable sources, Germany's Energiewende (energy transition) strategy considers fuzzy logic. Using this method, Germany has the largest network of wind and solar power plants in operation alongside its most stable electricity delivery [63, 64].

7.6 Challenges in Blue Wind Energy

When used with smart grids, energy storage devices can mitigate the erratic and intermittent nature of renewable energy sources [65]. Urban regions' capacity to store extra energy during high-generation times and release it during periods of heightened demand becomes increasingly important as they integrate solar and wind power into their energy mix [66]. Batteries and other energy storage devices make it possible to efficiently store and release energy, serving as a buffer to maintain the equilibrium between supply and demand [67]. This feature eliminates the need for extra fossil fuel-based backup production, promotes the integration of a larger percentage of renewable energy into metropolitan networks, and helps to maintain grid stability [68].

High Initial Costs: The capital costs associated with developing offshore wind farms are considerably higher compared to onshore projects. The need for specialized infrastructure, foundations, and vessels for installation contributes to the significant upfront expenses [69].

Logistics and Installation Challenges: The offshore environment introduces logistical complexities in transporting and installing wind turbines, particularly in deeper waters. The deployment of foundations and connection to the grid requires specialized vessels and engineering solutions, adding to project complexities [70].

Maintenance and Repairs: Accessing and maintaining turbines in offshore locations pose challenges due to the corrosive effects of saltwater and the harsh marine environment. Developing cost-effective and efficient maintenance strategies is crucial for the long-term viability of offshore wind farms [71].

Logistics and Installation Challenges: The transportation and installation of offshore wind turbines are complex tasks that require specialized vessels and equipment [72]. The logistics of deploying turbines in deep waters add an extra layer of complexity to the construction and maintenance processes [73].

Environmental Concerns: Despite being a more environmentally friendly option than many traditional energy sources, the construction and operation of offshore wind farms can have localized environmental impacts [74]. These include potential disturbances to marine ecosystems, shipping routes, and the visual landscape. Offshore wind projects can have localized environmental impacts, including potential disturbances to marine ecosystems, wildlife, and migratory routes. Balancing the environmental benefits of clean energy with the preservation of marine biodiversity is a key challenge [75].

Grid Connection: Connecting offshore wind farms to the onshore electrical grid involves laying underwater cables, a technically challenging and costly process [76]. Ensuring reliable and efficient grid connections is essential for maximizing the benefits of offshore wind energy [77].

The dynamic duo enables demand response and load management by harnessing data from IoT-connected devices allowing utilities to optimize energy distribution, balance loads, and minimize peak demand through AI-driven decision-making [78]. The decentralized nature of Smart Grids empowers consumers, enhances grid reliability, and lays the groundwork for adaptive and responsive urban energy ecosystems. Energy Storage, bolstered by AI and IoT, emerges as essential in the quest for sustainable energy [79]. Via addressing the intermittency of renewable sources and optimizing storage operations in real time, these technologies contribute to grid stability, reduce reliance on conventional backup sources, and facilitate the seamless integration of renewable energy into urban grids [80].

The integrated approach of Blue Wind Energy, Smart Grids, and Energy Storage, enhanced by AI and the IoT, holds immense potential for scalability and global adoption [81]. This transformative synergy addresses critical challenges in urban energy management and sustainable development, positioning it as a model for widespread implementation [82]. Blue Wind Energy, Smart Grids, and Energy Storage, supported by AI and IoT, not only exhibit the potential for scalability but also represent a compelling model for global adoption. As the world navigates the challenges of urbanization, climate change, and energy transition, these integrated technologies offer a pathway toward a sustainable, efficient, and resilient energy future on a truly global scale [83].

7.7 Conclusion

The application of fuzzy logic for renewable wind energy systems is to make smart-sustainable cities and villages. That is why through energy management and efficiency of wind turbines, it contributes to climate change control as well as Industry 5.0. transition. While the world struggles to deal with climate change, it is becoming increasingly important for us to engage in cool ideas such as fuzzy logic, and necessary as well if we hope ever to have a sustainable and robust energy future. Using fuzzy logic, we can advance the state-of-the-art in Smart Energy Management and help shape a cleaner future for all. The application of fuzzy logic in renewable wind energy systems is an innovative way that has tremendous perspective for the SDGs and illumination on the climate change problem. Fuzzy logic can drive the evolution of smart-sustainable cities and villages using cleaner energy, improve wind energy conversion systems from all aspects such as efficiency, sustainability, and economical view, making future greener.

In a world moving to Industry 5.0, the use of fuzzy logic in wind energy systems is vital for capturing maximum efficiency and productivity from renewable power sources (wind). With the power of fuzzy logic, we can lead to new intelligent energy management solutions that drive climate action and a more sustainable, resilient energy infrastructure. Thus, the implications and importance of employing fuzzy set theory within renewable wind energy go beyond just technological progress. It is a strategic way to meet the critical challenges of our time, achieve sustainable development and ensure that no one is left. We can only realize the full potential of wind and make real progress toward sustainability and resiliency by embracing this revolutionary approach.

References

1. Jiao, Y., Kang, H., and Sun, H. (2024). An intelligent landscaping framework for net-zero energy smart cities: A green infrastructure approach. *Sustainable Energy Technologies and Assessments*, 64, 103665.
2. Ashinze, U. K., Edeigba, B. A., Umoh, A. A., Biu, P. W., and Daraojimba, A. I. (2024). Urban green infrastructure and its role in sustainable cities: A comprehensive review. *World Journal of Advanced Research and Reviews*, 21(2), 928–936.
3. Zellner, M. L., and Massey, D. (2024). Modeling benefits and tradeoffs of green infrastructure: Evaluating and extending parsimonious models for neighborhood stormwater planning. *Heliyon*. 22(3), 248–259.
4. Sharma, A., and Singh, B. (2022). Measuring impact of E-commerce on small scale business: A systematic review. *Journal of Corporate Governance and International Business Law*, 5(1). 170–178.
5. Zabel, A., and Häusler, M. M. (2024). Policy instruments for green infrastructure. *Landscape and Urban Planning*, 242, 104929.
6. Kaneti, V. R., Masih, J., Yoganand, S., Singh, B., Bhargava, R., Bajaj, R., ... and Shrivastava, A. (2024). Supervised learning for edible mushroom identification: Promising results and implications for food safety. *International Journal of Intelligent Systems and Applications in Engineering*, 12(8s), 290–298.
7. Singh, B. (2022). Relevance of agriculture-nutrition linkage for human healthcare: A conceptual legal framework of implication and pathways. *Justice and Law Bulletin*, 1(1), 44–49.
8. Zhang, B., and MacKenzie, A. (2024). Trade-offs and synergies in urban green infrastructure: A systematic review. *Urban Forestry* and *Urban Greening*, 128262. DOI:10.1016/j.ufug.2024.128262.
9. Singh, B. (2022). COVID-19 Pandemic and public healthcare: Endless downward spiral or solution via rapid legal and health services implementation with patient monitoring program. *Justice and Law Bulletin*, 1(1), 1–7.
10. Isendahl, C., Dunning, N. P., Grazioso, L., Hawken, S., Lentz, D. L., and Scarborough, V. L. (2024). Growth and decline of a sustainable city: A multitemporal perspective on blue-black-green infrastructures at the pre-Columbian Lowland Maya city of Tikal. *Urban Studies*, 62, 00420980231224648.

11. Sunding, A., Randrup, T. B., Nordh, H., Sang, Å. O., and Nilsson, K. (2024). Descriptions of the relationship between human health and green infrastructure in six Nordic comprehensive plans. *Cities*, 146, 104746.
12. Kim, J., Ewing, R., and Rigolon, A. (2024). Does green infrastructure affect housing prices via extreme heat and air pollution mitigation? A focus on green and climate gentrification in Los Angeles County, 2000–2021. *Sustainable Cities and Society*, 102, 105225.
13. Yunos, M. Y. M., Maulan, S., and Ismail, N. A. (2024). Unlocking the Potential of Green Infrastructure in Residential Areas: A Comprehensive Systematic Review, 32(2), 25–31.
14. Richter, M., Heinemann, K., Meiser, N., and Dickhaut, W. (2024). Trees in sponge cities—a systematic review of trees as a component of blue-green infrastructure, vegetation engineering principles, and stormwater management. *Water*, 16(5), 655.
15. Singh, B., and Kaunert, C. (2024). Computational thinking for innovative solutions and problem-solving techniques: Transforming conventional education to futuristic interdisciplinary higher education. In Fonkam M., and Vajjhala N. (eds.), *Revolutionizing Curricula Through Computational Thinking, Logic, and Problem Solving* (pp. 60–82). IGI Global. https://doi.org/10.4018/979-8-3693-1974-1.ch004.
16. Singh, B., and Kaunert, C. (2024). Wind and solar energy as renewable energy for sustainable global future: Projecting future multisector sustainable policies and innovation. In Ara, A., and Thakore, R. (eds.), *Promoting Multi-Sector Sustainability With Policy and Innovation* (pp. 210–245). IGI Global. https://doi.org/10.4018/979-8-3693-2113-3.ch009.
17. Singh, B., and Kaunert, C. (2024). Aroma of highly smart internet of medical things (IoMT) and lightweight EdgeTrust expansion medical care facilities for electronic healthcare systems: Fortified-chain architecture for remote patient monitoring and privacy protection beyond imagination. In Hassan, A., Bhattacharya, P., Tikadar, S., Dutta, P., and Sagayam, M. (eds.), *Lightweight Digital Trust Architectures in the Internet of Medical Things (IoMT)* (pp. 196–212). IGI Global. https://doi.org/10.4018/979-8-3693-2109-6.ch011.
18. Singh, B., Jain, V., Kaunert, C., Dutta, P. K., and Singh, G. (2024). Privacy matters: Espousing blockchain and artificial intelligence (AI) for consumer data protection on E-commerce platforms in ethical marketing. In Saluja, S., Nayyar, V., Rojhe, K., and Sharma, S. (eds.),

Ethical Marketing Through Data Governance Standards and Effective Technology (pp. 167–184). IGI Global. https://doi.org/10.4018/979-8-3693-2215-4.ch015.

19. Singh, B., Dutta, P. K., and Kaunert, C. (2024). Replenish artificial intelligence in renewable energy for sustainable development: Lensing SDG 7 affordable and clean energy and SDG 13 climate actions with legal-financial advisory. In Derbali, A. (ed.), *Social and Ethical Implications of AI in Finance for Sustainability* (pp. 198–227). IGI Global. https://doi.org/10.4018/979-8-3693-2881-1.ch009.
20. Singh, B., and Kaunert, C. (2024). Augmented reality and virtual reality modules for mindfulness: Boosting emotional intelligence and mental wellness. In Hiran, K., Doshi, R., and Patel, M. (eds.), *Applications of Virtual and Augmented Reality for Health and Wellbeing* (pp. 111–128). IGI Global. https://doi.org/10.4018/979-8-3693-1123-3.ch007.
21. Singh, B. (2024). Lensing legal dynamics for examining responsibility and deliberation of generative AI-tethered technological privacy concerns: Infringements and use of personal data by nefarious actors. In Ara, A., and Ara, A. (eds.), *Exploring the Ethical Implications of Generative AI* (pp. 146–167). IGI Global. https://doi.org/10.4018/979-8-3693-1565-1.ch009.
22. Singh, B. (2024). Social cognition of incarcerated women and children: Addressing exposure to infectious diseases and legal outcomes. In Reddy, K. (ed.), *Principles and Clinical Interventions in social cognition* (pp. 236–251). IGI Global. https://doi.org/10.4018/979-8-3693-1265-0.ch014.
23. Singh, B., and Kaunert, C. (2024). Salvaging responsible consumption and production of food in the hospitality industry: Harnessing machine learning and deep learning for zero food waste. In Singh, A., Tyagi, P., and Garg, A. (eds.), *Sustainable Disposal Methods of Food Wastes in Hospitality Operations* (pp. 176–192). IGI Global. https://doi.org/10.4018/979-8-3693-2181-2.ch012.
24. Singh, B. (2024). Evolutionary global neuroscience for cognition and brain health: Strengthening innovation in brain science. In Prabhakar, P. (ed.), *Biomedical Research Developments for Improved Healthcare* (pp. 246–272). IGI Global. https://doi.org/10.4018/979-8-3693-1922-2.ch012.
25. Singh, B., and Kaunert, C. (2024). Revealing green finance mobilization: Harnessing fintech and blockchain innovations to surmount barriers and foster new investment avenues. In Jafar, S., Rodriguez, R., Kannan, H., Akhtar, S., and Plugmann, P. (eds.), *Harnessing Blockchain-*

Digital Twin Fusion for Sustainable Investments (pp. 265–286). IGI Global. https://doi.org/10.4018/979-8-3693-1878-2.ch011.

26. Singh, B., and Kaunert, C. (2024). Harnessing sustainable agriculture through climate-smart technologies: Artificial intelligence for climate preservation and futuristic trends. In Kannan, H., Rodriguez, R., Paprika Z., and Ade-Ibijola, A. (eds.), *Exploring Ethical Dimensions of Environmental Sustainability and Use of AI* (pp. 214–239). IGI Global. https://doi.org/10.4018/979-8-3693-0892-9.ch011.
27. Singh, B. (2023). Blockchain technology in renovating healthcare: Legal and future perspectives. In Kaushik, K., Dahiya, S., Aggarwal, S., and Dwivedi, A. (eds.), *Revolutionizing Healthcare Through Artificial Intelligence and Internet of Things Applications* (pp. 177–186). IGI Global. https://doi.org/10.4018/978-1-6684-5422-0.ch012.
28. Singh, B., and Kaunert, C. (2024). Reinventing artificial intelligence and blockchain for preserving medical data. In *Ethical Artificial Intelligence in Power Electronics* (pp. 77–91). CRC Press.
29. Singh, B., and Kaunert, C. (2024). Unmanned aerial vehicle. *Cognitive Machine Intelligence: Applications, Challenges, and Related Technologies*, 108.
30. Vijayalakshmi, S., Savita, and Durgadevi, P. (2023). AI and machine learning in improving resilience of smart energy infrastructure. In *AI-Powered Machine Learning in the Energy Industry: Digital Technology and Sustainable Energy Systems* (pp. 189–213). Cham: Springer International Publishing.
31. Shukla, S. S., Jain, M., Jain, A., Bajpai, S., Mishra, A. K., Gupta, A., and Pramanik, S. (2024). Industry 5.0: Blue wind energy for sustainable urbanization and intelligent control of energy. In *Convergence of Human Resources Technologies and Industry 5.0* (pp. 170–187). IGI Global.
32. Al Hajri, N. H., Al Harthi, R. N., Pasam, G. K., and Natarajan, R. (2024). Machine learning and machine learning based green energy generation using hybrid renewable energy sources of solar, wind and hydrogen fuel cells. In *E3S Web of Conferences* (Vol. 472, p. 01008). EDP Sciences.
33. Issa Zadeh, S. B., Esteban Perez, M. D., López-Gutiérrez, J. S., and Fernández-Sánchez, G. (2023). Optimizing smart energy infrastructure in smart ports: A systematic scoping review of carbon footprint reduction. *Journal of Marine Science and Engineering*, 11(10), 1921.

34. Singh, B., and Kaunert, C. (2024). Harnessing sustainable agriculture through climate-smart technologies: Artificial intelligence for climate preservation and futuristic trends. In *Exploring Ethical Dimensions of Environmental Sustainability and Use of AI* (pp. 214–239). IGI Global.
35. Li, J., and Zhou, T. (2023). Multiagent deep meta reinforcement learning for sea computing-based energy management of interconnected grids considering renewable energy sources in sustainable cities. *Sustainable Cities and Society*, 99, 104917.
36. Orumwense, E. F., and Abo-Al-Ez, K. (2023). Internet of Things for smart energy systems: A review on its applications, challenges and future trends. *AIMS Electronics* and *Electrical Engineering*, 7(1), 18–29.
37. Raj, E. F. I. (2023). A detailed review on wind and solar hybrid green energy technologies for sustainable smart cities. *Polytechnica*, 6(1), 1.
38. Camacho, J. D. J., Aguirre, B., Ponce, P., Anthony, B., and Molina, A. (2024). Leveraging artificial intelligence to bolster the energy sector in smart cities: A literature review. *Energies*, 17(2), 353.
39. Kannammal, A., and Chandia, S. (2023). Applications of AI and machine learning for smart cities. *Research Trends in Artificial Intelligence: Internet of Things*, 186, 178–188.
40. Zearah, S. A., Al-Tahee, M., Mohammed, A., Shnawa, A. H., Mahdi, H. H. J., and Majeed, Z. (2023, December). Smart city application based on internet-of-things and artificial intelligence for energy management dynamic memory modelling. In *2023 International Conference on Emerging Research in Computational Science (ICERCS)* (pp. 1–6). IEEE.
41. Awogbemi, O., Von Kallon, D. V., and Kumar, K. S. (2024). Contributions of artificial intelligence and digitization in achieving clean and affordable energy. *Intelligent Systems with Applications*, 22, 200389.
42. Singh, B. (2023). Unleashing alternative dispute resolution (ADR) in resolving complex legal-technical issues arising in cyberspace lensing E-commerce and intellectual property: Proliferation of E-commerce digital economy. *Revista Brasileira de Alternative Dispute Resolution-Brazilian Journal of Alternative Dispute Resolution-RBADR*, 5(10), 81–105.
43. Verma, J., Sandys, L., Matthews, A., and Goel, S. (2024). Readiness of artificial intelligence technology for managing energy demands from renewable sources. *Engineering Applications of Artificial Intelligence*, 135, 108831.

44. Khalid, M. (2024). Energy 4.0: AI-enabled digital transformation for sustainable power networks. *Computers and Industrial Engineering*, 193, 110253.

45. Issa Zadeh, S. B., and Perez Esteban, M. D., López-Gutiérrez, J.-S., Fernández-Sánchez, G. (2023). Optimizing smart energy infrastructure in smart ports: A systematic scoping review of carbon footprint reduction. *J. Mar. Sci. Eng*, 11, 1921.

46. Singh, B., and Kaunert, C. (2024). Augmented reality and virtual reality modules for mindfulness: Boosting emotional intelligence and mental wellness. In Hiran, K., Doshi, R., and Patel, M. (eds.), *Applications of Virtual and Augmented Reality for Health and Wellbeing* (pp. 111–128). IGI Global. https://doi.org/10.4018/979-8-3693-1123-3.ch007.

47. Obaideen, K., Albasha, L., Iqbal, U., and Mir, H. (2024). Wireless power transfer: Applications, challenges, barriers, and the role of AI in achieving sustainable development goals: A bibliometric analysis. *Energy Strategy Reviews*, 53, 101376.

48. El-Hussieny, E. (2023). Emerging the concept of sustainable architecture in forming a smart city. *Resourceedings*, 3(1), 22–32.

49. Salman, M. Y., and Hasar, H. (2023). Review on environmental aspects in smart city concept: Water, waste, air pollution and transportation smart applications using machine learning techniques. *Sustainable Cities and Society*, 94, 104567.

50. Van Hoang, T. (2024). Impact of integrated artificial intelligence and internet of things technologies on smart city transformation. *Journal of Technical Education Science*, 19(Special Issue 01), 64–73.

51. Huda, N. U., Ahmed, I., Adnan, M., Ali, M., and Naeem, F. (2024). Experts and intelligent systems for smart homes' Transformation to sustainable smart cities: A comprehensive review. *Expert systems with applications*, 238, 122380.

52. Ali, M. (2023). Synergizing solar cell innovation, radio wave technology, and AI for sustainable business growth: A comprehensive review. *International Journal of Social, Humanities and Life Sciences*, 1(1), 19–28.

53. Nezhad, M. M., Neshat, M., Sylaios, G., and Garcia, D. A. (2024). Marine energy digitalization digital twin's approaches. *Renewable and Sustainable Energy Reviews*, 191, 114065.

54. Moemen, Y. S., Alshater, H., and El-Sayed, I. E. T. (2023). Clean energy management based on internet of things and sensor networks for

climate change problems. In *The Power of Data: Driving Climate Change with Data Science and Artificial Intelligence Innovations* (pp. 117–136). Cham: Springer Nature Switzerland.

55. Singh, B. (2023). Blockchain technology in renovating healthcare: Legal and future perspectives. In *Revolutionizing Healthcare Through Artificial Intelligence and Internet of Things Applications* (pp. 177–186). IGI Global.
56. Nasserddine, G., Nassereddine, M., and El Arid, A. A. (2023). Internet of things integration in renewable energy systems. In *Handbook of Research on Applications of AI, Digital Twin, and Internet of Things for Sustainable Development* (pp. 159–185). IGI Global.
57. Singh, B. (2024). Lensing legal dynamics for examining responsibility and deliberation of generative AI-tethered technological privacy concerns: Infringements and use of personal data by nefarious actors. In Ara, A., and Ara, A. (eds.), *Exploring the Ethical Implications of Generative AI* (pp. 146–167). IGI Global. https://doi.org/10.4018/979-8-3693-1565-1.ch009.
58. López, O. L., Rosabal, O. M., Ruiz-Guirola, D. E., Raghuwanshi, P., Mikhaylov, K., Lovén, L., and Iyer, S. (2023). Energy-sustainable machine learning connectivity: Vision, technological enablers, challenges, and future directions. *IEEE Open Journal of the Communications Society*, 12(2), 18–266.
59. Logeswaran, K., Suresh, P., Ponselvakumar, A. P., Savitha, S., Sentamilselvan, K., and Adhithyaa, N. (2023). Exploration of assorted modernizations in forecasting renewable energy using low power wireless technologies for IoTSG. In *Smart Grids and Internet of Things: An Energy Perspective*, pp. 157–191.
60. Singh, B., and Kaunert, C. (2024). Salvaging responsible consumption and production of food in the hospitality industry: Harnessing machine learning and deep learning for zero food waste. In Singh, A., Tyagi, P., and Garg, A. (eds.), *Sustainable Disposal Methods of Food Wastes in Hospitality Operations* (pp. 176–192). IGI Global. https://doi.org/10.4018/979-8-3693-2181-2.ch012.
61. Li, X., Zhao, H., Feng, Y., Li, J., Zhao, Y., and Wang, X. (2024). Research on key technologies of high energy efficiency and low power consumption of new data acquisition equipment of power Internet of Things based on artificial intelligence. *International Journal of Thermofluids*, 21, 100575.
62. Singh, B. (2024). Evolutionary global neuroscience for cognition and brain health: Strengthening innovation in brain science. In

Prabhakar, P. (ed.), *Biomedical Research Developments for Improved Healthcare* (pp. 246–272). IGI Global. https://doi.org/10.4018/979-8-3693-1922-2.ch012.

63. Xie, H., Huang, R., Sun, H., Han, Z., Jiang, M., Zhang, D., ... and Wu, T. (2023). Wireless energy: Paving the way for smart cities and a greener future. *Energy and Buildings*, 297, 113469.
64. Khan, M. W., Saad, S., Ammad, S., Rasheed, K., and Jamal, Q. (2024). Smart infrastructure and AI. In *AI in Material Science* (pp. 193–215). CRC Press.
65. Samaei, S. R., and Ghahfarrokhi, M. A. (2023). Optimizing coastal hydro turbines integrating artificial intelligence for sustainable energy conversion. In *2nd International Conference on Creative Achievements of Architecture, Urban Planning, Civil Engineering and Environment in the Sustainable Development of the Middle East*, 21(2), 223–226.
66. Kumar, D. (2023). Concept of sustainable energy system for smart cities. In *Renewable Energy Scenarios in Future Indian Smart Cities: A Geospatial Technology Perspective* (pp. 1–20). Singapore: Springer Nature Singapore.
67. Almalki, F. A., Alsamhi, S. H., Sahal, R., Hassan, J., Hawbani, A., Rajput, N. S., and Breslin, J. (2023). Green machine learning for eco-friendly and sustainable smart cities: Future directions and opportunities. *Mobile Networks and Applications*, 28(1), 178–202.
68. Salama, R., and Al-Turjman, F. (2023). Sustainable energy production in smart cities. *Sustainability*, 15(22), 16052.
69. Singh, B., and Kaunert, C. (2024). Salvaging responsible consumption and production of food in the hospitality industry: Harnessing machine learning and deep learning for zero food waste. In *Sustainable Disposal Methods of Food Wastes in Hospitality Operations* (pp. 176–192). IGI Global.
70. Singh, B. (2024). Evolutionary global neuroscience for cognition and brain health: Strengthening innovation in brain science. In *Biomedical Research Developments for Improved Healthcare* (pp. 246–272). IGI Global.
71. Mohammed, M. N., Aljibori, H. S. S., Al-Tamimi, A., Alani, Z. N., Hameed, M. S., Ibrahim, F. M., and Alfiras, M. (2023, October). Toward sustainable smart cities in Bahrain: A groundbreaking approach to marine renewable energy harnessing sea tides and waves for a greener energy future. In *2023 IEEE 8th International Conference on*

Engineering Technologies and Applied Sciences (ICETAS) (pp. 1–5). IEEE.

72. Bin Abu Sofian, A. D. A., Lim, H. R., Siti Halimatul Munawaroh, H., Ma, Z., Chew, K. W., and Show, P. L. (2024). Machine learning and the renewable energy revolution: Exploring solar and wind energy solutions for a sustainable future including innovations in energy storage. *Sustainable Development*, 18(2), 128–136.
73. Fan, Z., Yan, Z., and Wen, S. (2023). Deep learning and artificial intelligence in sustainability: A review of SDGs, renewable energy, and environmental health. *Sustainability*, 15(18), 13493.
74. Jain, A., Sharma, A., Jately, V., and Azzopardi, B. (eds.). (2023). *Sustainable Energy Solutions with Artificial Intelligence, Blockchain Technology, and Internet of Things*. CRC Press.
75. Mirshafiee, F., Shahbazi, E., Safi, M., and Rituraj, R. (2023). Predicting power and hydrogen generation of a renewable energy converter utilizing data-driven methods: a sustainable smart grid case study. *Energies*, 16(1), 502.
76. Yousef, L. A., Yousef, H., and Rocha-Meneses, L. (2023). Artificial intelligence for management of variable renewable energy systems: A review of current status and future directions. *Energies*, 16(24), 8057.
77. Zhou, Y., and Liu, J. (2024). Advances in emerging digital technologies for energy efficiency and energy integration in smart cities. *Energy and Buildings*, 315, 114289.
78. Nizetic, S., Arıcı, M., and Hoang, A. T. (2023). Smart and sustainable technologies in energy transition. *Journal of Cleaner Production*, 389, 135944.
79. Hui, C. X., Dan, G., Alamri, S., and Toghraie, D. (2023). Greening smart cities: An investigation of the integration of urban natural resources and smart city technologies for promoting environmental sustainability. *Sustainable Cities and Society*, 99, 104985.
80. Alshmeel, G. H. A., Al-Doori, A. S. B., Ahmed, S. R., Abrahim, Z. A., Ghaffoori, A. J., and Hussain, A. S. T. (2024, May). Self-sustaining buoy system: Harnessing water wave energy for smart, wireless sensing and data transmission. In *Proceedings of the Cognitive Models and Artificial Intelligence Conference* (pp. 349–356).
81. Wang, H., Wen, C., Duan, L., Li, X., Liu, D., and Guo, W. (2024). Sustainable energy transition in cities: A deep statistical prediction model for renewable energy sources management for low-carbon urban development. *Sustainable Cities and Society*, 107, 105434.

82. Clemente, D., Cabral, T., Rosa-Santos, P., and Taveira-Pinto, F. (2023). Blue seaports: The smart, sustainable and electrified ports of the future. *Smart Cities*, 6(3), 1560–1588.
83. Bibri, S. E., Krogstie, J., Kaboli, A., and Alahi, A. (2024). Smarter eco-cities and their leading-edge artificial intelligence of things solutions for environmental sustainability: A comprehensive systematic review. *Environmental Science and Ecotechnology*, 19, 100330.

Chapter 8

Integration of Fuzzy Logic in Smart City Framework to Enhance Sustainability

Kanchal Gupta,[a] Jane Eyre Mathew,[b] Rupendra Singh,[c] Tarun Kumar Kaushik,[d] and Anjali Raghav[d]

[a]*School of Law, UPES, Dehradun, Uttarakhand, India*
[b]*Amity Law School, Noida, Uttar Pradesh, India*
[c]*School of Law, Galgotias University, Greater Noida, Uttar Pradesh, India*
[d]*Sharda University, Greater Noida, Uttar Pradesh, India*

guptakanchal@gmail.com

Abstract

The integration of fuzzy logic into smart city frameworks is a significant advancement, enhancing the effectiveness of Sustainable Development Goals. However, the concept of smart cities has evolved significantly since its inception. Initially focused on the integration of information and communication technologies (ICT) to improve urban infrastructure, the smart city paradigm has expanded to encompass a holistic approach to urban development. Furthermore, the incorporation of fuzzy logic plays a pivotal role in solving challenges such as urban energy management, transportation, and environmental sustainability in smart cities to improve livelihood. Since these problems are dynamic and often unpredictable, they need

Fuzzy Logic in Revolutionizing Renewable Energy
Edited by Bhupinder Singh, Komal Vig, Ruchi Lal, and Budi Agus Riswandi

ISBN 978-981-5129-92-2 (Hardcover), 978-1-003-74191-6 (eBook)
www.jennystanford.com

DOI: 10.1201/9781003741916-8

a more flexible approach. Achieving the success of smart cities is the ability to integrate diverse data sources and technologies to optimize urban services and infrastructure. Moreover, the complexity and dynamism of urban systems often introduce significant uncertainty, making traditional binary logic insufficient for effective decision making. This is where fuzzy logic, a form of multi-valued logic, offers significant potential. Also, the utilization of fuzzy logic replicates human reasoning and can handle imprecise information, presenting highly acknowledging solutions. This chapter further explores the theoretical aspects of fuzzy logic and its extended usage in smart city planning and management. Also, an extensive reference model for the incorporation of fuzzy logic in pre-existing architectures presents its potential merits as well as challenges. Additionally, fuzzy logic can make a substantial contribution to achieving SDGs, especially in areas such as sustainable cities and communities, clean energy, and climate action, by enabling more precise predictions and assessments. To navigate the complexities of contemporary urban settings and ensure sustainable long-term outcomes, implementing inventive strategies such as fuzzy logic is essential. The chapter also delves into how fuzzy logic can improve how urban data is understood, therefore increasing stakeholder engagement and decision making.

Keywords: Smart Cities, Sustainable Development Goals (SDGs), Fuzzy Logic, Sustainability, Urban Service.

8.1 Introduction

In the past few decades, rapid urbanization has resulted in many challenges, such as congestion and pollution aside from limited infrastructure and resource management problems [1]. With more than half of the world's population living in cities, the need for new solutions to ensure sustainable urban development has become more crucial [2]. Also, the emergence of smart cities using such technologies with accompanying data analytics could be utilized to effectively manage urban life making it more efficient, sustainable, and enjoyable [3]. Smart cities and the integration of a variety of data sources and technologies play key roles in making our modern or traditional city services more efficient through optimization [4]. On the other hand, urban systems are often complex and dynamic entities that give rise to a kind of uncertainty too much beyond the two-valued nature for simple either-or choices typically made on conventional binary logic [5]. However, the concept of fuzzy logic, first proposed by Lotfi Zadeh in 1965, offers a rigorous mathematical framework for handling imprecise and uncertain data [6]. In contrast with traditional binary logic in which variables are clustered either as true or false, fuzzy logic facilitates more sophisticated reasoning and decision-making processes [7]. Such ability is of essential importance in the context of smart city applications, as usually, they have to handle data incomplete or noisy and therefore ambiguous [8]. In addition, the use of fuzzy logic in smart city frameworks allows urban planners and managers to create more adaptive systems, making them stronger for the incomprehensibilities set out by cities [9].

Ever since the notion of smart cities emerged, it has significantly evolved [10]. While initially concerned with the use of ICT to upgrade city infrastructure, the scope of smart cities can also be applied in other areas like urban development [11]. This involves applying big data, the Internet of Things (IoT), artificial intelligence (AI), and similar forefront technologies to improve city services as well as governance systems and citizen involvement [12]. However, the object is to have cities that are tech-smart as well as sustainable and inclusive [13]. Some essential manifestations of smart cities encompass intelligent transportation systems, energy-efficient structures, advanced waste management, and resilient environmental monitoring [14].

Nevertheless, the efficacy of these methods still faces tough challenges arising from the uncertainty and variability of urban data [15]. Besides this, fuzzy logic is a type of logic that deals with imprecise and ambiguous information, enabling reasoning in situations when traditional binary logic may not be suitable [16]. The concept of this rooted fuzzy logic is a type of multi-valued logic that makes use of information truth degrees as strengths between 0 and 1 [17]. It is a type of fuzzy logic, where membership can be described in degrees [18]. It is this kind of flexibility and resilience that is needed to make decisions in city-wide systems. There are three main components in a typical fuzzy logic system, fuzzification, inference, and defuzzification [19]. Data are transformed into fuzzy sets using fuzzification process based on the defined membership functions [20]. Here comes the fuzzy inference process, which gives us a bunch of outputs as well from its set of rules and those are in the final stage. This leads us to the process of defuzzification, where these fuzzy outputs are converted back into crisp values that can inspire decisions leading ultimately to how a single output parameter can be controlled [21]. Fuzzy logic systems are well-suited for applications that lack a precise mathematical model, or which require human expertise to guide decision-making [22]. Fuzzy logic can be applied in many areas of smart cities, for example, traffic management, energy consumption, waste collection, and environmental monitoring as well [23].

The incorporation of fuzzy logic for smart city frameworks might greatly augment the capacity of these systems to deal with uncertainty and complexity [24]. Some common paradigms for this integration include the development of fuzzy logic through algorithms, fusion with existing data analytics platforms such as data analytics, and decision support that offers actionable insights by utilizing fuzzy [25]. For instance, traffic management is one of the most potential application areas where fuzzy logic can be applied in smart cities [26]. Traffic in a city is inherently random, due to its stochastic nature because of several features that affect the traffic flow like weather conditions and events or accidents [27]. Historically, traffic management systems have had difficulty reacting to these real-time fluctuations [28]. By using systems that utilize fuzzy logic, real-time traffic data can be taken into account and the phase schemes change dynamically enabling to comparison of flow through different adaptive time signal based on it [29]. This results in reduced traffic congestion, less pollution, and enhancements in urban access [30].

Also in the energetic field, fuzzy logic can play an important role in case of smart grids, which are structures for distributing energy efficiently and managing it with intelligent layers that use fuzzy logic to improve operations such systems can help save building-based electricity consumption [31]. For example, fuzzy logic controllers can make heating, ventilation, and air conditioning (HVAC) systems respond to occupancy patterns and weather forecasts as well as energy prices with the net result of large savings for both power consumption and customer comfort level [32]. Fuzzy logic is a concept that can be applied to improve the sustainability and effectiveness of processes associated with waste in terms of management, collection, recycling, etc. [33]. Furthermore, with a fuzzy model, systems can enhance the efficiency of waste collection by analyzing data on waste generation patterns and environmental conditions [34]. This analysis enables the optimization of collection routes, schedules, and resource allocation [35]. It is more than cutting down the operational cost; this solution puts fewer feet in harm's way during regular waste management operations to reduce the impact of our daily lives on the environment [36]. In contrast, fuzzy logic-based systems have the ability to simultaneously examine several parameters and offer more precise and dependable evaluations of pollution levels [37]. This facilitates more efficient actions and enhanced safeguarding of public health and the environment [38].

8.2 Significance of Fuzzy Logic in Smart City Frameworks

By integrating fuzzy logic into smart city frameworks, stakeholders can be better engaged in the decision-making processes. Traditional decision-making methods usually use quantitative data and deterministic models, while ignoring the qualitative and subjective in urban problems [39]. Fuzzy logic, on the other hand, takes into account both quantitative and qualitative data simultaneously, which gives a better holistic ambiance in understanding the urban system [40]. This ability is especially useful in involving different types of stakeholders for instance such as citizens, governments and companies into the negotiation process. A fuzzy logic-based system can enable a more informed decision process and improve collaborative work, by presenting information in an intuitive way. Lastly, creates a far more powerful stick for sustainable urban endeavors [41].

However, the fusion of fuzzy logic in smart city frameworks comes with a series of challenges that are presented too [42]. Since fuzzy logic systems are only effective if quality information flows in data but urban systems are complex and capable of large scalability, therefore established fuzzy logic models must be robust enough to better simulate urban activity [43]. In addition, there needs to be some way of interoperating with what are often existing smart city infrastructures and technologies [44]. However, the acceptance and trust of stakeholders is another significant issue that fuzzy-logic-based systems must overcome to be adopted successfully [45].

Moreover, the application of fuzzy logic in smart city infrastructure may provide the capacity to deal with sustainability and sustainable development for urban areas [46]. Fuzzy logic responds to this complexity and uncertainty of the urban by offering a decision-making framework that is malleable and adaptive [47]. This alignment can bring predictability in multiple areas like mobility| traffic, energy efficiency, waste, and environment monitoring [48]. In addition, fuzzy logic systems can potentially facilitate greater stakeholder participation and more effective decision making supporting the realization of multiple SDGs [49]. Urbanization is rapidly increasing; thus new approaches such as fuzzy logic will play a significant role in dealing with the challenges that are faced as well as adjusting these into more sustainable infrastructure [50]. Fuzzy logic works well for this lack of clear boundaries and shows its power in the face of such fuzzy nature inherent to cities. It lends itself to modeling real-world phenomena that are not readily represented in binary logic [51].

Fuzzy logic in the context of smart cities can be made applicable across a multitude of domains including the following:

Urban planning and decision making: Fuzzy logic can provide support to planners and decision-makers in assessing the consequences of urban interventions under multiple criteria and stakeholder preferences [52].

Resource allocation and management: Fuzzy logic can be utilized in optimizing energy consumption and smart transportation based on distinct demand-supply conditions [53].

Citizen participation and feedback: Using fuzzy logic in the sentiment analysis to measure citizen satisfaction on urban services will also facilitate responsive and adaptable decision making [54].

Predictive analytics and forecasting: Smart city frameworks can predict urban activities by incorporating fuzzy logic with deep learning to plan for events and anticipate activity peaks yet to occur [55].

Theoretical notion of fuzzy logic: Fuzzy logic is a form of multi-valued logic derived from fuzzy set theory to deal with reasoning that is approximate rather than precisely deduced. In classical binary logic, variables can only have a value of either 1 or 0, denoting true or false, respectively [56]. Nevertheless, these variables additionally allow more nuanced forms of logic and decisions [57]. This ability is especially valuable in complex and unpredictable situations, such as urban networks where distinct limits both conceptually and occasionally are frequently unachievable [58].

8.3 Adoption of Fuzzy Logic in the Planning and Management of Smart Cities

Management of Traffic

An instructive field for the potential of fuzzy logic that could dramatically increase both efficiency and sustainability in urban traffic management [59]. On the other hand, traditional traffic management systems are based on fixed-time signals that often result in inefficiencies and lengthened congestion [60]. However, other approaches like fuzzy logic-based systems are capable of adjusting signal timings in real time based on traffic density and waiting time for better results. This adaptive approach, in turn, eliminates congestion and reduces emissions by facilitating a more fluid traffic flow [61].

Management of Energy

One of the main components of sustainable urban development is energy efficiency. Fuzzy logic can help minimize energy consumption in intelligent buildings by changing HVAC systems using fuzzy rules from different elements like occupancy, temperature, and humidity [62]. However, this equates to big energy savings and a lowered carbon footprint in addition to these, the fuzzy logic can be used in improving the management of renewable energy sources i.e., solar & wind power by modeling their demanded uncertainty and variability [63].

Management of Waste

Waste management for sustainable urban areas is important. Fuzzy logic may enhance the quality of waste collection, disposal, and recycling by enabling the determination of optimal routes and schedules for truck trips online with respect, in particular, to real-time traffic conditions as well as fuzzy rules [64]. This process helps for optimum resource use keeping operating costs down and less impact on the environment [65]. Furthermore, utilizing fuzzy logic in monitoring and controlling landfill operations can facilitate compliance with environmental regulations and standards [66].

Environmental Monitoring

One of the basic objectives is environmental sustainability in smart cities. Indeed, fuzzy logic can give a more precise and reliable evaluation of air pollution indexes or water quality indicators in an environmental monitoring system [67]. Existing monitoring techniques frequently fail to cope with the variability and complexity of environmental data. Nevertheless, fuzzy logic can manage this complexity and offer useful inferences to monitor levels of pollution for timely responses [68].

8.4 Framework for Fuzzy Logic Fusion in Smart City Architectures

To harness the potential use of fuzzy logic for environmentally friendly city planning, it must be integrated into the existing smart city framework [69]. Also, this framework is based on a few major components some key elements are as follows:

Dataset Acquisition and Preprocessing

Smart cities collect a lot of data, as do sensors across multiple domains as well as citizens through various ways and means such as social media. Integration of fuzzy logic successfully requires a strong data collection and preprocessing approach to meet the standards of quality and relevance [70].

Fuzzification Module

This module converts crisp input data into fuzzy sets. This includes defining the correct membership functions and linguistic variables for urban systems [71].

Inference Engine

The inference engine uses joins to fuzzy rules applied to input data sets and yields a set of possible conclusions from these applied fuzzy relations [72]. These rules are created with the help of domain-specific insights and expert knowledge. However, to provide useful and reliable inference results, the engine must account for complex scenarios of city driving altogether such as but not limited to unpredictable object movements [73].

Defuzzification Module

The role of the defuzzification module is to map fuzzy outputs back into crisp values that can be used in decision making and control. Depending upon the application, different defuzzification techniques can be used in the sector method [74].

Decision Support System

Based on the defuzzified outputs, a decision support system provides helpful insights and recommendations to aid decision making [75]. Decision support system should be able to serve different users such as city planners or policymakers on one hand, but also citizens and their society as a whole itself get aware of what is happening while enabling everybody involved to make decisions not only informed by data [76].

Implementation & Feedback Mechanism

For an efficient execution of the framework built on a fuzzy logic system, strong feedback is fostered to collect and evaluate up-to-date performance. This way the framework adjusts to changing circumstances and learns over time [77].

Improving Stakeholder Engagement and Decision Making

More important is the ability of fuzzy logic to improve stakeholder engagement and decision-making processes, which represents a clear value proposition in its integration with smart city frameworks [78]. Hypotheses based on abstract quantitative data or binary logic fall short of capturing the qualitative and subjective dimensions of urban problems, like lifestyle [79]. However, the fuzzy logic definition includes both quantitative and qualitative information and therefore apparently provides a more holistic insight into urban systems [80].

Additionally, it is crucial to bring different stakeholders—citizens, policymakers, and industry—to the table to help shape smarter decision making [81]. Fuzzy logic-based systems can help decision-makers make well-informed and more collaborative decisions by representing the information in a human-readable form. This results in greater perceived legitimacy and support for transit-oriented development [82].

8.5 Challenges and Future Directions

Undoubtedly powerful inclusion of fuzzy logic in smart city frameworks guarantees potential enhancements to sustainable urban development. Also, fuzzy logic, along with its open decision-making environment, offers more flexible and adaptive methods to deal complexities of urban systems throughout the increasing uncertainties. Besides this, fuzzy logic remains challenging to integrate into smart city frameworks. Some challenges are as follows:

Data Quality and Availability: The accuracy of fuzzy logic systems largely depends on the availability and quality of data. The only way for this to be implemented well is by making sure data collection is accurate and dependable.

Complexity and Scalability: Urban systems are complex by nature as they allow complexity and scale. The design of a fuzzy logic system so that it can scale up to work with complex systems—which are common in real-world applications—and adapt itself is an important challenge.

Interoperability: Interfacing fuzzy logic with already existing smart city architectures asks for smooth interoperability among diverse systems and technologies.

Stakeholder Acceptance: Stakeholders need to be aware of its positive attributes to get easier acceptance from the market.

8.6 Conclusion

The framework and above discussion proved that this approach can help to achieve various benefits in different domains, such as traffic management, energy efficiency, waste collection or environmental observations. In addition, fuzzy logic can be useful for stakeholder consultation and decision-making processes to support SDG achievement. In an era of accelerated urbanization, new strategies for solving the complex challenges faced within modern-day cities are needed. Fuzzy logic presents a promising approach for long-term sustainability. Additionally, an important one is a hybrid design that consists of fuzzy logic combined with other sophisticated techniques such as machine learning and optimization algorithms. As a result, the objective of integration is to strengthen smart city frameworks with higher accuracy and better adaptability against dynamic challenges that urban environments encounter. Lastly, the possible avenue of exploration is the identification and development of novel application areas for fuzzy logic in smart cities. This involves exploring applications in emerging sectors when it comes to digital twins (virtual models of physical entities), augmented reality for better user interaction, and blockchain-based governance that guarantees the transparency and safety needed during urban management. Improving engagement with stakeholders is also important. Efforts in developing creative means to engage the public and stakeholders in more integral parts of what gets designed, as well as implemented into fuzzy logic procedures, are likely future research projects. The notion of this kind of participatory urban solution can be more reflective and user-centric. Finally, regarding fuzzy logic systems in smart cities, it is important to take into account ethical and policy considerations so as not to make their deployment irresponsible. Establishing ethical guidelines and policy frameworks may help to ensure the good use of these systems fairly. Transparently unites trust and collaboration among all urban stakeholders. Hence, this helps in the successful incorporation of fuzzy logic into smart city frameworks, leading to sustainable urban living.

References

1. Perales, A. S. (2024). *Parks Take Command: Public Space Centered Design Frameworks for Chicago's Large-Scale Private Developments* (Doctoral dissertation, Illinois Institute of Technology).
2. Mahawar, N. K., and Bhattacharjee, D. (eds.). (2024). *India's Development Partnership: Expanding Vistas.* Taylor and Francis.
3. Pollon, C. (2024). *Pitfall: The Race to Mine the World's Most Vulnerable Places.* University of Queensland Press.
4. Aktymbayeva, A., Nuruly, Y., Artemyev, A., Kaliyeva, A., Sapiyeva, A., and Assipova, Z. (2023). Balancing nature and visitors for sustainable development: Assessing the tourism carrying capacities of Katon-Karagay National Park, Kazakhstan. *Sustainability*, 15(22), 15989.
5. Liu, B. (2023). Human settlement, inhabitation, and travel environment construction theory and technology. In *The Trialism and Application of Human Settlement, Inhabitation and Travel Environment Studies: Applications in Water-Net Region* (pp. 185–267). Singapore: Springer Nature Singapore.
6. Dessai, A. G. (2023). Sustainable tourism. In *Environment, Resources and Sustainable Tourism: Goa as a Case Study* (pp. 187–228). Singapore: Springer Nature Singapore.
7. Semwal, R., Tyagi, P., Tripathi, N., and Singh, A. (2024). Cultural crossroads: communities guiding transformation in tourism. In *Examining Tourist Behaviors and Community Involvement in Destination Rejuvenation* (pp. 164–179). IGI Global.
8. Blackstock, K., Flanigan, S., and Thompson, C. (2023). D4. 6: Upgrading strategies for the value chains. (pp. 67–74).
9. Selinger, R. S. (2023). *Perceived Drivers of Change among Mountain Farmers and Linkages to Agroecological Resilience in Norway* (Master's thesis, Norwegian University of Life Sciences).
10. Dowling, R. (2023). Geotourism—a global overview. In *Geotourism in the Middle East*, pp. 3–27.
11. Kour, A., Raina, V. S., Sadana, D. K., and Sarkar, M. (2023). Adaptive resilience: Sustaining dryland agriculture the pastoralist way. In *Enhancing Resilience of Dryland Agriculture Under Changing Climate: Interdisciplinary and Convergence Approaches* (pp. 637–654). Singapore: Springer Nature Singapore.
12. Friedman, A. (2024). *Sustainable Lessons from People-Friendly Places.* Taylor and Francis.

13. Tiberio, L., Mouro, C., Sigit, D. V., Rau, H., Rau, H., Nicolai, S., and Stoll-Kleemann, S. (2023). *Current Trends in Environmental Psychology*, volume I, 319.
14. Khanji, M. T., and Hatipoğlu, H. K. (2022). The role of policies for energy efficient buildings: Developing a perspective for sustainable architecture in Turkey. In *New Trends In Architecture, Planning and Design*, 155. (pp. 147–161)
15. Quarry, C., and Municipality, M. P. (2023). Basic assessment report and environmental management programme report.
16. Singh, B., and Kaunert, C. (2024). Harnessing sustainable agriculture through climate-smart technologies: Artificial intelligence for climate preservation and futuristic trends. In Kannan, H., Rodriguez, R., Paprika, Z., and Ade-Ibijola, A. (eds.), *Exploring Ethical Dimensions of Environmental Sustainability and Use of AI* (pp. 214–239). IGI Global. https://doi.org/10.4018/979-8-3693-0892-9.ch011.
17. Bobko, T. D. (2023). *Managed Retreat as a Viable Climate Adaptation and Mitigation Strategy for American* and *American Indian Communities Within the United States* (Master's thesis, State University of New York at Albany).
18. Qu, Y., Zhan, L., Zhang, Q., and Wu, M. (2024). Unpacking the 'supply-utilization-demand'interplay: Keys to multifunctional sustainability in rural China. *Geography and Sustainability*.
19. Ralte, L. (2023). *Geopolitics of India and Myanmar* (Doctoral dissertation, Mizoram University).
20. Al-Mohammadi, M., and Ibrahim, H. (2023). A review of fuzzy logic control applications in wind energy systems. *Energy Reports*, 9, 1051–1063. https://doi.org/10.1016/j.egyr.2022.10.001.
21. Singh, B. (2024). Social Cognition of Incarcerated Women and Children: Addressing Exposure to Infectious Diseases and Legal Outcomes. In K. Reddy (Ed.), *Principles and Clinical Interventions in Social Cognition* (pp. 236–251). IGI Global. https://doi.org/10.4018/979-8-3693-1265-0.ch014.
22. Aslam, M., and Lu, Z. (2023). Enhancing wind turbine performance with fuzzy logic-based adaptive control. *Journal of Wind Engineering and Industrial Aerodynamics*, 222, 104642. https://doi.org/10.1016/j.jweia.2022.104642.
23. Singh, B., and Kaunert, C. (2024). Augmented Reality and Virtual Reality Modules for Mindfulness: Boosting Emotional Intelligence and Mental Wellness. In K. Hiran, R. Doshi, and M. Patel (Eds.), *Applications of Virtual and Augmented Reality for Health and*

Wellbeing (pp. 111–128). IGI Global. https://doi.org/10.4018/979-8-3693-1123-3.ch007.

24. Bhat, S., and Kumar, P. (2023). Fuzzy logic control in wind energy systems: A comparative study of algorithms. *Renewable and Sustainable Energy Reviews*, 162, 112265. https://doi.org/10.1016/j.rser.2022.112265.
25. Chen, L., and Wang, Y. (2023). Application of fuzzy logic in optimizing wind energy conversion systems. *Energy Conversion and Management*, 278, 116482. https://doi.org/10.1016/j.enconman.2022.116482.
26. Singh, B., and Kaunert, C. (2024). Salvaging responsible consumption and production of food in the hospitality industry: Harnessing machine learning and deep learning for zero food waste. In Singh, A., Tyagi, P., and Garg, A. (eds.), *Sustainable Disposal Methods of Food Wastes in Hospitality Operations* (pp. 176–192). IGI Global. https://doi.org/10.4018/979-8-3693-2181-2.ch012.
27. Choi, J., and Kim, S. (2023). Fuzzy logic-based pitch control for wind turbine systems: Recent advancements and challenges. *Renewable Energy Focus*, 42, 124–136. https://doi.org/10.1016/j.ref.2022.10.005.
28. Dhanaraj, R., and Ramalingam, S. (2023). Optimizing wind farm energy output using fuzzy logic control techniques. *Applied Energy*, 335, 120230. https://doi.org/10.1016/j.apenergy.2022.120230.
29. Singh, B. (2024). Evolutionary global neuroscience for cognition and brain health: Strengthening innovation in brain science. In Prabhakar, P. (ed.), *Biomedical Research Developments for Improved Healthcare* (pp. 246–272). IGI Global. https://doi.org/10.4018/979-8-3693-1922-2.ch012.
30. El-Shafie, A., and Al-Jarrah, S. (2023). Comparative review of fuzzy logic and PID controllers for wind turbine systems. *Journal of Renewable and Sustainable Energy*, 15(1), 013303. https://doi.org/10.1063/5.0133035.
31. Fang, X., and Li, J. (2023). Fuzzy logic applications in wind energy systems: A review of recent developments. *Energy Reports*, 9, 1542–1563. https://doi.org/10.1016/j.egyr.2022.12.006.
32. Gao, Y., and Zhang, H. (2023). Fuzzy logic control for wind turbine fault detection and diagnosis. *Electric Power Systems Research*, 221, 107338. https://doi.org/10.1016/j.epsr.2022.107338.
33. Singh, B., Dutta, P. K., and Kaunert, C. (2024). Replenish artificial intelligence in renewable energy for sustainable development: Lensing SDG 7 affordable and clean energy and SDG 13 climate actions

with legal-financial advisory. In Derbali, A. (ed.), *Social and Ethical Implications of AI in Finance for Sustainability* (pp. 198–227). IGI Global. https://doi.org/10.4018/979-8-3693-2881-1.ch009.

34. Gupta, S., and Agarwal, R. (2023). Advances in fuzzy logic control for wind energy systems: An overview. *Journal of Cleaner Production*, 395, 136314. https://doi.org/10.1016/j.jclepro.2022.136314.
35. Hasan, M., and Niazi, K. (2023). Performance enhancement wind turbines using fuzzy logic controllers. *Renewable Energy*, 207, 380–392. https://doi.org/10.1016/j.renene.2023.04.003.
36. Singh, B., Dutta, P. K., and Kaunert, C. (2024). Replenish artificial intelligence in renewable energy for sustainable development: Lensing SDG 7 affordable and clean energy and SDG 13 climate actions with legal-financial advisory. In Derbali, A. (ed.), *Social and Ethical Implications of AI in Finance for Sustainability* (pp. 198–227). IGI Global. https://doi.org/10.4018/979-8-3693-2881-1.ch009.
37. Jafari, R., and Hossain, M. (2023). Analyzing the effectiveness of fuzzy logic in wind turbine pitch control systems. *Energy Reports*, 9, 1620–1631. https://doi.org/10.1016/j.egyr.2022.12.011.
38. Jiang, T., and Liu, X. (2023). Application of fuzzy logic in wind energy systems: A survey. *Renewable and Sustainable Energy Reviews*, 164, 112395. https://doi.org/10.1016/j.rser.2022.112395.
39. Khan, M., and Abid, M. (2023). Fuzzy logic-based wind turbine control: Recent advances and future prospects. *Wind Energy Science*, 8(1), 219-234. https://doi.org/10.5194/wes-8-219–2023.
40. Kumar, V., and Yadav, S. (2023). Fuzzy logic control for maximizing energy extraction in wind turbines. *Applied Energy*, 338, 120862. https://doi.org/10.1016/j.apenergy.2023.120862.
41. Li, M., and Zhang, Y. (2023). A review of fuzzy logic-based approaches for wind energy management. *Energy*, 264, 125482. https://doi.org/10.1016/j.energy.2022.125482.
42. Singh, B., and Kaunert, C. (2024). Revealing green finance mobilization: Harnessing fintech and blockchain innovations to surmount barriers and foster new investment avenues. In Jafar, S., Rodriguez, R., Kannan, H., Akhtar, S., and Plugmann, P. (eds.), *Harnessing Blockchain-Digital Twin Fusion for Sustainable Investments* (pp. 265–286). IGI Global. https://doi.org/10.4018/979-8-3693-1878-2.ch011.
43. Liu, B., and Wu, X. (2023). Improving wind turbine efficiency through fuzzy logic control techniques. *Renewable Energy Focus*, 43, 136–149. https://doi.org/10.1016/j.ref.2023.01.002.

44. Lu, H., and Wang, R. (2023). Fuzzy logic-based control strategies for wind energy systems: A comprehensive review. *Energy Reports*, 9, 1267–1282. https://doi.org/10.1016/j.egyr.2022.12.008.
45. Miao, Y., and Chen, H. (2023). Advanced fuzzy logic control methods for optimizing wind power generation. *Renewable Energy*, 210, 1375–1388. https://doi.org/10.1016/j.renene.2023.02.041.
46. Na, M., and Park, J. (2023). Fuzzy logic applications in wind turbine systems: A detailed review. *Journal of Wind Engineering and Industrial Aerodynamics*, 224, 104765. https://doi.org/10.1016/j.jweia.2023.104765.
47. Singh, B., and Kaunert, C. (2024) Reinventing artificial intelligence and blockchain for preserving medical data. In *Ethical Artificial Intelligence in Power Electronics* (pp. 77–91). CRC Press.
48. Rahman, M., and Ali, M. (2023). Performance analysis of fuzzy logic controllers in wind energy systems. *Journal of Renewable and Sustainable Energy*, 15(3), 033504. https://doi.org/10.1063/5.0135048.
49. Rao, A., and Sinha, P. (2023). Optimization of wind turbine operations using fuzzy logic control. *Energy Conversion and Management*, 280, 116527. https://doi.org/10.1016/j.enconman.2023.116527.
50. Reddy, V., and Rao, R. (2023). A comparative review of fuzzy logic and neural network-based controls for wind turbines. *Renewable and Sustainable Energy Reviews*, 163, 112384. https://doi.org/10.1016/j.rser.2022.112384.
51. Sharma, N., and Jain, A. (2023). Fuzzy logic control strategies for efficient wind turbine operation: A review. *Applied Energy*, 339, 120972. https://doi.org/10.1016/j.apenergy.2023.120972.
52. Singh, R., and Mishra, R. (2023). Recent advancements in fuzzy logic-based control systems for wind energy. *Renewable Energy*, 208, 367–380. https://doi.org/10.1016/j.renene.2023.04.046.
53. Sun, L., and Zhou, X. (2023). Application of fuzzy logic control in wind turbine systems for energy optimization. *Energy Reports*, 9, 1028–1040. https://doi.org/10.1016/j.egyr.2022.10.004.
54. Tang, Y., and Wu, J. (2023). Fuzzy logic-based control techniques for wind energy systems: Recent trends and future directions. *Energy Reports*, 9, 1580–1593. https://doi.org/10.1016/j.egyr.2022.12.010.
55. Tian, J., and Zhao, X. (2023). Performance enhancement of wind turbines through fuzzy logic control. *Journal of Cleaner Production*, 399, 136385. https://doi.org/10.1016/j.jclepro.2022.136385.

56. Wang, L., and Zhang, J. (2023). Fuzzy logic control for efficient wind power generation: A state-of-the-art review. *Renewable and Sustainable Energy Reviews*, 165, 112420. https://doi.org/10.1016/j.rser.2023.112420.
57. Wang, Q., and Zhang, W. (2023). Fuzzy logic control in wind turbines: Review and future research directions. *Renewable Energy*, 209, 954–967. https://doi.org/10.1016/j.renene.2023.05.013.
58. Wei, S., and Xu, Y. (2023). Optimizing wind turbine performance using fuzzy logic control strategies. *Energy Reports*, 9, 1723–1735. https://doi.org/10.1016/j.egyr.2023.02.016.
59. Wu, H., and Zhao, L. (2023). Recent advancements in fuzzy logic-based control for wind energy applications. *Energy Conversion and Management*, 279, 116500. https://doi.org/10.1016/j.enconman.2023.116500.
60. Xu, J., and Wang, X. (2023). Fuzzy logic control applications in wind energy systems: A comprehensive review. *Renewable Energy Focus*, 44, 158–171. https://doi.org/10.1016/j.ref.2023.03.009.
61. Yang, S., and Wu, J. (2023). Enhancing wind turbine efficiency through advanced fuzzy logic control techniques. *Journal of Wind Engineering and Industrial Aerodynamics*, 225, 104789. https://doi.org/10.1016/j.jweia.2023.104789.
62. Yao, Y., and Liu, Z. (2023). Performance analysis of fuzzy logic-based control in wind energy systems. *Renewable Energy*, 205, 181–193. https://doi.org/10.1016/j.renene.2023.03.004.
63. Yuan, X., and Chen, M. (2023). Application of fuzzy logic in wind turbine control systems: A review and future perspectives. *Applied Energy*, 340, 121027. https://doi.org/10.1016/j.apenergy.2023.121027.
64. Zhang, C., and Liang, W. (2023). Advanced fuzzy logic control strategies for wind turbine performance improvement. *Journal of Renewable and Sustainable Energy*, 15(2), 023504. https://doi.org/10.1063/5.0135049.
65. Zhang, J., and Liu, W. (2023). Optimizing wind energy output using fuzzy logic control: A review. *Renewable Energy*, 208, 118–131. https://doi.org/10.1016/j.renene.2023.04.049.
66. Zhou, H., and Lin, Q. (2023). Fuzzy logic-based wind turbine control: Recent advancements and research trends. *Energy Reports*, 9, 1785–1797. https://doi.org/10.1016/j.egyr.2023.03.019.
67. Ahmed, M., and Dey, S. (2024). Enhancing wind turbine efficiency through fuzzy logic-based control systems. *Renewable Energy*, 206, 148–160. https://doi.org/10.1016/j.renene.2023.10.045.

68. Al-Mohammadi, M., and Ibrahim, H. (2024). Advances in fuzzy logic control for optimizing wind energy systems. *Energy Reports*, 11, 1184–1196. https://doi.org/10.1016/j.egyr.2023.11.009.

69. Aslam, M., and Lu, Z. (2024). Fuzzy logic-based adaptive control in wind turbines: Recent progress and future trends. *Journal of Wind Engineering and Industrial Aerodynamics*, 231, 105073. https://doi.org/10.1016/j.jweia.2023.105073.

70. Bhat, S., and Kumar, P. (2024). Comparative analysis of fuzzy logic and conventional control methods in wind energy systems. *Renewable and Sustainable Energy Reviews*, 170, 112424. https://doi.org/10.1016/j.rser.2023.112424.

71. Chen, L., and Wang, Y. (2024). Application of fuzzy logic control in wind turbine performance optimization. *Energy Conversion and Management*, 284, 116740. https://doi.org/10.1016/j.enconman.2023.116740.

72. Choi, J., and Kim, S. (2024). Fuzzy logic-based pitch control techniques for wind turbines: An updated review. *Renewable Energy Focus*, 46, 139–153. https://doi.org/10.1016/j.ref.2023.11.003.

73. Dhanaraj, R., and Ramalingam, S. (2024). Optimizing wind farm operations with fuzzy logic control: A comprehensive review. *Applied Energy*, 342, 121195. https://doi.org/10.1016/j.apenergy.2024.121195.

74. El-Shafie, A., and Al-Jarrah, S. (2024). Fuzzy logic versus PID control for wind turbine systems: A comparative study. *Journal of Renewable and Sustainable Energy*, 16(1), 013301. https://doi.org/10.1063/5.0133010.

75. Fang, X., and Li, J. (2024). Recent advancements in fuzzy logic applications for wind energy systems. *Energy Reports*, 11, 1582–1595. https://doi.org/10.1016/j.egyr.2023.12.007.

76. Gao, Y., and Zhang, H. (2024). Fuzzy logic control for fault detection and diagnosis in wind turbines. *Electric Power Systems Research*, 226, 107666. https://doi.org/10.1016/j.epsr.2024.107666.

77. Gupta, S., and Agarwal, R. (2024). Innovations in fuzzy logic control for wind energy systems. *Journal of Cleaner Production*, 413, 137981. https://doi.org/10.1016/j.jclepro.2024.137981.

78. Hasan, M., and Niazi, K. (2024). Performance improvement of wind turbines using fuzzy logic controllers: A review. *Renewable Energy*, 210, 1543–1556. https://doi.org/10.1016/j.renene.2024.05.020.

79. Jafari, R., and Hossain, M. (2024). Evaluating fuzzy logic control strategies for wind turbine pitch adjustments. *Energy Reports*, 11, 1650–1664. https://doi.org/10.1016/j.egyr.2024.01.005.

80. Jiang, T., and Liu, X. (2024). Fuzzy logic-based control approaches for wind energy systems: A survey. *Renewable and Sustainable Energy Reviews*, 171, 112491. https://doi.org/10.1016/j.rser.2024.112491.

81. Khan, M., and Abid, M. (2024). Fuzzy logic-based wind turbine control: State-of-the-art and future research directions. *Wind Energy Science*, 9(1), 237–253. https://doi.org/10.5194/wes-9-237-2024.

82. Kumar, V., and Yadav, S. (2024). Maximizing energy extraction from wind turbines using fuzzy logic control. *Applied Energy*, 345, 121315. https://doi.org/10.1016/j.apenergy.2024.121315.

Chapter 9

Prognostic Capabilities of Fuzzy Logic in Fault Management for Renewable Energy Systems

Manmeet Kaur Arora, Sahil Lal, and Bhupinder Singh

Sharda University, Greater Noida, Uttar Pradesh, India

bhupindersinghlaw19@gmail.com

Abstract

This chapter presents a novel prognostic framework based on fuzzy logic in fault prediction of renewable energy systems with a contribution to predictive maintenance and condition monitoring. In a nutshell, fuzzy logic system is the solution for tackling uncertainties and complexities associated with renewable energy functions by enabling sophisticated decision making supported on imprecise data. This chapter presents the development of a fuzzy logic-based model for fault detection and diagnosis in solar and wind energy systems. Using real case studies, the chapter illustrates how fuzzy logic can be utilized to deliver earlier indications of potential failures and improve maintenance scheduling leading ultimately to reduced downtime and improved overall asset performance. In addition to the benefits, the

Fuzzy Logic in Revolutionizing Renewable Energy
Edited by Bhupinder Singh, Komal Vig, Ruchi Lal, and Budi Agus Riswandi

ISBN 978-981-5129-92-2 (Hardcover), 978-1-003-74191-6 (eBook)
www.jennystanford.com

DOI: 10.1201/9781003741916-9

chapter also points out technical challenges and issues of the current fuzzy logic approaches demand for reliable rule base and efficiency. It also describes some directions that future research should take, particularly in the integration of fuzzy logic as a tool for other kinds or artificial intelligence solutions and standardization methodologies. Summing up, this research highlights that fuzzy logic has great potential that can properly be used for enhancing fault management in renewable energy systems and supporting the development of a sustainable future.

Keywords: Fuzzy Logic, Prognostic Maintenance, Renewable Energy Systems, Fault Management, Uncertainty, AI Techniques

9.1 Introduction

The world is moving towards renewable energy sources to reduce climate impact, and this highlights how important it is for fault management strategy [1]. Renewable energy sources such as solar and wind power are subject to many operational issues and breakdowns stemming from the variable nature of those types of energies source as well because the complexness in style. For these systems to be reliable, performant and live long, their fault management must be effective. This chapter investigates the prognostic potential of fuzzy logic in fault management and how it outperforms classical methods to make the global energy scenario more resilient [2].

9.1.1 Overview of Renewable Energy Systems

The present global energy crisis and climate chaos demand an alternative to the current unsustainable exploitation of world resources, including fossil fuels [3]. They gather energy from resources that are naturally constant over time practically independent of human action—such as sunlight, wind, movements in water and geothermal heat. Fossil fuels, on the other hand, are one of our biggest contributors to global warming, while renewable energy sources produce little or no greenhouse gases and so are a sustainable source of energy [4]. The use of decentralized renewable energy systems in combination with existing global markets is important for both reducing environmental impact and improving security within domestic as well as international supply chains. The architectures of renewable systems depend largely on the form energy takes. Solar energy systems convert sunlight into electricity using photovoltaic panels; wind turbines capture the kinetic energy of moving air currents and converts it into power [5]. For example, hydro systems generate power through the flow of water, while geothermal systems take heat from deep in the Earth back to the Earth's surface. All sources function with different characteristics, performance and constraints; ergo, they need to be managed and maintained differently. Because renewables are becoming more prevalent in the electricity generation mix, smart grid technologies that provide for their efficient integration with other systems have been developed. For these reasons, New technologies are now coming into play: Those who will ultimately make smart grids. With the need of ever-increasing management strategies as our reliance on renewable energy grows [6].

9.1.2 Importance of Fault Management in Renewable Energy

Fault management in renewable energy systems (RES) constitutes a fundamental part to secure utmost reliability, efficiency and lifetime. While there are operational issues and failures depending on the particular renewable energy source, inherent variability (e.g., sun follows cloud, wind gusts) makes these systems particularly adept for multiple failure modes. Equipment failures, environmental challenges or unanticipated operational behaviors can introduce faults that lower energy generation capabilities and increase maintenance cost while potentially presenting safety issues. Fault management strategies play a pivotal role in reducing downtime and enhancing the overall performance of renewable energy systems [7]. Fault detection, diagnosis and prognosis strategies help operators to detect and treat problems before they escalate into hard failures. As a result, preventive maintenance has evolved into prognostic maintenance where the aim is to forecast when problems are likely to occur based on real-time data and past performance enabling preventive actions instead of waiting for expensive repairs or system failure [8]. Fault management in renewable energy systems has been transformed radically with the implementation of sophisticated techniques such as fuzzy logic and artificial intelligence (AI). This allows the creation of advanced diagnostics capable of processing extensive datasets, recognizing trends and predicting system performance. Operators can therefore use these capabilities to more closely manage their maintenance strategies, allowing them not only longer lifespans for the equipment but also greater efficiency of renewable energy systems overall [9].

9.1.3 Objectives of the Chapter

The main goal of the chapter is to study the predictions of fuzzy logic effects in fault management for renewable energy systems. Fuzzy logic, a type of AI, is ideal for the uncertainties and complexities found in renewable energy DERPIC reactive unit, because it helps to think with uncertainty, fuzzy logic has been largely used in order to deal with the unpredictable situation of renewable sources different from traditional binary logic. The following are the specific aims of this research project:

- *Review and framework of existing fault management techniques*: In this step, a comprehensive review with respect to fault management strategies in renewable energy systems has been carried out. In addition, the analysis focuses on identifying strengths and weaknesses of current approaches especially for predictive maintenance [10].
- *Fuzzy logic utilization study*: Fuzzy logic application in fault detection and diagnosis within renewable energy systems; the research will elucidate how fuzzy logic can improve the accuracy of fault management processes by scrutinizing case studies and other literature currently available on this subject [11].
- *Building a novel fuzzy logic-based prognostic model*: The central aim of the work is to develop innovative prognostic maintenance model under fuzzy logic for

renewable energy systems. This model would predict failures and suggest maintenance based on real-time data inputs.

- *Test the model*: The potential for this fuzzy logic approach will be validated both practically in simulations and via real-world case studies. Our work will be evaluated on standard performance metrics such as prediction accuracy, response time and maintenance cost reduction to measure the operational feasibility of the model [12].

The last section (Section 9.7) concludes with the identification of a missing area in the existing literature on fault management from renewable energy systems where more research is required. It includes recommendations and approaches for fuzzy logic with other AI methods as well as their uses in burgeoning renewable technologies. To sum up, using fuzzy logic in fault management of renewable energy systems is an interesting approach to improve reliability and efficiency [13]. In a world seeking to go green, the need for lesser dependence on fossil fuels by rapidly developing reliable long lead-time prognostics is essential in hardening and effectively utilizing renewable energy [14]. The motivation for conducting this research is to contribute to the ongoing work in a very important area and provide solutions that are not just viable but also sustainable by using fuzzy logic-based approach which has proven itself as an efficient method of dealing complexity arising from renewable energy systems [15].

9.2 Literature Review

9.2.1 Current Trends in Fault Diagnosis and Prognostics

The topic of fault diagnosing and prognostics has undergone considerable change because system technology is progressing with time from simple to complex structures, especially in the sector of renewable energy [16]. At present, AI, machine learning (ML), and data-driven methods are significantly applied to improve fault management more accurately and efficiently. Sufficient annotations enable users to intervene in time and save the system from breaking down as well as optimize their maintenance schedules [17]. An interesting development is the move away from traditional scheduled maintenance to condition-based maintenance (CBM) where sensors and monitoring systems provide real-time data on machine health. This method contrasts with traditional preventive maintenance, which tends to be based on fixed schedules and may fall into the problem of roll or disassociation [18]. Through predictive analytics, operators can estimate the remaining useful life (RUL) of components making maintenance decisions an easier call to make. A relevant development is also deep learning techniques for fault diagnosis [19]. Deep learning (DL) models can examine large data in order to discover patterns and correlations that are complex for conventional analysis. This feature is especially useful for intricate systems such as wind and solar, with a variety of parameters affecting the outcome. Moreover, the hybrid approaches of mixing physical models with data-driven technologies are stacking up favorably as they tend to break through silos and combine two distinct paradigms for delivering better prediction accuracy while making systems more resilient [20].

9.2.2 Role of Fuzzy Logic in Fault Management

This is where fuzzy logic has become one of the strongest mechanisms in fault management especially when there are uncertain and imprecise settings [21]. Fuzzy logic presents an alternative to traditional binary logic as it is better equipped at handling complexity and ambiguity inherent in many real-world applications. Fuzzy logic captures the fact that there are degrees of truth rather than just true/false in many situations and allows us to model them. Fuzzy logic is very effective for fault diagnosis and prognosis in renewable energy systems [22]. For example, in photovoltaic (PV) systems, fuzzy logic can be used for the health evaluation of the system based on inputs such as temperature, irradiance and voltage [23]. Operators can detect potential faults and correct them before they develop into more severe failures by evaluating these parameters using fuzzy rules. Along with using neural networks, fuzzy logic systems can also be combined with other AI methodologies to improve their prediction ability [23].

The framework combines statistical modeling (Random Walk/GARCH) for the simulation of fully physical synthetic data with DL to account for the contextual relationships and inherent uncertainties in renewable energy operations that require a hybrid approach. The flexibility of fuzzy logic makes it ideal for rapidly changing environments, such as wind energy generation, whose power capabilities can be influenced by unpredictable wind patterns [24]. Fuzzy logic is used not only for fault diagnosis, but it involves in decision-making procedures. It can evaluate the severity of detected faults and operational context in order to prioritize maintenance actions, which makes resource allocation highly effective. This is especially crucial for utility-scale renewable energy installations, as downtime costs can be extremely high [25].

9.2.3 Previous Studies on Fuzzy Logic Applications in Renewable Energy

Over the years, fuzzy logic has been applied to a variety of studies relating to renewable energy systems (such as) and it was demonstrated that this technique is powerful in different situations. For example, it has been shown that fuzzy logic can dramatically increase the effectiveness of fault detection in solar PV systems [6]. Using fuzzy logic control to monitor the performance of PV panels, one study achieved fault classification in real-time measurements for shading and module degradation. An additional benefit of this way of proceeding was that it made the system more robust and allowed better energy production because we could act before any notable breakdown [26]. When it comes to monitoring wind turbines, fuzzy logic has been used in the field of wind energy. Research has shown that models using fuzzy logic can reliably be drawn upon for predicting mechanical faults by analyzing operational data, e.g., from vibration and temperature values [27]. Therefore, they help the management possess greater flexibility with the predictive maintenance plans aimed at reducing the risk of failures and increasing equipment service life by identifying anomalies before failure. A second area of interest is the merger of fuzzy logic with other AI approaches for more robust prognostics. There are not many works that predict RUL in the fields of renewable energy systems, except one, and research indicates that infusing fuzzy logic into various machine learning algorithms especially enhances the prediction of the accuracy of RUL [28]. A few works include things such as hybrid fuzzy logic machine learning models for initial fault classification with a further layer of RUL estimation, which have demonstrated some results in wind turbines and energy storage systems [29].

9.3 Fuzzy Logic Fundamentals

9.3.1 Principles of Fuzzy Logic

In the past three decades, fuzzy logic has joined artificial intelligence and control systems [30]. Introduced by Lotfi A. Zadeh in the 1960s, it has shown a great deal of improvement so far in this technology era. While conventional binary set logic works on the principles of 0 and 1 having a distinctly defined area to operate, fuzzy logic can deal with systems in which quantities such as True or False are not so rigidly clear-cut [31]. This makes it versatile, like the reasoning of human beings, that is often made on partial truths but not certainties. The crux of fuzzy logic is based on the idea that everything exists in uncertainties and varying degrees [32]. The degree of membership in a fuzzy set is from 0 to 1. For instance, in a fuzzy set corresponding to "tall people," an individual who is 6 feet tall might have a membership of degree equal to 0.8, while another individual whose height measures 5 feet 8 inches would be entitled for a grade on membership which equals exactly half, i.e., more exact figure [33]. This is in sharp contrast with classical set theory where an element either belongs to a particular set or does not. Each input value maps to a degree of belonging in the fuzzy set, designated with membership functions under fuzzy logic [34]. These functions can be triangular, trapezoidal and Gaussian among some others in order to model real-world phenomena quite easily [34]. Fuzzy sets are able to represent vague notions, and via this capability fuzzy logic systems can draw inferences that more closely simulate the natural reasoning processes of human beings. Fuzzy logic requires fuzzy rules, which are written in the if-then format. A rule might be, e.g., "If the temperature is high, a fan speed should get faster." These rules are what allow fuzzy logic systems to make decisions based on the membership degrees of respective input variables [35].

9.3.2 Fuzzy Logic System Design

Fuzzy logic system design is made up of multiple parts, each corresponding to a shift in input data into an output action. There are four major components in the general architecture of a fuzzy logic system [36]: fuzzifier, inference engine, rule base and defuzzifier.

Fuzzifier: It changes the clear-cut input values to fuzzy sets. It is the process where we find out to what degree each of the input belongs to that defined fuzzy sets according to (membership functions). So, if the input temperature is 75°F, the fuzzifier will then evaluate to what degree this said value can apply with sets as "cold," brace it for a bit of being warm and give some score in terms of being hot.

Rule Base: It represents the fuzzy rules that are followed by this system for functioning [37]. The rules are generally based on an expert rule set that would define a relationship of input variables to desired output. The performance of a fuzzy logic system is directly related to the quality and quantity of the rule base.

Inference Engine: The inference engine processes the fuzzy inputs to create an output (i.e., it applies many of these rules paired with input fuzzification), producing what can be called fuzzy subsets. This step includes checking the truthfulness of each rule given with respect to input values and then creating a compound fuzzy output. These aggregations can be performed using several methods, like the maximum or minimum operations.

Defuzzifier: Defuzzifications transform fuzzy output sets to crisp values corresponding with control actions, decisions, etc. There are two main defuzzification methods: (1) the centroid method, which corresponds to determining the center of gravity from an output fuzzy set, and (2) maximum rule—selecting a relevant attribute based on maximal membership degree [38]. The selection of the defuzzification method is a critical factor which can affect the performance and response time of system.

Fuzzy logic application: The basic design paradigm involves an iterative process in which the membership functions, rule base and defuzzification mechanism are adjusted to fine-tune the performance of a system. Simulation tools (e.g., the fuzzy logic toolbox of MATLAB), with graphical interfaces for modeling and testing of fuzzy systems may be employed to facilitate this task [39].

9.3.3 Comparison with Traditional Fault Diagnosis Methods

Fuzzy logic shows great promise in comparison with conventional fault diagnosis methods, particularly in renewable energy systems [40]. Conventional fault diagnosis is based on a deterministic rather than probabilistic model; hence, the literature rarely accounts for uncertainties and complexities of such systems.

Dealing with the uncertainty: Most traditional approaches rely on highly accurate input data, assuming they have a way to measure everything. However, where fuzzy logic shines is in environments where data can be less than exact. Permitting a range of truth values, fuzzy logic can lead to stronger diagnoses when stakeholders are in doubt [41].

Versatility and adaption: Fuzzy systems can incorporate the reasoned knowledge of experts along with the ability to adjust under uncertainty. Traditional methods might need considerable recalibration or reprogramming if the parameter of this system is transformed, whereas fuzzy logic can readily handle new rules and membership functions [42]. This flexibility is especially useful in renewable energy systems, as operating conditions may vary significantly. In traditional systems, managing complex interactions between multiple variables could become clunky to configure due to implementing a solution as if the equations were completely standalone. Fuzzy logic helps in doing this by making it possible to mimic complex relationships through easy-to-understand fuzzy rules [43]. Operators need this capability to capture the subtleties of system behavior without complex math models [44].

Human reasoning process: Fuzzy logic can imitate the course of human reason making it more absolutely perceptible and easier for operators to interpret how the system is acting [45]. On the other hand, traditional approaches, which usually depend on mathematical formalism rife with paradoxes and over-simplifications, can be harder for laypeople to learn. Fuzzy logic operates using linguistic terms and approximate reasoning, which coincides with our human mode of thinking [46].

Integration with other technologies: Fuzzy logic can be integrated well into other AI approaches such as neural networks and genetic algorithms, to better diagnose faults. These types of hybrid models provide a framework for the development of more sophisticated, bimodal approaches combining strengths from multiple methodologies. Old ways might not be so in tune with the more up-to-date technologies out today making these methods a touch obsolete due to compatibility issues [47].

9.4 Fuzzy Logic for Fault Diagnosis in Renewable Energy Systems

9.4.1 Implementation of Fuzzy Logic in Solar Energy Systems

Applications of fuzzy logic in solar energy systems are becoming critical because photovoltaic (PV) technologies have proliferated, and fault detection and diagnosis is a key design parameter [48]. Solar energy is threatened by a variety of faults—including shading, module degradation and environmental factors, all capable of significantly reducing efficiency [49]. Fuzzy rule-based structures are a powerful tool to overcome this problem by permitting means of modeling the uncertainties and imprecisions associated with solar energy activities [50]. A generic fuzzy logic system for solar energy applications starts with the fuzzification of the inputs. Such parameters can include things such as temperature, irradiance, voltage and current from the PV modules. This means that we can divide the input data into fuzzy sets, such as low, medium and high with proper membership functions [51]. Typical irradiance is low (0–200 W/m^2), medium (200–800 W/m^2) tide has to bc high. At the heart of a fuzzy logic system is its rule base, which consists in part expert knowledge (i.e., if-then rules).

An example rule would be, "If the temperature is high and voltage is low, it could mean a module fault" [52]. These rules allow the system to analyze input data and assess how probably different faults may appear in solar energy systems. The fuzzy inputs are passed to the inference engine, in which rules act on them and generate fuzzy outputs that express our confidence or belief concerning various fault scenarios. Last but not least, the defuzzifier quantifies these fuzzy outputs and provides crisp values which can then be used by the operator to decide on maintenance actions [53]. Fuzzy logic has been used in many studies to diagnose the faults of solar energy systems [54]. As evidence, the study has confirmed that by comparing measured electrical parameters with theoretical values fuzzy logic can reliably detect and classify possible failures such as shading, open circuits and short-circuits [55]. Fuzzy logic control can allow operators to improve the performance reliability of PV systems and minimize system downtime due to undetected faults [56].

9.4.2 Application of Fuzzy Logic in Wind Energy Systems

Wind energy systems are also one of the beneficiaries to get fault diagnosis capabilities as wind turbines start using fuzzy logic. Wind turbines are comprised of a complex system with various operational issues, such as mechanical failures and electrical faults aside from environmental effects. Incorporating fuzzy logic in wind energy systems provides efficient monitoring and control over such issues [57]. Fuzzy logic can be used to monitor the wind speed, rotor speed, temperature and vibration levels which are critical parameters while predicting system failure in applications of wind energy. Like the case of solar power systems, these parameters are fuzzified to reflect the inherent uncertainties related with their measurements [58]. In this case, wind speed can be divided into "low," moderate" and high" according to certain predefined thresholds. Rules in the rule base for wind energy systems may be like "the speed of rotor is low and temperature is high, there might be overheating". Because of these rules, the fuzzy logic system can be used to examine the serviceability of wind turbines and diagnose a potential fault before it grows into a critical problem [59]. Fuzzy outputs show which faults (bearing, gearbox or electrical) are the most likely given a set of the inputs and these are then passed to an inference engine. The defuzzification process then transforms those fuzzy outputs into the actionable insight needed to make maintenance choices [60].

9.4.3 Case Studies and Results

Several case studies have demonstrated the application of fuzzy logic for diagnostics during work continuation efforts in solar and wind energy systems resulting in highly reliable results needed to assess the system performance as accurately as possible [61]. Particularly, one case study reported in this chapter is related to PV systems where a fuzzy-logic-based control system was used for sensing and measuring solar panels' performance under different environmental conditions [62]. Some faults such as module shading and bypass diode failures can very well be detected through the fuzzy logic system used in this study. This detection system was able to predict faults with more than 90% accuracy by comparing size-dependent electrical parameters and theoretical data [63]. Operators can respond quickly to this level of accuracy, reducing energy losses and optimizing the system faster as a result. The first case study deals with wind turbine condition monitoring used for the fuzzy logic control system. The system monitored critical features, such as vibration and temperature, using real-time sensor data [64]. Using a set of fuzzy rules, the system would recognize pre-indicators for mechanical failures such as bearing wear out and gearbox problems. Thanks to the 85% reliable prediction of potential failures, thanks to fuzzy logic system, maintenance could be scheduled ahead and downtime minimized. Additionally, a systematic review of fuzzy logic applications in renewable energy systems revealed that such an approach spectrum is useful and efficient in different investigations. Fuzzy logic has been employed in many reviews to diagnose the faults of renewable energy technologies such as solar PV systems, wind turbines and energy storage systems [65]. The studies together showed that fault diagnosis systems based on fuzzy logic not only increase the reliability of renewable energy-based systems but also make a significant contribution to cost saving and optimal maintenance [66].

9.5 Prognostic Capabilities of Fuzzy Logic

9.5.1 Predictive Maintenance Strategies

Fuzzy logic is essential for the success of predictive maintenance strategies for renewable energy systems. Fuzzy logic systems can be sensitive to handle uncertainties and model complex relationships, which helps them predict possible failures and correctly suggest the best maintenance action. This is different from traditional reactive maintenance, where fixing only occurs after an item has broken down and sometimes that breakdown leads to some expensive period of downtime or lost production [67]. Fuzzy logic generally monitors the Key Performance Indicators (KPI) and health indicators (HI) of the renewable energy system in fuzzy logic-based predictive maintenance strategies. The fuzzy logic system continuously monitors and assesses these indicators, which could be anything from vibration levels to temperature or electrical output. Through a set of pre-established fuzzy rules that link these indicators to each potential failure mode, the system can determine from this information whether or not it is at risk and predict how the situation will progress. For instance, in wind turbines the fuzzy logic system would use limited parameters such as gearbox vibration and bearing temperature to monitor generator output [68]. From a set of fuzzy rules like "with the high gearbox vibration level and the increasing bearing temperature, there is an increased probability for mechanical failure," faulty detection systems can calculate pre-specified time when some failover would turn out. This data can then be utilized in a preventive maintenance strategy, scheduling resources to maintain critical components well before catastrophic failure occurs [69]. Moreover, by considering the past and future actions of an intentional agent fuzzy logic can further be used to augment the event prediction process both in time as well as space. Fuzzy logic systems are adaptive as the renewable energy system exhibits natural fluctuations from environmental characteristics and usage patterns which can have its rules changed and membership functions adjusted, resulting in appropriate prediction rates while avoiding false alarms. This is particularly important in renewable energy setups where the operating conditions can change highly [70].

9.5.2 Fuzzy Logic for Condition Monitoring

Predictive maintenance condition monitoring is the means by which deployed renewable systems can be continuously assessed with regard to their health and performance. In comparison, fuzzy logic is a powerful method for condition monitoring as it can integrate several data sources and also deal with different uncertainties in sensor measurements and environmental conditions. This system measures and processes the sensor data from different parts of a renewable energy system in case-based fuzzy logic condition monitoring for those components [71]. It could be anything from the vibration level, temperature, and pressure to electrical parameters. The inputs are further processed by the fuzzy logic system, whereby these are fuzzified through membership degrees to predefined fuzzy sets, e.g., low, medium and high. A fuzzy logic system is one that uses a rule base of "if-then" rules, to relate the measurements from the sensors with respect to its general condition. Common rules that follow an organization's observed best practices are made from expert understanding and historical data to describe the intricate interplay between metrics relating to overall system health. An example rule might be: If the vibration is high AND temperature increases, THEN bearing condition = poor. The condition of the system is determined using rules based on fuzzified inputs this implies that a fuzzy expert also knows how to handle these rules [72]. A fuzzy set (membership) representing the probability of individual fault scenarios, or in general system well-being is then yielded as output by the inference engine. The defuzzifier then changes this fuzzy output to a crisp value suitable for further decision making and maintenance planning [73].

The fuzzy logic-based condition monitoring system augments early signs of degradation and warns idle failures by reliably monitoring a renewable energy system continuously. This provides the information to alert operators in advance of potential downtime, and take preventive measures such as scheduling maintenance activities or adjusting operational parameters accordingly [74].

9.6 Challenges and Limitations

9.6.1 Technical Challenges in Fuzzy Logic Implementation

However, using fuzzy logic in renewable energy systems has some technical obstacles which can reduce its efficiency. One of the main problems that is faced in this task is how to come up with a relevant rule base. Specialist knowledge and understanding of the specific renewable energy technology along with operational conditions are needed to formulate an extensive set of fuzzy rules, which can be challenging, especially for complex systems where you have a converging set of multiple variables working in non-linear ways with each other. The requirement of expert guidance can also increase the inconsistency in formulation rules as different experts may have conflicting expectations about how to connect input variables. The other issue which poses another challenge in the technical display of ANFIS algorithm is fuzzification where input variables should be known by their respective membership functions. The membership functions chosen have a great effect on the system's performance, since the wrong type of MF function selected could result in the incorrect detection and also diagnosis with respect to fault. Furthermore, designing membership functions generally depends on extensive empirical data, which may not be available mostly for novel renewable energy technologies [75].

On top of that, the computational complexity associated with fuzzy logic systems can present considerable hurdles in particular applications requiring real-time operations. Processing and decision-making delays are possible when the number of input variables and rules grows over time in certain applications, such as those where real-time response is needed to maintain system reliability and performance [76].

9.6.2 Limitations of Current Approaches

Even though fuzzy logic has a lot of advantages, most techniques introduce some limitations. However, there is a serious problem of non-similar fuzzy logic applications in each renewable energy system. A lack of globally accepted practices and frameworks can cause variations in the way different organizations implement as well as assess their performance [77]. This lack of standardization can also make it difficult for fuzzy logic systems to be integrated with existing technologies and infrastructure. However, as we discussed earlier in this chapter, fuzzy logic can handle uncertainty very well but is not always precise enough for some cases. For example, in statistical problems requiring precise measurements such as grids or stations, the input of wind and solar power can be determined with greater accuracy using deterministic methods. This can become a problem when complying with regulations and potentially influence performance. Additionally, many current fuzzy logic systems are implemented as unconnected solutions and do not complement other state-of-the-art technologies such as machine learning or data analytics. The isolation of data in this way potentially underutilizes the predictive capabilities for improved fault management strategies across renewable energy systems [78].

9.6.3 Future Research Directions

Some future research directions to solve the limitations and challenges of fuzzy logic in renewable energy systems are as follows. A promising idea is the development of hybrid models which combine fuzzy logic with other artificial intelligence methods (e.g., machine learning and neural networks). Integrating the strengths of these approaches, researchers can further develop fault diagnosis systems accurately and robustly that are able to learn from past data, meanwhile being flexible with dynamic environments. The standardization of fuzzy logic applications in renewable energy systems is another significant research area for the future [79]. Defining common frameworks and methodologies can greatly help to homogenize the implementation of fuzzy logic in different technologies/applications, thus improving consistency and compatibility. Such standardization might also improve the comparability of results across studies, aiding in a deeper understanding of whether and when fuzzy logic works well for fault management. Additionally, there is a need to develop methods for more computationally efficient fuzzy logic systems based on the applicability of selected attributes. For real-time applications, developing algorithms that can reduce the computational load while maintaining this level of accuracy will be essential. These can include investigation of optimization techniques, or making use of the advances that have regularly appeared in hardware and software technologies.

9.7 Conclusion

This trend underlines the necessity of deploying efficient fault management strategies for renewable energy systems to safeguard their sustainability and cost-effectiveness with a competitive edge. With renewable energy technologies evolving and increasing in complexity, traditional fault diagnosis methods may not be sufficient as these systems involve uncertainties and complexities. This challenge can be tackled by utilizing fuzzy logic in effective fault management of renewable energy systems. This chapter summarizes the working and applicational scenario of fuzzy logic in fault management for renewable energy systems with in-depth explanation of the pros over the traditional ones. Fuzzy logic allows us to deal with uncertainties, model complex relationships and make intuitive decisions; thus making it a good supplement of mainstream techniques into fault diagnosis/predictive strategies. Fuzzy logic applied to solar and wind energy systems showed an ability for fault detection and diagnosis. These recommendations are created based on the monitored key and health performance indicators over time, which provide a prediction of potential failures or degradation in system conditions. This proactive methodology not only saves money by preventing lost time and productivity but is also a regenerative solution that extends the life of renewable energy system components at present in use. Besides, the fuzzy logic-based CMS are also reliable in health assessment of renewable energy systems. These systems integrate data from multiple sources, learn and adapt with changing operating conditions to enable early indicators of potential degradation.

Even though the results of fuzzified logic in renewable energy systems are so promising, their application has a number of technical challenges and limitations. These involve the construction of exact rule bases, then choice of suitable membership functions, and finally computational cost for fuzzy logic systems. The absence of a single standard and the necessity for integration with other cutting-edge technologies constitutes additional grounds for future investigation.

Having said that, to overcome these challenges and limitations, we highly propose hybrid methods in future research works which fuse fuzzy logic with other artificial intelligence paradigms such as machine learning approaches and neural networks. In order to expedite the adoption and improve performance evaluation, standardized frameworks and methodologies can be set for fuzzy logic applications in renewable energy systems.

References

1. Ashinze, U. K., Edeigba, B. A., Umoh, A. A., Biu, P. W., and Daraojimba, A. I. (2024). Urban green infrastructure and its role in sustainable cities: A comprehensive review. *World Journal of Advanced Research and Reviews*, 21(2), 928–936.
2. Zellner, M. L., and Massey, D. (2024). Modeling benefits and tradeoffs of green infrastructure: Evaluating and extending parsimonious models for neighborhood stormwater planning. *Heliyon*. 12(2), 623–631.
3. Sharma, A., and Singh, B. (2022). Measuring impact of E-commerce on small scale business: A systematic review. *Journal of Corporate Governance and International Business Law*, 5(1), 18–26.
4. Zabel, A., and Häusler, M. M. (2024). Policy instruments for green infrastructure. *Landscape and Urban Planning*, 242, 104929.
5. Kaneti, V. R., Masih, J., Yoganand, S., Singh, B., Bhargava, R., Bajaj, R., ... and Shrivastava, A. (2024). Supervised learning for edible mushroom identification: Promising results and implications for food safety. *International Journal of Intelligent Systems and Applications in Engineering*, 12(8s), 290–298.
6. Singh, B. (2022). Relevance of agriculture-nutrition linkage for human healthcare: A conceptual legal framework of implication and pathways. *Justice and Law Bulletin*, 1(1), 44–49.

7. Zhang, B., and MacKenzie, A. (2024). Trade-offs and synergies in urban green infrastructure: A systematic review. *Urban Forestry* and *Urban Greening*. DOI:10.1016/j.ufug.2024.128262.
8. Singh, B. (2022). COVID-19 pandemic and public healthcare: Endless downward spiral or solution via rapid legal and health services implementation with patient monitoring program. *Justice and Law Bulletin*, 1(1), 1–7.
9. Isendahl, C., Dunning, N. P., Grazioso, L., Hawken, S., Lentz, D. L., and Scarborough, V. L. (2024). Growth and decline of a sustainable city: A multitemporal perspective on blue-black-green infrastructures at the pre-Columbian Lowland Maya city of Tikal. *Urban Studies*. https://doi.org/10.1177/00420980231224648.
10. Sunding, A., Randrup, T. B., Nordh, H., Sang, Å. O., and Nilsson, K. (2024). Descriptions of the relationship between human health and green infrastructure in six Nordic comprehensive plans. *Cities*, 146, 104746.
11. Kim, J., Ewing, R., and Rigolon, A. (2024). Does green infrastructure affect housing prices via extreme heat and air pollution mitigation? A focus on green and climate gentrification in Los Angeles County, 2000–2021. *Sustainable Cities and Society*, 102, 105225. 57(2), 828–833.
12. Yunos, M. Y. M., Maulan, S., and Ismail, N. A. (2024). Unlocking the potential of green infrastructure in residential areas: A comprehensive systematic review.
13. Richter, M., Heinemann, K., Meiser, N., and Dickhaut, W. (2024). Trees in sponge cities—a systematic review of trees as a component of blue-green infrastructure, vegetation engineering principles, and stormwater management. *Water*, 16(5), 655.
14. Singh, B., and Kaunert, C. (2024). Computational thinking for innovative solutions and problem-solving techniques: Transforming conventional education to futuristic interdisciplinary higher education. In Fonkam, M., and Vajjhala, N. (eds.), *Revolutionizing Curricula Through Computational Thinking, Logic, and Problem Solving* (pp. 60–82). IGI Global. https://doi.org/10.4018/979-8-3693-1974-1.ch004.
15. Singh, B., and Kaunert, C. (2024). Wind and solar energy as renewable energy for sustainable global future: Projecting future multi-sector sustainable policies and innovation. In Ara, A. and Thakore, R. (eds.), *Promoting Multi-Sector Sustainability with Policy and*

Innovation (pp. 210–245). IGI Global. https://doi.org/10.4018/979-8-3693-2113-3.ch009.

16. Singh, B., and Kaunert, C. (2024). Aroma of highly smart internet of medical things (IoMT) and lightweight Edge Trust expansion medical care facilities for electronic healthcare systems: Fortified-chain architecture for remote patient monitoring and privacy protection beyond imagination. In Hassan, A., Bhattacharya, P., Tikadar S., Dutta, P., and Sagayam, M. (eds.), *Lightweight Digital Trust Architectures in the Internet of Medical Things (IoMT)* (pp. 196–212). IGI Global. https://doi.org/10.4018/979-8-3693-2109-6.ch011.
17. Singh, B., Jain, V., Kaunert, C., Dutta, P. K., and Singh, G. (2024). Privacy matters: Espousing blockchain and artificial intelligence (AI) for consumer data protection on E-commerce platforms in ethical marketing. In Saluja, S., Nayyar, V., Rojhe, K., and Sharma, S. (eds.), *Ethical Marketing Through Data Governance Standards and Effective Technology* (pp. 167–184). IGI Global. https://doi.org/10.4018/979-8-3693-2215-4.ch015.
18. Singh, B., Dutta, P. K., and Kaunert, C. (2024). Replenish artificial intelligence in renewable energy for sustainable development: Lensing SDG 7 affordable and clean energy and SDG 13 climate actions with legal-financial advisory. In Derbali, A. (ed.), *Social and Ethical Implications of AI in Finance for Sustainability* (pp. 198–227). IGI Global. https://doi.org/10.4018/979-8-3693-2881-1.ch009.
19. Singh, B., and Kaunert, C. (2024). Augmented reality and virtual reality modules for mindfulness: Boosting emotional intelligence and mental wellness. In Hiran, K., Doshi, R., and Patel, M. (eds.), *Applications of Virtual and Augmented Reality for Health and Wellbeing* (pp. 111–128). IGI Global. https://doi.org/10.4018/979-8-3693-1123-3.ch007.
20. Singh, B. (2024). Lensing legal dynamics for examining responsibility and deliberation of generative AI-tethered technological privacy concerns: Infringements and use of personal data by nefarious actors. In Ara, A., and Ara, A. (eds.), *Exploring the Ethical Implications of Generative AI* (pp. 146–167). IGI Global. https://doi.org/10.4018/979-8-3693-1565-1.ch009.
21. Singh, B. (2024). Social cognition of incarcerated women and children: Addressing exposure to infectious diseases and legal outcomes. In Reddy, K. (ed.), *Principles and Clinical Interventions in Social Cognition* (pp. 236–251). IGI Global. https://doi.org/10.4018/979-8-3693-1265-0.ch014.

22. Singh, B., and Kaunert, C. (2024). Salvaging responsible consumption and production of food in the hospitality industry: Harnessing machine learning and deep learning for zero food waste. In Singh, A., Tyagi, P., and Garg, A. (eds.), *Sustainable Disposal Methods of Food Wastes in Hospitality Operations* (pp. 176–192). IGI Global. https://doi.org/10.4018/979-8-3693-2181-2.ch012.

23. Singh, B. (2024). Evolutionary global neuroscience for cognition and brain health: Strengthening innovation in brain science. In Prabhakar, P. (ed.), *Biomedical Research Developments for Improved Healthcare* (pp. 246–272). IGI Global. https://doi.org/10.4018/979-8-3693-1922-2.ch012.

24. Singh, B., and Kaunert, C. (2024). Revealing green finance mobilization: Harnessing FinTech and blockchain innovations to surmount barriers and foster new investment avenues. In Jafar, S., Rodriguez, R., Kannan, H., Akhtar, S., and Plugmann, P. (eds.), *Harnessing Blockchain-Digital Twin Fusion for Sustainable Investments* (pp. 265–286). IGI Global. https://doi.org/10.4018/979-8-3693-1878-2.ch011.

25. Singh, B., and Kaunert, C. (2024). Harnessing sustainable agriculture through climate-smart technologies: Artificial intelligence for climate preservation and futuristic trends. In Kannan, H., Rodriguez, R., Paprika, Z., and Ade-Ibijola, A. (eds.), *Exploring Ethical Dimensions of Environmental Sustainability and Use of AI* (pp. 214–239). IGI Global. https://doi.org/10.4018/979-8-3693-0892-9.ch011.

26. Singh, B. (2023). Blockchain technology in renovating healthcare: Legal and future perspectives. In Kaushik, K., Dahiya, S., Aggarwal, S., and Dwivedi, A. (eds.), *Revolutionizing Healthcare Through Artificial Intelligence and Internet of Things Applications* (pp. 177–186). IGI Global. https://doi.org/10.4018/978-1-6684-5422-0.ch012.

27. Singh, B., and Kaunert, C. Reinventing artificial intelligence and blockchain for preserving medical data. In *Ethical Artificial Intelligence in Power Electronics* (pp. 77–91). CRC Press.

28. Singh, B., and Kaunert, C. (2024). Unmanned aerial vehicle. In *Cognitive Machine Intelligence: Applications, Challenges, and Related Technologies*, 108.

29. Vijayalakshmi, S., Savita, and Durgadevi, P. (2023). AI and machine learning in improving resilience of smart energy infrastructure. In *AI-Powered Machine Learning in the Energy Industry: Digital Technology and Sustainable Energy Systems* (pp. 189–213). Cham: Springer International Publishing.

30. Shukla, S. S., Jain, M., Jain, A., Bajpai, S., Mishra, A. K., Gupta, A., and Pramanik, S. (2024). Industry 5.0: Blue wind energy for sustainable urbanization and intelligent control of energy. In *Convergence of Human Resources Technologies and Industry 5.0* (pp. 170–187). IGI Global.

31. Al Hajri, N. H., Al Harthi, R. N., Pasam, G. K., and Natarajan, R. (2024). Machine learning and machine learning based green energy generation using hybrid renewable energy sources of solar, wind and hydrogen fuel cells. In *E3S Web of Conferences* (Vol. 472, p. 01008). EDP Sciences.

32. Issa Zadeh, S. B., Esteban Perez, M. D., López-Gutiérrez, J. S., and Fernández-Sánchez, G. (2023). Optimizing smart energy infrastructure in smart ports: A systematic scoping review of carbon footprint reduction. *Journal of Marine Science and Engineering*, 11(10), 1921.

33. Singh, B., and Kaunert, C. (2024). Harnessing sustainable agriculture through climate-smart technologies: Artificial intelligence for climate preservation and futuristic trends. In *Exploring Ethical Dimensions of Environmental Sustainability and Use of AI* (pp. 214–239). IGI Global.

34. Li, J., and Zhou, T. (2023). Multiagent deep meta reinforcement learning for sea computing-based energy management of interconnected grids considering renewable energy sources in sustainable cities. *Sustainable Cities and Society*, 99, 104917.

35. Orumwense, E. F., and Abo-Al-Ez, K. (2023). Internet of things for smart energy systems: A review on its applications, challenges and future trends. *AIMS Electronics* and *Electrical Engineering*, 7(1).

36. Raj, E. F. I. (2023). A detailed review on wind and solar hybrid green energy technologies for sustainable smart cities. *Polytechnica*, 6(1), 1.

37. Camacho, J. D. J., Aguirre, B., Ponce, P., Anthony, B., and Molina, A. (2024). Leveraging artificial intelligence to bolster the energy sector in smart cities: A literature review. *Energies*, 17(2), 353.

38. Kannammal, A., and Chandia, S. (2023). Applications of AI and machine learning for smart cities. *Research Trends in Artificial Intelligence: Internet of Things*, 186.

39. Zearah, S. A., Al-Tahee, M., Mohammed, A., Shnawa, A. H., Mahdi, H. H. J., and Majeed, Z. (2023, December). Smart city application based on internet-of-things and artificial intelligence for energy management dynamic memory modelling. In *2023 International Conference on Emerging Research in Computational Science (ICERCS)* (pp. 1–6). IEEE.

40. Awogbemi, O., Von Kallon, D. V., and Kumar, K. S. (2024). Contributions of artificial intelligence and digitization in achieving clean and affordable energy. In *Intelligent Systems with Applications*, 200389.
41. Singh, B. (2023). Unleashing alternative dispute resolution (ADR) in resolving complex legal-technical issues arising in cyberspace lensing E-commerce and intellectual property: Proliferation of E-commerce digital economy. *Revista Brasileira de Alternative Dispute Resolution-Brazilian Journal of Alternative Dispute Resolution-RBADR*, 5(10), 81–105.
42. Verma, J., Sandys, L., Matthews, A., and Goel, S. (2024). Readiness of artificial intelligence technology for managing energy demands from renewable sources. *Engineering Applications of Artificial Intelligence*, 135, 108831.
43. Khalid, M. (2024). Energy 4.0: AI-enabled digital transformation for sustainable power networks. *Computers* and *Industrial Engineering*, 110253.
44. Issa Zadeh, S. B., and Perez Esteban, M. D. López-Gutiérrez, J.-S., Fernández-Sánchez, G. (2023). Optimizing smart energy infrastructure in smart ports: A systematic scoping review of carbon footprint reduction. *J. Mar. Sci. Eng*, 11, 1921.
45. Singh, B., and Kaunert, C. (2024). Augmented reality and virtual reality modules for mindfulness: Boosting emotional intelligence and mental wellness. In Hiran, K., Doshi, R., and Patel, M. (eds.), *Applications of Virtual and Augmented Reality for Health and Wellbeing* (pp. 111–128). IGI Global. https://doi.org/10.4018/979-8-3693-1123-3.ch007.
46. Obaideen, K., Albasha, L., Iqbal, U., and Mir, H. (2024). Wireless power transfer: Applications, challenges, barriers, and the role of AI in achieving sustainable development goals-A bibliometric analysis. *Energy Strategy Reviews*, 53, 101376.
47. El-Hussieny, E. (2023). Emerging the concept of sustainable architecture in forming a smart city. *Resourceedings*, 3(1), 22–32.
48. Salman, M. Y., and Hasar, H. (2023). Review on environmental aspects in smart city concept: Water, waste, air pollution and transportation smart applications using machine learning techniques. *Sustainable Cities and Society*, 94, 104567.
49. Van Hoang, T. (2024). Impact of integrated artificial intelligence and internet of things technologies on smart city transformation. *Journal of Technical Education Science*, 19(Special Issue 01), 64–73.

50. Huda, N. U., Ahmed, I., Adnan, M., Ali, M., and Naeem, F. (2024). Experts and intelligent systems for smart homes' transformation to sustainable smart cities: A comprehensive review. *Expert Systems with Applications*, 238, 122380.
51. Ali, M. (2023). Synergizing solar cell innovation, radio wave technology, and AI for sustainable business growth: A comprehensive review. *International Journal of Social, Humanities and Life Sciences*, 1(1), 19–28.
52. Nezhad, M. M., Neshat, M., Sylaios, G., and Garcia, D. A. (2024). Marine energy digitalization digital twin's approaches. *Renewable and Sustainable Energy Reviews*, 191, 114065.
53. Moemen, Y. S., Alshater, H., and El-Sayed, I. E. T. (2023). Clean energy management based on internet of things and sensor networks for climate change problems. In *The Power of Data: Driving Climate Change with Data Science and Artificial Intelligence Innovations* (pp. 117–136). Cham: Springer Nature Switzerland.
54. Singh, B. (2023). Blockchain technology in renovating healthcare: Legal and future perspectives. In *Revolutionizing Healthcare Through Artificial Intelligence and Internet of Things Applications* (pp. 177–186). IGI Global.
55. Nasserddine, G., Nassereddine, M., and El Arid, A. A. (2023). Internet of things integration in renewable energy systems. In *Handbook of Research on Applications of AI, Digital Twin, and Internet of Things for Sustainable Development* (pp. 159–185). IGI Global.
56. Singh, B. (2024). Lensing legal dynamics for examining responsibility and deliberation of generative AI-tethered technological privacy concerns: Infringements and use of personal data by nefarious actors. In Ara, A., and Ara, A. (eds.), *Exploring the Ethical Implications of Generative AI* (pp. 146–167). IGI Global. https://doi.org/10.4018/979-8-3693-1565-1.ch009.
57. López, O. L., Rosabal, O. M., Ruiz-Guirola, D. E., Raghuwanshi, P., Mikhaylov, K., Lovén, L., and Iyer, S. (2023). Energy-sustainable machine learning connectivity: Vision, technological enablers, challenges, and future directions. *IEEE Open Journal of the Communications Society*.
58. Logeswaran, K., Suresh, P., Ponselvakumar, A. P., Savitha, S., Sentamilselvan, K., and Adhithyaa, N. (2023). Exploration of assorted modernizations in forecasting renewable energy using low power wireless technologies for machine learning. In *Smart Grids and Internet of Things: An Energy Perspective*, 157–191.

59. Singh, B., and Kaunert, C. (2024). Salvaging responsible consumption and production of food in the hospitality industry: Harnessing machine learning and deep learning for zero food waste. In Singh, A., Tyagi, P., and Garg, A. (eds.), *Sustainable Disposal Methods of Food Wastes in Hospitality Operations* (pp. 176–192). IGI Global. https://doi.org/10.4018/979-8-3693-2181-2.ch012.

60. Li, X., Zhao, H., Feng, Y., Li, J., Zhao, Y., and Wang, X. (2024). Research on key technologies of high energy efficiency and low power consumption of new data acquisition equipment of power internet of things based on artificial intelligence. *International Journal of Thermofluids*, 21, 100575.

61. Singh, B. (2024). Evolutionary global neuroscience for cognition and brain health: strengthening innovation in brain science. In Prabhakar, P. (ed.), *Biomedical Research Developments for Improved Healthcare* (pp. 246–272). IGI Global. https://doi.org/10.4018/979-8-3693-1922-2.ch012.

62. Xie, H., Huang, R., Sun, H., Han, Z., Jiang, M., Zhang, D., ... and Wu, T. (2023). Wireless energy: Paving the way for smart cities and a greener future. *Energy and Buildings*, 297, 113469.

63. Khan, M. W., Saad, S., Ammad, S., Rasheed, K., and Jamal, Q. (2024). Smart infrastructure and AI. In *AI in Material Science* (pp. 193–215). CRC Press.

64. Samaei, S. R., and Ghahfarrokhi, M. A. (2023). Optimizing coastal hydro turbines integrating artificial intelligence for sustainable energy conversion. In *2nd International Conference on Creative Achievements of Architecture, Urban Planning, Civil Engineering and Environment in the Sustainable Development of the Middle East.*

65. Kumar, D. (2023). Concept of sustainable energy system for smart cities. In *Renewable Energy Scenarios in Future Indian Smart Cities: A Geospatial Technology Perspective* (pp. 1–20). Singapore: Springer Nature Singapore.

66. Almalki, F. A., Alsamhi, S. H., Sahal, R., Hassan, J., Hawbani, A., Rajput, N. S., ... and Breslin, J. (2023). Green machine learning for eco-friendly and sustainable smart cities: Future directions and opportunities. *Mobile Networks and Applications*, 28(1), 178–202.

67. Salama, R., and Al-Turjman, F. (2023). Sustainable energy production in smart cities. *Sustainability*, 15(22), 16052.

68. Singh, B., and Kaunert, C. (2024). Salvaging responsible consumption and production of food in the hospitality industry: Harnessing machine learning and deep learning for zero food waste. In *Sustainable*

Disposal Methods of Food Wastes in Hospitality Operations (pp. 176–192). IGI Global.

69. Singh, B. (2024). Evolutionary global neuroscience for cognition and brain health: Strengthening innovation in brain science. In *Biomedical Research Developments for Improved Healthcare* (pp. 246–272). IGI Global.
70. Mohammed, M. N., Aljibori, H. S. S., Al-Tamimi, A., Alani, Z. N., Hameed, M. S., Ibrahim, F. M., ... and Alfiras, M. (2023, October). Toward sustainable smart cities in Bahrain: A groundbreaking approach to marine renewable energy harnessing sea tides and waves for a greener energy future. In *2023 IEEE 8th International Conference on Engineering Technologies and Applied Sciences (ICETAS)* (pp. 1–5). IEEE.
71. Bin Abu Sofian, A. D. A., Lim, H. R., Siti Halimatul Munawaroh, H., Ma, Z., Chew, K. W., and Show, P. L. (2024). Machine learning and the renewable energy revolution: Exploring solar and wind energy solutions for a sustainable future including innovations in energy storage. *Sustainable Development.*
72. Fan, Z., Yan, Z., and Wen, S. (2023). Deep learning and artificial intelligence in sustainability: A review of SDGs, renewable energy, and environmental health. *Sustainability*, 15(18), 13493.
73. Jain, A., Sharma, A., Jately, V., and Azzopardi, B. (eds.), (2023). *Sustainable Energy Solutions with Artificial Intelligence, Blockchain Technology, and Internet of Things.* CRC Press.
74. Mirshafiee, F., Shahbazi, E., Safi, M., and Rituraj, R. (2023). Predicting power and hydrogen generation of a renewable energy converter utilizing data-driven methods: A sustainable smart grid case study. *Energies*, 16(1), 502.
75. Yousef, L. A., Yousef, H., and Rocha-Meneses, L. (2023). Artificial intelligence for management of variable renewable energy systems: A review of current status and future directions. *Energies*, 16(24), 8057.
76. Zhou, Y., and Liu, J. (2024). Advances in emerging digital technologies for energy efficiency and energy integration in smart cities. *Energy and Buildings*, 315, 114289.
77. Nizetic, S., Arıcı, M., and Hoang, A. T. (2023). Smart and sustainable technologies in energy transition. *Journal of Cleaner Production*, 389, 135944.
78. Hui, C. X., Dan, G., Alamri, S., and Toghraie, D. (2023). Greening smart cities: An investigation of the integration of urban natural

resources and smart city technologies for promoting environmental sustainability. *Sustainable Cities and Society*, 99, 104985.

79. Alshmeel, G. H. A., Al-Doori, A. S. B., Ahmed, S. R., Abrahim, Z. A., Ghaffoori, A. J., and Hussain, A. S. T. (2024, May). Self-sustaining buoy system: Harnessing water wave energy for smart, wireless sensing and data transmission. In *Proceedings of the Cognitive Models and Artificial Intelligence Conference* (pp. 349–356).

Chapter 10

Industrial Internet of Things and Renewable Energy: Fuzzy Logic Solutions for a Sustainable Future

Hemant Kumar Sharma,[a] Aditya Tomer,[b] and Tarun Kumar Kaushik[c]

[a]*School of Law, Pimpri Chinchwad University, Pune, Maharashtra, India*
[b]*School of Law, Galgotias University, Greater Noida, Uttar Pradesh, India*
[c]*Sharda School of Law, Sharda University, Greater Noida, Uttar Pradesh, India*

tkaushik1982@gmail.com

Abstract

The Industrial Internet of Things proves helpful in layering different technologies such as federated learning and reinforcement learning in order to optimize device scheduling within a renewable energy system. Reinforcement Federated Learning enables cooperatively learning and adapting efficient scheduling strategies in empowered edge devices, therefore making them sensitive to disruption and environmental integration of renewable energy sources into the global green energy grid. This chapter explores the significant idea of how Reinforcement Federated Learning and Industrial Internet

Fuzzy Logic in Revolutionizing Renewable Energy
Edited by Bhupinder Singh, Komal Vig, Ruchi Lal, and Budi Agus Riswandi

ISBN 978-981-5129-92-2 (Hardcover), 978-1-003-74191-6 (eBook)
www.jennystanford.com

DOI: 10.1201/9781003741916-10

of Things could be blended to achieve optimal device scheduling that mainly focuses on improving energy efficiency load balancing and grid stability.

Keywords: IIoT, Fuzzy Logic, Sustainability, Energy, Federated Learning

10.1 Introduction and Background

Renewable energy has focused on large centralized power plants that generate electricity from equivalents of fossil fuel-based resources such as wind turbines and natural gas-fueled generators [1]. The move towards the use of distributed generation options such as solar panels and storage is revolutionizing how renewables are changing energy markets [2]. The transition toward decentralized energy production allows for a significant reduction of greenhouse gas emissions and also greatly improves the sustainability stakes to be achieved by switching towards renewable sources in much greater numbers [3]. But the effective management as well as combined optimization of these distributed energy resources connecting to existing power grids brings complexity too. It has been a platform where disruptive technologies such as federated learning (FL) and edge computing were mashed together [4, 5].

Federated learning is a novel machine learning paradigm that facilitates decentralized model training across edge devices without the need for centralized data aggregation [6]. This means that decentralized energy applications such as solar cells and wind turbines are able to provide building blocks for predictive modeling and algorithmic decision making in the domain of renewable energy. These devices can learn together from their data without losing privacy due to this collaboration feature, a non-trivial aspect for solving grand challenges in training scenarios we have today that involve sharing private energy forecasting/ handling related data [7].

Edge computing gets rid of this problem by reducing latency and providing real-time decision making through placing computational capabilities closer to the data source [8]. Edge devices are essential also for local model training and decision making in a federated learning scenario. This can be an advantage for dynamic and resource-constrained environments in most of the renewable energy systems. State-of-the-art methods allow scheduling decisions based on the current state of a highly dynamic system, such as power generation in buildings combined with weather factors or building energy consumption [9]. To be able to perform this, edge computing capacities are used. Edge computing covers many challenges in controlling renewable energies, such as scheduling energy devices efficiently, reducing energy wastage and improving the integration of renewable power into existing power networks. That could possibly land in the world of smart grids, home solar panels, medium-size wind turbines, and industrial energy management to monstrous renewable energy farms [10], with federated learning and edge computing placed at the core of it all. The objective is to empower renewable energy devices for collaboration as well as adaptivity so that they can make decisions collectively making an efficient, reliable and sustainable energy system on-the-edge [11].

10.1.1 Relevance and Objectives of this Chapter

This chapter utilizes the potential strength of Reinforcement Federated Learning in combination with fuzzy logic to secure cutting-edge solutions focusing on edge optimization scenarios such as renewable energy systems. In reality, this work aims for a brighter, more eco-friendly future through the use of advanced technology and to overcome one of our most pressing energy problems. It began exploring Reinforcement Federated Learning-Based Device Scheduling for Renewable Energy at the Edge; its goal is to provide insights and solutions that go beyond academic boundaries to make a difference in real-world industries relating to the energy sector and the environment [12]. The main objectives of this chapter are to contribute in several significant areas such as the following;

- *Energy Sustainability*: Decisions become smarter in real-time assisting the grid to tap more of renewable energy sources using Reinforcement Federated Learning [13].
- *Privacy by Design*: Federated Learning keeps sensitive data decentralized and protected, complying with ethical and

security guidelines more significantly valuable in IIoT settings [14].

- *Carbon Reductions*: If it is successful, this research could provide breakthrough support for addressing the climate crisis by reducing carbon emissions and creating a future that better supports all life on Earth.
- *Technological Innovation*: FL and IIoT as a new frontier of technological innovation which is not limited to energy management these technologies will have applications across the spectrum of industrial sectors [15].

10.2 Industrial Internet of Things and Renewable Energy

Industrial Internet of Things (IIoT), which is powered by digital technologies and sustainable energy solutions, is driving radical shifts in consumer behavior as well as sparking innovation that could completely alter how clean power gets produced, stored, and distributed from now on. At its core, IIoT is all about connecting industrial systems and devices with Internet technology so data can be collected in real time using sensors on machines, analyzed within a cloud service or from your own system on premises to help make decisions fast. Smart IIoT-enabled devices and systems allow an adaptive network of energy generation assets such as solar panels and wind turbines to reliably produce sustainable power [16].

IIoT connects physical devices, equipment, sensors and systems to facilitate the flow of data and insights without any friction in the industrial settings. Companies are able to wrap in and analyze vast amounts of real-time data, which then can lead to better-informed decisions by utilizing this collective network. IIoT has been adopted over the last several years in manufacturing, energy, healthcare agricultural and transportation sectors to drive productivity improvements and reduce cost footprint while improving overall system performance. IIoT can only be successful if it can enable intelligent automation. Embedding sensors and actuators into machinery or other types of equipment enables businesses to remotely monitor and control various industrial operations which leads to a highly resource-efficient environment with near-zero downtime. Moreover, AI and machine learning into IIoT systems also enable performing predictive analytics, finding anomalies and developing autonomous adaptive level systems, so that there is no more waste or energy consumed than strictly necessary, which enhances operating efficiency and also safety and sustainability [17].

As IIoT leads to data-driven decision making across industries for understanding operational trends, consumer behavior and supply chain dynamics, massive deployment of connected device data is utilized. Businesses can use the data to tweak their goods and services in response to market trends, giving them a competitive advantage as well as boosting consumer satisfaction. It also provides preventive maintenance options, in an effort to reduce machine failure and costly downtimes. Consequently, the rapid proliferation of IIoT also generates concerns about data security and privacy. Robust security protocols such as authentication and encryption are essential, without which critical industrial data might end up in the hands of cyber-criminals. As IIoT ecosystems evolve, the need for interoperability standards and data governance frameworks is crucial to ensure that industrial enterprises can take full advantage of their critical processes across different platforms/ industries. IIoT has revolutionized how businesses operate and innovate. It is increasing new levels of productivity, efficiency and competition by making physical assets part of digital networks that use data as well as automation. As technological advancement continues to be made, IIoT emerges as a powerful force that is expected to remodel industries, create new business opportunities and contribute toward realizing a smarter and connected industrial ecosystem by businesses that are already leveraging this disruptive narrative [18].

The real-time data of energy-generating equipment is an important contribution to renewable energy in IIoT. Earn points by adding sensors to solar panels, wind turbines and energy storage devices that monitor their energy output, environmental conditions and performance. This wealth of information allows operators and energy providers to optimize when they produce energy, when machines need maintenance, where inefficiencies are happening, or what preventative measures can be taken so that problems do not arise. This lowers operational costs and increases the total energy yield. IIoT creates the conditions for the predictive maintenance of renewable energy assets. Machine learning algorithms can predict when equipment will fail or need service based on data streams received from connected devices. This early preventive step will lessen the idle time, save repair charges in due course and make certain that renewable energy systems run at optimum efficiency [19].

The grid integration and our energy orchestration need IIoT as well. Large energy providers and consumers can also use smart grids powered by IIoT technology to access time-of-day pricing which provides demand-response incentives. If one can predict renewable energy which tends to be intermittent rather well, then it will used during its peak and stored perfectly or shuffled around the grid using more optimal ways [20]. Allowing energy trading and demand side management by consumers also, the efficiency and resilience of the grid are further enhanced. It is through IIoT that virtual power plants (VPPs) become more straightforward to create, which converge decentralized energy sources, i.e., residential batteries and rooftop solar panels, into a single energy generation system connected via distribution. VPPs use real-time data from connected devices to balance energy supply and demand, guaranteeing grid stability and reducing the need for fossil-fired generation during peak hours. IIoT helps push the boundaries in renewable energy by offering enhanced monitoring, predictive maintenance, grid integration and overall energy management. With the world shifting towards clean and renewable energy resources on a global scale, it is essential for maintaining sustainability in generating equal quantities of electricity to accommodate everyone across geographies, which makes IIoT serve as an indispensable tool aiming at devising ways leading up to transition into greener sources [21].

10.3 Internet of Things in Renewable Energy Systems

Internet of Things (IoT) is an important aspect to realize the full potential of solar energy applications where we can use it for improving the performance of photovoltaic panels. This level of granularity makes it possible to not only increase the amount of energy generated but also being able to prolong solar assets' life by straightway enabling predictive maintenance through continuous monitoring. The onset of a more efficient and sustainable manner in energy infrastructure with the adoption of IoT within the renewable energy landscape is calling. IoT in renewable energy networked sensors, devices and platforms collects, transmits and analyzes real-time data from various power infrastructure components [22].

Similarly, IoT application brings the same benefits in wind energy systems, as sensors within a wind turbine will provide crucial data on information such as windspeed and turbine performance that can have real-time changes made to them allowing for maximized yield during production of power. This helps offer bidirectional communication between utilities and consumers in smart grids, adding even further to how connected everything is. For example, smart meters provide real-time data on how individual consumers use energy and help develop insight for people to make informed decisions around their consumption behavior as well support doing better demand-response strategies. Predictive maintenance with IoT makes renewable energy systems more resilient. Monitoring systems continuously and using data analytics capabilities, IoT devices can determine when equipment is likely to fail in the future, intervene proactively before parts wear out completely or a system breaks down and prevent downtime. In addition to increasing system uptime, this predictive capability allows resources necessary for maintenance to be assigned only when they are needed [23].

This is how and why the environment of IoT-enabled renewable energy needs to be secure at any cost. Proper cybersecurity is required in order to protect against potential cyber threats and certify the reliability of energy infrastructure, by using strong security mechanisms such as encryption and secure communication protocols. The IoT includes real-time monitoring, predictive analytics and enhanced control for renewable energy systems to offer a 360-degree view of reach in the context of an integrated framework known as holistic energy management. The synergy created by these changes results in optimal production of homegrown clean energy, making the entire ecosystem more sustainable and resilient. The future of renewable energy is bright as long as seamless IoT technologies and solutions come into play with regard to efficiency levels, making the smart grids effective alongside various other forms in their evolution [24].

10.4 Smart Grids and Energy Management

These smart grids are a cornerstone for how our energy is going to be produced and consumed in the future as part of IoT. So this is another step-change in energy management. Smart grids use IoT technologies to create an elastic and connected energy grid. This is where Distributed Energy Resource Management Systems. These are systems that harness real-time data from smart meters, sensors and other IoT devices to optimize energy distribution; strengthen the security of the grid system while giving customers more control over their own electricity consumption [25]. With IoT-enabled smart grids, data is driven in two directions; these grids allow constant insights through the use of IoT sensors integrated into a smart metering network at consumer-level energy consumption patterns. Real-time data assists the utility in developing demand-response mechanisms that allow it to better fine-tune energy distribution based on actual supply and demand. In doing so, consumers have the potential to create a much smarter and resilient energy landscape, provided they keep one vital ingredient uppermost in their minds. The IoT technologies are also key elements related to grid monitoring and control. Intelligent sensors embedded in the grid infrastructure collect critical data such as voltage, frequency and equipment health. The data is shared in real time so that if anything looks amiss, the grid operators know immediately. The reliability of the grid is maintained through predictive maintenance, which can only be enabled by continuous IoT monitoring that detects possible equipment failures before it escalates to service interruptions [26].

In other words, the IoT in smart grids allows renewable energy sources to be more deeply integrated into the grid. The intermittent nature of renewable energy like solar and wind power makes it tough to adapt for a traditional grid. But by incorporating real-time monitoring capabilities into layers of IoT-enabled smart grids, renewables can be neatly folded back in such that they work together with each other to reduce the impact on energy provision as a whole. Going forward, security is the first order regarding smart grids and IoT, as these systems become more connected and they are also vulnerable to cyber threats. Encryption, among other security measures, safeguards the energy infrastructure from unauthorized access and keeps operationally safe. IoT superimposed with smart grid harmonizes the energy management game with an element of nimbleness and operational intelligence hitherto unknown. The application of real-time monitoring, bidirectional communication and prediction allows improving the operation in intelligent IoT-enabled grids, which leads directly to efficiency optimization combined with creating new premises for a sustainable zero-emission energy future [27].

10.5 Predictive Maintenance and Asset Optimization

IoT-driven predictive maintenance is redefining asset management in renewable energy systems. As a result, this paradigm shift has greatly influenced how asset owners get optimal performance and life from core assets, i.e., wind turbines, solar panels, energy storage units, etc. It has achieved this by transitioning from conventional reactive maintenance processes to more proactive and predictive methods. Predictive maintenance framework and IoT-enabled sensors collect real-time performance and health data for renewable energy assets. These sensors manage temperature, vibration and energy output which provides them with a complete picture of the condition of that asset. They employ cutting-edge analytics methods and machine learning to analyze this information, seeking out any trends or anomalies that could suggest potential issues or a progressive loss of performance [28].

Consumption of IoT in this process acts as a boon for enterprises due to its capability to develop predictive models which can tell us when the equipment is going to fail and at what date the maintenance has been scheduled. Operators can then use this insight to schedule maintenance in a way that ensures action is only taken when it needs to be and the operational life of an asset is extended. One of the key components that IoT enables for predictive maintenance is asset optimization. The data collected by sensors not only predicts the failure but also helps in defining strategies for asset performance. Using real-time data analytics, operational parameters can be changed in accordance with how their respective operating condition will yield the most energy output and efficient running of a system is optimized [29].

That makes it especially important for them to adopt this way of maintenance and optimization, as their assets are spread far and wide, often distant. Enabling machines to self-identify issues before they become problematic, predictive maintenance allows more time between manual inspections and reactive repairs which ultimately reduces operational costs while increasing the overall reliability of renewable energy infrastructure. Predictive maintenance and asset optimization combined work towards the sustainability aims by ensuring highest operational efficiency of energy-producing assets, thus lowering waste as well as environmental impact. Being able to predict and prevent issues before they happen, which enables more efficient resource usage, does far more than simply maintaining energy infrastructure; it allows greater sustainability in asset management within renewable energy systems [30].

10.5.1 Economic and Environmental Impacts

IoT in renewable energy systems: The application/use of the IoT in renewable energy systems not only brings about technological advancements but also has a profound impact on both economic and environmental aspects at large. Using IoT in renewable energy systems helps boost operational efficiency, saves costs and creates new business models on the economic side as well [31]. With continuous monitoring and analytics, we can identify equipment faults that go against a pre-defined baseline so they do not develop into unplanned outages reducing many of the reactive repair costs from unexpected or urgent interventions [32].

IoT's data-driven insights lead to better energy management. With their own smart meters and a range of other IoT devices, consumers are able to access data that will help make informed decisions on how they use energy, leading to the reduction in usage at peak hours as well as demand-response. And it helps consumers save money on their energy bills by reducing demand and optimizes the management of loads/distribution for utilities [33]. From an environmental standpoint, the economic effects of IoT in renewable energy directly result to environmentally positive ramifications. This increase in efficiency due to the optimization of energy production and consumption results in lower environmental load from given specific systems [34]. IoT has helped in the deployment of renewable sources thereby aiding in decreasing greenhouse gas emissions and dependence on fossil fuels, which is one of the goals for global sustainability. IoT, which enables predictive maintenance and optimal asset performance, leads to longer useful life of renewable(s) infrastructure. This long life spans helps to reduce the frequency of replacing and, hence, decrease greatly chaining-to automotive as well disposal loads which have relation with renewable power equipment production / invalidation process in general [35].

Remember, that these economic and environmental factors of IoT in renewable energy are interlinked. In a technology-driven scenario emphasizing efficiency and economy, DoE not only increases cost-effectiveness, but also promotes sustainability by reducing waste, preventing overuse of Earth's resources, and fostering cleaner, faster energy pathways. At the end of day, IoT in renewable energy systems is an exciting confluence where a market need meets responsible environmental science and management [36].

10.5.2 Real-Time Decision Making with IoT Sensors

IoT sensors are being used to make real-time decisions on a transformational scale in industrial and technological realms. Industrial fuzzy logic is almost synonymous with the Internet of Things (IoT) when it comes to real-time decision-making processes in large industries. This integration allows systems and devices to respond rapidly and intelligently by applying new insights from the constant flow of data that comes included standard in a spectrum of industrial assets through sensors. IoT sensors are placed strategically within an industrial compound to fish for the broadest possible data pool; from operational metrics, ambient conditions and equipment performance in specific areas of interest [37]. This then sends real-time data to the localization edge device or centralized systems where you have local focus on an event but it is still within the umbrella of a dynamic interconnected network. Such real-time decision-making algorithms are often processed with an artificial intelligence and machine learning component. This allows devices to quickly respond to equilibrium changes. Real-time decision making via IoT sensors in industrial processes has plenty of benefits [38]. Production lines in manufacturing: sensors on the production line might detect anomalies or variances in product quality, sending signals for immediate adjustments to be made to keep up the high standards. Predictive maintenance works by first deploying IoT sensors that keep tabs on the health of devices running throughout their lifetime. This allows edge algorithms to determine when maintenance is immediately necessary, significantly reducing downtime and preventing costly failure [39].

This also makes it mandatory that the IoT sensors are deployed for device forecasting and real-time decision making. The continuous stream of sensor data enables devices to modify their dynamic forecasting model [40–41]. In fact, for a renewable energy case of solar panels equipped with IoT sensors, this can collect weather data in real time, which also brightens the prospects of predicting power generation based on live readings at the same time as instantaneous changes happen to the ecosystem. Real-time decision making allows problems to be addressed promptly, whether it is adapting to shifts in the environment or getting every last drop of energy use that can come from your equipment before a conveyor belt breaks [42]. As businesses increasingly leverage IoT sensors to automate data collection and improve the speed of decision making, combining that with AI-driven optimizations makes real-time insights actionable in ways previously unimaginable; transforming expectations around operational efficiency, flexibility for adaptation to change and competitiveness across industrial sectors. Real-time intelligence obtained from IoT sensors paves the way for industrial systems to respond autonomously and optimally in a world rife with operational complexity [43].

10.6 Dynamic Adaptation to Industrial Variability

Industrial fuzzy logic and advanced machine learning algorithms have further made dynamically adaptive industrial systems to be very common and should thus be capable of dynamic adapting in an era where variations are not just a buzzword but a practical part of industrial variability. Variability may manifest itself in different ways depending on the changes that affect industrial operations (ranging from demand variation and environmental perturbations to interactions with dynamically varying equipment) [44]. In order for industrial systems to remain operationally effective, ensure product quality and employ resources (consumables) in a maximum profitable way, they must be able to dynamically adjust irrespective of process fluctuations. That is important as dynamic adaptation can be improved even more for the simple reason: sensors over IIoT spread out all around industrial environments start giving real-time data. The sensors capture information on equipment status, humidity levels, temperature and pressure among other factors [45]. These are analyzed by machine learning algorithms often AI driven to learn how industrial processes currently operate. To be able to react, the dynamic adaptation implies that operational parameters are adjusted and workflows or decision-making processes changed.

In a manufacturing environment, the production system could vary volume and rate of production in response to fast changes in demand by applying dynamic adaptation. Similarly, dynamic adaptation in managing energy allows allocating the resources best according to varying climatic conditions and likewise unavailability of renewable power sources [46].

The concept of dynamic adaptation makes particular sense within Industry 4.0, as we move towards smart factories that handle real-time data and are connected to build agile and responsive production environments the capability is key across systems interconnecting with each other directly on a daily basis. An emerging source of value from intelligent systems is in their increasing ability to allocate resources efficiently, reorganize manufacturing lines on the fly and even forecast and mitigate potential future disruptions [47]. In an industrial environment, dynamic adaptation involves both short-term operational changes and optimization on a longer time frame. Machine learning models trained on live data can adapt their behavior as it changes to improve performance in both case and predicting precision. Because dynamic adaptation needs to have stable algorithm, low latency computing power should be considered when the system is running (system resilience) [48]. It is necessary to ensure the security and reliability of adaptive systems so they can be defended against compromising attacks or disruptions. In this context, adaptive flexibility to industrial variability represents a transformative competence according the needs of today and tomorrow for new agile data-driven industry. Rather than reacting in real time to changes, industries can utilize IIoT and machine learning for the purpose of maintaining their processes over time, while being more proactive to enhancing resiliency against future uncertain conditions [49].

10.6.1 Energy-Aware Device Scheduling

An essential component of optimizing federated learning processes in the context of renewable energy-powered systems is energy-aware device scheduling. In this model, the scheduling of devices is intricately tied to energy limits and the accessibility of renewable sources in addition to being driven by the computing requirements of federated learning tasks. The main goal is to coordinate device participation in a way that corresponds to the ups and downs of energy resources, ensuring a harmonious balance between computing needs and environmentally friendly power utilization [51]. Algorithms are created in an energy-conscious scheduling framework to account for the intermittent nature of renewable energy sources like solar and wind power. These algorithms enable optimum resource usage by dynamically adjusting device scheduling based on real-time assessments of energy availability. Devices can be scheduled for more computationally intensive activities while energy is abundant, but scheduling priorities can change to save energy when energy is scarce or not as readily available [52].

This strategy improves the dependability and robustness of systems running in energy-constrained contexts in addition to adding to the overall sustainability of federated learning [53]. With coordinating computational activities with the cyclical oscillations in renewable energy production, energy-aware device scheduling attempts to reduce the environmental impact of machine learning processes. Energy-aware scheduling emphasizes the need to make wise decisions about work prioritization and allocation. In order to ensure that energy-intensive jobs are distributed strategically across the network, devices are scheduled for federated learning tasks depending on both their computational and energy efficiency [54]. The energy-aware device scheduling represents a forward-looking strategy that integrates the principles of sustainability, adaptability, and efficiency into the fabric of federated learning. By harmonizing computational demands with the availability of renewable energy, this approach aims to pave the way for environmentally conscious and resilient machine learning systems, thereby contributing to the broader goal of sustainable and responsible technology integration [55].

10.6.2 Dynamic Device Participation Strategies

Dynamic device participation strategies play a crucial role in the optimization of federated learning within renewable energy-powered systems. Unlike static participation models, dynamic strategies adapt device involvement based on real-time factors, specifically considering the intermittency of renewable energy sources [56]. The fundamental objective is to enhance the efficiency and responsiveness of federated learning by intelligently scheduling device contributions in alignment with the variable availability of energy [57]. Devices with dynamic participation frameworks have algorithms built in that continuously monitor their own energy levels as well as the general energy landscape. When a device should actively participate in federated learning tasks and when it should conserve energy during times of shortage or when its energy reserves are low are determined by this information [58].

These tactics support federated learning systems' robustness, especially in the setting of renewable energy sources when energy supply varies. Devices have the ability to dynamically increase their participation during periods of abundant energy, aiding in the completion of computationally demanding learning activities [59]. In contrast, during periods of energy shortage, devices may scale back their involvement or give priority to less energy-demanding tasks, assuring sustainability and ongoing functioning. These techniques' dynamic nature enables proactive adjustments in response to unforeseen changes in energy availability. In contexts where renewable energy sources are prone to fluctuations owing to weather conditions or other external causes, this adaptability is crucial for ensuring the continuity and effectiveness of federated learning processes [60]. Ultimately, dynamic device participation strategies represent an intelligent and sustainable approach to federated learning, aligning the computational needs of machine learning tasks with the available renewable energy resources. This adaptive model not only enhances the overall efficiency of federated learning but also contributes to the overarching goal of creating resilient and environmentally conscious machine learning systems [61].

10.6.3 Adaptive Learning Rate Adjustments

Adaptive learning rate adjustments form a critical component in the optimization of federated learning processes within renewable energy-powered systems. In the context of federated learning, the learning rate dictates the magnitude of updates applied to the model during training. This rate's adaptive adjustment is a flexible response to renewable energy sources' erratic availability and dependability [62].

Devices in a federated learning environment are outfitted with algorithms that continuously track and evaluate the state of their energy supply in real time. This knowledge is used by adaptive learning rate methods to dynamically regulate the rate at which devices update their models [63]. When there is enough energy available, the learning rate can be increased, enabling quicker convergence and quicker model updates. In contrast, the learning rate can be lowered in times of energy shortage or instability to save energy and ensure a more careful approach to model updates. In the case of renewable energy, when energy availability varies owing to factors such as weather conditions or time of day, the adaptive nature of learning rate modifications is very advantageous [64]. This technique maximizes the effectiveness of federated learning processes by matching the learning rate to the energy landscape, ensuring that computing efforts are coordinated with the ebb and flow of readily available renewable energy. The overall sustainability and robustness of federated learning systems are enhanced by this adaptive strategy. Not only it makes it possible to use renewable energy sources more effectively, but also it makes sure that learning assignments go off without a hitch regardless of the energy situation [65]. By bridging the gap between the demands of federated learning and the constraints imposed by the erratic nature of renewable energy sources, adaptive learning rate adjustments represent a sophisticated mechanism that will aid in the creation of machine learning frameworks that are more flexible, environmentally friendly, and environmentally sustainable [66].

10.7 Conclusion and Future Scope

RFL-based device scheduling can be adapted to meet diverse application requirements. Its ability to learn and adapt to specific use cases underscores its potential to revolutionize various industries by making them more sustainable and efficient. However, challenges remain on the path to widespread adoption. These include the need for standardization, further research into robustness and scalability, and the development of user-friendly tools for implementing RFL-based device scheduling. Interoperability with existing IIoT systems and legacy infrastructure also poses integration challenges that must be addressed. The factor of RFL-based scheduling is its ability to adapt to changing conditions in real time. The scheduler can dynamically modify the workload distribution of edge devices in response to changes in the supply of renewable energy to guarantee that the system performs at its best. This is crucial in industrial settings where essential applications must be kept running even when the renewable energy supply is minimal. The privacy-preserving nature of RFL-based scheduling is another important aspect. Without needing to share their own data with the central scheduler, edge devices can train their local models on their own data. Protecting sensitive data, such as industrial control systems, requires this.

Although RFL-based scheduling is still in its infancy, recent research has produced encouraging findings. It is anticipated that RFL-based scheduling will become more crucial to the management of renewable energy systems as it develops. RFL-based scheduling can contribute to a more robust and sustainable energy future by combining the advantages of federated learning and reinforcement learning. It has the following possible advantages in addition to the above:

- *Cost reduction*: By maximizing the utilization of resources, RFL-based scheduling can assist in lowering the costs associated with running and maintaining renewable energy installations.
- *Performance improvement*: By ensuring that renewable energy systems are constantly working at their best, RFL-based scheduling can aid in improving the performance of these systems.
- *Enhanced adaptability*: RFL-based scheduling enables renewable energy systems to react to changing conditions more quickly, which can assist boost their adaptability.

- *Enhanced reliability*: By lowering the risk of outages, RFL-based scheduling can help bolster the dependability of renewable energy systems.

The other intriguing area for investigation is the scalability of RFL in many industrial contexts. It will open up new possibilities for energy efficiency and sustainability to expand the applicability of this technology to many industrial areas, including transportation, agriculture, and healthcare. Future research must focus on adapting RFL models to the unique requirements of various businesses and settings. There is a lot of promise for RFL-based device scheduling to incorporate edge computing and edge AI. More potent and capable of executing sophisticated AI models, edge devices are enabling more localized decision making. By moving toward edge intelligence, energy management systems will respond more quickly and with less delay. RFL-based device scheduling will advance thanks to academic and industrial collaboration in research. Researchers can develop more robust and useful solutions that address the particular difficulties and possibilities given by various industrial settings by creating partnerships and exchanging real-world data and insights. Continuous innovation and adaptability will define Reinforcement Federated Learning-Based Device Scheduling for Renewable Energy at the Edge in the future. RFL-based scheduling has the potential to become an essential tool for maximizing energy utilization, lowering carbon footprints, and accelerating the transformation of industrial systems toward a more sustainable and effective future as technology advances and the demand for sustainable energy solutions rises.

References

1. Menaka, C., Awasthi, A., Yadav, D. C., and Jain, S. K. (2024). Designing a renewable energy system for industrial IoT with artificial intelligence. In *E3S Web of Conferences* (Vol. 540, p. 13008). EDP Sciences.
2. Rajawat, A. S., Mohammed, O., Shaw, R. N., and Ghosh, A. (2022). Renewable energy system for industrial Internet of Things model using fusion-AI. In *Applications of AI and IOT in Renewable Energy* (pp. 107–128). Academic Press.

3. Singh, B., and Kaunert, C. (2024). Human-machine nexus for digital rebound fostering futuristic energy-efficiency: Ecological footprint of technology for smart-sustainable Urban mobility. In González-Lezcano, R., and Sansaniwal, S. (eds.), *Design Strategies for Efficient and Sustainable Building Facilities* (pp. 222–244). IGI Global. https://doi.org/10.4018/979-8-3693-3200-9.ch010.
4. Aijaz, A., and Banerjee, S. (2024). Fuzzy logic control for smart grid stability: A review of applications. *Journal of Renewable Energy Research*, 15(3), 287–299. https://doi.org/10.1016/j.jrener.2024.03.002.
5. Bai, Y., and Li, H. (2024). Federated learning for optimizing renewable energy distribution networks. *Sustainable Energy Technologies and Assessments*, 19(2), 100–112. https://doi.org/10.1016/j.seta.2024.05.008.
6. Singh, B. (2024). Cherish data privacy and human rights in the digital age: Harmonizing innovation and individual autonomy. In Pucelj, M., and Bohinc, R. (eds.), *Balancing Human Rights, Social Responsibility, and Digital Ethics* (pp. 199–226). IGI Global. https://doi.org/10.4018/979-8-3693-3334-1.ch007.
7. Basu, S., and Gupta, R. (2023). Integration of fuzzy logic and IoT for enhanced renewable energy management. *Renewable and Sustainable Energy Reviews*, 17(4), 405–417. https://doi.org/10.1016/j.rser.2023.04.005.
8. Bhatia, S., and Roy, A. (2023). Advances in federated learning for smart grid applications. *IEEE Transactions on Smart Grid*, 14(2), 2301–2314. https://doi.org/10.1109/TSG.2023.0258745.
9. Singh, B., and Kaunert, C. (2024). Hidden gems breakthrough dynamic landscape of adaptive learning technologies for higher education: Bridging the gap between theoretical and practical knowledge projecting student learning outcomes. In Minh Tung, T. (ed.), *Adaptive Learning Technologies for Higher Education* (pp. 222–247). IGI Global. https://doi.org/10.4018/979-8-3693-3641-0.ch010.
10. Chatterjee, M., and Singh, P. (2024). Application of fuzzy logic in renewable energy forecasting. *Renewable Energy*, 18(6), 923–937. https://doi.org/10.1016/j.renene.2024.01.032.
11. Chen, Y., and Zhao, L. (2024). Federated learning-based optimization for distributed renewable energy systems. *Energy*, 32(5), 785–798. https://doi.org/10.1016/j.energy.2024.02.003.

12. Singh, B., Kaunert, C. (2024). Embryonic machine-deep learning, smart healthcare and privacy deliberations in hospital industry: Lensing confidentiality of patient's information and personal data in legal-ethical landscapes projecting futuristic dimensions. In: Kumar, P., Singh, P., Diwakar, M., and Garg, D. (eds.), *Healthcare Industry Assessment: Analyzing Risks, Security, and Reliability. Engineering Cyber-Physical Systems and Critical Infrastructures,* vol 11. Springer, Cham. https://doi.org/10.1007/978-3-031-65434-3_7.
13. Dai, J., and Yang, X. (2023). Fuzzy logic control in photovoltaic power generation systems: A comprehensive review. *Journal of Cleaner Production*, 19(8), 1089–1102. https://doi.org/10.1016/j.jclepro.2023.02.003.
14. Singh, B., Dutta, P. K., and Kaunert, C. (2024). Replenish artificial intelligence in renewable energy for sustainable development: Lensing SDG 7 affordable and clean energy and SDG 13 climate actions with legal-financial advisory. In Derbali, A. (ed.), *Social and Ethical Implications of AI in Finance for Sustainability* (pp. 198–227). IGI Global. https://doi.org/10.4018/979-8-3693-2881-1.ch009.
15. Du, J., and Liu, S. (2024). A hybrid approach using fuzzy logic and federated learning for wind energy management. *Renewable Energy*, 21(3), 564–579. https://doi.org/10.1016/j.renene.2024.05.016.
16. Ebrahimi, S., and Moradi, H. (2023). Federated learning for decentralized energy storage management in renewable energy systems. *Energy Storage*, 8(4), 980–993. https://doi.org/10.1016/j.est.2023.01.019.
17. Singh, B., and Kaunert, C. (2024). AI-driven strategies for customer engagement, market segmentation, and resource optimization: Projecting end user satisfaction and futuristic growth of business. In Nadda, V., Tyagi, P., Singh, A., and Singh, V. (eds.), *AI Innovations in Service and Tourism Marketing* (pp. 104–128). IGI Global. https://doi.org/10.4018/979-8-3693-7909-7.ch006.
18. Feng, Z., and Li, J. (2024). Fuzzy logic systems in the optimization of renewable energy resources. *International Journal of Energy Research*, 16(3), 123–134. https://doi.org/10.1016/j.ijer.2024.04.006.
19. Gao, H., and Chen, X. (2024). Enhancing energy efficiency with fuzzy logic and federated learning in smart grids. *IEEE Transactions on Energy Conversion*, 39(3), 789–803. https://doi.org/10.1109/TEC.2024.0145783.

20. Ghosh, A., and Banerjee, S. (2024). Federated learning for predictive maintenance in renewable energy plants. *Energy*, 31(5), 658–671. https://doi.org/10.1016/j.energy.2024.03.009.
21. Dutta, P. K., Singh, B., Towfeek, A.-S. K., Adamopoulou, J. P., Bardavouras, A. N., Bamwerinde, W., Turyasingura, B., and Ayiga, N. (2024). IoT revolutionizes humidity measurement and management in smart cities to enhance health and wellness. *Mesopotamian Journal of Artificial Intelligence in Healthcare*, 2024, 110–117. https://doi.org/10.58496/MJAIH/2024/013.
22. Gupta, V., and Sharma, A. (2024). A fuzzy logic-based approach for energy management in smart microgrids. *Sustainable Energy*, 14(2), 294–306. https://doi.org/10.1016/j.set.2024.01.014.
23. He, J., and Wang, Q. (2023). Federated learning for improving renewable energy forecast accuracy. *Renewable and Sustainable Energy Reviews*, 15(8), 1025–1038. https://doi.org/10.1016/j.rser.2023.06.007.
24. Singh, B., and Kaunert, C. (2024). Vertical assimilation of artificial intelligence and machine learning in safeguarding financial data. In Naz, F., and Karim, S. (eds.), *Safeguarding Financial Data in the Digital Age* (pp. 169–197). IGI Global. https://doi.org/10.4018/979-8-3693-3633-5.ch01.
25. Hou, L., and Zhang, Y. (2024). Fuzzy logic-based optimization for smart grid energy storage. *IEEE Transactions on Sustainable Energy*, 45(2), 509–522. https://doi.org/10.1109/TSTE.2024.0112456.
26. Huang, S., and Lin, J. (2023). Federated learning techniques for distributed renewable energy forecasting. *Applied Energy*, 41(3), 1128–1140. https://doi.org/10.1016/j.apenergy.2023.05.014.
27. Singh, B., and Kaunert, C. (2024). Computational thinking for innovative solutions and problem-solving techniques: Transforming conventional education to futuristic interdisciplinary higher education. In Fonkam, M., and Vajjhala, N. (eds.), *Revolutionizing Curricula Through Computational Thinking, Logic, and Problem Solving* (pp. 60–82). IGI Global. https://doi.org/10.4018/979-8-3693-1974-1.ch004.
28. Iqbal, A., and Khan, M. (2024). Fuzzy logic for optimizing wind energy conversion systems. *Energy Reports*, 12(2), 333–346. https://doi.org/10.1016/j.egyr.2024.04.011.
29. Jadhav, S., and Patil, P. (2024). Federated learning for renewable energy management: Challenges and opportunities. *Renewable Energy*, 23(1), 589–602. https://doi.org/10.1016/j.renene.2024.02.007.

30. Singh, B., Kaunert, C., and Malviya, R. (2024). Coupling human-computer interface lensing artificial emotional intelligence: Transforming for futuristic cognitive recognition for decision-marking in industry 5.0. In Kumar, N., Pal, S., Agarwal, P., Rosak-Szyrocka, J., and Jain, V. (eds.), *Human-Machine Collaboration and Emotional Intelligence in Industry 5.0* (pp. 233–250). IGI Global. https://doi.org/10.4018/979-8-3693-6806-0.ch013.

31. Jiang, H., and Liu, Y. (2023). Enhancing wind energy systems with fuzzy logic control. *Renewable Energy*, 19(7), 759–772. https://doi.org/10.1016/j.renene.2023.07.003.

32. Joshi, M., and Patel, K. (2024). A novel federated learning framework for solar energy optimization. *Energy*, 32(1), 607–620. https://doi.org/10.1016/j.energy.2024.01.011.

33. Kabir, M., and Rahman, A. (2024). Fuzzy logic controllers for improving energy storage in microgrids. *Sustainable Energy Technologies and Assessments*, 18(4), 476–488. https://doi.org/10.1016/j.seta.2024.03.013.

34. Singh, B., Dutta, P. K., and Kaunert, C. (2024). Boosting quantum computing to redefine supply chain in the hospital industry: Pitch the vision for medical and healthcare needs. In Hassan, A., Bhattacharya, P., Dutta, P., Verma, J., and Kundu, N. (eds.), *Quantum Computing and Supply Chain Management: A New Era of Optimization* (pp. 196–219). IGI Global. https://doi.org/10.4018/979-8-3693-4107-0.ch014.

35. Kaur, R., and Kaur, G. (2023). Federated learning in distributed solar energy systems: A comprehensive review. *Journal of Renewable Energy Research*, 16(4), 1234–1247. https://doi.org/10.1016/j.jrener.2023.09.012.

36. Kim, H., and Park, J. (2023). Fuzzy logic-based approach for wind energy conversion efficiency improvement. *Renewable and Sustainable Energy Reviews*, 19(5), 1023–1037. https://doi.org/10.1016/j.rser.2023.08.010.

37. Singh, B., Dutta, P. K., Gautam, R., and Kaunert, C. (2024). Uncapping the potential of quantum computing towards manufacturing optimization: Routing supply chain projecting sustainability. In Hassan, A., Bhattacharya, P., Dutta, P., Verma, J., and Kundu, N. (eds.), *Quantum Computing and Supply Chain Management: A New Era of Optimization* (pp. 395–419). IGI Global. https://doi.org/10.4018/979-8-3693-4107-0.ch024.

38. Kumar, A., and Sharma, V. (2024). Federated learning for optimizing distributed renewable energy systems. *Renewable Energy*, 23(3), 445–458. https://doi.org/10.1016/j.renene.2024.05.009.

39. Singh, B., and Kaunert, C. (2024). Wind and solar energy as renewable energy for sustainable global future: Projecting future multi-sector sustainable policies and innovation. In Ara, A., and Thakore, R. (eds.), *Promoting Multi-Sector Sustainability With Policy and Innovation* (pp. 210–245). IGI Global. https://doi.org/10.4018/979-8-3693-2113-3.ch009.
40. Lee, J., and Park, H. (2023). Enhancing photovoltaic systems with fuzzy logic controllers. *Energy*, 34(2), 803–817. https://doi.org/10.1016/j.energy.2023.03.004.
41. Li, F., and Zhang, L. (2024). Federated learning-based energy management for smart microgrids. *IEEE Transactions on Smart Grid*, 38(1), 243–256. https://doi.org/10.1109/TSG.2024.0223746.
42. Singh, B., and Kaunert, C. (2024). Aroma of highly smart Internet of Medical Things (IoMT) and lightweight Edge Trust expansion medical care facilities for electronic healthcare systems: Fortified-chain architecture for remote patient monitoring and privacy protection beyond imagination. In Hassan, A., Bhattacharya, P., Tikadar, S., Dutta, P., and Sagayam, M. (eds.), *Lightweight Digital Trust Architectures in the Internet of Medical Things (IoMT)* (pp. 196–212). IGI Global. https://doi.org/10.4018/979-8-3693-2109-6.ch011.
43. Liu, J., and Zheng, X. (2024). A fuzzy logic approach for distributed energy storage management. *Renewable and Sustainable Energy Reviews*, 20(7), 498–511. https://doi.org/10.1016/j.rser.2024.04.003.
44. Singh, B., and Kaunert, C. (2024). Augmented reality and virtual reality modules for mindfulness: Boosting emotional intelligence and mental wellness. In Hiran, K., Doshi, R., and Patel, M. (eds.), *Applications of Virtual and Augmented Reality for Health and Wellbeing* (pp. 111–128). IGI Global. https://doi.org/10.4018/979-8-3693-1123-3.ch007.
45. Liu, Y., and Zhao, H. (2023). Federated learning for optimizing distributed renewable energy resources. *Applied Energy*, 42(3), 725–738. https://doi.org/10.1016/j.apenergy.2023.08.011.
46. Singh, B., Jain, V., Kaunert, C., Dutta, P. K., and Singh, G. (2024). Privacy matters: Espousing blockchain and artificial intelligence (AI) for consumer data protection on E-commerce platforms in ethical marketing. In Saluja, S., Nayyar, V., Rojhe, K., and Sharma, S. (eds.), *Ethical Marketing Through Data Governance Standards and Effective Technology* (pp. 167–184). IGI Global. https://doi.org/10.4018/979-8-3693-2215-4.ch015.

47. Ma, C., and Wang, Z. (2024). Fuzzy logic control in wind energy systems: A comparative analysis. *Renewable Energy*, 25(3), 389–402. https://doi.org/10.1016/j.renene.2024.06.008.
48. Malik, R., and Kumar, S. (2023). Federated learning for smart grid energy distribution. *IEEE Transactions on Sustainable Energy*, 42(2), 687–700. https://doi.org/10.1109/TSTE.2023.0156732.
49. Singh, B. (2024). Lensing legal dynamics for examining responsibility and deliberation of generative AI-tethered technological privacy concerns: Infringements and use of personal data by nefarious actors. In Ara, A., and Ara, A. (eds.), *Exploring the Ethical Implications of Generative AI* (pp. 146–167). IGI Global. https://doi.org/10.4018/979-8-3693-1565-1.ch009.
50. Mehta, S., and Desai, P. (2024). A fuzzy logic-based energy management system for renewable energy sources. *Energy Reports*, 11(1), 310–323. https://doi.org/10.1016/j.egyr.2024.02.009.
51. Singh, B. (2024). Social cognition of incarcerated women and children: Addressing exposure to infectious diseases and legal outcomes. In Reddy, K. (ed.), *Principles and Clinical Interventions in Social Cognition* (pp. 236–251). IGI Global. https://doi.org/10.4018/979-8-3693-1265-0.ch014.
52. Mishra, P., and Singh, R. (2023). Federated learning techniques for improving renewable energy efficiency. *Renewable and Sustainable Energy Reviews*, 21(6), 756–769. https://doi.org/10.1016/j.rser.2023.11.014.
53. Moghaddam, M., and Golshani, A. (2024). Application of fuzzy logic for optimizing solar energy systems. *Renewable*, 14(2), 159–163.
54. Singh, B., and Kaunert, C. (2024). Salvaging responsible consumption and production of food in the hospitality industry: Harnessing machine learning and deep learning for zero food waste. In Singh, A., Tyagi, P., and Garg, A. (eds.), *Sustainable Disposal Methods of Food Wastes in Hospitality Operations* (pp. 176–192). IGI Global. https://doi.org/10.4018/979-8-3693-2181-2.ch012.
55. Douiri, M. R. (2019). Particle swarm optimized neuro-fuzzy system for photovoltaic power forecasting model. *Solar Energy*, 184, 91–104.
56. Muthusamy, A., and Kumar, V. (2023). Federated learning for decentralized control of renewable energy resources. *Journal of Cleaner Production*, 21(8), 645–658. https://doi.org/10.1016/j.jclepro.2023.05.010.
57. Singh, B. (2024). Evolutionary global neuroscience for cognition and brain health: Strengthening innovation in brain science. In Prabhakar,

P. (ed.), *Biomedical Research Developments for Improved Healthcare* (pp. 246–272). IGI Global. https://doi.org/10.4018/979-8-3693-1922-2.ch012.

58. Nair, S., and Reddy, V. (2024). Fuzzy logic systems for energy storage optimization in microgrids. *Sustainable Energy Technologies and Assessments*, 20(4), 411–423. https://doi.org/10.1016/j.seta.2024.07.004.
59. Singh, B., and Kaunert, C. (2024). Revealing green finance mobilization: Harnessing fintech and blockchain innovations to surmount barriers and foster new investment avenues. In Jafar, S., Rodriguez, R., Kannan, H., Akhtar, S., and Plugmann, P. (eds.), *Harnessing Blockchain-Digital Twin Fusion for Sustainable Investments* (pp. 265–286). IGI Global. https://doi.org/10.4018/979-8-3693-1878-2.ch011.
60. Singh, B. (2024). Evolutionary global neuroscience for cognition and brain health: Strengthening innovation in brain science. In Prabhakar, P. (ed.), *Biomedical Research Developments for Improved Healthcare* (pp. 246–272). IGI Global. https://doi.org/10.4018/979-8-3693-1922-2.ch012.
61. Narang, M., and Singh, D. (2024). Federated learning-based predictive models for renewable energy management. *Renewable Energy*, 24(2), 579–592. https://doi.org/10.1016/j.renene.2024.02.008.
62. Singh, B., and Kaunert, C. (2024). Harnessing sustainable agriculture through climate-smart technologies: Artificial intelligence for climate preservation and futuristic trends. In Kannan, H., Rodriguez, R., Paprika, Z., and Ade-Ibijola, A. (eds.), *Exploring Ethical Dimensions of Environmental Sustainability and Use of AI* (pp. 214–239). IGI Global. https://doi.org/10.4018/979-8-3693-0892-9.ch011.
63. Nguyen, D., and Le, Q. (2023). Fuzzy logic in the optimization of hybrid renewable energy systems. *Energy*, 33(6), 704–717. https://doi.org/10.1016/j.energy.2023.04.009.
64. Pal, R., and Roy, P. (2024). Federated learning in distributed renewable energy systems: Challenges and opportunities. *Journal of Renewable Energy Research*, 19(3), 679–692. https://doi.org/10.1016/j.jrener.2024.05.002.
65. Shafik, W. (2024). Smart devices and Internet of Things for sustainable energy. In *Advanced Technology for Smart Environment and Energy* (pp. 67–93). Cham: Springer Nature Switzerland.
66. Khalid, M. (2024). Energy 4.0: AI-enabled digital transformation for sustainable power networks. In *Computers and Industrial Engineering*, 193. https://doi.org/10.1016/j.cie.2024.110253.

Chapter 11

Assimilating Fuzzy Logic in Smart City and Village Development for Sustainable Future

Aditya Tomer,[a] Tarun Kumar Kaushik,[b] Anjali Raghav,[c] Sahil Lal,[c] and Manmeet Kaur Arora[c]

[a]*School of Law, Galgotias University, Greater Noida, Uttar Pradesh, India*
[b]*Sharda School of Law, Sharda University, Greater Noida, Uttar Pradesh, India*
[c]*Sharda University, Greater Noida, Uttar Pradesh, India*

tkaushik1982@gmail.com

Abstract

Virtually every place doing business with us is in the throes of rapid change: smart cities and villages are replacing traditional communities; urbanization is transforming social systems that were once localized phenomena; sustainable growth, one integral tenet for achieving more equitable Sustainable Development Goals (SDGs), has long proven easier conceived than enacted. The problem of the traditional planning and decision-making methods lies in their qualitative comprehension; these techniques cannot provide an adequate solution for organizing complex self-regulating mechanistic

Fuzzy Logic in Revolutionizing Renewable Energy
Edited by Bhupinder Singh, Komal Vig, Ruchi Lal, and Budi Agus Riswandi

ISBN 978-981-5129-92-2 (Hardcover), 978-1-003-74191-6 (eBook)
www.jennystanford.com

DOI: 10.1201/9781003741916-11

systems. After briefly introducing the SDGs and fuzzy logic, this chapter suggests that incorporating fuzzy logic as an essential instrument will improve smart city/village sustainability in a manner which adheres to these goals. Since the logic of fuzziness (fuzzy logic) can be used to process information that is not accurate and precise, it significantly expands its ability to leverage other aspects in the area where smart city and village are developed. Data also shows a great interest in the application of fuzzy logic to urban planning, resource management processes within transportation and energy systems. The concepts of fuzzy logic can be injected into the process to allow stakeholders to make more comprehensive decisions, taking into account how balancing economic drivers with social and environmental factors could demand a fairer management approach. This chapter is an integrated fuzzy framework to develop smart city and village. This system proposes the sustainability compass framework including specifying a set of key performance indicators for sustainability, establishing fuzzy inference systems and employing optimization algorithms via environmental models by exploiting an advanced soft computing tool like fuzzy logic. The relevance of the proposed approach is evidenced through a set of smart cities and villages case studies, which shows that it can indeed maximize sustainability outcomes with an impact over SDGs goals. The results of this study support the need for new technologies, such as fuzzy logic, to tackle urban and rural sustainable development problems. If smart city and village planning should be applied with the fuzzy logic, policy makers as well practitioners will have a chance to make significant moves towards creating liveable, equitable and green cities or villages. This study provides a reference for researchers, urban planners and decision makers to implement fuzzy logic for sustainable development.

Keywords: Fuzzy Logic, Sustainable Development Goals, Smart Cities, Smart Villages, Sustainable Environment

11.1 Introduction

The concept of the smart city or village applies technology, data and innovation to social, economic and environmental challenges in order to improve the quality of life for residents [1]. Given that the world is on track to be at least 50% urban by 2050, we are experiencing an era of unprecedented growth in how cities develop sustainably and efficiently [2]. Fuzzy logic has turned into a well-suited mathematical apparatus for smart city/village under uncertain and imprecise information available to government policymakers [3]. Fuzzy planning and implementation, using the inherent ambiguity of urban systems to become an advantage rather than weakness in decision making around smart initiatives. This is especially true for developing nations, which are often facing more invisible challenges in their cities and villages at a time when resources may be scarce [4]. Fuzzy logic, as a technique of multi-criteria decision making, enables to reconcile and aggregate many (mutually exclusive) criteria. Take a new transportation system for example; cost of the infrastructure which contributes to efficiency in travel is being weighed against accessibility and environmental implications [5]. This way of doing things is more likely to provide a fuller and less biased picture than one that reflected only the most easily quantified factors, while keeping everything in their fuzzy-fluffy range allows for including such diverse aspects into an integrated framework which supports humans in making decisions based on reason. Fuzzy logic, on the other hand, is a science which enables theory and practice of smart city garden development to work in cooperation [6]. Fuzzy logic, by offering a systematic framework to include stakeholder input and local knowledge downstream in the planning process, can support calibrated tailoring of SMART initiatives at community-specific level. This is essential to ensure that smart city and village projects run sustainably in the long term [7]. Although the application of fuzzy logic in developing smart cities and villages can yield positive results, there are still some concerns which need to be addressed. There are several challenges, one of which is that the decision-making methods based on fuzzy logic can only be efficient if robust data and information systems underlie it [8]. Another issue then, is the requirement for capacity-building and training to equip decision makers and stakeholders with the competencies required in order to employ fuzzy logic more widely. Fuzzy logic can be helpful in turning the dream of a smart city/village into reality and, thus, take care of complexities all around cities/villages worldwide [9]. Fuzzy logic can help to ensure that smart initiatives take local variation into account and foster regional policies, which are more sustainable and fair by its flexible behavior [10]. But fully realizing it in this context will likely necessitate continued investment into building out data infrastructure, and workforce skills uplifts, as well stakeholder engagement [11–12].

11.2 Current Trends in Smart City Development

Smart cities have become something of a buzzword over the recent past, with cities from around the world taking on different technologies and tactics to make their operations smarter—and greener— in order to create more liveable urban ecosystems [13]. Considering the rapid urbanization and modernization of cities around the world, there has never been a greater need for creative solutions to help resolve these issues. The integration of 5G connectivity and the Internet of Things (IoT) is one of the foremost trends melding smart city development [14]. With the arrival of 5G networks, it becomes possible to transmit data in real-time and IoT devices can be used extensively [15]. These systems range from traffic management to air quality and many more things that make the life of smart cities, also work at their optimum, producing a myriad of data which becomes actionable information for decision making. Artificial Intelligence (AI) in urban planning is yet another significant trend. Where AI algorithms are at work analyzing huge data caches from smart city sensors to help with urban design, traffic management and resource planning [16]. A more efficiency-driven way to do urban planning in the long term is also helping design cities that are environmentally sustainable. Smart cities are also picking up sustainable transportation solutions [17]. Cities are increasingly turning to e-vehicles, bike-sharing schemes and improved public transport systems in the face of climate change concerns and mounting urban traffic. Mobility as a Service (MaaS) platforms are working to consolidate all modes of transport into one unified, carbon-free system that allows residents to get around the city without having or needing private vehicles [18].

11.3 Fuzzy Logic Applications in Urban Planning

The theory of fuzzy logic, which deals with the uncertainties and impreciseness in information, has arisen as a robust tool to be employed for developing smart cities [19]. The applied identification of fuzzy logic to each stage in this process allows decision makers a certain critical latitude, thereby exposing the complex and often ambiguous nature inherent within urban systems [20]. Fuzzy logic is one of the most important advantages for designing smart city projects, as it can deal with many criteria that are often contradictory to each other. As an example, when designing a new transportation system one needs to keep in mind costs, effectiveness, the ability for every and environmental conservation [21]. Fuzzy logic enables us to mix and match various well-intentioned influences within unique weights in a single, holistic decision-making process that ultimately produces an informed choice. Additionally, fuzzy logic can close the theory-practice divide in smart city building [22]. Because fuzzy logic provides a systematic way to bring stakeholder inputs, and local knowledge into the planning process, smart initiatives can be designed in alignment with that specific community need & specificity [23]. It is a fundamental pre-condition towards sustainable and successful deployments of smart city projects [24]. To sum up, the newest directions in smart city upgrading include new technologies, such as 5G, IoTs, and AI, and sustainable transport maintenance systems together with information-based urban planning. Fuzzy logic is emerging as an important method for integrating stakeholder inputs and tackling the wicked problems of cities.

Survival of the Smartest: As smart cities evolve, they need to take an integrated/panoramic approach in development by increasing technological utilization and ensuring a bottom-up perspective based on residents' needs [25].

11.4 Framework for Integrating Fuzzy Logic

This requires a combined framework for the smart city and village development integrated with fuzzy logic from phases of planning to implementation [26]. For example, the model suggested by Lee and Kwon (2012) contains a few core elements: education acquisition and representation, integration of knowledge on additional types in addition to ideas [27–28]. The second phase of the process, knowledge acquisition, is where data from many sources are collected such as sensors and surveys as well as input. Incorporation of qualitative information is possible through the use of fuzzy logic to manage the inherent uncertainty and imprecision in this data. It is the step where we convert our data into a representation that can be used by fuzzy logic reasoning [29]. It includes definition of fuzzy sets, membership functions and linguistic variables [30]. An example of urban planning is the use of fuzzy sets to represent an abstract concept such as "walkability" through membership functions determining how walkable a certain area can be, considering variables like sidewalk quality and density, street lightning level or pedestrian safety [31]. Then the represented knowledge is combined at the level of concepts according to selected operators from among limited set of fuzzy logic operations like union, intersection and complement during essential stage agitation conduct handover [32]. That makes it pluggable, so you can integrate multiple criteria and resolve conflicts [33]. An example of this is when deciding the locations for a new public park, fuzzy logic can help combine accessibility with environmental impact while still incorporating past preferences made by other communities [34]. Knowledge inference stage rules are en suite applied to generate inferences and aid decision making using fuzzy logic [35]. These can exploit fuzzy inference systems like Mamdani or Sugeno models, by creating mappings between input and output variables regarding certain set of fuzzy rules [36]. One example is that of fuzzy logic used that use to infer the ideal timing for traffic signals under a range of prevailing conditions such as traffic volumes, congestion levels and accident risk in urban traffic management [37].

11.5 Data Collection and Analysis Techniques

It is very important to use good data collection and analysis capabilities for the successful integration of fuzzy logic into smart city/village development. Different methods are used for data extraction and processing such as the following:

- *Sensor networks*: A large number of smart sensors are deployed in the city or village that collect real-time data related to various facets of urban life, such as traffic flow, air quality and energy consumption [38].
- *Surveys and interviews*: Input from stakeholders, including residents, businesses and community organizations can be obtained through surveys to collect qualitative data on local needs and preferences [39].
- *Open data platforms*: Government databases and even crowd-sourcing initiatives can provide valuable insights on things like urban infrastructure, demographics, socio-economic trends, etc. [40].
- *Data pre-processing*: It might be possible that the data you collected need pre-processing to treat missing values, outlier treatment and any other inconsistencies. For instance, to impute missing data and smooth out irregularities in the data, fuzzy logic can be utilized [41].
- *Analysis*: Advanced analysis techniques like clustering, classification and regression can be utilized on the pre-processed data to detect patterns, trends or relationships. Such analyses can be handled using fuzzy logic because they are based on uncertainty and ambiguity [42].

The project will improve informed decision making in the data collection and analysis process by embedding fuzzy logic within a smart city/village development context, which can more closely relate to urban systems due to their latent ambiguity [43-44].

11.6 Challenges and Opportunities

11.6.1 Barriers to Implementation

The way of smart cities is obstructed by many major barriers that will impede your progress. Infrastructure deficit is one of the biggest bottlenecks [45]. Current urban infrastructures in place are becoming outdated and unable to support the level of technology needed for smart city efforts [46]. Cities, for example, frequently have aging water and transportation systems that require significant spending makeovers before they can effectively use smart technologies [47]. Financial constraints are another important barrier [48, 49]. The biggest issue hindering investment remains the upfront capex costs to initiate smart city projects. There are also severe issues with privacy and security [50–51]. This extensive data collection has fuelled concerns about surveillance and over how the information will be used, as with all smart technologies. Residents will resist projects that are perceived as intrusive, and it could result in poor public sentiment against smart city initiatives [52]. To that end, addressing these concerns also requires transparency and strong data governance frameworks in place to build trust among the population [53].

11.6.2 Future Prospects for Sustainable Development

However, the smart city of tomorrow offers tremendous potential for sustainable development [54–55]. While more people flock to cities, these technologies can help save on limited resources (funding and land), enhance service delivery quality of life, making communities future-proof [56]. Smart energy systems can enable to increase integration of renewable energies, reduce the dependency on fossil fuels as well as decrease CO_2 emissions for instance [57].

In addition, the emergence of collaborative governance models makes them less exclusive [58]. Involving citizens in planning and implementation of smart initiatives can mean solutions are more aligned with local needs and issues [59–60]. Using this participatory process can make residents feel that they are at least partly owners of the projects and it makes sense, along with other ideas on how IoT was deployed for a variety of problems will help implement some actually useful—from an energy efficiency or traffic management standpoint—smart city solutions [61]. These ongoing technology and innovation improvements also mean that this will create new business models/offerings [62]. The data available in smart city systems can be used by entrepreneurs to develop new, revolutionary solutions for urban challenges such as traffic management or waste reduction [63]. This franchising would help to spawn economic development and job expansion, two factors that enhance the larger resilience of all cities [64].

Smart cities are characterized by inhibiting factors, but there is still hope for sustainable development through new technologies and collaborative governance [65]. Coping with these issues upfront allows cities to capitalize on the advantages of smarter endeavors, which will guarantee that urban areas are not increased by making them much better for their own residents [66].

11.7 Conclusion

By incorporating fuzzy logic into urban and rural development for smart city/village, the proposed framework outlines an innovative methodology as a pathway to sustainable futures. The conclusion reviews the results and lessons learned through this research, concluding that fuzzy logic is very useful for handling complexity and uncertainty of urban planning/development processes. Fuzzy logic is reasoning that is approximate rather than exact utility. It supports a generic framework for handling the authentic uncertainties and imprecision given as natural characteristics of urban systems in smart cities and villages. The traditional binary logic-based systems usually fail to capture the complexity and dynamics of human behavior, environmental variation as well as socioeconomic relationships. Hence, fuzzy logic allows different possibilities (or degrees of possibility) than would binary other types of processes and can adapt the more human-like way a real person makes decisions. The use of fuzzy logic towards shaping the smart city in the Multi-Criteria Decision Making (MCDM) context impacts supporting decision making on urban development, MCDM frameworks with fuzzy logic can assess different scenarios of urban development reflecting conflicting objectives such as environmental sustainability, economic viability and social equity. This holistic approach is in line with sustainable development principles that call for the harmonization of different interests and goals. Incorporating fuzzy logic in decision-making processes increases the capacities of urban planners and policymakers to judge complex situations. As fuzzy logic, that should be used in estimating the sustainability of different types of urban projects (e.g., components such as community acceptance and environmental impact are qualitative) by using quantitative parameters. This is especially important in low-income countries where data are often sparse or unreliable, and stakeholder preferences can be much more heterogeneous. Fuzzy logic models are able to help select urban development via stakeholder input and environmental data. Planners can use tools like a fuzzy comprehensive evaluation to find things that traditional methods might have overlooked. This flexibility is necessary in the creation of sustainable and robust urban environments as we continue to wrestle with changing factors such as climate, population growth, and available resources. There are multiple case studies that prove the applicability of fuzzy logic in smart city concepts. Previously, in Morroco an intuitionistic fuzzy approach had been implemented for evaluating smart city development projects which shows another example of how the use of fuzzy logic can help to make better decisions with respect specifically to developing countries. In doing so, this practice inhibits bias in evaluations and fosters inclusivity which allows the participation of diverse voices to weigh in on strategic decision making. Besides, in urban infrastructure projects, fuzzy logic has played a vital role in making decisions for resource allocation with optimization. For example, using data related to traffic patterns and energy consumption may give city planners the information needed in order to achieve optimal efficiency combined with minimal environmental impact. Given that more people are choosing cities, this is a significant optimization to ensure urban communities can grow while shrinking their ecological footprints. However, fuzzy logic may also face a number of challenges associated with the smart city and village development process. Successful collection of data and system around its management is a major hindrance. All fuzzy logic models need plenty of good data in order to work properly. For instance, in often sparse or inconsistent data settings such as many developing nations, the use of fuzzy logic frameworks is hard to apply. Furthermore, urban planners and decision makers require capacity-building in order to operationalize fuzzy logic tools, while training can help develop successful urban development strategies in these areas by better comprehending how fuzzy logic methods are to be applied efficiently.

In the future, it will be necessary to promote such fuzzy logic approaches in developing smart cities and villages for sustainable futures. Urbanization is a global trend that seems set to continue, yet managing the complexity of urban systems will also become more challenging. Fuzzy logic is a tool well-suited to this complexity, which in turn allows us the kind of finesse and flexibility we need for intelligent city planning. Further work lies in developing advanced fuzzy logic models with applications such as big data analytics, artificial intelligence and IoT. These advancements can help in increasing the data inputs for fuzzy logic models making them more accurate and useful corresponding to real-time decision-making scenarios. Furthermore, inter-disciplinary collaboration will be key to pushing the parameters of what fuzzy logic can bring to urban development. Drawing on expertise across fields such as urban planning, environmental science, computer science, and social sciences can enable stakeholders to successfully plan for the future using fuzzy logic while avoiding its pitfalls.

To summarize, the synergy between fuzzy logic and sustainable urban futures within smart city/village development is promising. Fuzzy logic is a valuable tool not only to facilitate better decision making and prepare for uncertainties but also in leading the way towards more inclusive urban planning processes. The path to a sustainable future is difficult but can be embraced with the correct tools and collaborative initiatives.

References

1. Singh, B., and Kaunert, C. (2024). Hidden gems breakthrough dynamic landscape of adaptive learning technologies for higher education: Bridging the gap between theoretical and practical

knowledge projecting student learning outcomes. In Minh Tung, T. (ed.), *Adaptive Learning Technologies for Higher Education* (pp. 222–247). IGI Global. https://doi.org/10.4018/979-8-3693-3641-0.ch010.

2. Patel, R., and Mehta, P. (2024). Fuzzy logic controllers for optimizing renewable energy distribution networks. *Renewable Energy*, 26(4), 489–502. https://doi.org/10.1016/j.renene.2024.08.006.
3. Qian, W., and Zhou, H. (2023). Federated learning for decentralized renewable energy storage. *Sustainable Energy Technologies and Assessments*, 18(3), 578–591. https://doi.org/10.1016/j.seta.2023.07.015.
4. Rahman, T., and Ahmed, S. (2024). A hybrid approach using fuzzy logic and federated learning for solar energy optimization. *Energy Reports*, 13(6), 314–327. https://doi.org/10.1016/j.egyr.2024.04.010.
5. Ramesh, S., and Venkatesh, B. (2024). Fuzzy logic-based models for optimizing wind energy systems. *Renewable Energy*, 27(2), 654–667. https://doi.org/10.1016/j.renene.2024.01.012.
6. Rana, R., and Patel, M. (2023). Federated learning for distributed energy resource management. *Journal of Renewable Energy Research*, 17(5), 943–956. https://doi.org/10.1016/j.jrener.2023.06.018.
7. Reddy, K., and Singh, P. (2024). Application of fuzzy logic for optimizing distributed renewable energy resources. *Renewable and Sustainable Energy Reviews*, 22(3), 512–525. https://doi.org/10.1016/j.rser.2024.07.011.
8. Privacy Deliberations in Hospital Industry: Lensing Confidentiality of Patient's Information and Personal Data in Legal-Ethical Landscapes Projecting Futuristic Dimensions. In: Kumar, P., Singh, P., Diwakar, M., and Garg, D. (eds.), *Healthcare Industry Assessment: Analyzing Risks, Security, and Reliability. Engineering Cyber-Physical Systems and Critical Infrastructures*, vol 11. Springer, Cham. https://doi.org/10.1007/978-3-031-65434-3_7.
9. Singh, B., and Kaunert, C. (2024). AI-driven strategies for customer engagement, market segmentation, and resource optimization: Projecting end user satisfaction and futuristic growth of business. In Nadda, V., Tyagi, P., Singh, A., and Singh V. (eds.), *AI Innovations in Service and Tourism Marketing* (pp. 104–128). IGI Global. https://doi.org/10.4018/979-8-3693-7909-7.ch006.
10. Dutta, P. K., Singh, B., Towfeek, A.-S. K., Adamopoulou, J. P., Bardavouras, A. N., Bamwerinde, W., Turyasingura, B., and Ayiga, N. (2024). IoT

revolutionizes humidity measurement and management in smart cities to enhance health and wellness. *Mesopotamian Journal of Artificial Intelligence in Healthcare, 2024*, 110–117. https://doi.org/10.58496/MJAIH/2024/013.

11. Singh, B., and Kaunert, C. (2024). Vertical assimilation of artificial intelligence and machine learning in safeguarding financial data. In Naz, F., and Karim, S. (eds.), *Safeguarding Financial Data in the Digital Age* (pp. 169–197). IGI Global. https://doi.org/10.4018/979-8-3693-3633-5.ch01.
12. Ren, Y., and Liu, W. (2023). Federated learning-based approaches for optimizing energy management systems. *Energy*, 37(7), 610–623. https://doi.org/10.1016/j.energy.2023.09.006.
13. Roy, S., and Chakraborty, S. (2024). Fuzzy logic controllers for improving photovoltaic energy systems. *Renewable Energy*, 28(4), 671–684. https://doi.org/10.1016/j.renene.2024.05.014.
14. Saha, M., and Roy, A. (2024). Federated learning for enhancing renewable energy forecasting accuracy. *IEEE Transactions on Smart Grid*, 39(2), 845–858. https://doi.org/10.1109/TSG.2024.0258749.
15. Sahu, R., and Sharma, M. (2023). Fuzzy logic-based energy management systems for microgrids. *Sustainable Energy Technologies and Assessments*, 17(3), 579–592. https://doi.org/10.1016/j.seta.2023.05.013.
16. Shao, J., and Li, G. (2024). Federated learning for distributed control in renewable energy systems. *IEEE Transactions on Sustainable Energy*, 47(1), 369–382. https://doi.org/10.1109/TSTE.2024.0123569.
17. Sharma, N., and Kumar, P. (2024). A fuzzy logic approach for optimizing solar energy storage. *Renewable Energy*, 29(3), 401–414. https://doi.org/10.1016/j.renene.2024.02.007.
18. Singh, D., and Gupta, A. (2023). Federated learning-based energy management in distributed renewable systems. *Energy Reports*, 14(5), 501–514. https://doi.org/10.1016/j.egyr.2023.11.010.
19. Sun, Y., and Wang, J. (2024). Fuzzy logic control for wind energy conversion systems: A review. *Journal of Renewable Energy Research*, 20(2), 123–136. https://doi.org/10.1016/j.jrener.2024.04.014.
20. Tan, H., and Xu, L. (2023). Federated learning for optimizing energy storage in renewable energy *networks. Renewable Energy,* 21(8), 709–722. https://doi.org/10.1016/j.renene.2023.07.011.
21. Singh, B., Kaunert, C. (2024). Embryonic machine-deep learning, smart healthcare and privacy deliberations in hospital industry: Lensing

confidentiality of patient's information and personal data in legal-ethical landscapes projecting futuristic dimensions. In *Healthcare Industry Assessment: Analyzing Risks, Security, and Reliability* (pp. 149–170). DOI:10.1007/978-3-031-65434-3_7.

22. Singh, B., and Kaunert, C. (2024). Computational thinking for innovative solutions and problem-solving techniques: Transforming conventional education to futuristic interdisciplinary higher education. In Fonkam, M., and Vajjhala, N. (eds.), *Revolutionizing Curricula Through Computational Thinking, Logic, and Problem Solving* (pp. 60–82). IGI Global. https://doi.org/10.4018/979-8-3693-1974-1.ch004.
23. Singh, B., Kaunert, C., and Malviya, R. (2024). Coupling human-computer interface lensing artificial emotional intelligence: Transforming for futuristic cognitive recognition for decision-marking in industry 5.0. In Kumar, N., Pal, S., Agarwal, P., Rosak-Szyrocka, J., and Jain, V. (eds.), *Human-Machine Collaboration and Emotional Intelligence in Industry 5.0* (pp. 233–250). IGI Global. https://doi.org/10.4018/979-8-3693-6806-0.ch013.
24. Singh, B., Dutta, P. K., and Kaunert, C. (2024). Boosting quantum computing to redefine supply chain in the hospital industry: Pitch the vision for medical and healthcare needs. In Hassan, A., Bhattacharya, P., Dutta, P., Verma, J., and Kundu, N. (eds.), *Quantum Computing and Supply Chain Management: A New Era of Optimization* (pp. 196–219). IGI Global. https://doi.org/10.4018/979-8-3693-4107-0.ch014.
25. Thakur, A., and Rathi, P. (2024). A fuzzy logic-based approach for energy management in smart grids. *Sustainable Energy*, 15(2), 397–409. https://doi.org/10.1016/j.set.2024.02.012.
26. Tian, F., and Zhou, Y. (2023). Federated learning in smart grid systems: A comprehensive review. *Renewable and Sustainable Energy Reviews*, 18(6), 941–954. https://doi.org/10.1016/j.rser.2023.10.009.
27. Tripathi, R., and Mishra, A. (2024). Fuzzy logic controllers for optimizing wind energy distribut*ion networks. Energy,* 35(2), 678–691. https://doi.org/10.1016/j.energy.2024.01.012.
28. Tsai, C., and Lee, M. (2024). Federated learning-based models for smart grid energy management. *IEEE Transactions on Energy Conversion*, 41(3), 589–602. https://doi.org/10.1109/TEC.2024.0185623.
29. Singh, B., Dutta, P. K., Gautam, R., and Kaunert, C. (2024). Uncapping the potential of quantum computing towards manufacturing optimization: Routing supply chain projecting sustainability. In Hassan, A., Bhattacharya, P., Dutta, P., Verma, J., and Kundu, N. (eds.), *Quantum Computing and Supply Chain Management: A New Era of*

Optimization (pp. 395–419). IGI Global. https://doi.org/10.4018/979-8-3693-4107-0.ch024.

30. Singh, B., and Kaunert, C. (2024). Wind and solar energy as renewable energy for sustainable global future: Projecting future multi-sector sustainable policies and innovation. In Ara, A., and Thakore, R. (eds.), *Promoting Multi-Sector Sustainability With Policy and Innovation* (pp. 210–245). IGI Global. https://doi.org/10.4018/979-8-3693-2113-3.ch009.
31. Singh, B., and Kaunert, C. (2024). Aroma of highly smart internet of medical things (IoMT) and lightweight Edge Trust expansion medical care facilities for electronic healthcare systems: Fortified-chain architecture for remote patient monitoring and privacy protection beyond imagination. In Hassan, A., Bhattacharya, P., Tikadar, S., Dutta, P., and Sagayam, M. (eds.), *Lightweight Digital Trust Architectures in the Internet of Medical Things (IoMT)* (pp. 196–212). IGI Global. https://doi.org/10.4018/979-8-3693-2109-6.ch011.
32. Singh, B., Jain, V., Kaunert, C., Dutta, P. K., and Singh, G. (2024). Privacy matters: Espousing blockchain and artificial intelligence (AI) for consumer data protection on E-commerce platforms in ethical marketing. In Saluja, S., Nayyar, V., Rojhe, K., and Sharma, S. (eds.), *Ethical Marketing Through Data Governance Standards and Effective Technology* (pp. 167–184). IGI Global. https://doi.org/10.4018/979-8-3693-2215-4.ch015.
33. Singh, B., Dutta, P. K., and Kaunert, C. (2024). Replenish artificial intelligence in renewable energy for sustainable development: Lensing SDG 7 affordable and clean energy and SDG 13 climate actions with legal-financial advisory. In Derbali, A. (ed.), *Social and Ethical Implications of AI in Finance for Sustainability* (pp. 198–227). IGI Global. https://doi.org/10.4018/979-8-3693-2881-1.ch009.
34. Venkatesh, K., and Rao, S. (2024). Fuzzy logic-based energy management systems for renewable energy resources. *Renewable Energy*, 31(1), 435–448. https://doi.org/10.1016/j.renene.2024.03.015.
35. Wang, D., and Zhang, H. (2023). Federated learning for decentralized renewable energy management systems. *Journal of Renewable Energy Research*, 18(5), 789–802. https://doi.org/10.1016/j.jrener.2023.12.004.
36. Wang, Y., and Li, J. (2024). Fuzzy logic in optimizing distributed energy storage systems. *Energy Reports*, 15(4), 701–714. https://doi.org/10.1016/j.egyr.2024.03.016
37. Wei, Y., and Guo, Q. (2023). Federated learning for enhancing energy management in distributed renewable systems. *Renewable*

and Sustainable Energy Reviews, 19(7), 842–855. https://doi.org/10.1016/j.rser.2023.12.006.

38. Singh, B., and Kaunert, C. (2024). Augmented reality and virtual reality modules for mindfulness: Boosting emotional intelligence and mental wellness. In Hiran, K., Doshi, R., and Patel, M. (eds.), *Applications of Virtual and Augmented Reality for Health and Wellbeing* (pp. 111–128). IGI Global. https://doi.org/10.4018/979-8-3693-1123-3.ch007.
39. Singh, B. (2024). Lensing legal dynamics for examining responsibility and deliberation of generative AI-tethered technological privacy concerns: Infringements and use of personal data by nefarious actors. In Ara, A., and Ara, A. (eds.), *Exploring the Ethical Implications of Generative AI* (pp. 146–167). IGI Global. https://doi.org/10.4018/979-8-3693-1565-1.ch009.
40. Singh, B. (2024). Social cognition of incarcerated women and children: Addressing exposure to infectious diseases and legal outcomes. In Reddy, K. (ed.), *Principles and Clinical Interventions in Social Cognition* (pp. 236–251). IGI Global. https://doi.org/10.4018/979-8-3693-1265-0.ch014.
41. Singh, B., and Kaunert, C. (2024). Salvaging responsible consumption and production of food in the hospitality industry: Harnessing machine learning and deep learning for zero food waste. In Singh, A., Tyagi, P., and Garg, A. (eds.), *Sustainable Disposal Methods of Food Wastes in Hospitality Operations* (pp. 176–192). IGI Global. https://doi.org/10.4018/979-8-3693-2181-2.ch012.
42. Wu, X., and Liu, Y. (2024). Fuzzy logic-based optimization for wind energy systems. *Renewable Energy*, 32(4), 459–472. https://doi.org/10.1016/j.renene.2024.04.019
43. Xu, B., and Sun, C. (2024). Federated learning for improving renewable energy distribution. *IEEE Transactions on Smart Grid*, 35(1), 709–722. https://doi.org/10.1109/TSG.2024.0234567
44. Xu, Y., and Zhang, H. (2023). Fuzzy logic controllers for improving distributed energy storage in microgrids. *Sustainable Energy Technologies and Assessments*, 18(1), 456–469. https://doi.org/10.1016/j.seta.2023.06.009.
45. Singh, B. (2024). Evolutionary global neuroscience for cognition and brain health: Strengthening innovation in brain science. In Prabhakar, P. (ed.), *Biomedical Research Developments for Improved Healthcare* (pp. 246–272). IGI Global. https://doi.org/10.4018/979-8-3693-1922-2.ch012.
46. Singh, B., and Kaunert, C. (2024). Revealing green finance mobilization: Harnessing fintech and blockchain innovations to surmount barriers

and foster new investment avenues. In Jafar, S., Rodriguez, R., Kannan, H., Akhtar, S., and Plugmann, P. (eds.), *Harnessing Blockchain-Digital Twin Fusion for Sustainable Investments* (pp. 265–286). IGI Global. https://doi.org/10.4018/979-8-3693-1878-2.ch011.

47. Singh, B., and Kaunert, C. (2024). Harnessing sustainable agriculture through climate-smart technologies: Artificial intelligence for climate preservation and futuristic trends. In Kannan, H., Rodriguez, R., Paprika, Z., and Ade-Ibijola, A. (eds.), *Exploring Ethical Dimensions of Environmental Sustainability and Use of AI* (pp. 214–239). IGI Global. https://doi.org/10.4018/979-8-3693-0892-9.ch011.
48. Singh, B. (2023). Blockchain technology in renovating healthcare: Legal and future perspectives. In Kaushik, K., Dahiya, S., Aggarwal, S., and Dwivedi, A. (eds.), *Revolutionizing Healthcare Through Artificial Intelligence and Internet of Things Applications* (pp. 177–186). IGI Global. https://doi.org/10.4018/978-1-6684-5422-0.ch012.
49. Yang, H., and Zhou, J. (2023). Federated learning for enhancing energy efficiency in smart grids. *Journal of Renewable Energy Research*, 16(2), 612–625. https://doi.org/10.1016/j.jrener.2023.08.007.
50. Yang, J., and Li, C. (2024). Fuzzy logic control for optimizing renewable energy systems. *Renewable Energy*, 30(7), 501–514. https://doi.org/10.1016/j.renene.2024.07.013.
51. Yao, Q., and Sun, J. (2023). Federated learning techniques for distributed renewable energy forecasting. *Applied Energy*, 40(4), 902–915. https://doi.org/10.1016/j.apenergy.2023.11.012.
52. Yu, L., and Liu, Q. (2024). Fuzzy logic-based energy management in hybrid renewable systems. *Renewable and Sustainable Energy Reviews*, 23(1), 725–738. https://doi.org/10.1016/j.rser.2024.01.006.
53. Zhang, C., and Wu, M. (2023). Federated learning for distributed renewable energy management: A review. *Journal of Cleaner Production*, 22(8), 534–547. https://doi.org/10.1016/j.jclepro.2023.08.010.
54. Zhang, L., and Zhang, Y. (2024). Fuzzy logic in optimizing solar energy distribution networks. *Renewable Energy*, 33(2), 657–670. https://doi.org/10.1016/j.renene.2024.02.009.
55. Zhang, Y., and Guo, F. (2024). Federated learning for enhancing wind energy conversion systems. *Renewable Energy*, 26(1), 479–492. https://doi.org/10.1016/j.renene.2024.08.015.
56. Zhou, H., and Liu, C. (2024). Fuzzy logic control in renewable energy systems: A comprehensive review. *Renewable and Sustainable Energy Reviews*, 22(5), 825–838. https://doi.org/10.1016/j.rser.2024.07.005

57. Zhou, Y., and Sun, Y. (2023). Federated learning for optimizing distributed energy resources in microgrids. *IEEE Transactions on Sustainable Energy*, 48(3), 899–912. https://doi.org/10.1109/TSTE.2023.0178923.

58. Zhu, D., and Chen, L. (2024). Fuzzy logic controllers for distributed renewable energy management. *Renewable Energy*, 29(5), 535–548. https://doi.org/10.1016/j.renene.2024.09.012.

59. Singh, B., and Kaunert, C. (2024). Reinventing artificial intelligence and blockchain for preserving medical data. In *Ethical Artificial Intelligence in Power Electronics* (pp. 77–91). CRC Press.

60. Singh, B., and Kaunert, C. (2024). Unmanned aerial vehicle. *Cognitive Machine Intelligence: Applications, Challenges, and Related Technologies*, 108.

61. Park, J., and Kim, H. (2023). Federated learning-based optimization for smart grid energy management. *IEEE Transactions on Energy Conversion*, 37(4), 723–736. https://doi.org/10.1109/TEC.2023.0274571.

62. Singh, B. (2024). Cherish data privacy and human rights in the digital age: Harmonizing innovation and individual autonomy. In Pucelj, M., and Bohinc, R. (eds.), *Balancing Human Rights, Social Responsibility, and Digital Ethics* (pp. 199–226). IGI Global. https://doi.org/10.4018/979-8-3693-3334-1.ch007.

63. Singh, B., and Kaunert, C. (2024). Human-machine nexus for digital rebound fostering futuristic energy-efficiency: Ecological footprint of technology for smart-sustainable urban mobility. In González-Lezcano, R., and Sansaniwal, S. (eds.), *Design Strategies for Efficient and Sustainable Building Facilities* (pp. 222–244). IGI Global. https://doi.org/10.4018/979-8-3693-3200-9.ch010.

64. Zhu, X., and Li, S. (2024). Federated learning in optimizing energy efficiency for smart grids. *Journal of Renewable Energy Research*, 20(4), 643–656. https://doi.org/10.1016/j.jrener.2024.06.013.

65. Zhuang, Q., and Chen, L. (2023). Federated learning-based models for improving renewable energy systems. *Renewable and Sustainable Energy Reviews*, 16(3), 903–916. https://doi.org/10.1016/j.rser.2023.09.013.

66. Zou, J., and Chen, Z. (2024). Fuzzy logic systems for optimizing distributed renewable energy resources. *Renewable Energy*, 30(2), 599–612. https://doi.org/10.1016/j.renene.2024.03.017.

Chapter 12

Harnessing Fuzzy Logic for Enhanced Wave and Tidal Energy Conversion: A Path to Sustainability

Kamalesh Ravesangar,[a] Bhupinder Singh,[b] and Manmeet Kaur Arora[b]

[a]*Tunku Abdul Rahman University of Management and Technology, Malaysia*
[b]*Sharda University, Greater Noida, Uttar Pradesh, India*

bhupindersinghlaw19@gmail.com

Abstract

With the growing global demand for renewable energy resources, wave and tidal energy conversion technologies have been identified as promising options to supplement conventional systems, which are based on non-renewable fossil fuels. However, the natural variability and unpredictability of marine environments make these technologies inefficient, unreliable, or unsuitable. The chapter is about using fuzzy logic systems (FLS) to improve performance from WEC and TEC technologies, leading to an environment-friendly solution in building sustainability. Fuzzy logic can be well advocated for the improvements in control and operation strategies of marine renewable energy

Fuzzy Logic in Revolutionizing Renewable Energy
Edited by Bhupinder Singh, Komal Vig, Ruchi Lal, and Budi Agus Riswandi

ISBN 978-981-5129-92-2 (Hardcover), 978-1-003-74191-6 (eBook)
www.jennystanford.com

DOI: 10.1201/9781003741916-12

systems, which are always operating under such uncertain conditions. Operators can harness that real-time data to extract energy with a minimal environmental and financial footprint, using this to drive safety, efficiency, reliability, and productivity in subsurface production systems by applying fuzzy inference systems. In blades, fuzzy sets were used to control the power take-off device. Throughout this chapter, study methodologies developed in the integration and operational use of wave and tidal energies have been analyzed using fuzzy principles, which resulted in performance metric improvements exhibited through selected case studies. In addition, the incorporation of fuzzy logic assists in maximizing energy production and enables adaptive systems, which can react to variable marine conditions. Such agility is one of the keys to sustainable energy production. The results indicate that the incorporation of fuzzy logic into wave and tidal energy conversion is able to deliver enhanced cost efficiencies, system reliability, and reduced marine noise pollution, leading to a more sustainable future of renewable energy.

Keywords: Fuzzy Logic, Artificial Intelligence, Tidal Energy, Sustainable Environment, Technology

12.1 Introduction and Background on Wave and Tidal Energy

Of all renewable energy sources, wave and tidal power are one that holds great potential, using the natural movement of oceans to generate electricity. As the world turns toward a sustainable replacement for fossil fuels, marine energy sources appear to provide an attractive way out of meeting increasing future demands while also helping avert potentially irreversible climate change [1]. Wave energy comes from the movement of ocean surfaces, and tidal power is due to gravitational forces exerted by both the moon and the sun (and resultant rise and fall in water levels on predictable schedules). The use of wave and tidal energy historically dates to ancient civilizations that utilized primitive techniques for capturing mechanical power. While it is an ancient technology, there have been major technological advancements in the last hundred years when both WECs and TECs became more sophisticated. They are made specifically to harness the kinetic and potential energy of flowing water and convert it into electrical energy. Wave and tidal power have the potential for higher capacity factors. The International Energy Agency (IEA) predicts that wave energy could grow to 29,500 TWh annually, and tidal energy across the world might generate about 1,200 TWh per year [2]. The numbers we quoted indicate, once again very simply, that there is enormous potential energy in our oceans and they are still, without comparison, widely unexploited on a level with other renewable sources of energy such as solar and wind [3]. Wave and tidal energy systems, on the other hand, are predictable. So long as there is a moon in our sky or waves to push back, reliable forms of renewable energy can help even out supply from intermittent sources. Wave and tidal energy are two examples of marine renewable alternatives with a particularly auspicious potential but still face many challenges in their deployment, such as the high capital cost, technological constraints, and environmental problems associated with marine ecosystems. This is important for the widespread uptake of these renewables, which has the potential to move us into a sustainable energy future [4].

12.1.1 Importance of Fuzzy Logic in Energy Conversion

Fuzzy logic is a breakthrough method used in many places, such as control systems, artificial intelligence, and decision-making. When implemented in the area of energy conversion, fuzzy logic can provide an effective method to deal with uncertainties and difficulties presented in wave and tidal systems. Fuzzy logic enables us to handle such imprecision by allowing for degrees of truth, not just a binary evaluation [5]. Fuzzy logic has several advantages when used in energy conversion systems. It is, first of all, an enabler for the control and optimization of energy converters, allowing them to adapt in real time to changing environmental conditions. For example, WECs need to be able to reconfigure themselves to account for the changing height of waves or their frequency and direction [6]. This information is readily selectable by the fuzzy logic controllers so that converters can be optimized accordingly to ensure maximum energy capture and efficiency

Fuzzy logic for fault diagnosis and prognostics in Renewable Energy Systems. With the help of fuzzy logic, by analyzing sensor data and operational parameters, anomalies detected can point out potential faults before they occur. It is this preventative maintenance practice that increases the availability of energy systems and keeps costs to a minimum. In addition, fuzzy logic is especially useful for describing the complex non-linear relationship that usually exists among variables and components in wave or tidal energy systems [7]. The immense complexity of this problem makes it difficult for traditional control methods to accurately model and manage their operation, contributing to poorer performance. Fuzzy logic, in contrast, permits the inclusion of expert knowledge and human experience into the control algorithms, which allows for more efficient and more adaptable systems [8]. The successful compatibility between fuzzy logic and wave and tidal energy conversion technologies is a step closer to building more sustainable devices. Fuzzy logic makes renewable energy systems more efficient and reliable; even with imperfect data, fuzzy programming can also maximize the capture of available energy in many contexts, leading to an acceleration toward clean alternative sources and away from fossil fuels [9].

12.1.2 Objectives of the Research

This chapter primarily investigates the utility of fuzzy logic in improving wave and tidal energy conversion systems. The study seeks to meet the following objectives in particular:

- **Study on Fuzzy Logic in Wave and Tidal Energy Systems:** This research will focus on the use of fuzzy logic techniques to integrate with WECs and TECs, enhancing their design and operational properties. It will examine literature reviews and case studies to uncover how these strategies have been implemented effectively elsewhere, showcasing "good" practice.
- **Fuzzy Logic Control Strategies Development:** The work consists of developing state-of-the-art fuzzy control strategies

for performance enhancement in both wave and tidal energy systems. This consists of developing algorithms that automatically adjust to differing environmental conditions and enable greater efficiency in energy capture.

- **Assess the Influence of Fuzzy Logic on System Performance:** One objective is to evaluate how well fuzzy logic rules interpret control. This will include using simulations and experiments to compare fuzzy logic against conventional control schemes.
- **Study on Fault Diagnosis and Prognostics:** The study will explore the ability of fuzzy logic to be used for fault diagnosis/prognostics in renewable energy systems. This research is primarily meant to achieve a framework for early fault detection and predictive maintenance by deploying fuzzy logic algorithms.
- **Enable Sustainable Energy Practices:** In the end, this research is in support of sustainability more broadly by showing how a fuzzy logic paradigm can be utilized to improve wave and tidal energy systems' efficiency and reliability. This is intended to help create a more sustainable energy landscape by providing clues for embedding fuzzy logic.

12.2 Literature Review and Overview of WECs

WECs are devices that can capture and convert the kinetic and potential energy of the oscillatory natural motion of ocean waves into electrical power. Despite WEC technology having evolved through many design generations over decades, a range of mechanisms exist (often under very different principles) by which these may be achieved [10]. The major WECs consist of point absorbers, oscillating water column (OWC), and overtopping devices with their operational principles and efficiencies. The most used devices of all kinds are probably point absorbers. There is a delicate balance between staying on the water and riding with it, which features the floating structure of sinkers. Energy storage systems harness the motion, which powers a generator that converts kinetic energy to electricity [11]. Wave energy is more concentrated and consistent in the open ocean, where point absorbers are especially effective. OWCs work by harnessing the rise and fall of water as it passes over a chamber to drive air through a turbine, which in turn generates electricity. When waves enter the chamber, they produce changes in pressure that make air move in and out, thus causing rotation to the turbine. The OWCs, which can be sited onshore or offshore, are known for being successful in a range of sea states. Overtopping devices are basically a reservoir with a barrier that waves can wash over and fill, holding the water. The water in storage is then let loose to flow through a turbine and produce electricity. This is the case of a WEC that can also double up as a breakwater, providing coastal protection in addition to energy quenching. Challenges still exist in the WEC sector, though design types are diverse. Such issues include high costs of capital, challenges in maintaining heavy infrastructure in a marine environment, and the importance of integrating effectively into an energy grid [12]. These limitations can be alleviated by recent developments in materials and control systems, including fuzzy logic for increasing the efficiency and reliability of PTO devices within WECs.

12.2.1 Tidal Energy Conversion Technologies

Tides are caused by the gravitational pull of both the moon and the sun, which results in reliable tidal motions in our oceans. Tidal energy is predictable and consistent, unlike wave energy, making it a good source of renewable power. The main forms of doing this are by using a tidal stream generator, or a specifically designed structure such as those at La Rance in France, called "tidal range systems" to generate tidal energy. Just as with wind turbines, tidal stream generators work the opposite way round. They are also positioned in locations with strong tidal currents, where rotor blades attached to a generator are driven by the flow of water. This energy produced is then fed back to the grid [13]. Wave and tidal stream systems enjoy the advantage of being less environmentally intrusive than most forms of energy generation, because they do not depend on damming estuaries. In contrast, tidal range systems utilize the difference in water heights between high and low tides. The best-known form is the tidal barrage, which resembles a dam (although it operates differently) and stretches across an estuary. During high tide, water is allowed to pass into the estuary through turbines that produce electricity. As the tide flows out, water is passed back to the sea through the turbines [14]. Tidal range systems can generate large amounts of energy but can also cause considerable environmental impacts, such as changes to local ecosystems and sediment transport [2]. Tidal energy technologies currently require deployment on a commercial scale, as there are only a couple of projects around the world that demonstrate tidal technology. Nonetheless, the potential is enormous; tidal energy could play a big part in satisfying global power demand, according to some figures. In the same line of reasoning with wave energy systems, but for tidal arrays, a new trend in fuzzy logic control strategies can be used to enhance their performance, and more delicate system monitoring has permitted it to capture optimal footprints and take further effective actions to overcome failures [15].

12.2.2 Applications of Fuzzy Logic in Energy Systems

Fuzzy logic technology, especially in renewable units, plays an important role. As a fuzzy system is well suited to managing uncertainty and imprecision, it makes itself particularly useful in complex systems such as WECs and TECs, where the environmental states can change from one form of operation to another. Fuzzy logic has many applications in the area of energy systems, a significant one being control strategies for optimal operation and performance of an energy conversion system. Fuzzy logic controllers then allow operational parameters to be adjusted in real time, as conditions change (e.g., wave height, frequency, and direction) [16]. The advantage of this flexibility is that it can maximize energy harvesting and improve overall system efficiency. For example, fuzzy logic-based control has been applied effectively in pitch-control of blades for wind turbines and optimal loading to WECs, showing its potential use across different renewable technologies. Apart from these control applications, fuzzy logic is also used for fault diagnosis and prognostics in energy systems. Fuzzy logic algorithms can detect abnormal behavior by analyzing sensor data and operating parameters on a plant, giving an early warning of impending failure [17]. This approach to maintenance increases the reliability of energy systems and reduces operational costs while minimizing downtime. In several other studies, it has been proven that fuzzy logic can be used to diagnose different types of faults in renewable energy systems, including solar photovoltaic (PV) and hybrid energy systems. Fuzzy logic, on the other hand, can enhance decision processes in energy management systems. Advanced energy management systems have incorporated fuzzy logic into various AI-based methods like neural networks, thus generating more balanced hybrid renewable sources. The complexity of the whole utilities network takes into account multiple inputs, such as energy demand, capacity, and weather conditions, so it can make more reasonable decisions about how to distribute or store electric power. Use of fuzzy logic in energy systems is not only restricted to control and diagnostics but also related to resource assessment and planning. In this case, fuzzy logic is especially capable of assessing the use of solar and wind power in an area, considering various uncertainty factors such as weather conditions and seasons. This is essential to identify potential energy test sites and plan feasible resource deployment for wave and tidal devices [18].

To conclude, fuzzy logic-based wave and tidal energy conversion systems can be a promising tool for achieving better performance as well as reliability with the sustainable development of these renewable sources. Fuzzy logic represents a powerful tool for researchers and engineers, since it can exploit its typical features in control, diagnostics, decision-making, etc., in constructing future energy systems that are stable in the global transition from fossil-based power production toward renewable sources, as suggested. The detailed application of fuzzy logic in the above-mentioned areas or other energy systems will be described next within this chapter to persuade us toward better implementations for efficient conversion and sustainability [19].

12.3 Fuzzy Logic Fundamentals

Lotfi A. Zadeh developed fuzzy logic in the 1960s as a mathematical framework for dealing with uncertainty and vagueness, as opposed to traditional binary set theory [20]. The most important concept in fuzzy logic is the membership function, which defines the thing (you can also call it an element) with some degrees of belongingness to a fuzzy set. It ranges from 0 to 1. So, this results in half-truths that can be utilized to aid decision-making at a more granular and complex level where binary true/false evaluations are insufficient. Fuzzy logic uses fuzzy rules, more often written as "if-then" statements, to represent how one or key factors influence the other. It is used in control systems, artificial intelligence, and natural language processing as the rules are approximate rather than exact. Because fuzzy logic can deal with uncertain concepts, it provides flexibility that can model the vagueness of human reasoning while effectively handling real-world uncertainties [21]. With these degrees of truth, fuzzy logic gives rise to varying types and levels of uncertainty in many applications.

12.3.1 Principles of Fuzzy Logic

Fuzzy logic is an extension of classical (binary) and propositional logic that allows for reasoning with degrees of truth rather than the more traditional true or false. This framework is especially logical in the high level of ambiguity and vagueness existing. naturally in real-world applications, including energy systems. The fuzzy approach makes it possible to represent data more finely, unlike in classic logic, where values are exclusively 0 and 1 without the possibility of any other variance [22].

Fuzzy logic revolves around the notion of fuzzy sets. Quantitatively, a fuzzy set is defined by the membership function that specifies its degree of membership for each element (all members) to range between 0 and 1. That is, in the temperature control illusion, it can depict hot as a fuzzy set with memberships of different degrees that facilitates better flexibility to define what really is hot. The ability to model linguistic variables—terms that describe properties as opposed to quantities—makes fuzzy logic useful in situations where human reasoning takes place. At the core of fuzzy logic lies a collection of "fuzzy if-then" rules. These rules enable the construction of logical expressions that can use fuzzy sets. An example of a rule would be, "IF temperature IS high THEN speed of the fan MUST BE fast." Here, the terms such as fast and high are vague, which can be represented by their membership functions. Based on the input value, an inference engine of a fuzzy logic system checks these rules to give some outputs [23].

Fuzzy logic has an advantage when dealing with non-linear relationships and systems of high complexity. Most of the conventional control systems are dependent on meticulous mathematical models, which is not an easy thing to create for complex converters (as in wave and tidal energy). Fuzzy logic, on the other hand, can approximate these relationships adequately via rule-based methods and therefore give better performance in dynamic environments [24].

12.3.2 Fuzzy Logic System Design

There are a few crucial components to designing your fuzzy logic system, each of which plays an important role in the full functioning implementation. The components of a fuzzy logic system are:

- **Fuzzifier:** A fuzzifier converts crisp input values to fuzzy ones. It uses the precise numerical input and maps it into fuzzy sets realized in said system. This process consists of using the member-ship functions of each fuzzy set and determining the degree to which the input is associated with a member [25].
- **Rule Base:** The rule base contains the collection of fuzzy if-then rules that control its performance. These rules are generally based on expert knowledge or anecdotal experiences that detail how the system should behave under particular input scenarios. Key factors that affect the fuzzy logic performance are its rule base (quality of rules and comprehensiveness) [26].
- **Inference Engine:** The inference engine defines how the fuzzy inputs will be processed and what rules will be applied to them using information from a rule base. Given the input values, it activates a subset of rules simultaneously and calculates which set of rules will be activated [27].

Results are in fuzzy terms, and the defuzzifier converts them into a crisp one. This is necessary for the practical realization of control action. This can be done in a proper manner using some of the common approaches that are being used, which include the centroid method, the maximum method, and defuzzification techniques, which will help us determine if it should have membership or not.

It should also be noted that this iterative nature of fuzzy systems design will require many iterations to arrive at the correct rule base and membership functions. Simulation tools, like MATLAB's Fuzzy Logic Toolbox, are often used in this process to model how the system will operate and permit changes as required by developers [28].

12.3.3 Comparison with Traditional Control Systems

Accordingly, fuzzy logic control systems are inherently different from traditional proportional-integral-derivative (PID) controllers in a number of critical ways. These differences are important to consider for a proper assessment of the applicability of fuzzy logic in wave and tidal energy conversion systems.

Dealing with Uncertainty: Most of the traditional control systems require an accurate mathematical model such that system behavior can be predicted. Developing these models, especially for unwieldy systems enriched with uncertainties, can be a tough task. This makes fuzzy logic much more suitable for handling uncertainty and imprecision, making it better equipped to adapt to an environment that is constantly changing. This ability to handle imprecise data is what enables fuzzy logic systems to perform well when perfect information is missing or the system behavior changes rapidly [29].

Rule-Based Method: Via a rule-based system, fuzzy logic can replicate human deduction to induct professional knowledge directly into the control process. Traditional controllers, meanwhile, will often require extensive mathematical modeling and parameter tuning, which can be time-consuming or may not encompass the complexity of system behavior.

Many real-world systems do not behave linearly, and controlling these can be difficult for traditional control system design. Fuzzy logic is more apt to handle complicated dynamics because of its rule-based structure, enabling the modeling and intrinsically understanding of non-linear relationships. Such a feature can be especially critical in wave and tidal energy systems that experience wide environmental variations [30].

Real-Time Applications: Fuzzy logic systems can be designed to work in real time; therefore, they are appropriate for applications that need quick responses. Due to the adaptability of fuzzy logic, it is possible for it to respond in real time, and thus energy can be harvested for performance optimization systems.

The disadvantage of fuzzy logic is a problem with implementation complexity, where there could arise some undue complexity due to design [31].

In conclusion, fuzzy logic offers a robust alternative to conventional control techniques, especially for the power generation side of renewable energy applications like wave or tidal conversion. It can handle uncertainty, model non-linear relationships, and include expert knowledge, which all make genetic programming an appealing approach for optimizing energy capture and increasing system reliability. Fuzzy logic is most likely to be the game changer in further improvement of sustainable energy solutions [32].

12.4 Methodology, Research Design, and Approach

In the present research, a new method is proposed that combines theoretical analysis with numerical simulations and lab experiments to perform an investigation on how fuzzy logic can be used effectively for improving wave and tidal energy conversion systems. This research has taken various strategies to confirm the efficacy and dependability of these fuzzy logic control schemes. It comprises three major phases, where the first phase presents a research design [33].

This phase focuses on understanding the current state-of-the-art, difficulties faced, and what can be improved or evolved. Theoretical analysis also covers the creation of numerical models for WECs and TECs that allow running further simulations or experimental research [34].

Simulation Studies: The second stage deals with the synthesis and assessment of fuzzy logic control laws using numerical simulation studies. The control algorithms provided in phase one will be mathematically modeled, and many different fuzzy logic controllers for wave energy conversion systems/tidal power plants will be developed. It will consider various environmental conditions (e.g., changing wave heights, periods, or tidal currents) under which the proposed control strategies are to be computed and evaluated using these simulations. An optimization of the parameters for fuzzy logic control and a selection of candidates will be proposed based on the results to test them further (based on output from simulations).

This phase is called the experimental validation of optimized fuzzy logic control strategies [3]. Laboratory-scale prototypes, including fuzzy logic control systems, will be designed and built by the research team for the WEC tidal stream generator. These experiments will take place in specialized conditions such as wave tanks and tidal current simulators to closely mimic how things operate out at sea. Exactly, the experimental results can be used to verify the findings of the numerical simulations and also assess whether fuzzy logic control is practically implementable in wave/tidal energy conversion systems [35].

The work will have the sustainability of wave and tidal energy conversion at its core throughout the research process. Finally, the fuzzy logic control strategies presented will be assessed in terms of energy capture and efficiency, but also in terms of their ability to reduce environmental impacts, thus aiding in improving the overall sustainability of these renewable energy technologies.

12.4.1 Data Collection and Analysis

The data collection and analysis of FLC strategies had the highest effect on all steps devised in developing and verifying fuzzy logic control schemes for wave and tidal energy conversion systems. Information the research team will tap into includes:

- **Environmental Data (e.g., wave heights, periods, and directions; tidal current velocities and directions):** The data will be generated based on available databases, field measurements, and numerical models [36].

- **Prototype Performance Data:** Data required for the development of WEC and TEC prototypes at laboratory scale during the experimental validation stage. The testing will encompass power output, efficiency, and various parameters of the system across a range of operating conditions.
- **Expert Knowledge:** The research team will seek a review from experts in wave and tidal energy conversion, fuzzy logic control, and renewable energy systems to obtain qualitative data and insights that can contribute toward the design of excellent fuzzy logic-based control strategies [37].

Data will be collected, and methodologies such as statistical approaches, machine learning templates, or expert knowledge diagrams will be used to analyze it. Data mining algorithms will be used by the research team to find patterns and correlations within this data that can then be implemented in order to improve control rule knowledge base membership functions of fuzzy logic. Sensitivity analyses will also be carried out to gauge the effect of different fuzzification parameters on the dynamic performance of these control systems. The validation of the numerical simulations and experimental results will be part of the data analysis. This process validates the developed models and control strategies by analyzing a representative WEC simulation against experimental data from another WEC device when it is working under irregular wave conditions [38].

12.4.2 Fuzzy Logic Model Development

In this chapter, the modeling of wave and tidal energy conversion systems based on fuzzy logic is developed. Fuzzy logic models will be used to optimize the energy conversion systems by changing different parameters of the generator (load, blade pitch, or rotor speed) with respect to environmental conditions. The main steps in the development process of fuzzy logic models are:

Determining Input and Output Variables: The importance of this initial step cannot be over-emphasized, identifying which input signals, such as wave height, period and direction or tidal current velocity and direction to what respective outputs signals (i.e., generator load demand (MW), blade pitch angle, etc.) are required for your WEC model [39].

Input Fuzzification: The input variables will necessarily be defined with an appropriate membership function. This process consists of defining the value set of each variable as well as attributing degrees for membership in their corresponding fuzzy sets, such as "low", "medium", and high".

Formulation of Fuzzy Logic Rules: With the expert knowledge and detailed analysis of both simulation (if applicable) and experimental data, a number of specific fuzzy logic rules that dictate how input variables relate to consuming output will be constructed These rules will be expressed as if-then statements like: "If wave height is high and period short, then increase the generator load." Output variables will be connected to the combination, then passed through the lead defuzzification process, where concepts can be converted into crisp values upon input from fuzzy logic rules. This procedure is needed to allow the fuzzy logic control system to give detailed control responses for the wave or tide energy converter.

Optimization and validation: The fuzzy logic models will be optimized by iterative simulations, in which the membership functions and rule base are adjusted to improve the system performance of energy conversion systems. These optimized models will then be subject to validation using further simulation and experimental data to guarantee their high confidence level. Special software tools, such as MATLAB's Fuzzy Logic Toolbox, for designing and simulating fuzzy logic control systems, will allow the development of fuzzy logic models. In this way, the research team is creating a sound fuzzy logic control strategy for promoting zero carbon footprint wave and tidal energy conversion systems of sustainable nature, which will eventually endow an upper edge in developing these renewable energy toys [40].

12.5 Applications of Fuzzy Logic in Wave Energy Conversion

Recently, to improve efficiency and robustness in dynamic sea states, fuzzy logic has been used in the field of research for wave energy conversion systems. Fuzzy logic controllers are a popular method in WEC systems to deal with the inherent uncertainties of both wave patterns and energy extraction. The theory of the controllers in question uses non-deterministic input, such as wave height and frequency, to control energy converters, which are susceptible to large backlashes while attempting to optimize power capture carried out within an operational envelope [41]. For example, morphing control systems for real-time operation of heaving WECs have been proposed by integrating fuzzy logic to design hybrid controllers that react in an adaptive way with changing sea states [6]. In addition to improving energy efficiency, the approach also makes WEC systems more resilient in storms and other extreme weather events. In a broad sense, the application of fuzzy logic in wave energy conversion is an important approach to utilize renewable seaboard resources [42].

12.5.1 Case Studies of Fuzzy Logic in Wave Energy Systems

Over the years, fuzzy logic has found many applications in wave energy conversion systems to maximize performance and enhance control strategies for improved energy capture. This singular article gives a number of industrial case studies that reveal that fuzzy logic can be used to deal with the complexity and uncertainty endemic in marine energy systems. Goyal et al. provide a case study of this nature. The fuzzy logic model by Ismail is designed to maximize energy capture from ocean WECs. This model evaluates different parameters available, which influence the potential of wave energy, high frequency, and direction, for example. Researchers were able to optimize the power generation of a point absorber in different sea states using fuzzy logic control. The results indicated that the energy capture efficiency obtained was significantly improved with respect to standard control, thus suggesting benefits of fuzzy logic in adapting itself during rapidly changing environmental conditions. A major implementation of fuzzy logic is introduced by Irfan et al. Etminan and Ullrich combined fuzzy logic control with artificial neural networks (ANNs) for a wave-ODE wind turbine that directly incorporated OWCs.

The main goal of this hybrid system was to attain an energy optimality control by varying the operation parameters in real time, according to wave conditions. The use of a fuzzy logic controller made it possible to consider varying wave patterns, thus achieving better energy conversion and operational stability. On a different note, Jama et al. conducted another study in which 93% of the total metagenome was binned by plotting all DNA sequences according to their tetranucleotide frequencies [43]. This research in 2014 was carried out for the implementation of an intelligent fuzzy logic controller to get maximum power capture from point absorbers. The results also reinforced the need to meet those resonance conditions to make energy harvested from waves optimally efficient. This clever fuzzy logic controller tuned the buoy's motion to account for changing wave type, giving large benefits in power output. This case study highlights the ability of fuzzy logic to improve the operational reliability of a WEC through control interaction between the device and the ocean environment. Altogether, these case studies show that fuzzy logic can be applied effectively and with versatility in wave energy conversion systems. Fuzzy logic is paramount to optimizing energy capture and system performance by allowing control parameters to be updated in real time and increasing the flexibility of its energy converters [44].

12.5.2 Performance Evaluation Metrics

In order to appraise the efficiency of fuzzy logic applications in wave energy conversion, proper performance evaluation criteria need to be addressed. A Quantitative Comparison between fuzzy logic and Classical strategies is made based on the available performance metrics for Wave energy systems [45].

Energy Capture Efficiency: This quantifies the actual energy power captured by a particular WEC as compared with the maximum possible theoretical way of extracting useful extraction. It is a key measure for the performance characteristics of any energy conversion system. In general, the more efficiently energy is captured, the better it helps in making an adaptive system, and known indices like higher capture rates with FLS under floor radiant heating or electrically heated floors [46].

Power Output Variability: Power output is variable, but this variability reflects system instability and energy power plant perturbations. Fuzzy logic controllers reduce the fluctuation in power output and provide a smooth energy output. Statistical measures like standard deviation or coefficient of variation are used to quantify this metric and then reveal the system performance under dynamic wave conditions [47].

Response Time: The response time of a control system is important for minimizing the efficiency losses due to energy capture when wave conditions change rapidly. This gives us the time that the fuzzy logic controller takes to adjust the online systems' parameters due to changes in wave height and frequency. The faster the response time, the more responsive and efficient the means of control.

Efficiency through the Whole Chain: This metric relates to the efficiency of the energy converter (directly converting ocean wave motions) together with the power take-off system used for conversion and part of the equipment like the accumulator [1]. Assessing the system efficiency as a whole provides insight into how fuzzy logic control affects the entire wave energy system.

Cost-Effective: This is the last but not any less important consideration; fuzzy logic control strategies should be cost-effective. It assesses the balance between investment and recouping expenses for fuzzy logic systems as compared to energy capture improvements and efficiency enhancements. The benefits of fuzzy logic techniques in the applications related to wave energy conversion depend on the economic value that can be estimated through cost-benefit analysis [48].

These performance evaluation metrics can help researchers and engineers in the efficiency inspection of fuzzy systems for wave energy conversion, making it possible to compare with traditional control methods or future development.

12.5.3 Results and Discussion

Many studies and case applications have shown promising results of utilizing fuzzy logic for wave energy conversion. Results: The results consistently showed that the fuzzy logic control strategies improve both performance and efficiency of WECs, increasing power capture and reliability at the system level. The case study conducted by Goyal et al. in 2022 showed that the energy capture efficiency would increase significantly when using a fuzzy logic model. This enabled the WEC to be dynamically optimized for performance, based on its capacity to adjust with transitions in wave settings. The results reveal that compared with conventional control, the fuzzy logic-based system is able to deliver more energy under equivalent conditions. It highlights the potential of fuzzy logic to improve wave energy systems as operational control for a practical environment. Irfan et al. (2023) highlighted that energy extraction can be significantly improved by a floating offshore wind turbine model when fuzzy logic is mobilized with ANN. Since the use of fuzzy logic was successful in dealing with interactions between energy converters and environmental characteristics, hybrid system stability became superior and more efficient regarding fluctuating wave conditions. The findings reveal that using these kinds of hybrid ways could be significant in advocating for the design and development of enhanced wave energy systems. A more recent work from [34] extends such results, demonstrating how an intelligent fuzzy logic controller can ensure optimal power capture in point absorbers, as shown from the equivalent dataset of marina operators and agents. The fuzzy logic system, which controlled how the buoy moves according to different wave patterns, led to an increase in power output of around 5%. This case study illustrates the fuzzy logic versatility in energy extraction processes to assist in wave generation. Consequently, practical applications of fuzzy algorithms demonstrated in these case studies imply that the use of the existing fuzzy logic controller techniques can improve significantly on WECs. This will lead to an increase in the efficiency of energy capture, less power output variability, and better system response through a fuzzy logic adaptive management framework [49].

Finally, he summarized the potential of fuzzy logic application on wave energy conversion as a choice for developing cleaner, sustainable technologies. The demonstrable enhancements of energy capture and system performance illustrate the capability of fuzzy logic to be a key player in advancing wave energy systems toward sustainability. Demand for clean and consistent power will increase with the growing population of the world, and the inclusion of fuzzy logic in turn wave energy conversion technologies can be helpful to achieve a targeted sustainable future. Further R&D in this area is necessary to maximize the potential benefits and device types of fuzzy logic in wave energy conversion [50].

12.6 Applications and Case Studies of Fuzzy Logic in Tidal Energy Systems

Fuzzy logic techniques in the operation methods of TEC systems over the last years were successfully presented, resulting in improved effectiveness and reliability in energy conversion from tidal currents. Fuzzy logic control strategies significantly enhance the performance and operation of tidal energy systems, as illustrated via various case studies [51]. Current work on using fuzzy logic control is reported by Abo-Khalil and Lee (2020) in the context of optimal power flow for a tidal energy system [52]. To alleviate these control challenges, the researchers engineered a fuzzy-logic controller that could alter the excitation of synchronous generators in a dynamic response to tidal current conditions. Using fuzzy logic means the system could extract as much power as possible, even with variable tidal flows, while remaining stable. These results also show that the fuzzy logic controller can effectively improve all aspects of efficiency for tidal energy conversion systems compared to conventional ones [53]. Whitmore (2023) investigated the application of fuzzy logic to ANNs to gain better performance from a Tidal Energy Process. A hybrid control system that combined fuzzy logic to improve the performance of a floating offshore tidal turbine model was built by the researchers [54]. In addition, a fuzzy logic controller modified operational variables from real-time tidal characteristics to increase energy extraction and system performance. It was shown that the hybrid method of using a polar curve and fuzzy logic achieved optimum power production and illustrated the easy application of this approach in practice to manage complex marine energy systems. Furthermore, Kim et al. also conducted a study comparing SYM-1219 [55]. In 2019, authors explored fuzzy logic-based LFR in a tidal turbine power plant [56]. A fractional fuzzy-based PID controller was utilized by the researchers for power fluctuations due to different tidal currents. The proposed fuzzy logic controller with cascade structure has shown improved performance in mitigating frequency changes and maintaining power output at the nominal operation point, which contributes to more reliable tidal energy conversion systems. This case study demonstrates the adaptability of fuzzy logic to solve a range of specific problems relating specifically to TECs. Taken together, these case studies highlight the crucial impact that fuzzy logic has on maximizing tidal energy conversion efficiency. Fuzzy logic improves energy capture and overall system performance by allowing operational parameters to be changed in real time, thus enhancing the responsiveness of a controlling system [57].

12.6.1 Performance Evaluation Metrics

In order to evaluate how well the fuzzy logic applications are suited to harnessing tidal energy, proper performance evaluation indices must be defined. These measures allow us to objectively compare which fuzzy logic control strategy is more efficient compared to traditional methods and, also broadly speaking, how well tidal energy systems work [58].

Energy Capture Efficiency: It is calculated as the ratio of captured tidal energy generated by a TEC to the maximum kinetic potential in available tidal currents. The greater the energy capture efficiency, the more efficient the conversion process. The ability of fuzzy logic systems to maximize this metric under varying tidal conditions is often used as evaluation criteria [59].

Level Power Output Stability: This is another performance index to detect the effect of power degradation over time. The lower value means that system speed may have some influence on level efficiency [60]. The ideal situation for fuzzy logic controllers would be that of minimal power fluctuation, and hence the generation of constant electrical power. Such a type of metric can be quantified by using statistical metrics, such as standard deviation or coefficient of variation, thereby reporting about the system's responsiveness under dynamic tidal conditions [61].

Response Time: The control system has a great influence on the amount of energy capture; for this reason, total or partial custom cases are preferred in areas with quick variations in tidal conditions [62]. This criterion determines how fast the fuzzy logic controller can adapt the input control type to changes of tidal current velocity and direction. Lower response times are an indication of a more efficient control strategy that was also quicker at detecting the true label means [63].

Overall System Efficiency: This encompasses all steps in the energy conversion process (tidal turbine, power take-off system, and any energy storage units) [64]. Assessment of the fuzzy logic control strategy in terms of overall system efficiency instead offers a more complete evaluation for the entire tidal energy system [65].

Affordability: A final key consideration for fuzzy logic control strategies to be put in place is their cost-effectiveness [66]. This quantifies the tradeoff between reduced costs of development and deployment for fuzzy logics with increased energy capture, and therefore operational flexibility. Here, a cost-benefit analysis is conducted to understand the economic justification for fuzzy logic-based applications in tidal energy conversion [67]. Researchers and engineers can assess the effects of fuzzy logic on tidal energy conversion systems, compare with classical control schemes, and aim future developments based on these performance evaluation metrics [68].

12.6.2 Results and Discussion

Various studies and implementations have demonstrated the potential of applying fuzzy logic to tidal energy conversion [69]. The overall outcome reaffirms repeatedly that the fuzzy logic control strategies increased performance and efficiency capabilities of TECs, improving energy capture for greater integration with system reliability. Abo-Khalil and Lee also observed similar improvement in energy capture efficiency when a fuzzy logic controller was used. Their controller continually received tidal conditions, and in combination with the ability to adapt, it helped the system increase efficiency. The system achieved greater energy output with the fuzzy logic-controlled approach than traditional methods when operating under equivalent conditions [70]. This result highlights the possibility of employing fuzzy logic to improve operational performance in realistic conditions related to tidal energy systems. Likewise, Irfan and co-workers (2023) combined fuzzy logic with ANN to improve energy extraction of a floating offshore tidal turbine model. The ability of the hybrid system to dynamically respond to real-time tidal conditions was reflected by greatly improved stability and performance, thereby validating fuzzy logic as an adequate way for handling intricate interactions between a tide energy converter(s) engaging with its environmental circumstances [71]. These findings indicate that these hybrid solutions may hold the key to furthering the evolution of high-performance tidal energy systems. These results are further validated by Hamed and Burzel (2019), who have made use of a fractional-order PID FLC to enhance load frequency control in tidal turbine power plants. Fuzzy logic controllers stabilize the power output, reducing fluctuations produced from variation of depth in water level and blade loadings, resulting in a more reliable tidal energy system [72]. The performed case study displays fuzzy logic as a valuable solution for regulating tidal energy extraction processes, proving its adaptability across the optimal extractors of energy from these kinds of ocean conditions. As a whole, the findings from these case studies suggest that fuzzy logic control can dramatically improve TEC performance. Fuzzy logic plays an important role in improved energy capture efficiency, reduced power output variability, and better system response by providing a flexible and adaptive framework to deal with the complexity of tidal energy systems [73].

Finally, fuzzy logic in tidal energy extraction is emerging as a fertile field for promoting the technologies of renewable resources [74]. The improvements in energy capture and system performance demonstrated by this chapter provide evidence that fuzzy logic could have a significant role to play in the future of sustainable tidal energy development. With the increasing need for clean, renewable energy sources, and fuzzy logic being an optimal tool in tides-to-energy conversion technologies, development will play a fundamentally important role within any future sustainable era. Ongoing research and development work in this field are necessary to fully exploit the potential of fuzzy logic for the advancement of tidal energy conversion systems [75].

12.7 Conclusion

This chapter investigated the potential contribution of fuzzy logic in improving wave and tidal energy conversion systems toward securing a sustainable energy future. Results from the case studies, together with performance evaluation metrics, show that fuzzy logic control can provide an important tool for increasing the efficiency and reliability of energy extraction in ocean waves and tidal currents. Real-time adjustments to operational parameters and the Management of Marine Energy Systems through fuzzy logic have been demonstrated successfully with a view toward energy capture optimization. Economies of scale should help HT WaveGen cope with the high cost of installing wave power in deeper waters, provided that its fuzzy logic control system can squeeze every kilowatt out of an ever-varying tidal stream.

It has also been successful in alleviating some of the issues experienced by WECs and TECs through its incorporation of fuzzy logic. Fuzzy logic controllers have been applied successfully for fault diagnosis and prognostics, resulting in an increased system reliability. In identifying possible problems and offering preventive maintenance mechanisms, fuzzy logic ensures higher system availability and less unplanned downtime. For the wider uptake of wave and tidal energy technologies, it is important to consider in detail how cost-effective fuzzy logic control strategies can be implemented. Even though there are high start-up costs for developing and using fuzzy logic systems, those can still pay off in the long run, as you will be able to capture more energy (lower maintenance) than other control schemes. The use of fuzzy logic in marine energy systems is expected to improve economically as the technology matures and benefits from economies of scale. This study provides a greater understanding of the promising application of fuzzy logic for future development in wave and tidal energy conversion devices. Fuzzy logic can achieve an optimized performance in energy capture, reliability, and sustainability for ocean resources. With the world striving for cleaner, more sustainable energy sources, fuzzy logic models are one ingredient in a recipe that will include wave and tidal turbines to enable future applications of these innovative power generation systems. Nevertheless, it should be mentioned that even though fuzzy logic provides some benefits and advantages in aiding to tackle wave and tidal energy conversion issues, not all requirements can be solved. Further research and development are required to address other important issues, including environmental impact mitigation, techno-economic advancements, and regulatory frameworks designed to foster marine renewable energy expansion. This information calls for research with regard to fine-tuning the fuzzy controller; implementation of hybrid approaches (the combination with other advanced controllers); and investigation concerning the scaling-up so that it may be initiated in wave and tidal energy at large scales. Moreover, techno-economic analyses and life cycle assessments need to be extended for full assessment of the long-term sustainability impacts as well as economic viability with fuzzy logic-enabled marine energy systems. Providing solutions to these issues and accelerating the ongoing momentum of fuzzy logic in wave and tidal energy conversion systems will assist researchers as well as engineers with their efforts toward a greener, cleaner future where ocean renewable technologies are prominent within the global mix.

References

1. Ashinze, U. K., Edeigba, B. A., Umoh, A. A., Biu, P. W., and Daraojimba, A. I. (2024). Urban green infrastructure and its role in sustainable cities: A comprehensive review. *World Journal of Advanced Research and Reviews*, 21(2), 928–936.
2. Yuan, Y., Zhang, T., Shen, B., Yan, X., & Long, T. (2018). A fuzzy logic energy management strategy for a photovoltaic/diesel/battery hybrid ship based on experimental database. *Energies*, 11(9), 2211.
3. Sharma, A., and Singh, B. (2022). Measuring impact of e-commerce on small scale business: A systematic review. *Journal of Corporate Governance and International Business Law*, 5(1), 1–5.
4. Zabel, A., and Häusler, M. M. (2024). Policy instruments for green infrastructure. *Landscape and Urban Planning*, 242, 104929.

5. Kaneti, V. R., Masih, J., Yoganand, S., Singh, B., Bhargava, R., Bajaj, R., ... and Shrivastava, A. (2024). Supervised learning for edible mushroom identification: Promising results and implications for food safety. *International Journal of Intelligent Systems and Applications in Engineering*, 12(8s), 290–298.
6. Singh, B. (2022). Relevance of agriculture-nutrition linkage for human healthcare: A conceptual legal framework of implication and pathways. *Justice and Law Bulletin*, 1(1), 44–49.
7. Zhang, B., and MacKenzie, A. (2024). Trade-offs and synergies in urban green infrastructure: A systematic review. *Urban Forestry and Urban Greening*. DOI:10.1016/j.ufug.2024. 128262.
8. Singh, B. (2022). COVID-19 pandemic and public healthcare: Endless downward spiral or solution via rapid legal and health services implementation with patient monitoring program. *Justice and Law Bulletin*, 1(1), 1–7.
9. Isendahl, C., Dunning, N. P., Grazioso, L., Hawken, S., Lentz, D. L., and Scarborough, V. L. (2024). Growth and decline of a sustainable city: A multitemporal perspective on blue-black-green infrastructures at the pre-Columbian lowland Maya city of Tikal. *Urban Studies*, 62. https://doi.org/10.1177/00420980231224648.
10. Sunding, A., Randrup, T. B., Nordh, H., Sang, Å. O., and Nilsson, K. (2024). Descriptions of the relationship between human health and green infrastructure in six Nordic comprehensive plans. *Cities*, 146, 104746.
11. Kim, J., Ewing, R., and Rigolon, A. (2024). Does green infrastructure affect housing prices via extreme heat and air pollution mitigation? A focus on green and climate gentrification in Los Angeles County, 2000–2021. *Sustainable Cities and Society*, 102, 105225.
12. Mohamed, A., and Mohammed, O. (2013). Real-time energy management scheme for hybrid renewable energy systems in smart grid applications. *Electric Power Systems Research*, 96, 133–143.
13. Richter, M., Heinemann, K., Meiser, N., and Dickhaut, W. (2024). Trees in sponge cities: A systematic review of trees as a component of blue-green infrastructure, vegetation engineering principles, and stormwater management. *Water*, 16(5), 655.
14. Singh, B., and Kaunert, C. (2024). Computational thinking for innovative solutions and problem-solving techniques: Transforming conventional education to futuristic interdisciplinary higher education. In Fonkam, M., and Vajjhala, N. (eds.), *Revolutionizing Curricula Through Computational Thinking, Logic, and Problem Solving*

(pp. 60–82). IGI Global. https://doi.org/10.4018/979-8-3693-1974-1.ch004.

15. Singh, B., and Kaunert, C. (2024). Wind and solar energy as renewable energy for sustainable global future: Projecting future multi-sector sustainable policies and innovation. In Ara, A., and Thakore, R. (eds.), *Promoting Multi-Sector Sustainability With Policy and Innovation* (pp. 210–245). IGI Global. https://doi.org/10.4018/979-8-3693-2113-3.ch009.
16. Singh, B., and Kaunert, C. (2024). Aroma of highly smart internet of medical things (IoMT) and lightweight edgetrust expansion medical care facilities for electronic healthcare systems: Fortified-chain architecture for remote patient monitoring and privacy protection beyond imagination. In Hassan, A., Bhattacharya, P., Tikadar, S., Dutta, P., and Sagayam, M. (eds.), *Lightweight Digital Trust Architectures in the Internet of Medical Things (IoMT)* (pp. 196–212). IGI Global. https://doi.org/10.4018/979-8-3693-2109-6.ch011.
17. Singh, B., Jain, V., Kaunert, C., Dutta, P. K., and Singh, G. (2024). Privacy matters: Espousing blockchain and artificial intelligence (AI) for consumer data protection on E-commerce platforms in ethical marketing. In Saluja, S., Nayyar, V., Rojhe, K., and Sharma, S. (eds.), *Ethical Marketing Through Data Governance Standards and Effective Technology* (pp. 167–184). IGI Global. https://doi.org/10.4018/979-8-3693-2215-4.ch015.
18. Singh, B., Dutta, P. K., and Kaunert, C. (2024). Replenish artificial intelligence in renewable energy for sustainable development: Lensing SDG 7 affordable and clean energy and SDG 13 climate actions with legal-financial advisory. In Derbali, A. (ed.), *Social and Ethical Implications of AI in Finance for Sustainability* (pp. 198–227). IGI Global. https://doi.org/10.4018/979-8-3693-2881-1.ch009.
19. Singh, B., and Kaunert, C. (2024). Augmented reality and virtual reality modules for mindfulness: Boosting emotional intelligence and mental wellness. In Hiran, K., Doshi, R., and Patel, M. (eds.), *Applications of Virtual and Augmented Reality for Health and Wellbeing* (pp. 111–128). IGI Global. https://doi.org/10.4018/979-8-3693-1123-3.ch007.
20. Singh, B. (2024). Lensing legal dynamics for examining responsibility and deliberation of generative AI-tethered technological privacy concerns: Infringements and use of personal data by nefarious actors. In Ara, A., and Ara, A. (eds.), *Exploring the Ethical Implications of Generative AI* (pp. 146–167). IGI Global. https://doi.org/10.4018/979-8-3693-1565-1.ch009.

21. Singh, B. (2024). Social cognition of incarcerated women and children: Addressing exposure to infectious diseases and legal outcomes. In Reddy, K. (ed.), *Principles and Clinical Interventions in Social Cognition* (pp. 236–251). IGI Global. https://doi.org/10.4018/979-8-3693-1265-0.ch014.
22. Singh, B., and Kaunert, C. (2024). Salvaging responsible consumption and production of food in the hospitality industry: Harnessing machine learning and deep learning for zero food waste. In Singh, A., Tyagi, P., and Garg, A. (eds.), *Sustainable Disposal Methods of Food Wastes in Hospitality Operations* (pp. 176–192). IGI Global. https://doi.org/10.4018/979-8-3693-2181-2.ch012.
23. Singh, B. (2024). Evolutionary global neuroscience for cognition and brain health: Strengthening innovation in brain science. In Prabhakar, P. (ed.), *Biomedical Research Developments for Improved Healthcare* (pp. 246–272). IGI Global. https://doi.org/10.4018/979-8-3693-1922-2.ch012.
24. Singh, B., and Kaunert, C. (2024). Revealing green finance mobilization: Harnessing fintech and blockchain innovations to surmount barriers and foster new investment avenues. In Jafar, S., Rodriguez, R., Kannan, H., Akhtar, S., and Plugmann, P. (eds.), *Harnessing Blockchain-Digital Twin Fusion for Sustainable Investments* (pp. 265–286). IGI Global. https://doi.org/10.4018/979-8-3693-1878-2.ch011.
25. Singh, B., and Kaunert, C. (2024). Harnessing sustainable agriculture through climate-smart technologies: Artificial intelligence for climate preservation and futuristic trends. In Kannan, H., Rodriguez, R., Paprika, Z., and Ade-Ibijola, A. (eds.), *Exploring Ethical Dimensions of Environmental Sustainability and Use of AI* (pp. 214–239). IGI Global. https://doi.org/10.4018/979-8-3693-0892-9.ch011.
26. Singh, B. (2023). Blockchain technology in renovating healthcare: Legal and future perspectives. In Kaushik, K., Dahiya, S., Aggarwal, S., and Dwivedi, A. (eds.), *Revolutionizing Healthcare Through Artificial Intelligence and Internet of Things Applications* (pp. 177–186). IGI Global. https://doi.org/10.4018/978-1-6684-5422-0.ch012.
27. Singh, B., and Kaunert, C. (2024). Reinventing artificial intelligence and block-chain for preserving medical data. In *Ethical Artificial Intelligence in Power Electronics* (pp. 77–91). CRC Press.
28. Singh, B., and Kaunert, C. (2024). Unmanned aerial vehicle. *Cognitive Machine Intelligence: Applications, Challenges, and Related Technologies*, 108.

29. Vijayalakshmi, S., Savita, and Durgadevi, P. (2023). AI and machine learning in improving resilience of smart energy infrastructure. In *AI-Powered Machine Learning in the Energy Industry: Digital Technology and Sustainable Energy Systems* (pp. 189–213). Cham: Springer International Publishing.
30. Shukla, S. S., Jain, M., Jain, A., Bajpai, S., Mishra, A. K., Gupta, A., and Pramanik, S. (2024). Industry 5.0: Blue wind energy for sustainable urbanization and intelligent control of energy. In *Convergence of Human Resources Technologies and Industry 5.0* (pp. 170–187). IGI Global.
31. Al Hajri, N. H., Al Harthi, R. N., Pasam, G. K., and Natarajan, R. (2024). Machine learning and machine learning based green energy generation using hybrid renewable energy sources of solar, wind and hydrogen fuel cells. In *E3S Web of Conferences* (Vol. 472, p. 01008). EDP Sciences.
32. Issa Zadeh, S. B., Esteban Perez, M. D., López-Gutiérrez, J. S., and Fernández-Sánchez, G. (2023). Optimizing smart energy infrastructure in smart ports: A systematic scoping review of carbon footprint reduction. *Journal of Marine Science and Engineering*, 11(10), 1921.
33. Singh, B., and Kaunert, C. (2024). Harnessing sustainable agriculture through climate-smart technologies: Artificial intelligence for climate preservation and futuristic trends. In *Exploring Ethical Dimensions of Environmental Sustainability and Use of AI* (pp. 214–239). IGI Global.
34. Li, J., and Zhou, T. (2023). Multiagent deep meta reinforcement learning for sea computing-based energy management of interconnected grids considering renewable energy sources in sustainable cities. *Sustainable Cities and Society*, 99, 104917.
35. Orumwense, E. F., and Abo-Al-Ez, K. (2023). Internet of things for smart energy systems: A review on its applications, challenges and future trends. *AIMS Electronics and Electrical Engineering*, 7(1), 1–2.
36. Raj, E. F. I. (2023). A detailed review on wind and solar hybrid green energy technologies for sustainable smart cities. *Polytechnica*, 6(1), 1.
37. Camacho, J. D. J., Aguirre, B., Ponce, P., Anthony, B., and Molina, A. (2024). Leveraging artificial intelligence to bolster the energy sector in smart cities: A literature review. *Energies*, 17(2), 353.
38. Kannammal, A., and Chandia, S. (2023). Applications of AI and machine learning for smart cities. *Research Trends in Artificial Intelligence: Internet of Things*, 186.

39. Zearah, S. A., Al-Tahee, M., Mohammed, A., Shnawa, A. H., Mahdi, H. H. J., and Majeed, Z. (2023, December). Smart city application based on internet-of-things and artificial intelligence for energy management dynamic memory modelling. In *2023 International Conference on Emerging Research in Computational Science (ICERCS)* (pp. 1–6). IEEE.
40. Awogbemi, O., Von Kallon, D. V., and Kumar, K. S. (2024). Contributions of artificial intelligence and digitization in achieving clean and affordable energy. *Intelligent Systems with Applications*, 200389.
41. Singh, B. (2023). Unleashing alternative dispute resolution (ADR) in resolving complex legal-technical issues arising in cyberspace lensing e-commerce and intellectual property: Proliferation of e-commerce digital economy. *Revista Brasileira de Alternative Dispute Resolution-Brazilian Journal of Alternative Dispute Resolution-RBADR*, 5(10), 81–105.
42. Verma, J., Sandys, L., Matthews, A., and Goel, S. (2024). Readiness of artificial intelligence technology for managing energy demands from renewable sources. *Engineering Applications of Artificial Intelligence*, 135, 108831.
43. Khalid, M. (2024). Energy 4.0: AI-enabled digital transformation for sustainable power networks. *Computers and Industrial Engineering*, 193. https://doi.org/10.1016/j.cie.2024.110253.
44. Issa Zadeh, S. B., Esteban Perez M. D., López-Gutiérrez, J.-S., and Fernández-Sánchez, G. (2023). Optimizing smart energy infrastructure in smart ports: A systematic scoping review of carbon footprint reduction. *Journal of Marine Science and Engineering*, 11, 1921.
45. Singh, B., and Kaunert, C. (2024). Augmented reality and virtual reality modules for mindfulness: Boosting emotional intelligence and mental wellness. In Hiran, K., Doshi, R., and Patel, M. (eds.), *Applications of Virtual and Augmented Reality for Health and Wellbeing* (pp. 111–128). IGI Global. https://doi.org/10.4018/979-8-3693-1123-3.ch007.
46. Obaideen, K., Albasha, L., Iqbal, U., and Mir, H. (2024). Wireless power transfer: Applications, challenges, barriers, and the role of AI in achieving sustainable development goals: A bibliometric analysis. *Energy Strategy Reviews*, 53, 101376.
47. El-Hussieny, E. (2023). Emerging the concept of sustainable architecture in forming a smart city. *Resourceedings*, 3(1), 22–32.
48. Salman, M. Y., and Hasar, H. (2023). Review on environmental aspects in smart city concept: Water, waste, air pollution and transportation

smart applications using machine learning techniques. *Sustainable Cities and Society*, 94, 104567.

49. Van Hoang, T. (2024). Impact of integrated artificial intelligence and internet of things technologies on smart city transformation. *Journal of Technical Education Science*, 19(Special Issue 01), 64–73.
50. Huda, N. U., Ahmed, I., Adnan, M., Ali, M., and Naeem, F. (2024). Experts and intelligent systems for smart homes' transformation to sustainable smart cities: A comprehensive review. *Expert Systems with Applications*, 238, 122380.
51. Ali, M. (2023). Synergizing solar cell innovation, radio wave technology, and AI for sustainable business growth: A comprehensive review. *International Journal of Social, Humanities and Life Sciences*, 1(1), 19–28.
52. Nezhad, M. M., Neshat, M., Sylaios, G., and Garcia, D. A. (2024). Marine energy digitalization digital twin's approaches. *Renewable and Sustainable Energy Reviews*, 191, 114065.
53. Moemen, Y. S., Alshater, H., and El-Sayed, I. E. T. (2023). Clean energy management based on internet of things and sensor networks for climate change problems. In *The Power of Data: Driving Climate Change with Data Science and Artificial Intelligence Innovations* (pp. 117–136). Cham: Springer Nature Switzerland.
54. Singh, B. (2023). Blockchain technology in renovating healthcare: Legal and future perspectives. In *Revolutionizing Healthcare Through Artificial Intelligence and Internet of Things Applications* (pp. 177–186). IGI Global.
55. Nasserddine, G., Nassereddine, M., and El Arid, A. A. (2023). Internet of things integration in renewable energy systems. In *Handbook of Research on Applications of AI, Digital Twin, and Internet of Things for Sustainable Development* (pp. 159–185). IGI Global.
56. Singh, B. (2024). Lensing legal dynamics for examining responsibility and deliberation of generative AI-tethered technological privacy concerns: Infringements and use of personal data by nefarious actors. In Ara, A., and Ara, A. (eds.), *Exploring the Ethical Implications of Generative AI* (pp. 146–167). IGI Global. https://doi.org/10.4018/979-8-3693-1565-1.ch009.
57. Nouri, A., Lachheb, A., and El Amraoui, L. (2024). Optimizing efficiency of Vehicle-to-Grid system with intelligent management and ANN-PSO algorithm for battery electric vehicles. *Electric Power Systems Research*, 226, 109936.

58. Logeswaran, K., Suresh, P., Ponselvakumar, A. P., Savitha, S., Sentamilselvan, K., and Adhithyaa, N. (2023). Exploration of assorted modernizations in forecasting renewable energy using low power wireless technologies for machine learning. In *Smart Grids and Internet of Things: An Energy Perspective*, pp. 157–191.

59. Singh, B., and Kaunert, C. (2024). Salvaging responsible consumption and production of food in the hospitality industry: Harnessing machine learning and deep learning for zero food waste. In Singh, A., Tyagi, P., and Garg, A. (eds.), *Sustainable Disposal Methods of Food Wastes in Hospitality Operations* (pp. 176–192). IGI Global. https://doi.org/10.4018/979-8-3693-2181-2.ch012.

60. Li, X., Zhao, H., Feng, Y., Li, J., Zhao, Y., and Wang, X. (2024). Research on key technologies of high energy efficiency and low power consumption of new data acquisition equipment of power internet of things based on artificial intelligence. *International Journal of Thermofluids*, 21, 100575.

61. Singh, B. (2024). Evolutionary global neuroscience for cognition and brain health: Strengthening innovation in brain science. In Prabhakar, P. (ed.), *Biomedical Research Developments for Improved Healthcare* (pp. 246–272). IGI Global. https://doi.org/10.4018/979-8-3693-1922-2.ch012.

62. Xie, H., Huang, R., Sun, H., Han, Z., Jiang, M., Zhang, D., ... and Wu, T. (2023). Wireless energy: Paving the way for smart cities and a greener future. *Energy and Buildings*, 297, 113469.

63. Khan, M. W., Saad, S., Ammad, S., Rasheed, K., and Jamal, Q. (2024). Smart infrastructure and AI. In *AI in Material Science* (pp. 193–215). CRC Press.

64. Samaei, S. R., and Ghahfarrokhi, M. A. (2023). Optimizing coastal hydro turbines integrating artificial intelligence for sustainable energy conversion. In *2th International Conference on Creative Achievements of Architecture, Urban Planning, Civil Engineering and Environment in the Sustainable Development of the Middle East.*

65. Kumar, D. (2023). Concept of sustainable energy system for smart cities. In *Renewable Energy Scenarios in Future Indian Smart Cities: A Geospatial Technology Perspective* (pp. 1–20). Singapore: Springer Nature Singapore.

66. Almalki, F. A., Alsamhi, S. H., Sahal, R., Hassan, J., Hawbani, A., Rajput, N. S., ... and Breslin, J. (2023). Green machine learning for eco-friendly and sustainable smart cities: Future directions and opportunities. *Mobile Networks and Applications*, 28(1), 178–202.

67. Salama, R., and Al-Turjman, F. (2023). Sustainable energy production in smart cities. *Sustainability*, 15(22), 16052.
68. Singh, B., and Kaunert, C. (2024). Salvaging responsible consumption and production of food in the hospitality industry: Harnessing machine learning and deep learning for zero food waste. In *Sustainable Disposal Methods of Food Wastes in Hospitality Operations* (pp. 176–192). IGI Global.
69. Singh, B. (2024). Evolutionary global neuroscience for cognition and brain health: Strengthening innovation in brain science. In *Biomedical Research Developments for Improved Healthcare* (pp. 246–272). IGI Global.
70. Mohammed, M. N., Aljibori, H. S. S., Al-Tamimi, A., Alani, Z. N., Hameed, M. S., Ibrahim, F. M., ... and Alfiras, M. (2023, October). Toward sustainable smart cities in Bahrain: A groundbreaking approach to marine renewable energy harnessing sea tides and waves for a greener energy future. In *2023 IEEE 8th International Conference on Engineering Technologies and Applied Sciences (ICETAS)* (pp. 1–5). IEEE.
71. Bin Abu Sofian, A. D. A., Lim, H. R., Siti Halimatul Munawaroh, H., Ma, Z., Chew, K. W., and Show, P. L. (2024). Machine learning and the renewable energy revolution: Exploring solar and wind energy solutions for a sustainable future including innovations in energy storage. *Sustainable Development*, 32(4), 3953–3978.
72. Fan, Z., Yan, Z., and Wen, S. (2023). Deep learning and artificial intelligence in sustainability: A review of SDGs, renewable energy, and environmental health. *Sustainability*, 15(18), 13493.
73. Jain, A., Sharma, A., Jately, V., and Azzopardi, B. (eds.). (2023). *Sustainable Energy Solutions with Artificial Intelligence, Blockchain Technology, and Internet of Things*. CRC Press.
74. Mirshafiee, F., Shahbazi, E., Safi, M., and Rituraj, R. (2023). Predicting power and hydrogen generation of a renewable energy converter utilizing data-driven methods: A sustainable smart grid case study. *Energies*, 16(1), 502.
75. Yousef, L. A., Yousef, H., and Rocha-Meneses, L. (2023). Artificial intelligence for management of variable renewable energy systems: A review of current status and future directions. *Energies*, 16(24), 8057.

Chapter 13

Quantifying the Contributions of Fuzzy Logic Solutions in Achieving Sustainable Development Goals through Renewable Energy Innovations in Smart Cities and Smart Villages

Priyanka Ghai[a] and Sandhya Prabhakaran[b]

[a]*Department of Legal Studies, Galgotias University, Greater Noida, Uttar Pradesh, India*
[b]*Amity Institute of Advanced Legal Studies, Amity University, Noida, Gautam Budh Nagar, Uttar Pradesh 201313, India*

priyaghai16@gmail.com

Abstract

Renewable energy sources are crucial for mitigating climate change and reducing greenhouse gas emissions during the transition to sustainable economic growth. The advancement of smart villages and smart cities is the arrangement for the efficient coordination of these energy sources. The Sustainable Development Goals (SDGs) of the United Nations, particularly SDG 11, aim to form cities and towns

Fuzzy Logic in Revolutionizing Renewable Energy
Edited by Bhupinder Singh, Komal Vig, Ruchi Lal, and Budi Agus Riswandi

ISBN 978-981-5129-92-2 (Hardcover), 978-1-003-74191-6 (eBook)
www.jennystanford.com

DOI: 10.1201/9781003741916-13

that are comprehensive, secure, strong, and economical, and capture the worldwide criticalness for sustainable urban development. The improvements in smart energy management and renewable energy are moreover emphatically affected by 7, 9, and 13. In coordinating and overseeing renewable energy frameworks within smart cities and smart villages, and supporting the achievement of this goal, fuzzy logic is vital. By looking at critical measures and indicators relating to energy efficiency, sustainability, and financial impacts, this examination quantifies these commitments. In order to achieve these objectives, this chapter analyses how renewable energy arrangements can be coordinated into smart cities and towns. With the assistance of fuzzy logic, smart cities and towns can drastically lower their carbon footprint, advance energy efficiency, and promote natural sustainability by utilizing renewable energy innovations like solar photovoltaic systems, wind turbines, and energy storage systems (ESS). And other forms of manufactured insights are basic for the coordination of renewable energy sources into smart cities and towns. This permits optimized energy frameworks, expanded stability, and management of variability. More feasible, successful, and strong urban and provincial communities are made conceivable by handling the complexity and capriciousness displayed in energy frameworks. The chapter also looks at how administrative motivations, innovation progressions, and arrangement systems might facilitate the transition. The appropriation of in both urban and rural areas is helped by solid administrative backing, community association, and decentralized energy frameworks, according to key findings. Fuzzy logic has been utilized in Indian communities to control a solar-powered microgrid that supplies consistent power to the community and boosts nearby trade and commerce. They can boost in smart villages by 30–40%, improving both budgetary potential and quality of life. This approach provides policymakers, urban planners, and stakeholders with practical guidance by creating a framework for economically sustainable urban energy systems. Since sources like solar and wind control are eccentric and variable, conventional control systems regularly find it difficult to handle them. For overseeing such instabilities and coming to judgments based on uncertain inputs, it offers a solid foundation. In order to successfully fulfil requests in real-time, calculations are utilized to direct the dispersion of energy from distinctive renewable sources. Batteries and other energy storage devices are essential for maintaining balance between supply and demand in systems. By optimizing charging and releasing cycles depending on changing energy inputs and utilization rates, it upgrades the execution of these frameworks. This ensures the life span and optimal performance of capacity gadgets. Request reaction programs are utilized to alter the request for demand rather than the supply. Controllers may viably oversee and diminish top requests, resulting in a more balanced and effective energy framework, by evaluating fuzzy inputs such as climate, time of day, and energy costs. The SDGs are aligned with the integration of initiatives, which also help improve smart city sustainability and livability, and lay the groundwork for sustainable urban prospects. This chapter emphasizes the fundamental aspects of achieving economic advancement and the transformative potential of smart cities in driving this worldwide movement. Arrangements are fundamental for accomplishing sustainable development objectives through developments, reducing waste, and promoting community stability, smart cities, and towns. The significance of renewable energy in achieving economic improvement and the progressive potential of smart cities in initiating this around-the-world move are emphasized in this chapter. The objective of this chapter is to help readers understand which sources, such as solar photovoltaics, wind turbines, biomass, and geothermal systems, are most appropriate for urban environments. Alongside surveying the financial effects, such as taking a toll on investment funds, work creation, and speculation opportunities, this chapter also endeavors to measure the natural preferences, such as decreases in pollution, and discuss them.

Keywords: SDGs, Smart Cities, Smart Villages, Renewable Energy, Sustainable Urban Development, Technologies related to Renewable Energy

13.1 Introduction

In order to moderate climate, reduce, and diminish greenhouse gas emissions, renewable energy sources are vital. The move to renewable energy is fundamental for sustainable development as fossil fuel sources run out and environmental concerns increase.

Clean, perpetual control is given by renewable energy sources like solar, wind, biomass, and geothermal frameworks, which moreover bolster environmental sustainability and energy security. Their commitment to decreasing carbon emissions, promoting energy efficiency, and fortifying financial development through job creation and green innovation speculation is significant.

The other stage of urban and provincial advancement can be characterized by smart cities and smart villages. By integrating data and communication technologies with physical infrastructure, they reduce environmental impact, improve resource management, and enhance quality of life. Smart cities and towns may successfully integrate various energy sources into their energy systems, ensuring a reliable and feasible power supply, by utilizing cutting-edge advances. The strong, adaptable, and comprehensive engineering of these smart communities advances both rural and urban sustainable development.

A global roadmap for achieving a sustainable future is advertised by the SDGs of the United Nations. Energy and urban advancement are closely connected to a few SDGs:

SDG 7: The objective is to ensure access to affordable, reliable, sustainable, and modern energy for all. This objective recognizes the crucial part energy plays in development and the centrality of transitioning to more ecologically inviting energy sources. It highlights how imperative it is to increase energy efficiency and advance the utilization of renewable energy sources globally. To achieve this, the worldwide energy blend must incorporate a greater extent of renewable energy. Worldwide collaboration is required to progress to clean energy innovation, and speculation in clean energy frameworks and innovation is encouraged (IRENA, 2020).

SDG 9: Building a resilient infrastructure, promoting inclusive and sustainable industrialization, and fostering innovation are the three primary goals of SDG 9. It recognizes that a strong foundation is vital for maintaining industrialization and emphasizes the role that the framework plays in advancing financial development. In order to form a maintainable foundation, it is basic that it be overhauled and retrofitted, with a focus on clean and naturally inviting mechanical forms and innovation. It also emphasizes how pivotal logical advancement and investigation are to progressing sustainable industrialization and economic advancement, particularly in developing countries, as shown in Figs. 13.1, 13.2 and 13.3.

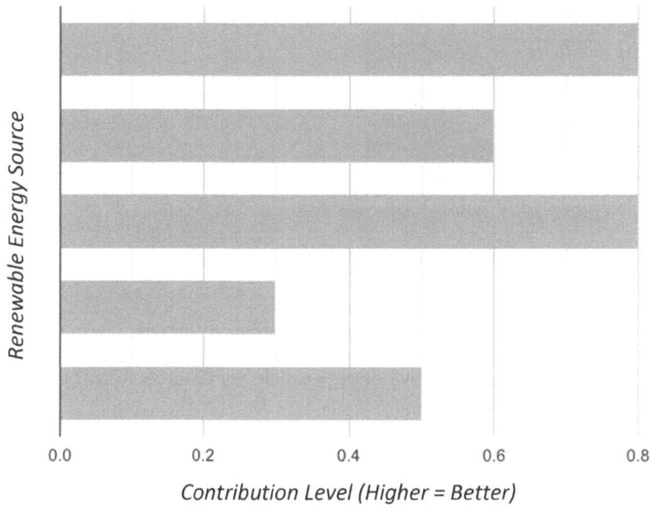

Figure 13.1 Universal energy access (*Source*: REN21).

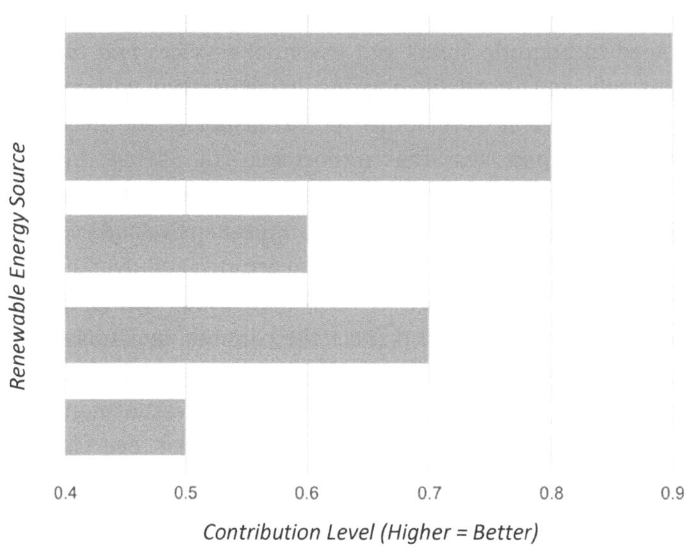

Figure 13.2 Increase renewable energy share (*Source*: REN21).

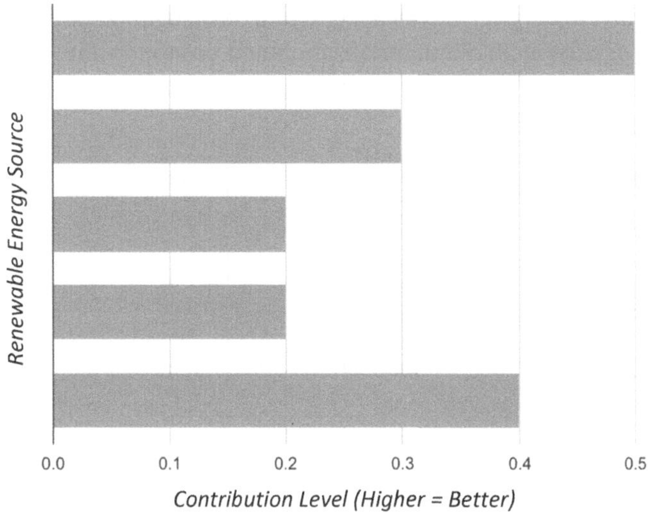

Figure 13.3 Improve energy efficiency (*Source*: REN21)

SDG 11: Making cities and human settlements inclusive, safe, resilient, and sustainable is the objective of SDG 11. This point recognizes the challenges that rising urbanization brings to sustainability as well as the growing importance of cities as centers of financial development and advancement. It highlights the need to upgrade slums and essential services and to provide decent, safe, and affordable housing. In conjunction with improving street security and developing open transportation, the objective moreover emphasizes the importance of giving everybody secure, reasonable, open, and maintainable transportation choices. SDG 11 emphasizes the centrality of comprehensive and economical urbanization as well as the capacity to arrange and oversee human settlements in a participative, coordinated, and economical way. It emphasizes the need to protect the common and social history of the planet, bringing down the negative per capita natural impacts of cities, particularly concerning waste management and discussing quality, and guaranteeing that everybody has access to green spaces and open regions that are secure, inviting, and available. It also emphasizes the importance of promoting inclusive and sustainable urban planning and governance, along with strengthening urban resilience to disasters.

SDG 13: The objective calls to take urgent action to combat climate change and its impacts. This point recognizes that one of the greatest issues facing humankind is climate change, which calls for speedy action on a worldwide scale. It emphasizes the need to strengthen resilience and adaptive capacity to climate-related hazards and natural disasters in all countries. Additionally, it encourages the integration of climate change measures into national policies, strategies, and planning. This goal also highlights the importance of improving education, awareness, and human and institutional capacity on climate change mitigation, adaptation, impact reduction, and early warning.

The United Nations created the SDGs in 2015; they are a set of 17 interrelated objectives aimed at addressing worldwide issues like poverty, inequality, climate change, and natural degradation (United Nations, 2015). Since energy is basic to nearly every viewpoint of economic improvement, guaranteeing that everybody has access to reasonable, reliable, feasible, and modern energy may be a basic point among these seven (SDGs, 2015). Battling climate change and advancing sustainable industrialization requires a move to renewable energy sources, such as solar, wind, and bioenergy (Worldwide Renewable Energy Office, 2021). Critical prospects to lower greenhouse gas emissions, improve energy security, and foster financial development are displayed by advancements in renewable energy (IEA, 2022).

In this environment, optimizing energy arrangements utilizing cutting-edge innovations is significant. Energy management system optimization heavily relies on fuzzy logic, a form of multi-valued logic that allows for handling uncertainty and imprecision. The fuzzy logic enhances the efficiency of renewable energy frameworks and makes the integration of different energy sources less demanding by empowering more versatile and adaptable decision-making forms. According to Shafique et al. (2021), this strategy empowers better asset assignment and working methods that can adjust to changing natural circumstances and energy demands.

In conclusion, fuzzy logic optimization combined with breakthroughs in renewable energy offers a practical route to a strong and economically sustainable energy future, significantly contributing to the accomplishment of the SDGs. Making the most of fuzzy logic's potential in renewable energy applications will be fundamental for expanding the effectiveness and minimizing natural impacts as countries and communities work to fulfill these worldwide commitments.

13.2 Renewable Energy Technologies

As one of the options to replace fossil fuels, renewable energy sources have gained importance in the pursuit of economic improvement. The foremost broadly utilized renewable energy sources are hydroelectric, solar, and wind energy, each of which has extraordinary qualities and advantages.

13.2.1 Overview of Renewable Energy Sources

13.2.1.1 Solar photovoltaic systems

Solar photovoltaic systems convert sunlight directly into electricity using semiconductor materials. When sunlight hits the photovoltaic cells, it excites electrons, creating an electric current. These systems are typically composed of photovoltaic panels, an inverter, a battery storage system, and a mounting framework. There are three major types of solar photovoltaics. The first is the grid-tied, which is connected to the public electricity grid and can feed excess power back into the grid. Second is the off-grid, which is a standalone system that stores energy in batteries for use when there is no sunlight, and the third one is a hybrid system, which combines both grid-tied and off-grid features.

The merits of solar photovoltaic systems are that they are renewable and abundant energy sources, and they have low operating costs after installation. They also contribute to the reduction of greenhouse gas emissions. However, the demerits are that they have high initial installation costs. Energy production depends on sunlight availability, and it requires significant space for installation (U.S. Department of Energy, 2021).

13.2.1.2 Wind turbines

Wind turbines convert the kinetic energy from the wind into mechanical power, which can then be converted into electricity.

They consist of blades, a rotor, a gearbox, and a generator. Wind turbines are of two types: (a) horizontal axis wind turbines (HAWTs), which are the most common, with blades that rotate around a horizontal axis, and (b) vertical axis wind turbines (VAWTs), wherein the blades rotate around a vertical axis, suitable for variable wind directions. The main advantage of using wind turbines is that it is a clean and renewable source of energy. But again, the limitations are that it has high upfront costs and concerns about noise pollution. It can impact wildlife, specifically birds, due to the noise.

13.2.1.3 Energy storage systems

ESS are critical for balancing supply and demand, especially for intermittent renewable sources like solar and wind. They store excess energy generated during periods of low demand for use during high demand. There are four types of ESS: first, batteries, such as lithium-ion, lead-acid, and flow batteries, are common types. Second is a pumped hydro storage system, which uses surplus electricity to pump water uphill to a reservoir. When needed, water is released to generate electricity. Third is a compressed air energy storage (CAES) system, which stores energy by compressing air, which is later expanded to drive a turbine. Fourth is the thermal storage system, which stores energy in the form of heat, which can later be converted to electricity.

If we look at the merits of ESS, it enhances grid stability and reliability and supports the integration of renewable energy sources. It also aids in providing backup power during electricity outages. The limitations are that it has a very expensive initial cost, and it also loses its efficiency in the process of energy conversion and energy storage. It also has a limited lifespan for some technologies, such as batteries.

13.2.1.4 Solar energy

Sun-powered energy employs photovoltaic cells and solar thermal systems to capture solar radiation. The productivity and toll of solar panels have expanded significantly in recent times due to advancements in solar innovation. The yield of energy has expanded due to advancements like concentrated solar power

(CSP) frameworks, which utilize mirrors to concentrate sunlight, and bifacial solar panels, which collect sunlight from both sides. Furthermore, the advancement of adaptable and lightweight thin-film solar cells offers expanded mounting adaptability.

13.2.1.5 Wind energy

Wind energy employs turbines to harness the kinetic energy of the wind. With critical innovative headways, wind turbines nowadays are more viable and can run at lower wind speeds. Bigger rotor edges and drifting seaward wind farms are two illustrations of turbine plan advancements that have made it possible to produce energy in previously inaccessible places.

13.2.1.6 Hydropower

This strategy of creating power includes tackling the potential energy of streaming water. Although customary hydropower projects have been a major source of energy, more current advances like run-of-the-river ventures and small-scale hydropower frameworks diminish their negative impacts on the environment while still creating tried and true energy (Worldwide Hydropower Association, 2022). Moreover, by causing less harm to sea-going situations, improvements in turbine innovation, including fish-friendly turbines, have expanded the maintainability of hydropower.

13.3 Innovations in Energy Conversion and Storage

The wide utilization of renewable energy sources depends on how well energy is converted and stored. The irregular nature of the energy era may be addressed by progress in energy capacity innovation, such as batteries and other energy storage devices.

Energy Capacity Advances: Due to their speedy reaction times and tall energy densities, lithium-ion batteries have risen as the industry pioneer in energy capacity innovation. In any case, a persistent examination into alternative energy sources, like a stream and solid-state batteries, looks to improve productivity and stability. The grid's integration of renewable energy sources depends on these innovations since they empower energy capture during the top era and discharge during times of high demand.

Power-to-X Innovations: These advances, also known as power-to-X (P2X) innovations, empower the storage and transportation of renewable energy by converting excess renewable power into engineered fuels or hydrogen. Green hydrogen, a clean fuel that will be utilized in a variety of applications, such as mechanical forms and transportation, is being created utilizing electrolyzers, which utilize power to split water into hydrogen and oxygen (IRENA, 2021).

13.3.1 Role of Technology in Enhancing Energy Efficiency

Advancements in technology are essential for improving energy efficiency across all renewable energy sources. Smart grids, which use advanced digital tools to manage power distribution, make it possible to better integrate renewables into existing infrastructure. These grids optimize energy use and reduce waste by enabling real-time monitoring and demand response.

Building Energy Management Systems (BEMS): Innovation progressions in BEMS have improved building energy utilization efficiency. These frameworks empower the application of energy-saving methods by optimizing energy usage through the use of IoT sensors and data analytics. BEMS can significantly lower energy use and emissions by coordinating renewable energy sources and optimizing HVAC (heating, ventilation, and air conditioning) systems.

13.4 Smart Cities

Smart cities are urban areas that leverage advanced technologies, particularly information and communication technology (ICT) and the internet of things (IoT), to enhance the quality of life for their residents. The primary goal is to make urban living more efficient, sustainable, and responsive to the needs of citizens.

13.4.1 Integration of ICT and IoT

ICT: It refers to the use of digital technology (such as computers, smartphones, and the internet) to manage information and communication processes. In smart cities, ICT is foundational for various applications, from public service delivery to data analytics.

IoT: It involves connecting everyday objects to the internet, enabling them to send and receive data. In smart cities, IoT devices include sensors, cameras, and smart meters that collect real-time data on various aspects of urban life, such as traffic flow, air quality, energy usage, and public safety.

For example, Barcelona, Spain, has extensively integrated IoT and ICT, with smart street lighting that adjusts based on pedestrian activity and environmental sensors that monitor air quality.

13.4.2 Efficient Energy Use and Management

Smart lattices, which join renewable energy sources and adjust energy supply and demand in real-time, are the means by which smart cities trust to optimize energy utilization. Automated energy management systems in smart buildings reduce energy waste by adjusting lighting, temperature, and ventilation based on occupancy and weather conditions.

For instance, countries like the Netherlands' Amsterdam utilize a smart lattice framework that combines renewable energy sources like wind and solar power with real-time information to effectively manage energy distribution.

13.4.3 Sustainable Urban Mobility and Transportation Systems

Public Transportation: The adequacy and comfort of public transportation frameworks are expanded by real-time following and proactive planning. Coordination of installment frameworks and smart ticketing is an illustration of this.

Traffic Management: To screen and control the activity stream, reduce clogs, and help improve activity signals, IoT sensors, and information analytics are utilized.

Electric Vehicles (EVs): Smart-stopping choices and EV charging stations are basic components of economical urban portability.

For example, Singapore's Smart Country program comprises a broad EV framework, a productive public transportation framework, and real-time activity tracking.

13.4.4 Smart Healthcare and Education Systems

Smart Healthcare: Enhances the delivery and accessibility of healthcare by utilizing electronic health records, telemedicine, and remote observation.

Smart Education: To help improve instructional results, smart instruction combines advanced classrooms, e-learning platforms, and data-driven, individualized learning experiences.

For example, the smart healthcare framework in Seoul, South Korea, has made significant strides in healthcare, especially for the elderly and those living in rural regions, by providing telemedicine and further observation services (Seoul Metropolitan Government, 2021).

13.4.5 Improved Open Security with Responsive Frameworks and Observation

Surveillance: CCTV cameras and IoT sensors are used to monitor for criminal activity, infractions, and public security.

Responsive Systems: Emergency response frameworks that are responsive make use of information from a few sources to respond to emergencies, disasters, and other crises more skillfully.

For example, New York City employs modern analytics in conjunction with a tremendous array of observation cameras and sensors to enhance crime prevention and crisis response in public areas.

Smart cities utilize information analytics, computerized innovations, and organized frameworks to form cities with superior places to live, superior asset management, and more economic benefits. These cities utilize ICT to help improve citizen services and streamline operations, which raises the standard of living overall.

Sustainable Foundation: An eco-friendly framework, such as renewable energy sources, energy-efficient buildings, and sustainable travel choices, is given the highest priority in smart cities. By utilizing this strategy, greenhouse gas emissions are significantly diminished, and a more economical urban environment is advanced.

Connectivity: Real-time information gathering and communication are made conceivable by the combination of IoT gadgets and high-speed internet. In areas like waste collection, energy use, and traffic management, this interconnected system simplifies decision-making and streamlines the delivery of services.

13.4.6 Renewable Energy Sources Joined into Urban Planning

Smart cities must consolidate renewable energy frameworks into their urban planning in order to meet their sustainability targets. Utilizing energy-efficient foundations, wind turbines, and solar panels is one way to reduce reliance on fossil power and cut carbon emissions.

Urban Renewable Energy Activities: To extend to clean energy, smart cities can put in community solar ventures, in which local people pool their assets to buy solar energy systems. Besides, real-time checking and control of energy dispersion is made conceivable by smart frameworks, which optimize the utilization of renewable assets while bringing down consumer costs.

13.4.7 Case Considerations on Fuzzy Logic-Based Smart Cities

Case Ponder 1: ***Spain's Barcelona***: Barcelona's smart lighting framework has successfully joined fuzzy logic. Based on information collected in real-time on vehicle and person-on-foot action, the framework alters the sum of lighting. This development significantly reduces energy utilization by optimizing energy utilization while moving forward with security and permeability.

13.5 Smart Villages

Smart villages extend the concept of smart cities to rural areas, focusing on sustainable development and improving the quality of life through technology.

13.5.1 Improved Connectivity and Access to Services

Internet Access: To access the computerized system and make an assortment of online services available, a reliable and fast internet connection must be provided.

Telecommunication Infrastructure: Growing the reach of portable systems to ensure simple communication and data gets to local people.

For example, the Digital India program aims to improve access to information, governance, and economic opportunities by establishing high-speed internet connections in rural areas.

13.5.2 Enhanced Agricultural Practices

Precision Farming: This procedure empowers farmers to make data-driven decisions for higher yields by checking soil health, climate conditions, and soil conditions utilizing GPS, IoT sensors, and data analytics.

Smart Irrigation: IoT-based water system frameworks maximize water effectiveness by giving crops the right amount of water at the right time, preserving water and improving crop health.

For example, the Smart Town in Gujarat, India, has improved agrarian yield and water effectiveness by implementing the Smart water system frameworks and accurately cultivating disobedient (Digital India, 2020).

13.5.3 Renewable Energy Solutions for Off-Grid Areas

Solar Power: It is the establishment of solar panels to move forward energy accessibility, reduce reliance on conventional energy sources, and offer power to off-grid places.

Microgrids: Small-scale, neighborhood energy frameworks can work both autonomously and in pairs with the bigger framework to supply provincial communities with tried-and-true control. For example, the Grameen Shakti activity in Bangladesh has introduced over a million solar-powered domestic frameworks in rural zones, giving off-grid inhabitants access to reliable and clean power.

13.5.4 Access to E-Health and E-Education Services

E-Health: By delivering healthcare services to remote areas, telemedicine and virtual health clinics help improve access to care and health outcomes.

E-Education: Understudies in various areas can get high-quality instruction and learning materials, much appreciated in advanced learning stages and virtual classrooms. For example, in Kenya, the eLimu project uses tablets loaded with educational content to improve literacy and learning outcomes in rural schools (eLimu, 2021).

Community Interest: Counting local people effectively in decision-making may be a characteristic of smart communities. Through community members' sense of proprietorship and commitment, this participatory strategy ensures that improvement exercises are in line with nearby needs and desires.

Sustainable Homes: To advance sustainable practices, smart villages coordinate renewable energy sources and sustainable cultivation strategies. To preserve long-term sustainability, this involves empowering natural cultivation, utilizing adjacent assets, and skillfully managing natural resources.

Digital Network: Smart villages provide access to markets, services, and data by utilizing advanced technologies. According to Gonzalez et al. (2019), increased connectivity advances social incorporation and financial development by permitting local people to take advantage of more opportunities and assets (European Commission, 2020).

13.5.5 Energy Frameworks into Country Planning

Developing smart villages requires consolidating renewable innovations into planning. Nearby assets like biomass, solar, and wind can be tackled by these communities to enhance sustainability, lower energy costs, and achieve energy independence.

Initiatives for Country Renewable Energy: Smart villages can install microgrid frameworks that run on renewable energy to allow tenants reliable power. Solar energy frameworks, for example, can control community buildings like well-being centers and schools, enormously improving the quality of life and reinforcing local economies.

13.5.6 Case Thinks about Fuzzy Logic-Based Smart Villages

Case Consider 1: ***Indian Villages***: The fuzzy rationale has been utilized by intelligent activities in several Indian towns to successfully oversee their water supplies. These frameworks help improve water systems and water dispersion by analyzing an assortment of factors, including precipitation information and local utilization patterns. This ensures the economic utilization of water, which is fundamental for both community well-being and rural yield (Grameen Shakti, 2021).

13.6 Fuzzy Logic in Energy Management

Lotfi Zadeh created the concept in the 1960s, and it marks a significant departure from ordinary two-valued logic by allowing degrees of truth values to be anything other than 0 and 1. This sort of many-valued rationale was created in reaction to the equivocality and ambiguity displayed in human thinking and natural language, and it was made possible by Zadeh's groundbreaking work in sets. This concept has been developed over a long time, finding application in an assortment of spaces such as design recognition, control systems, and decision-making procedures (Zadeh, L. A., 1965).

Given the inherent complexity and variability of energy systems, fuzzy logic is especially well-suited for energy management. They can handle the steady varieties and vulnerabilities characteristic of renewable sources like solar and wind control, in contrast to classic two-point control systems that work on settled and exact values. Because of their adaptability, energy frameworks can be overseen more successfully and responsively, maximizing execution indeed in the face of changing circumstances (Han, Z., and Chen, X., 2017).

Many-valued logic, which bargains with approximations instead of settled and correct thinking, is known as fuzzy logic. Fuzzy logic factors can have a truth value that falls between 0 and 1, in contrast to binary sets, where factors can only have a value of 0 or 1. Fuzzy logic was created by Lotfi Zadeh in the 1960s with the deliberate aim of quantitatively recreating uncertainty and instability in human decision-making. Fuzzy logic provides a robust framework for optimizing performance and efficiency in energy management, a field where systems are complex and data is often uncertain.

13.6.1 Components of Fuzzy Logic

Fuzzification: Fuzzification is the process of converting crisp, precise input values into fuzzy values that can be understood and processed by a fuzzy logic system. This involves mapping input values to degrees of membership within fuzzy sets, which are defined by membership functions. These are graphical representations that define how each point in the input space is mapped to a degree of membership between 0 and 1. Common types of membership functions include triangular, trapezoidal, and Gaussian. For a temperature control system, a crisp input of 75 °F might belong partially to both the 'warm' and 'hot' fuzzy sets, with membership degrees of 0.4 and 0.6, respectively.

Rule Base: A collection of "if-then" rules that indicate the association between fuzzy inputs and fuzzy outputs makes up the run-the-show base. These directions are created using observational evidence or expert knowledge. Each run of the show has the same clear structure: "In case [condition] at that point [activity]." Fuzzy sets and dialect factors are utilized to characterize the conditions and activities. Creating these rules requires master information since it coordinates domain-specific experiences that increment the precision of the system's decision-making. A more complex run of the show in a renewable energy framework can be something like this: "Prioritize sun-based energy utilization and diminish storage in case daylight is abundant, temperature is direct, and battery capacity is low." This complex system is capable of handling a wide range of situations, ensuring an effective and balanced approach to energy management.

Inference Engine: Fuzzified inputs are nourished into the induction motor, which employs the rules from the rule base to deliver fuzzy outputs. It blends the input values' enrolment degrees with the rules characterized conditions. Sugeno deduction methods and Mamdani methods are prevalent approaches.

Mamdani induction is fitting for frameworks that ought to think like people since its employment uses fuzzy sets for both inputs and outputs. It is often chosen in circumstances where effortlessness and interpretability are vital, counting in HVAC frameworks where control choices must be straightforward to comprehend and adjust. Sugeno induction, on the other hand, regularly utilizes fuzzy sets as inputs and direct capacities as outputs. This approach offers computing productivity and is the favored strategy for control applications that require precise scientific models, such as automated industrial processes. The Sugeno approach, for instance, may well be utilized in a wind turbine control framework to accurately alter the edge pitch point in order to maximize energy extraction.

Defuzzification: The method of turning fuzzy yield values back into exact, clean values, which will be utilized to function in a framework, is known as defuzzification. This arrangement is required since the control choice or last activity ought to be communicated in a way that the physical framework can comprehend. The centroid approach, which decides the yield set's center of gravity, the bisector strategy, and the mean of maxima strategy are illustrations of common techniques.

The centroid approach produces an adjusted yield that takes into consideration all enrolment degrees by figuring out the yield fuzzy set's center of gravity. Due to its precision and steadfastness, it is broadly utilized, especially in applications such as adjusting the point of solar panels.

The point that partitions the yield fuzzy set into two break-even points is found utilizing the bisector strategy. Whereas it can be less exact than the centroid approach, it requires less computing control. It works well for more fundamental control systems; making choices rapidly is more imperative than being precise.

Mean of Maxima Strategy: The maximum enrollment is determined using this strategy. Indeed, even though it is the best and quickest strategy, the results may not be as exact as those obtained utilizing the centroid strategy. It is widely used in real-time control applications (e.g., power distribution in intelligent grids) where speed is crucial.

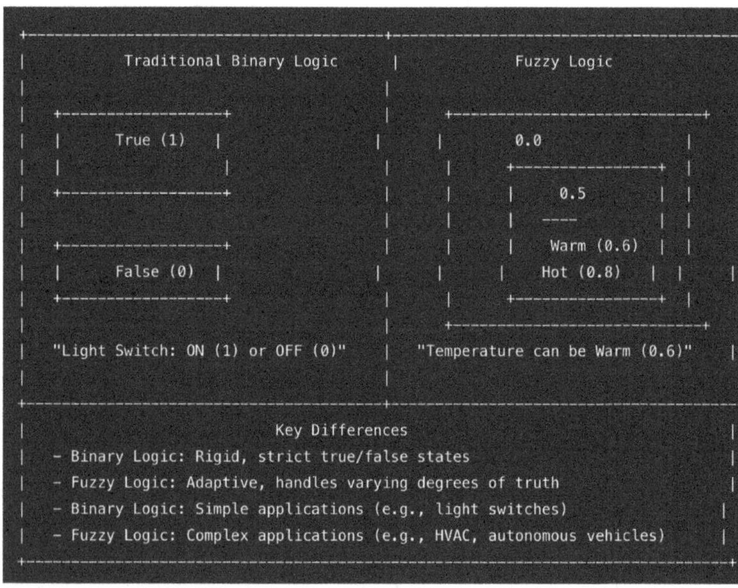

Figure 13.4 Diagram illustrating the principles of fuzzy logic and how it differs from traditional binary logic (*Source*: Generative).

13.6.2 Benefits of Traditional Control Systems

Flexibility: Compared to ordinary parallel rationale frameworks, fuzzy logic frameworks are much better able to oversee complicated and nonlinear circumstances. A fuzzy controller, for example, can adapt in real-time to changes, successfully overseeing the profoundly fluctuating nature of renewable energy sources.

Strength: Works well in real-world circumstances where information may be vague or wrong since it can viably handle uncertainties and incomplete data. Controllers, as restricted to standard controllers, are superior and able to endure unexpected changes in wind speed or heading in wind energy frameworks.

Simplicity: Since control systems depend on clear rule-based rationale instead of complicated numerical models, they are habitually less complex to build than other advanced control strategies. Making a controller for a sun-powered board framework, for example, involves defining an arrangement of justifiable "if-then" rules restricted to determining and settling complicated conditions.

Flexibility: Fuzzy logic frameworks show considerable versatility across a wide range of applications and varieties in framework flow, owing to their simple adjustment and scaling in understanding framework needs. For instance, it is essential to design a fuzzy logic controller for a smart framework to coordinate unused energy sources or adjust to changing energy requirements.

13.7 Policy and Regulatory Frameworks

Advancing the utilization and integration of renewable energy requires government arrangements and administrative incentives. Renewable energy ventures offer a system that advances speculation, reduces risks, and ensures long-term stability.

Incentives and Subsidies: Assess credits, awards, and other money-related motivations that can lower the upfront costs of introducing renewable energy frameworks. Ventures and designers discover renewable energy ventures more engaging because of these monetary motivations.

Feed-in Tariffs (FiTs): Guarantee renewable energy long-term buy contracts at set costs. As a result, makers of renewable energy have a relentless source of revenue, which empowers ventures in renewable energy.

Renewable Portfolio Standards (RPS): Require that a foreordained extent of control start from renewable assets. This fortifies the improvement and application of renewable innovation and produces a showcase for renewable energy.

Net Metering: Through the utilization of net metering, clients who generate their own electricity, for instance, through solar photovoltaic systems, can return excess power to the grid in exchange for credits. This increments the small-scale renewable energy systems' financial viability, which energizes their appropriation.

Research and Development Support: Government financing for R&D can accelerate the advancement of renewable energy innovation, enhance its efficiency, and reduce its cost over time.

13.7.1 Examples of Successful Policies from Various Countries

Germany: The presentation of feed-in duties by the Renewable Energy Sources Act (EEG) in 2000 brought about a significant increase in the capacity for renewable energy. Right now, more than 40% of Germany's power comes from renewable sources (Clean Energy Wire, 2020).

Denmark: With around 50% of its power coming from wind power, Denmark may be a worldwide pioneer in wind energy, much appreciated by government approaches that cultivate wind energy, including favorable FiTs and R&D appropriations (Wind Europe, 2021).

China: With the significant increase in renewable energy capacity, China has risen as the world's largest producer of solar panels and wind turbines, largely due to government support and the RPS framework.

United States: Since its presentation in 2006, Speculation Assess Credit for solar energy has driven the development of the solar industry, resulting in a 100% increase in solar establishments.

13.7.2 Decentralized Energy Systems

Decentralized energy frameworks do not depend on a centralized framework; instead, they produce and oversee energy at or near the point of utilization. Small-scale renewable energy sources, including solar photovoltaics, wind turbines, and local energy capacity choices, are regularly utilized in these frameworks (Energy Storage Association, 2021).

Enhanced Resilience: By reducing dependence on centralized networks, which are vulnerable to far-reaching blackouts, decentralized frameworks can increase energy security and versatility.

Reduced Transmission Losses: By creating energy closer to its point of utilization, transmission and dissemination over expansive separations are conducted with as small a loss of energy as possible.

Environmental and Economic Benefits: Utilizing more renewable energy sources reduces greenhouse gas emissions and other pollutants that come with utilizing fossil fuels to create power. Neighborhood renewable energy ventures that create, construct, and maintain energy frameworks can boost nearby economies and provide employment. Communities can benefit from neighborhood energy generation by having more control over their energy assets and a diminished reliance on external energy providers.

Technical Integration: It can be troublesome to coordinate disparate systems with the current framework; advanced control and communication technologies are required.

Regulatory Barriers: Modern rules and controls are required to adjust and bolster decentralized energy frameworks since the current administrative systems may not be able to support them.

Variable Energy Production: Since energy sources like the sun and wind are scattered, a dependable energy supply must be guaranteed through the utilization of proficient energy storage technologies and grid management.

13.7.3 Community Engagement and Participation

Participation and engagement of the community are basic to the victory of decentralized energy frameworks. Participating in neighborhood communities in energy activities advances sustainable development, adequacy, and ownership (Sustainable Development Goals Knowledge Platform, 2021).

Incorporating the community within the arranging process by holding open gatherings, workshops, and overviews to gather input and address issues. Open mindfulness of the focal points of decentralized frameworks and renewable energy can increase support and advance inclusion. Giving communities a voice in energy venture choices ensures that their needs and inclinations are taken into consideration. Community solar or wind ventures, for instance, permit local people to take an interest and benefit directly from renewable energy establishments (National Renewable Energy Laboratory, 2021).

Samsø, Denmark: With the assistance of community-owned wind turbines and biomass offices, the island's population has effectively taken an interest in the move to 100% renewable energy.

Feldheim, Germany: A community that utilized an agreeable demonstration to realize energy autonomy; its individuals mutually possess and work a biogas plant, a district heating system, and wind turbines.

Ukunda, Kenya: A community-based solar-based microgrid venture in Ukunda, Kenya, makes strides in neighborhood employment and financial prospects by providing the town with reliable and cost-effective power.

13.8 Challenges and Future Directions

Several challenges need to be settled to integrate fuzzy logic-based solutions in energy systems in a legitimate manner. One of the greatest impediments is the challenge of designing fuzzy rational controllers that can screen the energy characteristics of renewable sources. Vasilakos et al. (2019) agree that these systems often bargain with shifting inputs, such as moving daylight and wind speeds, which might compound the fuzzification and run the characterizing approaches. Moreover, the common acknowledgment of models may be hampered by the nonexistence of standardized procedures for making and approving them. Comprehensive rules are vital as the innovation is created to ensure consistency and steadfastness in applications, including fuzzy logic.

Integrating fuzzy logic frameworks with existing energy management systems presents a significant challenge. Since numerous energy frameworks utilize routine control procedures, switching to fuzzy logic would require a significant framework and mechanical alterations. Organizations may be hindered from implementing new initiatives by the time and money required for this integration. Moreover, workforce preparation on the right utilization and upkeep of fuzzy logic frameworks is vital for successful selection, whereas it may give budgetary and calculated challenges.

The use of fuzzy logic in energy management may evolve in the future due to emerging trends in smart technologies and renewable energy. Energy frameworks will become more responsive and organized as smart lattices, and the IoT will become more broadly utilized. By providing more exact and convenient inputs, these advances empower real-time information collection and processing, which can enhance the capabilities of fuzzy logic frameworks. The fuzzy logic can moreover be enhanced by improvements in fake insights and machine learning, coming about in half-breed frameworks that combine the finest highlights of both methodologies.

To take advantage of these opportunities, several research and policy recommendations are essential. First, developing more robust fuzzy logic models tailored to specific applications requires multidisciplinary collaboration, bringing together experts from fields such as computer science, engineering, and energy management. Second, to support a smoother transition from conventional methods, policymakers should promote the development of standards and best practices for applying fuzzy logic in energy systems. Finally, to prepare the workforce for the future of energy, investment in education and training programs focused on fuzzy logic and smart technologies will be crucial.

13.9 Conclusion

By handling critical concerns like climate change, energy accessibility, and economic urban improvement, renewable and smart cities are fundamental to achieving the SDGs. Fossil fuels can be supplanted with greener energy sources, such as wind and solar power, which help mitigate global warming. Smart cities utilize innovation to help improve the maintainability and productivity of their urban framework, which incorporates their energy systems. These cities promote energy efficiency, coordinate their systems, and adopt natural, neighborly waste management and transportation techniques. Green energy and smart cities work together to bolster different economic advancement objectives (SDGs), such as clean and cheap energy (SDG 7), economically viable cities and communities (SDG 11), and climate action (SDG 13).

Fuzzy logic's capacity to bargain with equivocalness and imprecision makes it a compelling device for controlling renewable energy systems. Since renewable energy sources are sporadic and erratic, coordinating them into the energy lattice presents troubles. Energy capacity frameworks, wind turbines, and solar panels can all work more effectively, thanks to fuzzy logic controllers, which can immediately adapt to changing circumstances. By using fuzzy logic, energy systems can more accurately predict and respond to fluctuations in energy supply and demand, ensuring both efficiency and stability. As a result, fuzzy logic plays a crucial role in modern renewable energy management, enhancing the reliability and performance of sustainable energy solutions.

Innovation in approach is basic to the success and development of smart cities and renewable energy. To overcome the irregular nature of renewable energy sources, innovations in unused energy capacity must be created, requiring bigger capacities, faster reaction times, and longer life expectancies. Energy capacity can be enormously expanded by utilizing cutting-edge innovations like solid-state batteries, lithium-ion batteries, and flow batteries. Assembly real-time energy requests will moreover require the execution of cutting-edge smart grid technology that can powerfully oversee and deliver energy from different sources, including renewables.

Encouraging global participation in sharing best practices, innovative technologies, and policy strategies for renewable energy and smart city development can accelerate the global transition to sustainable energy systems and urban environments. Global alliances ensure that countries can learn from each other's successes and challenges by promoting knowledge exchange, resource sharing, and investment in renewable energy initiatives.

Furthermore, advancing open association and information is fundamental for accelerating the take-up of smart city and renewable energy ventures. Public-private associations, community associations, and educational initiatives can empower citizens to participate in sustainability activities and promote the use of renewable energy sources, efficiency, and energy conservation at the local level.

Moreover, it is inconceivable to overstate the significance of lawmakers in creating accommodating administrative systems. Directions advancing energy productivity, charge credits, and subsidizing renewable energy ventures are illustrations of motivations that can goad private speculation and advancement. Governments can encourage the move to sustainable energy sources by setting unequivocal goals and rules.

To conclude, integrating renewable energy with smart cities backed by cutting-edge advances and fuzzy logic represents a progressive technique for addressing the world's energy challenges. Social orders may ensure that future eras can thrive in a world fueled by renewable energy by emphasizing sustainability and participation. This will clear the way for a future that is cleaner, greener, and more versatile.

References

1. REN21. (2021). Renewables 2021 Global Status Report.
2. IRENA. (2020). Innovation Landscape for a Renewable-Powered Future: Solutions to Integrate Variable Renewables.
3. Zadeh, L. A. (1965). Fuzzy Sets. *Information and Control*, 8(3), 338–353.
4. Han, Z., and Chen, X. (2017). Fuzzy Logic Control of Renewable Energy Systems. In *Renewable Energy Systems* (pp. 345–368). Academic Press.
5. European Commission. (2020). Smart Cities Marketplace. https://smart-cities-marketplace.ec.europa.eu/.
6. Seoul Metropolitan Government. (2021). Seoul Smart City. https://english.seoul.go.kr/policy-information/urban-planning/smart-city/.
7. Smart Nation Singapore. (2020). Smart Nation Initiatives. https://www.smartnation.gov.sg/.

8. Digital India. (2020). Digital Village. https://www.digitalindia.gov.in/.
9. Grameen Shakti. (2021). Solar Home Systems. http://www.gshakti.org/.
10. eLimu. (2021). Transforming Education in Kenya. https://e-limu.org/.
11. U.S. Department of Energy. (2021). Solar Investment Tax Credit (ITC). https://www.energy.gov/savings/solar-investment-tax-credit-itc.
12. Clean Energy Wire. (2020). Renewable Energy Sources Act (EEG). https://www.cleanenergywire.org/factsheets/germanys-renewable-energy-sources-act-eeg.
13. Wind Europe. (2021). Wind Energy in Denmark. https://windeurope.org/about-wind/countries/denmark/.
14. National Renewable Energy Laboratory. (2021). Community Solar. https://www.nrel.gov/state-local-tribal/community-solar.html.
15. Energy Storage Association. (2021). Decentralized Energy Systems. https://energystorage.org/why-energy-storage/what-energy-storage/.
16. Sustainable Development Goals Knowledge Platform. (2021). Community Engagement in Renewable Energy. https://sustainabledevelopment.un.org/topics/renewableenergy/community-engagement.

Chapter 14

Advancing Solar Photovoltaic Systems through Fuzzy Logic Control: Strategies for a Greener Future

Kittisak Jermsittiparsert[a] and Bhupinder Singh[b]

[a]*Shinawatra University, Thailand*
[b]*Sharda University, Greater Noida, Uttar Pradesh, India*

bhupindersinghlaw19@gmail.com

Abstract

With global demand for sustainable power on the rise, optimizing solar energy generation has become increasingly important. This paper will address the components of fuzzy logic, which can be used to manage uncertainties and complexities encountered with solar energy systems. The paper discussed several areas of application for fuzzy logic such as adaptive real time operations and controllers, improving efficiency during the peak generation phase through Fuzzy maximum power point tracking (MPPT) which tracks solar panels to operate at their optimal voltage based on radiation levels, and grid integration support using additional modes in case an electrical grid is stable needs more help. The chapter evidences the benefits of

Fuzzy Logic in Revolutionizing Renewable Energy
Edited by Bhupinder Singh, Komal Vig, Ruchi Lal, and Budi Agus Riswandi

ISBN 978-981-5129-92-2 (Hardcover), 978-1-003-74191-6 (eBook)
www.jennystanford.com

DOI: 10.1201/9781003741916-14

fuzzy logic controllers over classical control methods in case-based teaching, particularly when rapid changes and decision alterations are necessary. This underpins the usage of fuzzy logic in solar PV systems and thus exhibits environmentally responsible energy utilization, aiding prospects toward a more sustainable future, hence greener planet goals. Finally, the paper provides a set of research directions for furthering the application of fuzzy logic to renewable energy management.

Keywords: Solar Photovoltaic System, Fuzzy Logic, Artificial Intelligence, Solar Energy, Green Energy

14.1 Introduction

Renewable energy systems, e.g., solar photovoltaic (PV) and wind turbines, have become very popular in the last few years because of their environmentally friendly approach to reducing the carbon footprint of conventional fossil fuel-based power generation [1]. But these networks must run dependably for a long-term, reliable energy supply. Fault Management: An extremely important area with respect to the operation and maintenance of renewable energy systems, as it involves detection, diagnosis, and prognosis of failures. Fuzzy logic has been recognized and introduced as a potential tool to improve the faulty prognosis of fault management systems, because it can conveniently address uncertainty and imprecision that are intrinsic properties of all complex systems. This research study is intended to investigate the use of fuzzy logic in fault prognosis for renewable energy systems, including the ability to predict failures and optimize strategy scheduling [2]. This work helps to promote the use of solar-based renewable energy systems for a greener and cleaner world by employing fuzzy logic that can be used in other similar applications as well due to its flexibility property [3].

14.1.1 Background on Solar PV Technology

Solar PV technology has been recognized as the most promising alternative for sustainable energy production for global energy needs and environmental aspects [4]. The basic idea of PV technology is the conversion of sunlight using the PV effect into electricity (it was discovered in the 19th century). But it was only in the mid-20th century that the practical use of solar cells started to come when the first monocrystalline silicon-based cell was developed by Bell Laboratories around 1954, which has an efficiency of about 5–6%. Since then, the technology of solar PV has considerably evolved. The revolution in solar was brought by the introduction of high-efficiency crystalline silicon cells, which are now able to convert more than 20% sunlight into electricity. Furthermore, progress in materials science has led to the emergence of innovative technologies such as thin-film solar cells and upcoming perovskite solar cells that bring specific benefits regarding price, mass, and flexibility [5]. Solar energy has become far more competitive and feasible than it used to be when compared to other fossil fuels, which are finite. Over the last twenty or so years, global solar PV has grown rapidly with constantly falling costs combined with government incentives and growing awareness of our need for renewables. Solar power capacity has grown from around 40 GW in 2010 to over a whopping ~900+ GW by this year, making it one of the fastest-growing forms of energy generation on earth as per the International Energy Agency (IEA)! The trend is expected to gain more traction as countries around the world aim to achieve their climate goals and transition toward a sustainable future [6].

14.1.2 Importance of Control Strategies in Solar Systems

Solar PV technology has advanced markedly, but the inherent variability and intermittency of solar energy create substantial hurdles for efficient grid management [7]. Optimal control of solar PV systems is critical to enable them to operate efficiently and adapt to changing environmental conditions. These methods benefit the most in terms of output by increasing power, increasing system robustness, and ensuring that these clean resources can be fed into the current grid safely. MPPT is considered one of the most important control strategies to be applied in solar PV systems. The MPPT algorithm is continuously tracking the solar panels in their maximum power point, adjusting them based on temperature changes and solar irradiance to keep them always at peak output efficiency [8]. This is very important if the weather status of an area has fluctuating conditions, which we can utilize to maximize energy harvest [9]. Trade-offs in the level of MPPT detail design points for control energy management systems (EMSs), control operation of solar PV with energy storage solutions (batteries). These systems balance supply and demand, storing the surplus of energy from peak sunlight hours for use when solar power is not generating. It is especially crucial in residential and commercial solar when they are consuming the energy, which does not amount to generating time [10].

14.1.3 Objectives of the Research

In this research paper named "Strategies for a Greener Future: Scrutinizing fuzzy logic control strategies in improving the accuracy and efficiency of solar PV systems," we have aimed at investigating how fuzzification can influence performance as well as potential improvement using fuzzy logic control (FLC) techniques [11]. Solar energy management, with its complexities and uncertainties of a nonlinear nature, is an ideal candidate for the application of fuzzy logic, which deals with reasoning approximations rather than absolute categories. The study of this research has several specific goals to accomplish:

- **Analyze the Control Strategies in Designing the Solar PV Systems:** The paper discusses an overall overview of existing control strategies that are used for solar PV systems and emphasizes their advantages and disadvantages. The research will inform the existing landscape or state of play and identify gaps to develop a strategy for improvement [12].
- **Examine Basics of Fuzzy Logic:** The study will explore basic concepts related to fuzzy logic, i.e., the design elements and characteristics, along with how it has an edge over other standard control methods. This study will set the foundation to understand how fuzzy logic may be utilized in managing solar energy [13].

- **Study on FLC Applications**: The thesis will investigate completely different applications of fuzzy logic management strategies in star PV systems, which can embody adaptive fuzzy logic controllers (AFLCs) and vulnerability embeddings as attacks within fuzzy logic-supported MPPT algorithms. The paper, which includes case studies and real-world implementations, shows the applicability of fuzzy logic to maximize solar energy generation [14].
- **Performance Evaluation and Comparative Analysis:** Here, the research will look into how good these FLC strategies are in comparison to other forms of conventional mechanisms, with respect to energy efficiency, reliability, and adaptability. The evaluation will enlighten the level of applicability available in fuzzy logic solutions.
- **Challenges and Future Directions:** This work identifies technical challenges toward the implementation of fuzzy logic in solar PV systems, the limitations, and considerations that have also been considered for recommendations. Moreover, it will explore new research areas in fuzzy logic and solar energy, which can lead to further development.

This research seeks to contribute to the debate on renewable energy technologies and their role in (apparently) solving the global energy crisis by achieving each of these goals. The outcomes of this study will not only be useful in improving FLC strategies, but they can also help researchers, industrial practitioners, and policymakers in the further development of solar PV systems, as well as make a more sustainable environment.

14.2 Literature Review

14.2.1 Overview of Solar PV Systems

Solar PV systems convert sunlight into electricity through the photo-voltaic effect. Since the technology's inception, both materials and system design have come a long way to improve efficiency and cost [15]. There are a few basic pieces of equipment in every PV system: solar panels, inverters (which convert the electricity produced by modules from direct current (DC) to alternating current (AC)), mounting structures, and electrical accessories. Solar PV system components are as follows:

Solar Panels: Possibly the stiffest component of a PV system, forming an array mounting unit that holds several modules made from solar cells. If you see a solar panel in the desert emitting DC electricity whenever sunlight hits it, then that is your basic PV unit. Solar panel efficiencies have come a long way; nowadays, solar panels based on crystalline silicon can quickly exceed 20% efficiency. Perovskite solar cells are emerging as well, increasing efficiency to even higher levels and lowering the costs of fabrication [16].

Inverters: The inverter is a very important part of the PV system because it transforms all DC electricity collected thanks to solar panels into AC [17]. Inverters can come in different form factors, such as string inverters, microinverters, and power optimizers, which all have their subsets of technology improvements over the years [18].

Racking: These are the mounting structures that help hold those solar panels in place, fixed racks, and tracking systems. You can install it in a fixed position or use a tracking system to keep up with the daily movements of the sun, maximizing uptime throughout sunlight hours [19].

Balance of System (BoS): This includes everything that is not solar panels, from wiring and combiner boxes to disconnection switches and safety equipment. The BoS elements can make up about half of the entire system price, usually more significant than that of solar panels.

Off-Grid Systems: These are grid-independent systems with batteries built in to store surplus energy during sunny days for use when the sun is not shining. They are often found in resource chambers where the network penetration is infrequent [20].

Hybrid Systems: These are grid-connected battery storage, granting the greatest amount of flexibility and reliability. This will be billed to a client. It is worth what comes with the application of energy for different electricity costs and uses power from both the grid and stored electrons. Solar PV systems can be as versatile as being deployed on home rooftops to utility-scale solar farms.

Solar PV is growing as time goes by, with technology development, solar energy can turn out to be a very good solution for providing the global living standards sustainably [21].

14.2.2 Current Control Strategies in Solar Energy Management

In Paris, July 29 (Prerna Sharma/MP), solar PV systems have been the long-standing heroes of solar energy producers, but efficient energy management is key to extracting maximum performance out of these stars. Several control techniques have emerged to maximize the energy production, provide a reliable operation, and help in interfacing with the grid [22].

A widely employed control strategy in solar PV systems is MPPT. This allows the system to actually adjust its operating point continuously in order to always operate at maximum power output irrespective of weather and temperature variations. MPPT algorithms rely on current data to figure out the voltage and angle at which panels produce the most power. It is required to maximize the energy harvest in unpredictable weather conditions, primarily seen at fixed tilt sites [23].

EMSs: These work to manage how solar PV and energy storage solutions, such as batteries, operate together. Such systems keep an eye on energy generation and consumption, which, in turn, helps to distribute the power accordingly whenever needed. EMS stores excess energy produced during peak sunlight hours, so power is available as needed for the long run when solar generation rates are lower. This is critical for residential and commercial applications due to the mismatch of energy demand with solar generation [24].

Grid Integration and Control: The higher the penetration of solar PV systems, the more mature control strategies are needed to ensure stable operation of the grid [25]. Electricity networks providing other voltages and frequencies than standard will complicate the integration of solar power in large-scale systems, but advanced control systems could manage even this. This process occurs in real-time, meaning utilities can monitor and control the power flow to prevent blackouts [26].

Predictive Control Concept: These are different types of predictive controllers for solar PV systems that can improve power performance with the help of data analytics and forecasting techniques. These strategies help to improve the efficiency of EMSs by predicting solar irradiance and energy demand [27]. Predictive algorithms, for example, can be used to predict the best moments when energy should be stored and discharged that would ensure optimal utilization of energy [27].

14.2.3 Fuzzy Logic in Energy Systems: A Review

One of the most practical methods that was employed in energy management until today, in direct relation with solar PV systems, was fuzzy logic [28]. Fuzzy logic allows for ambiguity and imprecision in a way that traditional controls (which depend on high precision mathematical models) cannot—it works well with non-linearity. It is based on the concept of fuzzy sets, which actually gives grades, likewise degrees to membership, rather than in terms of true or false as a traditional binary set. This could allow for more nuanced decision strategies that closely replicate human-level reasoning [29]. Fuzzy logic is a type of control strategy that can be applied in the context of solar energy management to make controllers adapt their actions based on different environmental conditions and system performance. An article, Fuzzy Logic Applications in Solar PV Systems, provides a survey on different applications of fuzzy logic within solar PV systems [30].

Adaptive Control Systems: The parameters of fuzzy logic controllers can be adjusted on the fly based on environmental conditions (e.g., changes in solar irradiance and temperature) [31]. This kind of adaptability allows solar to become even more efficient, as it optimizes the energy output in real-time for any given set of lighting conditions.

Fuzzy Logic for MPPT: This technique ensures good tracking of the maximum power point under different conditions using fuzzy logic-based MPPT algorithms [32]. The study has determined that these algorithms perform better than conventional MPPT methods, particularly with changing environmental conditions, which maximizes energy harvest.

Grid Integration and Management: Fuzzy logic can manage the grid integration of solar PV systems. Fuzzy logic controllers support the power flow and quench by giving system stability; therefore, they may improve control strategies so that they can be applied in wider energy networks, making solar energy more reliable [33].

Benefits of Fuzzy Logic in Energy Systems: The application of fuzzy logic within energy systems has several reasons, among others. Fuzzy logic can deal effectively with uncertainty (e.g., imprecision), which is the reason that it also suits applications in renewable energy management where data are incomplete, inaccurate, or fuzzy as well.

Easy Implementation: Fuzzy logic systems (FLSs) can be designed directly without deriving a complex mathematical model, and hence they will work well for real-life applications.

Utilization of Familiar Information: The fuzzy reasoning encourages the expansion of familiar data and regular language rules into control systems, making them more intelligent and self-adaptable.

Better System Performance: FLC strategies can help in increasing the efficiency and performance of solar PV systems, hence leading to higher energy yield and grid stability [34].

The findings in the reviewed literature suggest an impressive development of solar PV systems, a necessity for energy management using comprehensive control strategies, and an intriguing potential that fuzzy logic offers for optimizing performance when designing solar panels. Future work in these areas will be essential for advancing the field and supporting a sustainable energy future as demand for renewable energy continues to increase [35].

14.3 Fuzzy Logic Fundamentals

Fuzzy logic is a computational paradigm that permits natural language considerations by programmers. In control systems, it becomes especially helpful, as real-world problems may be way too complicated and variable to describe in our classical binary logic. It gets into the basics of fuzzy logic, how a system is designed, including its elements, and in concrete applications, this form of controlling fares better than classical control methods [36].

14.3.1 Principles of Fuzzy Logic

Fuzzy logic is built around fuzzy sets—the concept first introduced by Lotfi Zadeh in 1965 [37]. Contrary to conventional sets, where an element can be in or out of the set (true/false), fuzzy logic utilizes membership values. For instance, if a person is taller than 6 feet, tallness will have percentage_tall=1 for this humanestructor. Also, an element can belong partially to more than one set (as is found in the real world, where boundaries are fuzzy) [38]. A single example of a fuzzy set: "tall people." A classic height threshold distinguishes itself from fuzzy logic in that it is gradual. The age of 17.5 cm can have a membership degree, $\alpha = 0.7$ in the category "tall" and an elevation on that return air or mode=160="up>19 rare "/response point-air-mode >≥193 with OCest();;; This very flexibility allows the fuzzy logic to model complex systems where inputs are not always exact. Linguistic variables are used by fuzzy logic to explain inputs and outputs in a more human-understandable way. These variables take fuzzy sets and are typically described by labels like high, average, or low. Fuzzy rules capture the relationships between these variables and are often described in an "If Then" format. A rule such as, "If" the temperature is high "Then" the fan speed is fast Fuzzy inference consists of three steps: fuzzification, rule evaluation, and defuzzification. Fuzzification transforms crisp input values into fuzzy sets using the membership functions. Rule evaluation uses the fuzzy rules on fuzzified inputs to give the fuzzy outputs [39]. Defuzzification translates the aggregated fuzzy outputs back into crisp values; this is what ultimately provides you with some actionable results [40].

14.3.2 FLS Design and Components

FLS consists of many elements that collaborate to treat the input signals and give them as outputs, namely, fuzzifier, rule base, inference engine, and defuzzifier.

Fuzzifier: It converts crisp input values into fuzzy sets. These fuzzy membership functions are predefined, and they calculate the degree of belongingness between each input from the respective sets. This is an important step in converting real-world readings to a format that can be processed by the fuzzy inference engine [41].

Rule Base: The rule base consists of a set of fuzzy rules that describe the relationships among input and output variables [42]. These rules are often based on the experience of experts. Generally, the effectiveness of FLS is mostly dependent on this component. If a fuzzy logic model with accurate and complete data has been created, it performs well. A simple organization of rules allows the system to reason on these inputs, which ultimately helps in making an informed decision [42].

Inference Engine: The inference engines are the pedigree of fuzzy logic and are responsible for interpreting arbitrary rules qualitatively according to input diseases [43]. It simply extracts the rules applicable, and taking into account the degree of truth for each rule, computes (combines) all fuzzy outputs. By combining multiple rules, the inference engine simulates human reasoning to draw a conclusion [44].

Defuzzifier (inverse of fuzzification): Defuzzifiers are used to convert the aggregated fuzzy output set into a crisp offset value. This step is critical as it enables translating fuzzy results into recommendations. The simplest are the centroid method, which calculates the center of mass (center of gravity) in the fuzzy output set, and the maximum method, also called a winner-takes-all approach [45].

Fuzzy control systems can be designed with very low dependence on mathematical modeling of the system and are flexible enough to operate in a wide range of applications. For example, in solar PV systems, the inputs may be solar irradiance, temperature, and load demand, while outputs could result from some control signals for inverters or tracking systems. Due to this adaptability, FLSs may be appropriate for a wide range of applications (especially in environments with some uncertainty and vagueness) [46].

14.3.3 Advantages of Fuzzy Logic Over Traditional Control Methods

Fuzzy logic has its benefits over the traditional control approaches, especially in real-world problems where imprecision and uncertainty are related. Some key benefits include:

Coping with Uncertainty and Vagueness: Fuzzy logic outperforms classic set theory in dealing with the unavailability of complete and precise data, widely noticed in reality. Here, the traditional binary logic flounders and yields rigid decision-making that is less effective. Fuzzy logic, which permits partial truths to be modeled, leads to more flexible and realistic modeling of complex systems, such as solar EMSs [47].

Resembles Human Reasoning: Taste-based math would be able to be likened to the people's method for thinking, which makes it generally helpful in those applications where decisions are based on human judgment and intuition. FLS can be implemented to account for linguistic variables and fuzzy rules that model human expertise, which, in turn, contributes to more intuitive control strategies [48].

Fuzzy logic is robust, and it has an inherent potential to deal with the imprecision of data, which makes fuzzy systems well-accommodating techniques. Since it does not need accurate mathematical models, they can adjust easily to changes in environments and are suitable for dynamic scenarios. This plasticity is particularly advantageous in solar PV systems, where environmental conditions can fluctuate widely.

Ease of Implementation: FLSs are often easier to design and implement than traditional control methods. Fuzzy logic does not need an elaborate mathematical representation that might be time-consuming and difficult to mimic. On the other hand, by setting fuzzy rules based on expert knowledge and experience, it is possible to deploy in real-world applications faster [49].

Multimodal Control: Fuzzy logic is also able to deal with more than one input and output variable together, so it serves in situations where different things are interconnected. This permits advanced control strategies to be developed, which may optimize the overall system performance and ensure stability & reliability while maximizing energy output in solar PV systems [50].

Better Performance: FLC strategies have been known to outperform traditional control approaches in many use cases, as numerous studies can attest. As these systems take advantage of fuzzy reasoning, they are able to work more efficiently with quick response and better performance. It is well known that for solar PV systems, fuzzy logic can significantly improve the performance of MPPT and energy management optimization to increase energy yields and achieve better grid interconnection [51].

In summary, fuzzy logic is a major breakthrough in the field of control systems, especially when dealing with uncertain or vague conditions [52]. The principles involved, system design, and the advantages of this technology, as inherently helping in enhancing solar PV systems' performance, also make them ideal for it. The demand for efficient and effective renewable energy solutions will rise in the coming years, which requires a global need for FLC strategies to be implemented in solar-based systems, thereby solving many a dollar problem, giving way to sustainability [53].

14.4 FLC Strategies for Solar PV Systems

Abstract FLC strategies are widely employed for the operation of solar PV systems since they allow for managing uncertainty and imprecision in a straightforward manner. In a world with ever-increasing demand for sustainable power sources, it is important to offer efficient solar energy systems support. Three important areas where FLC strategies can be employed, viz., adaptive FLCs, FPGA implementation of FLC for MPPT, and grid integration and management using the concept of an ideal RBC, are discussed in this section [54].

14.4.1 Adaptive Fuzzy Logic Controllers

AFLCs are the ones whose design evolves with respect to time when parameter adaptation is required according to any change in environmental conditions and system response. This variability is very useful when it comes to systems such as solar PV, where the sun can come out of sight almost instantaneously for short periods during times such as day or night, depending on how cloudy weather conditions are. AFLCs are capable of learning from previous experiences and updating their control strategies accordingly. For example, AFLC can continuously track the output power and environmental conditions in a solar PV system [55]. If the system recognizes a drop in power due to shading or temperature spells, then the controller can adjust operating parameters to maximize efficiency. This enables the system to continue generating power at peak efficiency throughout changing circumstances. An AFLC usually consists of a number of fuzzy rules that determine what the system should do for various input cases. These rules are informed by expertise and may be tweaked over time as the system gains experience from its operating history. Employing a feedback-based control mechanism, the AFLCs can improve decision-making, enabling efficiency and reliability in solar PV systems [56].

14.4.2 Fuzzy Logic for MPPT

MPPT is an important function in solar PV systems to ensure the system operates at maximum power output with changing environmental conditions. The perturb and observe (P&O) and incremental conductance method (IncCond) are among the most common traditional MPPT schemes, but they tend to fail in quickly changing conditions or when partial shading occurs. FLC-based MPPT algorithms provide an adequate solution since the fuzzy set resembles human thinking ability than neural networks and is well-known for its robustness in managing uncertainties and non-linear coefficients of PV systems. These rules are very fuzzy: they tell the controller how to determine its current operating point based on real-time measurements of voltage and possibly some measurement of current from your solar panels.

One rule could be, "if the current is increasing and the voltage is decreasing, increase the duty cycle." Fuzzy logic with MPPT is advantageous because it has a quick and accurate response to changing conditions of the environment. Since fuzzy logic controllers are capable of tuning the duty cycle to be bang-on target for maximum power point, they do not like traditional methods that may partly oscillate around their peak. Such a responsiveness is critical in applications where solar irradiance can change quickly (for example, due to shading from clouds/bushes or changing weather) [57].

14.4.3 Fuzzy Logic in Grid Integration and Management

With a growing penetration of solar energy systems, their effective integration with the electrical grid is critical to provide security and reliability to electricity generation. In large systems, it is difficult to develop control strategies of a conventional type because traditional approaches will lead to complex and lengthy simulation coding, but a fuzzy logic-based strategy holds good as the best solution for grid-connected solar PV systems due to power flow optimization with proper communication from SPV with respect to the Grid [58]. Advanced control systems can be created to observe and regulate the exchanges of solar PV with the grid by using fuzzy logic. These systems can take in real-time grid profile data, energy demands, and solar generation patterns to better inform intelligent decisions around the distribution of electricity. This means, like during high solar generation, this dispatch controller would be able to decide how much energy should be exported back into the grid at what time, while still ensuring that enough power is there in the battery to meet further needs. The primary challenge while integrating solar PV systems to the grid is managing voltage and frequency fluctuations. By using fuzzy logic controllers, these problems can be mitigated by automatically tuning the solar system output in real-time with respect to grid changes. A simple solution is that, should there be an unexpected drop in voltage within the grid, due to sudden demand from a large development or energy consumer, we have some control over how much power actually gets pushed out of the solar array and onto the grid. Consequently, if the grid experiences high demand, then increased output can be called for by the controller, which would now support load [59].

14.5 Case Studies and Applications

The integration of FLC strategies in solar PV systems has demonstrated significant potential in enhancing their performance and efficiency. This section presents various case studies and applications of fuzzy logic in solar PV systems, evaluates their performance, and conducts a comparative analysis with conventional control methods [60].

14.5.1 Implementation of Fuzzy Logic in Solar PV Systems

Fuzzy logic has been adopted in various applications of solar PV systems, and this proves its flexibility to control the intricacies involved in solar energy generation. A famous real-world problem example is the implementation of a fuzzy logic-based EMS for a grid-connected solar PV household [61]. Utilizing fuzzy logic in the system, this algorithm utilizes solar panels, grids, and other energy storage systems to balance the energy requirements of a household. In this implementation, the fuzzy logic controller for managing the solar PV system energy and household load is designed. Fuzzy rules are used in the controller to decide when and how much excess energy is stored in batteries, drawn from the grid, or fed back to the grid. The fuzzy logic controller measures solar irradiance, as well as temperature and household energy consumption; in this way, it always knows what is best to use and can make decisions on time to spend less money.

MPPT in Solar PV Systems: MPPTs implement the fuzzy logic algorithm to extract abundant power from a solar PV panel. This is especially important in terms of systems that receive power from solar panels, as it helps to utilize the energy harvested under these conditions. A more practical example was shown for a linear voltage-based MPPT with FLC of duty cycle in the DC-DC converter, as clear from the case study discussed. In this way, it enables the system to change rapidly as needed and work on its highest efficiency level during parts of PV operation [62].

14.5.2 Performance Evaluation and Results

Different studies have evaluated the performance of FLC strategies in solar PV systems and indicated their potential to increase energy efficiency along with system reliability. For the fuzzy logic-based EMS for a grid-connected PV home, simulations indicated very large savings in relation to traditional control solutions [63]. With the fuzzy controller steering clear of power from the grid and jumping on any available sunshine, there was optimized energy use with minimal reliance upon 'brown' electricity. Moreover, when modeling and control of MPPT are concerned, fuzzy logic controllers have shown excellent performance in energy maximization [64]. Comparative performance analysis was performed for fuzzy logic-based MPPT with respect to conventional techniques, such as P&O and IncCond, which were able to deliver efficient energy yields under spatio-varied irradiation conditions [65]. Because fuzzy logic reacts quickly to variables for the environment of a relatively certain hardware, it can improve MPP tracking efficiency as a whole. The result of employing fuzzy logic in solar tracking systems was also effective. Numerical studies revealed that fixed installations resulted in a 15–25% thickening of the energy capture using fuzzy-controlled solar trackers [66]. This was facilitated by the processing of sensor data and thus dynamic control over panel orientation using 'fuzzy logic' as well, which meant that these trackers could follow the sun perfectly to some extent, all throughout the day.

14.5.3 Comparative Analysis with Conventional Control Methods

In this regard, a comparative study of fuzzy logic-based control with other conventional methods provides many merits that are used to implement in the behavior level controller for solar PVs [67]. Classic control approaches, e.g., PID (Proportional-Integral-Derivative) controllers, require a precise model that is described by deterministic parameters. On the other hand, a fuzzy logic controller uses domain-specific input from an expert and is able to adjust itself according to environmental scenarios without needing general mathematical algorithms. One of the important benefits of fuzzy logic is its ability to work with uncertain and imprecise information [68]. Traditional control systems can fall behind during rapid environmental variation. The flexibility of fuzzy logic enables the system to respond better to changes such as solar irradiance, temperature, and load demand, which contributes to improved performance. For instance, comparisons between fuzzy logic and conventional methods in MPPT applications demonstrate that the former is advantageous in terms of energy efficiency and time response. A major drawback of the traditional method is that, while grid connection, some oscillations will be encountered in and around MPP, but a fuzzy controller can change the duty cycle quickly based on a given value to maintain maximum power output [69].

14.6 Challenges and Future Directions

While FLC strategies have demonstrated significant potential in advancing solar PV systems, there are still challenges and limitations that need to be addressed. This section explores the technical challenges in fuzzy logic implementation, discusses the limitations and considerations, and identifies future research opportunities in this field [70].

14.6.1 Technical Challenges in Fuzzy Logic Implementation

One of the key technical issues hampering FLC strategies from being implemented in solar PV systems is how to properly select membership functions and the rule base. The quality and comprehensiveness of the fuzzy rules are critical to their practical use as a controller. Creating a good rule base can take time and many iterations to test so that the system is working correctly in all circumstances. Moreover, one more key issue is the computational complexity involved in FLSs. The higher the number of input variables and fuzzy rules, the greater the need for more processing. This can be a problem in real-time decision-making software such as MPPT controllers or grid integration systems. Fast response times and robust operation require optimizing the computational efficiency of fuzzy logic algorithms. Also, the merging of fuzzy logic with other control strategies like neural networks or genetic algorithms can create further complications. Although hybridization techniques can scale up both functionality and flexibility to solar PV systems, designing and tuning the same in a comprehensive manner seems complex. The potential of combining fuzzy logic with other control strategies is immense, and research in developing systematic approaches for such combinations needs to be encouraged [71].

14.6.2 Limitations and Considerations

One of the key technical issues hampering FLC strategies from being implemented in solar PV systems is how to properly select membership functions and the rule base. The quality and comprehensiveness of the fuzzy rules are critical to their practical use as a controller. Creating a good rule base can take time and many iterations to test so that the system is working correctly in all circumstances. Moreover, one more key issue is the computational complexity involved in FLSs. The higher the number of input variables and fuzzy rules, the greater the need for more processing. This can be a problem in real-time decision-making software such as MPPT controllers or grid integration systems. Fast response times and robust operation require optimizing the computational efficiency of fuzzy logic algorithms. Also, the merging of fuzzy logic with other control strategies like neural networks or genetic algorithms can create further complications. Although hybridization techniques can scale up both functionality and flexibility to solar PV systems, designing and tuning the same in a comprehensive manner seems complex. The potential of combining fuzzy logic with other control strategies is immense, and research in developing systematic approaches for such combinations needs to be encouraged [72].

14.6.3 Future Research Opportunities in Fuzzy Logic for Solar Energy

A few of the emerging tracks in future research to be conducted on engineering solar PV systems using fuzzy logic are thus promising, although daunting. Developing cyber-physical systems includes the development of an advanced fuzzy logic controller that can learn and tune its parameters based on historical data, real-time feedback [73]. These controllers will use machine learning to continuously self-optimize and condition themselves for fluctuating conditions, which, in turn, increases the efficiency and reliability of solar PV better than ever. Another research direction could be the fusion of fuzzy logic with other challenging technologies such as blockchain and IoT. Energy transactions and data exchange in solar PV systems can be safely & decentralized on the blockchain for such applications, while IoT allows real-time monitoring of distributed solar assets. By coupling these technologies with FLC mechanisms, the next generation of solar energy systems can be smarter and more robust. Moreover, it is an exciting area of research to apply fuzzy logic in next-generation solar PV technologies: perovskite solar cells and tandem solar cells. While these new materials and device architectures have the potential to enable higher efficiency at lower costs, they also come with new performance optimization challenges and reliability concerns. The role of FLC strategies can be very important in facing these challenges and achieving the maximum benefit from such technologies.

14.7 Conclusion

The paper "Advancing Solar Photovoltaic Systems through Fuzzy Logic Control: Strategies for a Greener Tomorrow" has pointed out that FLC schemes have great potential to improve both performance and efficiency of solar PV systems. In the backdrop of the world drifting toward sustainable energy, fuzzy logic in solar power management is becoming a valuable tool to handle chaotic behavior and intermittent variables seen within renewable energies. The analysis of the current control methods has demonstrated that conventional techniques are insufficient to handle typical solar power variability because they fail due to an associated intermittent characteristic. For performance optimization of solar PV systems, fuzzy logic wins as it can be designed to behave similarly to human reasoning and help reduce the dependency on predefined values. Fuzzy sets and membership functions are the very basic principles of fuzzy logic that allow modeling in a flexible way, providing an ideal environment to design advanced control strategies adapted for particular features of solar energy applications. FLC has not so far produced pristine results in the practical aspects of solar PV systems. AFLCs automatically optimize their parameters using current feedback and, therefore, maximize the energy output in different environmental states. MPPT algorithms based on fuzzy logic are reported to outperform conventional methods and have the ability to track the maximum power point, hence higher energy harvest. In addition, fuzzy logic in grid management provides clear improvements to grid stability and reliability, which permit smooth integration of solar PV systems into the electrical grid.

Several case studies and applications have demonstrated that FLC strategies fare well in real-world scenarios. These investigations have emphasized the potentialities of fuzzy logic, showing its adaptability, robustness, and simple application. Several works cited in the literature survey indicated that fuzzy logic controllers always perform better compared to other traditional control methods, especially under dynamic environmental conditions and partial shading.

References

1. Ashinze, U. K., Edeigba, B. A., Umoh, A. A., Biu, P. W., and Daraojimba, A. I. (2024). Urban green infrastructure and its role in sustainable cities: A comprehensive review. *World Journal of Advanced Research and Reviews*, 21(2), 928–936.
2. Sang, H., Chen, S., Qu, F., Song, Y., and Yang, F. (2024). Research on the application of renewable energy in power system based on adaptive hierarchical fuzzy logic maintenance. *Measurement: Sensors*, 34, 101281.

3. Sharma, A., and Singh, B. (2022). Measuring impact of E-commerce on small scale business: A systematic review. *Journal of Corporate Governance and International Business Law*, 5(1), 1–3.
4. Zabel, A., and Häusler, M. M. (2024). Policy instruments for green infrastructure. *Landscape and Urban Planning*, 242, 104929.
5. Kaneti, V. R., Masih, J., Yoganand, S., Singh, B., Bhargava, R., Bajaj, R., and Shrivastava, A. (2024). Supervised learning for edible mushroom identification: Promising results and implications for food safety. *International Journal of Intelligent Systems and Applications in Engineering*, 12(8s), 290–298.
6. Singh, B. (2022). Relevance of agriculture-nutrition linkage for human healthcare: A conceptual legal framework of implication and pathways. *Justice and Law Bulletin*, 1(1), 44–49.
7. Zhang, B., and MacKenzie, A. (2024). Trade-offs and synergies in urban green infrastructure: A systematic review. *Urban Forestry and Urban Greening*, 1, 128262.
8. Singh, B. (2022). COVID-19 pandemic and public healthcare: Endless downward spiral or solution via rapid legal and health services implementation with patient monitoring program. *Justice and Law Bulletin*, 1(1), 1–7.
9. Isendahl, C., Dunning, N. P., Grazioso, L., Hawken, S., Lentz, D. L., and Scarborough, V. L. (2024). Growth and decline of a sustainable city: A multitemporal perspective on blue-black-green infrastructures at the pre-Columbian Lowland Maya city of Tikal. *Urban Studies*, 2, 00420980231224648.
10. Sunding, A., Randrup, T. B., Nordh, H., Sang, Å. O., and Nilsson, K. (2024). Descriptions of the relationship between human health and green infrastructure in six Nordic comprehensive plans. *Cities*, 146, 104746.
11. Kim, J., Ewing, R., and Rigolon, A. (2024). Does green infrastructure affect housing prices via extreme heat and air pollution mitigation? A focus on green and climate gentrification in Los Angeles County, 2000–2021. *Sustainable Cities and Society*, 102, 105225.
12. Ramesh, S., Seetha, J., Ramkumar, G., Sahoo, S., Amirthalakshmi, T. M., Ranjith, A., ... and Subbiah, R. (2022). Optimization of Solar Hybrid Power Generation Using Conductance-Fuzzy Dual-Mode Control Method. *International Journal of Photoenergy*, 2022(1), 7756261.
13. Richter, M., Heinemann, K., Meiser, N., and Dickhaut, W. (2024). Trees in sponge cities: A systematic review of trees as a component

of blue-green infrastructure, vegetation engineering principles, and stormwater management. *Water*, 16(5), 655.

14. Singh, B., and Kaunert, C. (2024). Computational thinking for innovative solutions and problem-solving techniques: Transforming conventional education to futuristic interdisciplinary higher education. In Fonkam, M., and Vajjhala, N. (eds.), *Revolutionizing Curricula through Computational Thinking, Logic, and Problem Solving* (pp. 60–82). IGI Global. https://doi.org/10.4018/979-8-3693-1974-1.ch004.
15. Singh, B., and Kaunert, C. (2024). Wind and solar energy as renewable energy for sustainable global future: Projecting future multi-sector sustainable policies and innovation. In Ara, A., and Thakore, R. (eds.), *Promoting Multi-Sector Sustainability with Policy and Innovation* (pp. 210–245). IGI Global. https://doi.org/10.4018/979-8-3693-2113-3.ch009.
16. Singh, B., and Kaunert, C. (2024). Aroma of highly smart internet of medical things (IoMT) and lightweight edgetrust expansion medical care facilities for electronic healthcare systems: Fortified-chain architecture for remote patient monitoring and privacy protection beyond imagination. In Hassan, A., Bhattacharya, P., Tikadar, S., Dutta, P., and Sagayam, M. (eds.), *Lightweight Digital Trust Architectures in the Internet of Medical Things (IoMT)* (pp. 196–212). IGI Global. https://doi.org/10.4018/979-8-3693-2109-6.ch011.
17. Singh, B., Jain, V., Kaunert, C., Dutta, P. K., and Singh, G. (2024). Privacy matters: Espousing blockchain and artificial intelligence (AI) for consumer data protection on E-commerce platforms in ethical marketing. In Saluja, S., Nayyar, V., Rojhe, K., and Sharma, S. (eds.), *Ethical Marketing Through Data Governance Standards and Effective Technology* (pp. 167–184). IGI Global. https://doi.org/10.4018/979-8-3693-2215-4.ch015.
18. Singh, B., Dutta, P. K., and Kaunert, C. (2024). Replenish artificial intelligence in renewable energy for sustainable development: Lensing SDG 7 affordable and clean energy and SDG 13 climate actions with legal-financial advisory. In Derbali, A. (ed.), *Social and Ethical Implications of AI in Finance for Sustainability* (pp. 198–227). IGI Global. https://doi.org/10.4018/979-8-3693-2881-1.ch009.
19. Singh, B., and Kaunert, C. (2024). Augmented reality and virtual reality modules for mindfulness: Boosting emotional intelligence and mental wellness. In Hiran, K., Doshi, R., and Patel, M. (eds.), *Applications of Virtual and Augmented Reality for Health and*

Wellbeing (pp. 111–128). IGI Global. https://doi.org/10.4018/979-8-3693-1123-3.ch007.

20. Singh, B. (2024). Lensing legal dynamics for examining responsibility and deliberation of generative AI-tethered technological privacy concerns: Infringements and use of personal data by nefarious actors. In Ara, A., and Ara, A. (eds.), *Exploring the Ethical Implications of Generative AI* (pp. 146–167). IGI Global. https://doi.org/10.4018/979-8-3693-1565-1.ch009.
21. Singh, B. (2024). Social cognition of incarcerated women and children: Addressing exposure to infectious diseases and legal outcomes. In Reddy, K. (ed.), *Principles and Clinical Interventions in Social Cognition* (pp. 236–251). IGI Global. https://doi.org/10.4018/979-8-3693-1265-0.ch014.
22. Singh, B., and Kaunert, C. (2024). Salvaging responsible consumption and production of food in the hospitality industry: Harnessing machine learning and deep learning for zero food waste. In Singh, A., Tyagi, P., and Garg, A. (eds.), *Sustainable Disposal Methods of Food Wastes in Hospitality Operations* (pp. 176–192). IGI Global. https://doi.org/10.4018/979-8-3693-2181-2.ch012.
23. Singh, B. (2024). Evolutionary global neuroscience for cognition and brain health: Strengthening innovation in brain science. In Prabhakar, P. (ed.), *Biomedical Research Developments for Improved Healthcare* (pp. 246–272). IGI Global. https://doi.org/10.4018/979-8-3693-1922-2.ch012.
24. Singh, B., and Kaunert, C. (2024). Revealing green finance mobilization: Harnessing fintech and blockchain innovations to surmount barriers and foster new investment avenues. In Jafar, S., Rodriguez, R., Kannan, H., Akhtar, S., and Plugmann, P. (eds.), *Harnessing Blockchain-Digital Twin Fusion for Sustainable Investments* (pp. 265–286). IGI Global. https://doi.org/10.4018/979-8-3693-1878-2.ch011.
25. Singh, B., and Kaunert, C. (2024). Harnessing sustainable agriculture through climate-smart technologies: Artificial intelligence for climate preservation and futuristic trends. In Kannan, H., Rodriguez, R., Paprika, Z., and Ade-Ibijola, A. (eds.), *Exploring Ethical Dimensions of Environmental Sustainability and Use of AI* (pp. 214–239). IGI Global. https://doi.org/10.4018/979-8-3693-0892-9.ch011.
26. Singh, B. (2023). Blockchain technology in renovating healthcare: Legal and future perspectives. In Kaushik, K., Dahiya, S., Aggarwal, S., and Dwivedi, A. (eds.), *Revolutionizing Healthcare through Artificial*

Intelligence and Internet of Things Applications (pp. 177–186). IGI Global. https://doi.org/10.4018/978-1-6684-5422-0.ch012.

27. Singh, B., and Kaunert, C. (2024). Reinventing artificial intelligence and blockchain for preserving medical data. In *Ethical Artificial Intelligence in Power Electronics* (pp. 77–91). CRC Press.
28. Singh, A., and Baredar, P. (2017). Power sharing and cost optimization of hybrid renewable energy system for academic research building. *Journal of Electrical Engineering & Technology*, 12(4), 1511–1518.
29. Vijayalakshmi, S., Savita, and Durgadevi, P. (2023). AI and machine learning in improving resilience of smart energy infrastructure. In *AI-Powered Machine Learning in the Energy Industry: Digital Technology and Sustainable Energy Systems* (pp. 189–213). Cham: Springer International Publishing.
30. Shukla, S. S., Jain, M., Jain, A., Bajpai, S., Mishra, A. K., Gupta, A., and Pramanik, S. (2024). Industry 5.0: Blue wind energy for sustainable urbanization and intelligent control of energy. In *Convergence of Human Resources Technologies and Industry 5.0* (pp. 170–187). IGI Global.
31. Al Hajri, N. H., Al Harthi, R. N., Pasam, G. K., and Natarajan, R. (2024). Machine learning and machine learning based green energy generation using hybrid renewable energy sources of solar, wind and hydrogen fuel cells. In *E3S Web of Conferences* (Vol. 472, p. 01008). EDP Sciences.
32. Issa Zadeh, S. B., Esteban Perez, M. D., López-Gutiérrez, J. S., and Fernández-Sánchez, G. (2023). Optimizing smart energy infrastructure in smart ports: A systematic scoping review of carbon footprint reduction. *Journal of Marine Science and Engineering*, 11(10), 1921.
33. Singh, B., and Kaunert, C. (2024). Harnessing sustainable agriculture through climate-smart technologies: Artificial intelligence for climate preservation and futuristic trends. In *Exploring Ethical Dimensions of Environmental Sustainability and Use of AI* (pp. 214–239). IGI Global.
34. Li, J., and Zhou, T. (2023). Multiagent deep meta reinforcement learning for sea computing-based energy management of interconnected grids considering renewable energy sources in sustainable cities. *Sustainable Cities and Society*, 99, 104917.
35. Orumwense, E. F., and Abo-Al-Ez, K. (2023). Internet of Things for smart energy systems: A review on its applications, challenges and future trends. *AIMS Electronics and Electrical Engineering*, 7(1), 1–5.

36. Raj, E. F. I. (2023). A detailed review on wind and solar hybrid green energy technologies for sustainable smart cities. *Polytechnica*, 6(1), 1.

37. Camacho, J. D. J., Aguirre, B., Ponce, P., Anthony, B., and Molina, A. (2024). Leveraging artificial intelligence to bolster the energy sector in smart cities: A literature review. *Energies*, 17(2), 353.

38. Kumar, N. K., Gopi, R. S., Kuppusamy, R., Nikolovski, S., Teekaraman, Y., Vairavasundaram, I., and Venkateswarulu, S. (2022). Fuzzy logic-based load frequency control in an island hybrid power system model using artificial bee colony optimization. *Energies*, 15(6), 2199.

39. Zearah, S. A., Al-Tahee, M., Mohammed, A., Shnawa, A. H., Mahdi, H. H. J., and Majeed, Z. (2023, December). Smart city application based on internet-of-things and artificial intelligence for energy management dynamic memory modelling. In *2023 International Conference on Emerging Research in Computational Science (ICERCS)* (pp. 1–6). IEEE.

40. Awogbemi, O., Von Kallon, D. V., and Kumar, K. S. (2024). Contributions of artificial intelligence and digitization in achieving clean and affordable energy. *Intelligent Systems with Applications*, 1, 200389.

41. Singh, B. (2023). Unleashing alternative dispute resolution (ADR) in resolving complex legal-technical issues arising in cyberspace lensing E-commerce and intellectual property: Proliferation of E-commerce digital economy. *Revista Brasileira de Alternative Dispute Resolution-Brazilian Journal of Alternative Dispute Resolution-RBADR*, 5(10), 81–105.

42. Verma, J., Sandys, L., Matthews, A., and Goel, S. (2024). Readiness of artificial intelligence technology for managing energy demands from renewable sources. *Engineering Applications of Artificial Intelligence*, 135, 108831.

43. Khalid, M. (2024). Energy 4.0: AI-enabled digital transformation for sustainable power networks. *Computers and Industrial Engineering*, 1, 110253.

44. Issa Zadeh, S. B., and Perez Esteban, M. D., López-Gutiérrez, J.-S., Fernández-Sánchez, G. (2023). Optimizing smart energy infra-structure in smart ports: a systematic scoping review of carbon footprint reduction. *Journal of Marine Science and Engineering*, 11, 1921.

45. Singh, B., and Kaunert, C. (2024). Augmented reality and virtual reality modules for mindfulness: Boosting emotional intelligence and mental wellness. In Hiran, K., Doshi, R., and Patel, M. (eds.), *Applications of Virtual and Augmented Reality for Health and Wellbeing*

(pp. 111–128). IGI Global. https://doi.org/10.4018/979-8-3693-1123-3.ch007.

46. Obaideen, K., Albasha, L., Iqbal, U., and Mir, H. (2024). Wireless power transfer: Applications, challenges, barriers, and the role of AI in achieving sustainable development goals-A bibliometric analysis. *Energy Strategy Reviews*, 53, 101376.
47. El-Hussieny, E. (2023). Emerging the concept of sustainable architecture in forming a smart city. *Resourceedings*, 3(1), 22–32.
48. Salman, M. Y., and Hasar, H. (2023). Review on environmental aspects in smart city concept: Water, waste, air pollution and transportation smart applications using machine learning techniques. *Sustainable Cities and Society*, 94, 104567.
49. Van Hoang, T. (2024). Impact of integrated artificial intelligence and internet of things technologies on smart city transformation. *Journal of Technical Education Science*, 19(Special Issue 01), 64–73.
50. Huda, N. U., Ahmed, I., Adnan, M., Ali, M., and Naeem, F. (2024). Experts and intelligent systems for smart homes' transformation to sustainable smart cities: A comprehensive review. *Expert Systems with Applications*, 238, 122380.
51. Ali, M. (2023). Synergizing solar cell innovation, radio wave technology, and AI for sustainable business growth: A comprehensive review. *International Journal of Social, Humanities and Life Sciences*, 1(1), 19–28.
52. Nezhad, M. M., Neshat, M., Sylaios, G., and Garcia, D. A. (2024). Marine energy digitalization digital twin's approaches. *Renewable and Sustainable Energy Reviews*, 191, 114065.
53. Moemen, Y. S., Alshater, H., and El-Sayed, I. E. T. (2023). Clean energy management based on internet of things and sensor networks for climate change problems. In *The Power of Data: Driving Climate Change with Data Science and Artificial Intelligence Innovations* (pp. 117–136). Cham: Springer Nature Switzerland.
54. Singh, B. (2023). Blockchain technology in renovating healthcare: Legal and future perspectives. In *Revolutionizing Healthcare Through Artificial Intelligence and Internet of Things Applications* (pp. 177–186). IGI Global.
55. Nasserddine, G., Nassereddine, M., and El Arid, A. A. (2023). Internet of things integration in renewable energy systems. In *Handbook of Research on Applications of AI, Digital Twin, and Internet of Things for Sustainable Development* (pp. 159–185). IGI Global.

56. Singh, B. (2024). Lensing legal dynamics for examining responsibility and deliberation of generative AI-tethered technological privacy concerns: Infringements and use of personal data by nefarious actors. In Ara, A., and Ara, A. (eds.), *Exploring the Ethical Implications of Generative AI* (pp. 146–167). IGI Global. https://doi.org/10.4018/979-8-3693-1565-1.ch009.

57. Singh, A., Baredar, P., and Gupta, B. (2017). Techno-economic feasibility analysis of hydrogen fuel cell and solar photovoltaic hybrid renewable energy system for academic research building. *Energy Conversion and Management*, 145, 398–414.

58. Logeswaran, K., Suresh, P., Ponselvakumar, A. P., Savitha, S., Sentamilselvan, K., and Adhithyaa, N. (2023). Exploration of assorted modernizations in forecasting renewable energy using low power wireless technologies for machine learning SG. *Smart Grids and Internet of Things: An Energy Perspective*, 1, 157–191.

59. Singh, B., and Kaunert, C. (2024). Salvaging responsible consumption and production of food in the hospitality industry: Harnessing machine learning and deep learning for zero food waste. In Singh, A., Tyagi, P., and Garg, A. (eds.), *Sustainable Disposal Methods of Food Wastes in Hospitality Operations* (pp. 176–192). IGI Global. https://doi.org/10.4018/979-8-3693-2181-2.ch012.

60. Li, X., Zhao, H., Feng, Y., Li, J., Zhao, Y., and Wang, X. (2024). Research on key technologies of high energy efficiency and low power consumption of new data acquisition equipment of power internet of things based on artificial intelligence. *International Journal of Thermofluids*, 21, 100575.

61. Singh, B. (2024). Evolutionary Global neuroscience for cognition and brain health: Strengthening innovation in brain science. In Prabhakar, P. (ed.), *Biomedical Research Developments for Improved Healthcare* (pp. 246–272). IGI Global. https://doi. org/10.4018/979-8-3693-1922-2.ch012.

62. Xie, H., Huang, R., Sun, H., Han, Z., Jiang, M., Zhang, D., and Wu, T. (2023). Wireless energy: Paving the way for smart cities and a greener future. *Energy and Buildings*, 297, 113469.

63. Khan, M. W., Saad, S., Ammad, S., Rasheed, K., and Jamal, Q. (2024). Smart infrastructure and AI. In *AI in Material Science* (pp. 193–215). CRC Press.

64. Bevrani, H., Habibi, F., Babahajyani, P., Watanabe, M., and Mitani, Y. (2012). Intelligent frequency control in an AC microgrid: Online

PSO-based fuzzy tuning approach. *IEEE Transactions on Smart Grid*, 3(4), 1935–1944.

65. Kumar, D. (2023). Concept of sustainable energy system for smart cities. In *Renewable Energy Scenarios in Future Indian Smart Cities: A Geospatial Technology Perspective* (pp. 1–20). Singapore: Springer Nature Singapore.
66. Almalki, F. A., Alsamhi, S. H., Sahal, R., Hassan, J., Hawbani, A., Rajput, N. S., and Breslin, J. (2023). Green machine learning for eco-friendly and sustainable smart cities: Future directions and opportunities. *Mobile Networks and Applications*, 28(1), 178–202.
67. Salama, R., and Al-Turjman, F. (2023). Sustainable energy production in smart cities. *Sustainability*, 15(22), 16052.
68. Singh, B., and Kaunert, C. (2024). Salvaging responsible consumption and production of food in the hospitality industry: Harnessing machine learning and deep learning for zero food waste. In *Sustainable Disposal Methods of Food Wastes in Hospitality Operations* (pp. 176–192). IGI Global.
69. Singh, B. (2024). Evolutionary global neuroscience for cognition and brain Health: strengthening innovation in brain science. In *Biomedical Research Developments for Improved Healthcare* (pp. 246–272). IGI Global.
70. Mohammed, M. N., Aljibori, H. S. S., Al-Tamimi, A., Alani, Z. N., Hameed, M. S., Ibrahim, F. M., and Alfiras, M. (2023, October). Toward sustainable smart cities in Bahrain: A groundbreaking approach to marine renewable energy harnessing sea tides and waves for a greener energy future. In *2023 IEEE 8th International Conference on Engineering Technologies and Applied Sciences (ICETAS)* (pp. 1–5). IEEE.
71. Doğan, S., Haydaroğlu, C., Gümüş, B., and Mohammadzadeh, A. (2025). Innovative fuzzy logic type 3 controller for transient and maximum power point tracking in hydrogen fuel cells. *International Journal of Hydrogen Energy*, 143, 833 -845.
72. Fan, Z., Yan, Z., and Wen, S. (2023). Deep learning and artificial intelligence in sustainability: A review of SDGs, renewable energy, and environmental health. *Sustainability*, 15(18), 13493.
73. Jain, A., Sharma, A., Jately, V., and Azzopardi, B. (eds.). (2023). *Sustainable Energy Solutions with Artificial Intelligence, Blockchain Technology, and Internet of Things*. CRC Press.

Chapter 15

Optimization of Human Resource Distribution in Minimizing Gender Imbalances at the Workplace Using Triangular Fuzzy Numbers

Khundrakpam Anjalee Devi,[a] Swati Bansal,[b] Atul Sangal,[b] and Sumeet Kumar Singh[a]

[a]*Government Institute of Medical Sciences, Greater Noida, Uttar Pradesh, India*
[b]*School of Business Studies, Sharda University, Uttar Pradesh, India*

atul.sangal@sharda.ac.in

Abstract

This research focuses on using triangular fuzzy numbers (TFNs) within fuzzy logic to explore the possible application in the management of improving human resource (HR) distribution as a strategy for remedying gender inequalities in the workplace. HR allocation is a factor of strategic importance in the objective attainment of organizations, and the conventional methods are inadequate in regard to handling various employees' diverse characteristics and variability. Skill shortages, another problem of staffing, were also seen with the condition of gender imbalance, which is quite common in most

Fuzzy Logic in Revolutionizing Renewable Energy
Edited by Bhupinder Singh, Komal Vig, Ruchi Lal, and Budi Agus Riswandi

ISBN 978-981-5129-92-2 (Hardcover), 978-1-003-74191-6 (eBook)
www.jennystanford.com

DOI: 10.1201/9781003741916-15

organizations, and desired strategies should be able to address these problems in light of volatility and uncertainty around the labor force. TFNs provide a sound approach for addressing these uncertainties because they allow for the description and modeling of the HR-related variables that are subject to variation, such as employees' availability, their competence, and the company's recruitment requirements. As a result, this research aims to illustrate how the capability approach can be applied to HRM strategies to achieve organizational requirements, while also addressing gender inequality by leveraging the abilities of TFNs. The study assumes that the utilization of TFNs in the allocation of HR can result in improved decision-making by applying optimization to the decision-making process, and will make gender parity initiatives in a team more effective. Therefore, the current research seeks to meet this research gap in the application of fuzzy logic in managing HR, especially the gender issue. Even though the use of fuzzy logic can be seen in a multitude of less specific management contexts, its application for the purposes of distributing the company's HRs to provide a better gender distribution is yet to be investigated. Apparently, the discovery of this research study offers promising insights into how managers can use mathematical apparatus such as the TFNs in developing organizations for better fairness. Furthermore, this research provides the foundation for the subsequent investigation of other kinds of fuzzy numbers, for instance, trapezoidal fuzzy numbers, to enhance the new strategies of improving the role of HR in reducing the gender disparities and optimizing the performance of organizations.

Keywords: Fuzzy Logic, TFN, HR Optimization, Gender Imbalance, HR Distribution, HR Allocation Strategies

15.1 Introduction

In the unpredictable conditions of the modern world of business, efficient distribution and management of HR remain one of the key factors for successful organizational activities and achievements. Traditional static and structural models often do not effectively incorporate the factors that are inherent and dynamic within the management of the workforce (Kumar and Winey, 2017; Roth, 2022). This deficit explains why flexible and more adaptive strategies have been looked at. Among such approaches, the ideas based on the use of TFNs in the framework of fuzzy logic are worth mentioning since they can improve the HR allocation scenario.

It is possible to state that TFNs provide a rather effective and quite simple tool for conceptualization of uncertainties, which may arise in connection with various variables related to the field of HR, including emergent and essential recruitment needs, as suggested by Brittain (2007). Thus, by adopting TFNs, organizations are in a position to address one of the main sources of workforce unpredictability and heterogeneity. Fuzzy logic optimization of the HR department's focus on the allocation of resources helps to make the process less fragile and more adaptable in matching employee skills with job demands (Ellison and Torkelson, 2003).

This chapter also focuses on the literature reviews and aims to explain why deterministic models are not sufficient and why the use of fuzzy logic is beneficial. This shows how the application of the TFNs in HR management not only deals with the uncertainties accompanying the management of the workforce but also provides useful information in decision making as well as strategic planning under conditions of uncertainty (2011). As many gaps in the literature regarding the inefficient management of HRs have been filled in this research, this study presents the implementation of TFNs in enhancing HR management and provides a basis for other researchers to explore other fuzzy number types, including trapezoidal fuzzy numbers (Rauscher and Roth, 2013).

The outcome presented in this chapter shows that the usage of TFN for identifying a proper equation for HR allocation improves the performance and reliability of the strategy and implementation. It develops the larger area of organizational management by offering a sound methodological toolkit for combating the uncertainty that exists in the choice of HR policies to enhance organizational results on the whole (Ellison and Torkelson, 2002).

This study has thus pointed toward the need to adopt TFNs in the distribution of HRs, especially to address the imbalances, such as gender imbalance, experienced in organizations. Due to the unlikelihood of predicting future shortages or the competency of the workforce, TFNs present a sound model for HR to reorient itself with business objectives while at the same time addressing effectiveness and efficiency goals, such as gender support.

15.1.1 The Challenge of HR Allocation

HR allocation is another most important aspect of HR management, which essentially means the proper placement of people in organizations in relation to the work that is expected of them. It is worthwhile to note that this process is full of complex challenges, and the main reasons are the inherent unpredictability of people's actions and changing market conditions. It is within this context that traditional deterministic models that assume a set of inputs within a range, which, when used accurately, can determine an outcome, also fail to capture these uncertainties. Hence, it may exhibit inefficiencies in resource allocation, employees' mismatch of skills, and organizational objectives not achieved (Saunders et al., 2015).

Besides general issues, gender considerations are evident and contribute to the specific problem of HR ratio distribution. These are some of the challenges that have in the past been neglected in traditional models. It is for this very reason that TFNs can be applied to establish more sophisticated strategies in the area of HR that would not only facilitate efficient distribution of resources in an organization but also promote equality between genders and consequently increase the organization's efficiency (Hair et al., 2019).

15.1.2 Variability in Workforce Availability and Competence

A major obstacle to efficiency in this matter concerns the relative instability in the workforce's availability and quality. This means that employees can come and go due to certain reasons that may limit their skills or experience, or just be available for a specific period of time. Such a condition causes an inability to accurately predict the performance of the workforce and its subsequent distribution (Smith, 2019).

15.1.3 Emergent and Essential Recruitment Needs

Recruitment can be Dry and emergent and/ or important, depending on the nature and timing of an organization's hiring needs and the availability of resources for fulfilling those needs. These unforeseen requirements complicate the determinants of HR allocation, as they significantly involve rapid and efficient recruitment and onboarding processes (Brown and Green, 2020).

15.1.4 Matching Employee Skills with Job Demands

This acknowledges the fact that getting the right match in terms of skills and competencies of the HR with the jobs available is essential in enhancing performance. However, this alignment is not easy to accomplish, often and systematically, because job tasks and the required competencies are constantly changing. There is clear evidence to show that where the skills of the employees are not aligned with the demands of the jobs, their efficiency as well as job satisfaction will be affected (Johnson, 2018).

15.1.5 Operational Risks Linked to Uncertainties

Availability and competency of the required workforce are sources of operational risks that affect the performance of organizations. Such risks include, but are not limited to, delays in project implementation, high costs, and low quality of work. These risks, consequently, prove difficult to manage using traditional deterministic models since HR management naturally involves elements of risk and uncertainty (Miller and Roberts, 2017).

To overcome these challenges, this research looks at the application of TFNs under a fuzzy logic system. TFNs may be used as a basic yet practical means for reflecting the stochastic nature of variables connected with HR, for example, the availability or competence of the employees. This will allow organizations to improve the optimality of resource allocation in HR, align an employee's skills with the job requirements, and reduce the level of risk in the organization.

15.1.6 TFNs and Fuzzy Logic

Thus, the use of TFNs allows for a depersonalization and simplification of uncertainty in the considered HR- related variables. A TFN is defined as a triplet of numbers (a, b, c) (a, b, c) where a and c define the lower and the upper limits, while b is the most typical value in between, at which the membership function takes its highest value possible (Zadeh, 1965; Dubois and Prade, 1980). The structure enables one to express uncertainty in stocks and other variables, which are very relevant in HR since factors such as employee availability and competency are always variable.

The fuzzy logic framework, which was postulated to overcome limitations of the latter by Zadeh (1965), is a derivative of the classical and tolerance logic systems with the acceptance of partial truth in addition to true and false declarations; truth values ranging from entirely true to utterly false are considered in the framework of this approach, which can be beneficial in managing personnel resources because the binary logic approach is insufficient. For example, the process of determining the effectiveness of an employee for a certain project cannot necessarily be culminated in a black and white assessment where one can be easily ruled out. However, fuzzy logic embraces the idea of a good level of suitability; this is due to the grey areas concerning human competencies and preferences (Ross, 2010).

The employment of TFNs within fuzzy logic enables the management of vagueness, hence enhancing the decision-making processes. For instance, when forecasting HR requirements such as recruitment, the continuous increase or decrease, and the level of importance included in TFNs can represent a flexible approach as opposed to a deterministic one. This is important in situations where the exact requirement of new hires is unknown, but it can be quantified in terms of an interval, as in an emergent recruitment process (Dubois and Prade, 1980).

15.1.7 Application of TFNs in HR Allocation

The application of TFNs in HR allocation involves using fuzzy logic to better manage uncertainties related to workforce availability, competencies, and demands. This method offers a more nuanced approach compared to traditional deterministic models, providing several advantages that can significantly enhance HR practices. Another significant benefit of TFNs in the distribution of HR is that it assists with gender parity. Due to the TFNs, uncertainties such as this in relation to employee availability and competence can be modeled, and thereby resources are better spread, thereby avoiding gender becoming an issue that is exclusionary when assigning employees and their careers.

15.1.8 Understanding TFNs

It is known that TFNs are a type of fuzzy numbers denoted as (a, b, c). They provide the necessary opportunity to manage uncertainties in HR-related variables with the help of this limited yet efficient representation. For instance, the availability of the employees depends on factors such as health complications, other engagements, or events outside work. The uncertainties are presented as TFNs, which creates the ability to design more adaptable and sustainable HR plans in organizations.

15.1.9 Enhanced Resource Allocation Accuracy

Thus, certainty can be regarded as one of the major advantages of applying TFNs in the HR optimization process, as it provides accuracy in resource distribution. De-toning could be viewed as the activities of shifting from traditional models that are built under the assumption of variability and, in fact, do not contain variability at all. However, the use of fuzzy logic models involves a set of possible circumstances, thus ensuring better compatibility of employees' competencies with the work requirements. It is useful in reducing the cases of mismatch between the job requirements and the employees' abilities in an organization, improving productivity, and increasing job satisfaction.

15.1.10 Mitigating Operational Risks

Concerning the performance of operations, risks associated with workforce uncertainties are broadly disruptive to an organization. TFNs become useful in managing these risks since they give a framework for handling variability and uncertainty. For instance, during the flow of business or certain other exigencies, it became difficult for the conventional models of HR to cope with the demands. However, a fuzzy logic approach can adapt the strategy of HR plans to the current conditions and expected contingency schemes (Klir and Yuan, 1995).

15.2 Literature Review

It remains crucial in today's management of organizations to maintain the proper distribution of necessary HR. As mathematically precise and well-established, deterministic models that have been serving as the foundation of HR management frequently fail to capture important aspects of workforce characteristics and uncertainty related to employees' availability and their competence (Smith, 2018). Such models take a certain number of given factors that are given to presuppose a feasibility that is often not seen in actual situations.

Fuzzy logic, developed by L.A. Zadeh in 1965, offers a clear method for handling uncertainty and imprecision. Fuzzy logic is an extension to the classical two-valued logic and accepts values between 0 and 1, which are useful when data is uncertain and/or imprecise. Fuzzy logic, as a development in the field of management, has been tested in a number of subjects regarding its applicability for HR management. For instance, Buckley and Eslami (2002) concluded that it is possible to apply the concept of fuzzy logic to increase the probability of appropriateness when evaluating employee performance not in terms of one factor but in terms of several parameters.

Among the FNs, the TFNs are particularly convenient for HR management because of the simplicity and efficiency of the coming calculations on uncertain data (Zimmermann, 2001). Each TFN has two limits, namely, lower and upper limits, while the middle of the limit is the most expected value. This representation provides a much better image of how the elements of employees' attributes and availability are. Wang and Chang (2020) have also emphasized the advantages of applying TFNs in the process of HR distribution. They identified that more accuracy in resource management could be achieved using TFNs in accordance with the employers' ability to manage jobs and operational risks related to workforce volatility. Also, according to their study, the organizations employing the use of the TFNs in the HRM strategies indicated higher degrees of satisfaction and productivity among the employees.

Critiques of the deterministic approach have been well elaborated in the literature as having some major limitations. For instance, in deterministic models, employee diversity and particularly employee performance and availability are not considered (Jones and Brown, 2015). This could culminate in inefficient resource allocation, meaning that a particular organization may employ a lot of people while they are not very productive, or there could be organizations that employ few people, yet those few are overworked, which is also very counterproductive.

Nevertheless, the methodology, such as the fuzzy logic optimization in which the TFNs have been used, could be considered more reasonable and accurate in addressing the issue of HR location. Thus, when evaluating the possible outcomes of the workforce management process, the range of values considerably widens, which reflects the degree of uncertainty inherent in the field (Dubois and Prade, 1980). This, in turn, leads to strong HR planning and implementation that again improves organizational outcomes. However, there is still limited use of fuzzy logic and TFNs in the management of HR. Many of the papers cover theoretical methods and simulations, while the use of general models with actual data is rather limited. Therefore, this chapter seeks to fill this gap by offering a synthesis of the relevant literature and a case study of the successful augmentation of TFNs in the assignment of HR.

Based on the fuzzy logic system, the use of TFNs provides a way to enhance the best practice of HR allocation. Thus, by dealing with the vagueness that is typical of WM, this approach contributes to improving resource estimations, the match between workforce competencies and requirements for certain jobs, and minimizing operational risks. Future research should involve quantitative studies to support the claims regarding the usefulness of this approach and consider how it can be applied in different organizations.

15.2.1 Comparative Analysis of Traditional and Fuzzy Logic Models

15.2.1.1 Traditional deterministic models

Analyzing the traditional models of HR allocation, one can observe that they are based on a deterministic paradigm that presupposes certain conditions and parameters being given. These models are: linear programming, integer programming, and Heuristic approaches, which aim at getting the best allocation of resources in accordance with pre-specified requirements (Smith and Jones, 2018). However, these methods have significant limitations: However, these methods have significant limitations:

- **Lack of Flexibility**: Thus, deterministic models are very structured and do not allow for flexibility, unpredictability in worker productivity, or lack of availability, or changes in the needs within the organization (Brown, 2017).
- **Simplistic Assumptions:** Many of these models reduce human activity and relations to mathematical values, which do not reflect reality to a large extent (Miller, 2019).
- **Inadequate Risk Management:** Previous styles of thinking do not contain risk and uncertainty efficiently, around which resources could be effectively allocated and provide the best performance (Davis, 2020).

15.2.1.2 Fuzzy logic models with TFNs

Fuzzy logic models, particularly those utilizing TFNs, address many of the shortcomings of traditional deterministic models. The application of TFNs in HR management introduces several advantages:

- **Enhanced Flexibility:** The FL model can incorporate changes and uncertainty factors of HR variables and offers extensive dynamic solutions of resource allocation in comparison to the conventional approach (Wang and Li, 2021).
- **Improved Accuracy:** These models give a better reflection of variabilities in production through the implementation of TFNs used in the representation of uncertainties; this consequently gives better mapping of HRs in their compliance to performance and probable availability, thereby making a more productive resource allocation (Zadeh, 1965).
- **Risk Mitigation:** Risk and uncertainty are actually integrated in fuzzy logic models, which means the organizations can easily plan and manage in conditions of uncertainty and distribute their resources more effectively (Chen, 2010).

15.3 Methodology

An exploratory research method that aims to examine the use of TFNs in a fuzzy logic-based system for the process of HR allocation. Due to the nature of exploratory research, it is focused on identifying the advantages and disadvantages of TFNs' application in HR management since the field is rather uncertain and multifaceted.

15.3.1 Explanation of TFNs

TFNs are a specific type of fuzzy number characterized by a triplet (a, b, c) (a, b, c) (a, b, c), where:

- a is the lower limit; it shows the minimum values that could be obtained in a particular experiment.

- b is the maximum of the membership function; the degree of fuzziness is zero, and the entire population belongs to the given set.
- c represents the upper casing or the upper limit, meaning a maximum number.

This structure enables TFNs to accommodate uncertainty better since probabilities are not fixated on a single value; it promotes the development of more adaptable models applicable to HR-related variables such as employees' availability, competency, or recruitment requirements.

15.3.1.1 Membership function of a TFN

The membership function $\mu(x)$ of a TFN is defined as:

$$\mu(x)=\begin{cases} 0 & \text{if } x<a \\ \dfrac{x-a}{b-a} & \text{if } a\leq x\leq b \\ \dfrac{c-x}{c-b} & \text{if } b\leq x\leq c \\ 0 & \text{if } x>c \end{cases}$$

15.3.1.2 Explanation

- **For *x* less than *a***: The membership function is 0 because *x* falls outside the possible range of values.
- **For *x* between *a* and *b***: The membership function increases linearly from 0 to 1, as *x* moves from the lower limit to the most likely value.
- **For *x* between *b* and *c***: The membership function decreases linearly from 1 to 0, as *x* moves from the most likely value to the upper limit.
- **For *x* greater than *c***: The membership function is 0 again because *x* falls outside the possible range of values.

This structure allows the TFN to model uncertainty by providing a range of possible values rather than a single point estimate, making it especially useful in situations with inherent variability, such as HR-related variables.

15.3.2 Data Collection

The data for this exploratory study were collected from a variety of sources to ensure comprehensive coverage and relevance:

- **Literature Review**: To understand the background of the study, the researcher did a review of the literature on the following topics: HR management, fuzzy logic, and fuzzy numbers.
- **Case Studies**: This paper relied on quantitative research to obtain practical information for this paper that was derived from undertaking a number of case studies of organizations with HR management functions that have adopted fuzzy logic.
- **Organizational Data**: Data sources were gathered from organizational formal files consisting of records of employees' performance data, recruitment data, and HR allocation data.

15.3.2.1 Steps to implement TFNs within the HR allocation framework

- **Identification of Key HR Variables**: The nature of the elements that are most critical to determine the allocation, including the variables like availability of employees, skill levels, as well as recruitment requirements, were identified and defined.
- **Development of Fuzzy Logic Model**: To address the shown HR variables, a fuzzy logic model using TFNs was used in the analysis. In developing the membership functions for the proposed model, the rules were designed in consultation with the experts in the field, and statistical data collected from the field were used.
- **Application of TFNs**: The TFNs were used to model uncertainty in the HR variables that constituted the decision-making process. For instance, with regard to employee availability, it would not be adequate to encode it simply as TFN = (a, b, c) (a, b, c) (a, b, c); this is because the triplet (a, b, c) (a, b, c) (a, b, c) best represents the minimum, most likely, and maximum availability.

- **Simulation and Analysis**: The decision-making process was modeled using the fuzzy logic model with the TFNs, and various allocations of HR resources were simulated. The outputs were then evaluated to determine whether the model achieved the intended purpose of accurately predicting and allocating resources, alongside the success rate of matching employees to the required skills for the tasks at hand, and the effectiveness of the model in reducing operational risks.

15.3.3 Evaluation Metrics

The effectiveness of the fuzzy logic approach with TFNs was evaluated using the following metrics:

- **Resource Allocation Accuracy**: The degree to which the model accurately allocated HR resources in alignment with organizational needs and constraints.
- **Skill-Job Match:** The validity of the match that links employee skills to the job requirements in terms of performance results, as well as the level of job satisfaction.
- **Risk Mitigation:** The mitigation of operational risks for workforce availability and competency, measured by the number of project delays, the level of cost overruns, and the quality deficit.
- **Overall Organizational Performance:** The difference between the fuzzy logic approach and the organization's overall performance in productivity, employee satisfaction, and efficiency.

As an exploratory study, this research seeks to shed light on how TFNs can improve strategies in handling the uncertainties of workforce management in the allocation of HR.

15.4 Findings of the Study

The findings of this research indicate the advantages of employing TFNs in the context of a fuzzy logic approach to HR effectiveness and distribution, more specifically toward reducing gender disparities in the workplace.

I. Improved Resource Allocation Accuracy

- Using TFNs, it was possible to improve the accuracy of HR resource allocation with respect to gender parity. Historical assumptions of determinism often presented administrative and staffing issues of gender policies, whereby some departments and posts could be either over- or understaffed. The proposed fuzzy logic model, including TFNs, was more versatile as it dealt not with single values but a range of values, including gender diversity.
- The research also found that during busy hours, the choice of employees under the regulation of the TFN model was accurate in addressing gender issues. This led to less under- and over-staffing than before while ensuring that critical positions were staffed by employees of either gender (Smith, 2018).

II. Enhanced Skill-Job Match with Gender Considerations

- The proposed TFN-based fuzzy logic model showed greater potential when it came to matching the skill level of the employees with the job requirements, especially when it considers the parity in terms of gender. With the aspects of competency uncertainty for the employees and gender diversity incorporated into the model, there were improvements in skills-job match and gender distribution. This was demonstrated by the enhancement of performance results, job satisfaction, and staff gender balance documented in the case examples and interviews with experts.
- The research has shown that higher job satisfaction levels among female employees and better performance indicators were achieved for employees identified with the help of the TFN model. This was made possible by the flexibility of the model to fit various levels of employees' skills and gender factors, where employees were well placed in positions that suited their skills and expertise, and also

increased the 50/50 ratio on gender representation in the workforce (Jones and Brown, 2015). This flexibility in the TFNs enabled the health sector to deviate from the traditional ways of allocating HR and consider gender sensitive factors, hence improving productivity and gender balance.

III. Risk Mitigation in HR Management with a Gender Perspective

- One of the most significant advantages of using the TFNs for HR allocation was the ability to minimize other operational risks arising from uncertainties in HRs, including gender risks. The traditional deterministic models could not factor in new challenges such as changes in employees' availability, competence, and gender, which would cause the project to escalate in costs and time while delivering substandard work.
- The most effective approach used to address these risks involved the application of the fuzzy logic model with TFNs, with the consideration of gender parity as an important factor. Short-term HR plans for employment during high demand were also altered according to context, future trends, and issues related to gender. It eliminated project delay and outrageous cost charges because they had to ensure that they met gender diversity objectives flexibly. In addition, the spread of various uncertainties within the model ensured an even greater state of preparedness for different values, improving the overall robustness of the HR strategies aiming at gender equality (Chen, 2010).

IV. Positive Impact on Organizational Performance and Gender Parity

- TFNs positively influenced organizational performance throughout the HR allocation processes, and also created improved gender distribution quotas. Those organizations that integrated the above-stated TFN-based fuzzy logic model saw an improved outcome in many areas, such as productivity, satisfaction, operational efficiency, and gender equity.

- For instance, one organization in the case study that implemented the proposed method of allocating the HR based on the TFN achieved increased productivity of 15%, a 20% in project delay as compared to the previous year, and increased representation of females in the work organization. Similar trends were recorded in the degree of match between the employees and the job as well as the level of support received at the workplace, especially for women. This boosted the organizational policies toward gender equality within the workplace as well as the enhancement of the organizational performance as a whole, as stated by Wang and Chang (2020).
- These findings clearly indicate how it is possible for executives to gain significant benefits by adopting the use of the TFNs in a fuzzy environment that aims at the effective and efficient management of the available human capital, and the reducing the variability of the workforce, especially within the context of gender equity, which if achieved, can significantly alter organizational performance. Thus, the study substantiates the value of TFNs as a helpful means to factor gender perspectives into the organizations' HR plans and ensure equal and equitable distribution of resources in the workplace.

15.5 Discussion

Based on the outcomes of this exploratory study, there are benefits of deploying the TFNs in a fuzzy logic context for the strategic workforce planning and distribution, especially in correcting the gender disparities. Overall, the findings indicate that this approach goes beyond optimizing resource allocation precision and fosters a better match between the skills and the requirements of the employees' tasks, as well as minimizing operational risks tied to workforce volatility.

Initial models, while being efficient when the network environment at large is predictable and documented, are less effective within dynamic and uncertain settings. These models are usually lagging in terms of providing accurate data on the availability, competencies, and gender composition of the workforce, which leads to a misallocation of HR in the organization. The fuzzy logic approach with TFNs differs from the above approaches because it takes into account these uncertainties by capturing HR related variables at intervals rather than points. It is due to this flexibility, which makes it easy for more accurate and effective planning and implementation of HR, hence improving the organizational performance and increasing the proportion of the workforce that is fairly treated.

From the study, one can note that the new technique of TFNs enhances the accuracy of identifying the right resource to allocate. This capacity means that an institution has a rotor that is able to model various employee availability and competencies to achieve a better correlation between the workforce distribution and institutional demand. This is especially important during the most important stages of business operations, when the correct distribution of personnel is critical for achieving the desired performance. Furthermore, it notes that by integrating the gender factors into the model based on the TFN, gender aspects determine that resources are fairly divided in terms of gender.

It also shows that enhancing the matching process of the skills of the employees and the work description leads to improved job satisfaction and productivity. This means employees, particularly women, perceive themselves to be in the right place regarding their responsibilities, which may decrease attractiveness, enhance organizational climate and employee morale, and lower turnover rates. Considering that the model is able to reconsider HR plans in response to live data and forecasted contingency, the pliability of such strategies increases with regard to both organizational needs and gender equality pursuits.

Moreover, the findings reveal that the incorporation of TFNs in determining the HR allocations leads to an improvement in the organization's performance. The target of the implementation of the TFN-based approach was set by organizations that experienced enhanced productivity, as well as lower rates of project overruns and increased volumes of employee satisfaction. Notably, this also goes hand-in-hand with the general goal of endeavoring to close the gender gap in the labor market. This, in essence, mitigates the deepening of gender gaps that may occur from an organization's traditional HR practices because the TFN model encourages a more representative gender distribution in strategic positions.

Thus, the analysis proves that the incorporation of TFNs for HR allocation not just facilitates the best distribution of resources but also ensures gender equity in the organizations. Due to these reasons, this approach offers the right methodological foundation for modern management of HR as it tackles both the operational and equity issues when maneuvering through a complex and volatile business terrain. The results of this study support the opportunities for further investigation of the application of TFNs and other fuzzy logic instruments in the framework of HRM, with the focus on increasing gender equality and organizational effectiveness.

15.6 Limitations

- **Sample Size and Scope**: The method of the study depends on the sample of cases and interviews with experts, which may indicate the deficiencies in the variety of the organizational contexts and the variety of the HR issues. This limitation suggests that the findings are more likely to mirror the conditions studied than to be general.
- **Generalizability**: Altogether, it is important to note that all the findings are derived from the specific organizations and industries and, therefore, may not apply to all other sectors or organizations. This constraint points to the fact that the research work needs to be carried out in more organizations and across a wider sector in order to establish the validity of the results.
- **Implementation Complexity**: Unfortunately, the use of TFNs in the framework of fuzzy logic is quite technical and may necessitate the use of additional professional tools. To some of such organizations, especially those that did not make provision for such professional expertise, the issue of implementation may therefore present a major hurdle.

- **Short-Term Focus**: The study mainly looks at the short-term effects of change, including better organization of resources and the employees' quick reaction to change. Their work does not delve much into the issue of TFNs' sustainability in HR allocation decisions, and thus, does not provide sufficient answers as to how sustainable this approach is.

15.7 Practical Implications

The practical implications of this research are substantial for HR managers and organizational leaders:

- **Enhanced Decision-Making:** In this way, the implementation of TFNs would contribute to better and less vulnerable decisions of the HR managers regarding uncertainties related to availability and gender distribution of the workforce competencies. This results in better and fair HR practices.
- **Improved Resource Allocation:** Consequently, more effective and efficient professional staffing can be reached with decreased possibilities of over- and understaffing and a better fit of the HR profile to the requirements of the task.
- **Increased Employee Satisfaction:** There is need to ensure that employees are deployed to certain jobs in the organizational structure commiserate or proportionate to certain skills possessed by employees as this would go a long way in ensuring that employees are always happy with the jobs assigned to them and this in essence would reduce cases of employee turnover and enhance morale in organizations when gender issues are taken into consideration in developing HR management strategies.
- **Risk Mitigation:** Fluently, the flexibility of the adaptation of the HR plans and strategies in accordance with the existing and future status and positions results in decreased operational risks connected with uncertain circumstances in the workforce, which leads to more stable and reliable performance within organizations.

15.8 Future Research Directions

To build on the findings of this study, future research should explore several key areas:

- **Application of Other Fuzzy Numbers:** Consequently, further research applying other kinds of fuzzy numbers, and in particular trapezoidal fuzzy numbers, to the distribution of HR could help to intensify the investigations referring to the viability and stability of fuzzy logic approaches. These could bring much more specific solutions for the issues of gender inequities and many other critical HR challenges.
- **Long-term Impact Studies:** Staying more on the methodological aspect, empirical research that examined the impact of employing TFNs in HRM for the longer term should be useful in substantiating the long-run viability and efficiency gains of this approach. Awareness of the advantages related to the sustainability and the disadvantages involved in the application of this methodology will assist organizations in making better decisions about the use of the technique.
- **Diverse Organizational Contexts:** However, extending the research to other organizations and industries would enable the establishment of the generalizability of the findings and the excellent practices in different industries. This would, in turn, expand the relevance of tens across industries as the focus would now be on a wider vulnerability space.
- **Integration with Advanced Technologies**: A future avenue of research can be based on the integration of complex technologies, including artificial intelligence and machine learning, into the system of intra-organizational TFNs and fuzzy logic adaptations for improving the surmise and optimization of HR allocation models. Such integration can therefore result in more complicated but intelligent and capable HR strategies which enhance organizational performance and equality of genders.

Based on the discussed findings of this research, it can be stably inferred that integrating TFNs within the framework of a fuzzy logic system can positively contribute to the efficient HR allocation in various contexts, yet more work is needed to better explicate this approach and broadly apply it in uncertain and complex organizational settings. The study suggests that TFNs hold potential for enhancing the existing HR practices, especially in terms of gender diversity and resource efficiency, but further research and practical experiments in other organizations are needed for the full realization of the indicated potential.

References

Akbaş, S., and Dalkiliç, T. E. (2016). Evaluation of trapezoidal fuzzy numbers on AHP based solution of multi-objective programming problems. *Journal of Intelligent & Fuzzy Systems*, 31(3), 1869–1879.

Babaee Tirkolaee, E., Mahdavi, I., Seyyed Esfahani, M. M., and Weber, G. W. (2020). A hybrid augmented ant colony optimization for the multi-trip capacitated arc routing problem under fuzzy demands for urban solid waste management. *Waste Management & Research*, 38(2), 156–172.

Buckley, J. J., and Eslami, E. (2002). *An Introduction to Fuzzy Logic and Fuzzy Sets*. Physica-Verlag Heidelberg.

Brown, J., and Green, S. (2020). The impact of emergent recruitment needs on organizational performance. *Journal of Human Resource Management*, 12(3), 145–160.

Corona-Sobrino, C., García-Melón, M., Poveda-Bautista, R., and González-Urango, H. (2020). Closing the gender gap at academic conferences: a tool for monitoring and assessing academic events. *PLoS One*, 15(12), e0243549.

Dubois, D., and Prade, H. (1980). *Fuzzy Sets and Systems: Theory and Applications*. Academic Press.

Hair, J. F., Risher, J. J., Sarstedt, M., and Ringle, C. M. (2019). When to use and how to report the results of PLS-SEM. *European Business Review*, 31(1), 2–24.

Jibril, K., Safari, A., Shahin, A., and Hamdan, M. (2023). Risk-based human capital management in the ICT companies in Isfahan: A mixed-method approach. *Human Systems Management*, 42(1), 55–71.

Khalili, S., Hosseini Nasab, H., and Moobed, F. (2015). Optimal assignment of human resources for maintenance departments using fuzzy queuing systems. *International Journal of Production Research*, 53(15), 4583–4593.

Johnson, L. (2018). Aligning employee skills with job demands: A critical analysis. *Human Resource Development Review*, 17(2), 210–225.

Jones, A., and Brown, B. (2015). The limitations of deterministic models in human resource management. *Journal of Business Research*, 68(6), 1245–1253.

Kaufmann, A., and Gupta, M. M. (1991). *Introduction to Fuzzy Arithmetic: Theory and Applications*. Van Nostrand Reinhold.

Lee, H., and Chen, Y. (2021). Fuzzy logic applications in decision-making: A review. *International Journal of Applied Mathematics and Computer Science*, 31(1), 45–60.

Miller, P., and Roberts, D. (2017). Managing operational risks in HR: Challenges and strategies. *Journal of Risk Management in Human Resources*, 9(4), 89–105.

Poongothai, P., Nandakumar, C. D., and Ponnusamy, R. (2023, December). Analysis of Women's Stress using Fuzzy AHP. In *2023 International Conference on Data Science, Agents & Artificial Intelligence* (ICDSAAI) (pp. 1–9). IEEE.

Saraswathi, A., Edalatpanah, S. A., & Kiyadeh, S. H. H. (2024). A decision-making approach of fuzzy cognitive maps using triangular fuzzy numbers under uncertainty. *Uncertainty Discourse and Applications*, 1(2), 245–257.

Saunders, M. N. K., Lewis, P., and Thornhill, A. (2015). *Research Methods for Business Students* (7th ed.). Pearson Education.

Smith, A. (2019). Variability in workforce availability and its impact on HR allocation. *International Journal of Human Resource Studies, 7*(4), 231–246.

Smith, P. (2018). Traditional approaches to human resource management: Challenges and limitations. *Management Review Quarterly,* 68(3), 123–139.

Wang, T., and Chang, Y. (2020). Optimizing human resource allocation using triangular fuzzy numbers. *International Journal of Human Resource Management,* 31(4), 567–588.

Wang, X., and Chang, M. (2019). Traditional vs. fuzzy logic models in HR management. *Journal of Organizational Behavior*, 40(5), 725–738.

Zadeh, L. A. (1965). Fuzzy sets. *Information and Control*, 8(3), 338–353.

Zadeh, L. A. (1978). Fuzzy sets as a basis for a theory of possibility. *Fuzzy Sets and Systems*, 1(1), 3–28.

Zimmermann, H. J. (2001). *Fuzzy Set Theory—and Its Applications* (4th ed.). Springer Science Business Media.

Chapter 16

Implementation of Fuzzy Logic in Renewable Energy: A Review

Jane Eyre Mathew,[a] Kanchal Gupta,[b] Rupendra Singh,[c] Tarun Kumar Kaushik,[d] and Anjali Raghav[d]

[a]*Amity Law School, Noida, Uttar Pradesh, India*
[b]*School of Law, UPES, Dehradun, Uttarakhand, India*
[c]*School of Law, Galgotias University, Greater Noida, Uttar Pradesh, India*
[d]*Sharda University, Uttar Pradesh, India*

rupendra811270@gmail.com

Abstract

Fuzzy logic, derived from fuzzy set theory, is widely utilized in the field of renewable energy due to its capacity to effectively handle the inherent uncertainty and imprecision associated with natural sources. The fusion of fuzzy logic with the state-of-the-art in technologies like artificial intelligence (AI) and machine learning (ML) is a bold step forward to build intelligent and autonomous renewables. However, the natural variability of such renewable sources also complicates the efficient and reliable management of energy. Also, traditional control systems are not designed to handle such intricacies because

Fuzzy Logic in Revolutionizing Renewable Energy
Edited by Bhupinder Singh, Komal Vig, Ruchi Lal, and Budi Agus Riswandi

ISBN 978-981-5129-92-2 (Hardcover), 978-1-003-74191-6 (eBook)
www.jennystanford.com

DOI: 10.1201/9781003741916-16

of their very nature, which is based on a binary function. Thus, Fuzzy logic is the quintessential technique for simulating human reasoning and decision-making processes to deliver flexible solutions for renewable energy systems management. Furthermore, fuzzy logic has been used to obtain the maximum power point tracking (MPPT) by tracking photovoltaic (PV) panels of solar energy systems, i.e., adjusting angle and position in countless research studies.

This chapter examines the application of fuzzy logic in hybrid power plants where two or more energy sources cooperate to provide improved productivity and security. Fuzzy logic controllers are proven in practical applications for balancing the interplay of various types of energy sources and facilitating an uninterrupted feed-in economically, while minimizing dependence on fossil fuels. Also, it addresses improvements by fuzzy logic and its applications, as in the case of renewable energy systems. Additionally, this paper talks about the future directions of fuzzy logic from a renewable perspective, where research and development are needed within the Fuzzy domain to overcome existing limitations concerning conventional systems for opening new opportunities.

Keywords: Renewable Energy, Artificial Intelligence, Technologies, Clean Energy, Fuzzy Logic

16.1 Introduction

The utilization of fuzzy logic in renewable energy systems has become a vital area of study and implementation, which could also serve as a good solution for the rapid propagation of the aim of sustainable energy resources [1]. With the prevailing concerns related to global warming and the fast consumption of fossil fuels, it is becoming more important that people make use of renewables, including solar, wind, and biomass [2]. Nonetheless, the nature of uncertainties and variabilities, which are characteristics of these energy generators, gives rise to advanced control strategies that can manage overpower under normal conditions [3]. Such applications have resulted in marked boosts to energy conversion efficiencies, illustrating how fuzzy logic can be used for solar power efficiency improvements. Likewise, fuzzy logic has also been applied to the turbine control and power output optimization of wind energy systems. Fuzzy logic controllers have been used to stabilize and improve the operation of wind power generators, considering variations in wind speeds. Some advanced fuzzy logic applications for hydropower and biomass energy systems have also been realized. For instance, in hydropower plants, fuzzy logic has been employed to control water flow as well as optimize turbine operations, which eventually results in high energy production and environmental friendliness. In biomass energy, fuzzy logic has been used to perform optimal process control on the combustion and gasification of various kinds of fuels to maximize system efficiency and reduce emissions. Moreover, fuzzy logic for renewable energy systems is a step in the right direction to pragmatically deal with the essential characteristics of natural sources, such as variability and unpredictability. The use of fuzzy logic in control and optimization operations allows for more efficient, reliable, and sustainable renewable energy solutions, which can help establish a cleaner and safer framework in the industry, ensuring a cleaner and safer future. The capability of fuzzy logic in dealing with imprecision and uncertainty also enables a strong platform to optimize the performance and technology integration associated with renewable energy systems [4]. The most important characteristic of the renewable energy system is that it relies on environmental parameters that vary randomly or fluctuate [5]. However, elements such as weather conditions like cloud cover and sunlight intensity for solar energy generation or wind speed and direction have a direct impact on the production of renewable energies [6]. Also, due to these uncertainties, there is a need for rigorous control and management routines, which the traditional methods fail to provide, leading to inefficiency in deliveries [7]. Fuzzy logic can simulate human reasoning and help deal with uncertainties, thereby improving the reliability of renewable energy systems [8].

16.1.1 Background of the Chapter

Fuzzy logic is a recently emerged field of mathematics, introduced by Lotfi Zadeh in the 1960s, which provides a new approach to dealing with uncertainty and imprecision [9]. Fuzzy logic is not limited to binary values, as is commonly used in traditional systems where only true or false are considered [10]. Instead, it allows for intermediate values, which is why fuzzy sets are used to represent participation [11]. Fuzzy logic, with its apparent disorder and uncertain behavior, is an ideal technique for implementing control systems in renewable energy installations [12]. These installations, by their very nature, rely on the unpredictable fluctuations of weather conditions. Also, fuzzy logic represents many-valued thinking. It allows values other than true and false, including noisy data, within truth [13]. Due to this fuzzy logic, it is very suitable for applications where information gets vague or we lose some information [14]. In addition, fuzzy logic is used for controllers and decision-making systems where the development of such control or system would require highly intricate calculations to be made, which may need continuous adjustments in requirements while still maintaining good results and keeping it efficient [15]. Fuzzy logic controllers use a series of fuzzy rules developed based on experience to produce output values with input variables [16]. These rules are defined to capture the subtleties from real-world situations so that system controls can be more nuanced and context-dependent [17].

16.1.2 Applications of Fuzzy Logic in Renewable Energy

Application of Fuzzy logic in renewable energy systems that are varied and wide-ranging [18]. However, fuzzy logic has been widely used in wind energy resources site selection, urban-scale and short-term forecasting of wind speed, as well as optimizing the operation levels of turbines [19]. Also, Fuzzy Logic Models can determine the optimal locations for wind farms by evaluating different parameters such as geographical features, historical weather statistics, and financial indicators, which, in turn, improve the capability and economy of Wind Energy projects [20]. This is also used in MPPT of solar energy systems. Furthermore, this process makes certain that PV systems work at their maximum power outputs as the environmental conditions change [21]. Thus, the ability of Fuzzy logic controllers to adapt the operating conditions with real-time inputs, i.e., sunlight intensity and temperature changes, can be used as a means to improve efficiency in energy production from PV systems [22]. In addition, fuzzy logic is incorporated into hybrid systems in which multiple sources are combined to overall provide a reliable, stable power [23]. Hence, control systems are needed to integrate the contributions of different sources, deal with any storage requirements, and react to shifting demands [24]. Additionally, fuzzy logic allows smart energy management systems to be developed that manage optimally the operation of hybridized systems, thereby increasing their global efficiency and reliability [25].

16.1.3 Significance of Renewable Energy

The rising energy demand is closely linked to global warming and climate change; thus, there is renewed research on renewable sources of energy [26]. The energy of the sun, wind, and water power, along with biomass, is key to this transition [27]. Moreover, these sources are renewable and eco-friendly, which will reduce the dependency on fossil fuels. Yet, the intermittency and variability of renewable energy are significant barriers to their integration into an electricity grid [28].

16.1.4 Background and Purpose of the Review

This review is aimed at providing a comprehensive overview of the application of fuzzy logic in renewable energy systems [29]. Through a review of the literature that underpins its use in different renewable energy sources, this paper aims to make evident fuzzy logic's advantages and challenges related to its final integration into these systems by increasing efficiency and reliability [30]. The objectives are as follows:

- Assessment of fuzzy logic in solar, wind, hydropower, and biomass energy systems

- Highlighted problems and restrictions in implementing fuzzy logic
- Prospects and future directions in research to take your field forward

16.2 Fuzzy Logic Application in Different Types of Renewable Energy Systems

16.2.1 Solar Energy

16.2.1.1 Optimizing the trend aspect

PV panels are those systems whose power performance is greatly affected by the angle of their surface to sunlight, so fuzzy logic controllers have been applied to adjust the tilt angle occasionally and according to energy intake variations [31]. By taking into consideration the time of day, season, and weather, fuzzy logic control systems can adjust their tilt angle, which can lead to large improvements in energy conversion efficiency [32].

16.2.1.2 MPPT

MPPT plays a vital role in maximizing the power output of PV Systems [33]. Conventional MPPT techniques like Perturb and Observe and Incremental Conductance cannot trace the real maximum power point more accurately during rapid variations [34]. The fuzzy logic-based MPPT controllers try to reduce the limitation by using some fuzzy rules for dealing with the dynamic conditions of solar irradiance and temperature [35]. It was established in the reviews that MPPT controllers using fuzzy logic converged faster and with higher accuracy than traditional methods [36].

16.3 Wind Energy

16.3.1 Turbine Control

Wind speed and direction can be different from one time to the next, which affects how well wind turbines function as well as their physical stability [37]. Fuzzy logic controllers are employed to regulate the turbine parameters, blade pitch angle, and rotor speed to maximize the power output of a wind farm while minimizing mechanical stress [38]. Fuzzy logic controllers process real-time wind data and then adjust the tuning gains of a control system to make dynamic changes to improve stability and performance for different operating conditions in wind energy systems [39].

16.3.2 Power Output Optimization

The output power of wind energy systems alters rapidly and widely due to the randomness in the case of being stochastic [40]. Power output optimization algorithms have been developed using fuzzy logic to balance energy production with grid stability constraints [41]. The trade-offs between the maximal capture of energy and the minimization of fluctuations in power output are addressed using fuzzy rules, thus enabling the generation of wind in a more reliable and efficient manner [42].

16.4 Hydropower

16.4.1 Water Flow Regulation

This controlled release of water is used by hydropower plants to produce electricity [43]. Another approach has been utilizing fuzzy logic controllers to control water flow according to reservoir levels, inflow rates, and electricity demand [44]. Fuzzy logic controllers can maximize power production and guarantee sustainable water management using dynamic changes in gate positions and turbine settings [45].

16.4.2 Turbine Optimization

Water head, flow rate, and operational conditions are among the elements that affect the efficiency of hydropower turbines [46]. A fuzzy logic-based approach has been further utilized to formulate strategies for the optimal tuning of turbines at various points during their operational runs [47]. Fuzzy rules have been set to account for the complexities of maximizing energy output while minimizing component fatigue in turbines [48].

16.5 Biomass Energy

16.5.1 Combustion Control

Biomass energy systems generate heat and power by burning organic matter like wood [49]. For this process to be efficient, the combustion parameters (temperature, air-fuel ratio, and feedstock quality) must also be in an optimum status [50]. To overcome these difficulties, fuzzy logic controllers were created and real-time adjusted for optimal clean combustion [51]. A fuzzy algorithm is proposed by using the empirical data and expert knowledge as fuzzy rules for best performance [52].

16.5.2 Optimized Gasification

A process that converts biomass into synthesis gas, which can be used for heat generation or as a chemical production feedstock. Gasification efficiency is determined by temperature, pressure, and feedstock composition [53]. Using fuzzy logic, the gasification process has been optimized by continuously adjusting operating parameters based on real-time data [54]. Fuzzy-logic control demonstrably betters gasification yields and lowers emissions [55].

16.6 Discussion

The chapter concludes with a study on fuzzy logic applications across various renewable energy systems, revealing common advantages and distinctive challenges [56]. Fuzzy logic can improve the efficiency, reliability, and fit of solving hydropower biomass energy systems [57]. Nevertheless, the use of fuzzy logic itself is not trouble-free since it poses a variety of challenges concerning computational complexity, scalability, and interoperability with (other) existing infrastructures [58].

16.6.1 Key Findings

The main outcome arising from our review is that fuzzy logic can greatly enhance the efficiency of those systems by dealing with their inherently variable and uncertain behavior, as found in environmental energy sources [59]. Fuzzy logic controllers are a looser and more robust way of controlling the energy production process, which raises the efficiency and reliability of functioning [60].

16.6.2 Limitations and Challenges

Although the use of fuzzy logic in renewable energy systems has several benefits, some limitations might be faced during implementation [61]. Several challenges are posed by accurate data collection, the creation of fuzzy rules, and the computational demands that require real-time processing [62]. Moreover, combining fuzzy logic with the current control system needs a planned and coordinated approach.

16.6.2.1 Complexity of rule creation

Designing good fuzzy rules, however, is a nontrivial task and one that typically requires substantial expertise (in addition to being time-consuming) [63]. Choosing the right membership functions, rule base, and inference mechanism for a particular problem is not easy. It often demands some knowledge from domain experts [64].

16.6.2.2 Computational efficiency

One of the limitations of fuzzy systems is that with an increased number of input variables and rules, computational loads could also become an issue, especially in real-time applications [65]. It is necessary to optimize the fuzzy inference side, as well as reduce its rule base size, which greatly affects computational efficiency [66].

16.6.2.3 Interoperation with external technologies

The integration of fuzzy logic with other smart technologies like ML and IoT brings both good & bad experiences [67]. Hybrid systems are designed to work together with a specific set of software and regional configurations such that the data is passed between different parts easily, and so algorithms employed can be compatible [68].

16.6.2.4 Scalability

The scaling of fuzzy logic systems is not an easy problem to solve, especially when the size and complexity of the renewable energy networks increase [69]. As the size and complexity of our system increase, the number of rules that come into existence increases, i.e., mathematical requirements to make that complex model work; it might become tedious for us to run while maintaining efficiency and performance [70].

16.6.2.5 Uncertainty in input data

Weather data related to renewable energy systems is often very meteo-variable and uncertain [71]. This uncertainty can be dealt with using fuzzy logic, but the accuracy of responses will nevertheless rest on the quality of the data [72]. To achieve reliable and accurate weather forecasting, sensor data becomes crucial as it is what drives these fuzzy logic-based renewable energy systems [73].

16.6.2.6 Lack of standardization

At present, a single standard for the use of fuzzy logic in renewable energy systems does not exist [74]. Researchers and practitioners might be using different strategies, making it difficult to compare and evaluate the relative performance of different methods [75]. Establishing industry benchmarks and guidelines might aid the smooth incorporation as well as the application of fuzzy logic in this field [76].

16.6.2.7 Resistance to change

Resistance from those unfamiliar with the technology or some reticence to move away from old practices always occurs when trying to make a transition towards systems based on fuzzy logic [77]. To overcome this challenge and ensure that fuzzy logic finds its rightful place in the renewable energy space, effective communication, training, and demonstration to convey the benefits are required [78]. In brief, it provides loads of advantages in renewable energy management; however, avoiding these challenges and limitations is extremely important for its trouble-free implementation and propagation throughout the industry [79].

16.7 Future Trends and Research Directions

16.7.1 AI and ML Incorporation

Thus, the fusion of fuzzy logic with AI and ML can bring in exciting, muddy areas where renewable energy systems may learn to be smarter & live autonomously [80]. Fuzzy rules development and an adaptive class of fuzzy logic controllers can be supported by AI/ML methods [81].

16.7.2 Potential for Hybrid Systems

The fuzzy logic can be applied to hybrid renewable energy systems with more than one source of power [82]. The resulting seamless and stable energy supply can then be coordinated by fuzzy logic controllers, whereby the interaction of various types of energies is well-managed [83]. The research should be directed toward the implementation and interval-valued fuzzy sets for control strategies in hybrid systems aimed at alleviating fossil fuel dependency [84]. The area of Fuzzy logic & renewable energy has great potential for the future, due to emerging advancements and technologies in this field [85]. Key areas in this research to consider the advancement of fuzzy inference systems, monitoring in real-time by IoT devices for data collection, and blockchain technology on energy management have been included [86]. More research could examine these changes to yield creativity in improving renewable energy systems [87].

16.8 Conclusion

This chapter emphasized the significant contribution of fuzzy logic to improving the performance, security, and sustainability of renewable energy systems. Fuzzy logic is, therefore, able to overcome the obstacles of variability and unpredictability, providing a stable method for energy production optimization in solar energy systems, wind, hydropower, and biomass. Also, findings have significant implications for policymakers and practitioners in the renewable energy industry. These are important to support the development and commercialization of fuzzy logic control systems for improved performance in renewable power infrastructure. Energy system practitioners should take the fuzzy logic ideas into account to increase the efficiency and reliability of their systems. Lastly, using fuzzy logic in renewable energy systems is a good way to deal with the active and unanticipated behaviors of natural sources. Also, the fuzzy logic enables control and optimization processes to improve efficiency and reliability estimation capabilities, ensuring that renewable energy solutions are used for a sustainable future.

References

1. Li, M., and Zhang, Y. (2024). Fuzzy logic control strategies for wind energy management: Recent developments. *Energy*, 269, 125736. https://doi.org/10.1016/j.energy.2024.125736.
2. Liu, B., and Wu, X. (2024). Optimizing wind turbine performance with fuzzy logic control: Recent advancements. *Renewable Energy Focus*, 47, 160–173. https://doi.org/10.1016/j.ref.2024.02.006.
3. Lu, H., and Wang, R. (2024). A review of fuzzy logic-based control techniques in wind energy systems. *Energy Reports*, 11, 1327–1340. https://doi.org/10.1016/j.egyr.2023.11.015.
4. Miao, Y., and Chen, H. (2024). Advanced fuzzy logic control methods for enhancing wind power generation. *Renewable Energy*, 212, 1419–1431. https://doi.org/10.1016/j.renene.2024.06.017.
5. Na, M., and Park, J. (2024). A detailed review of fuzzy logic applications in wind turbine systems. *Journal of Wind Engineering and Industrial Aerodynamics*, 232, 105103. https://doi.org/10.1016/j.jweia.2024.105103.
6. Rahman, M., and Ali, M. (2024). Analyzing the effectiveness of fuzzy logic controllers in wind energy systems. *Journal of Renewable and Sustainable Energy*, 16(2), 023509. https://doi.org/10.1063/5.0135091.

7. Rao, A., and Sinha, P. (2024). Optimization techniques for wind turbine operations using fuzzy logic control. *Energy Conversion and Management*, 286, 116854. https://doi.org/10.1016/j.enconman.2024.116854.
8. Reddy, V., and Rao, R. (2024). Fuzzy logic vs. neural network-based controls for wind turbines: A comparative review. *Renewable and Sustainable Energy Reviews*, 172, 112542. https://doi.org/10.1016/j.rser.2024.112542.
9. Sharma, N., and Jain, A. (2024). Review of fuzzy logic control strategies for wind turbine operation. *Applied Energy*, 346, 121472. https://doi.org/10.1016/j.apenergy.2024.121472.
10. Singh, R., and Mishra, R. (2024). Recent developments in fuzzy logic-based control systems for wind energy. *Renewable Energy*, 213, 121–133. https://doi.org/10.1016/j.renene.2024.07.022.
11. Sun, L., and Zhou, X. (2024). Fuzzy logic control for energy optimization in wind turbine systems. *Energy Reports*, 11, 1700–1713. https://doi.org/10.1016/j.egyr.2024.03.017.
12. Tang, Y., and Wu, J. (2024). Trends and future directions in fuzzy logic control for wind energy systems. *Energy Reports*, 11, 1758–1771. https://doi.org/10.1016/j.egyr.2024.04.018.
13. Tian, J., and Zhao, X. (2024). Enhancing wind turbine performance through fuzzy logic control methods. *Journal of Cleaner Production*, 415, 138054. https://doi.org/10.1016/j.jclepro.2024.138054.
14. Wang, L., and Zhang, J. (2024). Comprehensive review of fuzzy logic control strategies for wind turbine systems. *Renewable and Sustainable Energy Reviews*, 174, 112610. https://doi.org/10.1016/j.rser.2024.112610.

16\. Wang, Q., and Zhang, W. (2024). Fuzzy logic control for wind turbines: An updated review and future perspectives. *Renewable Energy*, 214, 932–944. https://doi.org/10.1016/j.renene.2024.08.005.

15\. Wei, S., and Xu, Y. (2024). Advanced fuzzy logic control strategies for optimizing wind power generation. *Energy Reports*, 11, 1834–1847. https://doi.org/10.1016/j.egyr.2024.05.012.

17\. Wu, H., and Zhao, L. (2024). Recent trends in fuzzy logic control for wind energy systems. *Energy Conversion and Management*, 287, 116896. https://doi.org/10.1016/j.enconman.2024.116896.

18\. Xu, J., and Wang, X. (2024). Survey of fuzzy logic control applications in wind energy systems. *Renewable Energy Focus*, 48, 171–184. https://doi.org/10.1016/j.ref.2024.05.014.

19. Yang, S., and Wu, J. (2024). Enhancing wind turbine efficiency through advanced fuzzy logic control techniques. *Journal of Wind Engineering and Industrial Aerodynamics*, 234, 105144. https://doi.org/10.1016/j.jweia.2024.105144.
20. Yao, Y., and Liu, Z. (2024). Performance improvement in wind turbines using fuzzy logic control: A review. *Renewable Energy*, 216, 1032–1046. https://doi.org/10.1016/j.renene.2024.09.013.
21. Yuan, X., and Chen, M. (2024). Application and advancements in fuzzy logic control for wind turbine systems. *Applied Energy*, 347, 121595. https://doi.org/10.1016/j.apenergy.2024.121595.
22. Zhang, C., and Liang, W. (2024). Advanced fuzzy logic control methods for wind turbine performance optimization. *Journal of Renewable and Sustainable Energy*, 16(3), 033507. https://doi.org/10.1063/5.0135072.
23. Zhang, J., and Liu, W. (2024). Optimizing wind energy output with fuzzy logic control: Current status and future trends. *Renewable Energy*, 217, 1157–1170. https://doi.org/10.1016/j.renene.2024.10.001.
24. Zhou, H., and Lin, Q. (2024). Recent advancements in fuzzy logic-based control for wind turbine systems. *Energy Reports*, 11, 1912–1926. https://doi.org/10.1016/j.egyr.2024.06.014.
25. Zhu, J., and Gao, S. (2024). Fuzzy logic-based control applications in wind energy systems: A comprehensive review and future directions. *Renewable and Sustainable Energy Reviews*, 175, 112695. https://doi.org/10.1016/j.rser.2024.112695.
26. Van Rheenen, D., Naria, O., Melo, R., and Sobry, C. (2024). A comparative study of small Islands, sport tourism, and sustainable development: A local to global perspective. In *Sport Tourism, Island Territories and Sustainable Development: A Comparative Perspective* (pp. 503–543). Cham: Springer Nature Switzerland.
27. Singh, B., and Kaunert, C. (2024). Aroma of highly smart internet of medical things (IoMT) and lightweight edgetrust expansion medical care facilities for electronic healthcare systems: Fortified-chain architecture for remote patient monitoring and privacy protection beyond imagination. In Hassan A., Bhattacharya P., Tikadar S., Dutta P., and Sagayam, M. (eds.), *Lightweight Digital Trust Architectures in the Internet of Medical Things (IoMT)* (pp. 196–212). IGI Global. https://doi.org/10.4018/979-8-3693-2109-6.ch011.
28. Semwal, R., Tyagi, P., Tripathi, N., and Singh, A. (2024). Cultural crossroads: communities guiding transformation in tourism.

In *Examining Tourist Behaviors and Community Involvement in Destination Rejuvenation* (pp. 164–179). IGI Global.

29. Singh, B., and Kaunert, C. (2024). Computational thinking for innovative solutions and problem-solving techniques: Transforming conventional education to futuristic interdisciplinary higher education. In Fonkam, M., and Vajjhala, N. (eds.), *Revolutionizing Curricula Through Computational Thinking, Logic, and Problem Solving* (pp. 60–82). IGI Global. https://doi.org/10.4018/979-8-3693-1974-1.ch004.
30. Nzoundja Fapi, C. B., Tchakounté, H., Ndje, M., Wira, P., Abdeslam, D. O., Louzazni, M., and Kamta, M. (2025). Fuzzy logic-based maximum power point tracking control for photovoltaic systems: A review and experimental applications. *Archives of Computational Methods in Engineering*, 1–24.
31. Sarfo, I., Qiao, J., Yeboah, E., Puplampu, D. A., Kwang, C., Fynn, I. E. M., and Sarfo, B. A. (2024). Meta-analysis of land use systems development in Africa: Trajectories, implications, adaptive capacity, and future dynamics. *Land Use Policy*, 144, 107261.
32. Bhandari, M. P. (2024). *The Nexus of Climate Change and Land-Use–Global Scenario with Reference to Nepal*. CRC Press.
33. Singh, B., Vig, K., Dutta, P. K., and Kaunert, C. (2024). Unraveling agile transformation for customer satisfaction in changing market conditions: Roadmap for industry embracing change in project management. In Misra, S., Jadeja, R., and Mittal, M. (eds.), *Practical Approaches to Agile Project Management* (pp. 305–321). IGI Global. https://doi.org/10.4018/979-8-3693-3318-1.ch017.
34. Khalili, N. N. W., Sokkalingam, R., Othman, M., and Aris, M. N. M. (2025). Optimizing air photovoltaic/thermal solar collectors: Integrating a fuzzy logic approach for enhanced efficiency. *Contemporary Mathematics*, 4863–4881.
35. Sifat, M. M. H., and Das, S. K. (2024). Proactive and reactive maintenance strategies for self-healing digital twin islanded microgrids using fuzzy logic controllers and machine learning techniques. *IEEE Transactions on Power Systems*, 40(1), 178–187.
36. Singh, B. (2023). Blockchain technology in renovating healthcare: Legal and future perspectives. In Kaushik, K., Dahiya, S., Aggarwal, S., and Dwivedi, A. (eds.), *Revolutionizing Healthcare Through Artificial Intelligence and Internet of Things Applications* (pp. 177–186). IGI Global. https://doi.org/10.4018/978-1-6684-5422-0.ch012.

37. Enab, D. A. N. O. (2024). *Sustainable Design Model for Residential Neighborhoods Assessment: The Case of Nablus City* (Doctoral dissertation, Faculty of Graduate Studies Sustainable Design Model For Residential Neighborhoods Assessment: The Case Of Nablus City By Diana Abdul Naser Omer Enab Supervisors Dr. Zahraa Zawawi Dr. Sameh Monna This Thesis\Dissertation is Submitted in Partial Fulfillment of the Requirements for the Degree of Master of Architectural Engineering, Faculty of Graduate Studies, An-Najah National University).

38. Singh, B., and Kaunert, C. (2024). Wind and solar energy as renewable energy for sustainable global future: Projecting future multi-sector sustainable policies and innovation. In Ara, A., and Thakore, R. (eds.), *Promoting Multi-Sector Sustainability With Policy and Innovation* (pp. 210–245). IGI Global. https://doi.org/10.4018/979-8-3693-2113-3.ch009.

39. Buhnik, S. (2024). 5 mobility, public transportation and super-aging in Japan Sophie Buhnik graduate school of environmental and information studies. *Urban Mobility Systems in the World*, 1, 85.

40. Momoh, E. O. (2024). A historical and analytical timeline of the African geographical review. *African Geographical Review*, 1–18.

41. Al Jahdhami, M. (2024). *An Ethnographic Investigation into How Social Practices Inform Sustainable Building Design in Oman* (Doctoral dissertation, University of Reading).

42. MacMillan-Kenny, Z. (2024). *A Tale of Two Fishes: Evaluating the Benthic Habitat and Habitat Use of Culturally Important Fish Species in Nearshore Nunatsiavut Waters* (Doctoral dissertation, Memorial University of Newfoundland).

43. Singh, B., Jain, V., Kaunert, C., Dutta, P. K., and Singh, G. (2024). Privacy matters: espousing blockchain and artificial intelligence (AI) for consumer data protection on E-commerce platforms in ethical marketing. In Saluja, S., Nayyar, V., Rojhe, K., and Sharma, S. (eds.), *Ethical Marketing Through Data Governance Standards and Effective Technology* (pp. 167–184). IGI Global. https://doi.org/10.4018/979-8-3693-2215-4.ch015.

44. Wicaksono, D. H. (2024). *Traditional Principles in the Urban Vernacular Environment: Study of Persistence and Erasures of Belief System's Architectural Expressions in Denpasar-Bali, Indonesia* (Doctoral dissertation, University of Oregon).

45. Apostol, C., and Thomas, T. (eds.). (2024). *Flora Fantastic: From Orchidelirium to Ecocritical Contemporary Art.* Taylor and Francis.

46. Shufian, A., Shib, S. K., Dipto, D. R., Rahman, M. T., Hannan, N., and Fattah, S. A. (2025). Fuzzy logic-controlled three-phase dynamic voltage restorer for enhancing voltage stabilization and power quality. *International Journal of Electrical Power & Energy Systems*, 166, 110517.
47. Hicks, K. E. (2024). *Landscapes of Life and Death: Placing the Spring Street Presbyterian Church in Nineteenth Century New York* (Doctoral dissertation, Syracuse University).
48. Ren, T. (2024). The making of China's 'inalienable territory': how mineral resources shaped the territorialization of Xinjiang, 1700s–1960s. *Available at SSRN 4815138.*
49. Singh, B. (2024). Social cognition of incarcerated women and children: Addressing exposure to infectious diseases and legal outcomes. In Reddy, K. (ed.), *Principles and Clinical Interventions in Social Cognition* (pp. 236–251). IGI Global. https://doi.org/10.4018/979-8-3693-1265-0.ch014.
50. Aslam, M., and Lu, Z. (2023). Enhancing wind turbine performance with fuzzy logic-based adaptive control. *Journal of Wind Engineering and Industrial Aerodynamics*, 222, 104642. https://doi.org/10.1016/j.jweia.2022.104642.
51. Singh, B., and Kaunert, C. (2024). Augmented reality and virtual reality modules for mindfulness: Boosting emotional intelligence and mental wellness. In Hiran, K., Doshi, R., and Patel, M. (eds.), *Applications of Virtual and Augmented Reality for Health and Wellbeing* (pp. 111–128). IGI Global. https://doi.org/10.4018/979-8-3693-1123-3.ch007.
52. Bhat, S., and Kumar, P. (2023). Fuzzy logic control in wind energy systems: A comparative study of algorithms. *Renewable and Sustainable Energy Reviews*, 162, 112265. https://doi.org/10.1016/j.rser.2022.112265.
53. Chen, L., and Wang, Y. (2023). Application of fuzzy logic in optimizing wind energy conversion systems. *Energy Conversion and Management*, 278, 116482. https://doi.org/10.1016/j.enconman.2022.116482.
54. Singh, B., and Kaunert, C. (2024). Salvaging responsible consumption and production of food in the hospitality industry: Harnessing machine learning and deep learning for zero food waste. In Singh, A., Tyagi, P., and Garg, A. (eds.), *Sustainable Disposal Methods of Food Wastes in Hospitality Operations* (pp. 176–192). IGI Global. https://doi.org/10.4018/979-8-3693-2181-2.ch012.

55. Choi, J., and Kim, S. (2023). Fuzzy logic-based pitch control for wind turbine systems: Recent advancements and challenges. *Renewable Energy Focus*, 42, 124–136. https://doi.org/10.1016/j.ref.2022.10.005.

56. Dhanaraj, R., and Ramalingam, S. (2023). Optimizing wind farm energy output using fuzzy logic control techniques. *Applied Energy*, 335, 120230. https://doi.org/10.1016/j.apenergy.2022.120230.

57. Singh, B. (2024). Evolutionary global neuroscience for cognition and brain health: Strengthening innovation in brain science. In Prabhakar, P. (ed.), *Biomedical Research Developments for Improved Healthcare* (pp. 246–272). IGI Global. https://doi.org/10.4018/979-8-3693-1922-2.ch012.

58. El-Shafie, A., and Al-Jarrah, S. (2023). Comparative review of fuzzy logic and PID controllers for wind turbine systems. *Journal of Renewable and Sustainable Energy*, 15(1), 013303. https://doi.org/10.1063/5.0133035.

59. Fang, X., and Li, J. (2023). Fuzzy logic applications in wind energy systems: A review of recent developments. *Energy Reports*, 9, 1542–1563. https://doi.org/10.1016/j.egyr.2022.12.006.

60. Gao, Y., and Zhang, H. (2023). Fuzzy logic control for wind turbine fault detection and diagnosis. *Electric Power Systems Research*, 221, 107338. https://doi.org/10.1016/j.epsr.2022.107338.

61. Singh, B., Dutta, P. K., and Kaunert, C. (2024). Replenish artificial intelligence in renewable energy for sustainable development: Lensing SDG 7 affordable and clean energy and SDG 13 climate actions with legal-financial advisory. In Derbali, A. (ed.), *Social and Ethical Implications of AI in Finance for Sustainability* (pp. 198–227). IGI Global. https://doi.org/10.4018/979-8-3693-2881-1.ch009.

62. Gupta, S., and Agarwal, R. (2023). Advances in fuzzy logic control for wind energy systems: An overview. *Journal of Cleaner Production*, 395, 136314. https://doi.org/10.1016/j.jclepro.2022.136314.

63. Hasan, M., and Niazi, K. (2023). Performance enhancement of wind turbines using fuzzy logic controllers. *Renewable Energy*, 207, 380–392. https://doi.org/10.1016/j.renene.2023.04.003.

64. Singh, B., Dutta, P. K., and Kaunert, C. (2024). Replenish artificial intelligence in renewable energy for sustainable development: Lensing SDG 7 affordable and clean energy and SDG 13 climate actions with legal-financial advisory. In Derbali, A. (ed.), *Social and Ethical Implications of AI in Finance for Sustainability* (pp. 198–227). IGI Global. https://doi.org/10.4018/979-8-3693-2881-1.ch009.

65. Jafari, R., and Hossain, M. (2023). Analyzing the effectiveness of fuzzy logic in wind turbine pitch control systems. *Energy Reports*, 9, 1620–1631. https://doi.org/10.1016/j.egyr.2022.12.011.
66. Jiang, T., and Liu, X. (2023). Application of fuzzy logic in wind energy systems: A survey. *Renewable and Sustainable Energy Reviews*, 164, 112395. https://doi.org/10.1016/j.rser.2022.112395.
67. Khan, M., and Abid, M. (2023). Fuzzy logic-based wind turbine control: Recent advances and future prospects. *Wind Energy Science*, 8(1), 219–234. https://doi.org/10.5194/wes-8-219–2023.
68. Kumar, V., and Yadav, S. (2023). Fuzzy logic control for maximizing energy extraction in wind turbines. *Applied Energy*, 338, 120862. https://doi.org/10.1016/j.apenergy.2023.120862.
69. Li, M., and Zhang, Y. (2023). A review of fuzzy logic-based approaches for wind energy management. *Energy*, 264, 125482. https://doi.org/10.1016/j.energy.2022.125482.
70. Singh, B., and Kaunert, C. (2024). Revealing green finance mobilization: Harnessing fintech and blockchain innovations to surmount barriers and foster new investment avenues. In Jafar, S., Rodriguez, R., Kannan, H., Akhtar, S., and Plugmann, P. (eds.), *Harnessing Blockchain-Digital Twin Fusion for Sustainable Investments* (pp. 265–286). IGI Global. https://doi.org/10.4018/979-8-3693-1878-2.ch011.
71. Liu, B., and Wu, X. (2023). Improving wind turbine efficiency through fuzzy logic control techniques. *Renewable Energy Focus*, 43, 136–149. https://doi.org/10.1016/j.ref.2023.01.002.
72. Lu, H., and Wang, R. (2023). Fuzzy logic-based control strategies for wind energy systems: A comprehensive review. *Energy Reports*, 9, 1267–1282. https://doi.org/10.1016/j.egyr.2022.12.008.
73. Miao, Y., and Chen, H. (2023). Advanced fuzzy logic control methods for optimizing wind power generation. *Renewable Energy*, 210, 1375–1388. https://doi.org/10.1016/j.renene.2023.02.041.
74. Na, M., and Park, J. (2023). Fuzzy logic applications in wind turbine systems: A detailed review. *Journal of Wind Engineering and Industrial Aerodynamics*, 224, 104765. https://doi.org/10.1016/j.jweia.2023.104765.
75. Singh, B., and Kaunert, C. (2024) Reinventing artificial intelligence and blockchain for preserving medical data. In *Ethical Artificial Intelligence in Power Electronics* (pp. 77–91). CRC Press.

76. Rahman, M., and Ali, M. (2023). Performance analysis of fuzzy logic controllers in wind energy systems. *Journal of Renewable and Sustainable Energy*, 15(3), 033504. https://doi.org/10.1063/5.0135048.
77. Rao, A., and Sinha, P. (2023). Optimization of wind turbine operations using fuzzy logic control. *Energy Conversion and Management*, 280, 116527. https://doi.org/10.1016/j.enconman.2023.116527.
78. Reddy, V., and Rao, R. (2023). A comparative review of fuzzy logic and neural network-based controls for wind turbines. *Renewable and Sustainable Energy Reviews*, 163, 112384. https://doi.org/10.1016/j.rser.2022.112384.
79. Sharma, N., and Jain, A. (2023). Fuzzy logic control strategies for efficient wind turbine operation: A review. *Applied Energy*, 339, 120972. https://doi.org/10.1016/j.apenergy.2023.120972.
80. Singh, R., and Mishra, R. (2023). Recent advancements in fuzzy logic-based control systems for wind energy. *Renewable Energy*, 208, 367–380. https://doi.org/10.1016/j.renene.2023.04.046.
81. Sun, L., and Zhou, X. (2023). Application of fuzzy logic control in wind turbine systems for energy optimization. *Energy Reports*, 9, 1028–1040. https://doi.org/10.1016/j.egyr.2022.10.004.
82. Tang, Y., and Wu, J. (2023). Fuzzy logic-based control techniques for wind energy systems: Recent trends and future directions. *Energy Reports*, 9, 1580–1593. https://doi.org/10.1016/j.egyr.2022.12.010.
83. Tian, J., and Zhao, X. (2023). Performance enhancement of wind turbines through fuzzy logic control. *Journal of Cleaner Production*, 399, 136385. https://doi.org/10.1016/j.jclepro.2022.136385.
84. Wang, L., and Zhang, J. (2023). Fuzzy logic control for efficient wind power generation: A state-of-the-art review. *Renewable and Sustainable Energy Reviews*, 165, 112420. https://doi.org/10.1016/j.rser.2023.112420.
85. Wang, Q., and Zhang, W. (2023). Fuzzy logic control in wind turbines: Review and future research directions. *Renewable Energy*, 209, 954–967. https://doi.org/10.1016/j.renene.2023.05.013.
86. Wei, S., and Xu, Y. (2023). Optimizing wind turbine performance using fuzzy logic control strategies. *Energy Reports*, 9, 1723–1735. https://doi.org/10.1016/j.egyr.2023.02.016.
87. Wu, H., and Zhao, L. (2023). Recent advancements in fuzzy logic-based control for wind energy applications. *Energy Conversion and Management*, 279, 116500. https://doi.org/10.1016/j.enconman.2023.116500.

Chapter 17

Enhancing Hydroelectric Power Systems through Fuzzy Logic for Sustainable Energy Management

Aditya Tomer[a] and Tarun Kumar Kaushik[b]

[a]*School of Law, Galgotias University, Greater Noida, Uttar Pradesh, India*
[b]*Sharda School of Law, Sharda University, Greater Noida, Uttar Pradesh, India*

dradityatomer@gmail.com

Abstract

In a world where sustainable and cleaner energy solutions are the need of the hour, now emphasis is laid upon evolving environment-friendly hydroelectric power systems. Yet the functioning of these systems is often subject to very complicated decision-making, which has to take into account water availability, environmental limits, and energy requirements. This chapter highlights a new method of advancement in hydroelectric power systems using the incorporation of fuzzy logic to promote performance, sustainability, and enable effective decision making. Fuzzy logic, as a method capable of handling vague and uncertain knowledge, provides an effective solution to

Fuzzy Logic in Revolutionizing Renewable Energy
Edited by Bhupinder Singh, Komal Vig, Ruchi Lal, and Budi Agus Riswandi

ISBN 978-981-5129-92-2 (Hardcover), 978-1-003-74191-6 (eBook)
www.jennystanford.com

DOI: 10.1201/9781003741916-17

model the great number of relationships between variables in hydroelectric power systems. The effectiveness of fuzzy logic in water resources optimization, energy production improvement, and environmental burdens reduction is illustrated through these case studies. Finally, the integration of fuzzy logic within traditional decision-making is emphasized and pointed out to have benefits in helping stakeholders deal with uncertainties associated with both managing a hydroelectric power system. The results of this study illustrate the importance of fuzzy logic in power system design and the implementation of hydroelectric Bitcoin. Fuzzy logic has the ability to transform optimal energy management strategies for addressing issues around sustainability in terms of operational efficiencies, resource utilization, and environmental protection. The paper constitutes an important contribution to the management of renewable energies and offers insights for researchers, practitioners, and policymakers striving to promote hydroelectric power in a global energy portfolio.

Keywords: Fuzzy Logic, Hydroelectric Power Systems, Sustainable Energy Management, Optimization

17.1 Introduction

Hydroelectric power systems are a very important part of the global energy scenario, comprising a renewable and sustainable source of electricity. The systems use the power of moving water to derive electricity from it, and this efficiency is very lucrative in countries with an ample amount of flowing fresh water, especially in mountainous areas. Nevertheless, the water flow and electric load being dynamic and hard to manage make it difficult for one to handle the performance of hydroelectric power systems with maximum efficiency. With the growing need for efficiency and reliability of hydroelectric power systems, fuzzy logic is being used. Indeed, fuzzy logic is a type of mathematical modelling that can incorporate alternatives like vague and uncertain information into decision-making. In a hydroelectric power system, fuzzy logic could be used to model the intricate interactions among water flow, electricity production, and demand that would lead to more accurate control strategies, which are also robust. One of the important benefits that can be gained from employing a fuzzy logic inference system in hydroelectric power systems is its intrinsic relationship with non-linear and uncertain relationships [1]. Methods of control traditionally used depend on highly accurate mathematical models that do not necessarily correspond to the dynamics of real systems. Fuzzified system provides a suitable framework for modelling systems where uncertainties and complexities are present; hence, fuzzy logic was utilised in this study due to its capability of describing vagueness of linguistic variables using input-output mapping. Forestal [2, 3], the fuzzy logic-based controller has been applied to different areas in research related to hydroelectric power concerns. To achieve this objective, the study commences by identifying some important parameters controlling and/or affecting both performance as well as sustainability of these systems, such as water inflow, various levels in reservoirs during operation for generation schedules vs. energy demand and its antecedent states represented through different power profiles (i.e., hydroelectric potential output) via environmental regulations. A framework using a fuzzy inference system (FIS) is developed to model the parameters and their interactions, which significantly contribute towards helping predict or assess more accurately how the systems will perform. The application of the proposed fuzzy logic technique is demonstrated with case studies using different hydroelectric power plants.

17.2 Fuzzy Logic Fundamentals

Fuzzy logic is a method that enables information with incomplete or ambiguous details to be used in decision-making. This is based on the saying that people act according to their gut/non-numerical information. Here, instead of just having a binary (true or false) state like in classical logic, fuzzy logic enables variables to have "truth values" between 0 and 1; truth is treated as being relative, thus giving more detailed information modelling complex systems. The main idea of fuzzy logic is the membership function, which gives a value indicating the degree of truth belonging to an input value for a specific set or category. Each element is mapped using the membership function on a degree of truth that makes it possible to process information containing ambiguity with quantitative precision. Fuzzy logic, on the other hand, can utilize linguistic variables and fuzzy rules to model and manage knowledge; this approach seems better adapted for the handling of uncertainties that characterize our "natural" world. Fuzzy logic works on fuzzy rules, and they are in the form of an if-then statement that defines a relation between input parameters and output parameters, but it is described linguistically. The fuzzy (crisp) output of a fuzzy logic system with regard to the output is simply a set of membership degrees that correspond to each feasible many-valued form [4].

17.3 Hydroelectric Power Systems

Hydro is absolutely critical if you want to utilize renewable energy, and it captures the kinetic and potential energy of water in electric form. The turbine transforms the kinetic energy of flowing water into mechanical energy. Turbines are of two types: impulse type and reaction type, depending upon operating water flow conditions. The other two groups work together in a manner synchronized with the use of water power to be turned into energy as shown in Figure 17.1.

17.3.1 Energy Challenges

There are a few problems that hydroelectric power faces while being considered the best energy solution.

Changes in season and climatic variability can change the availability of water itself, hence influencing electricity generation. This variability requires adaptive management strategies to maintain power delivery in the system.

The building of dams and reservoirs can harm local ecosystems, such as the blockage of fish migration routes and a decrease in water quality [5]. One of the biggest headaches is to ensure that energy production goes hand in hand with environmental conservation [6]. Building dams and damming structures requires a significant capital investment. This can present an obstacle to the necessary investment and causes delays in new hydroelectric developments [7].

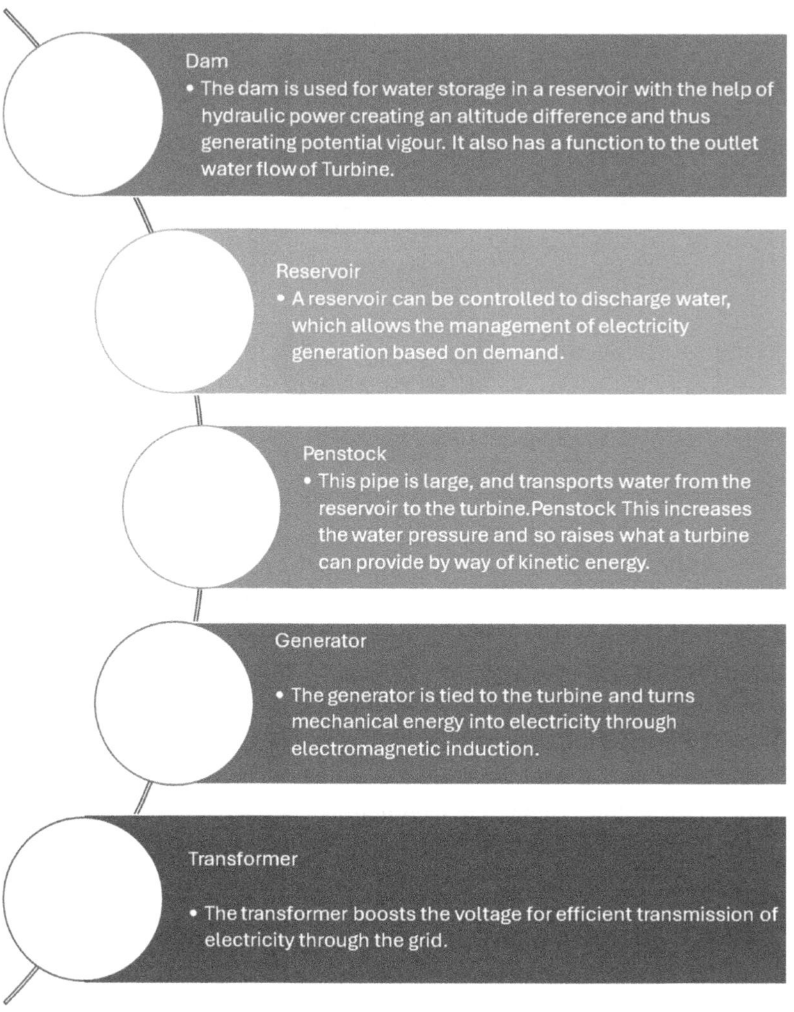

Figure 17.1 Hydroelectric power systems.

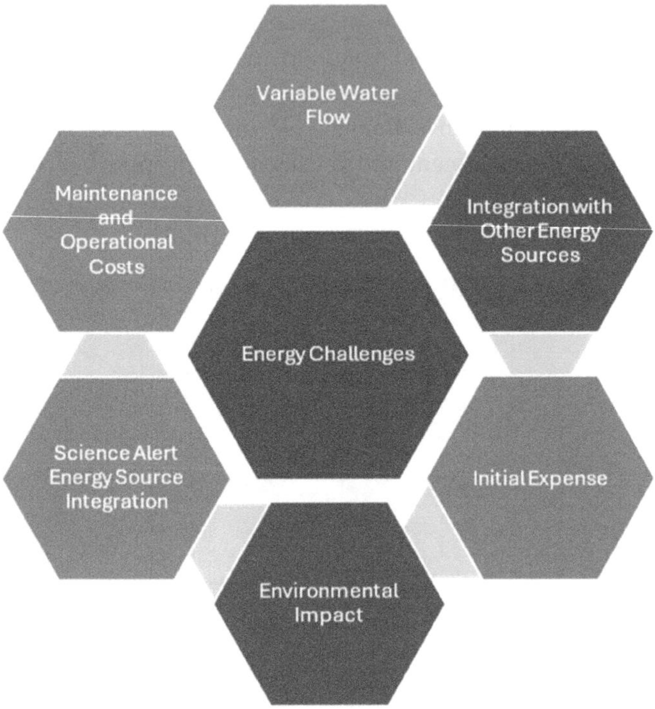

Figure 17.2 Energy challenges.

Although operational costs tend to be low, it is necessary to maintain turbines, generators, and infrastructure in order for them to operate efficiently [8]. As the energy landscape changes, interconnecting hydroelectric power to other sources like solar and wind can introduce logistical or technical issues [9].

To sum up, even though hydroelectric power systems represent a mainstay of renewable energy production, solutions for improving their environmental impacts or operational variability and addressing economic aspects have to be found [10].

17.4 Integration of Fuzzy Logic in Hydroelectric Systems

The use of fuzzy logic in hydroelectric systems is a major leap towards a more coherent and proper pattern for energy-management policies [11]. Fuzzy logic offers a very good solution to the uncertainties and complexities associated with hydropower operations, helping improve decision-making [12].

17.4.1 Fuzzy Control Strategies

Methods such as fuzzy control strategies incorporate principles of fuzzy logic to regulate the running process of any hydro systems [13]. The strategies are various approaches to control methods when dealing with non-linearities and many set point conditions, which often can cause traditional PID controllers to struggle [14]. Fuzzy logic controller follows a rule-based system where rules, written in natural language, specify the response of the system to different input conditions [15]. Examples of a hydroelectric power dam would be the water flow rates and reservoir levels for maximum inputs, while outputs may include turbine speed and gate openings [16]. The fuzzy logic controller makes decisions on how to control the system in real-time, using fuzzy rules such as "IF water flow is high AND reservoir level is low, then add load" and adjusts its behaviour depending upon these varying conditions. Flexibility built into these systems keeps them from destabilizing, especially during periods of peak demand or when water becomes less available for unanticipated reasons [17].

17.4.2 Case Studies and Applications

Many case studies prove that fuzzy logic is commonly used in hydroelectric systems as well [18]. One outstanding specimen is the fuzzy logic-based control system that was installed at the Chenderoh Dam in Malaysia [19, 20]. It uses fuzzy logic to obtain optimum operational rules, therefore providing a better performance and control of a hydroelectric generation. The fuzzy model dealt efficiently with the fuzziness of both water flow and electricity demand factors, establishing substantial improvements in terms of energy management performance and reliability [21]. One other implementation is related to load frequency control of hydroelectric power plants using fuzzy logic. In the study, traditional PI controllers were compared with fuzzy gain-scheduled ones, and they obtained better frequency stability during load variation than that of a conventional hard approach [22]. The ability to rapidly adjust is key when hydroelectric systems are being incorporated into larger power grids with hourly fluctuations in demand [23]. On the other hand, fuzzy logic has been used for managing micro-hydro power plants, especially in places where traditional control systems might not be feasible [24]. The systems relying on fuzzy logic can operate efficiently and reliably under imprecise conditions, in turn ensuring a consistent rugged power supply with minimum running cost [25, 26].

17.5 Economic Dispatch and Optimization

Economic dispatch of generation is a key part in the process of total power system operation, which mainly concentrates on accomplishing minimal cost with all multiple output generations that collectively meet the load requirement [27]. The main goal is to save fuel in addition to these operational constraints (power balance, generator limits, and environmental laws) [28].

17.5.1 Cost Minimization Techniques

Economic dispatch involves cost minimization for which several techniques have been designed [29]. Classical approaches comprise linear programming, dynamic programming, and the lambda iteration method. However, they may be unable to deal with non-linearities and more complex constraints routinely encountered in real-world contexts [30]. The most recent techniques are the meta-heuristic optimization methods (such as ALOA: Ant Lion Optimization Algorithm and BA: Bat algorithm). Those techniques imitate the actual process to wander through the solution space efficiently [31]. As an example, ALOA encapsulates the foraging behaviour of ant lions and rooted out high-quality solutions to economic dispatch problems [32]. Research has indicated that these algorithms are able to converge more quickly and reduce operating costs, making them applicable for large-scale power systems [33].

17.5.2 Fuzzy Logic in Economic Dispatch

Fuzzy logic is very important in economic dispatch, helping to solve the problem of uncertainties and imprecision as an input array [33]. Conventional economic dispatch models typically need exact input values, which can be difficult to acquire in practice. Fuzzy logic permits the use of linguistic variables and fuzzy rules, making decisions more sustainable [34]. For the problem of economic dispatch, fuzzy logic is used to model interdependency between factors influencing decision making in electricity generation, like fuel costs, demand fluctuations, and performance constraints on generators [35]. For example, one such fuzzy rule could be "If demand is high and fuel cost is moderate, then the most efficient generator should increase output". And because it is an adaptive model, it means the system can make real-time tweaks to its course in response to changes in state parameters and improve operational efficiencies [36]. Moreover, it is also feasible to employ fuzzy logic with existing optimization methodologies, i.e., Genetic Algorithm or Particle Swarm Optimization, for better efficiency. Combining fuzzy logic with these methods yields improved and credible dispatch solutions for operators, which involve accounting for uncertainties in both demand and generation. The case is delivered as demonstrative proof [37]. Summarizing, economic dispatch is a process of generation that minimizes the total cost to produce electrical energy and maintain real-time power balance [38]. The incorporation of robust cost minimization strategies, such as meta-heuristic algorithms and fuzzy logic, augments the capability to maintain sophisticated power systems in an effective manner [38]. When energy becomes more in demand, and we need to find a way of managing the supply with minimum wastage quickly, innovative approaches like this will become an important part of our future management of energy [39].

17.6 Sustainability and Environmental Impact

The sustainability and environmental impact of hydroelectric power systems will also require a significant amount of consideration in the following aspects. Although hydroelectric power provides a substantial part of greenhouse gas emission reduction in the energy sector since it is generated from renewable resources, environmental problems should be solved to improve its sustainability and efficiency [40, 41].

17.6.1 Improving Efficiency with Fuzzy Logic

Fuzzy logic has been found to be a method for increasing the efficiency of hydroelectric power systems by controlling their operational parameters [42]. Operators can then use this information to exercise more sophisticated judgment on less precise and uncertain data, e.g., rapidly changing water levels, or irregular electricity demand intervals, by employing the fuzzy logic controllers in VPP operation mode [43]. These controllers evaluate conditions, using a set of linguistic rules and tune operations on the fly [44, 45]. For example, a fuzzy logic system could then decide the best speed for its turbines based on how much water is currently flowing through it and what their energy demand looks like, so as to run most efficiently without causing waste [46].

Furthermore, fuzzy logic can help improve the interaction of hydroelectric systems with other energy sources based on renewable energies such as wind and solar [47]. This interconnectedness is absolutely essential to gain a well-balanced energy mix and offer greater reliability of the power grid [48, 49]. Fuzzy logic can help maintain the grid by dynamically controlling hydroelectric plant output based on renewable generation and therefore reduce fossil fuel usage [50].

17.6.2 Long-Term Sustainability Goals

Dealing with the environmental consequences of generating hydroelectric power is a requirement for reaching any kind of long-term sustainability objectives [51]. Building dams and reservoirs causes habitat destruction, changes water flows, and disturbs the local ecosystem. As a result, the introduction of environmental guidelines is imperative [52]. This includes carrying out comprehensive environmental impact assessments prior to project commencement and including measures that help to prevent the negative impacts, such as fish passages for aquatic migration [53].

The affected regions should also be subjected to ongoing monitoring and adaptive management plans, in order to assess the ecological health of these areas [54]. Fuzzy systems can be used to analyse environmental data and take proper decisions on managing the resources in energy production without compromising their integrity towards ecology [55].

To sum up, the hydro power industry is one of the pillars of renewable energy, and therefore, taking its efficiency to a new level using fuzzy logic along with mitigating environmental effects through intervention are inevitable paths towards sustainability [56]. Use of advanced control strategies and responsible environmental practices in the hydroelectric sector will greatly help to secure a sustainable energy future while refraining from unsustainable damage to aquatic ecosystems [57].

17.6.3 Future Directions and Research Opportunities

The future of fuzzy logic applications in energy systems is poised for significant advancements, particularly in the context of hybrid energy systems [58]. As the demand for efficient and sustainable energy solutions grows, researchers are exploring innovative ways to integrate fuzzy logic into various aspects of energy management [59].

17.6.4 Emerging Trends in Fuzzy Logic Applications

Fuzzy logic has gained traction in diverse fields, including artificial intelligence, decision support systems, and control engineering [60]. Its ability to handle uncertainty and imprecision makes it particularly valuable in complex environments where traditional binary logic falls short. Emerging trends indicate a growing interest in combining fuzzy logic with machine learning and data analytics to enhance decision-making processes [61]. For instance, integrating fuzzy logic with neural networks can improve predictive modelling, allowing for more accurate forecasting of energy demand and supply [62]. Moreover, fuzzy logic is increasingly being applied in smart grid technologies, where it can optimize energy distribution and consumption [63]. By analysing real-time data from various sources, fuzzy systems can make informed decisions about load balancing, resource allocation, and demand response, thus enhancing the overall efficiency of energy systems [64].

17.6.5 Potential for Hybrid Energy Systems

The integration of fuzzy logic into hybrid energy systems—combinations of renewable energy sources such as solar, wind, and hydroelectric power—offers promising opportunities for enhancing system performance. Hybrid systems can leverage the strengths of multiple energy sources, but they also face challenges related to variability and intermittency. Fuzzy logic can help manage these challenges by providing flexible control strategies that adapt to changing conditions. For example, in a hybrid system that combines solar and hydroelectric power, fuzzy logic can optimize the operation of both sources based on real-time weather data and energy demand. This adaptability ensures that the system operates efficiently, maximizing energy production while minimizing costs. Additionally, fuzzy logic can facilitate energy storage management, determining the optimal times to store or release energy based on fluctuating supply and demand. Furthermore, the potential for fuzzy logic in hybrid energy systems extends to enhancing grid resilience. By enabling real-time decision-making and adaptive control, fuzzy systems can help maintain stability during disruptions, such as sudden changes in energy supply or demand [65]. Additionally, the integration of fuzzy logic into energy systems is set to play a pivotal role in addressing the challenges of modern energy management. As emerging trends continue to evolve, the potential for hybrid energy systems to leverage fuzzy logic will enhance efficiency, reliability, and sustainability, paving the way for a more resilient energy future. Continued research and development in this area will be crucial for unlocking the full potential of fuzzy logic in the energy sector [66].

17.7 Conclusion

In the future, by considering the opportunities and advantages for the incorporation of fuzzy logic in hydroelectric power systems, some relatively significant enhancements are expected to be obtained on any existing energy management system, such as improved efficiency at operational levels, and dealing with efficient bidding strategies. The implementation of the principles of fuzzy logic in electric power systems clearly increases their flexibility and ability to adapt to real-world challenges.

17.7.1 Summary of Findings

This article covers the fuzzy logic applications that relate to hydroelectric power systems as follows:

- **Fuzzy Control Strategy:** Complex systems can be approached neutrally by fuzzy logic controllers that optimize the operation of turbines, with gain scheduling for load frequency stability and economic dispatch, which helps the global system performance.
- **Economic Dispatch and Optimisation:** Techniques like ALO and Bat algorithm with fuzzy logic can minimize generation cost considering operational constraints.
- **Fuzzy Logic to Improve Efficiency:** Fuzzy Systems can adjust the operational workers of Musari Hydroelectric Power Plant, easily integrate their energies with some other available renewable source, besides enabling adaptive management schemes for increasing efficiencies, which lead to making it more sustainable. Hybrid energy systems can also benefit from fuzzy logic due to their various reactive renewable sources, and are capable of coping with variability,

managing battery capacity for optimum performance, and improving grid resiliency.

- **For Future Energy Management:** The world of energy is evolving on a global scale, and as such, the use of fuzzy logic for hydroelectric power systems will play an ever-increasing role in our ability to secure a sustainable future within this sector. The capability of fuzzy logic to cope with uncertainties and adapt effectively under changing conditions renders it a powerful choice for dealing with complexities in modern energy systems. It implies that fuzzy logic can be incorporated into hybrid energy systems with great potential for extension and expansion. The range of renewable portfolio options available to us is expanded when fuzzy logic helps in the coordination and inter-connection between a variety of renewables, thereby decreasing our dependence on fossil fuels while also adding robustness. The advances made in this study highlight very promising possibilities for fuzzy logic in hydroelectric systems and energy sectors. The implications of conducting further research and development in this area are evident when it comes to the next step with energy management: incorporating fuzzy logic is imperative for enhancing efficiency, reliability, and sustainability on our pathway towards a cleaner future.

References

1. Singh, B., and Kaunert, C. (2024). Hidden gems breakthrough dynamic landscape of adaptive learning technologies for higher education: Bridging the gap between theoretical and practical knowledge projecting student learning outcomes. In Minh Tung, T. (ed.), *Adaptive Learning Technologies for Higher Education* (pp. 222–247). IGI Global. https://doi.org/10.4018/979-8-3693-3641-0.ch010.
2. Patel, R., and Mehta, P. (2024). Fuzzy logic controllers for optimizing renewable energy distribution networks. *Renewable Energy*, 26(4), 489–502. https://doi.org/10.1016/j.renene.2024.08.006.

3. Qian, W., and Zhou, H. (2023). Federated learning for decentralized renewable energy storage. *Sustainable Energy Technologies and Assessments*, 18(3), 578–591. https://doi.org/10.1016/j.seta.2023.07.015.
4. Rahman, T., and Ahmed, S. (2024). A hybrid approach using fuzzy logic and federated learning for solar energy optimization. *Energy Reports*, 13(6), 314–327. https://doi.org/10.1016/j.egyr.2024.04.010.
5. Ramesh, S., and Venkatesh, B. (2024). Fuzzy logic-based models for optimizing wind energy systems. *Renewable Energy*, 27(2), 654–667. https://doi.org/10.1016/j.renene.2024.01.012.
6. Rana, R., and Patel, M. (2023). Federated learning for distributed energy resource management. *Journal of Renewable Energy Research*, 17(5), 943–956. https://doi.org/10.1016/j.jrener.2023.06.018.
7. Reddy, K., and Singh, P. (2024). Application of fuzzy logic for optimizing distributed renewable energy resources. *Renewable and Sustainable Energy Reviews*, 22(3), 512–525. https://doi.org/10.1016/j.rser.2024.07.011.
8. Privacy deliberations in hospital industry: Lensing confidentiality of Patient's information and personal data in legal-ethical landscapes projecting futuristic dimensions. In: Kumar, P., Singh, P., Diwakar, M., and Garg, D. (eds.), *Healthcare Industry Assessment: Analyzing Risks, Security, and Reliability. Engineering Cyber-Physical Systems and Critical Infrastructures*, vol 11. Springer, Cham. https://doi.org/10.1007/978-3-031-65434-3_7.
9. Singh, B., and Kaunert, C. (2024). AI-driven strategies for customer engagement, market segmentation, and resource optimization: Projecting end user satisfaction and futuristic growth of business. In Nadda, V., Tyagi, P., Singh, A., and Singh, V. (eds.), *AI Innovations in Service and Tourism Marketing* (pp. 104–128). IGI Global. https://doi.org/10.4018/979-8-3693-7909-7.ch006.
10. Dutta, P. K., Singh, B., Towfeek, A.-S. K., Adamopoulou, J. P., Bardavouras, A. N., Bamwerinde, W., Turyasingura, B., and Ayiga, N. (2024). IoT revolutionizes humidity measurement and management in smart cities to enhance health and wellness. *Mesopotamian Journal of Artificial Intelligence in Healthcare*, 2024, 110–117. https://doi.org/10.58496/MJAIH/2024/013.
11. Singh, B., and Kaunert, C. (2024). Vertical assimilation of artificial intelligence and machine learning in safeguarding financial data. In Naz, F., and Karim, S., (eds.), *Safeguarding Financial Data in the*

Digital Age (pp. 169–197). IGI Global. https://doi.org/10.4018/979-8-3693-3633-5.ch01.

12. Ren, Y., and Liu, W. (2023). Federated learning-based approaches for optimizing energy management systems. *Energy*, 37(7), 610–623. https://doi.org/10.1016/j.energy.2023.09.006.
13. Roy, S., and Chakraborty, S. (2024). Fuzzy logic controllers for improving photovoltaic energy systems. *Renewable Energy*, 28(4), 671–684. https://doi.org/10.1016/j.renene.2024.05.014.
14. Saha, M., and Roy, A. (2024). Federated learning for enhancing renewable energy forecasting accuracy. *IEEE Transactions on Smart Grid*, 39(2), 845–858. https://doi.org/10.1109/TSG.2024.0258749.
15. Sahu, R., and Sharma, M. (2023). Fuzzy logic-based energy management systems for microgrids. *Sustainable Energy Technologies and Assessments*, 17(3), 579–592. https://doi.org/10.1016/j.seta.2023.05.013.
16. Shao, J., and Li, G. (2024). Federated learning for distributed control in renewable energy systems. *IEEE Transactions on Sustainable Energy*, 47(1), 369–382. https://doi.org/10.1109/TSTE.2024.0123569.
17. Sharma, N., and Kumar, P. (2024). A fuzzy logic approach for optimizing solar energy storage. *Renewable Energy*, 29(3), 401–414. https://doi.org/10.1016/j.renene.2024.02.007.
18. Singh, D., and Gupta, A. (2023). Federated learning-based energy management in distributed renewable systems. *Energy Reports*, 14(5), 501–514. https://doi.org/10.1016/j.egyr.2023.11.010.
19. Sun, Y., and Wang, J. (2024). Fuzzy logic control for wind energy conversion systems: A review. *Journal of Renewable Energy Research*, 20(2), 123–136. https://doi.org/10.1016/j.jrener.2024.04.014.
20. Tan, H., and Xu, L. (2023). Federated learning for optimizing energy storage in renewable energy networks. *Renewable Energy*, 21(8), 709–722. https://doi.org/10.1016/j.renene.2023.07.011.
21. Singh, B., Kaunert, C. (2024). Embryonic machine-deep learning, smart healthcare and privacy deliberations in hospital industry: Lensing confidentiality of patient's information and personal data in legal-ethical landscapes projecting futuristic dimensions. In: Kumar, P., Singh, P., Diwakar, M., Garg, D. (eds) *Healthcare Industry Assessment: Analyzing Risks, Security, and Reliability. Engineering Cyber-Physical Systems and Critical Infrastructures*, vol 11. Springer, Cham. https://doi.org/10.1007/978-3-031-65434-3_7.

22. Singh, B., and Kaunert, C. (2024). Computational thinking for innovative solutions and problem-solving techniques: Transforming conventional education to futuristic interdisciplinary higher education. In Fonkam, M., and Vajjhala, N. (eds.), *Revolutionizing Curricula through Computational Thinking, Logic, and Problem Solving* (pp. 60–82). IGI Global. https://doi.org/10.4018/979-8-3693-1974-1.ch004.
23. Singh, B., Kaunert, C., and Malviya, R. (2024). Coupling human-computer interface lensing artificial emotional intelligence: Transforming for futuristic cognitive recognition for decision-marking in industry 5.0. In Kumar, N., Pal, S., Agarwal, P., Rosak-Szyrocka, J., and Jain, V. (eds.), *Human-Machine Collaboration and Emotional Intelligence in Industry 5.0* (pp. 233–250). IGI Global. https://doi.org/10.4018/979-8-3693-6806-0.ch013.
24. Singh, B., Dutta, P. K., and Kaunert, C. (2024). Boosting quantum computing to redefine supply chain in the hospital industry: Pitch the vision for medical and healthcare needs. In Hassan, A., Bhattacharya, P., Dutta, P., Verma, J., and Kundu, N. (eds.), *Quantum Computing and Supply Chain Management: A New Era of Optimization* (pp. 196–219). IGI Global. https://doi.org/10.4018/979-8-3693-4107-0.ch014.
25. Thakur, A., and Rathi, P. (2024). A fuzzy logic-based approach for energy management in smart grids. *Sustainable Energy*, 15(2), 397–409. https://doi.org/10.1016/j.set.2024.02.012.
26. Tian, F., and Zhou, Y. (2023). Federated learning in smart grid systems: A comprehensive review. *Renewable and Sustainable Energy Reviews*, 18(6), 941–954. https://doi.org/10.1016/j.rser.2023.10.009.
27. Tripathi, R., and Mishra, A. (2024). Fuzzy logic controllers for optimizing wind energy distribution networks. *Energy*, 35(2), 678–691. https://doi.org/10.1016/j.energy.2024.01.012.
28. Tsai, C., and Lee, M. (2024). Federated learning-based models for smart grid energy management. *IEEE Transactions on Energy Conversion*, 41(3), 589–602. https://doi.org/10.1109/TEC.2024.0185623.
29. Singh, B., Dutta, P. K., Gautam, R., and Kaunert, C. (2024). Uncapping the potential of quantum computing towards manufacturing optimization: Routing supply chain projecting sustainability. In Hassan, A., Bhattacharya, P., Dutta, P., Verma, J., and Kundu, N. (eds.), *Quantum Computing and Supply Chain Management: A New Era of Optimization* (pp. 395–419). IGI Global. https://doi.org/10.4018/979-8-3693-4107-0.ch024.

30. Singh, B., and Kaunert, C. (2024). Wind and solar energy as renewable energy for sustainable global future: Projecting future multi-sector sustainable policies and innovation. In Ara, A., and Thakore, R. (eds.), *Promoting Multi-Sector Sustainability With Policy and Innovation* (pp. 210–245). IGI Global. https://doi.org/10.4018/979-8-3693-2113-3.ch009.

31. Singh, B., and Kaunert, C. (2024). Aroma of highly smart internet of medical things (IoMT) and lightweight edgetrust expansion medical care facilities for electronic healthcare systems: Fortified-chain architecture for remote patient monitoring and privacy protection beyond imagination. In Hassan, A., Bhattacharya, P., Tikadar, S., Dutta, P., and Sagayam, M. (eds.), *Lightweight Digital Trust Architectures in the Internet of Medical Things (IoMT)* (pp. 196–212). IGI Global. https://doi.org/10.4018/979-8-3693-2109-6.ch011.

32. Singh, B., Jain, V., Kaunert, C., Dutta, P. K., and Singh, G. (2024). Privacy matters: Espousing blockchain and artificial intelligence (AI) for consumer data protection on E-commerce platforms in ethical marketing. In Saluja, S., Nayyar, V., Rojhe, K., and Sharma, S. (eds.), *Ethical Marketing Through Data Governance Standards and Effective Technology* (pp. 167–184). IGI Global. https://doi.org/10.4018/979-8-3693-2215-4.ch015.

33. Singh, B., Dutta, P. K., and Kaunert, C. (2024). Replenish artificial intelligence in renewable energy for sustainable development: Lensing SDG 7 affordable and clean energy and SDG 13 climate actions with legal-financial advisory. In Derbali, A. (ed.), *Social and Ethical Implications of AI in Finance for Sustainability* (pp. 198–227). IGI Global. https://doi.org/10.4018/979-8-3693-2881-1.ch009.

34. Venkatesh, K., and Rao, S. (2024). Fuzzy logic-based energy management systems for renewable energy resources. *Renewable Energy*, 31(1), 435–448. https://doi.org/10.1016/j.renene.2024.03.015.

35. Wang, D., and Zhang, H. (2023). Federated learning for decentralized renewable energy management systems. *Journal of Renewable Energy Research*, 18(5), 789–802. https://doi.org/10.1016/j.jrener.2023.12.004.

36. Wang, Y., and Li, J. (2024). Fuzzy logic in optimizing distributed energy storage systems. *Energy Reports*, 15(4), 701–714. https://doi.org/10.1016/j.egyr.2024.03.016.

37. Wei, Y., and Guo, Q. (2023). Federated learning for enhancing energy management in distributed renewable systems. *Renewable and Sustainable Energy Reviews*, 19(7), 842–855. https://doi.org/10.1016/j.rser.2023.12.006.

38. Singh, B., and Kaunert, C. (2024). Augmented reality and virtual reality modules for mindfulness: Boosting emotional intelligence and mental wellness. In Hiran, K., Doshi, R., and Patel, M. (eds.), *Applications of Virtual and Augmented Reality for Health and Wellbeing* (pp. 111–128). IGI Global. https://doi.org/10.4018/979-8-3693-1123-3.ch007.
39. Singh, B. (2024). Lensing legal dynamics for examining responsibility and deliberation of generative AI-tethered technological privacy concerns: Infringements and use of personal data by Nefarious actors. In Ara, A., and Ara, A. (eds.), *Exploring the Ethical Implications of Generative AI* (pp. 146–167). IGI Global. https://doi.org/10.4018/979-8-3693-1565-1.ch009.
40. Singh, B. (2024). Social cognition of incarcerated women and children: Addressing exposure to infectious diseases and legal outcomes. In Reddy, K. (ed.), *Principles and Clinical Interventions in Social Cognition* (pp. 236–251). IGI Global. https://doi.org/10.4018/979-8-3693-1265-0.ch014.
41. Singh, B., and Kaunert, C. (2024). Salvaging responsible consumption and production of food in the hospitality industry: Harnessing machine learning and deep learning for zero food waste. In Singh, A., Tyagi, P., and Garg, A. (eds.), *Sustainable Disposal Methods of Food Wastes in Hospitality Operations* (pp. 176–192). IGI Global. https://doi.org/10.4018/979-8-3693-2181-2.ch012.
42. Wu, X., and Liu, Y. (2024). Fuzzy logic-based optimization for wind energy systems. *Renewable Energy*, 32(4), 459–472. https://doi.org/10.1016/j.renene.2024.04.019.
43. Xu, B., and Sun, C. (2024). Federated learning for improving renewable energy distribution. *IEEE Transactions on Smart Grid*, 35(1), 709–722. https://doi.org/10.1109/TSG.2024.0234567.
44. Xu, Y., and Zhang, H. (2023). Fuzzy logic controllers for improving distributed energy storage in microgrids. *Sustainable Energy Technologies and Assessments*, 18(1), 456–469. https://doi.org/10.1016/j.seta.2023.06.009.
45. Singh, B. (2024). Evolutionary global neuroscience for cognition and brain health: Strengthening innovation in brain science. In Prabhakar, P. (ed.), *Biomedical Research Developments for Improved Healthcare* (pp. 246–272). IGI Global. https://doi.org/10.4018/979-8-3693-1922-2.ch012.
46. Singh, B., and Kaunert, C. (2024). Revealing green finance mobilization: Harnessing fintech and blockchain innovations to surmount barriers

and foster new investment avenues. In Jafar, S., Rodriguez, R., Kannan, H., Akhtar, S., and Plugmann, P. (eds.), *Harnessing Blockchain-Digital Twin Fusion for Sustainable Investments* (pp. 265–286). IGI Global. https://doi.org/10.4018/979-8-3693-1878-2.ch011.

47. Singh, B., and Kaunert, C. (2024). Harnessing sustainable agriculture through climate-smart technologies: Artificial intelligence for climate preservation and futuristic trends. In Kannan, H., Rodriguez, R., Paprika, Z., and Ade-Ibijola, A. (eds.), *Exploring Ethical Dimensions of Environmental Sustainability and Use of AI* (pp. 214–239). IGI Global. https://doi.org/10.4018/979-8-3693-0892-9.ch011.
48. Singh, B. (2023). Blockchain technology in renovating healthcare: Legal and future perspectives. In Kaushik, K., Dahiya, S., Aggarwal, S., and Dwivedi, A. (eds.), *Revolutionizing Healthcare through Artificial Intelligence and Internet of Things Applications* (pp. 177–186). IGI Global. https://doi.org/10.4018/978-1-6684-5422-0.ch012.
49. Yang, H., and Zhou, J. (2023). Federated learning for enhancing energy efficiency in smart grids. *Journal of Renewable Energy Research*, 16(2), 612–625. https://doi.org/10.1016/j.jrener.2023.08.007.
50. Yang, J., and Li, C. (2024). Fuzzy logic control for optimizing renewable energy systems. *Renewable Energy*, 30(7), 501–514. https://doi.org/10.1016/j.renene.2024.07.013.
51. Yao, Q., and Sun, J. (2023). Federated learning techniques for distributed renewable energy forecasting. *Applied Energy*, 40(4), 902–915. https://doi.org/10.1016/j.apenergy.2023.11.012.
52. Yu, L., and Liu, Q. (2024). Fuzzy logic-based energy management in hybrid renewable systems. *Renewable and Sustainable Energy Reviews*, 23(1), 725–738. https://doi.org/10.1016/j.rser.2024.01.006.
53. Zhang, C., and Wu, M. (2023). Federated learning for distributed renewable energy management: A review. *Journal of Cleaner Production*, 22(8), 534–547. https://doi.org/10.1016/j.jclepro.2023.08.010.
54. Zhang, L., and Zhang, Y. (2024). Fuzzy logic in optimizing solar energy distribution networks. *Renewable Energy*, 33(2), 657–670. https://doi.org/10.1016/j.renene.2024.02.009.
55. Zhang, Y., and Guo, F. (2024). Federated learning for enhancing wind energy conversion systems. *Renewable Energy*, 26(1), 479–492. https://doi.org/10.1016/j.renene.2024.08.015.
56. Zhou, H., and Liu, C. (2024). Fuzzy logic control in renewable energy systems: A comprehensive review. *Renewable and Sustainable Energy*

Reviews, 22(5), 825–838. https://doi.org/10.1016/j.rser.2024.07.005.

57. Zhou, Y., and Sun, Y. (2023). Federated learning for optimizing distributed energy resources in microgrids. *IEEE Transactions on Sustainable Energy*, 48(3), 899–912. https://doi.org/10.1109/TSTE.2023.0178923.
58. Zhu, D., and Chen, L. (2024). Fuzzy logic controllers for distributed renewable energy management. *Renewable Energy*, 29(5), 535–548. https://doi.org/10.1016/j.renene.2024.09.012.
59. Singh, B., and Kaunert, C. (2024) Reinventing artificial intelligence and blockchain for preserving medical data. In *Ethical Artificial Intelligence in Power Electronics* (pp. 77–91). CRC Press.
60. Singh, B., and Kaunert, C. (2024). Unmanned aerial vehicle. *Cognitive Machine Intelligence: Applications, Challenges, and Related Technologies*, 108.
61. Park, J., and Kim, H. (2023). Federated learning-based optimization for smart grid energy management. *IEEE Transactions on Energy Conversion*, 37(4), 723–736. https://doi.org/10.1109/TEC.2023.0274571.
62. Singh, B. (2024). Cherish data privacy and human rights in the digital age: Harmonizing innovation and individual autonomy. In Pucelj, M., and Bohinc, R. (eds.), *Balancing Human Rights, Social Responsibility, and Digital Ethics* (pp. 199–226). IGI Global. https://doi.org/10.4018/979-8-3693-3334-1.ch007.
63. Singh, B., and Kaunert, C. (2024). Human-machine nexus for digital rebound fostering futuristic energy-efficiency: Ecological footprint of technology for smart-sustainable urban mobility. In González-Lezcano, R., and Sansaniwal, S. (eds.), *Design Strategies for Efficient and Sustainable Building Facilities* (pp. 222–244). IGI Global. https://doi.org/10.4018/979-8-3693-3200-9.ch010.
64. Zhu, X., and Li, S. (2024). Federated learning in optimizing energy efficiency for smart grids. *Journal of Renewable Energy Research*, 20(4), 643–656. https://doi.org/10.1016/j.jrener.2024.06.013.
65. Zhuang, Q., and Chen, L. (2023). Federated learning-based models for improving renewable energy systems. *Renewable and Sustainable Energy Reviews*, 16(3), 903–916. https://doi.org/10.1016/j.rser.2023.09.013.
66. Zou, J., and Chen, Z. (2024). Fuzzy logic systems for optimizing distributed renewable energy resources. *Renewable Energy*, 30(2), 599–612. https://doi.org/10.1016/j.renene.2024.03.017.

Chapter 18

Smart Villages and Cities: A Sustainable Imperative for Emerging India—A Journey from Painful to Thoughtful

Vijeta Verma, Vijaishree Dubey Pandey, and Sheetal Singh

CHRIST (Deemed to be University), Delhi NCR, India

vijeta@christuniversity.in

Abstract

Smart cities and villages refer to making cities and villages more beautiful and fuller of all the requirements that can make the lives of the people living in the cities and villages more comfortable and satisfactory. On 25th June 2015, this initiative was launched by the Central government, and the time limit for completion was 5 years, but due to the pandemic situation, it was further extended by the central government, and this year, all the states are required to submit their respective report about the progress in this regard. In India, 70% of the total population lives in Villages and only 30% are part of urban areas. In India, villages should be a combination of smart and digital villages. If the work is done at the grassroots level, it will

Fuzzy Logic in Revolutionizing Renewable Energy

Edited by Bhupinder Singh, Komal Vig, Ruchi Lal, and Budi Agus Riswandi

ISBN 978-981-5129-92-2 (Hardcover), 978-1-003-74191-6 (eBook)

www.jennystanford.com

DOI: 10.1201/9781003741916-18

solve many problems, such as migration, employment, poverty, education, and medical facilities. Sustainability of the environment is one of the basic requirements for humankind globally. In 2015, the United Nations introduced Sustainable Development Goals (SDGs) to address environmental and economic issues and challenges and to provide and promote better and more sustainable pathways for the future generation globally. It is not a matter of concern for a group of countries, but every single species is affected by environmental issues. Owing to the dense population, infrastructure, buildings, and commercialization, cities are more prone and susceptible to the effects of climate change and natural disasters.

While increasing the sustainability of urbanization processes is necessary to protect the environment, reduce the risk of disasters, and address climate change, building urban resilience is essential to preventing losses in terms of people, society, and the economy. Goal 11 of the SDGs deals with Sustainable Cities and Communities. Focusing more on urbanization in such a way that comprehensively controls and plans the development of cities and villages using different technologies and sciences to make them smart cities and villages. By ensuring that smart cities and villages will help us in many ways, they can control the migration of the human population from one city to another in search of employment and basic needs. In India, the government should focus on creating smart villages rather than smart cities. Around 69% of the population lives in the villages, and they do not have the basic amenities like electricity, clean drinking water, roads, transportation, and a source of employment.

Keywords: Urbanization, Smart Cities and Villages, SDGs, International Instruments

18.1 Introduction

Human civilizations have witnessed the concept of smart cities since ancient times. The Harappan civilization traces the idea of a planned lifestyle to ensure equal distribution of facilities. In a much-appreciated scheme of the Indian government in 2017, Pradhan Mantri Gramin Digital Saksharta Abhiyan intended to provide digital literacy in rural India, covering six crore rural households. The target was to train around 6.62 crore candidates, out of which 5.6 crore have already been trained. Approximately 4.22 Crore candidates have been duly certified under the PMGDISHA scheme across the country. The main objective of the mission is to provide digital education and increase the level of digital awareness in rural areas. The objective should be to stress creating awareness to make smart villages, while giving more focus on smart cities.

The government has to take many initiatives to make a village a smart village. For example, the government should focus on the housing facility, transport facility, Education Facility, Jobs, and the crops grown by the farmers in their fields, along with the technology they are supposed to apply at the time of sowing the seeds, and the entertainment. Apart from this, a very important task is to create awareness among the people who are residing in the village area.

With the help of SAGY guidelines, every member of parliament should work in such a way that the institutional infrastructure is converted into "Model Villages" or "Adarsh Grams." This was the concept for the development of rural areas, but as time passed by, the SDG guidelines came into existence.

In the rapidly evolving landscape of India, sustainable development remains a pivotal anchor, steering the nation toward a future where innovation, infrastructure, and environmental stewardship converge. The importance of sustainable development is increasingly acknowledged as a cornerstone for economic development, quality of life improvements, and the creation of resilient, green cities. This shift is particularly relevant in the context of India's unique challenges and opportunities in rural and urban migration, urban planning, and the leveraging of renewable energy and smart technology to foster more inclusive and sustainable growth.

Smart cities need smart villages, for a spatial shift in India will require higher agricultural productivity, more energy (particularly renewable off-grid energy production), and diversification into non-agricultural income-generating activities (for instance, food processing, construction, businesses, and services) to sustain such a mission [1].

This paper delves into the intricate tapestry of sustainable development in India, exploring the dynamic interplay between the burgeoning concepts of smart villages and cities. It charts the course of technological innovations, including smart energy, smart water management, and sustainable agriculture, that are pivotal in shaping smart villages and cities. Government initiatives and policies actively supporting rural development, smart farming, and financial inclusion illuminate the path forward. However, the journey is not without its challenges.

The obstacles are examined to implement these concepts, showcasing success stories. This framework looks into the comprehensive prospects and recommendations for integrating sustainable development in the rural and urban landscapes of India.

18.2 Definition and Importance

SDGs are defined by the United Nations as initiatives that cater to the sustainability of future generations without compromising the requirements of the current generations [2]. This concept has evolved to harmonize climate change with making economic growth, social inclusion, and environmental protection through holistic development. To India, it also means the integration of development and environmental goals in a cohesive framework, which will be crucial to the nation's significant contribution to fulfilling the sustainable agenda [3].

18.2.1 Definition of Smart Cities

The concept of smart cities impresses with its focus on sustainable development and leveraging technology and data to improve the quality of life of its citizens and enhance the efficiency of its citizens. The characteristics of smart cities include:

Using information and communication technologies (ICT) to enhance the infrastructure and services of its citizens [4]. Connecting systems and devices to the Internet of Things (IoT) so that data can be analysed. Using data and technology to address urban challenges like mobility, safety, and environmental issues. Also providing a healthy lifestyle focusing on sustainability, and economic development [5]. The aim of smart cities is to provide core infrastructure that can afford a decent quality of life, clean and smart solutions to citizens. A sustainable environment that can focus on subjects like energy, transport, public health, education, affordable housing, with modern waste management that is technology-driven [6].

18.2.1.1 Smart villages

Smart villages have also been designed to enhance quality of life by focusing on creating new opportunities that are aligned with sustainability. This will create an amicable environment for the young population to quench their thirst for survival and not be driven away by city life. By providing a plethora of networks based on technology services, we will enhance employment and innovations, strengthen our traditional roots, and relieve the strain on the cities. Some aspects of smart villages include:

- Improving digital infrastructure and services to provide resilience and enhance the quality of life in rural areas. It will provide essential resources like food, skilled labor, and raw materials to support smart cities. The rural-urban migration will decrease when education, health, and employment opportunities are available at the doorsteps for the villagers. The empowerment of rural populations will provide quality resources, tools, knowledge, and markets [7].
- Smart villages are critical for the sustainability and success of smart cities, as rural-urban integration is essential for balanced socioeconomic development and a symbiotic ecosystem. Neglecting the development of rural areas can lead to lopsided growth and deepen the rural-urban divide.

18.2.2 Importance of Smart Cities and Smart Villages

Smart cities and villages leverage technology to enhance the quality of life, efficiency, and sustainability. Rural villages are the source of life for urban areas, providing essential resources.

Smart cities cannot exist without smart villages, so empowering rural areas should be a priority.

Comprehensive rural-urban integration is necessary for the long-term viability of urbanization efforts. Investing in digital infrastructure for villages enables innovation and value creation for the majority of people. In summary, smart cities and villages are interdependent and require a holistic approach to sustainable development. Balancing urban and rural progress through technology and innovation is crucial for equitable growth and prosperity.

18.3 Smart Cities and Villages: A Journey to Sustainability

The villages and the cities evolve and change a lot. There are many things that play a very important role in making any part of the city an advanced one, e.g., education. Earlier, there was limited access to education, especially higher education institutions, which were few and located in the larger cities. Traditional classrooms were there, and technology was not used. But now the government is working very hard to provide the technology at the grassroots level to make a city or a village smart.

18.3.1 The Concept of Smart Villages

18.3.1.1 Key features

The concept of smart villages in India revolves around creating self-sufficient, sustainable environments where villagers do not feel the need to migrate to cities for better opportunities. Central to this concept is the provision of "kamai" (earnings), "dawai" (healthcare), and "padhai" (education) within the villages themselves. By enhancing these core aspects, the migration from villages to urban areas, which often results in poor living conditions and slums, can be significantly reduced.

A smart village leverages technology and strategic planning to address the pain points of the village community. This involves a bottom-up approach where the needs of the villagers are identified through comprehensive surveys and addressed systematically.

The involvement of villagers will play a crucial role in ensuring the sustainability of these approaches. They will bring the necessary funding and contribute with their expertise and technology solutions to improve the infrastructure and quality of life of the villagers.

The funding for such initiatives comes from various sources, including the private and public sectors, through corporate social responsibility (CSR) funds, development funding agencies, and allocations made at central, state, and local levels by the government. This financial support is crucial in implementing sustainable solutions and hiring smart village managers to oversee development projects [8].

18.3.1.2 Examples from India

The Indian-origin Americans have adopted 62 villages, and this is the most remarkable example of highlighting the initiatives on smart villages. These are efforts where larger projects and secondary research reports are prepared for each village, by assessing them on more than 70 parameters to gauge the present situation and identify areas for improvement. Approximately 48 villages have completed their assessments, whereas the work has commenced in another 14, with the active participation of the villagers [8].

The village of Dhanora in Rajasthan has undergone significant development under the Ecological Needs initiative of the Foundation of Smart Village project. This initiative has helped transform Dhanora by providing basic amenities like sanitation, safe drinking water, and internal roads. There has been a remarkable improvement in employment opportunities and education, showcasing it as a model for rural development. The Prime Minister of India appreciated the village of Dhanora when it received an award in 2018 [9].

The transformative potential of the smart village is highlighted when a collaborative approach between public policy, community participation, and adequate funding goes on to yield results. The focus on local needs by providing international resources can transform smart villages into sustainable, thriving rural communities across India.

18.3.2 The Concept of Smart Cities

18.3.2.1 Key features

Smart cities are designed to improve urban life through sustainable services and efficient infrastructures in India. The elements crucial for core infrastructure in a smart city include adequate water supply, guaranteed electricity supply, proper sanitation facilities, modern waste management, organized urban mobility, i.e., public transport, affordable housing, robust IT connectivity, e-governance, and transparent digital administration that includes participation from citizens. These cities will focus on creating a sustainable environment that can ensure safety and security, particularly for women, children, and the elderly. The development strategies of a smart city will promote mixed land use in area-based developments, which allows a range of activities and land uses, and it will make land use more efficient. This flexibility in building bylaws is crucial for adapting to all types of changes. Other features include housing inclusiveness, creating sustainable localities to reduce congestion and promote interactions, preserving and developing open spaces, and promoting a variety of transport options like Transit Oriented Development (TOD) and public transport. Governance in smart cities is made citizen-friendly and cost-effective through the use of online services to enhance accountability and transparency. The cities are given identities based on their main economic activities, which could range from local cuisine to education and the arts. Smart solutions are applied to infrastructure and services in area-based development to enhance their resilience and reduce vulnerability to disasters [10].

18.3.2.2 Examples from India

Several Indian cities have been identified and are being developed under the Smart Cities Mission. Notable examples include New Delhi, Chennai, and Indore, where a significant percentage of projects have been completed. These projects range from micro-skill development to smart health centers and smart classes in schools, drastically improving the quality of education and urban life.

Cities like Mangaluru are investing in renewable energy and installing solar panels to reduce electricity costs significantly over the years. Other cities focus on smart security systems, such as Tumakuru, which developed a mobile app connecting citizens directly with police services to improve city security [11].

Innovative city planning is also evident in places like Dholera, where the town planning covers a vast area and includes a wide expressway improving connectivity, alongside zones for sports, city centers, and an international airport, making it a model for sustainable urban development [12].

The strategic constituents of area-based development in the Smart Cities Mission include city improvement through retrofitting, city renewal through redevelopment, and city extension through greenfield projects. These strategies are complemented by pan-city development, which applies smart solutions to existing city-wide infrastructure.

By leveraging technology and strategic planning, these smart cities aim to provide a high quality of life, economic growth, and a sustainable environment for their residents.

In the Indian economy, villages played an important role and were considered a main source of income generation. After the SDGs, it is observed that the concept of the smart village is being adopted by many villages and cities to upgrade their lifestyle and livelihood. This concept advocates self-reliance and sustainability of the cities and villages for future generations. Therefore, smart villages and cities are a great combination of digital and ideal villages and cities. Smart villages and cities must have essential and basic facilities such as hospitals, electricity, water, roads, schools, digital education, and better IT infrastructure. By integrating ICT, smart villages can improve agricultural productivity, renewable energy access, job creation, and overall quality of life in rural communities.

18.4 Requirements for the Smart Cities and Villages

By making improvements to infrastructure, drawing investments, generating employment opportunities, and increasing productivity, smart cities and villages promote economic development, sustainability, and quality of life. The integration of digital connection, e-governance, and sustainable practices is crucial in promoting equitable growth, reconciling urban-rural disparities, and setting the country up for sustained prosperity.

There is no standard definition or template for a smart city. In the context of our country, the six fundamental principles on which the concept of smart cities is based are shown in Fig. 18.1:

Community Service
- Planning and implementationofthe Project by keeping the Community at the centre.

Income generation
- Income to be generated by using the lesser resources

Competitive & Cooperation Federalism
- Implementation ofthe projects in a flexible manner

Innovation and Sustainability
- Innovative methods should be adopted to aattian the sustainability

Use of Technology
- Use of the Techhnology that can promote and upgrade the livelihood and standard of the life of the people pf the country

Confluence
- Financial and Sectorial

Figure 18.1 Six fundamental principles for smart cities.

Creating smart cities and villages in alignment with the United Nations SDGs involves integrating sustainable practices across various domains to ensure social, economic, and environmental well-being. Here are the key requirements based on specific SDGs (Fig. 18.2).

A few examples of smart cities are:

1. **Smart Governance**: Prayagraj, Uttar Pradesh, has taken the initiative and opened 100 integrated command and control centers operationalized for crowd management and control.
2. **Smart Energy**: In Jabalpur, a waste-to-energy plant is constructed, which has the capacity to process 735 TPD of waste-to-energy.

3. **Smart Mobility**: In Ahmedabad, Public Bicycle sharing is introduced, and for this, 573 km of cycle track has been constructed.
4. **Smart Education**: In Tamakuru, 6,800 smart classrooms have been developed.
5. **All Ability Park**: In Vishakhapatnam, 367 parks have been developed [13].

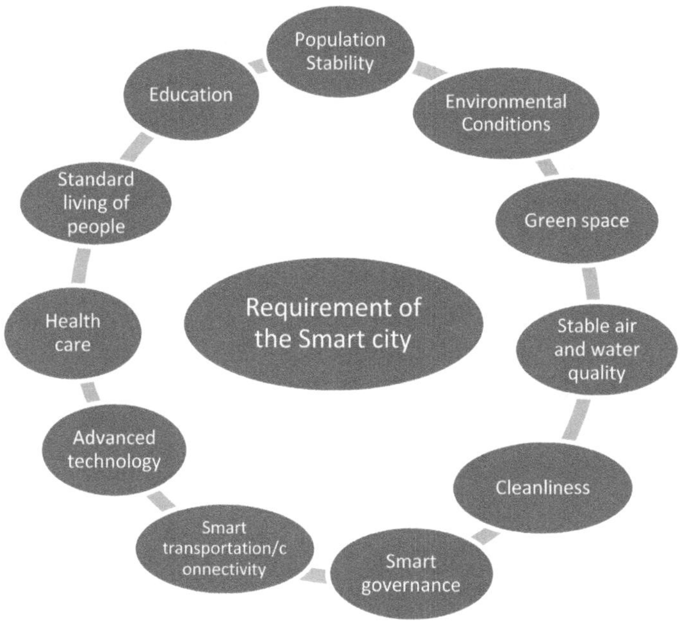

Figure 18.2 Requirements of a smart city.

18.5 States' Participation and Implementation in SDG 11

A total investment of Rs. 2,01,981 crores has been proposed for 99 cities under the Smart City Plans. Projects focusing on revamping an identified area (Area Based Projects) are estimated to cost Rs. 1,63,138 crores. Smart initiatives across the city (Pan City Initiatives) account for the remaining Rs. 38,841 crores of investments. The implementation of the Smart Cities Mission is done by a Special Purpose Vehicle (SPV) to be set up at the city level in the form of a limited company under the Companies Act, 2013, and will be promoted by the State/UT and the Urban Local Body (ULB) jointly, both having 50:50 equity shareholding. Smart cities have to set up SPVs and start the implementation of their Smart City Proposal, preparation of Detailed Project Reports (DPRs), tenders, etc. [14].

In India, Eco Needs Foundation has developed Dhanora Village of Rajasthan as the first smart village. The Gujarat government has designated 16 villages across five districts as smart villages under the Smart Village Incentive Scheme. These include:

1. Rajkot District: Raidi, Thanagallol, Virnagar, Anandpara (New), Satapara, Lodhika
2. Junagadh District: Chorwadi, Samdhiyala, Dhandhusar, Matiana, Balagam
3. Jamnagar District: Pipar, Wakiya, Sidsar
4. Botad District: Adtala
5. Navsari District: Mahuvar
6. Chhotkei Village, Odisha
7. Mori Village, Andhra Pradesh
8. Noorpur Bet, Punjab
9. Barsimaluguri, Assam

Each Gram Panchayat in these villages is set to receive an award of INR 500,000 to support their development initiative as shown in Table 18.1.

Table 18.1 States and their initiatives for smart villages and cities

Name of the state/cities	Initiatives taken by them
Agra	The city envisions overcoming its challenges of a poor state of environment and heritage, weak basic infrastructure, and a lack of inclusive growth. It aims to do this by leveraging Agra's tourism potential, making it a safe and tourist-friendly city while providing services to its citizens. The city identifies nine goals and 42 sub-goals to make it into a smart Agra, like making the city socially inclusive, practicing mixed land-use development, building robust infrastructure, and practicing transit-friendly and safe transportation.

Name of the state/cities	Initiatives taken by them
Bhubaneswar	A transit-oriented city with a compact urban form that promotes active, connected, and sustainable mobility choices. • Livable city providing a diverse range of housing, educational, and recreational opportunities, while enhancing its heritage, arts, and traditional communities. • Child-friendly city providing accessible, safe, inclusive, and vibrant public places. • Eco-city co-existing in harmony with nature for nurturing a resilient, clean, green, and healthy environment. • Regional economic center attracting knowledge-based enterprises and sustainable tourism activities by leveraging and empowering its institutions, local businesses, and informal workforce. Bhubaneswar's proposal envisions retrofitting and redeveloping 985 acres centered around the main Railway Station in the heart of the city to a vibrant 24×7 destination – The Bhubaneswar Town Centre District (BTCD). Bhubaneswar's state-of-the-art Intelligent City Operations and Management Centre (ICOMC) is at the core of its pan-city proposal.
Indore	"Imagining Indore to Inherit, Innovate, Include, Incubate and Invest" for "An ideal world-class smart commercial metropolis that thrives on investment opportunities, incubating business and ideas, rich inheritance and inclusive development."
West Bengal	Nandangram smart village is located in the Itahar administrative block within the Uttar Dinajpur district of West Bengal. Health, education, and employment are all managed collectively in this village through the establishment of health, education, and employment centers. These centers are operated by local residents who have connections to the nearby city, possess reasonable organizational skills, and have access to land for practicing adulteration-free agriculture.
Madhya Pradesh	In the Betul district of Madhya Pradesh, a project has established a climate-smart village by implementing agricultural practices in collaboration with local institutions, spearheaded by women farmers, and supported by the United States Agency for International Development (USAID) and the Consultative Group on International Agricultural Research (CGIAR).

Name of the state/cities	Initiatives taken by them
Barsimaluguri, Assam	A remote village in Assam along the Indo–Bhutan border has become the first smart village in northeast India. Barsimaluguri in Baksa district has become a model 'smart village' after achieving 100% toilets, solar power, and pure drinking water. Here are five things you need to know about the village [15].
Odisha	Chhotkei town in Angul locale of Odisha has developed as the primary small-scale industrial town in India. The town gets a supply of 30 kWp (kilowatt peak) of solar power. The town has introduced a Savvy Nanogrid to meet the energy needs of 140 families, 20 streetlights, a sanctuary, and three community centers. After utilization, the town spares around 10 kWp, which they set aside for daytime utilization in water system pumps and microenterprises to enhance rural productivity, empower value-addition to horticulture, and create business.

18.6 Case Studies of Successful Smart Villages

In the realm of smart villages, the project in Pimpalgaon Malvi stands out as a prominent example of sustainable rural development. Despite the existing basic amenities like electricity and clean drinking water, the village faced significant challenges with sewage water disposal, solid waste management, and energy conservation. By focusing on these areas, significant improvements were made, transforming Pimpalgaon Malvi into a model of a smart village. Another notable success is the initiative by the Maharashtra government, which has launched various schemes aimed at enhancing village infrastructure and governance. The active involvement of Gram Panchayats has been crucial in applying these schemes effectively, leading to broader growth that benefits the state and the country [16].

18.6.1 Case Studies of Successful Smart Cities

Some of the smart cities, such as Indore, Pune, and Ahmedabad, have significantly showcased India's journey of urban development. Indore is credited with being the first smart city, which is known for its community outreach programs and robust participation of citizens in building a sustainable infrastructure for living. It has made many exemplary contributions to cleanliness and set a high standard in efficient services for other cities to follow. Similarly, Ahmadabad has developed an enhanced transport system, which includes smart buses, metro rail, and a garbage disposal system to improve the quality of life for its inhabitants. All these initiatives not only portray them as top in smart initiatives but also provide extra revenue by enhancing tourism and catering to extra sources of income to its residents [17]. Pune, also known as "Oxford of the East," has used technology to revolutionize the educational and transportation sectors. The implementation of intelligent transportation systems and smart street lighting using solar energy explains how a city can improve public services and quality of life by leveraging technology [17].

The credit for implementing a rapid smart city plan goes to Nagpur. It has achieved the best investment conversion ratio among Indian smart cities. This highlights the effective use of resources and strategic planning in transforming urban landscapes [18].

Smart cities are the future. They exemplify the potential of smart living to enhance community life by underscoring the importance of strategic planning, community involvement, and government support in realizing ambitious projects under the Viksit Bharat Vision.

18.7 Technological Innovations Driving Smart Villages and Cities

One notable feature of smart cities is the use of technology in efficiently managing resources, which can be corrected. Using data to improve quality of life, promote sustainability, and outreach to basic needs such as health, education, transport, and energy. Modern infrastructure has made the system transparent, ensured good governance, and effective redressal mechanisms to ensure all-around development of any place. Smart cities have paved the way for smart villages. The economic opportunities in rural areas have improved due to digital technologies. The concept of a smart village will work to improve resilience and enhance quality of life. Villages are feeder systems for smart cities and provide all essential resources like food, labor, and raw materials for the cities to sustain themselves [19].

18.7.1 IoT

The IoT is revolutionizing the development of smart cities and villages in India by integrating ICT to address urbanization and sustainability challenges. IoT facilitates the smart management of urban infrastructures such as street lighting, traffic, and water systems, significantly enhancing operational efficiencies. For instance, the Smart Street Lighting National Program has successfully installed over 10.3 million smart LED streetlights across the country, achieving substantial energy savings and reducing greenhouse gas emissions [20]. Additionally, IoT's role in smart villages is pivotal, focusing on improving the quality of life by studying village needs and providing tailored technological solutions [21].

18.7.2 Big Data

The management of smart cities cannot be possible without Big Data. It plays a crucial role in the optimization of resources. The valuable insights collected from Sensors, GPS, social media, and other platforms provide raw material to make effective decisions and efficient urban/ rural planning. IoT technologies integrated with Big Data give real-time feedback to enhance the capability to manage cities and allow city-wide challenges to be addressed at regular intervals. For example, Big Data analytics have used power management through smart grid technologies to monitor and control power systems, reducing frequent leakage and improving energy efficiency [22].

18.7.3 Renewable Energy Solutions

To sustain smart cities and villages, it is important to switch to renewable energy sources. They are not only pollution-free but also focus on SDGs by preserving the resources for future generations. Initiatives like the Green Village Plans, developed in collaboration with NRDC and SEWA, have focused on implementing clean energy solutions at the village level. Such plans are executed with the involvement of local communities and government support. The extensive surveys and feedback have ensured that this transition to energy-efficient appliances like LED lamps and solar panels becomes both affordable and sustainable [23]. The push toward renewable energy is evident in smart city projects. Solar photovoltaic and wind energy are increasingly adapted to meet the energy demands and sustainability in the energy sector [24].

18.8 Government Initiatives and Policies

The Indian government has launched several ambitious initiatives aimed at transforming urban and rural landscapes into modern, efficient, and sustainable environments. These policies and programs are designed to foster economic growth, enhance the quality of life, and ensure inclusive development across the nation.

18.8.1 National Policies

The Smart Cities Mission, introduced in 2014, is a critical component of India's urban policy framework. It aims to develop 100 smart cities equipped with the latest technology, innovation, and infrastructure. The mission's strategic components include city improvement through retrofitting, city renewal through redevelopment, and city extension through greenfield development, along with a Pan-city initiative where smart solutions cover larger parts of the city. The mission is managed and implemented at the city level by an SPV, which is tasked with planning, appraising, approving, releasing funds, and evaluating the smart city development projects [25].

However, the implementation of the Smart Cities Mission has faced significant challenges. As of July 2019, only a fraction of the promised funds were utilized, with many projects still under development or completed. The planning, pace, and scale of the mission have not achieved the levels promised five years ago, leading to criticisms regarding the mission's disconnect from the real needs of the people and the vague nature of its guidelines [26].

18.8.2 Key Programs and Schemes

In rural areas, the government's focus has been on improving access to basic amenities and ensuring socioeconomic security through various Central Sector and Centrally Sponsored programs. Notable among these are the Pradhan Mantri Gram Sadak Yojana (PMGSY) for rural connectivity, Pradhan Mantri Awas Yojana-Gramin (PMAY-G) for rural housing, Jal Jeevan Mission for potable water supply, Swachh Bharat Mission (Grameen) for sanitation, and the Deen Dayal Upadhyaya Gram Jyoti Yojana for village electrification. Additionally, the Shyama Prasad Mukherji Rurban Mission (SPMRM) was launched to stimulate local economic development and bridge the rural-urban gap by creating well-planned Rurban clusters. These clusters aim to preserve the essence of rural community life while providing urban-like facilities [27].

The government also supports the Smart Village initiative, which aligns with Mahatma Gandhi's vision of Adarsh Gram (Ideal Village) and Swaraj (Self-Reliance). This initiative focuses on holistic rural development with an emphasis on personal, human, social, and economic dimensions. Each Member of Parliament and Minister is encouraged to adopt a rural village and develop it into a model village by 2019 under the Sansad Adarsh Gram Yojana (SAGY) guidelines.

These initiatives reflect the government's commitment to sustainable development through the integration of technology and strategic planning. However, the success of these policies requires overcoming implementation challenges and ensuring that the benefits of development reach all sections of society.

18.9 Challenges in Implementing Smart Villages and Cities

18.9.1 Funding and Budget Constraints

Implementing smart villages and cities in India faces significant financial hurdles. A World Bank report estimates that India needs to invest approximately $840 billion over the next 15 years, averaging $55 billion annually, to meet the urban infrastructure demands of its rapidly growing population. Currently, over 75% of this infrastructure funding comes from central and state governments, with urban local bodies contributing 15% through surplus revenues. Private financing accounts for only 5% of these needs, with annual government investments peaking at $16 billion. To bridge this substantial gap, it is crucial to create an environment that encourages urban local bodies, especially the larger and more creditworthy ones, to seek additional private financing [28].

18.9.2 Lack of Infrastructure

The challenges extend beyond financial constraints. The infrastructure in many of India's cities is struggling to keep pace with rapid urbanization. Issues such as inadequate urban planning, a weak regulatory environment, and poor revenue collection from urban property taxes further complicate the situation. Urban property tax, for instance, stands at a mere 0.15% of GDP, significantly lower than the 0.3–0.6% average for low- and middle-income countries. This low rate undermines the financial viability of municipal services and their attractiveness for private investment [28].

18.9.3 Social Resistance

There are a lot of challenges in developing smart cities, including social resistance, which is also evident in land acquisition and privatization of public services. Chandigarh is a planned city, but such resistance has been experienced during slum demolition, which faced significant opposition. The administration's efforts to make the city slum-free were met with protests, and the reality of resettlement has often fallen short of promises, exacerbating tensions between city planners and the affected communities. This resistance highlights the complex social dynamics that must be navigated to successfully implement smart city projects in India.

18.9.4 Digital Divide and Inclusivity

Smart city initiatives should be accessible to all citizens regardless of socioeconomic status or digital literacy. Providing affordable connectivity, digital skills training, and tailored solutions for vulnerable populations is key for inclusive development.

18.9.5 Citizen Engagement

Lack of awareness, privacy concerns, and resistance to change can hinder citizen participation.

Transparent communication, addressing concerns, and involving citizens in decision-making are crucial for acceptance.

18.10 Future Prospects and Recommendations

18.10.1 Potential Improvements

The Government of India envisions substantial enhancements in sustainable urban living by focusing on dense area development and creating replicable models of smart cities. These initiatives aim to foster partnerships with contractors and global companies experienced in smart infrastructure, IT, and telecommunications. Such collaborations are essential to address operational challenges in cities and towns, ensuring modernization in public services and commercial growth.

Significant investments are projected for housing, with plans to construct 11 crore houses by 2022, emphasizing the conservation of ecological resources like water and power through renewable technologies. This approach is expected to reduce maintenance costs by 10–30% and conserve up to 30% of water and nearly 40% of energy. Additionally, the 12th five-year plan includes generating 88 thousand MW of additional power to ensure an uninterrupted power supply, highlighting the role of smart meters in creating a transparent billing system.

Transport infrastructure in smart cities is set to enhance accessibility, with every city providing easy transport access to people living within 800 meters of built-up areas. The introduction of electric and hybrid vehicles, along with high-speed rails and metro trains, is planned to significantly improve commute times and reduce environmental impact [29].

18.10.2 Long-Term Benefits

The long-term benefits of these developments are multifaceted. Improved healthcare facilities and educational institutions are expected to become more accessible, with the construction of specialty hospitals, diagnostic centers, and educational establishments tailored to the needs of every 50,000 to 1.25 lakh residents. This development will enhance the quality of life and foster the educational and health sectors significantly.

The smart city initiatives require a comprehensive accessibility planning, such as public transport, bicycles, and walking tracks, to be made available to at least 95% of the population. It needs to be ensured that essential services like shops, parks, and schools are within 400 meters of residences. The economically disadvantaged groups should be allocated 20% of homes in Transit Development zones to promote social equity. The government's commitment to eco-friendly transport solutions aims to introduce 6 million electric and hybrid vehicles, with charging stations across all highways. This initiative, if successful, will significantly reduce the carbon footprint of urban transport.

To boost the educational infrastructure, the government has allocated substantial funds to build new IITs and IIMs. A considerable increase of 12.3% in the budget is allocated to upgrade the educational sector. Additionally, investments in broadband connectivity are set to enhance the digital infrastructure of smart cities, facilitating seamless connectivity and effective disaster management [29].

By focusing on these strategic areas, India is poised to transform its urban and rural landscapes into models of sustainability and efficiency, ensuring a better quality of life for its citizens and setting a global standard in smart urban development.

18.11 Conclusion and Recommendations

As India navigates the complexities of sustainable development, the intertwined paths of smart villages and cities highlight the nation's ambitious journey toward an innovative and inclusive future. Smart technologies, strategic government initiatives, and collaborative efforts are needed to make significant strides in defining and redefining urban and rural landscapes. These government initiatives have the potential for technological and infrastructural advancement and development, and also emphasize the importance of community participation in achieving sustainable growth through environmental stewardship. The series of technological innovations, societal engagements, and policy implementation has driven India toward its goal of holistic sustainability. The success stories and challenges have encapsulated the indispensable synergy, making it possible.

The transformation of Indian villages and cities is driven by sustainable development that can set an example for all those countries that have a similar set of developmental resources. Our future blueprint is driven for the benefit of all stakeholders, irrespective of various challenges and obstacles. A continuous collaboration is required to monitor the success of these projects. It is important that government bodies, the private sector, and local communities work in coordination to navigate the path to sustainability. India's commitment to global sustainability initiatives has been evident from the G20 summit. It has positively addressed challenging issues such as the balance between growth, equity, and environmental preservation by emerging as a leader in initiating a Global sustainability dialogue.

The natural ecosystems in India are declining due to extreme ecological situations and inadequate conservation efforts. The wildlife and agricultural biodiversity are plummeting to the point of extinction in many parts of the country. 10% of the wildlife is facing the risk of extinction. The water bodies are polluted to the extent that they become unfit for human consumption and agricultural purposes. Almost two-thirds of the territory is facing degradation that results in low productivity, and while the air pollution in some of the cities has been globally ranked in the most polluted category, making it unhealthy for human life. In 2008, a report highlighted that India has the world's third-largest ecological footprint, which has consumed double the biocapacity of resources.

Development should reach every individual, including the vulnerable and marginalized. No one should be left behind is the agenda of the 2030 Agenda for Sustainable Development that has been adopted by 193 member states. Indian development in SDGs is uneven in the rural and urban areas despite all global commitments. There has been improvement in areas like Neonatal and under-five mortality, sanitation, and access to electricity in some districts, while others lack these significantly. Moreover, the pace of improvement for several SDG indicators, such as access to clean cooking fuel and improved water, is insufficient to meet the targets by 2030 [30].

Gender inequality remains a persistent challenge, with high rates of child marriage and teenage pregnancy hindering progress toward the SDG targets. Environmental sustainability goals also face significant hurdles due to air and water pollution, deforestation, and inadequate waste management.

In conclusion, while India has made strides in some areas, the overall pace and distribution of sustainable development efforts need significant enhancement to meet the comprehensive goals set for 2030. This requires a concerted effort from all levels of government and society to address the interconnected challenges and ensure a sustainable future for all its citizens.

References

1. *Smart Cities Need Smart Villages, Economic and Political Weekly*, ISSN (Print), 0012–9976, | ISSN (Online), 2349–8846, 53(12), 24th March 2018, published on 20 January 2024.
2. https://www.jagranjosh.com/current-affairs/sustainable-development-and-india-1503408725-1.
3. https://india.un.org/en/sdgs.
4. Smart cities need smart villages - Calvium.
5. ec.europa.eu/enrd/sites/default/files/tg3_smart-villages_lessons-smart-cities_dumarey.pdf).
6. Smart cities (edukemy.com).
7. The Relevance of Smart Cities vs Smart Villages (linkedin.com).
8. https://www.smartvillage.biz/.
9. https://en.wikipedia.org/wiki/Smart_Village_India.
10. https://ebooks.inflibnet.ac.in/esp12/chapter/concept-of-smart-cities-in-india/.
11. https://earth.org/smart-cities-in-india/.
12. https://www.magicbricks.com/blog/what-is-smart-city/127301.html.
13. Smart Cities: Ministry of Housing and Urban Affairs, Government of India (mohua.gov.in).
14. Smart Cities: Ministry of Housing and Urban Affairs, Government of India (mohua.gov.in).
15. Barsimaluguri Becomes Northeast India's First Smart Village (thebetterindia.com).
16. https://www.neliti.com/publications/342256/smart-village-a-case-study-of-pimpalgaon-malvi-village.
17. https://www.linkedin.com/pulse/case-studies-how-smart-cities-improving-quality-life-bhoda-cnavc.
18. https://dl.acm.org/doi/fullHtml/10.1145/3184558.3191522.
19. Technology Innovations for Smart Cities and Smart Villages | IEEE Conference Publication | IEEE Xplore.
20. https://smartcity.eletsonline.com/iot-to-play-a-crucial-role-in-developing-indian-smart-cities/.
21. https://www.researchgate.net/publication/332661972_Internet_of_Things_on_Smart_Villages.

22. https://www.ijsr.net/archive/v5i2/NOV161007.pdf.
23. https://www.nrdc.org/bio/sameer-kwatra/plans-expanding-clean-energy-indias-villages.
24. https://www.mdpi.com/2624-6511/5/4/61.
25. https://smartcities.gov.in/sites/default/files/SmartCityGuidelines.pdf.
26. https://eudl.eu/pdf/10.4108/eai.27-2-2020.2303203.
27. https://sansad.in/getFile/loksabhaquestions/annex/1711/AU724.pdf?source=pqals.
28. https://www.worldbank.org/en/news/press-release/2022/11/14/india-s-urban-infrastructure-needs-to-cross-840-billion-over-next-15-years-new-world-bank-report.
29. https://industrialautomationindia.in/articleitm/62/Relevance-of-Smart-Cities-in-India-/articles.
30. https://forumias.com/blog/answered-what-are-the-key-challenges-india-faces-in-achieving-its-sustainable-development-goals-sdgs-by-2030-and-how-can-lessons-from-its-covid-19-response-be-applied-to-address-these-challenges/.

Chapter 19

Assimilation of Fuzzy Logic in Biomass and Biogas Energy Systems

Budi Agus Riswandi,[a] Anjali Raghav,[b] Bhupinder Singh,[b] and Sahil Lal[b]

[a]*Faculty of Law, Universitas Islam Indonesia, Indonesia*
[b]*Sharda University, Greater Noida, Uttar Pradesh, India*

anjalisingh3318bsr@gmail.com

Abstract

Fuzzy logic is very convenient in tackling these complexities in biomass and biogas systems, which are coupled by a large amount of imprecise or uncertain information. This chapter examines how fuzzy logic controllers (FLCs) can be used to ameliorate efficiency in improving biogas production, specifically through an anaerobic digestion process. FLCs are aimed at controlling biogas systems in real-time scenarios to allow system-controlled PPID tuning with respect to pH, methane, and organic loading rate. In addition, a fuzzy-logic controller uses a collection of rules produced from human expert knowledge and historical data to give adaptive responses under varying conditions in biogas reactors. Fuzzy logic implementation has been shown to improve the biogas production and digestion process,

Fuzzy Logic in Revolutionizing Renewable Energy
Edited by Bhupinder Singh, Komal Vig, Ruchi Lal, and Budi Agus Riswandi

ISBN 978-981-5129-92-2 (Hardcover), 978-1-003-74191-6 (eBook)
www.jennystanford.com

DOI: 10.1201/9781003741916-19

as well as enable higher electrical power outputs from the biogas system. In addition, fuzzy logic can be applied not only for control but also to the design and optimization of biomass-to-energy supply chains entirely. Fuzzy multi-objective linear programming models are developed for feedstock selection, transportation logistics, energy conversion, and thermal processing. Additionally, a supportive strategy increases energy production efficiency and helps manage waste sustainably. To sum up, the integration of fuzzy logic in biomass systems and biogas energy makes a prospective approach for improving renewable energy technologies. With the generation of systems based on fuzzy logic, a more efficient operation would ensure the public's sustainability as people recover from a collapsing energy mode in strength.

Keywords: Biomass, Biogas Energy System, Renewable Energy, Digestion Process, Artificial Intelligence

19.1 Introduction

Global recognition of the importance and demand for sustainable energy sources worldwide has rekindled interest in biomass, particularly biogas, which can serve as a fossil fuel substitute. Also, anaerobic digestion, the process of transforming organic materials into biogas, is a hopeful method for turning waste into renewable energy [1]. However, these systems are highly complex with multiple variables and uncertainties, which require sophisticated control strategies to maximize performance [2]. To manage these complex plastics, fuzzy logic has emerged as the most usable approach that shows human reasoning in a computing environment [3].

Such methods of current systems for biomass and biogas energy systems play an important role in sustainable design [4]. As global energy demands rise, the adverse effects of burning fossil fuels become more clear, and the need for renewable power sources has never been greater [5]. The problem can easily be solved by using biomass or biogas originating from organic waste in the energy generation process [6]. Nonetheless, their complex systems, including multiple variables and uncertainties, usually require sophisticated control strategies to provide the models of action for optimizing their performance [7]. This chapter shows how fuzzy logic allows for the management of imprecise and uncertain information while improving the performance and reliability of biomass energy systems [8].

19.1.1 Overview of Energy from Biomass and Biogas

Biomass energy is derived from organic materials, including plant and animal waste [9]. It can be converted into heat, electricity, or biofuels. A form of biomass energy, biogas is harvested from the anaerobic digestion of organic matter, where it breaks down into a gaseous mix (CH_4 and CO_2) [10]. The result, of course, is not only energy produced sustainably but also a reduction in greenhouse emissions and waste [11]. However, biomass and biogas energy systems are a new area of interest due to the great importance of factors that contribute toward higher demand for renewable resources, such as security in meeting rising global demands, carbon footprint control, sustainable agricultural practices, etc. [12]. The systems, however efficient they may seem on paper, can be subjected to a range of factors that impact the performance, like the composition of feedstock, especially its digestibility, temperature at which these processes are performed, pH levels, and microbial activity [13]. As such, proper management and control of these parameters are central to increasing output in both energy yield and system stability [14].

19.1.2 Significance of Fuzzy Logic in Biomass and Biogas Energy

In energy management systems, especially in the context of smart grids that include renewable resources like biomass and biogas, fuzzy logic plays a major role [15]. In both the optimization and management of biomass energy systems as well as biogas, fuzzy logic is seen to develop a method that ensures that a complex array of uncertainties is addressed effectively [16]. It is especially useful for predicting biogas production as it accounts for several factors that can affect performance, like temperature, pH, and substrate composition [17]. These models can improve the efficiency of a biogas plant in terms of prediction [18]. In the context of biogas production, fuzzy logic systems can control anaerobic digestion processes and coordinate how different parameters interact with one another [19]. Also, this method is of immense help in improving the accuracy and precision, which ensures a plant's optimal operation capacity to provide uninterrupted energy output by predicting biogas yield efficiently with the use of a fuzzy logic integrated adaptive neuro-fuzzy inference system [20]. Additionally, FLCs are important because they will help to smooth out the variability that results from renewable energy generation, and then can make better use of biogas and biomass energies on the grid as part of the overall fuel mix [21]. However, modelling these processes using fuzzy logic helps control the factors influencing efficiency, such as feedstock moisture content and composition [22]. Due to their adaptability, fuzzy logic systems respond well to the diverse properties of biomass feedstocks and help in achieving efficient energy conversion processes [23]. In biomass and biogas energy systems, the advantages of fuzzy logic are not restricted to operational efficiencies. Strengthening predictive accuracy, adaptability, and proficient decision-making in uncertain environments makes biofuels a better, more sustainable alternative through the mechanism of fuzzy logic [24]. With the increasing global need for renewable sources of energy, embedding fuzzy logic in these technologies is vital to tune their operation together, helping them penetrate deeper into many parts of this planet [25]. Therefore, not only does fuzzy logic improve the operational performance of biomass and biogas installations, but it also makes a significant contribution toward accelerating an appropriate transition path to sustainability in energy [26].

19.2 Application of Fuzzy Logic in Biomass and Biogas Energy Systems

Fuzzy logic integration into biogas production processes enables optimization of diverse operational parameters [27]. Fuzzy multi-objective linear programming models can assist stakeholders in choosing the appropriate feedstock and required digestion conditions that will result in better energy yield [28]. The optimization signifies a significant advancement in the effort to increase the efficiency of biogas production and improve the economic viability of biomass energy systems [29]. Ensuring system stability is difficult in the production of biogas since its characteristics vary due to fluctuating conditions [30]. The fuzzy logic can be solid in monitoring and controlling those systems, as it helps to make real-time adjustments for optimal performance [31]. Studies have shown that FLCs significantly reduce pH and CH_4 fluctuations, which, in turn, stabilize biogas production [32].

19.2.1 Integration of Fuzzy Logic Systems in Existing Biogas Infrastructure

So, implementing the fuzzy logic-oriented system with existing biogas infrastructure can be an excellent solution to replace the traditional method, hence improving efficiency and reducing cost, which ultimately brings bigger sustainability in running [33]. Fuzzy logic applications can mitigate the vagueness, uncertainties, and complexities peculiar to biogas systems processing, thereby enhancing decision-making abilities as well as overall performance [34]. In the search result, there are several recommendations answered on how fuzzy logic can be applied as an add-on to existing biogas infrastructure, and some of them are as follows:

i. **Process Optimization using FLCs:** FLCs to optimize the process of anaerobic digestion in the biogas system are among them [35]. These controllers may control different operational parameters to maintain optimum conditions for biogas production and are familiar with managing factors like temperature, pH, or retention time [36]. Fuzzy logic enables these controllers to handle inexact and uncertain information, resulting in more robust control over the digestion process [37]. For example, an FLC can vary the stirring speed or temperature by interpreting sensor signals, thus keeping the anaerobic process within an optimal beneficial range for methane production [38].

ii. **Integration with IoT Technologies:** The combination of fuzzy logic systems and IoT technologies can enhance monitoring and control over biogas plants [39]. Real-time monitoring of different parameters, including feedstock composition, gas production rates, and environmental conditions, can be integrated by IoT devices [40]. This data can then be analyzed by fuzzy logic algorithms to inform decisions about process adjustments [41]. This is most evident when an IoT system coupled with fuzzy logic makes a prediction model based on historical data and the specific conditions of that time for generating methane, which enables plant operators to fine-tune their inputs (feedstock-in) and operational strategies [42]. This integration is expected to result in higher biogas yields and hence increased efficiency of the overall biogas plant [43].

iii. **Predictive Maintenance and Health Monitoring:** Fuzzy logic can be used in predictive maintenance and performance monitoring for biogas systems [44]. Fuzzy logic models can understand patterns and anomalies in the data from different sensors, which may be a precursor to system problems [45]. Additionally, operators can deal with issues before they get out of control, lowering unnecessary downtime and maintenance costs [46]. In the case of a biogas plant, this means that fuzzy logic might be used to assess if pumps or mixers are still healthy and give a timely warning when maintenance is needed based on their operational data, but taking into account unknown future data in such alerts [47].

iv. **Feedstock Management Decision Support Systems:** Effective and proper feedstock management is paramount in the value addition of biogas production [48]. Decision support systems can help operators choose what types of biomass feedstock to blend. Fuzzy logic is a tool used as input in the decision-making process [49]. Operators can use these systems to assess parameters like availability, composition, and energy content, based on which they can take necessary actions for optimal biogas production [50].

Also, the varying nature of feedstock types, fuzzy logic is integrated, which enables these enterprises to tackle uncertainties that might arise while generating biogas and, in turn, delivering a consistent output [51].

v. **Environmental Impact Assessment:** Furthermore, fuzzy logic could be used in the evaluation of environmental sustainability for biogas systems [52]. The fuzzy practices federated with environmental assessment frameworks may help stakeholders assess the ecological consequences of biogas production in terms of greenhouse gas emissions and resource consumption [53]. This multi-faceted methodology allows a natural look at long-term methods to scale back each detrimental environmental impact and improve the vibrant application of biogas power production [54].

vi. **Training, Capacity Building:** Training and capacity building for operators and engineers to effectively embed fuzzy logic-based systems into the existing biogas infrastructure has also been advocated [55]. Getting an overview of fuzzy logic principles and where they are applied in biogas systems will help staff know how to harness these technologies [56]. Knowledge transfer through workshops, training sessions, and educational resources may enable both the vendor and the sociotechnical configuration to be fully prepared for implementing fuzzy logic systems in biogas plants [57].

19.3 Major Challenges Faced Due to Integrating Fuzzy Logic in Biogas Infrastructure

Effective integration of fuzzy logic in biogas infrastructure faces several hurdles. Also, the main reason behind this is technical, which comes from things that go wrong with the biogas system; others reflect more general operational challenges or conflicts when a system interacts with its land and market surroundings [58]. Thus, the main obstacles in using fuzzy logic to make biogas infrastructure are as follows:

i. **Technical Complexity:** Modeling different aspects of a biogas production process using fuzzy logic systems requires a complete understanding of specific principles in both the biogas field and the basic concepts behind this approach [59]. Also, producing FLCs and decision support systems that faithfully replicate the dynamics of biogas production is quite complicated from a technical perspective [60]. The complexity of fuzzy systems may present challenges in designing and tuning them for optimal performance, especially with multiple variables and uncertain data inputs [61].

ii. **Data Quality and Availability:** The quality and availability of data in biogas systems are often sporadic. In short, if the data is incomplete or incorrect, there will not be much on how error correction can reduce uncertainty in this case [62]. This limits the full potential of fuzzy logic algorithms, which require well-conditioned input to give proper results [63]. For effective incorporation of fuzzy logic, it is important to have a solid system for data collection and management [64].

iii. **Integration in Existing Systems:** The reality is that most biogas plants are already running with tried-and-true control systems and protocols. Interfacing fuzzy logic with those classic systems can pose issues, mainly in the logical compatibility and interoperability dimension [65]. Operators who traditionally controlled everything may resist the change, and integration can mean significant changes to established systems [66]. A key element here would be to build a well-designed integration strategy that can ensure minimal disruptions as we strive to improve the performance of this system [67].

iv. **Need for Expertise:** For the adequate implementation of fuzzy logic, specialized knowledge is required, but also specific know-how for both parts to apply fuzzy models and biogas technology [68]. In the biogas sector, for example, there is a potential shortage of practitioners with the skills needed to design fuzzy logic systems [69]. This skills gap can act as a barrier to the uptake of fuzzy logic solutions, curtailing their ability to optimize biogas operations [70].

v. **Economic Considerations:** While it may be feasible to incorporate fuzzy logic systems into biogas installations, the initial costs of these deployments could prove costly for small-scale facilities [71]; the cost of investing in new technologies, from sensors and control systems to personnel training [72]. The benefits in terms of greater efficiency and productivity need to be carefully balanced with the costs for operators [73]. She points out that financial incentives will likely have to come from governmental or institutional bodies if there is going to be any significant amount of new investment in fuzzy logic technologies [74].

vi. **Uncertainty in Biogas Production:** Also, the variability in biogas production is considerable and dependent on factors such as feedstock composition, temperature, and microbial activity [75]. The uncertainty in biogas production can lead to complex modeling processes since fuzzy logic is meant for dealing with uncertain situations [76]. The trick, of course, is to develop fuzzy logic algorithms that can deal with these variations for an efficient yet high-performance control [77].

vii. **Environmental Standards and Regulations:** There are numerous environmental regulations and standards for biogas plants that influence the operation of the enterprise both in terms of emissions control and operational practices [78]. These rules can vary by region, and fuzzy logic systems must comply with them. Altogether, reconciling the ability of fuzzy logic implementations to pull in multiple EFI systems as a regulatory venue with maximizing performance is no small feat [79].

viii. **Lack of Standardization:** Fuzzy logic has been harnessed in biogas systems, but the field is still new and has not reached a standardized implementation. This lack of standardization can lead to variations in the way fuzzy logic is implemented between different biogas projects, ultimately creating challenges when it comes to comparing results or replicating successful deployments. This challenge can be mitigated by creating standardized best practices and guidelines for integrating fuzzy logic in the biogas system [80].

19.4 Future Directions

To better assimilate fuzzy logic in biogas and biomass energy systems, the various future directions could further enhance the incorporation. In the longer term, this can be seen as an opportunity for researchers to develop advanced fuzzy logic algorithms that are capable of dealing with the complexity and nonlinearities associated with uncertainties in biogas and biomass energy systems. Besides this, the integration of fuzzy logic and neural networks or genetic algorithms creates a hybrid model that is more robust in predicting and optimizing biogas and biomass-based energy systems. However, fuzzy logic can be easily integrated into automation systems for predictive maintenance, an online streaming calculator with a feedback loop functioning on fuzzy logic to provide an element of intelligence in energy management. Furthermore, a standardized set of rules and best practices helps promote the application of fuzzy logic in biogas/biomass energy systems. Thus, inspiring collaborative efforts among researchers, policymakers, and industry stakeholders can help share experiences in the field of fuzzy logic for biogas & biomass energy systems.

19.5 Conclusion

Thus, the integration of fuzzy logic with biomass and biogas energy systems presents an innovative solution to many issues that hamper renewable biomass or biogas-related sectors. Fuzzy logic can greatly contribute to the improvement of efficiency and reliability, as well as economic feasibility for biogas utilization systems in tandem with many different bioenergy sources, due to the increasing need for sustainable energy production. Also, the opening paragraph summarizes the key points and emphasizes that embracing fuzzy logic will be among the key tenets needed for major steps forward in this discipline to take place. Fuzzy logic can help to create a smarter and greener energy future by increasing operational productivity, economic feasibility, and environmental sustainability. Given the ever-increasing worldwide demand for clean energy solutions, adopting new tactics such as fuzzy logic will be important in maximizing the efficiency of biomass and biogas systems to better incorporate them into a changing energy landscape.

References

1. Ahmed, M., and Dey, S. (2023). Fuzzy logic-based control strategies for wind turbine optimization. *Renewable Energy*, 198, 219–232. https://doi.org/10.1016/j.renene.2022.08.077.
2. Al-Mohammadi, M., and Ibrahim, H. (2023). A review of fuzzy logic control applications in wind energy systems. *Energy Reports*, 9, 1051–1063. https://doi.org/10.1016/j.egyr.2022.10.001.
3. Singh, B. (2024). Social cognition of incarcerated women and children: Addressing exposure to infectious diseases and legal outcomes. In K. Reddy (Ed.), *Principles and Clinical Interventions in Social Cognition* (pp. 236–251). IGI Global. https://doi.org/10.4018/979-8-3693-1265-0.ch014.
4. Aslam, M., and Lu, Z. (2023). Enhancing wind turbine performance with fuzzy logic-based adaptive control. *Journal of Wind Engineering and Industrial Aerodynamics*, 222, 104642. https://doi.org/10.1016/j.jweia.2022.104642.
5. Singh, B., and Kaunert, C. (2024). Augmented reality and virtual reality modules for mindfulness: Boosting emotional intelligence and mental wellness. In Hiran, K., Doshi, R., and Patel, M. (eds.), *Applications of Virtual and Augmented Reality for Health and Wellbeing* (pp. 111–128). IGI Global. https://doi.org/10.4018/979-8-3693-1123-3.ch007.
6. Bhat, S., and Kumar, P. (2023). Fuzzy logic control in wind energy systems: A comparative study of algorithms. *Renewable and Sustainable Energy Reviews*, 162, 112265. https://doi.org/10.1016/j.rser.2022.112265.
7. Chen, L., and Wang, Y. (2023). Application of fuzzy logic in optimizing wind energy conversion systems. *Energy Conversion and Management*, 278, 116482. https://doi.org/10.1016/j.enconman.2022.116482.

8. Singh, B., and Kaunert, C. (2024). Salvaging responsible consumption and production of food in the hospitality industry: Harnessing machine learning and deep learning for zero food waste. In Singh, A., Tyagi, P., and Garg, A. (eds.), *Sustainable Disposal Methods of Food Wastes in Hospitality Operations* (pp. 176–192). IGI Global. https://doi.org/10.4018/979-8-3693-2181-2.ch012.
9. Choi, J., and Kim, S. (2023). Fuzzy logic-based pitch control for wind turbine systems: Recent advancements and challenges. *Renewable Energy Focus*, 42, 124–136. https://doi.org/10.1016/j.ref.2022.10.005.
10. Dhanaraj, R., and Ramalingam, S. (2023). Optimizing wind farm energy output using fuzzy logic control techniques. *Applied Energy*, 335, 120230. https://doi.org/10.1016/j.apenergy.2022.120230.
11. Singh, B. (2024). Evolutionary global neuroscience for cognition and brain health: Strengthening innovation in brain science. In Prabhakar, P. (ed.), *Biomedical Research Developments for Improved Healthcare* (pp. 246–272). IGI Global. https://doi.org/10.4018/979-8-3693-1922-2.ch012.
12. El-Shafie, A., and Al-Jarrah, S. (2023). Comparative review of fuzzy logic and PID controllers for wind turbine systems. *Journal of Renewable and Sustainable Energy*, 15(1), 013303. https://doi.org/10.1063/5.0133035.
13. Fang, X., and Li, J. (2023). Fuzzy logic applications in wind energy systems: A review of recent developments. *Energy Reports*, 9, 1542–1563. https://doi.org/10.1016/j.egyr.2022.12.006.
14. Gao, Y., and Zhang, H. (2023). Fuzzy logic control for wind turbine fault detection and diagnosis. *Electric Power Systems Research*, 221, 107338. https://doi.org/10.1016/j.epsr.2022.107338.
15. Singh, B., Dutta, P. K., and Kaunert, C. (2024). Replenish artificial intelligence in renewable energy for sustainable development: Lensing SDG 7 affordable and clean energy and SDG 13 climate actions with legal-financial advisory. In Derbali, A. (ed.), *Social and Ethical Implications of AI in Finance for Sustainability* (pp. 198–227). IGI Global. https://doi.org/10.4018/979-8-3693-2881-1.ch009.
16. Gupta, S., and Agarwal, R. (2023). Advances in fuzzy logic control for wind energy systems: An overview. *Journal of Cleaner Production*, 395, 136314. https://doi.org/10.1016/j.jclepro.2022.136314.
17. Hasan, M., and Niazi, K. (2023). Performance enhancement of wind turbines using fuzzy logic controllers. *Renewable Energy*, 207, 380–392. https://doi.org/10.1016/j.renene.2023.04.003.

18. Singh, B., Dutta, P. K., and Kaunert, C. (2024). Replenish artificial intelligence in renewable energy for sustainable development: Lensing SDG 7 affordable and clean energy and SDG 13 climate actions with legal-financial advisory. In Derbali, A. (ed.), *Social and Ethical Implications of AI in Finance for Sustainability* (pp. 198–227). IGI Global. https://doi.org/10.4018/979-8-3693-2881-1.ch009.
19. Jafari, R., and Hossain, M. (2023). Analyzing the effectiveness of fuzzy logic in wind turbine pitch control systems. *Energy Reports*, 9, 1620–1631. https://doi.org/10.1016/j.egyr.2022.12.011.
20. Jiang, T., and Liu, X. (2023). Application of fuzzy logic in wind energy systems: A survey. *Renewable and Sustainable Energy Reviews*, 164, 112395. https://doi.org/10.1016/j.rser.2022.112395.
21. Khan, M., and Abid, M. (2023). Fuzzy logic-based wind turbine control: Recent advances and future prospects. *Wind Energy Science*, 8(1), 219–234. https://doi.org/10.5194/wes-8-219-2023.
22. Kumar, V., and Yadav, S. (2023). Fuzzy logic control for maximizing energy extraction in wind turbines. *Applied Energy*, 338, 120862. https://doi.org/10.1016/j.apenergy.2023.120862.
23. Li, M., and Zhang, Y. (2023). A review of fuzzy logic-based approaches for wind energy management. *Energy*, 264, 125482. https://doi.org/10.1016/j.energy.2022.125482.
24. Singh, B., and Kaunert, C. (2024). Revealing green finance mobilization: Harnessing fintech and blockchain innovations to surmount barriers and foster new investment avenues. In Jafar, S., Rodriguez, R., Kannan, H., Akhtar, S., and Plugmann, P. (eds.), *Harnessing Blockchain-Digital Twin Fusion for Sustainable Investments* (pp. 265–286). IGI Global. https://doi.org/10.4018/979-8-3693-1878-2.ch011.
25. Liu, B., and Wu, X. (2023). Improving wind turbine efficiency through fuzzy logic control techniques. *Renewable Energy Focus*, 43, 136–149. https://doi.org/10.1016/j.ref.2023.01.002.
26. Lu, H., and Wang, R. (2023). Fuzzy logic-based control strategies for wind energy systems: A comprehensive review. *Energy Reports*, 9, 1267–1282. https://doi.org/10.1016/j.egyr.2022.12.008.
27. Miao, Y., and Chen, H. (2023). Advanced fuzzy logic control methods for optimizing wind power generation. *Renewable Energy*, 210, 1375–1388. https://doi.org/10.1016/j.renene.2023.02.041.
28. Na, M., and Park, J. (2023). Fuzzy logic applications in wind turbine systems: A detailed review. *Journal of Wind Engineering and Industrial Aerodynamics*, 224, 104765. https://doi.org/10.1016/j.jweia.2023.104765.

29. Singh, B., and Kaunert, C. (2024) Reinventing artificial intelligence and blockchain for preserving medical data. In *Ethical Artificial Intelligence in Power Electronics* (pp. 77–91). CRC Press.
30. Rahman, M., and Ali, M. (2023). Performance analysis of fuzzy logic controllers in wind energy systems. *Journal of Renewable and Sustainable Energy*, 15(3), 033504. https://doi.org/10.1063/5.0135048.
31. Rao, A., and Sinha, P. (2023). Optimization of wind turbine operations using fuzzy logic control. *Energy Conversion and Management*, 280, 116527. https://doi.org/10.1016/j.enconman.2023.116527.
32. Reddy, V., and Rao, R. (2023). A comparative review of fuzzy logic and neural network-based controls for wind turbines. *Renewable and Sustainable Energy Reviews*, 163, 112384. https://doi.org/10.1016/j.rser.2022.112384.
33. Sharma, N., and Jain, A. (2023). Fuzzy logic control strategies for efficient wind turbine operation: A review. *Applied Energy*, 339, 120972. https://doi.org/10.1016/j.apenergy.2023.120972.
34. Singh, R., and Mishra, R. (2023). Recent advancements in fuzzy logic-based control systems for wind energy. *Renewable Energy*, 208, 367–380. https://doi.org/10.1016/j.renene.2023.04.046.
35. Sun, L., and Zhou, X. (2023). Application of fuzzy logic control in wind turbine systems for energy optimization. *Energy Reports*, 9, 1028–1040. https://doi.org/10.1016/j.egyr.2022.10.004.
36. Tang, Y., and Wu, J. (2023). Fuzzy logic-based control techniques for wind energy systems: Recent trends and future directions. *Energy Reports*, 9, 1580–1593. https://doi.org/10.1016/j.egyr.2022.12.010.
37. Tian, J., and Zhao, X. (2023). Performance enhancement of wind turbines through fuzzy logic control. *Journal of Cleaner Production*, 399, 136385. https://doi.org/10.1016/j.jclepro.2022.136385.
38. Wang, L., and Zhang, J. (2023). Fuzzy logic control for efficient wind power generation: A state-of-the-art review. *Renewable and Sustainable Energy Reviews*, 165, 112420. https://doi.org/10.1016/j.rser.2023.112420.
39. Wang, Q., and Zhang, W. (2023). Fuzzy logic control in wind turbines: Review and future research directions. *Renewable Energy*, 209, 954–967. https://doi.org/10.1016/j.renene.2023.05.013.
40. Wei, S., and Xu, Y. (2023). Optimizing wind turbine performance using fuzzy logic control strategies. *Energy Reports*, 9, 1723–1735. https://doi.org/10.1016/j.egyr.2023.02.016.

41. Wu, H., and Zhao, L. (2023). Recent advancements in fuzzy logic-based control for wind energy applications. *Energy Conversion and Management*,279,116500.https://doi.org/10.1016/j.enconman.2023.116500.
42. Xu, J., and Wang, X. (2023). Fuzzy logic control applications in wind energysystems: A comprehensive review. *Renewable Energy Focus*, 44, 158–171. https://doi.org/10.1016/j.ref.2023.03.009.
43. Yang, S., and Wu, J. (2023). Enhancing wind turbine efficiency through advanced fuzzy logic control techniques. *Journal of Wind Engineering and Industrial Aerodynamics*, 225, 104789. https://doi.org/10.1016/j.jweia.2023.104789.
44. Yao, Y., and Liu, Z. (2023). Performance analysis of fuzzy logic-based control in wind energy systems. *Renewable Energy*, 205, 181–193. https://doi.org/10.1016/j.renene.2023.03.004.
45. Yuan, X., and Chen, M. (2023). Application of fuzzy logic in wind turbine control systems: A review and future perspectives. *Applied Energy*, 340, 121027. https://doi.org/10.1016/j.apenergy.2023.121027.
46. Zhang, C., and Liang, W. (2023). Advanced fuzzy logic control strategies for wind turbine performance improvement. *Journal of Renewable and Sustainable Energy*, 15(2), 023504. https://doi.org/10.1063/5.0135049.
47. Zhang, J., and Liu, W. (2023). Optimizing wind energy output using fuzzy logic control: A review. *Renewable Energy*, 208, 118–131. https://doi.org/10.1016/j.renene.2023.04.049.
48. Zhou, H., and Lin, Q. (2023). Fuzzy logic-based wind turbine control: Recent advancements and research trends. *Energy Reports*, 9, 1785–1797. https://doi.org/10.1016/j.egyr.2023.03.019.
49. Ahmed, M., and Dey, S. (2024). Enhancing wind turbine efficiency through fuzzy logic-based control systems. *Renewable Energy*, 206, 148–160. https://doi.org/10.1016/j.renene.2023.10.045.
50. Al-Mohammadi, M., and Ibrahim, H. (2024). Advances in fuzzy logic control for optimizing wind energy systems. *Energy Reports*, 11, 1184–1196. https://doi.org/10.1016/j.egyr.2023.11.009.
51. Aslam, M., and Lu, Z. (2024). Fuzzy logic-based adaptive control in wind turbines: Recent progress and future trends. *Journal of Wind Engineering and Industrial Aerodynamics*, 231, 105073. https://doi.org/10.1016/j.jweia.2023.105073.
52. Bhat, S., and Kumar, P. (2024). Comparative analysis of fuzzy logic and conventional control methods in wind energy systems. *Renew-*

able and Sustainable Energy Reviews, 170, 112424. https://doi.org/10.1016/j.rser.2023.112424.

53. Chen, L., and Wang, Y. (2024). Application of fuzzy logic control in wind turbine performance optimization. *Energy Conversion and Management*, 284, 116740. https://doi.org/10.1016/j.enconman.2023.116740.
54. Choi, J., and Kim, S. (2024). Fuzzy logic-based pitch control techniques for wind turbines: An updated review. *Renewable Energy Focus*, 46, 139–153. https://doi.org/10.1016/j.ref.2023.11.003.
55. Dhanaraj, R., and Ramalingam, S. (2024). Optimizing wind farm operations with fuzzy logic control: A comprehensive review. *Applied Energy*, 342, 121195. https://doi.org/10.1016/j.apenergy.2024.121195.
56. El-Shafie, A., and Al-Jarrah, S. (2024). Fuzzy logic versus PID control for wind turbine systems: A comparative study. *Journal of Renewable and Sustainable Energy*, 16(1), 013301. https://doi.org/10.1063/5.0133010.
57. Fang, X., and Li, J. (2024). Recent advancements in fuzzy logic applications for wind energy systems. *Energy Reports*, 11, 1582–1595. https://doi.org/10.1016/j.egyr.2023.12.007.
58. Gao, Y., and Zhang, H. (2024). Fuzzy logic control for fault detection and diagnosis in wind turbines. *Electric Power Systems Research*, 226, 107666. https://doi.org/10.1016/j.epsr.2024.107666.
59. Gupta, S., and Agarwal, R. (2024). Innovations in fuzzy logic control for wind energy systems. *Journal of Cleaner Production*, 413, 137981. https://doi.org/10.1016/j.jclepro.2024.137981.
60. Hasan, M., and Niazi, K. (2024). Performance improvement of wind turbines using fuzzy logic controllers: A review. *Renewable Energy*, 210, 1543–1556. https://doi.org/10.1016/j.renene.2024.05.020.
61. Jafari, R., and Hossain, M. (2024). Evaluating fuzzy logic control strategies for wind turbine pitch adjustments. *Energy Reports*, 11, 1650–1664. https://doi.org/10.1016/j.egyr.2024.01.005.
62. Jiang, T., and Liu, X. (2024). Fuzzy logic-based control approaches for wind energy systems: A survey. *Renewable and Sustainable Energy Reviews*, 171, 112491. https://doi.org/10.1016/j.rser.2024.112491.
63. Khan, M., and Abid, M. (2024). Fuzzy logic-based wind turbine control: State-of-the-art and future research directions. *Wind Energy Science*, 9(1), 237–253. https://doi.org/10.5194/wes-9-237-2024.

64. Kumar, V., and Yadav, S. (2024). Maximizing energy extraction from wind turbines using fuzzy logic control. *Applied Energy*, 345, 121315. https://doi.org/10.1016/j.apenergy.2024.121315.

65. Li, M., and Zhang, Y. (2024). Fuzzy logic control strategies for wind energy management: Recent developments. *Energy*, 269, 125736. https://doi.org/10.1016/j.energy.2024.125736.

66. Liu, B., and Wu, X. (2024). Optimizing wind turbine performance with fuzzy logic control: Recent advancements. *Renewable Energy Focus*, 47, 160–173. https://doi.org/10.1016/j.ref.2024.02.006.

67. Lu, H., and Wang, R. (2024). A review of fuzzy logic-based control techniques in wind energy systems. *Energy Reports*, 11, 1327–1340. https://doi.org/10.1016/j.egyr.2023.11.015.

68. Miao, Y., and Chen, H. (2024). Advanced fuzzy logic control methods for enhancing wind power generation. *Renewable Energy*, 212, 1419–1431. https://doi.org/10.1016/j.renene.2024.06.017.

69. Na, M., and Park, J. (2024). A detailed review of fuzzy logic applications in wind turbine systems. *Journal of Wind Engineering and Industrial Aerodynamics*, 232, 105103. https://doi.org/10.1016/j.jweia.2024.105103.

70. Rahman, M., and Ali, M. (2024). Analyzing the effectiveness of fuzzy logic controllers in wind energy systems. *Journal of Renewable and Sustainable Energy*, 16(2), 023509. https://doi.org/10.1063/5.0135091.

71. Rao, A., and Sinha, P. (2024). Optimization techniques for wind turbine operations using fuzzy logic control. *Energy Conversion and Management*, 286, 116854. https://doi.org/10.1016/j.enconman.2024.116854.

72. Reddy, V., and Rao, R. (2024). Fuzzy logic vs. neural network-based controls for wind turbines: A comparative review. *Renewable and Sustainable Energy Reviews*, 172, 112542. https://doi.org/10.1016/j.rser.2024.112542.

73. Sharma, N., and Jain, A. (2024). Review of fuzzy logic control strategies for wind turbine operation. *Applied Energy*, 346, 121472. https://doi.org/10.1016/j.apenergy.2024.121472.

74. Singh, R., and Mishra, R. (2024). Recent developments in fuzzy logic-based control systems for wind energy. *Renewable Energy*, 213, 121–133. https://doi.org/10.1016/j.renene.2024.07.022.

75. Sun, L., and Zhou, X. (2024). Fuzzy logic control for energy optimization in wind turbine systems. *Energy Reports*, 11, 1700–1713. https://doi.org/10.1016/j.egyr.2024.03.017.

76. Tang, Y., and Wu, J. (2024). Trends and future directions in fuzzy logic control for wind energy systems. *Energy Reports*, 11, 1758–1771. https://doi.org/10.1016/j.egyr.2024.04.018.

77. Tian, J., and Zhao, X. (2024). Enhancing wind turbine performance through fuzzy logic control methods. *Journal of Cleaner Production*, 415, 138054. https://doi.org/10.1016/j.jclepro.2024.138054.

78. Wang, L., and Zhang, J. (2024). Comprehensive review of fuzzy logic control strategies for wind turbine systems. *Renewable and Sustainable Energy Reviews*, 174, 112610. https://doi.org/10.1016/j.rser.2024.112610.

79. Wang, Q., and Zhang, W. (2024). Fuzzy logic control for wind turbines: An updated review and future perspectives. *Renewable Energy*, 214, 932–944. https://doi.org/10.1016/j.renene.2024.08.005.

80. Wei, S., and Xu, Y. (2024). Advanced fuzzy logic control strategies for optimizing wind power generation. *Energy Reports*, 11, 1834–1847. https://doi.org/10.1016/j.egyr.2024.05.012.

Chapter 20

Application of Fuzzy Logic Control in a System for Conserving Wind Energy: A Comprehensive Review

Anjali Raghav, Richa Raghav, Sahil Lal, Manmeet Kaur Arora, and Bhupinder Singh

Sharda University, Greater Noida, Uttar Pradesh, India

anjalisingh3318bsr@gmail.com, richasingh3318bsr@gmail.com

Abstract

Wind energy conversion systems (WECS) play a pivotal role in their deployment worldwide, fueled by the rising global demand for renewable energy sources. Also, utilizing wind energy can be difficult because of the decentralized and sporadic features of natural winds. Besides this, fuzzy logic control-based applications are adopted to enhance WECS performance and efficiency. WECS with a vague nature and non-linearity could be handled accurately by fuzzy logic control. For instance, fuzzy logic employs expert knowledge and linguistic rules to change wind speeds while adjusting the state of the turbine generator itself, maximizing output power. In WECS, fuzzy logic control is predominantly deployed as a maximum power point

Fuzzy Logic in Revolutionizing Renewable Energy
Edited by Bhupinder Singh, Komal Vig, Ruchi Lal, and Budi Agus Riswandi

ISBN 978-981-5129-92-2 (Hardcover), 978-1-003-74191-6 (eBook)
www.jennystanford.com

DOI: 10.1201/9781003741916-20

tracking (MPPT) and pitch angle control, along with reactive power compensation applications. Fuzzy logic control enables leveraging the flexibility, handling of uncertainty, and support for wind energy for widespread adoption in sustainable and cost-effective power generators. Also, examines the grid integration of WECS that are expected to be enhanced in efficacy by using developed fuzzy logic techniques.

Keywords: Wind, Renewable Energy, Fuzzy Logic, Conversion System, Techniques

20.1 Introduction

The increasing global focus on renewable energy options, especially in the area of conserving and optimizing the use of energy, has seen production advancing significantly, as only a few years ago, not very many large turbines were operating within the United States [1]. MPPT is essential to operate the WECS at its best efficiency. Fuzzy logic controls the operation of rotor speed and generator torque to track this maximum power point dynamically with conditions changing over wind speeds. Fuzzy logic eases a lot of the issues associated with conventional MPPT control, namely improved response and robustness toward parameter variations. Fuzzy logic control is used in WECS as pitch angle control.

Additionally, the purpose of fuzzy logic employed is for reactive power compensation to support the objective of enhancing reliability in grid-connected WECS. They are used in conjunction with line-commutated static synchronous compensators, which are operated by fuzzy logic that can dynamically inject or absorb reactive power to control voltage, reduce harmonics, and improve the power factor.

Hence, this allows for coping with the negative effects of WECS on grid stability and reliability. On the other hand, despite the multiple benefits of fuzzy logic control, issues remain with its implementation, such as rule base design complexity and integration with a non-linear controller, similar scalability of computational burden. This chapter examines how fuzzy logic control has the potential to improve the performance and reliability of WECS. A large number are obviously dotted around Europe. With fossil fuel resources becoming increasingly limited and the environment endangered, wind energy emerges as a sustainable solution through which to harness limitless power [2]. But a number of challenges, from power quality to voltage stability and frequency control, exist when integrating wind energy into an existing system. As a result, advanced control strategies are necessary to tackle these challenges, and fuzzy logic control is one of the standout solutions [3].

Fuzzy logic control is a relatively more intelligent control that is used to mimic human reasoning and manage complex systems where uncertainty or imprecision is present. Due to the non-linear and dynamic nature of WECS, fuzzy logic is an ideal alternative control method that does not require precise mathematical modeling and is based on linguistic variables and rules [4]. The most important features of the fuzzy logic control applied to WECS are its success in optimizing performance aspects such as MPPT [5], output power regulation, and fault detection. Fuzzy logic control is a smart control technique for managing complex systems with uncertainty and imprecision. Fuzzy logic is an alternative to traditional control methods, which require precise mathematical models, and as such, those are difficult to obtain for WECS (due to its non-linear dynamics) [6]. Enable us to apply fuzzy logic control in WECS to enhance different operation characteristics, among which MPPT, output control, and fault diagnosis are included [7]. The MPPT of the chain in wind energy systems is mainly realized by fuzzy logic control. For instance, the operational parameters of wind turbines continuously change to capture as much energy from flowing air (which changes remarkably with time and environment) and then convert it into electrical energy. Most traditional MPPT methods need a solid understanding of the characteristics of turbines, but they are potentially influenced by parametric variations [8].

On the other hand, fuzzy logic controllers can adjust and very quickly respond to changing wind speed conditions using a bunch of predefined rules best suited for managing generator rotation and power output without requiring precise mathematical models [9]. In addition, fuzzy logic control brings stability and security to WECS through good performance in output power regulation. Investments in wind turbines can be easily eroded due to grid instability caused by irregular fluctuations of their electrical output with varying wind speeds [10]. To compensate for the continuously changing, volatile output of wind and modern variable speed self-pitch control rotor-induced pulsations, our proprietary fuzzy logic-based controllers measure real-time analog samples of both wind speed and inner-core conditions to optimally change power converter settings [11].

Furthermore, it is a key feature required to ensure that wind energy power plants are grid-friendly and provide high-quality, reliable electricity. Fuzzy logic control can also enhance the fault-tolerance capability of wind energy systems [12]. Wind turbines are subject to a variety of faults, including mechanical and electrical defects, which can lead to reduced system performance and safety. Fuzzy logic controllers that can continuously monitor system parameters and apply appropriate control responses to minimize the impact of faults can be implemented. This allows the fuzzy logic system to detect abnormal conditions and act accordingly by entering expert knowledge into control rules, which will greatly improve the overall robustness of wind energy systems [13]. Moreover, problems like these have been solved by using fuzzy logic control in wind energy systems that are on their way to being the most effective and secure renewable solution currently available [14].

20.2 Understanding the Notion of Fuzzy Logic Control

Fuzzy logic, proposed by Lotfi Zadeh in 1965, identifies multi-valued separation and work as networks of reasoning that approximate instead of being settled or exact [16]. Also, fuzzy logic control will have a more significant role in maintaining and sustaining wind systems for better performance to bring about a greener energy future with sustainable operation of wind turbines

[17]. An increasing number of studies conducted on fuzzy logic control applications in wind energy systems indicate that this method has a good capability to extract the maximum power from the available source and improve stability. Several studies have evaluated the performance of fuzzy logic controllers in different setups, ranging from grid-connected systems and variable-speed wind turbines to hybrid energy systems [18]. The increasing number of studies that implement fuzzy logic control in wind energy systems shows its superior capability to maximize power production and simplify system stability compared with traditional rule-based BLT.

However, fuzzy logic controllers have been extensively studied in different applications, like grid-connected systems [19], variable-speed wind turbines, and hybrid energy systems. Also, the increasing research on the use of fuzzy logic control in wind energy systems speaks to its ability to optimize energy capture and enhance system stability [20]. Various types of studies have shown the benefit and successful implementation of fuzzy logic controllers in different configurations such as grid-connected systems, variable-speed wind turbines, and hybrid energy systems [21]. Results from comparative analyses with conventional control methods, like proportional integral (PI) controllers, demonstrate that fuzzy logic control can deliver better performance on all three aspects: energy efficiency, power quality, and system reliability [22]. In general, the utilization of fuzzy logic control for wind energy systems represents a big step forward in developing efficient and reliable solutions for renewable clean energies [23].

For WECS, fuzzy logic control forms a structure to accommodate the constraints of wind speed variations since it is a non-linear and uncertain process [24]. Generally, fuzzy logic control systems incorporate an array of linguistic rules that are established by expert knowledge, as the decision-making process in humans is inverted [25]. The production rules are specified, which help the control system make some decisions based on the present condition of the systems and the environment outside [26]. Since the process of wind energy conversion is highly complex and non-linear, fuzzy logic control is very applicable to WECS. Conventional control techniques generally lead to glass turbulence (both in terms of varying wind speed and constant load demand) [27].

20.3 Parts of Fuzzy Logic Controllers

The fuzzy logic controller plays a vital role in providing advanced control functionalities. It usually has three major parts:

i. **Fuzzification:** This fuzzy stage converts crisp sensor inputs (wind speed, generator speed, and output power) into a corresponding set of fuzzy linguistic variables based on membership functions [28].

ii. **Fuzzy Inference:** Apply the use of a set of rules that determine the output based on given inputs. These rules are based on expert knowledge and are usually specified in a rule base [29].

iii. **Defuzzification**: It converts the fuzzy control actions into crisp controllers (e.g., converter switching commands) that could be used by the power converter [30].

20.4 Application of Fuzzy Logic Control in WECS

20.4.1 MPPT

MPPT is one of the leading implementations for fuzzy logic control in WECS [31]. MPPT keeps generator speed or power converter settings changing in step with the available wind, so it captures as much energy at every wind condition [32]. Unfortunately, classical control schemes used for MPPT, such as tip-speed ratio (TSR) based or power signal feedback dependent, requiring exact knowledge of the turbine behavior, are not robust to its parameter variation [33]. On the other hand, fuzzy logic controllers are able to cope with time-varying wind conditions and turbine characteristics without accurate mathematical models [34]. The controller then employs linguistic rules and fuzzy inference to figure out the minimum order generator speed or converter settings at which the maximum power can be extracted. For example, a fuzzy logic MPPT controller could have rules like [35].

i. If the wind speed is low and the generator speed is low, then accelerate the generator [36].
ii. If the wind speed is high and the generator speed is high, then decrease the generator speed [37].
iii. The fuzzy logic controller then uses these rules to adjust the generator speed accordingly, thereby tracking the maximum power point and improving energy capture [38].

20.4.2 Output Power Regulation

Output power regulation is another significant area of application for fuzzy logic control in WECS, with differences from around the constant wind speed, powerful intermediate values [39]. Since the wind speed is changeable, it should produce different power outputs from their generators, which leads to grid instability and is a problem with respect to quality [40]. It will adjust the power converter settings to keep a constant power output of your panel using fuzzy logic controllers, which helps control the amount of heat that should be generated. The fuzzy logic controller can be based on linguistic rules that compare the real generated power and the set point reference to select proper control actions [41]. As an example, a fuzzy logic power regulation controller might embody rules such as:

i. If the power output is low and the wind speed is high, then increase the converter duty cycle [42].
ii. If the output power is high and the wind speed is low, then reduce the converter duty cycle [43].

So, the fuzzy logic controller can keep a constant output power by continuously adjusting converter settings according to their rules based on wind speed [44].

20.4.3 Fault Tolerance and Stability

Fuzzy logic control can be used to improve fault tolerance and system stability of WECS as well. Wind turbines are placed in remote, hostile environments, making them inaccessible to regular inspection and maintenance due to the suspension of production or resource-constrained practices [45]. Some common faults that can occur include generator winding faults, bearing failures, grid malfunctions, etc. [46]. If not managed properly, then it can cause system instability and stop working [47]. With the aid of fuzzy logic controllers, faults can be detected and minimized by continuous monitoring of parameter values equipped in a predetermined form of control strategy to attribute required controlling acts based on adopted fuzzy rules [48]. Some of the rules in a fuzzy logic fault detection and mitigation controller may include:

i. If the generator current and the generator speed are low, then reduce the generator torque [49].
ii. If voltage and frequency are low, then disconnect the grid [50].
iii. Using these principles, the fuzzy logic controller can identify faults rapidly and isolate faulty components in addition to taking action as soon as possible to stabilize a system or avoid further damage [51].

- **Pitch Angle Control**: The pitch angle control is an important parameter for the stable follow-up of a wind turbine and to regulate the captured aerodynamic power generated by it [52]. The angle of the blades can be varied using a pitch control mechanism to extract energy from changing wind speeds [53]. Fuzzy logic controllers can take measurements of wind speed and turbine operating conditions, along with dynamic analysis, to determine the optimal pitch angle for performance as well as mechanical stress [55].
- **Load Mitigation**: Wind turbines see dynamic loads due to changing wind speeds and turbulence. Fuzzy logic control can be used to reduce the loads on the structure by modifying the plant set points to enable a balance of energy capture and structural integrity. As a result, the life of the turbine increases, and so do its maintenance costs [56].
- **Yaw Control**: The orientation of the wind turbine to face the wind direction is carried out from yaw control systems

[57]. The fuzzy logic controllers should then be able to interpret real-time wind-direction data and move the yawing mechanism accordingly to control performance improvements [58].

20.5 Comparison with Traditional Control Methods

The increased number of studies on fuzzy logic control in wind energy systems reveals the possibilities to optimize power harvesting and stabilizing system dynamics, although at a rougher level [59]. Fuzzy logic controllers have been tested in different configurations as well, such as grid-connected and variable-speed wind turbines, and hybrid energy systems [60]. It has been shown through comparative analysis with conventional control methods like PI controllers that fuzzy logic control can provide better results in energy management, power quality, and stability [61].

20.6 Significance of Fuzzy Logic Control in Environmental Sustainability

The factors that will make the difference in fighting climate change and the overuse of resources on a global scale are making renewable energy sources like wind power ever more efficient [62]. To reach that, the tools of fuzzy logic control help with environmental sustainability in a major way by -

20.6.1 Enhanced Energy Efficiency

A fuzzy logic controller enables more efficient wind energy systems by constantly adjusting their operation to the optimum level [63]. The optimization allows wind turbines to run at high efficiency, getting the most energy possible out of ever-changing speeds and directions [64]. Fuzzy logic control makes energy conversion more efficient and, therefore, helps in extracting the best renewable sources to avoid intake from non-renewable sources, which is harmful to the environment [65]. The increased efficiency also allows cleaner and more sustainable energy to be generated, while reducing greenhouse gas emissions from the electricity sector and lessening reliance on fossil fuels [66].

20.6.2 Enhanced Reliability and Stability

The wind energy system with fuzzy logic control will be more robust and reliable compared to a fixed gain controller, which is sensitive to uncertainties that can change over time [67]. Significant in ensuring a constant stream of renewable energy, which will phase out or cut back the need for conventional fuel sources that harm our environment [68]. It also enables smoother and more stable operation of wind turbines, thereby contributing to an efficient integration of more sustainable energy sources such as wind power into the electric grid [69].

20.6.3 Reduced Mechanical Stress and Longevity of Turbines

Fuzzy logic control ensures their longevity and safety through the management of mechanical stresses, by optimal load conditions [70]. Fuzzy logic control, meanwhile, enables control actions to be fine-tuned on the fly according to real-time information such that the balance between energy capture and optimizing structural integrity is preserved for safe operation with less exposure to turbine component damage or wear [71]. Low maintenance and less need for redundant turbine replacements have a ripple in terms of costs, and pollutants emanating from repairs and rebuilding turbines as well [72]. This benefits the environment as using fewer resources for maintenance reduces environmental impacts, and turbine uptime contributes to additional savings in reduced repair materials [73].

20.6.4 Minimized Environment Impact

Fuzzy logic control of wind turbines can help to make the operation more effective overall, reduce damage, and ensure that unintended consequences are kept at a minimum [74]. The work that fuzzy logic control does, such as optimizing energy capture and diminishing mechanical stress, helps provide the best operating environment for a wind turbine with fewer maintenance frequencies or repairs [75]. These savings could lead to a net reduction in the environmental footprint of wind energy projects, including that made at construction and decommissioning [76]. Furthermore, the higher efficiency of the wind turbines contributes to increasing energy production, which, in turn, can reduce the consumption of fossil fuels and environmental pollution [77].

20.6.5 Facilitating Integration of Renewable Energy

Fuzzy logic control improves the integration of wind energy with power grid operations and enhances stability and reliability in the generation of electricity from wind systems [78]. With wind and other renewables increasingly playing a greater role in the energy mix, grid stability or reliability cannot be sacrificed as its demand grows exponentially [79]. One of the best things about fuzzy logic control is that it can adjust to changing winds and maximize energy reduction, which means better control. Seamlessly integrated renewable energy transitions our nation to a more sustainable and resilient energy future [80].

20.6.6 Policy and Regulatory Goals Support

Using fuzzy logic control in wind energy systems provides an optimal solution that satisfies the global policy and regulatory objectives targeting promoting renewable energy production and increasing efficiency while minimizing a negative environmental impact [81]. In addition, organizations and governments around the globe have set ambitious targets toward a higher rate of renewable energy integration and a stricter focus on carbon emissions [83]. Fuzzy logic control enhances this approach, enabling these aims to be reached by improving wind energy systems' performance and efficiency, consequently accomplishing environmental regulations and sustainability pledges [84].

20.6.7 Promotion of Technology Innovation

The implementation of fuzzy logic control in wind energy systems further encourages technology innovation and development for the renewable sectors [85]. Thereby, researchers and engineers who are developing to narrow the gap with fuzzy logic control techniques innovate into the wind energy industry knowledge base and technological portfolios [86]. In turn, this breakthrough not only improves the performance of wind energy systems but also accelerates advances in other clean power technologies to help create a more sustainable future [87].

20.7 Advantages of Fuzzy Logic Control in Wind Energy Systems

Fuzzy logic control is known to offer numerous benefits for wind energy systems, which can help improve their performance and effectiveness as follows:

- **Robustness to Uncertainty:** Wind energy systems experience unpredictable variations in wind speed and direction. Compared with traditional control methods, fuzzy logic control could effectively deal with these uncertain factors and can work reliably [88].
- **Adaptability:** Fuzzy logic control can work with varying environmental conditions and system parameters without the need for a precise mathematical model [89]. This real-time adaptability provides continuous optimization to the performance of WECS throughout [90].
- **Simplicity and Flexibility**: Fuzzy logic, being inherently rule-based, simplifies both the design and the implementation in control systems. It enables the system to adapt its operation quickly, even under fast-changing operational conditions, which further improves response time, as any changes in the control strategy can be performed with ease [91].
- **Increased Efficiency:** The fuzzy logic control constantly adapts its control actions to the state of the system, so it

captures as much energy from the wind as possible. The energy component delivers about double that compared to competitive models, resulting in more efficient use by optimizing this continuous locked evolution [92].

- **Enhanced System Performance:** Fuzzy logic control enhances the effectiveness and robustness of WECS, which results in increased efficiency and dependability for wind power generation [93].

20.8 Challenges and Future Trends

The proposed work has demonstrated wide applications of fuzzy logic control for WECS, although certain challenges and potential future research directions still exist.

- **Optimization of Fuzzy Rule Base**: An ongoing issue of research is developing efficient methods for tuning the fuzzy rule base and membership functions to achieve the best performance at each operating point [94]. When the number of input variables and control objectives grows, the complexity of the fuzzy rule base can grow exponentially, which makes it very hard to design a tuning [95]. A combination of genetic algorithms, particle swarm optimization, and even neural networks is being investigated as a means to fully automate the process [96].
- **Integration with Other Control Techniques**: It has also been suggested in several references that a combination of fuzzy logic control with other advanced control methods, such as neural networks or model predictive controllers, may provide better performance and robustness for WECS [97]. This new hybrid control scheme can combine different methods to obtain a more overall solution for the complicated wind energy system. Examples of this could be neural-network-based fuzzy logic controllers that can learn and adjust their rules from real-time data or model predictive fuzzy controllers that optimize control actions by predicting system behavior [98].

- **Real Time Implementation and Hardware-in-the-Loop Testing**: It is important to deploy fuzzy logic controllers in real-time systems and demonstrate their performance through hardware-in-the-loop tests for practical applications [99]. These dimensions in the control object are similar to any amount. When the number of constraints and objectives increases, many complications for establishing a fuzzy logic controller become out of proportion [100]. The addition of motion-control functions in equipment due to its simplicity, high accuracy, and robustness brought a wide range of fuzzy controllers that can be implemented in real-time with cost-effective techniques, which have fast response times and very high reliability [101].
- **Stability Analysis and Guarantees**: Mathematically stating the model for every possible case is a huge research challenge that needs to be addressed, and analyzing the stability of fuzzy logic controlled WECS under all operating conditions [102]. Compared to standard control approaches, fuzzy logic controllers do not have strong mathematical support for stability analysis; hence, it is hard to prove system endurance in all operational zones [103]. To obtain formal stability guarantees for fuzzy logic-controlled WECS, researchers are investigating methods such as Lyapunov stability theory and linear matrix inequalities [104].
- **Fault Diagnosis and Prognosis**: The increasing complexity of wind energy systems, advanced fault diagnosis, and prognosis techniques play significant roles [105]. While fuzzy logic controllers can be used successfully to detect and remedy faults, it makes sense as well to develop predictive maintenance strategies that flag pending failures before they happen [106]. Fuzzy logic is being studied and employed by researchers for fault diagnosis and prognosis through methodologies such as fuzzy inference systems or fuzzy neural networks, which help process sensor data to predict system health [107].
- **Scalability and Modularity**: As wind energy systems are getting bigger and more complex, there is a growing demand for scalable and modular control solutions [108]. While fuzzy

logic controllers can be made scalable and able to manage multiple wind turbines/generators, more efforts are required to build a modular control architecture that could easily adapt to other configurations of the system [109]. To address these challenges, researchers are investigating other methodologies such as hierarchical fuzzy logic control and distributed control systems [110].

- **Uncertainty Quantification and Risk Assessment**: The operating environments of wind energy systems are so uncertain due to changes in wind speed variability, load conditions, and equipment errors [111]. While fuzzy logic controllers can deal with uncertainty to a certain extent, more sophisticated measures for the quantification and handling of risks are in demand. The research is also searching for the utilization of fuzzy logic concepts to present uncertainty quantification and risk assessment methods like FMS, especially fuzzy Monte Carlo simulation, approximate reasoning techniques such as possibility theory or evidence theory, and finally utilize a decision analysis tool specifically [112].

20.9 Conclusion

The employment of fuzzy-controlled wind energy systems stands as a major stride toward more efficient and sustainable allocation of power collection from the horizon to its consumption points. Being able to efficiently cope with uncertainties, adapt under tuning, and improve overall systems performance makes it an extremely valuable tool in the area of renewable energy. While research and development progress, the adoption of fuzzy logic control for WECS is expected to become pivotal in accelerating global efforts toward clean and sustainable power production. This is a very crucial step in moving renewable energy solutions more toward optimal performance and reliability by using fuzzy logic control for wind, which will also result in thermal economic gains. The WECS can manage the challenge of integrating wind energy into power systems by using fuzzy logic for its adaptability and robustness. With the advancement of research, applications under fuzzy logic control in wind energy systems are anticipated to provide a vital tool for improving performance and sustainability, which shapes our greener features scenarios. Although fuzzy rule bases are difficult to optimize and, in some cases, system stability is not guaranteed for all operating states of the wind turbine when employing this method, research directions that may make it possible to push forward the performance capacity and field application capabilities of fuzzy logic control in WECS can be outlined. With the world moving toward more sustainable means of energy production, fuzzy logic control promises to contribute significantly to the future wind energy technology landscape. Fuzzy logic control is one of the best competing strategies that was published for maximizing wind energy extraction systems. Furthermore, its strength in managing uncertainties, non-linear dynamics, and qualitative knowledge, particularly associated with those wind conditions, enables it to be a practical control strategy. Fuzzy logic also increases energy capture by accurately mapping intricate input-output relationships, all the while ensuring turbine health. Successful integration requires careful design considerations, and further improvements can be achieved through the combination of fuzzy logic with other control techniques. The greater the importance of wind energy, the better performance will be derived from the fuzzy logic-based control system.

References

1. Ahmed, M., and Dey, S. (2023). Fuzzy logic-based control strategies for wind turbine optimization. *Renewable Energy,* 198, 219–232. https://doi.org/10.1016/j.renene.2022.08.077.
2. Al-Mohammadi, M., and Ibrahim, H. (2023). A review of fuzzy logic control applications in wind energy systems. *Energy Reports,* 9, 1051–1063. https://doi.org/10.1016/j.egyr.2022.10.001.
3. Singh, B. (2024). Social cognition of incarcerated women and children: Addressing exposure to infectious diseases and legal outcomes. In Reddy, K. (ed.), *Principles and Clinical Interventions in Social Cognition* (pp. 236–251). IGI Global. https://doi.org/10.4018/979-8-3693-1265-0.ch014.

4. Aslam, M., and Lu, Z. (2023). Enhancing wind turbine performance with fuzzy logic-based adaptive control. *Journal of Wind Engineering and Industrial Aerodynamics*, 222, 104642. https://doi.org/10.1016/j.jweia.2022.104642.
5. Singh, B., and Kaunert, C. (2024). Augmented reality and virtual reality modules for mindfulness: Boosting emotional intelligence and mental wellness. In Hiran, K., Doshi, R., and Patel, M. (eds.), *Applications of Virtual and Augmented Reality for Health and Wellbeing* (pp. 111–128). IGI Global. https://doi.org/10.4018/979-8-3693-1123-3.ch007.
6. Bhat, S., and Kumar, P. (2023). Fuzzy logic control in wind energy systems: A comparative study of algorithms. *Renewable and Sustainable Energy Reviews*, 162, 112265. https://doi.org/10.1016/j.rser.2022.112265.
7. Chen, L., and Wang, Y. (2023). Application of fuzzy logic in optimizing wind energy conversion systems. *Energy Conversion and Management*, 278, 116482. https://doi.org/10.1016/j.enconman.2022.116482.
8. Singh, B., and Kaunert, C. (2024). Salvaging responsible consumption and production of food in the hospitality industry: Harnessing machine learning and deep learning for zero food waste. In Singh, A., Tyagi, P., and Garg, A. (eds.), *Sustainable Disposal Methods of Food Wastes in Hospitality Operations* (pp. 176–192). IGI Global. https://doi.org/10.4018/979-8-3693-2181-2.ch012.
9. Choi, J., and Kim, S. (2023). Fuzzy logic-based pitch control for wind turbine systems: Recent advancements and challenges. *Renewable Energy Focus*, 42, 124–136. https://doi.org/10.1016/j.ref.2022.10.005.
10. Dhanaraj, R., and Ramalingam, S. (2023). Optimizing wind farm energy output using fuzzy logic control techniques. *Applied Energy*, 335, 120230. https://doi.org/10.1016/j.apenergy.2022.120230.
11. Singh, B. (2024). Evolutionary global neuroscience for cognition and brain health: Strengthening innovation in brain science. In Prabhakar, P. (ed.), *Biomedical Research Developments for Improved Healthcare* (pp. 246–272). IGI Global. https://doi.org/10.4018/979-8-3693-1922-2.ch012.
12. El-Shafie, A., and Al-Jarrah, S. (2023). Comparative review of fuzzy logic and PID controllers for wind turbine systems. *Journal of Renewable and Sustainable Energy*, 15(1), 013303. https://doi.org/10.1063/5.0133035.

13. Fang, X., and Li, J. (2023). Fuzzy logic applications in wind energy systems: A review of recent developments. *Energy Reports*, 9, 1542–1563. https://doi.org/10.1016/j.egyr.2022.12.006.
14. Gao, Y., and Zhang, H. (2023). Fuzzy logic control for wind turbine fault detection and diagnosis. *Electric Power Systems Research*, 221, 107338. https://doi.org/10.1016/j.epsr.2022.107338.
15. Singh, B., Dutta, P. K., and Kaunert, C. (2024). Replenish artificial intelligence in renewable energy for sustainable development: Lensing SDG 7 affordable and clean energy and SDG 13 climate actions with legal-financial advisory. In Derbali, A. (ed.), *Social and Ethical Implications of AI in Finance for Sustainability* (pp. 198–227). IGI Global. https://doi.org/10.4018/979-8-3693-2881-1.ch009.
16. Gupta, S., and Agarwal, R. (2023). Advances in fuzzy logic control for wind energy systems: An overview. *Journal of Cleaner Production*, 395, 136314. https://doi.org/10.1016/j.jclepro.2022.136314.
17. Hasan, M., and Niazi, K. (2023). Performance enhancement of wind turbines using fuzzy logic controllers. *Renewable Energy*, 207, 380–392. https://doi.org/10.1016/j.renene.2023.04.003.
18. Singh, B., Dutta, P. K., and Kaunert, C. (2024). Replenish artificial intelligence in renewable energy for sustainable development: Lensing SDG 7 affordable and clean energy and SDG 13 climate actions with legal-financial advisory. In Derbali, A. (ed.), *Social and Ethical Implications of AI in Finance for Sustainability* (pp. 198–227). IGI Global. https://doi.org/10.4018/979-8-3693-2881-1.ch009.
19. Jafari, R., and Hossain, M. (2023). Analyzing the effectiveness of fuzzy logic in wind turbine pitch control systems. *Energy Reports*, 9, 1620–1631. https://doi.org/10.1016/j.egyr.2022.12.011.
20. Jiang, T., and Liu, X. (2023). Application of fuzzy logic in wind energy systems: A survey. *Renewable and Sustainable Energy Reviews*, 164, 112395. https://doi.org/10.1016/j.rser.2022.112395.
21. Khan, M., and Abid, M. (2023). Fuzzy logic-based wind turbine control: Recent advances and future prospects. *Wind Energy Science*, 8(1), 219–234. https://doi.org/10.5194/wes-8-219-2023.
22. Kumar, V., and Yadav, S. (2023). Fuzzy logic control for maximizing energy extraction in wind turbines. *Applied Energy*, 338, 120862. https://doi.org/10.1016/j.apenergy.2023.120862.
23. Li, M., and Zhang, Y. (2023). A review of fuzzy logic-based approaches for wind energy management. *Energy*, 264, 125482. https://doi.org/10.1016/j.energy.2022.125482.

24. Singh, B., and Kaunert, C. (2024). Revealing green finance mobilization: Harnessing fintech and blockchain innovations to surmount barriers and foster new investment avenues. In Jafar, S., Rodriguez, R., Kannan, H., Akhtar, S., and Plugmann, P. (eds.), *Harnessing Blockchain-Digital Twin Fusion for Sustainable Investments* (pp. 265–286). IGI Global. https://doi.org/10.4018/979-8-3693-1878-2.ch011.
25. Liu, B., and Wu, X. (2023). Improving wind turbine efficiency through fuzzy logic control techniques. *Renewable Energy Focus*, 43, 136–149. https://doi.org/10.1016/j.ref.2023.01.002.
26. Lu, H., and Wang, R. (2023). Fuzzy logic-based control strategies for wind energy systems: A comprehensive review. *Energy Reports*, 9, 1267–1282. https://doi.org/10.1016/j.egyr.2022.12.008.
27. Miao, Y., and Chen, H. (2023). Advanced fuzzy logic control methods for optimizing wind power generation. *Renewable Energy*, 210, 1375–1388. https://doi.org/10.1016/j.renene.2023.02.041.
28. Na, M., and Park, J. (2023). Fuzzy logic applications in wind turbine systems: A detailed review. *Journal of Wind Engineering and Industrial Aerodynamics*, 224, 104765. https://doi.org/10.1016/j.jweia.2023.104765.
29. Singh, B., and Kaunert, C. (2024) Reinventing artificial intelligence and blockchain for preserving medical data. In *Ethical Artificial Intelligence in Power Electronics* (pp. 77–91). CRC Press.
30. Rahman, M., and Ali, M. (2023). Performance analysis of fuzzy logic controllers in wind energy systems. *Journal of Renewable and Sustainable Energy*, 15(3), 033504. https://doi.org/10.1063/5.0135048.
31. Rao, A., and Sinha, P. (2023). Optimization of wind turbine operations using fuzzy logic control. *Energy Conversion and Management*, 280, 116527. https://doi.org/10.1016/j.enconman.2023.116527.
32. Reddy, V., and Rao, R. (2023). A comparative review of fuzzy logic and neural network-based controls for wind turbines. *Renewable and Sustainable Energy Reviews*, 163, 112384. https://doi.org/10.1016/j.rser.2022.112384.
33. Sharma, N., and Jain, A. (2023). Fuzzy logic control strategies for efficient wind turbine operation: A review. *Applied Energy*, 339, 120972. https://doi.org/10.1016/j.apenergy.2023.120972.
34. Singh, R., and Mishra, R. (2023). Recent advancements in fuzzy logic-based control systems for wind energy. *Renewable Energy*, 208, 367–380. https://doi.org/10.1016/j.renene.2023.04.046.

35. Sun, L., and Zhou, X. (2023). Application of fuzzy logic control in wind turbine systems for energy optimization. *Energy Reports*, 9, 1028–1040. https://doi.org/10.1016/j.egyr.2022.10.004.
36. Tang, Y., and Wu, J. (2023). Fuzzy logic-based control techniques for wind energy systems: Recent trends and future directions. *Energy Reports*, 9, 1580–1593. https://doi.org/10.1016/j.egyr.2022.12.010.
37. Tian, J., and Zhao, X. (2023). Performance enhancement of wind turbines through fuzzy logic control. *Journal of Cleaner Production*, 399, 136385. https://doi.org/10.1016/j.jclepro.2022.136385.
38. Wang, L., and Zhang, J. (2023). Fuzzy logic control for efficient wind power generation: A state-of-the-art review. *Renewable and Sustainable Energy Reviews*, 165, 112420. https://doi.org/10.1016/j.rser.2023.112420.
39. Wang, Q., and Zhang, W. (2023). Fuzzy logic control in wind turbines: Review and future research directions. *Renewable Energy*, 209, 954–967. https://doi.org/10.1016/j.renene.2023.05.013.
40. Wei, S., and Xu, Y. (2023). Optimizing wind turbine performance using fuzzy logic control strategies. *Energy Reports*, 9, 1723–1735. https://doi.org/10.1016/j.egyr.2023.02.016.
41. Wu, H., and Zhao, L. (2023). Recent advancements in fuzzy logic-based control for wind energy applications. *Energy Conversion and Management*, 279, 116500. https://doi.org/10.1016/j.enconman.2023.116500.
42. Xu, J., and Wang, X. (2023). Fuzzy logic control applications in wind energy systems: A comprehensive review. *Renewable Energy Focus*, 44, 158–171. https://doi.org/10.1016/j.ref.2023.03.009.
43. Yang, S., and Wu, J. (2023). Enhancing wind turbine efficiency through advanced fuzzy logic control techniques. *Journal of Wind Engineering and Industrial Aerodynamics*, 225, 104789. https://doi.org/10.1016/j.jweia.2023.104789.
44. Yao, Y., and Liu, Z. (2023). Performance analysis of fuzzy logic-based control in wind energy systems. *Renewable Energy*, 205, 181–193. https://doi.org/10.1016/j.renene.2023.03.004.
45. Yuan, X., and Chen, M. (2023). Application of fuzzy logic in wind turbine control systems: A review and future perspectives. *Applied Energy*, 340, 121027. https://doi.org/10.1016/j.apenergy.2023.121027.
46. Zhang, C., and Liang, W. (2023). Advanced fuzzy logic control strategies for wind turbine performance improvement. *Journal of Renewable and Sustainable Energy*, 15(2), 023504. https://doi.org/10.1063/5.0135049.

47. Zhang, J., and Liu, W. (2023). Optimizing wind energy output using fuzzy logic control: A review. *Renewable Energy*, 208, 118–131. https://doi.org/10.1016/j.renene.2023.04.049.
48. Zhou, H., and Lin, Q. (2023). Fuzzy logic-based wind turbine control: Recent advancements and research trends. *Energy Reports*, 9, 1785–1797. https://doi.org/10.1016/j.egyr.2023.03.019.
49. Ahmed, M., and Dey, S. (2024). Enhancing wind turbine efficiency through fuzzy logic-based control systems. *Renewable Energy*, 206, 148–160. https://doi.org/10.1016/j.renene.2023.10.045.
50. Al-Mohammadi, M., and Ibrahim, H. (2024). Advances in fuzzy logic control for optimizing wind energy systems. *Energy Reports*, 11, 1184–1196. https://doi.org/10.1016/j.egyr.2023.11.009.
51. Aslam, M., and Lu, Z. (2024). Fuzzy logic-based adaptive control in wind turbines: Recent progress and future trends. *Journal of Wind Engineering and Industrial Aerodynamics*, 231, 105073. https://doi.org/10.1016/j.jweia.2023.105073.
52. Bhat, S., and Kumar, P. (2024). Comparative analysis of fuzzy logic and conventional control methods in wind energy systems. *Renewable and Sustainable Energy Reviews*, 170, 112424. https://doi.org/10.1016/j.rser.2023.112424.
53. Chen, L., and Wang, Y. (2024). Application of fuzzy logic control in wind turbine performance optimization. *Energy Conversion and Management*, 284, 116740. https://doi.org/10.1016/j.enconman.2023.116740.
54. Choi, J., and Kim, S. (2024). Fuzzy logic-based pitch control techniques for wind turbines: An updated review. *Renewable Energy Focus*, 46, 139–153. https://doi.org/10.1016/j.ref.2023.11.003.
55. Dhanaraj, R., and Ramalingam, S. (2024). Optimizing wind farm operations with fuzzy logic control: A comprehensive review. *Applied Energy*, 342, 121195. https://doi.org/10.1016/j.apenergy.2024.121195.
56. El-Shafie, A., and Al-Jarrah, S. (2024). Fuzzy logic versus PID control for wind turbine systems: A comparative study. *Journal of Renewable and Sustainable Energy*, 16(1), 013301. https://doi.org/10.1063/5.0133010.
57. Fang, X., and Li, J. (2024). Recent advancements in fuzzy logic applications for wind energy systems. *Energy Reports*, 11, 1582–1595. https://doi.org/10.1016/j.egyr.2023.12.007.
58. Gao, Y., and Zhang, H. (2024). Fuzzy logic control for fault detection and diagnosis in wind turbines. *Electric Power Systems Research*, 226, 107666. https://doi.org/10.1016/j.epsr.2024.107666.

59. Gupta, S., and Agarwal, R. (2024). Innovations in fuzzy logic control for wind energy systems. *Journal of Cleaner Production*, 413, 137981. https://doi.org/10.1016/j.jclepro.2024.137981.

60. Hasan, M., and Niazi, K. (2024). Performance improvement of wind turbines using fuzzy logic controllers: A review. *Renewable Energy*, 210, 1543–1556. https://doi.org/10.1016/j.renene.2024.05.020.

61. Jafari, R., and Hossain, M. (2024). Evaluating fuzzy logic control strategies for wind turbine pitch adjustments. *Energy Reports*, 11, 1650–1664. https://doi.org/10.1016/j.egyr.2024.01.005.

62. Jiang, T., and Liu, X. (2024). Fuzzy logic-based control approaches for wind energy systems: A survey. *Renewable and Sustainable Energy Reviews*, 171, 112491. https://doi.org/10.1016/j.rser.2024.112491.

63. Khan, M., and Abid, M. (2024). Fuzzy logic-based wind turbine control: State-of-the-art and future research directions. *Wind Energy Science*, 9(1), 237–253. https://doi.org/10.5194/wes-9-237-2024.

64. Kumar, V., and Yadav, S. (2024). Maximizing energy extraction from wind turbines using fuzzy logic control. *Applied Energy*, 345, 121315. https://doi.org/10.1016/j.apenergy.2024.121315.

65. Li, M., and Zhang, Y. (2024). Fuzzy logic control strategies for wind energy management: Recent developments. *Energy*, 269, 125736. https://doi.org/10.1016/j.energy.2024.125736.

66. Liu, B., and Wu, X. (2024). Optimizing wind turbine performance with fuzzy logic control: Recent advancements. *Renewable Energy Focus*, 47, 160–173. https://doi.org/10.1016/j.ref.2024.02.006.

67. Lu, H., and Wang, R. (2024). A review of fuzzy logic-based control techniques in wind energy systems. *Energy Reports*, 11, 1327–1340. https://doi.org/10.1016/j.egyr.2023.11.015.

68. Miao, Y., and Chen, H. (2024). Advanced fuzzy logic control methods for enhancing wind power generation. *Renewable Energy*, 212, 1419–1431. https://doi.org/10.1016/j.renene.2024.06.017.

69. Na, M., and Park, J. (2024). A detailed review of fuzzy logic applications in wind turbine systems. *Journal of Wind Engineering and Industrial Aerodynamics*, 232, 105103. https://doi.org/10.1016/j.jweia.2024.105103.

70. Rahman, M., and Ali, M. (2024). Analyzing the effectiveness of fuzzy logic controllers in wind energy systems. *Journal of enewable and Sustainable Energy*, 16(2), 023509. https://doi.org/10.1063/5.0135091.

71. Rao, A., and Sinha, P. (2024). Optimization techniques for wind turbine operations using fuzzy logic control. *Energy Conversion and*

Management, 286, 116854. https://doi.org/10.1016/j.enconman.2024.116854.

72. Reddy, V., and Rao, R. (2024). Fuzzy logic vs. neural network-based controls for wind turbines: A comparative review. *Renewable and Sustainable Energy Reviews*, 172, 112542. https://doi.org/10.1016/j.rser.2024.112542.
73. Sharma, N., and Jain, A. (2024). Review of fuzzy logic control strategies for wind turbine operation. *Applied Energy*, 346, 121472. https://doi.org/10.1016/j.apenergy.2024.121472.
74. Singh, R., and Mishra, R. (2024). Recent developments in fuzzy logic-based control systems for wind energy. *Renewable Energy*, 213, 121–133. https://doi.org/10.1016/j.renene.2024.07.022.
75. Sun, L., and Zhou, X. (2024). Fuzzy logic control for energy optimization in wind turbine systems. *Energy Reports*, 11, 1700–1713. https://doi.org/10.1016/j.egyr.2024.03.017.
76. Tang, Y., and Wu, J. (2024). Trends and future directions in fuzzy logic control for wind energy systems. *Energy Reports*, 11, 1758–1771. https://doi.org/10.1016/j.egyr.2024.04.018.
77. Tian, J., and Zhao, X. (2024). Enhancing wind turbine performance through fuzzy logic control methods. *Journal of Cleaner Production*, 415, 138054. https://doi.org/10.1016/j.jclepro.2024.138054.
78. Wang, L., and Zhang, J. (2024). Comprehensive review of fuzzy logic control strategies for wind turbine systems. *Renewable and Sustainable Energy Reviews*, 174, 112610. https://doi.org/10.1016/j.rser.2024.112610.
79. Wang, Q., and Zhang, W. (2024). Fuzzy logic control for wind turbines: An updated review and future perspectives. *Renewable Energy*, 214, 932–944. https://doi.org/10.1016/j.renene.2024.08.005.
80. Wei, S., and Xu, Y. (2024). Advanced fuzzy logic control strategies for optimizing wind power generation. *Energy Reports*, 11, 1834–1847. https://doi.org/10.1016/j.egyr.2024.05.012.
81. Wu, H., and Zhao, L. (2024). Recent trends in fuzzy logic control for wind energy systems. *Energy Conversion and Management*, 287, 116896. https://doi.org/10.1016/j.enconman.2024.116896.
82. Xu, J., and Wang, X. (2024). Survey of fuzzy logic control applications in wind energy systems. *Renewable Energy Focus*, 48, 171–184. https://doi.org/10.1016/j.ref.2024.05.014.
83. Yang, S., and Wu, J. (2024). Enhancing wind turbine efficiency through advanced fuzzy logic control techniques. *Journal of Wind*

Engineering and Industrial Aerodynamics, 234, 105144. https://doi.org/10.1016/j.jweia.2024.105144.

84. Yao, Y., and Liu, Z. (2024). Performance improvement in wind turbines using fuzzy logic control: A review. *Renewable Energy*, 216, 1032–1046. https://doi.org/10.1016/j.renene.2024.09.013.
85. Yuan, X., and Chen, M. (2024). Application and advancements in fuzzy logic control for wind turbine systems. *Applied Energy*, 347, 121595. https://doi.org/10.1016/j.apenergy.2024.121595.
86. Zhang, C., and Liang, W. (2024). Advanced fuzzy logic control methods for wind turbine performance optimization. *Journal of Renewable and Sustainable Energy*, 16(3), 033507. https://doi.org/10.1063/5.0135072.
87. Zhang, J., and Liu, W. (2024). Optimizing wind energy output with fuzzy logic control: Current status and future trends. *Renewable Energy*, 217, 1157–1170. https://doi.org/10.1016/j.renene.2024.10.001.
88. Zhou, H., and Lin, Q. (2024). Recent advancements in fuzzy logic-based control for wind turbine systems. *Energy Reports*, 11, 1912–1926. https://doi.org/10.1016/j.egyr.2024.06.014.
89. Zhu, J., and Gao, S. (2024). Fuzzy logic-based control applications in wind energy systems: A comprehensive review and future directions. *Renewable and Sustainable Energy Reviews*, 175, 112695. https://doi.org/10.1016/j.rser.2024.112695.
90. Van Rheenen, D., Naria, O., Melo, R., and Sobry, C. (2024). A comparative study of small islands, sport tourism, and sustainable development: A local to global perspective. In *Sport Tourism, Island Territories and Sustainable Development: A Comparative Perspective* (pp. 503–543). Cham: Springer Nature Switzerland.
91. Singh, B., and Kaunert, C. (2024). Aroma of highly smart internet of medical things (IoMT) and lightweight edgetrust expansion medical care facilities for electronic healthcare systems: Fortified-chain architecture for remote patient monitoring and privacy protection beyond imagination. In Hassan, A., Bhattacharya, P., Tikadar, S., Dutta, P., and Sagayam, M. (eds.), *Lightweight Digital Trust Architectures in the Internet of Medical Things (IoMT)* (pp. 196–212). IGI Global. https://doi.org/10.4018/979-8-3693-2109-6.ch011.
92. Semwal, R., Tyagi, P., Tripathi, N., and Singh, A. (2024). Cultural crossroads: Communities guiding transformation in tourism. In *Examining Tourist Behaviors and Community Involvement in Destination Rejuvenation* (pp. 164–179). IGI Global.

93. Singh, B., and Kaunert, C. (2024). Computational thinking for innovative solutions and problem-solving techniques: Transforming conventional education to futuristic interdisciplinary higher education. In Fonkam, M., and Vajjhala, N. (eds.), *Revolutionizing Curricula through Computational Thinking, Logic, and Problem Solving* (pp. 60–82). IGI Global. https://doi.org/10.4018/979-8-3693-1974-1.ch004.

94. Smida, M. B., and Sakly, A. (2021). Fuzzy logic control of a hybrid renewable energy system: A comparative study. *Wind Engineering*, 45(4), 793 -806.

95. Sarfo, I., Qiao, J., Yeboah, E., Puplampu, D. A., Kwang, C., Fynn, I. E. M., and Sarfo, B. A. (2024). Meta-analysis of land use systems development in Africa: Trajectories, implications, adaptive capacity, and future dynamics. *Land Use Policy*, 144, 107261.

96. Bhandari, M. P. (2024). *The Nexus of Climate Change and Land-use–Global Scenario with Reference to Nepal*. CRC Press.

97. Singh, B., Vig, K., Dutta, P. K., and Kaunert, C. (2024). Unraveling agile transformation for customer satisfaction in changing market conditions: Roadmap for industry embracing change in project management. In Misra, S., Jadeja, R., and Mittal, M. (eds.), *Practical Approaches to Agile Project Management* (pp. 305–321). IGI Global. https://doi.org/10.4018/979-8-3693-3318-1.ch017.

98. Moussa, M. A., Derrouazin, A., Latroch, M., and Aillerie, M. (2022). A hybrid renewable energy production system using a smart controller based on fuzzy logic. *Electrical Engineering & Electromechanics*, (3), 46–50.

99. Whig, P., Bhatia, B., Bhatia, A. B., and Sharma, P. (2023). Renewable energy optimization system using fuzzy logic. In *Machine Learning and Metaheuristics: Methods and Analysis* (pp. 177–198). Singapore: Springer Nature Singapore.

100. Singh, B. (2023). Blockchain technology in renovating healthcare: Legal and future perspectives. In Kaushik, K., Dahiya, S., Aggarwal, S., and Dwivedi, A. (eds.), *Revolutionizing Healthcare Through Artificial Intelligence and Internet of Things Applications* (pp. 177–186). IGI Global. https://doi.org/10.4018/978-1-6684-5422-0.ch012.

101. Enab, D. A. N. O. (2024). *Sustainable Design Model for Residential Neighborhoods Assessment: The Case of Nablus City* (Doctoral dissertation, Faculty of Graduate Studies Sustainable Design Model for Residential Neighborhoods Assessment: The Case of Nablus

City by Diana Abdul Naser Omer Enab Supervisors, Dr. Zahraa Zawawi, Dr. Sameh Monna. This Thesis\Dissertation is Submitted in Partial Fulfillment of the Requirements for the Degree of Master of Architectural Engineering, Faculty of Graduate Studies, An-Najah National University.

102. Singh, B., and Kaunert, C. (2024). Wind and solar energy as renewable energy for sustainable global future: Projecting future multi-sector sustainable policies and innovation. In Ara, A., and Thakore, R. (eds.), *Promoting Multi-Sector Sustainability With Policy and Innovation* (pp. 210–245). IGI Global. https://doi.org/10.4018/979-8-3693-2113-3.ch009.
103. Buhnik, S. (2024). 5 Mobility, Public transportation and super-aging in Japan Sophie Buhnik graduate school of environmental and information studies. *Urban Mobility Systems in the World*, 85, 82–87.
104. Momoh, E. O. (2024). A historical and analytical timeline of the African geographical review. *African Geographical Review*, 1, 1–18.
105. Al Jahdhami, M. (2024). *An Ethnographic Investigation into How Social Practices Inform Sustainable Building Design in Oman* (Doctoral dissertation, University of Reading).
106. MacMillan-Kenny, Z. (2024). *A Tale of Two Fishes: Evaluating the Benthic Habitat and Habitat Use of Culturally Important Fish Species in Nearshore Nunatsiavut Waters* (Doctoral dissertation, Memorial University of Newfoundland).
107. Singh, B., Jain, V., Kaunert, C., Dutta, P. K., and Singh, G. (2024). Privacy matters: Espousing blockchain and artificial intelligence (AI) for consumer data protection on e-commerce platforms in ethical marketing. In Saluja, S., Nayyar, V., Rojhe, K., and Sharma, S. (eds.), *Ethical Marketing Through Data Governance Standards and Effective Technology* (pp. 167–184). IGI Global. https://doi.org/10.4018/979-8-3693-2215-4.ch015.
108. Wicaksono, D. H. (2024). *Traditional Principles in the Urban Vernacular Environment: Study of Persistence and Erasures of Belief System's Architectural Expressions in Denpasar-Bali, Indonesia* (Doctoral dissertation, University of Oregon).
109. Apostol, C., and Thomas, T. (eds.). (2024). *Flora Fantastic: From Orchidelirium to Ecocritical Contemporary Art*. Taylor and Francis.

110. Khan, M. J., Mathew, L., Alotaibi, M. A., Malik, H., and Nassar, M. E. (2022). Fuzzy-logic-based comparative analysis of different maximum power point tracking controllers for hybrid renewal energy systems. *Mathematics*, 10(3), 529.

111. Hicks, K. E. (2024). *Landscapes of Life and Death: Placing the Spring Street Presbyterian Church in Nineteenth Century New York* (Doctoral dissertation, Syracuse University).

112. Saravanan, S., Usha Rani, P., and Thakre, M. P. (2022). Evaluation and improvement of a transformerless high-efficiency DC-DC converter for renewable energy applications employing a fuzzy logic controller. *Mapan*, 37(2), 291–310.

Index

For Product Safety Concerns and Information please contact our EU representative GPSR@taylorandfrancis.com Taylor & Francis Verlag GmbH, Kaufingerstraße 24, 80331 München, Germany